# The Akbar Nama

Abul Fazl

VOLUME 1

*Translated by*

H. Beveridge (I.C.S.)

ATLANTIC
PUBLISHERS & DISTRIBUTORS (P) LTD

ATLANTIC
PUBLISHERS & DISTRIBUTORS (P) LTD
7/22, Ansari Road, Darya Ganj, New Delhi
Tel.: +91-11-4077 5252, 2327 3880
E-mail: orders@atlanticbooks.com
Web: www.atlanticbooks.com

Published by Atlantic Publishers & Distributors (P) Ltd.

Reprinted in 2015, 2017, 2019, 2021, 2022, 2024, 2025, 2026

First Published 1907



Printed & bound in India by Atlantic Print Services

# PREFACE TO THE FIRST VOLUME.

When the Asiatic Society of Bengal did me the honour of inviting me to translate the Akbarnāma, I replied that I doubted my ability to make a complete translation, and suggested that I might edit the manuscript version by Lieutenant Chalmers. My suggestion was accepted, and I accordingly obtained from the Royal Asiatic Society the loan of the Chalmers' manuscript and permission to print it. I soon found, however, that the translation was too abridged to be made the basis of my work, and that it was necessary to execute a new version. Chalmers' manuscript was of great service to Elphinstone and Count Noer, and it has also been of much use to myself, but there are many gaps in it, and Abul Faẓl's language has throughout been greatly compressed. One gap near the beginning extends to over ninety pages of the printed text, and has the effect of omitting the account of Akbar's birth, with the prognostics and horoscopes appertaining thereto, as well as the notices of his ancestors from Adam down to his grandfather (Bābar). The reader may judge of the extent to which abbreviation has been carried, when I state that the Chalmers MS. consists of two thinnish volumes of foolscap, and that the Bibliotheca Indica edition of the Persian text occupies three large quartoes which aggregate 1,600 pages.

The task of translation has occupied me several years, and the work has not been very congenial, for Abūl Faẓl is not an author for whom one can feel much sympathy or admiration. He was a great flatterer and unhesitatingly suppressed or distorted facts. His style, too, seems—at least to Western eyes—to be quite detestable, being full of circumlocutions, and both turgid and obscure. He is often prolix, and often unduly concise and darkly allusive. His one merit—and it is one which he specially claims for himself—is his laboriousness. He was an unwearied worker, and when we blame him and lament his deficiencies we shall do well to consider what a blank our knowledge of Akbar's reign would have been, had not Abūl Faẓl exerted himself during years of strenuous effort to chronicle events and institutions. His work also has the imperishable merit of being a record by a contemporary, and by one who had access to information at first hand.

I regret that the work of translation has not devolved upon a better Persian scholar than I am. I have endeavoured to do my best, and I have sought assistance in many quarters. I now desire to express my gratitude to my friends, Maulvi Abdul Haq Abid, the late Mr. J. Beames, Mr. A. G. Ellis of the British Museum, Mr. Irvine and Mr. Whinfield, and to the translation of the Āīn-i-Akbarī, by Professor Blochmann and Colonel Jarrett, and the works of Major Price. I am also indebted for much literary assistance to my elder brother, Mr. David Beveridge. There are, I am sure, many mistakes in my translation and notes, but there would have been many more but for the assistance of my friends. I regret that I have been obliged to make two long lists of Errata and Addenda. In part this has been due to the translations being made in England and printed in India, and in part to increase of knowledge. The translation of the second volume, which carries on the history of Akbar's reign to the middle of the seventeenth year, has been completed by me, and I am about to begin the translation of the third and last volume. The translation has been made from the Bibliotheca Indica edition of the text, but I have consulted many MSS. in the British Museum, the India Office, and the Royal Asiatic Society's Library, &c. The Bibliotheca Indica edition is by no means so good as it might have been, for the learned native editors* were destitute of geographical or historical knowledge. Hence they have often made mistakes in the names of persons and places. They have also no explanatory notes. In their preface they are severe upon the Lucknow edition. No doubt that edition has many faults, but it was the first in the field, and it is on the whole a creditable monument of the enterprise of the publisher, Munshi Newal Kishor, and of the liberality of the Maharajah of Patiala. The editor, Maulvī Ṣādiq 'Alī, also deserves honourable mention. He has added numerous notes, and though many of these are trivial, yet there are also many which are really enlightening.

Since completing the translation, I have seen a remarkable MS. of the first volume of the Akbarnama in the possession of Saiyid 'Alī

* It is stated in the Persian preface that nine MSS. and the Lucknow lithograph were used in the preparation of the edition. None of the MSS. was of an early date.

Bilgrāmī. This is evidently a rough draft and contains severa things which do not occur in the MSS. of the finished work. Among them are one or two letters of Humāyūn. I have given an account of this MS. in R.A.S.J. for January 1903, p. 115.

*4th September, 1902.* H. BEVERIDGE.

# AKBARNĀMA.

IN THE NAME OF GOD, THE MERCIFUL, THE COMPASSIONATE.

*Introduction.*

Almighty God![1] What a profound thought and glorious idea it 1
is that the subtle apprehenders of truth, whose bright minds are like the breath of morning, and who are keen-sighted students of the

---

1 *Allāh Akbar* (Arabic,—*Allāhu Akbar*) *God is very Great.* This expression is called the *takbīr*—the magnifying—and is often used at the commencement of undertakings. A.F. places it at the beginning of the *Akbarnāma* and also of the *Āīn.* Blochmann says, (168n.) "The words *Allāhu Akbar* are ambiguous; they may mean, 'God is Great,' or 'Akbar is God.' There is no doubt that Akbar liked the phrase for its ambiguity; for it was used on coins, the imperial seals and the heading of books, *farmāns*, etc." He then translates from Badāonī, (II, 210) as follows; "It was during these days "(A.H. 983=1575-6) that His Majesty "once asked how people would like "it, if he ordered the words *Allāhu* "*Akbar* to be cut on the imperial seal "and the dies of his coins. Most "said, people would like it very "much. But Ḥājī Ibrāhīm objected "and said, the phrase had an ambi-"guous meaning and the Emperor "might substitute the Koran verse "*Lazikru Allāhi akbaru—To think of* "*God is the greatest thing*—because "it involved no ambiguity. But His "Majesty got displeased and said, it "was surely sufficient that no man "who felt his weakness would claim "divinity; he merely looked to the "sound of the words and he had "never thought that a thing could "be carried to such an extreme." Mr. Lowe (230) has copied this translation but it seems to me that Mr. Blochmann meant to write "*self-evident*," and not "*sufficient*," for the Persian is خود معین است *khwud mu'aiyan ast*. Mr. Rehatsek ("Akbar's Repudiation of Islām," 14) translates: "But the Emperor was "not pleased and replied, 'It is self-'evident that no man can in his per-'fect weakness pretend to be God. 'Our intention is based on the literal 'meaning and there is no occasion

schedules[1] of Creation and drawers[2] of diagrams on the tablet of wisdom and perception, have not, with the exception of Speech which is but a vagrant breeze and fluctuating gale, found in the combinations[3] of the elements or in material[4] forms, anything so sublime, or a jewel so rare that it come not within the mould of price, that Reason's balance cannot weigh it, that Language's measure cannot contain it, and that it be beyond the scale of Thought;—and yet, how should it be otherwise? Without help of Speech, the inner world's capital could not be built, nor this evil outer world's civilization be conceived.

---

'to transfer it (to my name.)'" I think the passage might be rendered thus, "He (Akbar) did not approve, "and observed, 'It is self-evident 'that a humble slave cannot claim 'the Godhead; we are thinking only 'of the verbal coincidence (with our 'own name), there is no sense in put'ting such an interpretation (as you 'have suggested) on the phrase.'" The word مناسبت *manāsabat*—which I have translated *coincidence* occurs thrice in the beginning of the *Akbarnāma* in the sense of connection, *viz.*, Bib. Ind. ed. 2, ll. 2 and 9 fr. foot and 22, l. 6.

The conversation is, on the whole, creditable both to Akbar and Ḥājī Ibrāhīm. Akbar, I think, admitted that he chose the phrase on account of its consonance with his name but denied that he had any intention of claiming to be God. Probably Ḥājī Ibrāhīm's well-meant suggestion would not have mended matters, for people would still have remarked on the double significance of the words. See further on this point, Badāonī II. 268 (Lowe, 277). In Faiẓī's *Diwān*, there is a long poem in praise of Akbar, every couplet of which ends with the words, *Allāh Akbar*.

1 جد اول plural of جدول, *jadwal*, a column. The word is often used to signify astronomical tables or catalogues.

2 پرکار کشایان lit.: compass-openers.

3 تركّب عنصري, *tarakkub 'unṣurī*: lit.: elemental combination or insertion of one element in another. The similar phrase تركيب عنصري occurs in *Āīn*, No. 4 (13, 111.) *Tarakkub* is used in the *Akbarnāma* (22, l. 6) in opposition to *tajarrud*, *i.e.*, singleness or nudity. It appears that the phrase refers to the four compounds described in *Āīn* No. 13 about the origin of metals. There it is said that the Creator, by calling into existence the four elements, has raised up wondrous forms (*paikarhā*). Further on, we are told that four compounds (*murakkab*), are called into existence, *viz.*: 1st, *āṣār-i-'ulwī*, doings from on high, as rain, snow, etc.; 2nd, stones; 3rd, plants; 4th, animals. (Blochmann 39.)

4 پيكر هيولاني, *paikar haiyūlānī* material form. *Haiyūlānī* is from the Greek ὕλη, *matter*. I think the expression is synonymous or nearly so with *tarakkub 'anṣarī*. The ma-

VERSE.[1]

What a Word[2] was that whose utterance
Unveiled the eighteen thousand ![3]
No feast equals it in intoxicating power;
No rival comes nigh it in supremacy.
It is the initiator in the workshop;
It sits enthroned in the palace.
Whatever reaches the heart of the wise,
The heart utters to the tongue and the tongue rehearses to the ear.
Its path is from the *adit* to the *exit* of hearts;
Expression and audition are its arena.
In reason's observatory[4] the tongue and the ear
Are the rising[5] and setting of speech's moon.

We cannot reach its sublime foundation by the ladder[6] of the

---

terial forms must also be combinations of the elements.

1 These lines are Faiẓī's and in his *Markaẓi-adwār* (Centre of Circles) in the canto in praise of Speech. (B. M. Add. No. 7795, 25b. Rieu's Cat. II. 671). The MS. has *bar arbābi-hosh* in the last line in place of *bar raṣadgāhi-hosh*.

2 Meaning the word of two letters *kāf* and *nūn*, *i.e.*, *k* and *n*, كن, *Kun*, *Fiat*, Be, which God uttered at the Creation. "*Zi kāf wa nūn barūn āward kūnain.*" Exordium of *Gulshan-i-rāz*.

3 It is a Muhammadan idea that the number of created species was 18,000. See Badāonī II. 320 (Lowe, 330). Also *Akbarnāma* 9, l. 11. Meninski *s.v.* *'alam*, quoting from the Turkish says, "*Deus octodecim millia mundorum creavit.*" I cannot find any explanation of the choice of the number 18,000. Perhaps it was adopted as being a multiple of the mysterious number 9, and 9,000 was doubled to allow for male and female creations.

The *Majma'u-t-tawārīkh* (quoted by Anquetil du Perron, *Zendavesta*, II 352n.), says the first man was called Gilshāh—earth-lord—and that he had a son and daughter named Mesci and Mescianēh, and that after 50 years, they had 18 children. At least this is another instance of the use of the number 18 and perhaps a partial explanation of the "18,000."

4 *Raṣadgāh*. Observatories are described in the *Āīn* (II, 265) as wonderful buildings with upper and lower windows and placed on elevated spots where mists cannot reach them. See also l. c. 266 where the word *raṣad* is explained.

5 Lit. are its east and west.

6 Alluding, apparently, to the notion that there are nine heavens one above another.

skies nor can the swift foot of reason plant a step in its nature's mysterious wilderness. Its disposition[1] is fiery, its constitution aerial, its nature earthy but resembling water.[2] Its fount is the fire-temple of the heart; its culmination, the blissful abode of the atmosphere; it is as water in the flow of its traffic; earth's surface is its place of repose.

Judges of precedence in the ranks of glory, have in consonance with their knowledge and insight, recognized Speech as Commander-in-Chief[3] of Truth's army,—nay, as the true son and heir of the mind. They have felt it to be the Archimage[4] of knowledge, the fire-temple of the heart,—nay, to be the mind's first birth.[5] Espe-

---

[1] The reference is to the four elements. MS. No. 564 says that speech is compared to fire, on account of its vehemence; to air, because it is breath; to earth, because its place of utterance is the tongue which belongs to the visible world; and to water, because of its smoothness and mobility.

[2] آبنما, *ābnumā*, showing water or looking like water. *Āb* also means lustre and Chalmers translates "of liquid purity." But A. F. is evidently thinking of the element of water. See a similar passage in *Āīn* No. 4, (Bib. Ind. 13), where gold is compared to each of the four elements. There is a passage in A. F.'s preface to the *Āīn* where mankind is divided into four classes, corresponding to the four elements.

[3] *Sipah-sālār*, lit: Soldier-Chief; but the description in the *Āīn* of the duties and qualifications of the *Sipah-sālār* shows that he was rather a Vizier or Prime Minister. Indeed A. F. begins by calling him the Vicegerent of his Majesty. (Jarrett II, 37).

[4] *Mūbid mūbidāni-dānish*.

[5] ابو الاباي, *abū-l-ābāī*, father of fathers; but the meaning is not that Speech is the forefather or first-parent of mind but that it is the Adam or primeval ancestor engendered by the mind.

The passage from "Judges" to "birth" is a military metaphor, for *ṣufūf* (ranks) means lines of soldiers and *anjuman* may mean an army. The phrase which I have rendered "true son and heir" is *khalaf-aṣ-ṣidq* or *khalaf ṣidq* and means a successor or perhaps "Vicar worthy of his proto-type." The *tashdīd* and article of Text seem unnecessary, Lane 795c.

Chalmers translates, "Those who can appreciate the highest grandeur, have by means of their sense and penetration understood this exalted foundation of the Council Room of Reason to be even the son (the MS. has *sun*—clearly a clerical error) of the sincerity of the heart and the kindred of wisdom have supposed it to be the furnace of the soul or rather the Palladium of the affections of the mind."

cially preëminent is that Speech[1] which is the ornamented argument
of the splendid volume; adorned preface of the sublime code,
that is, is the praise of the Lord of heaven and earth; panegyric
of the Distributor of life and Creator of the body; which is at once 2
a stage of exaltation for the beginning and a heart-entrancing
ornament for the close; at once caravan-conductor[2] of the elo-
quent and prince of eloquence; chamber-lamp of the sitters in dark-
ness; solitude-adorning companion of the recluse; pain-increaser
of the lovers of the path of God-seeking; ulcer-plaster of the
wounded dwellers in the recess of impatience; cordial for the drinkers
of sorrow's bitter tears; embalmer[3] of the broken-hearted denizens
of the hermitage of silence; marshaller of the brave in the contests
of divine love; banquet-lamp of the beloved[4] ones in the palace of
peace; thirst-increaser[5] of thirsty-lipped inquirers; hunger-increaser

---

1 It is difficult to regard all these expressions as referring to speech only and Chalmers has, apparently, considered them as descriptive of the Almighty, for after the words "Creator of the body" (See *infra*) he translates, "He bestows the basis of exaltation to the commencement of eternity." But I think the reference is really to speech and that A. F. is thinking of the *logos*. I learn from the translation of the *Gulshani-rāz* of my friend Mr. Whinfield, that Sufis rendered the Neo-Platonic *logos* by the phrase *'aql-i-kull*, universal reason. A. F.'s language may be compared with Niẓāmī's address to Speech (*sukhan*) at the beginning of the *Makhzanu-l-asrār*. The author of the *Ma'āṣir-l-umara* (II. 622) says that A. F. has been called a Niẓāmī in prose.

2 The force of this antithesis or parallelism is not very clear, but apparently some such distinction as that between the Church militant and the Church triumphant is intended. While the eloquent are travelling, *i.e.*, marching on as praisers of God—and have not yet attained their goal, speech is their leader and when they have arrived at their resting place, *i.e.*, at perfection—speech becomes their sovereign. Chalmers translates. "He leads the Caravan of the Eloquent and He is the Prince of Oratory."

3 Properly, pissasphalt, or, as Chalmers has it, embalming drug. The word in the text is *momiāī* from which comes our word *mummy*. We might therefore translate, *mummifier*.

4 *Ma'shūq mizājān*, perhaps filled with love or excessively loving.

5 *Istisqābakhsh* lit. giver of dropsy. Thirst is often an accompaniment of dropsy. Sa'dī (*Gulistān* II. Story 33), speaks of a dropsical person as not being satisfied even by the Euphrates, and there is a similar reference in the *Būstān* (III, l. 26) to the condition of a dropsical person,

of hungry-hearted ones in the wilderness of search. Hence it is that wakeful-hea. ed sages,—with all their tumult of love and restless longing,—have stayed the hand of contemplation at the hem of the divine canopy [1] and with thirsty lips, and blistered feet, and the gulping down of thousands of agitations and cries, have set the seal of silence on their lips and—wisely wrapping the foot of respect in the skirt of humility,—have not attempted what has not been vouchsafed to them from the almonry of destiny.

VERSE.

Letters[2] and dots are the desert sand in Thy perfect path.
In the universe of Thy wisdom, the city of speech is but some market-booths.[3]
The warders of jealousy [4] at Thy door, smite the understanding,
With blows of astonishment in front, and strokes of ignorance [5] from behind.

---

on the banks of the Nile. The Romans had a similar notion. See Ovid's *Fasti* (I. l. 215) and Horace's *Crescit indulgens sibi dirus hydrops, Nec sitim pellit,*

A. F.'s meaning is that some knowledge of the Divine praise makes one thirst for more. Cf. A. F.'s *Inshā* where Sharafu-d-dī.. of Manīr is called a thirst-implanter. *Istisqā* also means praying for rain, and thus the epithet may mean that God puts a prayer for rain in the mouths of the thirsty, or that he grants their prayer for rain. The epithet following—*jū'-afzā*—may mean appetite-increaser.

1 *Ḥaudaj* (howdah) which also means a camel-litter. It is probably used in this sense in the *Akbarnāma*, I. 14, l. 12 from foot.

2 Lit. *points and letters*. By the dots are meant the diacritical points. The lines are Faiẓī's. See *Āīn* I. 236, and Blochmann, 550. Mr. Blochmann renders the lines, thus;—

"Science is like blinding desert-"sand on the road to Thy perfection; "the town of literature is a mere "hamlet, compared with the world "of Thy knowledge. Thy jealousy, "the guard of Thy door, stuns "human thought by a blow in the "face and gives human ignorance a "slap on the nape of the neck."

Chalmers has,—"The Viceroy of "dismay spurns our fancy from Thy "door;—With the blow of stupor "upon its front and the thrust of "ignorance from behind."

3 روستا *rūstā*, a market-town or hamlet.

4 Or pernaps, *the watchmen of Thy jealousy*. A. F. speaks (42, l. 10) of the Divine jealousy's preserving from public knowledge the true character of Akbar's horoscope.

5 The meaning seems to be that the human understanding is

In other words, praise of the incomparable Deity lies outside the field of possibility, and the panegyric of the unequalled God is beyond the field of existence.[1]

VERSE.

Wherever discourse[2] deals with the knowledge of God,
Our thoughts' praise becomes dispraise.
Behold rashness, how it boils over with daring!
Can a drop embrace the ocean?
Think not that it is even a single letter of the Book,[3]

---

encountered by amazement (Cf. Gray's "amazement in his van.") when it attempts to fathom the Divine mysteries and is also buffetted by its own ignorance.

1 اکوان *akwān.*—There is a Hindi word *akwān* signifying calculation but here, *akwān* seems to be the plural of کن *kun*, existence or world.

2 حدیث *ḥadīs*, which may either mean tradition or simply mention or discourse. It also means new or recent and perhaps the author of the lines wished to take advantage of these meanings. I think the primary meaning here is *talk* or *discourse* for the lines are Faiẓī's and we find him elsewhere using *ḥadīs* in the sense of discourse; *e.g.*, *Akbarnāma* III. 687, l. 10, where, addressing himself, the poet says. "Faiẓī! keep silent from this discourse!" The lines in our Text occur (but in other order) in the selection from Faiẓī's poems given in the *Akbarnāma*, III, 684, l, 2 and 683, last line.)

Chalmers thus translates the lines:—

"When our traditions could trace the knowledge of God,
"Our most grateful thoughts become ingratitude.
"Behold our arrogance in the ebullition of our daring
"When a drop would clasp the ocean in its embrace,
"Think not any volume contains a letter of it;
"For a letter is but as flax and it is the shining Moon.
"How long wilt thou arrange the harness of thy speech,
"Place thy step here with the offering of helplessness.

3 This difficult couplet receives illustration from the beginning of a letter to Shāh 'Abbās of Persia in the first book of the *Inshā*.' There it is said that, if all the dots of our intelligences and all the schedules of our thoughts were combined with the armies of knowledge and troops of sciences, their total would not represent one letter of the Book of Praise, or be one ray of the Sun. And then we are told, in evident allusion to Sa'dī's famous couplet about the leaves of the trees, that the works of creation praise God with a tongueless tongue. It is clear then that the word book (*kitāb*) is used in the above verse, in a mystical sense for the mysterious Record of the Divine Praise.

For the Letter is muslin[1] and the Book moonlight.
How long wilt thou be an embroiderer[2] of speech?
Stay thy foot here, with the acknowledgment[3] of humility.

So long as there is no link between terrestrials and celestials, and the path of speech between the earthly and the heavenly is closed, what intercourse can there be between the limited and the unlimited, so that an atom of the dust can have any lot in the pure, world-warming Sun? What goal in the boundless plains of necessity and eternity is possible for a prisoner in the subterraneous vault of accident and modernity; and what strength can he have to traverse them? What portion can a bewildered, headless and footless mote[4] have in the beams of the world-lighting Sun? It can only be tossed about in the wind. What is a dewdrop to the swelling ocean or to the cloud surcharged with rain? 'Tis but the vaunt of a parched lip. Pity it were that a mote should discourse about the Illuminator of the assemblage of existences and, though it know him not, and cannot address him, yet should speak of him and search for him!

What connection is there between the dark defile and the courts of light; between non-entity and absolute being? The creature may never attain such knowledge of the Creator, as to be able to draw even a few breaths in the rare atmosphere of the praise of His mysteries
3 (*maknūnāt*) or to plant some steps in the field of the comprehension
of the wonders[5] of His store-houses (*makhzūnāt*). How then can he

---

[1] كتان *katān*. The Lucknow editor says *katān* is a kind of cloth that goes to pieces when exposed to the moonlight. Blochmann (94) says (*katān*) "generally translated by *linen*. All dictionaries agree that it is exceedingly thin, so much so that it tears when the moon shines on it;—it is muslin." A. F. (*Āīn* I. 106.) calls it *katān-i-farangī*, i.e., European *katān*. (See Vullers s. v., and the *Burhāni-qāṭi'*. Apparently *katān* is our word cotton.

[2] محمل, *maḥmil*, means a camel-litter. It is also the term for the cloth which is sent annually from Egypt, as a covering for the *Ka'ba*. The lines are Faizī's. See *Akbarnāma* III. 684, l. 6.

[3] دستاويز, *dastāwīz*. This word which Chalmers translates *offering*, is commonly used in India to mean a document, voucher or exhibit.

[4] The mote is supposed to be in love with the sun. Blochmann 597 n. and 606 n.

[5] عجايب *'ajāib* does not occur in the Text after *idrāk*, but it is found in No. 564, in three MSS. of the R. A. S. and in three of the A. S. B. Chalmers' MS. also seems to have had it.

be fit to enter the courts of the Creator's praise? For him who has no right of approach, to speak of the Sultan's privy chamber, is only to be exposed to ridicule and to make himself a public laughing-stock.

VERSE.[1]

Though the foot of Speech be long of stride,
Thy curtain-stone[2] hath shattered it.
Though Speech be fat and lusty,
It is lean[3] when it reaches Thy table.

O Thou! Higher than our imaginary[4] heavens and more exalted than the plane of the elements and than the stars, inasmuch as Thou hast not bestowed on us knowledge of Thy essence and attributes, it is manifest that Thou regardest not thanksgiving as within our powers, and seeing that Thou hast conferred on us mercies which are infinite, it follows that Thou hast not laid upon us the obligation of adequate gratitude!

When I saw that the door of utterance was closed, I perceived that of action open and said to myself in ecstacy;—

"If thou hast not the power of utterance and canst not chaunt "panegyrics, be not cast down, for it is the smooth-tongued and "empty-handed who, by a fraudulent barter, traffic words at the "rate of realities. The praise which is laid upon mankind[5] as a "duty, by the commands of the Understanding,—that world-obeyed

1 Both couplets are from the *Makhzanu'l-asrār* of Niẓāmī. See Bland's ed. 3, 1.42 and 21. 1.380. Niẓāmī was a favourite author with Akbar. Blochmann, 104.

2 Qu. a stone placed upon the edge of a curtain to prevent its blowing aside. Perhaps simply stone of the threshold.

3 That is, from the length of the journey.

4 *Kursī-i-'aqūl ū awhām.* The *kursī* or throne is the crystalline or eighth heaven and below the *'arsh* which is the empyrean—the ninth heaven or the heaven of heavens. The *kursī* is supposed to be God's judgment seat and the author's meaning seems to be that God is higher than any such imaginary throne. Lane (*s. v. kursī*) quotes an authority as saying that the *kursī* is the place of the feet, and *s. v. 'arsh*, quotes a saying of Muhammad that the seven heavens and earths, by the side of the *kursī*, are naught but as a ring thrown down in a desert land; and such is the *kursī* with respect to the *'arsh* (the empyrean.)

5 خانوادۀ امکانی *khānwāda-i-imkānī lit.* the family of contingent existences.

"sovereign,—is that they make the night-illuminating jewel of "reason,—one of the bountiful Divine Ruler's greatest gifts,—into "a bright lamp, and employ it for sweeping and cleansing the courts "of their outer and inner man. Should the taskmasters[1] of fate's "workshop have attired a son of Adam in the garb of want and "solitude, let him first of all gird up his loins for self-culture and "afterward let him endeavour the improvement of others. Should "they have brought him into a crowd of associations and contacts— "as may be inevitable in the arrangements of this evil world,—let "him, if a ruler, prefer the betterment of others to his own; for "the duty of the shepherd is watching the flock, and the design "of sovereignty is universal guardianship. If he be a subject, "let him, first of all, show alacrity in obeying the orders of his "legitimate ruler,[2] and then let him cleanse the secret chambers "of his heart from the dust of heavy-pacing sensuality and nimble-"footed wrath, so that, by his life and conversation, he be a teacher "and a testimony of the incomparable Giver and Cherisher of his "outer and inner man."

When the communing with my heart had proceeded thus far, a resting-stage showed itself afar off to my bewildered mind, and my thoughts were pleasant for a while. My astonied heart was, it is true, saddened by the length and difficulty of the journey, but was cheered by the sound of the machinery of movement,[3] and by the good tidings of eventual arrival. Suddenly the thoughtful foot of my boding spirit came upon a stone; for the praise of God does not consist in comprehending His perfect attributes and assigning[4]

---

[1] *Mantazimān*, *lit.* arrangers or managers.

[2] اوامر من لّه الامر, *awāmiru mal-lahu al āmru*; -an Arabic phrase signifying the commands of him to whom is command, *i.e.*, who has right to command. See verse of the Koran in the document preserved by Badāonī. (II. 271, l. 9. Lowe 279. Koran, *Sura* IV. 62.)

[3] آهنگ ساز راه, *āhang-i-sāz-i-rāh*. *Āhang* means symphony and also intention or resolution. Perhaps the expression refers to the tinkling of the camels' bells. Chalmers has "the sweet-sounding of the instruments of travel." The meaning appears to be that, though the way is long and difficult, the mind of the pilgrim is cheered by the thought that he is moving on, and will eventually reach his goal.

[4] *Lit.* connect them with His court.

them to His Essence; nor is it the reckoning up of His benefits which are without beginning or end, and by dint[1] of these wares of new-fangled[2] praise, thrusting oneself forward; nor[3] should we regard praise as beyond human comprehension and so, stop short of the

1 *Lit.* alongside or abreast of.

2 حدوث آلود, *ḥadūṣ-ālūd*, stained with novelty. The text has an *iẓāfat* between *ḥaduṣ-ālūd* and the following *khudrā* which would, I think, be better away. It is not in No. 564.

3 I read يا *yā*, instead of تا *tā*, as this seems to me to make the better sense. It also appears to be the reading adopted by Chalmers. Most texts, however, read *tā*. The Elliot MS. (Bodleian 4a) has *yā* and the Walker MS. (Bodleian 115) had *yā* also but this has been altered into *tā*,—I suppose by the copyist. B.M. MS. Add. No. 6544 has also *yā*. B.M. MS. Add. No. 5610 has *tā*. *Tā* may be right and the meaning be that the result of attempting to number the Divine benefits, *etc.*, is that one finds the calculation beyond one's power and so gives up praise in despair. The translation, in this case, would run thus; "Until" (or "with the result that") "one recognizes that praise is beyond human comprehension and so joins those who have fallen short of the portico of praise." The author's meaning seems to be that for awhile he thought he had come to see what was "the chief end of man," *viz.*, to do his best in the situation in which he might be placed. This cheered him in spite of the path's being long and hard, but suddenly, a fresh difficulty presented itself, for he recognized that the praise of God which perhaps, we should call Theology and which the author regarded as man's prime care. Cf. the Shorter Catechism—"man's chief end is to glorify God and to enjoy him for ever" did not consist in either of the two following things;

1. Attempting to comprehend the inscrutable.

2. Much speaking about His bounties, hoping thereby to win God's favour and to have glory of men.

Nor again was it right to abandon the study of Theology as beyond our powers, and devote our energies to the improvement of our own miserable selves, even if such endeavour were after moral as well as material advancement. No! true Theology or Divine worship consisted in renouncing the attempt either to fathom the Divine mysteries or to recount His benefits and to take refuge in acknowledgment of our baseness and impotence. The author's view, in short, is that expressed in the parable of the Pharisee and the Publican, of which perhaps, he may have heard from his friend Aquaviva. These reflections led him to see that he must strive after worshipping God, though in a different fashion from that of the theologians, and eventually he found rest in the discovery that the highest form of Doxology was to record the achievements,—spiritual and temporal—of that Divine master-piece, the

porch of thanksgiving; nor should we style self-culture[1] the recital of the Divine praise, and growing weary-hearted[2] at the darkness of the road and the distance of the goal, regard such self-deception as a gain, and with abandonment of thanksgiving, set about whatever the cheatery of the hour represent as our true aim.

4 Rather the *note* of Praise is to lay this praise-loving, self-adorning, self-auctioning spirit[3] on the threshold of service, at the base of supplication and humiliation and to cast it down from the *arch*[4] of

---

Emperor Akbar. Unfortunately we may say of Abū-l-fazl what has been predicated of the poet Young—that he never gets hold of a thought that he does not tear it to pieces.

As the passage is difficult, I give Chalmers' translation below :—

"For the meaning of the giving "praise to the Almighty is neither "that we should inquire into the "qualities of His perfection and then "apply them to His Majesty—nor "that we should reckon up the "endless bounties of Eternity and "then offer up in return for them, "the fabricated wares of our own "commendations ; nor should we "suppose them too excellent for "human ken and thus despair of "reaching the portico of gratitude; "nor should we denominate the adorn-"ment of ourselves, the recital of "God's praises ; nor become sorrow-"ful of heart from the dimness of the "path and the delicacy of the under-"taking, and seizing the opportunity "of empty excuses, refrain from "shewing forth His praises by com-"mencing with the evasion which "may appear most plausible for the "purpose. But rather the true "intent of God's praise is this ;— "that our grateful soul should place "self-conceit and self-boasting on "the threshold of obedience at the "footstool of submission and devo-"tion, and thus expel them from the "palace of self-interest ; so that our "real helplessness may be decked "with the semblance of piety and our "inward and outward man may be "adorned with humility and poverty "which will thus suit the seemliness "of the breast of our purpose and "tend towards the praise of the "bounteous Creator of the Universe." Chalmers' MS. I. 7.)

1 *Khweshtan-arāī-i-khudrā.* I think this means self-improvement, rather than self-glorification. It refers, as No. 564 remarks, to the endeavours after a better life mentioned above. It may, however, mean self-advancement, *i.e.*, striving to "get on" without thinking of anything higher.

2 *Afgār-khāṭir, lit.* cripple-hearted, thus keeping up the metaphor of an exhausted wayfarer.

3 نفس سپاس, *nafs-i-sipās. Nafs* has many meanings but is generally rendered *spirit* or *breath.* Here perhaps, it means something more material and might almost be translated *body*; else how can the author speak of its being flung down, etc.?

4 طاق, *tāqt*, arch or archway, also alcove. *Tāqi-naẓr* appears to be a

self-consciousness and self-regard, so that its inward poverty may be adorned by outward submissiveness, and its inner and outer nature be decked with humility and lowliness till fitness[1] grace the bosom of purpose and be turned into praise of the Omnipotent Creator.

Now as such wares[2] of thanksgiving are abundant in the booths of men and are especially plentiful in my own stall, why do I withhold myself from Divine praise and why do I delay to laud the Eternal One? Under any circumstances, it is better for me to escape from this deceiving misery of self-pleasing and to address myself to the heights of lofty thanksgiving.

I was a long time in perplexity, having neither ability to speak nor power to remain silent, when suddenly a door of light was opened by the intellect, that glory of life, and my confused heart found the neck of hope fitted with the noose of resolution. This message came to the ear of guidance, "Artist in Truth's picture "gallery! dost thou not compose a book whose frontispiece thou "mayest adorn with praise? Thou art inditing the history of the "Lord of time and the terrene (*zamīn ū zamān*) and Crown-jewel of "monarchs, and praise to God will come into the writing, and thanks-"giving to the Almighty be part of the picture! praise of praise is "not right; the works of the Artificer are the perfect praise of the "pure God and acknowledge[3] him with a tongueless tongue."

"They (the works of creation) by conferring this knowledge, "grant to the soul-awakened and inwardly-cultured, possession of "Light absolute and bring them into the vast shadow of praise which "together with its delights, is the highest dignity (*mansab*) of celes-"tial existences."[4]

---

poetical phrase for the eye, *viz.*, the arch of sight.

[1] I omit the *iẓāfat* after *shaistagī*. If this be retained, the translation will be "until" (or "and") "it be fitted to the fitness of the bosom of its purpose."

[2] متاع سپاس, *matā'-i-sipās*, merchandise of praise. I suppose that this praise, like the *matā'-i-sitūdagī* on the previous page, must mean *words*, of which the author had no doubt a great stock.

[3] *Cf.* Addison's hymn.

[4] وجوب وجود, *wajūb-i-wajūd*, necessary existences. The reference is to the glorified spirits of saints and prophets. *Cf.* a passage in the letter to Shāh 'Abbās, already mentioned; *ẓall mahāmid kibriyā khudāwandī*, the shadow of the laudable qualities of the Almighty.

"Now[1] it is manifest that no nobler impress or sublimer jewel "is to be seen in the material world,[2] than the exalted presence of "powerful princes who by their holy energy, regulate the outer world "and knit it together. And assuredly, to make over a world to one "man and to consign to him the momentous affairs of a universe is "to incorporate in him the world of reality, or rather to make him its "soul. Especially if he be a world-adorner seized with the desire "of inhaling the fragrant breezes of Truth's spring-time and is seated "on the lofty throne of felicity. Still more if he be the Lord of "an Age who in addition to these two[3] endowments, has a heart "and mind fed from a hidden fountain. Above all, if he be that "altar of the pious who by the Divine aid, has risen above these
5 "degrees and has become colourist of the House of Truth, banquet-"illuminator of the Hall of Realities, confidant of the Presence "Chamber, intimate of the pure palace of unity, and is by auspicious "fate seated on the throne of fortune. Sway over the outer and inner "world and unravelment of knots, both spiritual and temporal, are "conspicuous in him. Therefore is he the adorner of the imperial "throne; the uplifter of the banner of God's shadow in our happy "age; aggregation of the artists of thought and wisdom, or rather "master-piece of the eternal artificers. With such vast stores of true "praise in thy keeping, why remainest thou distraught in search?"

On hearing this soul-refreshing message, the morning breeze of felicity arose; the stock of eternal bliss was collected; the eye of hope grew bright; the outer world became current coin; the inner world exulted; the skirt of success fell into my hand; the wished-for countenance came in sight.

Good God! What a strange mystery it is that in historical

---

1 The line of thought seems to be, that the works of the Creator are His highest panegyric and that the greatest of these works on earth is a king, consequently the description of a great king is the highest form of Divine praise. Evidently A. F. would not have agreed with Pope as to what was the noblest work of God.

2 عالم عنصر, *'ālam-i-unsur*, the elemential world, *i.e.*, the world made up of the four elements. The meaning is that even in the world of matter, there is no gem so precious as a king, much grander then is one who is not only a king but a saint, etc.

3 "Meaning love of truth and good fortune; the latter being considered a virtue of no mean order in the East." (Chalmers MS. n.)

writings, praise of the pure Giver is introduced as an adornment to the book, whereas here, the book is adorned in order to the praise of the Creator. In the pages of secularists, praise comes in as ancillary to the design of the book, but in this glorious history, the design is subservient to the praise. According to the old method, God's praise was effected by utterance; in this new rendezvous on Reason's highway, action is praise. My predecessors relied on speech for God's praise; in this exordium of rare writing, recourse is had to the perfect man[1] who is a God-worshipping king, *viz.*, that Lord of the World who, by virtue of his God-seeking and God-apprehending, has removed the veil from between the external and the internal and has established love between the sections of the recluse and the layman[2] and has lifted up the curtain from in front[3] of the apparent and the real.

Heedlessness which used to travel on the opposite road to discretion, has retraced his steps and become one of wisdom's servants. Formalism[4] which had left the regions of inquiry and was stirring up tumults, has now thrown inquiry's scarf on his shoulder and become a minister at the shrine. Blind self-worship which had abandoned the worship of God and adopted the worship of the creature, has now got eyes to see with and has come, ashamed and downcast, to the temple of divine worship.

Blear-eyed envy which had megrim[5] in the head and madness in the brain, and used to strive against the Allwise Lawgiver, has now got wisdom for his guide, and, having become enrolled as one of the pardoned of the shrine of grace,[6] has been ranked among the helpers of the kingdom. Painful longing—the health, indeed,

---

1 *Lit.* lords of abstraction (or nakedness) and masters of connexion.

2 Chalmers has, "from between the fleshly and the spiritual" and this may be the meaning, but the expression is "in front of both."

3 انسان كامل, *insān-i-kāmil*. This is a Sufistic phrase and is explained by Jorjānī. (*Notices et Extraits* X. 386, Silvestre de Saçy.) The phrase *perfect man* does not mean simply an impeccable person, in which sense the expression was used, I believe, by Whitfield. It rather means the essence or highest type of humanity. It is also explained as meaning the first intelligence, or,—in Arabic phrase,—the mother of the book. De Saçy says "L'homme parfait est la même chose que la première intelligence." (See also Badāonī, Lowe 266).

4 تقليد, *taqlīd*, imitation and also hypocrisy and superstition.

5 ماخوليا, *mā<u>kh</u>oliyā*, i.e., the Greek μελαγχολία.

6 عطية, *'atīyat*, gift or beneficence.

of Eternity—from being cripple has become a courier, and appears both as the runner and the winning-post. And why should this not be when we have, in this enlightened age, the chamber-lamp of the universe, the glory of Adam's race, the unveiler of hidden secrets, the revealer of faultless forms? Or how should these things appear strange in the eyes of the far-seeing and wise, when he is (at once) composer (*nāẓim*) of the institutes of sovereignty, distributor[1] of the riches of the servants of God, hairsplitting discerner of microscopic subtleties, the great lapidary and assaymaster?

So long as the spiritual supremacy over the recluse which is called Holiness and the sway over laymen which is called Sovereignty, were distinct, there was strife and confusion among the children
6 of Noah[2] (mankind). Now that in virtue of his exaltation, foresight, comprehensive wisdom, universal benevolence, pervading discernment and perfect knowledge of God, these two great offices (*manṣab*) which are the guiding thread of the spiritual and temporal worlds, have been conferred on the opener of the hoards of wisdom and claviger of Divine treasuries, a small portion at least,—if his holy nature grant the necessary faculty,—may be brought from the ambush of concealment to the asylum of publicity. Knowest thou at all who is this world-girdling luminary and radiant spirit? Or whose august advent has bestowed this grace? 'Tis he who by virtue of his enlightenment and truth, is the world-protecting[3]

---

[1] The meaning is not that Akbar was the almoner of God's servants, in which respect he was indeed, according to Badāonī, very deficient, but that he revealed spiritual mysteries as well as made rules for temporal administration. The word, *qāsim*, *lit.* divider, reminds us of St. Paul's phrase "rightly dividing the word of truth." In this group of four epithets, the first and the third relate apparently, to temporal matters and the second and fourth, to spiritual.

[2] Noah is called by Muhammadans, the second Adam.

[3] A. F.'s panegyric on Akbar is an extraordinary production, according to our western ideas. Probably, however, it was thought very fine by his countrymen. The original is full of *paronomasia* and parallellisms and these, as also the alliterations and cadenced clauses, make the Persian sound much better than the translation. The composition must have cost the author immense labour, though apparently, the task was not entirely his own, for in Faiẓī's preface to his *Diwān* we find the epithets here bestowed on Akbar, from *muqarrab* down to *'ālamjān ū jān 'ālam*, *i.e.*, for about eight lines of the text, and nearly in the same order.

sovereign of our age, to wit, that Lord (*Shāhanshāh*) of the hosts of sciences,—theatre of God's power,—station of infinite bounties,—unique of the eternal temple,—confidant[1] of the daïs of unity,—jewel of the imperial mine,—bezel of God's signet-ring,—glory of the *Gūrgān*[2] family,—lamp of the tribe of Timur,[3]—lord of incomparable mystery,—heir of Humāyūn's throne,—origin[4] of the canons of world-government,—author of universal conquest,—shining forehead of the morning of guidance,—focus[5] of the sun of holiness,—sublime[6] concentration of humanity,—heir-apparent of the sun,—anthology of the books of fate and destiny,—protagonist of triumphant armies,—quintessence of the commingling of nights and days,—cream of the progeny of the elements[7] and the heavenly bodies,—world's eye (sun) of benevolence and bounty,—cheek-mole

---

In the *Fundgrüben des Orients* (II. 271), may be found an interesting experiment, made by Joseph von Hammer, at preserving the oriental cadences in a German translation of the Turkish *Humāyūn-nāma*.

1 مقرّب, *muqarrab*, said to be from the same root as *cherub* and to mean, like it, one who is admitted or near to God's presence but the preferable opinion is that *cherub* is derived from the Chaldī and means the winged man-bull.

2 *Gūrgān* is said to mean son-in-law or near relation in Mongolian; (Blochmann 460*n*.) it was a title taken by Tīmūr to indicate his connection with the house of Cingīz Khān. (Sédillot, "*Materiaux*," 261, and Hyde's preface to Ulugh Beg's Tables, IV.)

3 *Ṣāḥib-i-qirān*, lord of conjunction;—a name given to Tīmūr, apparently because the planets (? Jupiter and Venus) were in conjunction at his birth, but Hyde says it merely means *dominus potentiae*. The three successive epithets are used in order to indicate that Akbar was, first, the glory of the house of Cingīz Khān; second, the lamp of the house of Timur; third, the heir of Humāyūn; and they lead up to a description of what he was in himself.

4 The Bib. Ind. ed. omits this phrase, but it occurs in Lucknow ed. and in No. 564 and is evidently genuine, for otherwise a paronomasia or cadence would be lost. The Persian is مبدع قوانين جهانباني, *mubdi' qawānīn-i-jahānbānī* and it rhymes with the next clause which is مخترع قواعد كشور ستاني, *mukhtari' qawā'id kishwar sitānī*.

5 *Lit.* eye-pupil.

6 Perhaps, harmonious blend of humanity. Maulvi A. Haq Abīd tells me it may also mean "exalting the offspring of Adam" or "elevating human nature." The original is *garāmī sāz-i-guhar-i-adam*.

7 The elements are called the earthly mothers, and the planets, the heavenly fathers.

of sovereignty and fortune,—back-bone[1] of the frame of the *Khilāfat*,[2]—bosom-joy of justice and mercy,—brightener (*farūzanda*) of the jewel of fortune and felicity,—exalter (*farāzanda*) of the throne and crown,—connoisseur of the gem of the wise,—appreciator of the pearl of lofty genius,—opening[3] the knots of those trammeled in business,—balm of ulcerated hearts,—clear-thoughted stoic,[4]—world-adorning life-giver,—a pictured soul and incarnate reason,—world of life and life of world,—enlightened truth-seër—lover of the way,—truth-chooser,—of discreet gait and constant intelligence,—wakeful occupant of the throne of morning,—sole tenant of light's *adytum*,—illuminating the Presence Chamber,—knowing the boundaries of the paths,—achiever of universal[5] peace,—site of wondrous gifts,—grandmaster of the grades of sanctity,—initiated in the mysteries of light[6] and darkness,—theatre of Divine and secular truths,—perceiver of the links between the visible[7] and invisible worlds,—knowing secrets, spiritual and temporal,—fountain for those athirst for the sweet waters of communion,—goal of the strayed from the path of perfection,—theatre of refined subtleties and exalted sciences,—resting place of infused knowledge and inspired mysteries,—adorning the travelling litter[8] while in his native land,—light of retirement in

---

[1] *Lit.* strength of the back. It is opposed to the next epithet which refers to the *ṣadr*, breast or bosom.

[2] *i.e.*, the being God's vicegerent.

[3] *i.e.*, solving their difficulties. A. F. applies this phrase to Faiẓī. (*Akbarnāma* III. 673), saying that those who were entangled in intricacies of business, were broken-hearted at Faiẓī's death because there was no longer anyone to explain their difficulties.

[4] *Ṣāḥib-dil*, which is often used to mean a Sufi: *lit.* master of one's heart or passions.

[5] *Ṣulḥ-i-kull.* The state of being at peace with every one, which A. F. regarded as the perfection of virtue. Cf. Hebrews XII. 14. "Follow after peace with all men."

[6] The Lucknow editor renders this "day and night;" Chalmers has, "acquainted with the mysteries of good and evil." A similar phrase, *viz.*, *nuktadān-i-ramūz safīdī ū siyāhī* —occurs in the *Inshā'*. (Part I, beginning of letter to Ḥakīm Hamām.)

[7] تقیدی و اطلاقی, *taqīdī ū iṭlāqī*, fixity and freedom,—meaning the temporal and spiritual world. *Āīn* III. 246. 1.10.

[8] The Bib. Ind. and Lucknow eds. have *maḥfal ārāī*, ornament of the assemblage, but No. 564 has *maḥmil*, camel-litter, and so had Chalmers' MS. This epithet and the next are repeated in the *Āīn* (III. 249) and are translated by Jarrett (III. 406) "who prepares the litters

society,—apprehending quickly,—retaining long,—giving much, getting little,—pilot of the ship[1] of the universe,—ark[1] of the boundless ocean,—keen-sighted guardian of degrees of honour,—subtle distributor of dignities,—of fortunate genius and auspicious glance,—of happy horoscope and exalted star,—bearer of heavy burdens,—brilliant master of lofty understanding,—ornament of wisdom,—cherisher of the wise,—world-adorning conqueror,—supporting friends,—scattering foes,—binding enemies,—opening countries, —exalter[2] of the thrones of majesty and awe,—uplifter of the cushions of pomp and prosperity,—warder of faith and state,—protector of throne and signet,—beautifier of the seven climes,—adorner of throne and diadem,—rank-breaking royal cavalier,[3]—tiger-throwing falcon,—champion of the battle-field of the Holy War,[4]—combatant stalking over the seven worlds,—bulwark builder

---

of travel while yet abiding in his native land,—a lamp for those who gather in privacy." In a note to the first epithet, Colonel Jarrett adds; "that is, preparing for the world to come while yet in this, or facilitating the salvation of others."

A. F. is never tired of insisting on the dualism of Akbar's nature, and his meaning here seems to be that Akbar had all the graces of a pilgrim while yet in his native land, and that he had the virtues of a hermit while still mingling with society. There can be no doubt that *maḥmil* is the right reading, for *maḥfal* can have nothing to do with travel. I find too, that it is *maḥmil* in the B. M. MSS. Or. Nos. 5610 and 6544.

1 The Persian word is *safīna* in both cases, but I take the second use of the epithet to refer to Noah's ark. However, *safīna* can also mean a memorandum book and this may be its sense in the first clause. In that case *dīdahbān* would signify *inspector* and the phrase be rendered "Inspector of the book of the universe."

2 ساعد, *ṣā'ad* from صعد, *ṣ'ad*. Chalmers seems to have read ساعد, *sā'ad* arm, for he translates "bracelet of the arm of magnificence and glory." ساعد is also a Sufistic expression for power generally. See Dic. of T. Ts., 640 l.4 fr. foot.

3 In *Āīn* No. 47 (Book I. Blochmann, 131) Akbar is called the "royal rider (*shāhsawār*) of the plain of auspiciousness." See also A. F.'s explanation of the word *shāhsawār* in his preface to the *Āīn*. (Blochmann ii.)

4 جهاد اکبر, *Jihād-i-akbar*, the Greater Holy War, *viz.*, that against one's lusts; the Crescentade or war against infidels being the *Jihād-i-asghar* or Lesser War. In the A. S. B. Per. MSS. Catalogue (170) there are entries of two treatises, one on the *Jihād-i-akbar* and the other on the *Jihād-i-asghar*. Cf. Bunyan's "Holy War" and Bābar's Mem., Erskine, 356, l.2.

of sovereignty and dominion,—base of the columns of instruction and discipline,—holding fast the strong handle of perfect reason,—riveter of the massy chain of universal justice,—all eye[1] in the
7 banquet-hall,—all heart in the battle-field,—in the joyous festival a refreshing cloud,[2]—in the triumphant battle, a blood-drinking sea,—in the fields of bravery, an unsheathed sword,—in the tournament, a polished lance,—a billowy ocean in the world of giving,—a lightning-darting cloud[3] in battle,—his breath, a swaying censer at the soul's feast,—his pleasantness, the waving fan of opening morn,—his justice, equable as *Farwardīn*[4] and of minute discernment,—his temper is like the zephyr of *Ardibihis̲h̲t*[5] and runs over with smiles,[6]—his nature is experienced and disciplined in the solution of problems,—his flawless intellect is a trusty counsellor in the explication of difficulties,—externally his splendour is that of Jams̲h̲īd,[7] and his glory that of Farīdūn,[8]—internally he is Socrates in wisdom, Plato in perception,—he is trained inwardly and outwardly,—his eye and heart are sources of liberality,—he has harmonized tongue and heart, and has made unity[9] partner with plurality,—his vigilance watches over appetite,—his genius treads lust under foot.—his fair-dealing

---

1 *Lit.* in the face of the banqueting room, all eye (or glance); in the heart of the battle-field, all liver (pluck.) *Dar rū-i-bazamgāh tamām naẓr, dar dil-ī-razmgāh tamām jigar.*

2 *Lit.* ocean-raining.

3 *Naisān*, a Syrian month, corresponding to April, and being the 7th month of the Syro-Macedonian Calendar, *i.e.*, Greek Era of A. F. It is the *Nisān* or *Abib* of the Jews and the first month of their sacred year, being that of the Passover. There is a saying that when the rain of the month of *Naisān* drops into shells, it produces pearls, and when it falls into the mouths of serpents, it produces poison. See Whinfield's *Guls̲h̲an-i-rāz* (57).

4 The first month of the Persian year, corresponding to March-April. It begins with the vernal equinox and hence, perhaps, the allusion to its equability.

5 The second month of the Persian year, corresponding to April-May.

6 Alluding to the sheet-lightnings of spring.

7 An early Persian king, celebrated for his cup or mirror (*jām*) which showed the world.

8 Another early Persian king, son or grandson of Jamshīd and said to have been the first tamer of elephants.

9 *i.e.*, has reconciled solitude and society. See opening of the *Gulshan-i-rāz*, l.27. *Cf.* also the Wisdom of Solomon, VII, 22, "Alone in kind, manifold."

has overturned the petty stalls of fraud and deception,—the touchstone[1] of his wisdom has separated the gold-encrusted lump[2] from the solid gold.

He rends the garment of contumacy[3] which wraps the faces of debts,[4] but draws the mantle of forgiveness over the heads of transgressions; the splendour of power streams from the brow of his benevolence; the lightning of benignity draws lambent[5] lights from the fires of his wrath. His fury melts adamantine boldness; his dread turns to water the courage of the iron-souled; the shrinking

---

[1] *'Ayār-dānish,* test of wisdom. This is the title of A. F.'s translation of the *Kalīlah Damnah* or rather of his revision of the *Anwāri Suhailī.* (Blochmann, 106 and S. de Saçy, "*Notices et Extraits,*" X. 197). There is here probably an allusion to *Āīn* No. 5 (Blochmann, Book I. 18), where we are told that Akbar had invented modes of purifying gold.

[2] *Qalb-i-sar-andūd az sar-i-gohar-āmūd.* The text has an *ū* after the second *sar* which would be better away and which does not occur in No. 564.

[3] تجبر, *tajabbur.* The word also means restitution or restoration of property, and we might give this meaning here and interpret the phrase to signify that Akbar releases debtors from the obligation of restitution which lies like a veil over their faces. But I think that the translation *contumacy* is right and that there is an antithesis between this and the following clause. A. F. means that Akbar compelled the contumacious to fulfil their obligations, *i.e.,* made them pay their fines, taxes, compensations for injuries and other debts but that, at the same time, he was forgiving to offenders. See *Āīn* No. 2 (Blochmann, Book II. 13). with the account of the distinction between exchequer-lands and fiefs, See also *Āīn* No. 19 (Blochmann Book II., 268).

[4] غرايم, *fines* or *mulcts* or *debts.* There are two *āīns* devoted to the subject of fines, *viz.,* Nos. 48 and 57 (Blochmann, Book I. 131 and 140) one being headed غرامت and the other تاوان. No. 564 explains the word غرايم by تاوان. Even grandees were fined and for certain offences elephant-drivers were liable to capital punishment. See Blochmann's note to *Āīn* No. 83 (217). For *tajabbur,* the B. M. MS. Or. No. 6544 has تحرير, writing, and Chalmers' MS. seems to have had this reading for he translates, "He tears the screen "of writing from the face of his "intent." Apparently, as Mr. Beames has suggested to me, Chalmers read عزايم *'azāīm,* intentions, instead of غرايم *gharāīm.*

[5] *Lit. tongues of light.* The two clauses are opposed; in spite of his benevolence, he is terrible; in spite of his wrath, he is lovely. Orientals regard lightning as an object of beauty rather than of terror.

of the age is the impress of the wrinkling of his brows; its expansion the reflex of his nature's blossoming.

Prayers for his permanence have stationed themselves on the tongue of small and great; love and belief in him repose in the hearts of young and old; the loftiness of his fame has lowered the glory of local magnates; the majesty of his dominion has put away the rulers of the quarters of the world; the echo of his fortune has opened the ears of the princes of the horizons; the ensign[1] of his glory has lifted up the eyes of provincial kings;[2] his mighty fame has mingled with the spheres; the sound of his glory has passed from shore to shore; the proclamation of his bounty has transgressed the boundaries of the world;[3] his glorious court has become the native land of the elect of the seven climes; his daily increasing dominion has become the masterpiece of epochs and cycles; his glorious ascension, the auspicious frontispiece of stars and planets.

VERSE.

That King of Kings, prop of the sky !
The umbrella of his fortune is the sky's shadow;
Adorning the garden-plot of wisdom and knowledge;
Exalting the throne and the diadem;—
The seat of his power is rich in liberality;
His fortune's shape has an open brow;
His presence is the truth-seekers' cynosure;
His pity a fountain-head for the thirsty;
By a single thought,[4] he has placed under foot

---

1 کوکبه, *kaukaba*, a steel ball suspended to a pole and carried as an ensign. (Blochmann, 50.)

2 *Mulūk-i-ṭawā'if*, tribal kings. It might be rendered kings of the Gentiles and was the name given to the satraps, established by Alexander and Tīmūr. (Albīrūnī's "Chronicle of Ancient Nations." Sachau, 116 and 401. Mas'ūdī, II. 132, Meynard et P. de Courteille). Cf. Isaiah, XIV., 9.

3 اقصاء شش جهة, *aqṣā'i shash jihat*; *lit.* the six sides of the surface, meaning the six sides of a cube, *i.e.*, the world. The regular Arabic expression for this appears to be مسدس عالم, *mussadasi 'ālam*, the six sides of the world, *viz.*, up and down, fore and aft, right and left. (Steingass, *s. v.*). The world is also called ششدری *shashdarī*, six-doored.

4 Or it may be, "He has placed under the foot of unanimity." The meaning is that he has united sovereignty and sanctity.

The royal divan and the dervish's carpet.
The nine heavens revolve for his purpose;
The seven stars[1] travel for his work;
By wisdom, he is the age's provider;
By vigilance, the world's watchman;
His love and his hate, in the banquet and the battle,
Are brimming cups of wine and blood;
The *khāqān*[2] fears his wrath; 8
Cæsar[3] is disturbed at his frown;
Heaven in glory, Earth in stability;[4]
Lord of universal reason,[5] *Jalālu-d-dīn.*[6]
Essence of sunlight and shadow of God,
Pearl of crown and throne is Akbar Shāh.
May this old world be renewed by him!
May his star be the sun's rays!

This empty-handed one, who, from lack of the capital of praise, had neither room to sit nor a leg to stand upon, became, through the above excellent idea and firm resolve, a treasury full of the Creator's praise; a marvellous treasury,—for its store increased by expenditure and diminished by hoarding. By force of sincerity, I became an alchemist, and enriched my poverty-stricken soul. I put forth the arm of fortune aud opened the door of the treasury. I was fortunate, I became rich. I was fluent, I became eulogistic. I crossed the threshold of allegory and opened the door of truth. I was simple, I became acute. The door of success which was shut in front of me, was divinely opened. My dejection became exalta-

---

1 *i.e.*, the five planets, Mercury, Venus, Mars, Jupiter and Saturn,—and the Sun and Moon. There is a similar passage in the *Āīn* (III. 249, 1.12).

2 Great Khān, the name given to the ruler of Chinese Tartary or of China.

3 The two titles stand for the rulers of the East and West. Turkish kings, *e.g.* Bāyazīd Ilderim, were styled *Qaisar-i-rūm* even before the capture of Constantinople. The lines are perhaps Faiẓī's. *Cf.* his *Nal Daman*. Bombay, 1831, p. 30. The literal rendering of the lines is "The *khāqān* dreads the heat of his sweat; Cæsar is disturbed at the fold of his brow."

4 A. F. did not know of the Copernican theory.

5 *'Aql-i-kull*, the phrase used by Sufis to express the *Logos* or first emanation from God.

6 One of Akbar's names, "the glory of faith."

tion; my inaction, flowing activity; my speechlessness, effective speech. I was taken from the public entrance to the royal apartments; a fluent tongue was granted to me, the tongueless one, and the right of speech was conceded to me.

I wished that before entering on my subject,—as it has been the usage of former writers of all nations to embellish the preambles[1] of their books (after praises of God) with general or special salutations to those great saints and masters of the divine mysteries who, after lighting up the lamp of guidance and effusion in the world's dark chamber, have gone down to the grave;—I too, might so adorn this collection of Divine praise and gratify my heart by saluting that Company which from its eminence and knowledge of God, occupies the intellectual fore-court of this humble individual. But inasmuch as this one who has left the path of semblance and followed after truth, is aware that if a distracted one should, on finding his way into the royal court, utter encomia on the field-marshals or wish by his intervention, to make the favour of the Lord of the Age fall upon the Prime Minister,[2] he would but prove his own folly and madness.

What strength has Sahā[3] to praise the shining Moon to the

---

[1] عنوان, *'anwān*, title-page or frontispiece.

[2] بگلر بیگي *baglarbegī*, a Turkish title meaning Bey of Beys, *i.e.*, Chief of Chiefs. Apparently it should be بگي *bagī* and not *begī*. It corresponds to *Āmīru-l-umarā* and was a title given to the Governor General of Rumelia and Anatolia and also to any Generalissimo. See Zenker's Turkish Dictionary.

[3] Sahā or Suhā is an obscure star in the Great Bear and used as a test of eyesight. It is also called الصدق, Al Ṣadiq. (Lane's Arabic Dictionary 1456*a*). Sahā and Suhail (Canopus) are often contrasted and apparently, this is not from their difference in brightness only, but also from their difference in position,—the one being a northern and the other a southern star. Sahā is also contrasted with the Sun. See *Anwārī Suhailī* (Hertford Introduction, 21,) Sahā is catalogued as "No. 80 by Zeta," which is the second star in the tail of the Great Bear and is called by the Arabs *El 'Anaq*, the Goat. Golius and others have wrongly described Sahā as being the southernmost star of the quadrilateral. Sahā is apparently called also Alcor. The name Sahā is said to come from *saho*, forgotten, but according to Albīrūnī (India. Sachau I. 389) Al Sahā was a pious woman who was a companion of the seven *Rishis*.

The Germans call Sahā, the *Reuter*, Cavalier, because, I suppose, he seems to ride on the second horse of the team of Charles' Wain. See Hyde's *Syntagma* I. 15 and Ideler's *Untersuchungen*, Berlin, 1809, 292 and 422.

glorious Sun? It is sufficient honour and glory to describe itself
in that Presence as an insignificant atom. In that Presence where
the favoured magnates of the Court to whom the power of recom-
mending a tiny ant has not been vouchsafed, have not received
permission to express their wishes, how can it be proper for one
who, like myself, is remaining on the threshold and is without right
of access, to solicit grace and favour for the chosen courtiers and to
ask pardon and paradise[1] for them. If he should, from inconsidera-
tion, lengthen the tongue of boldness, by what name would he be
called in the justice-hall of discernment, and what reproach would he
not receive from the Inquisitor of Justice? I therefore gave up
that idea and made myself ready, so that, if my abilities permitted
and the Divine aid were vouchsafed to me, I might reduce to writing
the auspicious description of the King of manifestation and reality,—
the leader of religion and realm (*dīn ū dunyā*),—and might bring
together his beautiful[2] and awful attributes and the praises of his
majesty and perfection; to wit,—the marvellous festivals, wondrous 9
wars, exalted devotions, and pleasant ways of this chosen one of
God, without the disagreeable admixtures of poetical[3] prose writers.
So that I might acquit myself of my duties of (1) worship, (2) loyalty,
(3) gratitude, and might also establish a claim to the regard of new-
comers to the world and of future travellers by life's caravans.

Though each one of those four points[4] was a powerful motive

[1] رضوان, *riẓwān*, the gate-keeper of Paradise and also Paradise itself. It also means blessing or benediction and may do so here.

[2] *Ṣifāt-i-jamāl ū jalāl*, in Sufistic language, the beautiful and the awful attributes.

[3] A. F. says, that on the fifth revision of his work, he inserted some couplets because good writers regard the admixture of verse as the salt (*lit. salt-cellar*) of prose. (Jarrett III. 415). He may also have been influenced by Akbar's remark that whoever introduced the verses of another into his writings or recited them aptly, displayed both his own merit and that of the author. (Jarrett III. 386). Perhaps the above passage was written before the thought occurred to him, and was retained because it meant that he would not interlard his prose with poetry in the manner of some previous writers of history, *e.g.*, 'Abdu-l-lāh (Waṣṣāf) who is even more rhetorical than A. F. There may also be a reference to the author of the *Ẓafarnāma* who has many bad verses.

[4] Chalmers, the Lucknow ed. and No. 564 substantially unite in saying that the four things or points are: 1. Akbar's beautiful and awful

for entering upon this great task, yet, as my aim was lofty and ability small, success was not attained nor my desire achieved until this light shone on the antechamber of my truth-reflecting heart; to wit—"In this noble enterprise, at the same time that you discharge your duty to the creature, you are also fulfilling your obligations to the Creator. While you are paying your devoirs of respect and gratitude, you are in reality, steadfastly engaged in praising God, the Creator of the world." Day by day, my purpose was growing confirmed and the materials of success were being collected, until at length, out of general good-will to the partakers of his felicity and from special favour to me, his charmed one,[1] a ray of intimation from the court of liberality reached this—as regards his sincerity,—forerunner on the highway of lo but—as regards attainment[2] of desires,—hindermost (member) the caravans of

attributes; 2. praise of his majesty and perfection; 3. his feasts and his wars; 4. his holiness and pleasant ways. But this seems wrong and to be partially occasioned by an erroneous reading. The text and one or two MSS. have *tā ḥaqq-i-'abūdīyat ū irādat-i-walī ni'mat guẕārda bāshām*. But nearly all the MSS. have *irādat ū ni'mat*, missing out the *walī* and this appears the true reading. We thus have three duties or points, *viz.*, worship, loyalty and gratitude which with the duty to posterity, make up the four points. The text, however, may be correct and the points be made up by regarding the "newcomers" and posterity as two distinct classes. The word *ḥaqqī* in the phrase *ū ham ḥaqqī bar nūrasān*, probably has two meanings, *viz.*, duty towards posterity and the establishment of a claim by the author to the gratitude of posterity. The phrase *ḥaqqī ṣābit gardānīda* is evidently used in antithesis to the *ḥaqq guẕārda*. Chalmers renders the passage "establish rectitude in the tender saplings of mortality and in the travellers of the caravans of existence." All these, however, were only duties towards or rights of the creature and so not sufficient to excite our author till he saw that in performing them, he would also be doing his duty to his Creator.

[1] *In naẓarkarda-i-khud, lit.* this one upon whom his glance had fallen, *i.e.*, his gazed one, protégé or client. See *Āīn* I. 24, for use of *naẓarkarda*, A. F. (*Akbarnāma* III. 114) describes how the glamour of Akbar's glance fell upon him in the mosque at Fatḥpūr Sikrī. *Cf.* Old English "overlooked."

[2] Perhaps, *the grandeur of his aspirations*, عزّ مراد *'izz-i-murād*. The meaning may be that his works did not equal his faith, *i.e.*, that the spirit was willing but the flesh weak.

felicity; and to Abu-l-faẓl, son of Mubārak, upon the crown[1] of whose heart is the quadripartite cap[2] of discipleship and whose seven times embroidered sleeve[3] of devotion is celebrated throughout the eighteen thousand creations, this sublime mandate was given. "Write with the pen of sincerity the account of the glorious events

---

1 "*Tārak,* properly the crown of the head." Blochmann 549*n*. It is used here for the sake of the assonance with *tark*.

2 كلاه چهار ترکی, *kulāh-i-cahār-tarkī*, the four-segmented cap. The reference seems to be to the symbolical caps worn by dervishes ("The Dervishes." J. P. Brown. Trübner, 1868, pp. 53, 88, 148). Speaking of the order of "*Bektashees,*" Mr. Brown says (148) "*Tāj* is the "name of the cap which all wear "in common. It is made of white "felt and is in four parts. The first "shows that the wearer has given up "the world; the second that he has "abandoned all hopes of Paradise; "the third that he disdains all hypo- "crisy and (it) means that the der- "vish cares not whether he is seen or "not, praying, and is wholly indiffer- "ent to public opinion; the fourth is "the total abandonment of all the "pleasures of life and that he belongs "to and is fully satisfied with Allah "alone. Their names also are *She- "ree'at, Tareekat, Hakeekat* and *Ma'ri- "fat.*" *Tark* means a segment, section or gore and also a string and a helmet. The Lucknow editor says that the four *tarks* signify the four elements, but this is doubtful. *Tark* has also the sense of abandonment and dervishes mean, by their *tarks*, the abandonment of the world, etc. The sect known as the Qādirīs, wear a fourfold cap, *i.e.*, one with four *tarks*. This may signify the abandonment of this world, of the next, of respect of men and, fourthly, of every thing except God. A. F. may also be referring to the four degrees of devotion mentioned by Blochmann (A. F.'s Preface vn.) and by Badāonī (Lowe, 299 and 314) and which consisted in the surrender of four things, *viz.*, Goods, Life, Fame, Faith. Hence the appropriateness of the word *cahār-tarkī*, as this may be rendered *the four abandonments* or *surrenders*. *Irādat* too may mean desire and inclination, as well as devotion and discipleship so that the whole phrase may signify *the cap of the fourfold abandonment of desires.* It is in such many-sided expressions that the author delights.

Writing of Maulavīs, Kaempfer in his valuable work on Persian customs, "*Amœnitates Exoticæ*" says, (p. 113), "*In vestitu nil peregrini habent, nisi mitram quatuor conspicuam plicis, ex fastigio ad oram decurrentibus.*"

3 آستین هفت طراز عقیدت بر هژده هزار عالم افشانده

*Āstīn-i-haft-ṭarāz-i-'aqīdat bar hazhda hazār 'ālam afshānda, lit.*, whose seven-broidered sleeve of devotion has been shed over the 18,000 species. Seven is a mystic number and there may here be a reference to the seven valleys of the *Manṭiqu-ṭ-ṭā'ir* of Farīdu-d-dīn 'Aṭṭār. The seven broideries may mean embroidery in seven different colours and be typical

and of our dominion-increasing victories." What shall I say was the effect of this order for describing the occurrences ?[1] Did it grant permission to undertake the task by bestowing on me the necessary genius ? or did it, by a grant of felicity to my heart, appoint me the

---

of the seven *Paths*, etc. See Brown l. c. 93. *Āstīn afs̲h̲āndan* means to applaud by clapping the hands, to dance, and to scatter gifts. It also has the contrary meaning of abandoning or refusing. See Vullers and the *Burhān-i-qāṭī‘ s. v.* A. F. seems here to play upon these meanings, but his primary intention probably was to signify that he was renowned throughout the world for his devotion. Chalmers perhaps read *anis̲h̲ānda* or *nis̲h̲ānda* and translates "who was re-"nowned among the 18,000 creatures "for the seven times embroidered "sleeve of trustiness." Perhaps we might translate, "whose seven em-"broidered sleeve of loyalty has show-"ered gifts over the 18,000 species," or, without the *iẓāfat*—"Whose "seven-broidered sleeve has showered "loyalty over the 18,000 species."

It would seem that the language was originally Faiẓī's, for we find it in the preface to his translation of the *Līlāvatī* (B. M. MSS. Or. No. 5649, p. 4). It is also in the printed edition of his translation. (Calcutta 1828, p. 2). In the MS. the phrase runs thus;—

بندهٔ کمترین درگاه سعادت و ذره خاک نشین آستان ارادت فیضي که کلاه چهار ترکي اخلاص چهارگوشه با سردل مانده و آستین هفت طراز عقیدت بر هژده هزار عالم افشانده.

*Banda-i-kamtarīn-i-dargāh-i-sa‘ād-at ū ẕara k̲h̲āk-nishīn-i-āstān-i-irādat Faiẓī ki kulāh-i-cahār-tarkī-i-ik̲h̲lāṣ-i-cahār-gōs̲h̲a bar sar-i-dil mānda ū āstīn-i-haft-ṭarāz-i-‘aqīdat bar haz̲h̲da hazār ‘ālam afs̲h̲ānda.*

It should be remembered that Faiẓī projected writing an *Akbar-nāma* on the model of the *Baḥrī-sikandarnāma* of Niẓāmī and that he, apparently, had begun its composition (*Ins̲h̲ā* III). It is probable that some of A. F.'s most flowery passages are borrowed from his brother's incomplete poem.

Possibly the expression about the 18,000 species, has reference to A. F.'s oft repeated assertions that he had arrived at the state of *ṣulḥ-i-kull*, perfect peace with all men. It may be noted that the sleeve mentioned is the wide sleeve of the Oriental which may be opened out and folded over the face. The expression *sleeve of devotion* has nothing in common with Shakespeare's "ravelled sleave of care," where *sleave* means an entangled skein.

The simplest rendering of the whole passage is something like this;—"Mubārak's son, Abu-l-faẓl, "in whose heart dwell the four "Renunciations, and the praise of "whose sevenfold devotion has gone "out to the ends of the earth."

[1] I think this must be the meaning, though the phrase might mean "What shall I say? Was this a "command for me to compose the "memoirs?" as Chalmers has translated it. The objection to this rendering is that we have just been told he had received a clear order.

recorder of glorious events? or did it bestow eloquence on one rude[1] of speech? Nay! nay! it gave wings to my words and feet to my pen. It was an invisible angel, conveying from the upper world, life-giving news of joy. It was the Archangel[2] Gabriel bringing down a revelation from the antechamber of Omnipotence.

Assuredly, I spent[3] much labour and research in collecting the records and narratives of his Majesty's actions and I was a long time interrogating the servants of the State and the old members of the illustrious family.[4] I examined both prudent, truth-speaking old

---

1 أعجمي, *a'jamī*. Chalmers seems to have read عجمي, *'ajamī* and so translates *zabān-i-'ajamī*, the Persian tongue. This is also the reading of the Lucknow ed. but *a'jamī* seems to be right. A. F. speaks of his having a stammering tongue, *kaj-maj zabān*. (*Āīn* II, 254).

2 ناموس اكبر, *nāmūs-i-akbar*, lit. the chief confidant of God. (Dozy 2725*b*.) A. F. also uses this phrase to mean reason. (*Āīn* I. 13). No doubt it is used here partly for the play upon the word *Akbar*. In a Circular Order preserved in the *Inshā'* (Part I.) we have the phrase *Nāmūs-i-akbar ū qānūn-i-ā'ẓam-i-sulṭānat*.

3 See for another account of the inception of the task and of his labours, the conclusion of the *Āīn* (Jarrett, 400–417).

4 Princess Gulbadan, the sister of Hindāl, aunt of Akbar, and widow of Khiẓr Khwāja, wrote her *Memoirs* in accordance with Akbar's request and apparently as material for the *Akbarnāma* (Rieu's Catalogue I. 227*a*. and MS. Or. No. 166). Her little book, called apparently the *Humāyūnnāma*, gives interesting details about Humāyūn's marriage with Akbar's mother and deserves publication and translation. She mentions that she was eight years old when her father Bābar died.

In the India Office, there is a MS. (No. 216) called the *Tārīkh-i-humāyūn* which was composed by Akbar's orders for the use of A. F. It was dictated by Bāyazīd, who had been *Mīr Sāmān*, steward or superintendent of the kitchen, under Humāyūn to a clerk of Abu-l-faẓl at Lahor. An examination of the book does not show that the author called it the *Tārīkh-i-humāyūn*, and such a title would be inadequate. Apparently the only name given to it by the author is that of *Mukhtaṣar* (Abridgment). It is in fact a book of Memoirs and comes down to the date of writing, *viz*., 999 (1590). It begins in 949 (1542), with Humāyūn's flight to Persia, and is a personal narrative of events from that date. Many events in Akbar's reign are described, *e.g.*, the murder of Shamsu-d-dīn by Adham Khān (105 *a* and *b*) and Khwāja Muaẓẓim's murder of his wife. (105*b* and 106*a*). A valuable feature of the book is its lists of officers, especially the long one of those who accompanied Humāyūn to India. The author was Bakāwal Begī (Superintendent of the Kitchen)

men and active-minded, right-actioned young ones and reduced their statements to writing. The royal commands were issued to the provinces, that those who from old service remembered, with certainty or with adminicle of doubt, the events of the past, should copy out their notes and memoranda and transmit them to Court. Inasmuch as this auspicious invitation was not fully responded to nor my wish fully accomplished, a second command shone forth from the holy Presence-chamber; to wit—that the materials which had been collected, should be faired out and recited in the royal hearing, and that whatever might have to be written down afterwards, should be introduced into the noble volume as a supplement, and that such details as on account of the minuteness of the inquiries and the *minutiae* of affairs, could not then be brought to an end,[1] should be inserted afterwards at my leisure. Being relieved by this royal order,—the interpreter of the Divine ordinance,—from the secret

in Akbar's time, and his full name appears to be Bāyazīd Sulṭān (158*b* last line). He was attached to Mun'im Khān and has many details about Kābul and the war in Bengal. Nine copies of the work were made, *viz.*, two (including one that got mislaid) for the King's Private Library, three for the Royal Princes, one for the library of Gulbadan whom the author calls the mother of the king's servants, and two for Abu-l-fazl's library. The ninth was probably the original, and remained with the author.

Bāyazīd, known as Bāyazīd Bāyat, is quoted by Raverty (Notes on Afghānistān) and the B. M. has a MS. (Add. No. 26, 610) which contains an apparently complete trs. of Bāyazīd's Memoirs by Erskine. (Rieu's Cat. II. Pref. XX). Both text and trs. merit publication.

1 Apparently *farū guzāshtan* here means to complete or bring to an end and not, to neglect or pass over. See Vullers *s. v. guzāshtan*, 954*b* and the quotation there given from the *Burhān-i-qāṭi'*. With regard to this account of the collection of materials, it should be remembered that the *Āīn* with all its wealth of tables and other statistics is part of the *Akbarnāma* and that the author was probably referring to his difficulties in getting full topographical details. What he seems here to mean is that he was disturbed in his mind at not getting full answers to his inquiries for local information and that Akbar relieved him by telling him to set to work on the material he had, and to leave other details to be inserted afterwards. We have (*Āīn* II. 14, Jarrett III. 23) the skeleton of an elaborate astronomical table which appears to be blank in all the MSS. Colonel Jarrett supposes that the entries were left to be made at a later time and that the matter was afterwards forgotten or the required information never obtained.

anxiety of my heart, I proceeded to reduce into writing the rough draughts which were void of the graces of arrangement and style.
I obtained the chronicle of events beginning at the nineteenth year 10
of the Divine Era, when the Record Office[1] was established by the enlightened intellect of his Majesty, and from its rich pages I gathered the accounts of many events. Great pains too, were taken to procure originals or copies of most of the orders[2] which had been issued to the provinces from the Accession up to the present day which is the dawn of Fortune's morning.[3] Their sacred contents yielded much material for the sublime volume. I also took much trouble to incorporate many of the reports which ministers and high officials had submitted, about the affairs of the empire and the events of foreign countries.[4] And my labour-loving soul was satiated by the apparatus of inquiry and research. I also exerted myself energetically to collect the rough notes and memoranda of sagacious and well-informed men. By these means, I constructed a reservoir

1 قانون واقعه نویسی, *qānūn-i-wāqi-'a-nawīsī*. (Blochmann 258, *Āīn* No. 10). There were 14 clerks employed in the Office, *viz.*, two for each day. It was established in the 19th year, 982 (1574). (*Akbarnāma* III. 118). In the same year A. F. entered the Emperor's service and we may reasonably suppose that the institution of the Record Office was partly due to his suggestion.

2 Two *dastūr-ul-'amal* (Circulars) to the local authorities are preserved in the first volume of *Inshā* and much of them (with modifications and additions) is to be found in the *Āīn* (Jarrett II. 37, 66, etc.).

3 We might here have expected A. F. to use this language with reference to the Accession and not to delay the "dawn of fortune's morning" till 40 years of the reign had passed away. But clearly he refers it to the time of his writing. There is a similar passage in Akbar's letter to 'Abdu-l-lāh Khān of Tūrān. (*Akbarnāma* III. 707, l. 8) where the phrase is used with reference to the 41st year and apparently to the completion of the conquest of the Deccan and the establishment of universal peace.

4 This passage might be compendiously rendered *Home and Foreign Affairs*. The phrase used for foreign countries is *Aknāf-i-wilāyat*, borders of foreign countries. Blochmann says (Prosody of the Persians, VI.) that *wilāyat*, in Indian prose writers and poets, means Kābul and Persia, and it is possible that Persia is intended here. But I should think Tūrān and Europe were also referred to. A. F. would not be likely to speak of Kābul as *wilāyat* because he regarded it as part of the empire and has described it among the *sūbas*.

for irrigating and moistening the rose garden[1] of fortune. But inasmuch as, notwithstanding all this apparatus and these rich treasures of information, the House of History[2] was become decayed from lapse of time, and there were contradictions and imperfections in the accounts and no sufficient means of clearing up difficulties,— I begged the correction of what I had heard from his Majesty who, by virtue of his perfect memory, recollects every occurrence in gross and in detail, from the time he was one year old—when the material[3] reason came into action—till the present day when he is, by his wisdom, the cynosure of penetrating truth-seekers. By repeated interviews I arrived at correctness and erased doubts and difficulties with the knife of investigation and ascertainment. When peace had possessed my soul, I made honesty and lavish labour, conductors of the lofty undertaking. I trust that I shall, by help of sincerity, accomplish my task, and that, having gathered such of the wondrous new fruit of the garden of creations, and catalogue of the Creator's masterpieces as my understanding can grasp, I may display them so that a lamp of vision may be set up at the head of Wisdom's Way for the darkened of heart, and that the store of the enlightened may be augmented. *Laus Deo!* What a blessed thing it is that I am paying my devotions to God behind the curtain of service to my sovereign, and that while setting forth the code of regulations of the outer and inner world and the duties of sovereignty and servitude for all mankind from the king to the beggar, I am acquiring a stock of eternal merit for myself.

## Author's Note.

As I consider it would be disrespectful to mention on every occasion in this book—which is a record of Divine praise—the sublime name of this King of the Horizons, I use the phrase *Ḥazrat Shāhanshāhī*, his Majesty, King of kings, and for the deceased[4] sovereign, his Majesty's illustrious father, I avoid prolixity, by using the phrase, *Jahānbānī*[5] *Jannat-āshiyānī*. I indicate the venerable mother of the holy one by the title

---

[1] Meaning the *Akbarnāma*.

[2] *Khāna-i-naql*. Cf. *Āīn* III. 193. "Whereas the City of History (*Shahristān-i-naql*) is in ruins."

[3] *'Aql-i-haiyūlānī*.

[4] غفران قباب, *Ghufrān-qibāb*, lit., cupola of pardon or absolution.

[5] Guardian of the world—whose nest is in Paradise. A. F. sometimes uses one and sometimes both epithets when referring to Humāyūn.

*Miryam-makānī*,[1] a majestic epithet which passed into the enlightened 11
mind of his Majesty, the king of kings. I style the revered grandfather of the Lord of the World, *Ḥazrat Gītī-sitānī-i-Fardōs-makānī*[2] and thereby abridge his designations.

## Note.

R. A. S. No. 117 has a curious addition to the account of the mandate (*ante* 27) which A. F. received to write the history of Akbar's achievements. After *afshānda*, it has "*Dar bīst-ū-dūyam Isfandārmaz māh, sana si-ū-siyūm-i-Ilāhī ḥukm shud*," etc. "On 22nd *Isfandārmaz*, 33rd of the Divine Era, an order was given." Lower down where it is stated that a second commandment was issued (ante page 29) the same MS. has "*Dar rūz isnād Ardibihisht sana si-ū-cahārum ki siyum Rajab nuh-ṣad-ū-nuwad-ū-haft ḥukm mujadd shud.*" "On 26th Ardibihisht of the 34th year, or 3rd Rajab 997. a second order was issued." I have not found these clauses in any other MS., but they are hardly likely to have been interpolated by the copyist and the first date appears to agree with A. F.'s other statements, for in the *Āīn* (Jarrett III. 416) he says that he was seven years employed on the history which with the year or so occupied in the collection of materials might bring the completion of the work to the 41st or 42nd of Akbar.

---

1 *Miryam* is Miriam or Mary and the epithet has been variously rendered—*she who dwells with Mary,*—*is of the household of Mary,*—and *who is of equal rank with Mary—viz.*, the Virgin Mary. (The Virgin is one of Muḥammad's four perfect women). Akbar did not invent the epithet, for it was borne by his great-grandmother, the mother of Bābar. (See Khafī Khān I. 35). Jahāngīr's wife, Jodh Bāi, was called *Miryam-i-zamānī*, the Mary of the Age. I think the word *Makānī*, in Ḥamīda Bānū's title must be translated, *rank* or *station*, and not *household*, for it was given to her in her life-time. It almost looks as though Akbar liked the title because it agreed with his resemblance to the Messiah. It was said that the two resembled one another in speaking in the cradle. See account of miracle wrought by the infant Akbar to comfort Jījī Anaga (*Akbarnāma* I. 187 and *Dabistān* III. 50, trs.). With reference to this incident A. F. calls Akbar *Masīḥā-wār*, Messiah-like.

2 Conqueror of the world, abiding in Paradise.

# CHAPTER I.[1]

## ACCOUNT OF SUNDRY SECRET ANNUNCIATIONS AND HOLY MANIFESTATIONS WHICH TOOK PLACE BEFORE HIS MAJESTY'S AUSPICIOUS BIRTH.

It is not hidden from the mirror-hearts of the quick-sighted and far-seeing—who know the mysteries of truth, and who show forth the secrets behind the divine veils, and are curtain-openers of elemental (*i.e.*, terrestrial and celestial) mysteries—that the profound wisdom and secret power of the Creator ordain that it is by the weddings of heavenly[2] sires with earthly mothers, and after various cycles of lunar[3] aspects, and of applications,[4] of syzygies and oppositions of the sun and moon, of conjunctions of the superior[5] and inferior planets, risings and settings, appearances and disappearances of stars, lunar and solar eclipses, qualities of exaltations and falls,[6] influences of zeniths and nadirs,[7] and the like, (which are architects in the workshop of production and change, and artists in the picture-gallery of invention and contrivance) that the unique one comes forth from the secret inner chambers into the palace of manifestation,

---

[1] Chalmers breaks off here, and does not resume his translation till page 102 of the text.

[2] The author here displays his learning by giving a string of astronomical and astrological terms. The planets and other heavenly bodies are the sires, and the four elements are the earthly mothers, though the latter may also be "elect ladies," such as Alang-goa (Alanqūā) and Maryam-makānī.

[3] امتزاج, *imtizāj*, union or mixture; but it appears to be also a term for the lunar aspects. See Dic. of T. T. 1323.

[4] اتصال, *ittiṣāl*, approximation or propinquity. It is an astrological term corresponding to the *continuation* or *application* of European astrologers and is the opposite of انصراف, *inṣirāf*, separation.

[5] The superior planets are Saturn, Jupiter and Mars,—as being above or beyond the orbit of the Sun,—and the inferior are Venus, Mercury and the Moon.

[6] A planet falls when it is in the house and degree opposite to those of its exaltation, *i.e.*, is six heavens, 180°, from them. Thus the Sun's exaltation is 19° Aries and his fall 19° Libra. The Sun is a planet, according to the Ptolemaic system.

[7] اوج و حضیض, *auj ū ḥaẓīẓ*. This may also mean the *apsides*, *i.e.*, the apogee and perigee or aphelion and perihelion. *Auj* (Pers. *auk* or *aug*), was used to signify the apogee of a planet.

and that Unity emerges from the veiled ones of the cabinet of non-existence and displays its glory in the sublime assembly of Being, to be the cause of the arrangement of the Universe and the means of discriminating between justice and oppression throughout the world. How can arrangement result from simple[1] matter? How will it make progress when the constitution of every individual is founded on a collection of opposite tendencies,[2] when there is colossal egotism in every brain, when justice is unattainable, love non-existent, appetite rampant, and concupiscence daily on the increase?

The wise and far-sighted man is aware that in every period it is indispensable that there be a ruler who shall be strengthened by God's help and made fortunate by eternal blessings. And the philosopher perceives that such a power must be spiritual as well as possessed of

---

1 تن واحد, *tan-i-wāḥid*. I understand this to signify matter only, *i.e.*, simple matter without the intervention of celestial influences. The author has been dwelling on the necessity of all sorts of combinations and influences to produce the Only One—the Unique,—and then winds up by exclaiming about the impotence of mere matter. In the *Āīn* (II. 966) the author uses تن, *tan*, in the sense of *matter* as opposed to *spirit* and has the phrase *tan gudākhtan*, to mortify—lit. to melt—the flesh.

I am, however, by no means sure of the meaning and possibly the phrase may, as has been suggested to me, be an exclamation of surprise at Akbar's greatness, "What an apparatus of arrangement from one man!" This rendering of *tan-i-wāḥid* receives support from the similar use of *tan* in page 4 (line 4 from foot); but then I do not see its connection with what follows. Possibly the correct reading would be to omit the *iẓāfat* after *tan* and to translate *wāḥid* as the Unique One. "What Cosmos can come out of flesh? How can the Unique One issue from it, seeing that every man is made up of contradictions?" See the corresponding passage in the *Āīn* (I. 290 l.12, Jarrett II. 51) and also in the beginning of the first letter to 'Abdu-l-lāh Khān of Tūrān, in the *Inshā*. Here we have the expression *qahr-i-waḥdat* which Jarrett translates *autocracy*. Finally I may point out that there is an Arabic word تن, *tinn*, signifying equality, and that possibly this is what A. F. wrote. His question then would be, "How can Cosmos result from equality (or equals)? How will the Unique One emerge from it?"

If it be objected that *wāḥid*, as an adjective, cannot mean the "Unique One," we might read *waḥdat*, unity; or, with still less violence, take the letter *w* to be *ū*, the conjunction and translate *ū aḥad*, "and the Unique One."

2 Alluding to the four warring and contradictory elements.

strength of arm. The man of experience knows that many years must elapse before a ruby[1] develop in the embryonic *sac* of the mine and arrive at maturity, so as to be fit for a royal diadem. How many revolutions of epochs then, and how many cycles, are required before such a priceless pearl and unique jewel,[2] lacking in naught, can obtain his special preparation, so that by ascending steps, he arrive at the fulness of perfection? Acute and experienced observers perceive that the length of the period is dependent on the number of the subjects,[3] for the greater their number, the greater are the opposition and incommensurability. The greatness of the Lord of an Age is more conspicuous when he takes the burden of the whole world and of mankind on the head (*farq*) of genius, and guards the flocks (*firq*) of the universe from strife, and arranges and completes, by virtue of his wisdom, the work of the world and of mankind. But whenever, in the plenitude of His desires, the Divine Workman wills, that the arrangement of things spiritual and temporal and the culture of the inner and outer worlds be placed in the hands of
12 one individual of the human race, how can the period of preparation of such a lofty comprehension and sublime intellect be calculated by the human understanding, and how can finite cycles contain it? Inasmuch as the enlightened and wise of our time find these two supreme gifts[4] in the writing on the luminous forehead of the Lord[5] of the World (Akbar), they quite justly admit their inability to expound his orbit.[6] To them, this very fact is bliss, that by the

---

[1] Alluding to the notion that the ruby is slowly developed from stone by the action of the Sun. Cf. Milton (Paradise Lost III. 608–12).

"With one virtuous touch
"The Arch-chimic Sun, so far from us remote,
"Produces with Terrestrial Humor mixt,
"Here in the dark, so many precious things
"Of colour glorious and effect so rare."

[2] As the perfect prince.

[3] رعايا, *ra'āyā*, subjects. The word primarily signifies a flock or herd and probably A. F. uses it here with a reference to this original meaning. We might therefore translate "the size of the flock."

[4] *Viz.*, the control of the worlds, *etc.*

[5] خديو, *khudēv*, lord or great king: it is the well-known word *Khedive*.

[6] مناقب, *manāqib* pl. of *manqab*, virtues, and also, a mountain-path. Here, I think, it means the path of Akbar's development, though A. F. probably has an eye to the double meaning of the word, as his manner is.

Divine aid, they have come to know him. For the comprehension of the stages of development of such a Lord is not within the compass of human calculation. They know that in venerating this Great One, they are doing reverence to the Divine power and are worshipping the very Godhead. They spend all their energies in acquiring his grace, as that necessarily includes the compassing of the grace of the incomparable God. What bliss can be greater than this? Or what fortune can be more exquisite than this boon? And the enlightened and far-seeing man whose visual ray has been strengthened by the antimony of rectitude, knows from the analogy[1] of an auspicious star, it was after thousands of years had been spent, womb after womb, in the cradle of preparation, that the broidery of existence was bestowed on her Majesty Ālanqūā,[2] so that she might become[3] worthy of that world-illuminating Light, which is the interpretation of that anthropomorphic Sun[4] which stands at the

---

1 Lit. by the guidance of an auspicious star but, I think, the verse quoted immediately afterwards, shows the meaning to be, that the length of time after which an auspicious star appears, proves how long a period is required for the development of a Light such as that of Akbar.

2 Her proper name appears to be Alang-goa. See Ssanang-Ssetzen's "History of the Eastern Mongols," (trs. J. J. Schmidt, St. Petersburg, 1829, 59). *Goa* or *Go* means *white* or *shining* and is a title given to noble ladies (l. c. 373). Ssanang-Ssetzen was a descendant of Cingīz Khān and completed his book in 1662 (l. c. 299). He describes Alang-goa as the daughter of Baraghodschin-goa, wife of Choritai-mergen. She became the wife of Dobo-mergen and bore him two sons. Then her husband died, and during her widowhood, she was visited by the Sun and became by him, the mother of three sons. She is the mythical ancestress of the Mongolian race by her supernaturally-born son, Budantsar Mong Khān. A. F. gives an account of her (*Akbarnāma,* 64). Both he and Ssanang-Ssetzen intimate that she was miraculously born as well as a miraculous mother, and the latter gives the name of her mother only.

3 The word is *gardīd,* became, but I think the past tense is used here for the future as is sometimes done in Persian. The elements of humanity traversed armies of martyrs,—thereby becoming purified,—and were eventually developed into Alanqūā.

4 شمسۀ پیشطاق, *shamsa-i-pēshṭāq.* In *Āīn* No. 19, (*Āīn,* Book I. 45), A. F. treats of the *insignia* of royalty and begins with the expression *shamsa-i-cahārṭāq.* He then adds that this *shamsa* is a Divine splendour which, without the intervention of human effort is the finger-mark

entrance-gate of ancient tradition and constitutes the basal inscrip-

---

of Divine power. Blochmann (50) translates, "The *shamsa* of the arch of royalty is a Divine light which God directly transfers to kings without the assistance of men, and kings are fond of external splendour because they consider it an image of the Divine glory." He adds, in a note, "*Shamsa* is a picture of the Sun, affixed to the gates or walls of the palaces of kings. At night, these pictures are illuminated." The expression *shamsa-i-cahārṭāq* must be connected with that of *shamsa-i-pēshṭāq* which occurs in the text (III. 184, 1.4). The expression there used is *shamsa-i-pēshṭāq-i-āgāhī*—the solar image of the arch of intelligence—and is applied to Akbar. Similarly Faiẓī, in the preface to his *Dīwān*, speaks of the *sham'-i-shashṭāq ū shāh-i-nuh-kharga*—meaning apparently, lamp of the six sides of the world and king of the nine vaults of heaven. *Cahārṭāq* which Blochmann translates *arch* is given by Steingass as meaning a kind of tent. Dozy (Supplement I. 786) defines *shamsa* as a round ornament or little ball in the shape of the Sun; he also says it is described as a sun-shaped button, by means of which a door is opened. It may apparently mean also a curtain or parasol. I think the *shamsa-i-pēshṭāq* in the passage before us, means in part, the solar images which were set up at the entrance-gates of royal palaces and here, we may quote the words of Quintus Curtius (III. Cap. 7) noticed in Hyde's "Religion of the Ancient Persians."

"Super tabernaculum unde ab omnibus conspici posset, imago solis crystallo inclusa fulgebat."

Perhaps, however, this rather refers to the *akāsdiya*. (Blochmann 50).

The following extract from Kaempfer's Amoenitates Exoticae, (Fasiculus V. 199), gives a nobler idea of the *Shamsa* than Mr. Blochmann's description. Kaempfer is describing the Gynaeceum Regium or Female Apartments of the Palace at Ispahan.

"Ambulacri superatâ longitudine (quam habet 150 passuum) portam contingimus primariam, extus, Janitoribus Sopi, intus, albis munitam spadonibus. Haec tota caeruleo imbuta, *iconem exhibit Mithrae*, i.e., *Solis* (detorta vox est ab obsoleto Mehiin quod Solem notat) *praegrandem, auream et sparso in orbem jubare radiantem*. Sanctitatem loci, non alii ornamenti species, mystici gentis judicio, gravius exprimebat quam Mithra, sive Sol, qui coelo decus, universitati lux et vitae focus praepositus est. Solem igitur pro summo Numine (verius pro larvâ Numinis) antiquitus colebat, ejusque simulacrum adoptabat absolutae potentiae suae insigne, quod et domi statuebat togatae Majestati praesidium, et in Campo signis praeferebat militaribus ita animas accensurum objectu rei, quae uno quasi complexa Divini Numinis imaginem, et Majestatis Regiae praesentiam innueret."

But I think A. F. chiefly means to refer to the solar being who came into Alang-goa's tent and that he wishes to indicate as the true explation[1] of true histories. And he perceives that the same Light which took shape, without human instrumentality or a father's loins, in the pure womb of her Majesty Ālanqūā, after having, in order to arrive at perfection, occupied during several ages the bodily wrappings of other holy witnesses, is manifesting itself at the present day, in the pure entity of this unique God-knower and God-worshipper (Akbar).

**Verse.**

How many ages have passed away !
How many planetary conjunctions occurred,
That this happy star might come forth from heaven !

It is an ancient custom and established institute that the messengers of the eternal city and the heralds of the opening of the gates[2] of munificence, before the appearance of an elect one,—such

---

nation of the mysterious figure which, according to the old tradition, came in as an image of the Sun and disappeared as a wolf,—that Alang-goa was made pregnant by the Divine Light, in the same way as the Virgin Mary. (*Akbarnāma* 64, ff.). It is believed by some writers that the story of Alang-goa is an imitation of the accounts of the incarnations of the Buddha and of Jesus Christ.

1 كتابهٔ مباني, *kitāba-i-mabānī*, epithet, inscription, foundation of (true records). I think the allusion must be to the title Nairūn which was given to Alang-goa's descendants by the Sun. (*Akbarnāma* 67, l.1). A. F. takes the epithet to be derived from *nūr* and says it means light-born; but the word does not seem to be Arabic and it is not likely that the rude forefathers of the Mughals would use an Arabic term. D'Ohsson (I. 25) says, "Nirūn, c'est-à dire *de la côte*, pour désigner la pureté de leur origine." Apparently then, he does not derive the word from *nūr* but connects it with the Turkī *narah*, a side or place. The legend about Alang-goa is mentioned in the *Shajratu-l-atrāk*. (Col. W. Miles' trs.) There may however, also, be a reference to the *Ṭabaqāt-i-nāṣirī* of Minhāj-i-sirāj, (Section XXI.) where the word *Shamsīa* is used as a title of a dynasty and where there is a passage not unlike A. F.'s. (Raverty 596 and Bib. Ind. Text 164). Possibly too, the word *tawārīkh* here means dates or chronology and the allusion (or at least, one of the allusions) is to the Divine Era, established by Akbar.

2 فتح الباب, *fatḥu-l-lāb*. I learn from the Dic. of T. T. (1104) that this is also an astrological term, meaning the coming together in the same house of two planets whose mansions are opposite to one another, *e.g.*, Saturn and the Sun and Moon, Jupiter and Mercury, Mars and Venus. Guido Bonatus has a chap-

that one only comes into existence after thousands of years,—rejoice the privileged and wakeful-hearted by the glad tidings of his approach. For every event is stationed[1] behind the veil of a time and the precise[2] moment (of its appearance) is concealed and hidden. Yet before it become a certainty, they open a wicket[3] in the invisible world in face of the senses, and the window-fronts hold a lattice[4] of indications.

Sometimes the manifestations occur in the visible world, and sometimes their lustre is exhibited in dreamland,—which is an image of the world of mortals,—so that the recipients may have hope while on the highway of desire, and may await the wished-for light and may be observing the ascension of the auspicious star, for expectation enhances joy, and joy is the ornament of felicity. And whatever takes form after longing and striving, and obtains its fulfilment after watching and waiting, has a charm about it which is not met with otherwise.

13 An instance of this is the circumstance that his Majesty Jahānbānī Jannat-āshiyānī (Humāyūn) after receiving an intimation of the advent of the glorious one (*ān ḥazrat*) was ever keeping the dust-stained head of supplication on the earth of humility; and placing the apex of beseechment on the threshold of the *Ka'ba* of requests, and turning the face of hope towards the altar of entreaty, used to pray with invocations and longing, for that living blessing, which in truth, is an auspicious ascension[5] and an increase of life.

---

ter headed *De apertione portarum.* (815*b*).

1 مرصود, *marṣūd.* This word, according to Lane, means lying in wait. It means also the station of a star and the act of observation and of being observed and is used in this sense in the *Āīn* (II, 1.5 fr. foot.)

2 Lit. "the knot (عقدة *'uqdat*) of the special time is veiled and hidden."

3 *Darīca*, a window or wicket.

4 شبکه, *shabaka.* (Dozy, Suppl. 722b). The name given to a part of the *astrolabe* known as the *cobweb*; Chaucer's Riet (*rete*); a moveable metal plate. See also Jarret, III. 315, *n.*1.

5 طالع همایون, *ṭāli'-i-humāyūn.* There is a play here upon the word Humāyūn; the phrase being capable of being rendered the *ascension* or *rising* of Humāyūn: perhaps too, there is an allusion to the etymology, real or supposed, of the Persian word *farzand*, son, from *far*, glory.

VERSE.

O Lord, by the lamplight of Thy Essence,
By the ocean pearls of Thy Attributes,
By those holy Ones (prophets and saints) who come forth
like pure roses,
Whose souls are washed by the fountains of the sun,
Grant a jewel to my fortune's crown;
Grant a star to my exaltation's heaven;
Grant a moonlight to my chamber[1],
Which may disperse the darknesses of the Universe;
Irradiate my existence by a sun,
That[2] the nine heavens may come within my adoration.
Give perpetuity to my afflicted soul,
So[3] that, if death come by a hundred ways, I may not die.

Of a truth, a son who will be one's successor and take one's place on the glorious throne, is something which is a compensation for life,—for which there is no compensation,—and is a substitute for bye-gone years. He is the fruit of life's garden and a celestial lantern, fed from the oil of the Divine bounty. He kindles the family lamp of the whole line of ancestors and fixes it firmly on the throne of fortune. He lengthens and broadens the shades of justice and glory over the heads of mortals. Especially, if he be such a rare and exquisite product and so consummately dutiful that, if he be called *Primus*[4] of the Poles of Saints, it is but proper, and if he be termed the knot in the grand chain of sovereignty,[5] Father of Fathers,[6] and Great Ancestor, it is but just and in accordance with

---

1 شبستان, *shabistān*. This is A. F.'s name for the harem or seraglio. See *Āīn* 39. The prayer is that there may be a moonlike son born in the harem.

2 This line is Faiẓī's. See *Akbarnāma* III, 683, 1.5.

3 This line is adapted from one of Faiẓī's. *Akbarnāma* III. 683, 1.4.

4 Lit. synopsis or title-page of the Poles of the saints.

5 The word *saltanat* does not occur in the text (Bib. Ind. ed.) but is in No. 564 and is probably genuine. It occurs after *silsila* and before *a'ẓima*. The word also occurs in B. M. No. 1709.

6 *Abu-l-ābā ū jadd-i-a'lā*. *Jadd* sometimes means maternal grandfather or ancestor and perhaps has this force here.

the real facts. It is exceptionally suitable that a king who in succession to a line of ancestors is placed on a throne of rule and sway, and is world-dominating and world-adorning, should have an illustrious successor and such an one is of all men, the most eager in this quest.

At length, on 4th Rabī'u-l-awwal, 947, of the lunar (Ḥijra) era (Friday, 10 July, 1540) his Majesty Jahānbānī Jannat-āshiyānī had, after paying his devotions to the Author of bounty, laid for a time his head on the pillow of repose and his limbs on the couch of tranquility, when, suddenly, under the auspicious veil of sleep,—hence called the cabinet of secrets—he became aware that God, (Glory be to Him) was bestowing on him an illustrious successor whose greatness shone from his forelock, and the lightning of whose splendour was flashing from his temples. From the light of his guidance, the dark regions of thoughts and opinions were illuminated, and the glory of his justice was lighting up the fields of night and day. It is in accordance with the communication which was made by the messengers of the invisible world regarding his Majesty (Akbar) that the glorious name of that divine masterpiece exalts at the present day, pulpits and proclamations. The superscriptions[1] of the gold and silver coins also tell of it.

14 When his Majesty awoke, he first returned thanks to God for the majestic message and splendid grace and then told the circumstance to the intimates of his harem and the servants of his threshold.[2]

---

[1] Lit. the faces of the *dirhams* and *dīnārs*. The *dirham* was a silver coin and the *dīnār* a gold one. They were in use before Akbar's time. See *Āīn* Nos. 10 and 11 (Book I. Blochmann). Akbar gave new names to the coins.

[2] This dream occurred about a year before Humāyūn's marriage with Akbar's mother. That marriage took place, according to Gulbadan, on Monday, (Dōshamba) 9th Jumāda-l-awwal 948. Gulbadan says the dream occurred at Lahor, and she gives a more poetical account of it. She says Aḥmad-i-jām himself appeared in a dream, as an old man dressed in green and with a staff in his hand, to Humāyūn when the latter was in great distress on account of the conflicts with Shēr Khān, and bade him not lose heart, for he would have a wonderful son whom he was to call Jalālu-d-dīn Muḥammad Akbar. Bībī Konor (qu. Gūnawar) was then pregnant and it was thought that she would have a son, but she bore a daughter, Bakhshī Bānū.

VERSE.

A[1] sleep which tore the veil from before the eyes of the soul,
Cannot be called sleep; it was the heart's waking.

Sh̲arīf Kh̲ān related that when his brother Sh̲amsu-d-dīn Mu. Kh̲ān Atga[2] was in Gh̲aznī, in the 22nd year of his age, he dreamt he saw the moon come into his arms.[3] He related the fact to his venerable father Mīr Yār Mu. Gh̲aznavī who was a spiritually-minded householder,[4] and the latter rejoiced at the happy appearance of the auspicious circumstance and interpreted it to mean that God would, one day, bestow a great privilege upon him which would be the means of exalting their family. And so it turned out, for by the blessings of that full Moon of glory of the heaven (Akbar) the family was raised from the nadir of the dust to the zenith of heaven.

Another circumstance was communicated by religious, right-thinking persons, *viz.* that when her Highness Miryam Makānī—may the shadows of her glory be eternal—was pregnant with the holy elements of his Majesty, a strange light was perceptible from her bright brows. Often her divine countenance had to observers, the appearance of mirrors such as are fastened by tirewomen[5] near the temples of secluded chaste ones.

And the star of fortune sang this strain with the tongue of ecstacy.

VERSE.

I placed the clouded brow on the path[6] of fortune,
I hung a thousand mirrors on the forehead.

---

1 These lines are Faiẓī's and occur in his *Dīwān*. B. M. MS. Add. No. 7794, 191*b*.

2 Blochmann 321. He was Akbar's foster-father and became a *wākil*, minister. He was assassinated by Adham Kh̲ān. The word *atga* is Turkish and properly اتاگا *atāgā*, the state of being a father.

3 Lit. armpit.

4 *Kadkh̲udā-i-darvīsh̲-manish̲.* This phrase is copied in the *Ma'āsiru-l-umarā* (II. 531), and is, apparently, that which Mr. Blochmann has rendered "a simple farmer." The context here shows its real meaning.

5 Jaffar, Herklots says nothing of mirrors being attached to the forehead, but states that they are placed on the thumb.

6 براه *barāh*. Possibly the word is *burā* and the translation should be, "I laid the *ornament* of fortune on the clouded brow."

One day, near the time[1] of the auspicious birth, her Highness Miryam Makānī was riding[2] on a camel. On the way, her eye fell on a mango-garden. As at such a time, there is an inclination for sub-acid drinks and for sour-sweet fruits, she bade her half-brother,[3] Khwāja Mu'azzam fetch some mangoes. The Khwāja brought some, and was giving them into her blessed hand when he saw a light upon her glorious brows like that from a mirror. He said, "Have you put a mirror on your forehead?" She replied, "I have not attached any mirror. What are you referring to?" Then the Khwāja looked narrowly and saw that her Highness' shining forehead was lighted by the light of God. He marvelled at the light eternal and mentioned the circumstance to several of the confidential courtiers. His statement was to the effect, that the glory of the divine light so streamed from the shining brows that he had not strength to gaze steadily at it.

The venerable mother of Khān A'ẓam Mīrzā 'Azīz Kokaltāsh,
who was his Majesty's nurse,[4] related the following anecdote. "One
15 " morning, before I had the good fortune to hold this supreme office,
" a great light approached me and entered my bosom. I felt as if
" the world-warming Sun had fallen into my breast. A strange
" condition supervened and a great astonishment laid hold of me so
" that all the parts and particles of my body were moved and shaken,

---

[1] The birth was on 15th October O.S., *i.e.*, 25th October N.S. There could hardly have been mangoes on the trees near that time, nor is it likely that there were any mango trees near Amarkōṭ.

[2] *Haudaj* (howdah), but here used, I think, to mean camel-litter.

[3] برادر مادری *barādar-i-mādarī* which can, apparently, mean either a maternal uncle or an uterine brother, *i.e.*, a brother on the mother's side. Here it must mean the latter, for A. F. (I. 221) speaks of the relationship as *akhūwat-i-akhyāfī* which the dictionaries explain as meaning brotherhood. The *Ma'āsir* (I. 618) describes the Khwāja as *barādar-i-a'yānī* of Miryam Makānī, *i.e.*, her full brother. Its author then, apparently, took *akhyāfī* to mean full brother.

Niẓāmu-d-dīn (*Ṭabaqāt*, Luck. ed. 263) speaks of the Khwāja as Akbar's maternal uncle and as the son of 'Alī Akbar, a descendant of the saint Aḥmad-i-jām. The Khwāja was a man of violent temper, if not wholly insane. He killed his wife and was imprisoned by Akbar in Gwalior. (Badāonī, Lowe, 71 and Noer's Akbar, A. S. Beveridge, I. 104).

[4] *Atagagī*. Apparently this ought to be *anagaji*, if it comes from *anaga* a nurse. (Blochmann 323*n*.)

"as by excess of joy and ecstacy. And the exquisiteness of that "delight still suffuses me (*lit.* still possesses every hair of me). And "from the time of that white dawn of the morning of majesty and "beauty and rose-blooming of fortune and glory, I was on the watch, "thinking, 'O God! what will be the result of this sublime feeling?' "At length, I was exalted to this lofty service which is the treasure "of realm and religion (*dīn ū dunyā*) and of trust."

HEMISTICH.

"Fortune[1] is what comes to our bosom without trouble."

"God be praised! What a blessing it was that came to my "bosom and what a fortune was received within my breast. "Though externally, I was strongly made for the service of that "sublimely-born pearl, yet in reality, it was Fortune who inclined her "face[2] towards me and supported me and my family. Whenever "I took his Majesty on my shoulder, auspiciousness raised me from "the dust. Accordingly, by the blessing of this service which was "destined for me, a great grace and a lucky star were conferred on me. "And I and my family became famous throughout the seven climes."

Another story was told by Maulānā[3] Nūru-d-dīn Tarkhān and some others who were in attendance on the Court, *viz.*, that near the emergence of the sun of fortune (Akbar), his Highness Jahānbānī was recreating himself in a room[4] which had latticed windows, and the formula of the *rectification*[5] of the glorious birth was before him.

---

1 This line is in the *Anwār-i-Suhailī* (Cap. 14, Story 2). The literal rendering is "Fortune is what comes into the bosom without the heart's blood" (being shed), and the nurse uses the line to indicate that she had not to undergo the pain and danger of parturition.

2 There is an antithesis between her strong back, *pusht-i-qawī* and Fortune's face.

3 See Blochmann 524 and 541, also long account in Badāonī (III. 197–200) and the *Ma'āsir* (I. 478). He died as custodian of Humāyūn's tomb in 994 (1586).

4 خانۀ مسقف *khāna-i-musaqqaf* a roofed apartment; apparently the word room expresses the meaning.

5 حرف نمودار *harf-i-namūdār* the "rectification" of English astrologers. The namūdār was a device for obtaining the date of birth. There is an account of it in Ulugh Beg's *Prolegomena* (Part IV. Cap. I. 146 and Sédillot's Trs. 201). The namūdār is also called *animoder* in European books on astrology. It was resorted to when the exact date of birth was not known; that is when there was doubt as to the correctness of clocks, *etc.* Apparently

Suddenly rays of divine light shone from the lattices, so that all who were privileged to be present, both small and great, perceived them. Those who were entitled to speak, asked his Highness Jahānbānī the meaning of the phenomenon, and he replied, "A rose of the rose-" garden of the Khilāfat will just now come into bloom, and a child "of light will emerge from the hidden chamber of magnificence and "glory, and from the gorgeous *sarāī* of Honour and Fortune and plant "his foot in the circle of existence. The refulgence[1] of his greatness "will melt the hearts of the enemies of the State in the crucible of "destruction, and confer new splendour and glory on our race and "family. Nay, rather, the night-chamber of the universe will acquire "grandeur and beauty from his world-lighting rays."

Mīr 'Abdu-l-ḥai Ṣadr,[2] one of the purely-born, related as follows:—"One morning, his Highness Jahānbānī Jannat-āshiyānī was bowed down in reverie, and seemed much distraught.[3] After a time, he raised his head and exclaimed, "Praise be to God the Gracious, the lamp of our royal family has been relit." On my asking the meaning of his giving thanks, his Highness replied, "While I was in a state of

---

it is here referred to as something used to calculate the time when a birth will take place. Ulugh Beg gives three namūdārs, *viz.*, Ptolemy's, Hermes' and Zoroaster's. Vullers (*s. v.* 1352*a*) gives a quotation from the *Bahāri-'ajam*, mentioning five namūdārs. The phrase *ḥarf-i-namūdār* probably means the formula of the namūdār. It would seem that the namūdār was also used to discover the nature of the coming child, *e.g.*, its sex.

1 *Kaukaba* means a star and is also the name of one of the royal ensigns, *viz.*, a polished steel ball suspended to a pole. (Blochmann, Plate IX).

2 Badāonī has an account of him (III. 273). He calls him *Mashhadī*, *i.e.*, from the town of Mashhad (Meshed) in Eastern Persia. He was a skilled penman and his brother, Mīr 'Abdu-l-lah was a performer on the *qānūn* (dulcimer). He is, apparently, the caligraphist mentioned in the *Āīn* (Blochmann, 101 and 103), but though Mr. Blochmann identifies him with Mīr 'Abdu-l-ḥai Mīr 'Adl, this seems doubtful. (Blochmann, 468, 471 and 480). The man who told the story of Humāyūn's dream was that monarch's *Ṣadr*,—Lord High Almoner. This office was higher than the Mīr 'Adl's (Blochmann 268) and it is not likely that a man whom Badāonī praises for sanctity would take part in a drinking bout. (Blochmann 468). However, this is not impossible, for Badāonī tells us (Lowe, 210) that the New Year festivities were too much for the sobriety of the Qāẓīs and Muftīs (Judges) and even of pious men.

3 Lit. it appeared as if his blessed eyes had become red (or inflamed).

"wakeful[1] sleep, a brilliant star emerged from a certain quarter (here 16
his Highness pointed to the region where the glorious parturient was) "and rose higher and higher every moment. And as it ascended, its "size and brilliance increased, until its light had embraced the greater "portion of the world. I asked a holy man what the luminous body "was, and he replied that it was the light incarnate of my successor, "and that whatever part of the earth had been shone upon by this "world-illuminating ray, would come under his dominion, and be "civilized by the light of his justice." Two days after this vision, the news came of the ascension of the auspicious star above the horizon of hope, and when the period of the spiritual manifestation and holy vision was compared,[2] it appeared that the auspicious birth and the delivery of the miraculous message had occurred at one and the same time." When such an illustrious progeny is the lot of an eminent man,[3] why should such a communication not be vouchsafed? And when such a boon followed, why should there not have been such a reverie, and such an interpretation? Such things may appear extraordinary to superficial observers and to materialists, but the pure-minded and far-seeing conjectured before the event, and knew with certainty afterwards that this was the shining of the world-lighting star and that the message betokened the darkness-destroying sun. And to those who have had the bliss of being long in the service of this Lord of the World and of understanding his glorious qualities, the appearance of such portents is no stumbling-block.

Nor is it hidden from the acute and scrutinising that though Maulānā Sharafu-d-dīn 'Alī-i-Yazdī has in the *Zafarnāma*[4] taken a superficial view of things and stayed Qācūlī Bahādur's[5] true vision and Tūmana Khan's interpretation at His Majesty the Lord of Conjunction (Timur) and has explained the eighth shining star that issued

---

[1] Meaning that his body was asleep but his soul awake.

[2] With that of the birth.

[3] *Buzurg*. This word often means a saint or holy person and may have that sense here.

[4] *Bib. Ind.* I. 11 and 12, but the full account of the dream is given in the *Muqaddama* or Preface to the Zafarnāma which has not been published in the *Bib. Ind.* edition. It is to be regretted that this Preface which Sharafu-d-dīn refers to at page 11,[5] has not been printed. See Rieu's Catalogue I. 174. Add. 6538.

[5] See later on, in the detailed account of Akbar's ancestors.

from Qācūlī Bahādur's breast[1] and lighted up the world, of the appearance of his Majesty the Lord of Conjunction who is the seventh[2] ancestor of his Majesty (Akbar), yet it is clear to the minds of those far-sighted light-dwellers who understand hermeneutics and the secrets of the dream-world that to explain seven stars as seven persons whose heads were not exalted by the diadems[3] of rule, nor were seen on the dominion-adorning Divan of excellence, is remote from the principles of interpretation and the significance of dreams. Rather those seven stars are seven world-adorning potentates, and the world-irradiating light is the holy personality of his Majesty the King of Kings who hath by the light of his Being illumined the terrene and terrestrials. It is the auspicious Akbar[4] who was the resplendent light which arose from the breast of that Jupiter of good fortune (Qācūlī Bahādur). Although the latter be, numerically his Majesty's fifteenth[5] ancestor, yet among those there are seven stars of the zodiacal Sign of greatness and having the light of this world-illuminating King of Kings emblazoned on the foreheads of their biographies. These seven
17 out of the fifteen[6] have been distinguished for greatness and world-adornment, and the eighth of the noble band is his Majesty the King of Kings. The light of their rectitude has made the horizons brilliant, and in the noble series of the fifteen[6] great ones, there has been given the glorious vesture of spiritual and temporal sovereignty to this perfect witness of Divine Power, and he has been made light-bestower of the inner and outer worlds. This explanation is not hidden from the subtle investigators of real significations. On this account a synopsis of the perfections of this series will be found in this noble volume, and

---

1 The word in the text is *jīb* or *jaib*. Later on (p. 68) the word used is *garībān*.

2 The text has eighth, but according to our idiom at least, the word should be seventh. Nor is A. F. consistent, for at p. 81 he calls Timur's son the sixth ancestor of Akbar.

3 The author means that none of Qācūlī's immediate descendants was a king. The first monarch of his race was Timur, and the seven stars are interpreted by A. F. to mean Timur and the six descendants who intervene between him and Akbar.

4 *Sa'd-i-Akbar.* The auspicious conjunction, *i.e.*, the conjunction of Jupiter and Venus, but here used with a play upon the Emperor's name. See the heading of next chapter and the horoscope Chapters *passim*.

5 It is sixteenth in the Text.

6 It is eighteen in the Text, but this, I think, must be a mistake for sixteen or rather for fifteen.

then the prudent and alert of mind will get proof of these words. Whoever at the present day shall peruse with the eyes of discernment and knowledge, the account of these illustrious magnates and understand the office of the Caliph[1] of the Age, and become acquainted with the stages of the degrees of greatness of the Lord of the World, will applaud the exposition. Away, Away! I am no word-seller,[2] seeking for approving glances from men. What more choice blessing can there be than this, that my truth-electing heart has been made a fount of true impressions,[3] and that my scrutinising reason has become an alighting-stage[4] for these divine subtleties? With these night-gleaming jewels[5] I frame glorious earrings as abiding ornaments for the understanding ears of the fortunate lovers of wisdom.

---

1 I am not sure if this expression applies to Akbar or to his predecessors. A. F. seems to regard Akbar as something higher than the Caliph or Vicar-General of the Age. He is the Khudēv-i-jahān, *i.e.*, the Lord or Khedive of the World.

2 The reproach of A. F. against Firdausī. Jarrett III. 401.

3 نکات *nikāt.* Apparently penmarks, *i.e.*, dots.*

4 مهبط *mahbiṭ* a place where one alights. Often, the descent of an angel.

5 Alluding to the phosphorescence of diamonds, etc.

* [نکات حقاني *nikāt-i-ḥaqqānī* means the same as دقائق رباني *daqā'iq-i-rabbānī* in the next sentence, *i.e.*, 'divine subtleties.' The above translation, no doubt, is wrong. T. B.]

## CHAPTER II.

### ACCOUNT OF THE RISE OF THE GREAT LUMINARY (THE SUN) AND OF THE DIFFUSION OF THE GREATER FORTUNE (JUPITER) FROM THE SKY OF AUSPICIOUSNESS—THE NATIVITY, TO WIT, OF HIS MAJESTY, THE KING OF KINGS AND SHADOW OF GOD.

The apparition of the result of hopes from the embryonic *sac* of desire, and emergence of the light of fortune from the auspicious ascension-point,—the most holy nativity,[1] to wit,—of his Majesty from the sublime veil and consecrated curtain of her Highness, cupola of chastity,—screen of modesty,—saint of seclusion,—scion of austerity,—holy one of the age,—dawn[2] of epochs,—mistress of the world,—perfect teacher,[3]—paragon of purity,—pattern of limpidity,—chosen one of pure disposition,—abounding in trustworthy fidelity,—pure-principled princess,—queen of celestial graces,—elect lady of time and the terrene,—world's bliss,—wave of eternal ocean,—mother[4]-o'-pearl of the ocean of bounty,—lamp of the holy family,—glory of the house of guidance,—lantern of the wall[5] of worship,—bridal chamber of the auspicious harem,—forefront of obedience to

---

[1] The sentence of which the word "nativity" is the subject, is continued after a series of epithets, by the verb "occurred," on page 54.

[2] بازغة *bāzigha* beginning to rise or come forth, (Lane). The Luck. ed. and No. 564 have بارع *bāriʻ* excellent. The *Muntakhabu-l-lughāt* (Taylor 51a) says that *bāzigha* was the name of a woman of the tribe of Ād who listened to Joseph and thereby attained great sanctity.

[3] *Āmozgār* also means pupil, but here probably teacher. It is used in the latter sense in the *Āīn*, I. 202, l.2.

[4] صدف *ṣadaf* pearl-shell.

[5] حطيم *ḥaṭīm*, properly the west wall of the *Ka'ba*.

God,—eye of eternal empire,—pillar of the celestial throne,—pedestal of the sublime seat,—lady of the exalted marriage-daïs,—princess of fortune's alcove,—chosen curtain of honour's litter,—exalter of chastity's coiffure,—glorious gift of heaven,—treasure of Divine mercy,—prime dainty of the Divine table,—supreme boon of heavenly gifts,—revolving-point of bounties and graces,—glorious pearl of dominion and prestige,—spring-flower of justice,—tablet of the gorgeous picture-gallery,—splendour of sanctity and love,—fire-flame of majesty and exaltation,—cream of abilities and accomplishments,—choice one[1] of the secrets[2] of hand and heart,—central node of wisdom and wakefulness,—linking the divine and the human,—goodly tree of peace and purity,—generous fruit of liberality and election,—truth-showing mirror,—countenance of certainty,—staircase of majesty,—ladder of realm and religion,—tap-root of the umbrageous trunk of
happiness,—noble palm of the garden of excellence,—veiled matron 18
of meekness and modesty,—screened and curtained one of honour and greatness,—glorious medium between hidden and revealed light,—opener of the morning of fortune and favour,—enveloped in celestial veils,—her Majesty Miryam Makānī, chaste one of church and state, Ḥamīda Bānū Bēgam —(may her glorious shadow be perpetuated !)—pure scion of that pattern of eminent saints,[3]—pole of the poles of greatness,—wanderer in the wilderness of humanity,—swimmer in the ocean of divinity,—lamp of spiritual secrets,—key of the treasures of conquests,—rose-gatherer[4] of the gardens of revelation,—garland-twiner of the fragrant herbs of truth,—abbot (*imām*) of the monastery of asceticism,—cup-bearer of the tavern of abundance,—ocean-hearted one of the baiting-place of privation,—ocean-drinker of the tavern of unity,—immersed in the seas of holy conflicts,—consumed by the lightnings of contemplation,—torch-bearer of the chamber of the Path,—caravan-conductor on truth's highway,—supreme theatre of the epiphanies of the divine essence,—illumination-

---

1 نخبه, *nakhba*. This may also mean *bumper* or *copious draught*.

2 سر, *sirr*, has for one of its meanings the lines of the palm of the hand or of the forehead. I think this is the meaning here.

3 The author here leaves Miryam Makānī and proceeds to eulogize he. remote ancestor, Aḥmad-i-jām.

4 *Gulcīn*; also a gardener.

spot[1] of the rays of the Attributes,—cambist[2] of the secrets of the masters of revelation and manifestation,—assayer of the hearts of the lords of divine transports,—observant traveller over hearts and spirits,—scrutinizer of the interiors of moulds and forms,—disperser[3] of the clouds of darkness,—procuring the blotting-out of the writings[4] of transgressions,—knowing the links between the seen and the unseen,—revealer of the splendours of the secrets of manifestation and concealment—

VERSE.

Pole[5] which salutes the two poles of heaven,
Bridling by discipline the tigers of lust,
Stalking as a lion in the forest of the heart,
Ocean-drinker of love, the premier elephant, Aḥmad-i-jām,[6]

---

1 اجلاي مجالي انوار صفاتية, *ijlā-i-majālī-i-anwār-i-ṣifātīya.* The *Ṣifātīya* or Attributists were a Muḥammadan sect. (See Hughes' Dict. of Islām;—Koran, Sale, Preface;—and the *Dabistān*, trans. II. 324 and 330). But I do not think A. F. is referring to them here. The occurrence of the word *ẕātīya* in the previous clause seems to show that *Ṣifātīya* is here used merely in the sense of attributes or of belonging to attributes. *Aḥmad-i-jām* was a Ṣūfī but it is not stated that he belonged to any particular sect. In the *Dabistān* (II. 270) we are told on the authority of the commentator on the *Gulshan-i-rāz* that there are four kinds of manifestations, and that "the third is *Ṣifātī*; belonging to attributes,—when the contemplative person sees the Absolute Being endowed with the attributes of his own essence such as science and life, and sees himself a real being or endowed with these attributes."

2 صراف, *ṣarrāf, shroff* or *money-changer*, one who puts philosophy into current coin.

3 انجلا, *injilā*, may also mean brightening. Cf. text 46, 1, 7.

4 Cf. Isaiah xliv. 22; and Colossians ii. 14.

5 قطب, *quṭb*, the pole, a common name for distinguished saints.

6 Jām is a town in Khurāsān (N.-E. Persia) and near Herāt. ("Jām—very near Herāt," says the *Dabistān* II. 334). For an account of Aḥmad-i-jām, see Rieu's Catalogue I. 551*b*, and the *Nafaḥātu-l-uns*. He is a very famous saint of the 11th and 12th centuries. His full name is Abū Naṣr Aḥmad ibn Abu-l-ḥasan. He bore the titles *Zhanda-pīl*, Raging, or perhaps Mighty, Elephant, and *Shaikhu-l-islām*. He is called *Nāmaqī* from his having been born in or at least, from his family's having sprung from the village of Nāmaq in the district of Jām. He was born 441 H. (1049), and died in 536 H. (1141). (Dr. Rieu states that according to the *Jawāhiru-l-asrār*

Holy be his tomb, (*i.e.*, *R. I. P.*)

---

(fol. 148) the date of his death is fixed by the chronogram احمد جامي قدّس سرّهٗ, *Aḥmad Jāmī quddisa sirruhu.* (See Richardson 718*a*.) The passage occurs at 148*a*. of Add. 7607, Rieu's Cat. I. 43*c*. and the words are تاريخ وفات احمد جامي ازقدس‌سرهٗ ميدان The letters give the date 536, *viz.*:—

| | | | |
|---|---|---|---|
| A = 1 | J = 3 | q = 100 | r = 200 |
| ḥ = 8 | ā = 1 | d = 4 | h = 5 |
| m = 40 | m = 40 | s = 60 | —— |
| d = 4 | ī = 10 | s = 60 | 536 Total. |

There is an account of the saint in Dārā Shikāh's *Ṣafīnatu-l-auliyā* and there the writer—the eldest son of Shāh Jahān—refers to his great-great-grandmother, Ḥamīda Bānū's descent from Aḥmad-i-jām. But the fullest account of Aḥmad is in Jāmī's *Nafaḥātu-l-uns*, Jāmī being a townsman of the saint. The life will Be found in Lees' ed. of the *Nafaḥāt*. ( l, 1859, 405–417) Aḥmad-i-jām is said To have converted 300,000 persons, and to have had 42 children, of whom 17 survived him. His *Dīwān* is in the B. M., and he wrote other works. There is an explanation of the term *Zhanda-pīl* by M. Pictet, in the *Journal Asiatique* for 1843, (Series IV., Vol. II., 141). He derives it from the Sanscrit *caṇḍa*. According to Fraser (Journey into Khorasan, Lond. 1825, App. B., 39), it means Elephant-reviver or animator, and was given to the saint because he, at the cost of his own life, restored to life the Governor's elephant. Fraser describes his tomb as a rough slab of marble, situated in a grove of pistadin trees, at *Turbat-i-jām*, half way between Mashhad and Herāt. According to A. F. Aḥmad-i-jām was the ancestor of Humāyūn's mother as well as of his wife (Ḥamīda Bānū). Humāyūn visited the South in 1544 and put up an inscription which still exists. (J. R. A. S. Jan. 1897).

Apparently the father of Ḥamīda Bānū was named 'Alī Akbar, for Niẓāmu-d-dīn says, Khwāja Mu'aẓẓam (whom he calls Akbar's maternal uncle) was the son of 'Alī Akbar. According to A. F. the Khwāja was only uterine or half-brother of Ḥamīda Bānū, but it seems probable that 'Alī Akbar was also her father, for Niẓāmu-d-dīn goes on to say that 'Alī Akbar was descended from Ḥaẓrat Shaikhu-l-islām, Zhanda-pīl Aḥmad-i-jām. Gulbadan calls Ḥamīda Bānū, the daughter of Mīr Bābā Dōst. Apparently Mīr Bābā is the Maulānā Bābā Dōst Ṣadr mentioned (*Akbarnāma* I. 315) as a servant for whom Hindāl had a special regard. Perhaps Mīr Bāba Dōst is not his full name—though it occurs in the *Akbarnāma*—and he may also have been named 'Alī Akbar. Gulbadan says that Mīr Abu-l-Baqā took part in the marriage and that two lakhs of rupees were paid (or promised) as dower by Humāyūn. Abu-l-Baqā is referred to in the *Akbarnāma* (I. 172). In the same volume, (I. 174, l.15) mention is made of Khwāja Hajrī Jāmī (qu. the Superintendent of Aḥmad Jāmī's cell?) as having been forward in promoting the marriage. Gulbadan's account of the marriage negotiations is minute and interesting.

........................ occurred[1] when the altitude of Procyon[2] was 88° and when 8hs. 20m. had passed from the beginning of the night of 8th Ābān[3] 464, Jalālī era, corresponding to 19th Isfandārmiẕ 911, of the old era,[4] and to night of Sunday (*shab-i-yak-shamba*) 5th Rajab, lunar era,[5] and to 6th Kārtik[6] 1599, Hindū era, and to 16th

---

[1] See Note 1, page 50.

[2] شعرای شامیه, *shi'rā-i-shāmīya*, the Syrian Dog-star, *i.e.*, Procyon or the Lesser Dog-star; Sirius or the Greater Dog-star being called *Shi'ra-l-yamānī* or Dog-star of Yamān, *i.e.*, S.-W. Arabia. Procyon is called also *Shi'ra-l-'abūr*, the Little Dog-star.

[3] Ābān is the eighth month in the Persian year. The Jalālī era is also called the Malikī because established by Sulṭān Jalālu-d-dīn Mālik Shāh Seljūkī. 'Umar Khayyām was one of the astronomers employed in settling this calendar. (Jarrett III. 29.) The era began on 5th Sha'bān, 468 (15th March, 1076,) according to one account and according to another, on 10th Ramaẓān 471 (15th March, 1079). Ulugh Beg says. "This is a difference of 1097 days, the cause of of which is unknown to us, but as the second is that generally adopted, we shall follow it." (Sédillot, Prolegomena, 27). The cause of the difference is explained by Sedillot at page 235. The initial date, 15th March, 1079, is that adopted by Gibbon and appears to be that followed by A. F. for 1079+468=1543 or nearly October 1542.

[4] This is the era of Yazdajird, so-called because it dates from the first year of his reign, *viz.*, A.D. 632. The era, however, began long before his time, and according to A. F. dates from the accession of Jamshīd. It began afresh with the accession of each king, and it has received the name of the Yazdajird era because he was the last king of Persia, he being great-grandson of the famous Nōshīrwān, and being vanquished by the Muḥammadans. (Jarrett III. 28.) A. F. makes the difference between the two eras 447 years. The Yazdajird era began on 16th June, 632 A.D. Isfandārmiẕ is the 12th month in the Persian year.

[5] A. F. here calls the Hijra era *Halālī*, lunar, but in the *Āīn*, he calls it Hijra. The date corresponds to Sunday, 15th October. 1542 O.S. and 25th October N.S. Gulbadan gives the date as 4th Rajab, but this must be a mistake, for 4th Rajab, 949 was a Saturday, and the birth took place on a Sunday. Sédillot (Prolegomena 240) says that 5th Rajab is tho day of Muḥammad's conception, but Ulugh Beg makes it 15th Rajab and calls it the feast of victory. It is possible that Akbar got his name of Muḥammad from his having been born on this festival.

[6] This era is the Samvat or Vikrāmaditya era. It began B.C. 57 so that its 1599=1542 A.D. The Bibl. Ind. ed. has 1519, but this is clearly wrong and for *nūzdahum*—we should read *nuwad ū nuhum*—as in the Lucknow ed. and No. 564 and all the other copies which I have consulted. According to Cowasji Patell's tables the Samvat year 1599 began on 10th October. The year began apparently with 1st Kartik so that 6th Kārtik=15th October.

Tis͟hrīnu'-l-awwal 1854, Greek era;—4hs. 22m.[2] of the said night (that of Saturday, or rather Sunday[3]) were remaining. The place was the auspicious city and fortunate fort, Amarkōṭ,[4] which belongs

1. Tis͟hrīn, the Tis͟hrī of the Jewish Calendar, was the first month of the Syrian year. It corresponds to our October. The era is that of the Seleucidæ and is also called Syro-Macedonian. It began 1st October B.C. 312, so that 16th Tis͟hrīnu-l-awwal = 16th October, 1542. It appears from Cowasji Patell's *Chronology* (162) that the Syro-Macedonian year of 1854 began on 2nd October so that 16th Tes͟hrīnu-l-awwal corresponds exactly with 15th October. A. F. calls the era *Rūmī* (Greek). In the *Āīn* (I. 279) he calls it the era of Alexander of Greece, but at p. 274 l.c. he calls it *Rūmī*. He says it took its origin from the death of Alexander II. Bicornutus, but that it did not come into effect till 12 years after his death. Ulug͟h Beg treats it as a Christian era and gives, under it, the dates of the Christian festivals. (See Sédillot, Text 54 and Trans. 62). Mas'ūdī, writing in the 10th century, does the same thing. (See French trans. III. 405)). Al-bīrūnī (*Chronology of Ancient Nations*, 282) also gives the Christian festivals and says that the Melkites, Nestorians and Jacobites observed them. In Golius' notes to *Al-farg͟hānī* (19) it is stated that the Jacobites and Nestorians use this era, but that the Malekites begin their year in January.

2 A. F. gives two statements of the number of hours—one taken from the beginning of the night and the other from its end. Probably he used two records. The sum of the two sets of figures, 8hs. 20m. and 4hs. 22m. is 12hs. 42m. which agrees with what apparently, would be the length of the night at Amarkōṭ on 25th October, 1542 (25th is the true date allowing for the difference between Old and New Styles). According to a communication with which I have been favoured by the Meteorological Department, Calcutta—sunset on 25th October in lat. 25 N. is at 5·23 and sunrise, on that day at 6·5. I presume there would be little difference between sunset on the 25th, and sunset on the 24th. The length of the night, then, on 24th October, would be from 5·23 P.M. to 6·5 A.M. or 13hs.-8m.= 12hs. 42m. exactly! On 15th October, sunset occurred at 5·59 P.M. and sunrise at 5·32 A.M. The 8th Ābān of the Persian era apparently corresponds to 26th October. It will be remembered that this era anticipated the corrections of the Gregorian Calendar. Apparently there is some mistake about the years 464 H. and 911 H. for when reduced to Christian years, they give 1543 and not 1542.

3 Properly Saturday, the birth occurring early on Sunday morning. Muḥammadans count their day or *nycthemeron* from sunset.

4 Amarkōṭ is a town in Scinde lat. 25° 21′ N. and long. 69° 46′ E. (Greenwich). Gulbadan spells it Amarkōṭ and in the *Imperial Gazetteer of India*, it appears as Umarkot. The *u* is short. Its latitude and

to the second climate and lies in latitude 25 N. and longitude 105 E. of the Fortunate Isles. At that time, the imperial army had marched to subdue the country of Tatta (Scinde) and the litter of fortune had been directed to halt in the pleasant country and fortunate fortress, on account of the time's drawing nigh for the appearance of the light of the world.

Among the strange circumstances which occurred near the time of the appearance of the light of fortune, there was this,—that before the auspicious moment above-mentioned, the mother felt a pressing urgency to bring forth the child. Maulānā Cānd, the astrologer, who by the king's order, had been stationed by the chaste threshold in order that he might cast the horoscope, was perturbed,
19 as the moment was inauspicious. "In a short time,[1] a glorious "moment will arrive, such as does not happen once in a thousand "years. What an advantage if the birth could be delayed." Those who were present made light of it and said, "What is the good of "your agitation? Such things are not under control."

At this very instant the impulse to bring forth passed off and the astrologer's mind was set at rest somewhat by the transit of the unlucky moment. The ostensible cause of this supreme blessing was that a country midwife had been just brought in to perform her office, and as her appearance was repulsive, the holy soul of Miryam Makānī felt disgusted and her even temper was rebuffed and so the urgency for parturition left her. But when the chosen time came, the Maulānā

---

longitude are also given in the *Āīn.* (Jarrett IV. 59 and text II. 32). The latitude there given is 24° and longitude 100°. In Gladwin's trans. the longitude is omitted, and the latitude given as 20° 40′. The statement in the *Akbarnāma* is more to be relied upon, as giving A. F.'s figures correctly, because the degrees are expressed in words. The *Fortunate Isles* are called by Ulugh Beg and A. F. the *Eternal Isles,* جزائر خالدات, *Jazā'ir-i-khālidāt.* There is an account of the Amarkōṭ (Omercote) district by Sir Bartle Frere. Bombay Selections XXI. 1855.

[1] The text has *ba'd az cand sā'at.* after some moments. The Luck, ed. and No. 564 have *ba'd az zamānī,* after some time. This is a considered reading in No. 564 for some other word has been erased and *zamānī* substituted. Probably *zamānī* is right for the next word to it is *sā'at* and it is not likely that the author would put two *sā'at*(s) in juxtaposition.

became disturbed, lest it should accidentally pass by. The confidants of the harem said to him, "Her Majesty,[1] has after much suffering, "got an interval of relief and is now slumbering. It would not be "right to waken her. Whatever Almighty God, in His good pleasure, "has determined, must happen." Just as they were speaking, the pains of travail came upon her Majesty, Miryam Makānī, and awoke her and in that auspicious moment, the unique pearl of the viceregency of God (*Khilāfat*) came forth in his glory.

They spread the carpet of joy under the canopy of chastity and curtain of honour, and made ready a feast of joy and exultation. The veiled ones of the pavilion, and the chaste inmates of the royal harem anointed the eye of hope with the collyrium of rejoicing and coloured the eyebrows of desire with the indigo[2] of merriness. They decked the ear of good tidings with the earring of success, painted the face of longing with the vermilion of pleasure, encircled the fore-arm of wish with the bracelet of purpose, and donning the anklet of splendour on the dancing foot, stepped into the theatre of delight and joy and raised the strain of praise and gratulation. Fan-wavers sprinkled otto of roses, and winnowed the air with sandal-scented arms. Dark-haired maidens freshened the floor by rubbing it with perfumes. Rose-cheeked damsels gave a new lustre to joy by sprinkling rose-water. Red-garmented, sweetly-smiling nymphs enveloped the silver-bosomed ones in gold, by scattering saffron. Rose-scented, jasmine-cheeked ones soothed the rapid dancers with camphorated[3] sandal-wood. Gold in thuribles on the borders of the carpet, gave off fumes of incense.[4] They uncovered the stoves which were filled with lign-aloes and ambergris. Musicians created enchanting ecstacy, and melodious minstrels breathed forth magic strains.

---

1 *Ḥaẓrat-i-mahd-i-ʿulyā* lit. her Highness of the sublime couch (or cradle).

2 وسمه, *wasma*, woad or indigo. In Zenker's Turkish Dict. this is described as a black dye made from indigo leaves, with which women colour their eyebrows. The dye is indeed of such a deep blue that it may be called black.

3 See the recipe for the powder called *argaja*. Blochmann 74.

4 بخور, *bakhūr*. A. F. gives a recipe for it. Blochmann 74, last line.

VERSE.

And soft-voiced Indian maids,
Glorious[1] as Indian peafowl,
And light-fingered Chinese musicians
Produced intoxication with wineless cups;
And dulcimer-players from Khurāsān
Brought ease to laden breasts,
And singers from the land of 'Irāq,[2]
Everlasting capturers[3] of joy.

In truth there was an assemblage like the communion of saints and recluses in the exquisiteness of its repose, and a carousal like a feast of spiritual beings in the absence of wine and cup. Celestial spectators took part in the rejoicings without the aid of bodily organs of vision, and sightseers from the upper world poured forth this strain with tongueless tongues:

VERSE.

What is this intoxication[4] without wine or bowl?
The wine which is drunk from cups is illicit here.

Trays of variously coloured fruits were spread, and tables laid out with different dainties. Robes of honour of divers colours were bestowed, and *khil'at*[5] upon *khil'at* was presented. What shall I say of the hilarity and rejoicing, for there is no need of explanation or description? Were it possible to give any idea of the completion of

[1] Probably the meaning is not that peacocks are melodious, but that the Indian maids were in beauty like peacocks and had the additional charm of being soft-voiced. The Muḥammadans have a tradition that the peacock was deprived of his voice as a punishment for having conducted Eve to where the forbidden fruit (i.e., wheat) was. See Ṭabarī's Chronicle, Zotenberg I, 82. When the peacock was expelled from paradise, he fell upon India.

[2] 'Irāq is a Persian province. A mode of music takes its name from it. *Gulistān* II. Story 19.

[3] Or it may be, "Song-makers for the banquet of everlasting life," or, "Capturers of joy for the rest of life."

[4] I suppose the reference is to the intoxicating power of music. See Blochmann 612, where A. F. speaks of the wine of harmony causing intoxication.

[5] A *khil'at* is more than a robe, for it consists of at least three articles, viz., the turban, the robe and the girdle.

the designs of the celestials, I might tell how, after long questing and searching, they clothed, with the glorious robe of existence, the Arranger of the world of reality and the Disposer of the outer world, and how they brought him from the hidden cradle of wondrous works and from the holy inner chambers, to the wondrous bridal-chamber of manifestation and splendid nuptial bed. But the description of heavenly exultation and of the joys of pure spirits is beyond the range of speech.

As soon as the light of glory deigned to emerge from the orient of fortune, they despatched swift couriers[1] and hard-riding horsemen to convey the life-increasing news and the heart-expanding tidings to the tents of fortune and encampment of glory. This had been sixteen[2] miles off, but on the morrow of the night which had been pregnant with the day of auspiciousness, the army marched at dawn from that station, and encamped about midday at a spot[3] which was very charming and salubrious, with clear water and delightful trees. There his Majesty Jahānbānī Jannat Āshiyānī had halted and a number of courtiers were assembled and in attendance.

---

1 Though A. F. speaks both of couriers and horsemen, I do not suppose he means that there were both foot and horse messengers.

2 "Four *farsakh*." فرسخ, Arabic form of فرسنگ, *farsang*, the *parasang* of Xenophon; about 4 miles.

3 Jauhar, according to Stewart's trans. (44) says that after leaving Amarkōṭ, Humāyūn marched 24 miles the first day to the banks of a large pond, and that the next day while the king was encamped there, a messenger arrived with the news. But according to A. F. Humāyūn did not arrive at the pond in one day. His camp was 16 miles off from Amarkōṭ and on the morning of the birth, he marched again at dawn and arrived at the halting place where the water was, at about midday. Apparently he did not get the news till the third day, for we are told that he heard of it two days after his vision which was simultaneous with the birth. Jauhar cannot be relied on. He began his Memoirs 45 years after Akbar's birth (995–1587) and he incorrectly states that the birth was on 14th Sha'bān. In Ilhāhad Faiẓ Sirhindī's rescension (No. 1890), this is altered to 14th Rajab. The late Kabī Rāj Çyāmal Dāṣ wrote a paper in the Asiatic Society's Journal (J. A. S. B. LV., Part 1. 1886, 80) to show that the date given by Jauhar was the correct one. I do not agree with his conclusions, but his paper is—like all the Kabī's productions—carefully written and interesting. He translates Jauhar from MSS. and his rendering is closer than Stewart's. He mentions that

VERSE.

Verdant trees with heaven-brushing tops,[1]
Casting shade o'er the head shadowed by the bird of paradise.[2]
The melodious singing of the birds of the meadow
Poured joyous notes over the banquet.

Suddenly a blackness was caused by the hoofs of galloping horses. Mehtar Sumbul,[3] an old slave (*ghulām*), of his Majesty

---

there is a stone two miles N.-W. of Amarkōṭ which professes to mark the spot of Akbar's birth, but the date on it (963) is that of the accession.

Stewart's trans. makes Jauhar's account more discrepant from A. F.'s than it really is, and Erskine has not fully amended Stewart here. On referring to the original, I find that Jauhar says nothing about "the first day" or the "next day." What he says is, that they marched thirty miles (12 *kōs*) and then encamped on the bank of a pond (*ḥauẓ*). No doubt, this place could be identified, It must lie between Amarkōṭ and Jūn, S. W. of the former (W. S. W. is perhaps more correct). The B. M. MS. is worm-eaten at the important place, but the words seem to be *dū shab*, two nights. It is not likely that Humāyūn would march 30 miles in one day and it is probable enough that he made his marches by night. Jauhar says that the news was brought by a *qāṣid* at early morning, *viz.*, at prayer-time. He gives Saturday, 14th Sha'bān as the birthday and says that Badru-d-dīn and Jalālu-d-dīn have the same meaning. But this is hardly correct and 14th Sha'bān 949, appears to have been a Thursday. Gulbadan says the birth took place three days after Humāyūn left Amarkōṭ and adds that the moon was in Leo and that the birth occurred under a fixed sign.

[1] *Lit.* rubbing their umbrellas against the sky.

[2] ظل هماي *ẓill-i-humāī*, the shadow of the *Humā*, a fabulous bird from which the name *Humāyūn* is derived. The *Humā* was supposed to prognosticate a crown to every head that it overshadowed. (No. 564 B. M. MS. Add. Nos. 5610 and 6544 have *ẓill-i-khudāī*, the shadow of God, which the Bib. Ind. gives as a variant). The meaning is said to be that the trees were so high that they even overshadowed the *Humā* or phœnix, high-soaring bird though it be.

[3] Sumbul means *hyacinth*. The name looks like that of an eunuch. Sumbul is mentioned in the *Akbarnāma* (I. 224) under the title of *Mīr Ātish* (Master of Ordnance) and also (263) as commanding a party of musketeers. *Mīr Ātish* means Artillery Officer or Head of the Ordinance Department, like the Corps of Fireworkers of the H.E.I.C.'s army, but it may also mean, head of the musketeers or marksman. (The *Ātish Sarkār* or *Fiery Department* was one of the divisions of offices

Jahānbānī and who was, subsequently raised by the kindnesses of his Majesty, the King of Kings, to the title of Ṣafdar Khān (rank-breaking chief), having perceived that blackness, in which the white sheen of two worlds was enveloped, reported the matter to his Majesty who said, "Should these horsemen bring tidings of the birth of the "light of the eyes of sovereignty, we will make you ruler over a "thousand."

VERSE.

Kings of the earth might well give the seven climes as a reward for such good news.

On that side too, the swift horsemen gave rein to their horses and galloped forward, and the riders[1] of the steeds[2] of auspicious-

made by Humāyūn, in accordance with the number of the elements.) Mehtar Sumbul was perhaps called Ṣafdar Khān because of the destructive effects of his muskets. (See also l. c. 266). He is mentioned by Bāyazīd (I.O.MS. No. 216, p. 186) as Sumbul Mīr Ḥazār and as Ṣafdar Khān Mehtar Ātish. This was in Humāyūn's reign, which might be taken to indicate, contrary to the text, that he got the title from Humāyūn.

In his first volume, A. F. does not give him the title of Ṣafdar Khān but calls him Khān and Mīr Ātish. He was one of those who accompanied Humāyūn to Persia. He is mentioned, as Ṣafdar Khān, in the 3th year of Akbar and as taking part in the siege of Rantanbhūr (*Akbarnāma* II. 330). We are told (l. c. III. 772) of a Ṣafdar Khān's being promoted to the command of 1,000 in the 45th year. He is also mentioned l. c. 184. Blochmann (532) notices a Ṣafdar Khān Khāṣa Khail as entered in the *Ṭabaqāt* list, but as Commander of 2,000. He does not appear in the *Āīn* list.

The title *Mehtar* is of common occurrence in Persian histories. In modern Persian, it is used to mean a groom, but in India it is the designation of a sweeper. In Meynard's Turkish Dict. it is explained as "Officier remplissant les functions de chambellan ou huissier; le Grand Vizier avait dans sa suite quarante *mehtar* faisant fonction de Suisses de son palais." D'Herbélot (*s. v.* Sanbal) says, "Ce mot est aussi un nom d'homme, et se donne plus ordinairement aux esclaves noirs, par ironie, comme ceux de Jasmin et de Cafur qui signifient le jasmin and le camphre dont la blancheur est parfaite."

1 Gulbadan says, as also does Niẓāmu-d-dīn, that the news was brought by Tardī Beg and that Humāyūn rewarded him by forgiving his past offences. See Jauhar for an account of his overbearing manners. He was afterwards put to death by Bairām Khān.

2 رخش, *rakhsh*, the famous horse of Rustam.

ness, having come near, uttered with loud voices the glad news to the sovereign of the world and to mortals, and proclaimed that the light of glory had risen from the horizon of hope, that the dawn of morning of desire had appeared in consonance with wishes, and that the cypress[1] of the spring of fortune had raised her head on the
21 stratum of hope. At the same instant his Majesty bowed his head in adoration and rubbed his forehead in the dust.

VERSE.

The crown of exaltation over the heavens,
The face of submission on the ground,
The foot of dominion on the *Dīwān*,
The head of praise in prostration.

After due rendering of thanks, he proceeded to the camp and entered the spacious hall[2] of audience. A feast was given to the world and the rites of prosperity were revived. The drums of joy and rejoicing raised a sound like the exultation of Kaiqubād. The pavilion was arranged after the manner of Humāyūn[3]—more delightful than the feast of Gayōmarṣ[4] and the banquet of Farēdūn.[4]

VERSE.

O eye! come and behold incomparable glory,
Observe this banquet-hall from without and within.
If you would appreciate the splendour of two worlds,
Look upon the array of Humāyūn's feast.

The old world put on anew the leaves and glory of youth, and rouse up the sad universe, grown forgetful of joy.

VERSE.

The[5] cupbearers seized the goblet of pure wine,
They made Elijah athirst for the fiery fount;—

1 Horace speaks of the *invisae cupressi*, but they are favourite trees with Orientals.

2 Perhaps all that is meant is that he entered the camp enclosure.

3 There is a play on the double meaning of this word which signifies also *august* or *sacred*.

4 These two and also Kaiqubād were early Persian kings. Gayōmarṣ is supposed to have been the first man who exercised regal powers.

5 These couplets are Faiẓī's (*Āīn* I. 239 and Blochmann 555 and 556). *Khiẓr* is the name given by Muhammadans to Elijah or Elias.

What was this wine that the cupbearer poured into the cup?
That the Messiah and Elijah grew envious and contended for it.

Melodious musicians and enchanting vocalists played on divers instruments and produced a variety of notes. Harpers smote[1] the strings of purpose,—lutanists buffetted the world's sorrows,—dulcimer-players bound the chords with the ringlet of success,—strong-breathed flautists drew out harmonious strains,—mandolin[2]-players suspended hearts on the curl of desire,—tambourinists[3] held up the mirror of fortune before their faces,—rare jesters made the tongue eloquent with ingenious conceits,—the jokes of merry buffoons caused the assemblage to break into peals of laughter. World-subduing generals and brigade-adorning captains saluted, with platoons of benedictions,—and crowds of great and small, of sages and servants, paid their respects.[4]

---

1 The Elliot MS. 4*a*. (Bodleian) has: *Cangiyān dast dar sīna-i-maqṣūd dar-zadand*—*i.e.*, harpers smote on the *breast* of purpose.

2 *Ghicak*, also called *kamānca*, a little bow, perhaps a guitar. It was evidently a small instrument, for we are told (Blochmann, 71) that the shell of the cocoa-nut was used for making *ghicaks*. Jarrett (III. 255 *n*. 2) says the *ghicak* is a kind of lute.

3 *Dā'ira-dastān*. The compound is not in the dictionaries, but apparently it means, tambourine-players. *Cymbal-players* would be the more appropriate, for the metallic cymbal might be compared to a metal mirror. A cymbal, however, is generally termed *sanj*. The Walker MS. (Bodleian) appears to read *dā'ira-sāzān*, which may also mean tambourine-players. The regular word for a tambourine-player appears to be *dā'iracī*.

4 It is unfortunate that our author did not for once leave grandiloquence and describe to us in simple language, the hardships and privations amid which his hero was born. *Rien n'est beau que le vrai* is a sentence which, as Gibbon says, should be nailed on the desk of every rhetorician. A. F.'s turgid descriptions of the magnificence of the natal celebrations at Amarkōṭ and the camp are as unpoetical as they are false, and the one touch of nature which he gives is the horror of the young mother at the hideous features of the village midwife. A. F.'s acquaintance with the Gospels and his manifest desire to liken Akbar to the Messiah, might have taught him that the solemnity of the birth-hour would have been deepened by surrounding it with images of distress and poverty. Jauhar, the illiterate old body-servant of Humāyūn, tells us that when the news of

Philosophers worthy of Alexander's approval, and astrolabe-knowing observers who were always seated in the council of mysteries and were confidants of the secrets of the heavens, made the horoscope of the auspicious birth a mirror for their enlightened intellects, and reported that the aspects of the planets and their complete or partial applications[1] prognosticated length of life and the high ascension of the Native on the steps of sovereignty and the degrees of the *khilāfat,* as witness the scheme[2] which has been taken from their tables and exhibited on a page of abridgment.

Likewise his Majesty Jahānbānī Jannat-āshiyānī who held high rank in mathematical sciences and had a heaven-embracing mind, and whose acute intellect was the heart-expanding mirror[3] of Alexander and the world-displaying cup of Jamshīd, made by his own lofty understanding, wondrous deductions and calculations from the indications of the horoscope of the divine masterpiece. He compared them with the results obtained by the other sages from the marks on the plains of the heavens, and the significations of the terrestrial and celestial bodies. He found that they all agreed and corroborated one another.

22 When the sublime festivities were over, he (Humāyūn) named that holy pearl—in accordance with the secret message and divine intimation already described,—by his lofty title and majestic appellation and caused it to be inscribed in the lists of auspiciousness and records of fortune. Thus the interpretation of the veracious vision was fulfilled after an interval of two years[4] and four months!

---

the birth was brought to the camp, there was no money to give away in presents, and Humāyūn sent for a pod of musk and broke it amongst his followers, saying it was all he had to bestow, and uttering the prayer that the child's renown might one day so fill the world as the perfume of the musk was pervading the tent. This story is worth all A. F.'s fustian.

1 اتّصالات, *ittiṣālāt.* This is a technical word and corresponds apparently to the astrological *applications.* (Dic. of T. T. 1508, near foot.) Guido Bonatus has a paragraph entitled *De alitisal planatarum.* (Basle 1550, p. 132). He says *alitisal sive continuatio.* I omit the *iẓāfat* after *tafāẓil.* The technical words for conjunction are *ijtimā'* and *qirān.*

2 Referring to Maulānā Cānd's horoscope, exhibited below.

3 Blochmann (553*n*). Alexander's mirror is a fable arising out of the Pharos at Alexandria.

4 From 4th Rabī'u-l-awwal, 947 to 5th Rajab, 949.

God be praised! Hail! celestial name and sublime talisman which came down from highest heaven and the realms of light and glory, whose splendour and whose rays have taken possession of the Orient and the Occident.

Among the excellencies of the name—which is full of wonders—there is one which my honoured elder brother, an encyclopaedia of inward and outward perfections, the poet-laureate,[1] Abū-l-faiẓ Faiẓī has brought out in various admirable writings, namely, that by the mysterious connections of letters which are lofty vocables[2] and which,—whether separately[3] or in combination,—display their influences, it appears that the indicatory letters (*baiyināt-i-ḥurūf*)[4] of the word *aftāb* (Sun) make the number 223 and thus correspond to the numerical value of the letters of the word ***Akbar***.

---

1 Faiẓī, the elder brother of A. F. was *Maliku-sh-shu'arā* or Poet Laureate; lit. Prince of Poets. Blochmann 491 and 548, and *Akbarnāma* III. 535.

2 *Kalimāt-i-'ālīyāt.* A cabalistic expression. See Dic. of T. T. 320, 1.8.

3 *Dar 'ālam-i-tajarrud ū tarakkub,* lit. world of solitude and combination. I think it means separate letters and letters in combination, and not the spiritual and temporal worlds.

4 بيّنات حروف, *baiyināt-i-ḥurūf*, indications or evidences of the letters, A. F. here enters on cabalistic lore. The Dic. of T. T. (Calcutta 1853. 128 *et seq.*) gives twelve *basaṭ* or modes of manipulating letters. (See also *l. c.* 156, 1.3). Faiẓī's seems to be the second mode, called the *basaṭ-i-talaffuẓ* and the *basaṭ-i-bāṭinī* and the *basaṭ-i-ẓāhirī* (*l. c.* 128, 1.7). It proceeds by pronouncing the letters and dividing them into *zabar* and *banīyāt*. Thus *āftāb* (the Sun) is composed of *alif, fā, tā, alif* and *bā*. The first letter of each of these words is called *zabar* and is discarded; thus, *(a)lif, (f)ā, (t)ā, (a)lif, (b)ā*. The remaining letters are the *baiyināt* or *banīyāt* and their value is calculated according to *abjad* as follows:—

l = 30 + f = 80 = 110
a = 1
a = 1
l = 30 + f = 80 = 110
a = 1

Total ... 223

The Editor of the Luck. *Akbarnāma* says there are nine letters in *āftāb*, *i.e.*, *alif, fē, tē, bē* = 9. He cuts off the *t* as being over 100 in value (its numerical value is 400) and the remaining eight give 223; *viz.*, *alif* = 111; *fē* = 90; *ē* = 10; and *bē* = 12; total 223. Thus he arrives at the same result, by a different road. Blochmann (237, Book II. *Āīn* No. 3) gives apparently another illustration of this process.

The word *Jalālah* is, I think made to yield 66 by cutting off the

VERSE.[1]

That very light which is yielded by the world-adorning Sun,
Is produced from the brows of the sublime *Shāhanshāh*,
That Akbar is allied to *Āftāb* (the Sun),
Is proved by the evidence (*baiyināt*) of the names.

Another of the delightful things about this glorious name is that those who are acquainted with the secrets of cabalistic[2] lore and who know the influences and combinations of letters, who are cognisant of the hidden stations of the divine essence[3] and of revelations,[4]

---

first letter of *Ja* and then counting the others; *viz.*, $a = 1$; $l = 30$; $a = 1$; $l = 30$; and $h = 5$. I do not see how the word *Allāh* could make 66 by *abjad* for a double letter, *i.e.*, one with *tashdīd*, is, according to rule, counted as one only. Perhaps, however, *Allāh* is regarded as containing three *lāms*.

The Lucknow editor says also that the words *āftāb* and *nūl*, *i.e.*, Nawal (Kishor), (his printer and publisher) harmonize if similarly treated; both yielding 612! See his note p. 19 folio ed. and pp. 9 and 10 (preface) ed. 1284 H. (1868 A.D.)

[1] This quatrain occurs on p. 3436 of Faiẓī's *Dīwān* (B.M.MS. Add., No. 7794) and is preceded by the following note by Faiẓī.

"Among the strange mysteries "which have been revealed to me, "who have placed on the head of my "heart the four-gored cap of four-"fold sincerity, there is this that the "*baiyināt-i-asmā-i-ḥurūf* (evidenti-"ary letters) of the sun (*āftāb*) agree "in number with the numerical value "of the word Akbar, which is 223."....

Probably Faiẓī plays on the double meaning of the word *asmā* which stands both for 'names' and 'attributes.' He has many other quatrains on the same subject.

[2] رموز جفر و تکسیر, *rumūz-i-jafar ū taksīr*. *Jafar* means cabalistic lore or the art of the mysteries of letters. It is said to take its name from Jafar Ṣadīq the 6th *Imām*, but no doubt, the art is much older and was in great vogue among the Jews. There is a learned article on the *Kabbala* by Dr. Ginsburg in the Ency. Brittanica. The literal meaning of *taksīr* is breaking in pieces, it coming from the root *kasr*. It is applied to the cabalistic science apparently because that partly consists in breaking up words into their component letters, which again are allocated to the four elements. The word seems to be often used as synonymous with *Jafar*. See Dic. of T. T. 1251, *s. v.* *taksīr* and Ibn Khaldūn, *Notices et Extraits*, XXI, 189.

[3] هويّت, *huwīyat*, ipseity. See Whinfield's *Gulshan-i-rāz*, 31 and Dic. of T. T. 1539.

[4] تنزّلات, *tanazzulāt*, lit. alightings or descendings.

and are aware of the illumination[1] and obscuration of alphabetical letters, according as they are with or without diacritical points, have assigned seven out of the twenty-eight letters of *abjad*[2] to each element. Now the equably-proportioned letters of this august name are a collection of the four-fold degrees (*i.e.*, the four elements), and tell of the collection of the four stages of Beauty, Majesty, Bounty and Perfection. Thus *alif* is Fire, *kāf* Water, *bā* Air and *rā* Earth. Whenever a name, by reason of the equality of its composition, is so made up of letters that no element is wanting in it and no element is redundant, that name is perfectly equipoised between its limits. This equipoise results in the name-bearer's being possessed of excellent qualities, bodily health, length of life, exaltation of sovereignty and lasting joy.

Another point in this matter becomes conspicuous in the window of intelligence, *viz.*, that although this Greater Fortune (*Sa'd-i-akbar,*—meaning Jupiter, and here taken for Akbar) may have enemies on various sides, yet they will be scattered and annihilated. For in the composition and arrangement of the letters of the name, there are two medial letters—*viz.*, *kāf* and *bā* (*k* and *b*) ; *kāf* is watery[3]

---

[1] عالمِ نورانیّت و ظلمانیتِ حروف *'ālam-i-nūrānīyāt u ẓulmānīyāt-i-ḥurūf* the universe of the lucidity and darkness of letters. These are divisions of letters made by practitioners of the art of *Jafar.* (Dic. of T. T. 320, l.6.) Apparently the mysterious letters which head most chapters in the Qur'ān are called *nūrānī*, lucid. Here, however, A. F bases the distinction upon letters being with or without diacritical points. His brother Faiẓī wrote a commentary on the Qur'ān in which he used undotted letters only. (Gladwin's *Dissertation on Persian Rhetoric, etc.* 19. Blochmann 549 and Dic. of T. T. *s. v. ḥarf,* 312). Composition without diacritical points is called *ta'ṭīl* and the opposite is *manqūṭ.* I conjecture from the arrangement of the words in the text and from the fact that Faiẓī called his undotted composition *shu'ā'u-l-ilhām*, rays of inspiration, that the lucid letters are those without diacritical points. Perhaps the name was given to them because they do not require to be lighted up or explained by dots. Dotted letters are styled also *mu'jama* and undotted *muhmala*.

[2] *Abjad*, the employment of the 28 letters of the Arabic alphabet as numerals.

[3] The letters of the alphabet are divided into four classes, corresponding to the four elements and *k* (*kāf*) belongs to the class representing water. See Dic. of T. T. 128. The Lucknow editor points out that *kāf* has also the meaning of *cleaving.*

and carries away the supernal[1] enemies, who are fire, and *bā* which is aerial, scatters the nether enemies, who are earthly. It is right that those who know the subtleties of secrets, should become cognisant of the mysterious *minutiae* of the import of the wondrous Name, and partake of the bounty of its auspiciousness and beneficence.

---

1 The "supernal enemies" are apparently, the *jinns* or demons who, according to Muḥammadan cosmogony, were made out of fire. They are represented by *a* (*alif*) which is a fiery letter. *R* (*ra*) is an earthy letter according to some classifications (Dic. of T. T., watery) and so, represents earthly enemies. In the I.O.MS. No. 3330, (which is a copy of *Akbarnāma*, Vol. I., given by Colonel Kirkpatrick), the explanation of the numerical value of the letters of *āftāb*, which I have already given, is stated in a marginal note. The annotator also arranges the 28 letters of the Arabic alphabet in four classes, as follows :—

| | |
|---|---|
| Fiery :—a, ẕ (ẕāl), sh, ṯ, f, m, h ... | 7 |
| Aerial :—b, t, s, ẓ, n, w, y ... | 7 |
| Earthy :—ḥ, kh, r, d, 'ain, ghain, l | 7 |
| Watery :—ṣ, j, z, ṣ, ṭ, q, k ... | 7 |
| Total ... | 28 |

The Dic. of T. T. gives a somewhat different classification.

## CHAPTER III.

### Description of the auspicious horoscope which was cast at the time of the glorious birth in accordance with the altitudes of the Greek astrolabe. 23

VERSE.

Approach heaven-weighing observer,
Regard with understanding the connexion of the spheres,
Look at the beautiful horoscope of the Lord of conjunction,[1]
Behold the auspicious charter of two worlds,
Contemplate this glorious rescript,
Fortune upon fortune, light upon light.

When the victory-grasping standards were leaving the fort of Amarkōṭ, Maulānā Cānd, the astrologer, who was possessed of great acuteness and thorough dexterity in the science of the astrolabe, in the scrutinizing of astronomical tables, the construction of almanacs, and the interpretations of the stars,—was deputed to be in attendance at the portals of the cupola of chastity (Miryam Makānī, Akbar's mother), in order that he might observe the happy time and ascertain exactly the period of birth. He[2] reported in writing to the exalted camp that, according to altitudes taken by the Greek

---

[1] *Ṣāḥib-qirān.* This title which properly belongs to Tīmūr and was afterwards bestowed on Shāh Jahān, seems to be applied here to Akbar because, according to the Indian horoscope (*viz.*, No. 2.), Jupiter and Venus were in conjunction at his birth. (See text 28, l.6.) The title may however, mean only Lord of epochs.

[2] Maulānā Cānd also cast the horoscope of Jahāngīr (Salīm) in the 14th year of Akbar, 977 = 1570. Text II. 346.) He is mentioned in Jai Singh's preface to the Muḥammad Shāhī Tables, under the name of Mullā Cānd, and as the author of the *Taṣhīlāt-i-Akbar Shāhī*. (Dr. Hunter, Asiatic Researches, V. 177.)

astrolabe, and by calculations based on the *Gurgānī* tables (Canon of Ulugh Beg[1]) the figure of the nativity was as follows :—

FIGURE[2] I.

AKBAR'S HOROSCOPE.

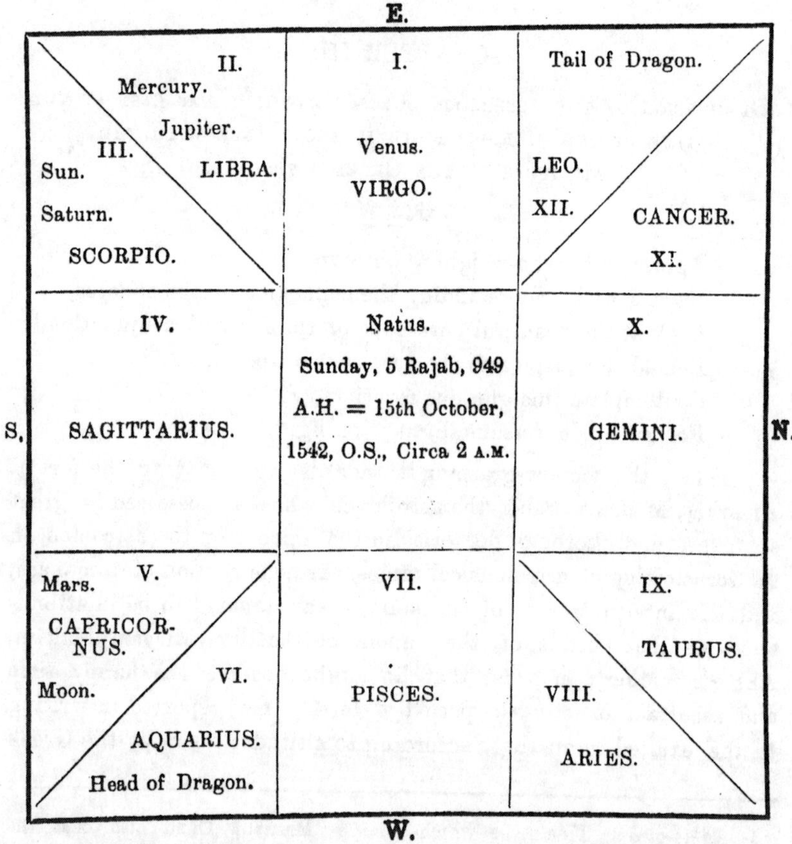


---

1 Ulugh Beg Mīrzā was a grandson of Tīmūr and son of Shāhrukh. For information about his Tables see the works of Hyde, Greaves and Sédillot. He was born in 1393 and put to death by his own son in 1449. His Tables were first published in 1437. See Jarrett II. 5n., and an interesting paragraph and note in Erskine's *Bābar* (51.)

2 I have added the numbers of the Houses to the diagram, and have inserted the date of birth. It will be seen that there is a difference of form between the horoscope as here given and the more elaborate dia-

Although Virgo is a Bicorporal[1] Sign, partly Fixed and partly Tropical, yet in this frontispiece of felicity, the fixity of the horoscope is, on close observation and careful consideration, indicated by 24

---

grams to be found in European books. In the latter, the observer is supposed to be looking south and the First House or Ascendant is on his left hand. In the horoscopes of the text, the observer appears to be looking east, for the First House or Ascendant is in front of him.

Although I have used capital letters for the designation of the Signs, it should be remembered that the Houses are those of the figure and not of the heavens, *i.e.*, they are mundane and not celestial. They do not correspond exactly with the celestial Houses, for the First House, *i.e.*, the Ascendant or horoscope, and which is that of life, begins at 7° of Virgo.

1 This is the Greek δισώματος. The signs of the Zodiac were divided into three groups, *viz.*, Tropical, Fixed and Bicorporal. Each group contained four Signs and the list is as follows :—

| *Tropical.* | *Fixed.* | *Bicorporal.* |
|---|---|---|
| Aries. | Taurus. | Gemini. |
| Cancer. | Leo. | Virgo. |
| Libra. | Scorpio. | Sagittarius. |
| Capricornus. | Aquarius. | Pisces. |

Astrologers also divided the Signs into three groups of four each, thus :—

| | | | | |
|---|---|---|---|---|
| *Tropical.* | Aries. | Cancer. | Libra. | Capricornus. |
| *Fixed.* | Taurus. | Leo. | Scorpio. | Aquarius. |
| *Bicorporal.* | Gemini. | Virgo. | Sagittarius. | Pisces. |

A. F. seems to say that the term *bicorporal*, like *common*, meant that a Sign possessed the properties of the Signs on either side of it; *e.g.*, Virgo was bicorporal because between the Fixed Leo and the Tropical Libra.

The Signs were also divided into Tropical, Fixed, Equinoctial and Bicorporal: and into Moveable, Fixed and Common. Acccording to Lilly's "Christian Astrology," the Bicorporal Signs were those represented by two bodies, such as Gemini and Pisces. Sagittarius is bicorporal because a centaur. But Virgo is also bicorporal, as may be seen from the table in Albīrūnī's *India* (Sachau, II. 218). Apparently this is because the figure was regarded as that of a hermaphrodite. Lilly (86. 2nd. ed. 1659) says "Signs are constituted between moveable and fixed and retain a property or nature partaking both with the preceding and consequential Sign." So also Ptolemy says, "The Bicorporal Signs severally follow the Fixed Signs; and being thus intermediately placed between the Fixed and Tropical Signs, they participate in the constitutional properties of both from their first to their last degree." (*Tetrabiblos*, Ashmand, 35.) This explains A. F.'s description of Virgo, for she is between the Fixed Leo and the Tropical Libra. Lilly (96) describes Virgo as a "barren Sign, but also human," and as "an earthly, cold, melancholy, barren, feminine, nocturnal, southern (northern?) Sign, the house and exaltation of ☿ (Mercury), of the earthly triplicity."

two circumstances. One is that the cusp[1] of the Ascendant is 7°,[2] and so belongs to the first third[3] (decanate) of the Sign which, astrologers are agreed, denotes fixity. The other is that Virgo is an earthy[4] Sign, and fixity[5] is the property of the earthy element. These are two proofs of the fixity of the throne of sovereignty and of the stability of the cushion (*masnad*) of the *Khilāfat*. Moreover, Mercury, the Lord of the Ascendant, is in this glorious nativity posited by the Greater Fortune,[6] for Jupiter, *i.e.*, the Greater Fortune, is beside him, and Mercury is a planet who makes good luck, better luck. Venus, the Lesser Fortune, is in Mercury's[7] House (Virgo) and Mercury, in hers, *viz.*, Libra.[8] He signifies wisdom,

---

1 جزو طالع, *juzw-i-ṭāli'*, *i.e.*, part or degree of the Ascendant or horoscope. I think it here means cusp, *i.e.*, the place where the House begins. The phrase occurs again in the text, 30. l.2.

2 Badāonī (Lowe, 269), mentions that on the festival of the 8th of Virgo, Akbar used to show himself marked on the forehead like a Hindu, and had strings of jewels tied on his wrists by Brahmans. Apparently this was because it was the anniversary of his birth. The 8th degree of Virgo might correspond to 8th Ābān.

3 Each Sign contains 30° and is divided into three parts of 10° each. It may be noted that 7° 7′ Virgo is said to be Mercury's term. A.F. here calls these parts thirds, but they are commonly called decanates or faces.

4 The Signs are also divided into four groups or triplicities, corresponding to the four elements. Taurus, Virgo and Capricornus constitute the earthy triplicity.

5 Referring to the Ptolemaic notion of the earth's being fixed and in the centre of the universe.

6 Jupiter is called *Sa'd-i-Akbar* or the Greater Fortune (*Fortuna Major*) and Venus *Sa'd-i-Asghar* or the Lesser Fortune (*Fortuna Minor.*) Saturn and Mars are called the Infortunes.

7 Mercury is regarded as a planet of mixed disposition and the character of his influence depends on his associate. Here, because he is near Jupiter, he is benefic. Virgo is his House and place of exaltation. According to the Lucknow editor, his culmination or highest point of exaltation is 7° 4′ Virgo, but according to the *Jyōtiṣa-Prakāça* it is 15°. Haly in his *De judiciis astrorum* says (16), *Mercurius fortunatus est cum fortunatis, et infortunatus, cum infortunatis.*

8 Libra is the diurnal House of Venus, while it is the *hubūṭ* or fall of the Sun. Hence the distich in the *Anwār-i-Suhailī* (Cap : IX. Story 3. 417. Hertford ed.) "Libra is the mansion of the star of amusement and joy, but the fall of the king of the planets." (*sc.* the Sun.) There is another astrological allusion in the same story, (416) where it is said that certain sailors made

knowledge, dexterity and ingenuity, and both by equal distribution of (mundane) Houses and by Sign, he is in the Second House which is connected[2] with the means of livelihood and the support of life. He bestows on the Native[3] amplitude of perfect reason and understanding, so that he adorns the universe with the light of intellect in the affairs of this life and the next, and opens knots, whether spiritual or temporal, with the very finger-tips of his understanding.

---

like the Moon, their mansion in a watery tower (*burj*). I believe this refers to the fact that the Moon's mansion is Cancer which is a watery Sign, *i.e.*, belongs to the watery triplicity of Cancer, Scorpio and Pisces.

1 تسوية *taswiyat.* In the dictionaries, this word is defined as meaning *making equal* or *parallel.* Here it refers to the division of the horoscope into twelve parts or Houses. "There are two kinds of Houses in astrology," says Wilson in his Dictionary of Astrology, "mundane and planetary. Mundane Houses are each a twelfth part of a figure (a horoscope) and begin their number at the east angle which is the First House (Ascendant), and proceed according to the order of the Signs. The Second House is the left, under the Earth, and is what they call Succedent, because it succeeds to the angle. The Third is to the left of the Second and is called Cadent, because it falls from the angle of the Fourth. The Fourth is the north angle or *Imum Coeli.*"

The full expression appears to be تسوية البيوت *taswiyatu-l-buyūt*—and not merely *taswiyat* as in the text. Chapter XII of 'Ulugh Beg's *Prolegomena* (Part III. Sédillot 141) is headed در معرفة تسوية البيوت and Sédillot translates this (198), "Déterminer la distribution régulière des douze maisons célestes." It appears from Rieu's Catalogue of Arabic MSS. (Suppl. 519*a*), that there is a chapter in Albīrūnī's *Canon Masudicus* (Fol. 242*b*), on the *Taswiyatu-l-buyūt.* See also, for the full expression, *Akbarnāma* II. 711. 2 and 4 fr. foot. Cf. also *Bādshāhnāma* of *'Abdu-l-ḥāmid* (99 1.4 fr. foot), where reference is made to the two *ḥisābs* or modes of calculation. But *taswiyat* alone also occurs there. (I. 103, 1.9.) Of course the Houses of a horoscope seldom or never exactly correspond with the Signs, for they are counted from the degree and minute which is ascending at the time of birth. The author means here that Mercury is in the Second House of the figure and also, in the Second Sign counting from Virgo, *viz.*, Libra,—for, as the mundane and celestial do not correspond, Mercury might have been in the Second House of the figure and yet in the Third Sign, counting from the Ascendant.

2 The Second House is that of fortune, wealth, or property, the First being that of life.

3 The technical name for the subject of a horoscope.

As Venus who is renowned for auspiciousness and prosperity and who signifies joy and pleasure,—is in this horoscope, (*i.e.*, the Ascendant or First House) she keeps ever ready the things of joy and gladness and the materials of magnificence and glory. It is a remarkable circumstance that whilst the lord of the Ascendant (Mercury) is in the House of wealth (the Second), the lord of the House of wealth (Venus)[1] is in the Ascendant (the First or House of Life.) Thus the two together signify personal and circumstantial felicity, and bestow a life of power and pleasure. Jupiter—the Greater Fortune—who signifies justice, integrity, magnanimity, firmness of soul and civilization,[2] is also in the Second House and, as he is in sextile[3] to the Fourth House which is that of finality, he keeps perfection of power and pleasure closely associated with the glorious condition of his Majesty, down to the very end. The double-natured (*dipsychus*) Mercury has acquired extreme auspiciousness, by reason of his vicinity to the Greater Fortune, and has heaped felicity upon felicity. He signifies that the Native will, by greatness of genius and loftiness of development, become the apex of mankind, and he indicates assemblages of the masters of understanding and reason and of the lords of perception and penetration. The philosophers of the age and sages of every sect will attend the wisdom-protecting Court, and ingenious wits of all countries will forsake their native lands, and donning the pilgrim's garb, will circumambulate his sublime threshold. Whatever the ray of illumination shall have darted into his inspired soul, will be consonant with
25 reason and reality. Having opened the gates of justice and equity to all mankind, he will in every action hold fast by the principles of rectitude and protection (*diyānat u ṣiyānat*). He will apply his genius to founding magnificent buildings such as have rarely been constructed in the times of former princes, and in those choice mansions he will pass his time in varieties of joys and happinesses and in all manner of ease and independence.

Among remarkable[4] circumstances we have this,—that Venus

---

[1] Though Venus be feminine, she is spoken of as *Ṣāḥib*, *i.e.*, lord or master.

[2] *Lit.* building up of the world.

[3] Sixty degrees or two Houses, *i.e.*, one-sixth of the heavens, apart.

[4] The author seems to have forgotten that he had already mentioned this circumstance. See *supra*.

is in the House of Mercury and Mercury in the House of Venus. Thus three happy influences are combined;—*viz.*, 1°. the happy influence of Jupiter,—2°. the happy influence of Venus;—3°. the happy influence which Mercury has imbibed from the fortunate twain. This is something very uncommon.

The Great Light (the Sun), the benefactor of the universe and moderator[1] of the affairs of mortals, and the special bestower of glory, power, pomp and prestige is in the Third House and in a Fixed Sign (Scorpio), signifying the grant of dignity, glory, greatness and magnificence. As he has come out of his *fall*[2] and his face is set toward his *exaltation*, he has made the Native's glory increase, day by day, and as he is in aspect[3] to the Ninth House (Taurus) which is that of travel. the standards[4] of victory and conquest will always be upraised on the march,[5] while he himself protects mankind from

---

1 Referring to the Sun's control of times, and seasons.

2 هبوط *hubūṭ*, fall, *i.e.*, the House opposite to, or six Houses apart from, the House of exaltation. Libra is the House of the Sun's fall, as being opposite to the House of exaltation, *viz.*, Aries. The author says that, as the Sun has emerged from Libra and entered Scorpio, he has left his fall and is proceeding towards his exaltation in Aries.

3 ناظر *Nāẓir*. The aspect is one of opposition or 180° which is regarded by astrologers as malefic. I do not therefore see the appropriateness of A.F.'s remark unless indeed, he is using the word *nāẓir* in a non-technical sense and merely as meaning one who beholds or inspects. There is a reference to the aspects in Paradise Lost X. 656.

To the blanc Moon
Her office they prescribed, to the other five
Their planetary motions and aspects
In Sextile, Square, and Trine and Opposite
Of noxious efficacy.

4 I do not feel sure of the meaning here. It is perhaps, the standards who are represented as illuminating the world,—the allusion being to the royal flag or standard's bearing a picture of the sun. See Blochmann Sayyid Aḥmad's Plates, IX. Figure I. The *kaukabah* (fig. 2) has a sphere suspended from it which apparently represents the Sun. See Blochmann's quotation from Terry IX.

5 سفر, *safar*. This word, like the German *Reise*, means both travel and war and A.F. probably intended to take advantage of the equivoque. There seems also an antithesis intended between the words *safar* and *kanaf*, كنف region or country. The standards of victory are abroad on the march while the Sun (Akbar) remains in the region of light-giving and protecting. The literal translation is "he (*i.e.*, the Sun or Akbar)

the confusions and calamities of the age and is the light-giver of the world.

As the Third House which is that of kindred, is Scorpio, it is significant of Scorpion-kinsmen.[1] (اقارب عقارب *aqārib-i-'aqārib.*) Saturn there sends those alien relatives (distant-near ones) by calamities and disasters, to the nethermost hell of destruction and perdition.

The Fourth angle[2] is Sagittarius and is the House of the final issue of things. Jupiter, its lord, is in sextile to it and is contiguous[3] to the ameliorated Mercury,[4] and in his own term[5] and triplicity.[6] Whatever the Native deigns to undertake, will be accom-

---

(is in) the region of protecting and guarding and is giving light to the world." There is a similar passage in the *Bādshāhnāma* (102 top line *et seq.*) but there is an interesting difference in the mode of treatment. The Ninth House is also that of religion. A.F. passes over this point but the caster of Shāh Jahān's horoscope lays stress on it and infers from the fact of Venus (whom he calls the planet of *Islām*) being in aspect towards the Ninth House that Shāh Jahān will be an upholder of religion and a faithful follower of Muḥammad. In Shāh Jahān's horoscope, the position noticed in Akbar's is reversed, the Third House being Taurus, *i.e.*, that of Venus, and the Ninth being Scorpio.

[1] There is a similar play on the two words in Badāonī. (Lowe 71.) The expression is used there with reference to Akbar's maternal uncle, Khwāja Mu'aẓẓam who certainly was a scorpion-relative.

[2] There are four angles or cardinal points, *viz.*, the First, Fourth, Seventh and Tenth Houses of a horoscope. The Arabic name is وتد *watad* lit.: tent-pole. They are the most important houses in a figure, the First being the Ascendant, the Fourth its nadir, *i.e.*, the north angle or *hypogeum*; the Seventh, the west or descendant angle, being opposite to the First, and the Tenth being the Mid-heaven. Sagittarius is Jupiter's House and gaudium.

[3] *Muttaṣil.* This is perhaps a technical term and refers to a planet's *applying to* another planet.

[4] *'Uṭārid-i-mas'ūd.* Mercury is called *mas'ūd*, benefited or auspicious, because he has become benefic by proximity to Jupiter and Venus. See Albīrūnī (Sachau II. 212.)

[5] حد *ḥadd.* The degrees of each sign are divided among the five planets, Saturn, Jupiter, Mars, Venus and Mercury, and those assigned to each are called its *term* (*terminus*). The term is one of a planet's essential dignities and tables of terms, showing the degrees assigned to each planet, are to be found in all astrological books.

[6] This is the fiery triplicity, consisting of Aries, Leo and Sagittarius. Jupiter is lord of this triplicity during the night and so, was its lord at the time of Akbar's birth.

plished with the greatest ease, and the terminations of his works will be prosperous.

The Fifth House is that of offspring and is Capricornus, a sign indicative of many[1] children. Mars, the soldier's planet, is there and is a *kadkhudā*[2] of the Ascendant which is the centre[3] of the laws of life. It is a glorious thing that this warlike planet is in his House of exaltation, and by face,[4]

[1] According to Haly (p. 2) Capricorn is a sign of few sons. It is Mars' House of exaltation. Haly's words are: *Signa multorum filiorum Pisces, Cancer, Scorpio; paucorum filiorum, Aries, Taurus, Sagittarius, Capricornus et Libra.*

[2] كدخداي طالع *kadkhudā-i-ṭāli'*. The word *kadkhudā* perhaps has the sense of the Alcochoden of medieval times. It seems to mean the planet in a horoscope which has most dignities in a hylegiacal place. Alcochoden is sometimes defined as the Arabic word for hyleg. (See note *infra* on hyleg.) According to Vullers' Dictionary, *s. v.*, *kadkhudā* means, in astrology, the soul or vital principle in opposition to *kadbānū*, the body. See *Mafātīḥu-l-'ulūm*, 331. It would seem that *kadkhudā* corresponds to the term "lord of the geniture," and means a planet in possession of all its dignities, essential and accidental. Such a planet is said to be *mubtazz* (from *ibtizāz*) Velschius in his *Commentarius in Roznāma Naurus* (1676) identifies *kadkhudā* with hyleg. The *Burhān-i-qāṭi'* states that *kadbānū* is equivalent to the Greek *hailāj* (hyleg). *Kadkhudā* means *paterfamilias* and *kadbānū*, *materfamilias* and so, Vullers suggests that *hailāj* may be the Greek ἄλοχος, but I believe the derivation from ὑλικός is correct.

Apparently what is meant here, by the Ascendant's being a centre of the laws of life, is that the Ascendant or First House is the House of Life.

[3] I take this expression to mean merely that the First House is that of life, but there may be an allusion to the Fardars,—the Alfridaria of Cardan, and the true translation may be, "a lord of the geniture who is the centre of the code of life,"—alluding to the fact of Mars' governing the years from 28 to 35.

[4] وجه *wajh*. This is the Greek πρόσωπον. It is the third part of a sign (10°) and thus corresponds to the decanate. The word *face* is also commonly used in English books on astrology. Dozy (II. 7852) says, *s.v.* *wajh*, "Les astrologues partagent chaque signe du zodiaque en trois faces, de dix degrés chacune. Les trente-six faces sont assignées, chacune à une des planètes ou au soleil ou à la lune." Salmon, however, in his *Horae Mathematicae* divides each Sign of the Zodiac into six faces of 5° each. See *Tetrabiblos*, Ashmand 28n. The above is what is meant by the term *face* as applied to a Sign, but the word has another meaning as applied to a planet. Ashmand

triplicity,[1] *darijān*,[2] *ādarjān*[3] and dodecatemorion[4] has endowed the Native with long life, and has given him the enjoyment of many sons and grandsons. His sons, too, will be fortunate and capable. He will also have world-traversing, victorious soldiers. It is a beautiful coincidence that in the horoscope of the Lord of Conjunction, (Timur) Mars is in the Fifth House, as mentioned in the *Ẕafarnāma*.[5] Experienced philosophers have laid stress on the

(l. c. 54) says, "Each planet is said to be in its proper face, when the aspect it holds to the Sun or Moon is similar to that which its own House bears to their Houses, for example, Venus is in her proper face when making a sextile aspect to either luminary, provided she be occidental to the Sun, but oriental to the Moon, agreeably to the primary arrangement of her Houses. And it follows that Saturn is in his proper face when he is five Signs, or in quintile, after the Sun or before the Moon; that Jupiter is so in trine; Mars when in quartile; Venus when in sextile; and Mercury when only one Sign (or, in modern phrase, semi-sextile) after the Sun or before the Moon." Similarly Wilson (Dic. of Astr.) says, "a planet is in its *face* when it is at the same distance from the Sun or Moon as its House is from their Houses and in the same succession of Signs." Probably when A. F. speaks of the *wajh* of a planet, he means this kind of face and not the third part of a Sign, which he designates by *darījān* decanate.

1 The earthy triplicity, consisting of Taurus, Virgo and Capricornus.

2 On the meaning of this word, see *Note* I. at the end of this Chapter, page 82.

3 On the meaning of this word, see *Note* II. at the end of this Chapter, page 82.

4 إثناعشريه *asnā'asharīah*, a twelfth part or two and a half degrees of a Sign; the δωδεκατημόριον of the Greeks. Scaliger refers to it in his notes on Manilius (Leyden ed. 179), and a table of Twelfths is given in Bengali books on astrology. The planet which rules the Sign is lord of the First Twelfth; the rulers of the two following Signs are lords of the second, and third, and so on. Thus Mars is lord of the first dodecatemorion of Aries, he being regent of Aries; Venus lord of the second, as being ruler of Taurus; and Mercury is ruler of the third, as regent of Virgo. The expression *twelfth part* is explained in Dict. of T. Ts. (I. 185). Ashmand (50) says the Twelfth of a Sign is technically called a *place*. The Persians call it دوازده بهره *duwāzda bahra*.

5 Bib. Ind. ed. I.14. The Fifth House is that of children. The Fifth House of Tīmūr's horoscope was Taurus, and Jupiter was there as well as Mars, while Venus was in the Third House (Pisces.) Tīmūr, like Augustus was born under Capricorn. His nativity, as cast by Ashmole, will be found in Hyde's *Syntagma* (II. 466) as pointed out by Gibbon.

power of Mars in the horoscopes of princes. The present powerful and holy horoscope excels that of the Lord of Conjunction in that this majestic planet is in his House of exaltation (Capricornus) and has the other dignities mentioned above. This signifies glory and greatness, lofty rank, victory and dominion, and that yet his glory will be greater and better from his youth upwards. The Moon who is the intermediary[1] between the celestial influences and the terrestrial elements, having come as an increaser[2] of light, points the way to daily increasing dominion.

She is also the hyleg,[3] which is the tabernacle of the soul and

---

[1] The heaven of the Moon is that nearest the earth, and therefore she is regarded as a link between the heavens and the earth. She is also the distributor of light from the heavenly bodies to the earthy ones. See *Akbarnāma* II. 8, l.14. Haly calls the Moon, the *Alguazil, i.e.*, the Vizier or Prime Minister of the Sun.

[2] زائد النور *zā'idu-n-nūr*. This is an epithet of the Moon. She is also called the swift-goer, *sarī'u-s-sair*, in opposition, perhaps, to Saturn who is called the slow-goer. (*Akbarnāma* II. 10 l.8.)

Hyleg is a word well-known in European astrology and comes from the Greek ὑλικός. It signifies the foundation or beginning of life and also the duration of life. Sédillot says (*Prolegomena*, Text 149). "Ce mot signifie le lieu de la vie; il est pris dans le sens de durée de la vie." Hyleg is also defined as the Moderator, Significator or Prorogator of life.

Moxon says (Mathematical Dictionary). "Hyleg or hylech, an Arabic word signifying the Giver of life; a planet or part of heaven which, in a man's nativity becomes, in an astrological sense, the moderator or significator of his life; hence hylegiacal places are such as when a planet happens to be posited therein, he may be said to be *hyleg* or to have the government of life attributed to him; which places are commonly reckoned five, *viz.*, the Ascendant, the Midheaven, the Seventh House, the Ninth and the Eleventh House. Also the Sun, Moon and Part of Fortune.

The question of hylegiacal places is one much discussed in astrological books. In the text the word is perhaps used as an equivalent for *kadbānū*, the body as opposed to the soul, *kadkhudā*. Sachau (Chronology of Ancient Nations) has translated it by *materfamilias*. There is a curious note in Schefer's *Chrestomatie Persane* (I. 102) where he says that hyleg is the Arabic form of the Persian *hailāj* which signifies master of the house or head of the family. And he mentions a book by Abu Mashar of Balkh bearing the title *Kitābu-l-Hailāj*. M. Schefer supposes that this book must have treated of domestic economy, but it is almost certain it was an astrological work. Haly says (147) that Ptolemy established five hylegs, *viz.*, the Sun, the Moon, the Ascendant, the Part of

26 guardian of the body, and is in the Fifth House. As she is separating (*munṣarif*) from Mars and is in trine to Venus, she is a cause of continual health, soundness of constitution and bodily strength.

The Sixth House is Aquarius and signifies armies. Saturn is the dominant and he is in the Third House which is that of allies and helpers. The Dragon's Head (*Rās*[1] or Anabibazon) is there and signifies soldiers of loyal and devoted clans.

The Seventh angle (*i.e.*, the Descendant or west angle) is Pisces at the seventh degree, which is the term[2] of Venus and belongs to her triplicity[3] and *ādarjān*.[4] She gives[5] chaste veiled ones who are constant in pleasing service and respects; and she makes the Native happy and prosperous by their good offices.

The Eighth House is Aries; Mars is its lord and his benefic influences have already been described. He is in trine to the Ascendant and signifies the Divine protection[6] in positions of fear and hidden dangers.

The Ninth House (Taurus) is that of travel. As its regent (Venus) is posited in the Ascendant—Virgo, she holds in readiness, tranquillity and pleasure in distant journies and makes them a cause of increase of territory.

---

Fortune and the Place of Conjunction or Opposition of the Sun and Moon prior to the birth. The Moon was probably the hyleg in Akbar's horoscope because his birth took place at night.

The hyleg was also called *aphēta* and was opposed to *anairēta*, destroyer.

[1] Anabibazon, the *ascending node* of the Greeks and *Rāhu* of the Hindus.

[2] Cardan (*De judiciis geniturarum.* Nuremburg 1547. 79b.) gives the first seven degrees of Pisces as the term of Venus.

[3] Venus is the noctural lord of the watery triplicity or *trigon, viz.*, Cancer, Scorpio and Pisces, for the last is her House of exaltation.

[4] If *ādarjān* be the same as decanate, I do not see how the seventh degree falls within the *ādarjān* of Venus, for the rule is that the first decanate of a Sign belongs to the lord of that Sign and the lord of Pisces is not Venus but Jupiter. Pisces is, however, the House of Venus' exaltation, and its 27th degree is said to be the *ὕψωμα, auj*, of Venus. Perhaps the reference is to this. Possibly A. F. used the word *ādarjān* without understanding it.

[5] The Seventh House is that of marriage.

[6] The Eighth House is one of misfortune and danger. Hence the need for the Divine protection. To be in *trine* is to be 120°, four Houses, apart.

The Part of Fortune (*Pars Fortunae*[1]) is in the Tenth angle which is that of dominion and prosperity (*iqbāl*). Its lord, the auspicious Mercury, is in trine to it. As the Greater Fortune (Jupiter) is also in trine to it, this signifies majestic sovereignty, perfect reason and justice, and brings the world's treasures into the powerful grasp of the Native.

The Eleventh House (Cancer) is that of Hope. Its lord is the crescent Moon. She is in the Fifth House of the horoscope, and as she is in trine to the Ascendant, she is a cause of safety and of the attainment of desires.

The Twelfth House (Leo) is that of enemies. The Dragon's Tail[2] (Ẕanab) being posited in it, makes the enemies of eternal fortune downcast and contemptible. It turns every wretch who averts his face from the altar of obedience, topsyturvy into the wilderness of annihilation. Its lord, the Sun, being posited in the Third House, *viz.*, that of allies and helpers, will bring many opponents to repentance and the path of submission and devotion. A wonderful thing in this horoscope is that the Tenth House, that of dominion and sovereignty, is in Gemini of which the lord of the Ascendant, (Mercury) is the regent. It is established that every lord of the Ascendant desires to promote his own signification (*or perhaps*, what is committed to him), but that he may be frustrated by obstacles to his power. Now in this auspicious horoscope, Mercury's House is also that of dominion and sovereignty. Seeing that dominion (*daulat*) is posited in his own (Mercury's) House, why should he (Mercury) hold back from carrying out his own signification (or, from what has been committed to him)?

---

1 "An imaginary point in the heavens supposed to contain equal power with the luminaries." (Wilson, 306). In the *Tetrabiblos* (Ashmand) we read that the Part of Fortune is calculated by counting the number of degrees between the Sun and Moon.

2 Katabibazon, the *descending node* of the Greeks; Kētu of the Hindus. It is where the Moon crosses the ecliptic on her way south.

NOTE I. (from page 78.)

دريجان *darījān*. Vullers describes this as an astrological rule according to which a Sign is divided into three parts and a planet assigned to each. The original Persian form is دريگان *darīgān*. It is the *dreshkāna* or *drekkāna* of the Hindus. Albīrūnī (II. 222) says, "Further, there are the triangles, called *drekkāna*. There is no use in enlarging on them, as they are simply identical with the so-called *draijānat* of our system." Unfortunately Albīrūnī did not foresee a time when Arabian and Persian astrology would be forgotten and his *Canon Masudicus* a sealed book. Sachau speaks of it (there are four copies in Europe and one in the Mullā Fīrōz Library at Bombay) as awaiting the combination of two editors a scholar and an astronomer, but probably, a third, an astrologer, would also be required. Colebrooke says (Asiatic Researches IX. 367) that the *dreshkāna* answer to the *decāni* of European astrologers. The *decāni* also correspond to the *wajh* of Arabian astrologers and according to the Lucknow editor of the *Akbarnāma*, are called by Hindus *ṣūrat*, face. *Decanus*, according to Scaliger's notes on Manilius, (329) comes from the Latin and not from the Greek. The Luck. ed. gives an explanation of the word *darījān* (27) and the corresponding term *drekkāna* is explained in Bengali books on astrology. It seems that every sign is divided into three parts each of 10°, that the planet who presides over the sign, is lord of the first 10°, that the next 10° are ruled by the planet who presides over the Fifth Sign from that under division, and that the third 10° or *drekkāna* is ruled by the planet presiding over the Ninth Sign from that under division.

(With reference to the "triangles" in the above quotation from Sachau, it should be observed that the word in the original is الاثلاث *alaṣlāṣ*, the plural of *ṣāliṣ* and should be translated *thirds* and not *triangles*. The *drekkāna* are not triangles but ten degrees or thirds of a Sign.)

---

NOTE II. (from page 78.)

آدرجان *ādarjān*. This word puzzled me for a long time. It is not to be found in the dictionaries except under the form آردجان or آردگان. They however do not explain even this word; saying only that it means "certain figures and mysteries in astrology." (See Vullers 78 and Steingass.) The Lucknow editor (27) says that *ādarjān* is the same as *wabāl*, and he repeats this explanation at page 30. He there says also that *ādarjān*, is a fortitude or dignity superior to that of the *darījān*, but inferior to that of the *wajh* face. It is clear therefore that it cannot bear the same meaning as *wabāl* which is a debility and corresponds to the English *detriment*. Perhaps the editor connected it with *auj*, *apsis* or exaltation. Another explanation was sent me from India, to the effect that when two planets were in the same *muṣallaṣat* or triplicity, each was said to be the *ādarjān* or partner of the other. If this were so, the word might be connected with the Arabic ادرج or ادراج *idraj* or *idrāj*, a fold or folding; but I now believe this explanation is quite incorrect. The fact seems to be that *ādarjān* or *ādarajān* is merely a form of the word *darījān* and is probably nothing but that word with the Arabic article *al* prefixed. The word occurs in the *Mafātīḥu-l-'ulūm* (ed. Vloten, Leyden 1895, 226) under the forms *aldahaj* and *aldaraj* and is there explained as synonymous with *wajh, ṣūrat* and *dārījān*. The editor says it is the same as the Greek δέκας. That this explanation is correct appears from the Latin translation of an early treatise on Astrology by an Eastern writer, commonly known as Alchabitius, but whose real name was 'Abdu-l-'azīz ibn 'Uṣmān Alqabīsī and who, according to the *Biographie Universelle* lived in the 10th century. He wrote a *Madkhal* or Introduction to Astrology which was translated into Latin by Johannis Hispalensis and was several times reprinted. Its Arabic title is given in Ḥājī Khalfa's Lexicon (V. 473) as *Madkhal fī 'ilm-al-nujūm*. In the *Differentia Quarta* (Cap. IV. The pages are not separately numbered, but this chapter is a few pages after *dd*4.) of this work, there is the following passage :—

"*Modus inveniendi dominum decani.*"

"*Et ex hoc adorogen, hoc est ut dividas ascendens in tres partes; et sit omnis divisio 10 graduum; dabisque divisionem primam domino ascendentis; et secundam domino quinti signi ab eo; et tertium domino noni; nam ascendens, 5, et 9 una semper sunt triplicitas. Verbi gratiâ, ab initio Arietis usque in decimum gradum ejus est dorogen i. (i.e.) decanus est Martis. Et si fuerit ex 10 gradu usque 20 gradum erit ejus dorongen sol, dominus Leonis. Et si fuerit 20 usque in finem ejus erit dorongen Jupiter, dominus Sagittarii.*"

The same volume contains a commentary on Alchabitius by John of Saxony and at M.M. 3, we have these words, "*Et ex hoc adoringen. Hic docet invenire decanum.*" This commentary, it seems, was written in 1331, though apparently not printed till 1485.

The book is in the British Museum, and there is another copy of Alchabitius and of John of Saxony's Commentary which was printed at Venice in 1521. In this, too, we have the expression, "*Et ex hoc adorogen*" and "*et ex hoc adorogen.*" This is the passage according to the Venetian editions of 1485 and 1521. In another edition, printed at Bologna in 1473 (B.M. press-mark 8610 d. 10.) we have the form *abdorungen*, but otherwise the wording is the same. It begins, "*Et ex hoc abdorungen*" and lower down has the important expression "*ejus abdorungen, id est, decanus, est Mars.*" The occurrence of the letter *b* certainly seems to favour the supposition that the first syllable is merely the Arabic article, the *b* being a misprint for *l*. As for the expression *et ex hoc*, the explanation is that the *Differentia Quarta* is a glossary of astrological terms and that *et ex hoc* seems a literal rendering of the Arabic ومنه *wa-minhu*. The difficulty arising from A.F.'s using the word as if it were of different meaning from *darījān*, his speaking, for instance, both of the *darījān* and *ādarjān* in the same passage.

This is due, I think, to the fact that each House of a horoscope consists of about 30° *i.e.*, of three decanates or *darījāns*. Hence, in mentioning the dignities or properties of a House, instead of saying *darījān* and *darījān* or using the word *wajh* (face) three times over, he varies the expression for the sake of euphony. What the exact etymology of the word *ādarjān* or *darījān* is, I am unable to say. The varieties of spelling lead one to suppose it a foreign word. It is clear from Alchabitius, that *ādarjān* or *ādarajān* is the proper spelling, and that the form *aradjān* of the *Bādshāhnāma* and the Dictionaries is incorrect.

Most probably the word comes from the Greek τρίγωνον, a triangle. I do not think it can come from δέκανος, for I do not see how the letter *r* came to be inserted. It appears, from Sachau's Albīrūnī, that the word which in our dictionaries is spelled *darījān* is in Arabic *draijān*. I have suggested above that the first syllable or letter of *ādarjān* is the Arabic article, but there may be another explanation. As Persian does not admit of conjunct consonants at the beginning of words, it is possible that when the word was borrowed from the Arabic or the Greek, the *dr* or the *tr* of the Greek necessitated either a prosthetic or a medial vowel. Thus *trīgonon* or *draijān* became in Persian, either *adrajān* or *darījān*. In a similar manner we have both Iskandar and Sekandar as transliterations of Alexander and *dirham* for the Greek *drachme*, *Firangi* for Frank, *etc.* But if *ādarjān* comes from *trigonon* and not from *decānus*, it must still be acknowledged that it came to have the same meaning as decanate in English or *drekkāna* in Sanscrit, and is stated by Alchabitius to be the equivalent of *decānus*.

If anything were necessary to prove that the word *ādarjān* is identical in meaning with *wajh*, *facies*, I think it is furnished by the fact that Haly, (*i.e.*, Abu-l-ḥasan ʻ Alī ibn Abī-'l Rajal al-Shaibānī) in his elaborate work on astrology, says nothing about *darījān* or *ādarjān*, though he has a chapter *De Faciebus* or, (as the Arabic has it) *Fi-l-wujūh*.

Moreover Guido Bonatus has this passage (ed. Basle 1550 825) *De dorungez non dico hic* (the passage occurs in a chapter on the triplicities) *aliquid quoniam videtur spectare ad considerationem facierum, de quibus latius ac sufficienter dictum est superius in Tractatu primo in cap. ed Faciebus.*

Scaliger has yet another spelling of *darījān;* he calls it *dorogen* and says the Arabs apply the term to the *dodecatemoria*. (Notes on Manilius 179 1.38.) This seems to be a mistake.

## CHAPTER IV.

SCHEME OF THE SKY-ADORNING NATIVITY OF HIS MAJESTY, THE KING OF KINGS; AND SUMMARY OF THE STELLAR INFLUENCES,[1] ACCORDING TO THE METHODS OF THE ASTROLOGERS OF INDIA.[2] 27

By the calculations of the Indian astrologers, his Majesty's auspicious horoscope falls under Leo which is a Fixed Sign and is significant of perfect supremacy, victory, energy and superiority. The Sun, which takes more note[3] of kings than of all the other objects in the universe, is the dominant, and this is a clear indication that the Native will be victorious and paramount over famous sovereigns and mighty rulers.

The pillars of his sovereignty and government will gain stability and strength, day by day, and the regulations of his exaltation and glory will be carried out firmly and with permanence. The rays[4] of his wrath will[5] consume the fore-arms[6] of stiff-necked, evil-disposed ones, and the beat of his war-drums will turn to water the courage of rank-breaking, tiger-hearted men.

The scheme of the holy nativity is hereby set down in accord-

---

[1] This appears to be a translation of the Greek ἀποτελέσματα. It may be rendered *judgments*.

[2] Later on, we find the horoscopes of the three princes, Salīm (Jahāngīr), Murād and Dānyāl, cast both according to the Greek and the Indian rules. There is also a horoscope of the Accession.

[3] Akbar said that the Sun specially favoured kings and that this was why they worshipped it,—thereby scandalizing the shallow-minded. (Jarrett III, 388. Blochmann 155. Text 154 l.16.)

[4] پنجه *panja*. There is a play on the double-meaning of this word, *panja* meaning both rays and paws and also footprints, *viz.*, those of Leo. *Punja* also means, in Hindi, a cluster, *e.g.*, of stars.

[5] *Lit.* have consumed, the past tense being used for the future in accordance with the Persian idiom.

[6] Perhaps this is an allusion to the story of Kṛṣṇa's having burnt off 998 of the 1,000 arms of Bāṇāsura at the place called Kardaha.

ance with the writing of the foremost of Indian astrologers, the Jotik[1] Rai who was one of the servants of the royal threshold.

FIGURE II.

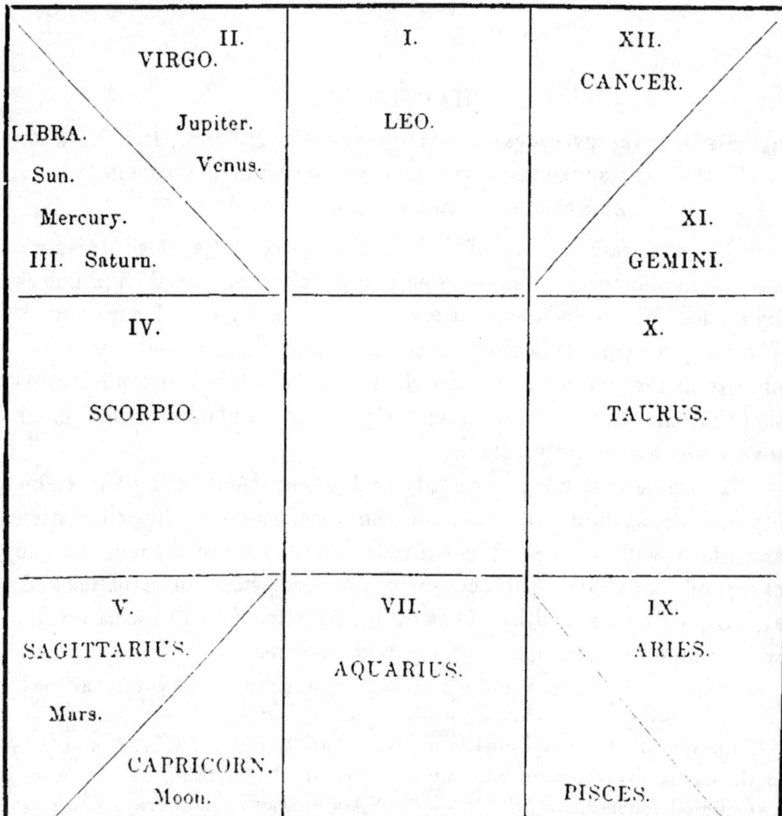


28 Notwithstanding[2] the perfect simplicity and unceremoniousness

---

[1] This seems to be a title and not the name of an individual. See Blochmann 404n. where he compares the title of *Jotik Rai*—Court Astrologer, to Birbal's title of *Kab Rai*—Poet Laureate. The Sanscrit word is *Jyautiṣika*—one who knows the *Jyōtiṣa*. The expression *Jyōtish Rai* is used in Jai Singh's preface and is translated *Astronomer Royal* by Dr. Hunter.

[2] *Or*, alongside of, *or*, together with.

of his Majesty, the King of Kings, such rays of glory and power[1] stream from the forehead of his might as to indicate that the Indian astrologers are not far from truth when they assert that his noble horoscope belongs to Leo. In their books of stellar influences, it is laid down that the Native of this Ascendant is wealthy, victorious over enemies, forgiving towards offenders, ruling according to just and equal laws, and accomplishing his purposes by force of his own reason and by firmness in his own opinions. He will be fond of travel[2] and will reap benefit from it. And he is lord of excellent and obedient children. The meeting[3] of Jupiter and Venus in the Second House makes the Native a guide in various arts and sciences.

As the Greater Fortune (Jupiter) is in the House of Mercury, he (the Native) will be endowed with beauty of form, proportional admixture of the elements, gravity of speech, social graces, lofty understanding, and sublime apprehension in theology and divine worship, and will be adorned with well-doing, and with ability to accomplish everything in accordance with propriety.

Venus in Virgo, takes charge of the adornment of virtuous veiled ones and provides for the increase of beauty[4] and elegance. As the Sun is in the Third House,[5] he (the Native) will accomplish whatever great undertaking he desires to compass, without reference to any other person. He will be powerful and his brethren will not attain to him. Indeed the star of the brothers' horoscope is occulted.[6] Men will be united and agreed in love of him. As Mercury is in the Third House, he (the Native) will be talented, versed in business, and disliking idleness, a subduer of difficulties, and a slayer of enemies (*maṣhaqqat-kaṣh u duṣhman-kuṣh*). His acute thoughts will revel in theology and other philosophies and will attain

[1] جبروت *jabrūt*, omnipotence, *etc.* It is a word used by Ṣūfīs.

[2] سفر *safar*. It is probably intended that this word should have its Sufistic meanings also, *viz.*, self-examination and thinking of the other world.

[3] *Farāham āmada.* This may mean conjunction or only that both planets are in the same Sign.

[4] There is here a sketch of Akbar's personal appearance but it is very vague. See later on in Amīr Fatḥu-l-lāh's horoscope.

[5] Apparently because the Sun is regent of the First House or Ascendant.

[6] The Third House is that of brethren. The meaning is that as the Sun is in the Third House, the star of brethren is occulted or combust.

the rank of ecstacy. And as (Mercury) is in Libra, he will be famed throughout the world, and his good deeds will be widely known. He will be world-conquering and world-ruling for lengthened periods of time, and excellent contrivances and ingenious plans are indicated. As Saturn is in the Third House, he (the Native) will enjoy repose and much tranquility, and will have attached servants innumerable, but he will act according to his own personal courage and his own ripe reason. As (Saturn) is in Libra, and in exaltation,[1] he (the Native) will be master of the treasures of the world, and as Saturn is under the shade of the venerable, world-warming Sun, his boundless treasures will last for lengthened periods and will remain unaffected by prolonged usage of them.

He will make delightful journeys with success and accomplishment of his objects. And there will not be a greater than he upon earth. Mighty[2] black beasts (elephants) will await at his gate. As he grows in years, his power will increase, and he will, without trouble or pains, acquire great armies and perfect dominion and glory. His power and his felicity will be lasting, for there is no slower[3] planet than Saturn, and among his gifts are extent of fortune, permanence of sovereignty, and length of days. The Sun, Saturn and Mercury are in one Sign. He will, therefore, be friend-cherishing, foe-subduing, well knowing the laws of amity and inimity. Mars being in Sagittarius, mankind will glorify him. For Mars is in the triplicity[4] of the ascendant; and in the house of his friend.[5]
29 This powerful friend is the Greater Fortune and puts away the sorrows and the apprehensions of the nations. And he will be happy and joyful. And by power visible and invisible, essential and accidental, he becomes Great of the Great and King of Kings. The glory of his renown embraces the world and the fame of his majesty

---

1 Libra is Saturn's House of exaltation.

2 The *nigri barri* of Horace. (*Āīn* III. 241 and Jarrett III. 395.) Akbar said that when he first came to India he looked upon his liking (*tawajjuh*) for elephants as a prognostic of his universal ascendency.

3 Alluding to the extent of his orbit which was then the largest known. *Çani* or *Çanaiçcara*, the Sanscrit name for Saturn means the slow (goer).

4 *I.e.*, apparently the fiery triplicity to which both Leo and Sagittarius belong.

5 According to Cardan, Jupiter is not friendly to Mars; but according to the *Jyōtiṣa Prakāça*, they are friends.

extends from shore to shore. Many princes and rulers will be subject to him, and, being afraid of him, will be obedient and submissive. And as Mars is in the House of Jupiter and the Sun is in sextile to him, the princes throughout the world will place their heads on the line of his command and make the dust of his threshold the adoration-spot of their obedience. The Moon is in the Sixth House; he may have powerful enemies but they will not reach him, nor be able to withstand the scorching lightning of his wrath and might, and they will always endeavour to gain his friendship so that by borrowing[1] the lights of his alliance, they may be in safety from evil.

As the Moon's detriment[2] is in Capricorn, the weakness of his enemies is signified. And there comes a sweet reasonableness to the Native which enables him to decide disputes according to equity and the real merits of the cases.

And having examined contradictory faiths, and different dispositions, he guides every sect in the way of good works. His desire is that men should leave the hollow of imitative routine, and emerge into the straight highway of inquiry. And as Jupiter is in aspect towards him,[3] the royal power and might will be beyond calculation. He will become possessed of tractable children and, as Venus is in aspect, high-minded chaste ones of excellent actions will serve him for long periods of life and he[4] will have obedient and amiable children

### Sundry rules of Indian Astrology.

There are certain principles, too, to be found in the books of Indian philosophers which prove the grandeur of this holy nativity. If a planet occupy the twelfth (dodecatemorion) of the Moon, the Native will have pleasure throughout a long life, and the dust of sickness will hardly touch the garment-hem of his health and, while in the fullness of his powers, and having become a manifestation

---

[1] *Iqtibās*. According to Sylvestre de Sacy, it originally meant to borrow fire from another's hearth.

[2] Being the opposite of her mansion which is Cancer.

[3] Apparently referring to the fact that Jupiter and Venus are in the House next to the Ascendant.

[4] Perhaps شوند, *they will have*.

of planetary dignities[1] and having attained the acme of felicity,—he will obtain a great kingdom, and will have long life and abundant blessings, and will be joyful in sublime stations and lofty palaces. Now, as in this horoscope Mars occupies the dodecatemorion of the Moon, all these things are fully proved and established. He will be lord of victorious armies, and be line-breaking and foe-scattering on the battle-fields, and everyone on whom the glance of his wrath shall fall, will be melted by his terrible majesty. And if an auspicious planet be in the dodecatemorion of the Sun, the honoured Native will be a mild prince, eloquent and wise, firm and fortunate. And in emergencies when the brave in battle and men of men may hesitate, the owner of these happy omens will never swerve, but will keep a steady foot on the skirt of fortitude and great-heartedness, and the trace[2] of doubt and the smallest vestige of change will not reach the court of his circumspection. Now in this holy horoscope, the meeting[3] of the two Fortunes in the dodecatemorion shows abundant auspiciousness. If the Sun be lord of the Ascendant, and be in the Third House, the noble Native will be advanced to lofty sovereignty. Now this glory is visible in the fortunate frontispiece (the diagram of the horoscope). If Jupiter, Mercury and Venus be
30 all three in aspect to the Moon, this signifies that the Native will open up countries and will rule over them. Now in this embellished tablet (the diagram) they (the three planets) are kindling the lamp of dominion.

If the cusp of the Ascendant or the Moon be in the *nuhbahr*[4] of a

---

[1] ابتزاز *ibtizāz*. A friend suggested to me that this was a mistake for ابتراز *ibtirāz*, superiority, and this view appeared to be confirmed by the fact that *ibtirāz* is the reading of MS. 564. It turns out, however, that *ibtizāz* is correct, it being an astrological term signifying a planet possessed of all its dignities and appearing in the horoscope (or perhaps in the First House). (See Dict. of T. Ts. I. 224 *s. v.* and the *Mafātīḥu-l-'ulūm* 229). The next clause of the text is also an astrological term, شرف *sharaf*, a planet in exaltation. The whole phrase is *shahādat-i-ibtizāz u sa'ādat-i-sharaf.*

[2] The text has *sā'ica*, horoscope, but the list of *errata* shows that this is a misprint for رائحه *rā'iḥat*, lit. odour or smell.

[3] Apparently Jupiter and Venus are meant. They have already been spoken of as meeting in the Second House, *viz.*, Virgo.

[4] *Nuhbahr*, nine parts. It means the dividing a Sign into nine parts of 3° 20′ each, and assigning a planet

**Sign** and four planets or more are in aspect to the Moon, the Native

to each part. *Albīrūnī* (Sachau. II. 222) gives a rule for calculating the *nuhbahrāt.*

***Nuhbahr*** is the Sanscrit *navāṁsa*. The Lucknow editor gives (27) a table shewing the arrangement of the *nuhbahr*. It seems to have been a refinement of Indian astrologers and is not, I believe, referred to by Ptolemy. Carden in the peroration of his work on Astrological Aphorisms, takes credit to himself for-discarding *nuhbahr*, etc. His words are "*Abjecimus partes, facies, novenaria, dodecatemoria, horas planetarias, atque caetera id genus nugamenta.*"

The Indian book to which A.F. refers, appears to be the ***Bṛhat** Jātaka* of *Varāha Mihira*. In N. Chidambaran Iyer's translation thereof, I find the following passage. (Madras, 1885, 114.) "The ***Lagna*** (Ascendant) or the Moon, being in *Vargōttama* position of (sic) all the planets, excepting the Moon, by the several groups of four, five and six planets, aspecting the *Lagna* or the Moon, the number of *Yōga* (s) obtained is 22." See also the *Bṛhajjātakam* (Rasik Mohan Chatterji's ed. Calcutta, 1300 B.S. 79a.) An explanation is there given of how the number 22 is arrived at and the *çlōka* is explained as giving a total of 44 kingdoms or *rājayōga*(s). There being seven planets,—the Sun is one of them,—and the Moon being excluded, we get the number, 6, mentioned above.

Monier Williams' Sanscrit Dictionary defines *rājayōga* as "a constellation under which princes are born, or a configuration of planets, *etc.*, at the birth of any person, indicating him to be destined to kingship."

The *Vargōttama* above referred to is defined as follows: (Iyer 10). "In the moveable and other Signs, the first, the central and the last" (*i.e.*, the First, Fifth and Ninth) "*navāṁsa* (s) are known as *Vargōttama* positions. Planets in such positions will produce good effects." The chapter in which this passage occurs, is that dealing with *rājayōga* or the birth of kings. *Yōga*, however, also means conjunction.

Blochmann (105) has the following passage:—"At the command of his Majesty, Muḥammad K͟hān of Gujrāt translated into Persian, the *Tājik*, a well-known work on astrology." (The original is at page 116 of the Bib. Ind. ed. and the notes give the various reading *nājak*). Gladwin similarly read *tājik*, but in a copy of his translation in the British Museum, Sir W. Jones has written the marginal emendation *jātak*. Probably this is correct. There is, it is true, a book or a—*Çāstra* on Hindu astrology, called the *Tājik-grantha*, but this was, as its name implies, a translation from the Persian. See Weber's *Indische Studien* II. 247. Dr. Weber is inclined to derive the word from *Tājik*—Arabian—and to suppose that the original language was Arabic, but there seems no reason to go further back than to Persian. *Tājik* is a well-known

will have 22 Kingdoms[1] and many countries will be permanently in his possession. Now, in this horoscope, not only are the cusp of the Ascendant and the Moon in their *nuhbahr*, but five planets are in aspect to the Moon, *viz.*, the Sun, Jupiter, Venus, Saturn and Mercury.

---

name for a Persian, hence probably the title of the Indian book. It is not likely that any Persian would take the trouble to translate from the Sanscrit a work which was itself a translation from the Persian. I therefore think the proper reading must be *Jātak*. The two words might easily be confounded in writing.

With reference to A. F.'s remark about the five planets being in aspect to the Moon, it may be pointed out that they are not all in one house, so that they all cannot have the same aspect. It will be remembered that the Sun was regarded as a planet by the ancients.

[1] It does not appear that Akbar ever possessed 22 kingdoms. His *ṣūbahs* (provinces) were originally twelve and became fifteen by the conquest of Berar, Khāndēsh, and Aḥmadnagar. (Jarrett II. 115). However on the same page, A. F. speaks of hoping to add Central Asia and Persia, *etc.*, to the list. It is curious that under Shāh Jahān, the provinces numbered 22. (Tieffenthaler Berlin, 1786. I. 66). Bernier's list makes the number 20 only, but he includes Bengal and Orissa as one.

In the *Bṛhajjātakam* referred to in the previous note, the Sanscrit *çlōka* is thus given :—

वर्गोत्तमगते लग्ने चन्द्रे वा चन्द्रवर्जितैः ।
चतुराद्यैर्ग्रहैर्दृष्टे नृपा द्वाविंशतिः स्मृताः ॥

This may, apparently, be translated as follows :—"If the Ascendant" (*i.e.*, the horoscope or point on the eastern horizon) "or the Moon be in *Vargōttama*, and four or more planets, exclusive of the Moon, be in aspect thereto, the Native will be king of two-and-twenty kingdoms."

The editor proceeds to explain in Bengali, how this figure is arrived at; *viz.*, by making different combinations of the planets. The figure 44 is reached by counting 22 for the case of the Ascendant's being in *Vargōttama* and being aspected by the planets, and 22 for the similar case of the Moon.

We are told that by some other manipulation of the figures, the number of kingdoms may rise to 528, *i.e.*, 22×24. Apparently A.F. claims more than 22 for Akbar and reaches at the least 44,—for he says that both the Ascendant and the Moon are in *nuhbahr*, though, to be sure, he does not say that both are aspected by five planets. Apparently he shrinks from specifying the number of the kingdoms just as he shrinks from telling us anything about the time of Akbar's death. It is a case of *Imperium sine fine dedi*. Nor does A.F. take notice of the fact that the *çlōka* speaks of "*Vargōt tama*,"—a word which means chief of a class and is only applied to three out of the nine *navāṁsa* positions.

And in this holy nativity, the lord of the ascendant (the Sun) is in the Third House. If the Native have a brother, the latter will not be long-lived[1] but many devoted friends will gather round him (the Native) and he will be beneficent, bounteous (or forgiving) and powerful and will enjoy sovereignty, free from calamity, and prosperity without end.

The lord of the Second House (Mercury) is in the Third and so, he (the Native) will do great things and will bring wondrous works to pass. He will devise laws of dominion and wisdom and be a terror to the evil-minded, and no alarm on this account will touch the hem of his lofty spirit.

The lord of the Third House is in the Second. The Native will assist the helpless and downcast, and deal benignantly with well-disposed kindred. And all those who walk rightly will experience his bounty and benevolence, and will gather fruits from the gardens of his bounties and liberalities. It is certain that if the lord of the Third House be auspicious, the Native will attain great sovereignty. Now in this holy nativity, the Lesser Fortune[2] (Venus) is lord

---

1 See to this effect the Bengali astrological work, *Jyotish Parkāsh*, Part II. 55.

2 The text has سعد اصغر *sa'd-i-asghar*, *i.e.*, the Lesser Fortune or Venus, but the editors admit that eight out of their nine authorities read *sa'd-i-akbar* (Jupiter.) They have adopted the reading of a single MS. because Venus and not Jupiter is lord of Libra, *i.e.*, the Third House. I think this reason sufficient for the emendation, although A. F.'s language where he speaks of the planet's signifying a "great *Khilāfat* and majestic Government" agrees better with Jupiter and would seem to imply that Jupiter was in his thoughts. However Venus is a much more respectable and important divinity with Orientals than she is in the West. She is called the planet of Islām (*Bādshāhnāma* 102, 1.2) and she ruled over Arabia—so the reference to the *Khilāfat* may not be inappropriate. According to the *Dabistān* (III. 107 trans.) Muḥammad worshipped Venus and for this reason, fixed Friday for the sacred day, "as he would not reveal the meaning to the common people, he kept it secret." This explanation of the choice of Friday for the sacred day is contrary to that commonly received, which is that Friday was the most excellent of days because the last of Creation and that on which man was made. Shāh Jahān's horoscope was under Libra and also Jahāngīr's. It is just possible that A. F. may have been thinking of Saturn who is in his exaltation in Libra.

of the Third House. This signifies a great *Khilāfat* and majestic Government.

The lord of the Fourth House is Mars and he is posited in the Fifth. His (Akbar's) venerable sire will help him from his place[1] in heavenly secret aids and his noble children will be long-lived and will be great and famous for dominion and fortune.

The lord of the Fifth House (Sagittarius) is Jupiter and he is in the Second. He (the Native) will have ample treasures and great countries will come under his sway. And as Venus is also in the Second House, he will be acute and discriminating in musical notes,[2] in subtle harmonies and in the secrets of melody.

Saturn,[3] the lord of the Sixth House (Capricornus) is in the Third; so some of his (the Native's) servants will put forth evil thoughts and be trodden under foot by his wrath.

Saturn, the lord of the Seventh (Aquarius), is in the Third House; he (the Native) will perform works of majesty and splendour by his own well-directed exertions. And there rises the longing in his heart, "Oh![4] that I might have a brother who would rise high in my service!"

Jupiter, the lord of the Eighth (Pisces) is in the Second House. He (the Native) will gather abundance of goods and incalculable

---

[1] I think وجدوِ اشرف او *wujūd-i-ashraf-i-ō* must mean Humāyūn's existence in heaven and not Akbar's birth, else why should the aid be secret or mysterious? Guido Bonatus mentions (636) that the second part of the Fourth House is that of the death of ancestors. A. F. alludes to the Fifth House because that is the House of children.

[2] According to A. F. (Blochmann 51) Akbar knew more about music than trained musicians and was an excellent performer, especially on the *naqqārah*, kettledrum.

[3] Saturn is an infortune. The Third House is that of brethren and the author infers from Saturn's presence in it that Akbar will be great through his own exertions and that his brethren will not help him. Akbar's half-brother, Muḥammad Ḥakīm (born 961=1553) the ruler of Afghānistān was ungrateful and rebellious and also a drunkard. See Akbar's remarks about him, Jarret III. 383. There was another half-brother, Ṣultān Ibrāhīm who died in infancy. (*Akbarnāma* I. 332.)

[4] I take نشد to be *nashd*, the verbal noun signifying information, etc., and also used as a form of adjuration and entreaty. It may, however, be *nashud*, "was not."

treasures by his own exertions. It may also happen that an inheritance[1] will enure to him.

Mars, the lord of the Ninth House (Aries) is in the Fifth, *viz.*, (Sagittarius) the House of Jupiter. This signifies strength of retention. He will have a powerful memory and whatever he transacts 31
with mortals, will be done in a becoming manner. Fitting worship of the Creater is also indicated. And he will excel in good regulations for the prosperity of his subjects and the administration of justice. He will have fortunate and truthful children and they will be respectful and obedient.

Venus the dominant of the Tenth House (Taurus) is in the Second. He (the Native) will be respectful and submissive to his parents and the elders of his family.

Mercury, the dominant of the Eleventh[2] House (Gemini) is in the Third. He (the Native) will love the attendants and servants of the Court and will protect mankind. His enemies will be turned into nothingness without any trouble or exertion on his part.

The Moon, the lord of the Twelfth House (Cancer) is in the Sixth (Capricornus). He (the Native) will have many blasphemers and opponents but they will be dispersed and scattered by the reverberating sound of his war-drums and the tumult of his majestic onset, and will descend with loss and frustration into the abode of annihilation. And if Jupiter or Saturn be in the Second House, the fortunate Native will be a great monarch and will prevail over his enemies. And whenever the Moon is in Capricorn, which is the House of Saturn and is in the *nuhbahr* of Saturn, this is a proof that much of the world will be submissive to the illustrious Native. His territories will be bounded by the ocean[3] and his auspicious reign be long. It is also certain that, if in the nativity, Saturn be in exaltation, the noble Native will attain great empire and have long life. Now all these principles and significations are illustrated in this auspicious horoscope.

---

[1] The Eighth House is that of inheritance. See *Bádsháhnáma* 84 1, 8 from foot.

[2] This is the House of friends.

[3] According to astrology, the Moon is lord of the ocean. A statement not without its truth.

## CHAPTER V.

### Description of the horoscope of auspicious characters which was cast by the erudite of the age, 'Azdu-d-daulah[1] Amīr Fatḥu-l-lāh of Shīrāz.

In the year in which the pattern of natural philosophers, sifted flour of erudition-amassing doctors, delicate balance of sciences, key of the locks of opinions, raised to lofty dignities, expounder of material truths, assayer[2] of the jewels of verity, solver of Greek problems, render of the curtain between light and darkness, discerner of the stations and motions of earthly and heavenly bodies, soaring phoenix (*'anqā*), very learned of the Age, 'Azdu-d-daulah Amīr Fatḥu-l-lāh of Shīrāz, under the guidance of good fortune, was elevated to the pedestal of the lofty throne and obtained a robe of honour, together with degrees of exaltation and steps of advancement,—the writer of this noble volume one day remarked to him that the horoscopes of the auspicious nativity were discrepant, and expressed the hope that he would examine them according to the true *namūdār*, and weigh them in the trutine of inquiry. The honoured Mīr, having after complete investigation, deduced the horoscope from the Persian rules and the Greek canon, found that the birth was in Leo. As in the opinion of the writer, this is the most reliable horoscope, he gives its figure here, together with some specimens of the prognostications.

---

1 *Arm of the State.* From Shīrāz, he went to the Deccan and joined Akbar's Court in 991=1583. We find Akbar consulting him as an astrologer, about the troubles in Gujrāt (*Akbarnāma* III, 431). Perhaps the title *'Azdu-d-daulah* was given to or assumed by Fatḥu-l-lāh in allusion to the Buyide prince, 'Azdu-d-daulah Alp Arslan, who reigned in Khurāsān in the 10th century and was a patron of astronomers. (See Sédillot). There is a *Canon* (Set of Tables) named after him, *'Azadī*. (See Jarrett II. 8 and Blochmann 33n).

2 He arranged the coinage in the 29th year, 1585 (Blochmann 33).

## ERRATA.

| Page | 2, | note | | line | 11, | *for* Manāsabat *read* Munāsabat. |
|---|---|---|---|---|---|---|
| „ | „ | „ | | „ | „ | 4 lines from end *read* Dīwān. |
| „ | 3, | „ | 2, | | | Delete the *i* after Z in Zi kāf and *read* birūn *for* barūn. |
| „ | „ | „ | 3, | | | *read* 'ālam. |
| „ | 7, | „ | 1, | „ | 4, | *read* کون kaun. |
| „ | 12, | „ | „ | „ | „ | ārāī. |
| „ | „ | „ | 4, | „ | 2, | ṭāq *for* ṭāqt. |
| „ | 13, | „ | 1, | „ | 1, | shayistagī. |
| „ | 17, | „ | | „ | „ | Fundgruben. |
| „ | „ | „ | 6, | | | Ādam. |
| „ | 18, | „ | „ | „ | 5, | rumūz. |
| „ | 20, | „ | 1, | „ | 4, | bazmgāh. |
| „ | „ | „ | „ | „ | 5, | naẓar. |

## NOTE to p. 7.

Dr. Bloch has kindly pointed out to me that there is an iẓāfat after *ḥarf* in the second hemistich of the third verse on p. 2 of text, and that the metre requires this. My translation therefore appears to be wrong and the true translation probably is — "For this is the case (*ḥarf*) of the Muslin and the moonlight."

If this be so, the preceding line should apparently be translated "Think not that there is a letter of it (*i.e.*, of God's Praise) in the (*i.e.* the writer's) book."

## FIGURE III. 32

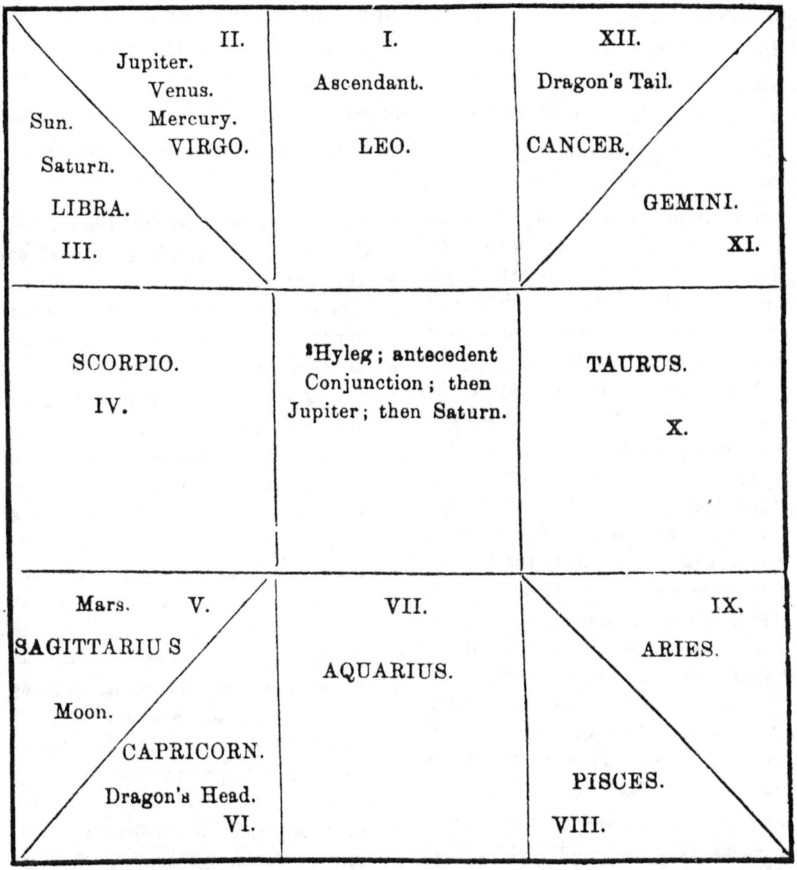


[1] At first sight, it appears as if the entries in this diagram were not correct, for Mercury is set down as being in Virgo, whereas the text (33 1.7.) describes him as in 25° 24′ Libra. Similarly the Dragon's Tail (Katabibazon) is in Leo, and not in Cancer; and the Sun (Text 33 1.9. fr. foot) in Scorpio and not in Libra.

But it should be remembered that the Houses or compartments of the figure are mundane Houses (Houses of the horoscope) and so, overlap the Signs. All that is meant by putting the name of a Sign into one of the Compartments is that the cusp or boundary of the House is in that Sign. The First House for example does not begin till nearly the last degree (*viz.*, 28°) of Leo. Apparently the entries in the figure misled Kavi Rāj Shyāmal Dās, for he speaks of some of the horoscopes as marking the Sun in Libra and others in Scorpio. But three out of the four put the Sun in Scorpio and probably the fourth (Jotik Rai's) does so, although details are not given. It is indeed stated in this that the Sun, Saturn and Mercury are all in one Sign, and we are told that the latter two are in Libra but perhaps all that is meant is, that the three are in the same House, *viz.*, the Third.

[2] [Persian script] *Hailāj awwal juzū-i-ijtimā'*. Apparently this means that the first hyleg is the degree or place where the conjunction of the Sun and Moon took

The cusp[1] of the glorious Ascendant in this holy horoscope which is a masterpiece of the revolutions of the stars and planets, is 28° 36′ Leo. The angles[2] are in Fixed Signs and as the cusp of the fortunate-starred Ascendant is in the Sun's House, no planet is its dominant. It is the term of Mars, and Jupiter is lord of the triplicity,[3] in companionship with the Sun and with Saturn in attendance.

---

place before the birth. Perhaps hyleg is here to be taken to mean duration of life. The Lucknow ed. and MS. 564 contain more details in this compartment and also in the other squares of the figure.

They write "Hyleg; first, the "degree of anterior conjunction; "then the Part of Fortune; then "the degree of the Ascendant's "*kadkhudā*; with reference to the "hyleg, Saturn is first, then Jupiter; "and with reference to the Part of "Fortune, Mercury, then Jupiter, "then Saturn: and with reference "to the degree of the Ascendant, "first the Sun, then Mars, then "Saturn." In fact they insert here the words of the beginning of p. 38 of the text. Perhaps A. F. or Fatḥu-l-lāh was referring to the *namūdār* of Zoroaster. (See *Prolegomena* text 149 and trans. 204). The central entry in the diagram of our text appears inconsistent with the description at page 38 where Saturn is placed before Jupiter as regards the hyleg.

The horoscope diagrams in the Lucknow ed. and in some of the MSS. contain many abbreviations. The Lucknow ed. explains some of them, but the best account of the subject that I have seen is the tract entitled "*Anonymus Persa de Siglis Arabum et Persarum astronomicis*" which was found at Constantinople by J. Greaves (*Gravius*) the Oxford Professor and published in 1648, at the end of his Persian Grammar. The tract might well be republished for it is rare. Dr. Weber was unable to meet with it.

[1] مرکز *markaz*. This ordinarily means centre. *Marākaz-i-muḥaqqaq*, true centres, is the name given to a method used by Albīrūnī for determining the limits of the twelve Houses. (See Ulugh Beg's *Prolegomena* 142, Sédillot 198.) But here the word means, I think, *cusp*, the boundary of a House. (See Dict. of T.Ts. I. 111. 1.4.) *Markaz* is derived, from *rakz* and, according to Lane means "a place where a spear or other thing is stuck in the ground upright." Apparently the word *cusp* which comes from *cuspis*, the point of a spear, is a translation of the Arabic term. There is no Greek astrological term corresponding to it, so far as I know.

[2] *Qā'imu-l-autād ittifāq uftāda*. The meaning is, apparently, that the four angles or cardinal points of the horoscope (*viz.*, the First, Fourth, Seventh and Tenth Houses) are Fixed Signs, *viz.*, Leo, Scorpio, Aquarius and Taurus.

[3] Apparently Jupiter and not the Sun, is lord of the triplicity (it is the fiery one) because the birth took place at night.

There are the face and *darījān*[1] of Mars, the *nuhbahr* of Jupiter, *ādarjān* and *haftbahr*[2] of Mars, twelfth of the Moon and detriment[3] of Saturn. The degree is masculine and lucid, free from misfortune. The Sun is dominant over the Ascendant with intent towards an alliance with Saturn. Venus is in 26° 23′ 37″ Virgo. Admittedly the Part[4] of children is 24° 23 (Virgo); that of wealth, 25° 7′; that of father's death 24° 23′; that of brethren 8° 47′; and that of the number of brethren 14° 12′ Virgo. 33

The cusp of the Second House is 28° 43′ Virgo; it is the House and exaltation of Mercury, and term of Saturn. The Moon is master of the triplicity in companionship with Venus and the *doryphory*[5] of Mars. There are the face and *nuhbahr* of Mercury, *darījān* of Venus, *ādarjān* of the Moon, twelfth of the Sun, *haftbahr* and fall of Venus and detriment of Jupiter. The Moon is dominant over the House. The degree is masculine, void of darkness or light, of good or bad fortune. Jupiter is posited in 15° 13′ 37″ and Mercury in 25° 24′ Libra. The Part of hope is 12° 53′; that of victory and conquest is 1° 17′ Libra. The place of anterior conjunction is 24° 50′ Libra.

The cusp of the Third House is 28° 1′ Libra. It is the House of Venus, exaltation of Saturn, term of Mars, and Mercury is lord of the (aerial) triplicity in companionship with Saturn and attended by Jupiter. There are the face of Jupiter, the *darījān*, *nuhbahr*,

---

[1] This is the third *darījān* or *drekkāna* (decanate) of Leo. A Table in the Bengali astrological work *Varāha Mihira* (38) gives a list of all the *drekkāna*.

[2] This is the Sanscrit *saptāṁça*. It is described in Bengali books on Astrology and is, apparently, an arrangement of the hours of the week. It is thus a form of the *ahargaṇa*.

[3] وبال *wabāl*. When a planet is in a Sign opposite to his House, he is said to be in his detriment. Thus Leo is the detriment of Saturn, because it is opposite to (six Houses, 180°, away from) his House, Aquarius. That *wabāl* corresponds to *detriment* appears, among other things, from the fact that the letter *lām* denotes the *opposite aspect* in astrology. This is because the Arabs use the last letter of a word as its abbreviation instead of its first as with us.

[4] سهم *sahm*, pl. سهام *sahām*, properly means an arrow, *sc.* a divining-arrow, and hence, a lot or part. European astrologers portion out the Signs of the Zodiac into *Parts*. Haly and Guido Bonatus have much to say about the various *partes* and especially about the *Pars Fortunae*. (See Dict. of T.Ts. 698, *s. v. Saham.*)

[5] I borrow this word from Ashmand. It seems to correspond to *k͟hidmat*.

twelfth and *haftbahr* of Mercury, *ādarjān* and fall of the Sun, and detriment of Mars. Saturn is paramount over this House. The degree is feminine, lucid, and void of good or bad fortune. Saturn is in 10° 40′ 33″ Scorpio. The Part of Fate is 17° 50′ Scorpio. The Part of good Fortune, according to Ptolemy [1] and Muḥyī'u-d-dīn Maghribī,[2] is 18° 9′ Scorpio. The Part of true friends and of welfare[3] (?) and that of servants are admittedly 23° 12.′ The Part of ailments is admittedly 17° 21′. The Sun is 0° 45′ 57″ Scorpio.

The cusp of the Fourth House is 27° 21′ Scorpio. This is a cardinal point (angle) and is the House of Mars, term of Saturn, face, twelfth and detriment of Venus. The Lord of the triplicity is Mars in companionship with Venus and attended by the Moon, and there are the *darījān* of Mercury and the *nuhbahr* and *haftbahr* of Jupiter. Mars is paramount over this House. The degree is masculine, fixed (*qayyima*) and void of good or bad fortune. The Part of land journeys is 12° 28′ Sagittarius. The Part of law-suits is 28° 32 Scorpio.

The cusp of the Fifth House is 27° 11′ Sagittarius. It is the House and *nuhbahr* of Jupiter and the exaltation of the Dragon's Tail (Katabibazon), the term of Mars and face of Saturn; the lord of the triplicity is Jupiter in companionship with the Sun and with Saturn in attendance. There are the Sun's *darījān*, the *ādarjān* of Venus,
34 the twelfth of Mars, the *nuhbahr* of Jupiter and *haftbahr* of Saturn, the fall of the Dragon's Head (Anabibazon) and the detriment of Mercury. Jupiter is paramount over the House with an inclination for the alliance of Saturn. This degree is masculine, fixed and void of good or bad fortune. The Part of sovereignty and territory is 28° 39′ Sagittarius. Cygnus and Aquila are in 25° Capricorn and Mars is in 10° 48′ 23″. The Moon is in 19° 48″ 14′ Capricorn.

The cusp of the Sixth House is 26° 46′ Capricorn. It is the House of Saturn, exaltation and term of Mars and face of the Sun. The Moon is master of the triplicity in companionship with Venus

---

[1] It is stated, later on, that most authorities put it in the 10th House.

[2] (See Jarret III. 20n.) Though originally from the West and hence called *Maghribī*, he eventually settled in Persia and assisted Naṣīru-d-dīn Ṭūsī. He belongs to the latter half of the 13th century.

[3] The Text is doubtful here.

and attended by Mars. There are the *darījān* and *nuhbahr* of Mercury, *ādarjān* and twelfth and fall of Jupiter, the *haftbahr* and detriment of the Moon. Mars is paramount over this House in companionship with Saturn and the Moon. The degree is masculine, lucid and unfortunate. The Dragon's Head is 27° 29′ 13″ Aquarius. The Part of war[1] and of captives is 24° 44′ Capricorn. The Part of the deaths of brethren is 2° 1′ Aquarius.

The cusp of the Seventh House is 28° 36′ Aquarius. It is the House and twelfth and term of Saturn. The lord of the triplicity is Mercury in companionship with Saturn and attended by Jupiter. There are the face of the Moon, the *darījān* of Venus, *ādarjān* and *nuhbahr* of Mercury, *haftbahr* of Jupiter and detriment of the Sun. Saturn is paramount over this House in companionship with Mercury and with inclination to the companionship of Jupiter. The degree is masculine, dark and void of good or bad fortune. The Part of friendship, constancy, firmness and love is 20° 8′ Pisces.

The cusp of the Eighth House is 28° 43′ Pisces. It is the House and *nuhbahr* of Jupiter, exaltation of Venus, term,[2] face, *darījān* and *ādarjān* of Mars who is lord of the triplicity in companionship with Venus and the *doryphory* of the Moon. It is the term, *haftbahr* and twelfth of Saturn and the fall of Mercury. Venus is paramount over this House in companionship with Mars and with inclination to alliance with the Moon. The degree is masculine, fixed, and void of good or evil fortune. The Part of excellence is 20° 8′ Aries and the Part of valour 2° 53′ of the same.

---

1 الجيش *aljaish*. The Lucknow ed. reads حبس *ḥabs*, 'prison.' So does MS. No. 564, and this is, perhaps, the correct reading, it being coupled with prisoners (*alasārā*). However, prisoners in the sense of captives or prisoners of war, may be meant and the reading in the text be right.

2 There appears to be a mistake in the text, for this same degree is said to be both the term of Mars and the term of Saturn. This coincidence is, I believe, impossible. Probably the second statement is wrong for, according to Bengali books on astrology, 28° Pisces falls within the term of Mars. The confusion may perhaps be due to A.F.'s use of two classifications of terms. According to the old classification, quoted by Cardan, the last two degrees of Pisces belong to the term of Saturn.

The cusp of the Ninth House is 28° 1′ Aries. It is the House of Mars, the exaltation[1] of the Sun, the term,[2] fall[3] and *ādarjān* of Saturn, and face and detriment of Venus. The lord of the triplicity is Jupiter, in companionship with the Sun, and the *doryphory* of Saturn. It is the *darījān, nuhbahr,* twelfth and *haftbahr* of Jupiter. Mars is paramount over this House in companionship with Jupiter and with inclination towards alliance with Saturn. The degree is masculine, light and belonging to the deep or pitted[4] degrees. The Part of male children is admittedly 23° 49 Taurus. The Part of sea-voyages is 2° 36′. The Part of messengers[5] is 5° Taurus.

The cusp of the Tenth House is 27° 21′ Taurus. It is the House and *ādarjān* of Venus, the exaltation of the Moon who is master

---

[1] Aries is the exaltation of the Sun, but it does not occur in this Ninth House which begins at 28° Aries. The Sun's exaltation is 19° Aries (according to Bengali books, it is 10°) and his fall is 19° Libra.

[2] The last five degrees of Aries are the term of Saturn, according to one classification and according to another, they are the term of Venus.

[3] There is some doubt what planet these designations are to be assigned to, but it is certain that Aries is the fall of Saturn as being opposite to Libra—his House of exaltation—and that, for a similar reason, it is the detriment of Venus, as being opposite to her Mansion, *viz.*, Libra.

[4] The text has ابار *abār*. MS. 564 reads آبار *ābār* and explains it as the plural of بئر *bi'r*, 'a well.' Either reading is right; Lane (145) gives both forms ابار and آبار as plural of بئر. See *Mafātīḥu-l-'ulūm*, 227, 1.4, (Cf. the Hebrew *Beersheba, i.e.*, the well of the oath.) It is difficult to see the connection of wells with degrees, but Wilson (Astrological Dict.) says that certain degrees are called deep or pitted because they subject the Native to deep marks of small-pox or scars, or, according to others, cause an impediment in speech, troubles and disputes in which he is sunk as in a deep pit. Lilly (Christian Astrology 116, 2nd. ed. 1659), gives a table of the various degrees, *viz.*, masculine and feminine, light, dark, smoky, void, deep or pitted, lame or deficient and says (118) that deep or pitted degrees "show the man at a stand in the "question he asks, not knowing "which way to turn himself and that "he had need of help to bring him "into a better condition for as a "man cast in a ditch cannot easily "get out without help so no more "can this querent in the case he is "without assistance." In the *Astronomia* (Guido Bonatus, 59) there is a table of kinds of degrees; *pitted* degrees are there called *gradus puteales*.

[5] الام *ulām*, 'messengers' and 'messages.' G. Bonatus mentions (646)

of the triplicity in companionship with Venus, and with attendance of Mars, the *darījān* of Saturn, the *nuhbahr* and *haftbahr* of Mercury; the twelfth term and detriment of Mars. Venus is paramount over this House in complete companionship with the Moon and in companionship with Mars. The degree is masculine, lucid and void of good or bad fortune. The Part of good fortune is admitted by all with the exception of Ptolemy and Muḥyī'u-d-dīn Maghribī to be 9° 22′ Gemini. The Part of reason and of speech is 9° 51′ Gemini. The Part of disease is 25° 27′ Gemini. The Part[1] of male offspring is admittedly 29° 40′ Taurus. The Part of abstinence (temperance) is 4° Gemini. The Part of possessions is 19° 36′. The Part of enemies is admittedly 25° 27′ Gemini.

The cusp of the Eleventh House is 27° 11′ Gemini. It is the House and *nuhbahr* of Mercury and he is lord of the triplicity in companionship with Saturn and with attendance of Jupiter. It is the exaltation of the Dragon's Head (*Anabibazon*) and the term and *darījān* of Saturn, the face of the Sun, *ādarjān* of Jupiter, twelfth and *haftbahr* of Venus. This degree is feminine and fixed, and void of good and evil fortune. The Part of the conclusions of actions and the Part of marriage are 14° Cancer. Mercury is paramount over this House in companionship with Saturn.

The cusp of the Twelfth House is 26° 46′ Cancer. It is the House and face of the Moon and the exaltation,[2] *nuhbahr* and the *darījān* of Jupiter. It is the term and detriment of Saturn. Mars is lord of triplicity in companionship with Venus and with the Moon in attendance. It is the *ādarjān, dodecatemorion, haftbahr* and fall of Mars. The Moon is paramount over this House with Jupiter, Mars, Venus and Saturn. The degree is feminine, lucid and void of good or evil fortune. The Dragon's Tail is in 27° 29′ 13″ Leo. The Part of knowledge and clemency (*al-'ilm wa-l-ḥilm*) of superiority and victory is 18° 22′. The Part of offspring is admittedly 2° 49′ The Part of fear and pain is 22° 15′. The Part of life is 2° 49′
The Part of the father is 18° 22′ Leo. 36

that the Seventh Part of the Ninth House is that of *Rumores*.

[1] There is, apparently, some mistake here for just above, in the account of the Ninth House, we are told that the Part of male children is 23° 49′ Taurus.

[2] Cancer is Jupiter's House of exaltation.

The hyleg[1] in this horoscope is;—firstly, the point[2] of anterior conjunction; secondly, the Part of Fortune; and thirdly, the Ascendant. As regards the hyleg, the *kadkhudā*[3] is Saturn and then Júpi-

[1] Apparently there may be more than one hyleg or prorogator of life in a figure, and the meaning of the text seems to be that the first or chief hyleg is the point of anterior conjunction; that the Part of Fortune is the second hyleg; and that the Ascendant, *lit.*, the degree of the Ascendant, is the third.

The meaning, however, may be that the hyleg is the first or most important thing in the horoscope. This agrees with the remark in the *Tetrabiblos* (Ashmand, 129.) "The "inquiry into the duration of life "takes precedence of all other "questions as to the events subse- "quent to birth." Obviously until it is known whether the Native will grow up to maturity, it is useless to inquire what his career will be in other respects.

[2] جزو اجتماع *juzū-i-ijtimā*, "point of conjunction." See the term explained in Dict. of T. Ts. 187 l.4, where the phrase is written جزء الاجتماع and where there is a quotation from Mullā 'Abdu-l-lāh Barjandī's Commentary on the Tables of Ulugh Beg. One of the hylegs in use was the last conjunction of the Sun and Moon (*syzygy*) before the birth, and another was the last antecedent opposition of the Sun and Moon. The full phrase in astrological books, as I find from a MS. in the B.A.S.'s Library called the *Jawāmi' aḥkāmu-n-nujūm* was جزو اجتماع یا استقبال مقدم بر ولادت *juzū-i-ijtimā' yā istiqbāl muqaddam bar wilādat*, 'the point to conjunction for opposition antecedent to the birth.' The point of conjunction was presumably, the hyleg in Akbar's case, because his birth took place on the 4th day of the month and consequently shortly after a conjunction, for the Muḥammadan months are lunar and begin with the new Moon, *i.e.*, conjunction. The phrase *awwal juzū-i-ijtimā'* also occurs in the diagram (Figure III.) (36 l.9. fr. foot and 37 l.3.). Sédillot (202) translates the phrase *juzū-i-ijtimā'*, (which occurs in Ulugh Beg's *Prolegomena* text 147 l.1.) by *le degré de la conjonction*, and the word متقدم *mutaqaddam* for which *muqaddam* is a variant, by *antérieure à la nativité*.

The point of anterior conjunction, we are told, is posited in the Second House of the horoscope, being 24° 50′ Libra and, as both Jupiter and Venus are in this House, it is possible that the conjunction referred to is that of Jupiter and Venus, *i.e.*, the two Fortunes, and not the conjunction of the Sun and Moon. According to the second or Indian horoscope, Jupiter and Venus were in conjunction in the Second House. (text 28 l.6.)

[3] The meaning seems to be that as regards the duration of life, Saturn is the *kadkhudā* 'lord of geniture,' as he is the planet with the largest orbit and his cycle is that of longevity, being a return to the Golden Age when men lived for centuries; (See Badāonī, Lowe 335.) but that as regards fortune and sovereignty, Jupiter is first; and as regards the Ascendant, the Sun is preëminent.

ter; as regards[1] the Part of Fortune, Jupiter comes first, then Saturn; as regards the Ascendant the Sun comes first, then Mars.

1. از ممر *az mamarr*. *Mamarr* has the technical meaning of *transit*, but apparently not here.

## CHAPTER VI.

### Explanation of the judgments contained in this wondrous horoscope which is a brachial amulet of the stars and heavens, and the crown-talisman of generations and cycles.

As the foundation of the holy horoscope has been firmly laid, it is indispensable that an explanation of a few out of its many wonderful judgments should be given.

### Judgments of the First House (*aḥkām*).

As the cusp of the Ascendant is Leo which is the Sun's House, this signifies lofty genius and excellence, and that the holy frame[1] will be strong and athletic, with a large head, broad forehead, wide chest, strength and length, courage, majesty, gravity, beauty of feature and powerful brain. As most of the degrees of the Ascendant (First House) belong to the Sign of Virgo, which is the House and exaltation of Mercury who is in the House of Venus (Libra) or Second House of the horoscope, and is near[2] Jupiter and in his own term and triplicity, it is fitting that the Native should fall back upon his own exquisite intellect in all affairs of finance and state, and should accomplish his momentous enterprises by his own excellent plans. As the Sun is regent of the noble Ascendant in alliance with Saturn, the Native will have complete sovereignty over all the countries of India and over part of the fourth[3] climate. And as,

---

[1] See Jahāngīr's *Memoirs*, Price 45. Jahāngīr states that his father was tall, and remarkable for the length of his arms and the breadth of his chest.

[2] متصل *muttaṣil*. This word, which occurs again a few lines lower down, appears to have a technical meaning, signifying that the planet is within the power of the rays of another planet. See Dict. of T.Ts. 1508. *s.v.* *ittiṣāl*.

[3] The Sun is supposed to have special sway over the *fourth climate* to which Kashmīr, Kābul and Badakhshān belong. Saturn rules the first climate and India. India belongs mostly to the second and third cli-

with reference to position,[1] the Sun comes after Saturn, the empire of Hindūstān will precede that of the fourth climate. And as the lord of the second cusp, *viz.*, Mercury, is near the lord of the Ascendant (the Sun), this is a proof that prosperity and principality (*māl u mulk*) will be easily acquired. As the Ascendant, the Part of Fortune and the place of prior conjunction of the Sun and Moon belong to Signs possessing many planets,[2] there is strong evidence of length of life and duration of sovereignty.

### Judgments of the Second House.

As the cusp of the Second House belongs to Virgo, which is the House of Mercury who is near the Sun, and most of it belongs to Libra, the House of Venus, and as Venus is in the Ascendant[3] which is the House and exaltation of Mercury,—this signifies that wealth and territory will be acquired by means of excellent contrivances and perfect reason, and that the Native will obtain the office of king. And Jupiter's being in this House in his own term, and Mercury's being near him, are a strong proof of this and

---

mates, though A. F. says it is an aggregate of the first four climates. Jarrett III. 44.

The first four climates extend from lat. 12°42′ to 39° N. In India A. F. includes Ceylon, the Moluccas, Malacca, etc. (Jarrett III. 7.) Bābar says India belongs to the 1st, 2nd and 3rd climates. (Erskine 312.) A.F. has no Indian places in his list of the countries of the fourth climate (Jarrett III. 76) though he makes it begin at 33°43′ N. The first climate must be held to begin much further south than 12° N. if Ceylon, etc., are to be included.

1 Apparently the meaning is that, as in this horoscope the position of the Sun is posterior to that of Saturn (the latter being in Libra and the former in Scorpio), the empire of India will be acquired before that of the fourth climate. It may, however, refer to the circumstance that according to the arrangement of *heavens*, Saturn has the first heaven and the Sun the fourth.

2 The translation is doubtful; the literal rendering seems to be, "Signs having many risings" (of stars and planets?). The Ascendant is Leo; the Part of Fortune is in the Tenth House, *viz:* in 9° 22′ Gemini and the degree of prior conjunction is in Libra. As according to Ptolemy and Muḥyī'u-d-dīn Maghribī, the Part of Fortune is 18° 9′ Scorpio and so is in the Third House, A.F.'s meaning may possibly be that the three things referred to all occur in the early Houses of the horoscope.

3 Venus is in 26° 23′ 37″ Virgo but as this part of Virgo falls into the First House of the horoscope, Venus is said to be in the Ascendant.

also that the Viziers will manage affairs by the abounding reason of the Native and not by their own plans. On the contrary, their ideas will not endure in the presence of the designs of the Lord of the Age. And as the lord of the Second House (Mercury [1]) is in the Ascendant, he (the Native) will collect countless treasures; and as Jupiter is in this House, he will spend his wealth in ways pleasing to
37 God, and will walk in God's paths and his property will increase daily.

And the fact of Jupiter's being in his own term, is a proof of long life, so that he will have honoured grandchildren and these fortunate ones will grow up under his discipline.

As Saturn is in the Second House and in exaltation, harm will never come to his (the Native's) treasures. The hyleg which is the degree of first conjunction (*qu.* conjunction prior to the nativity?) is in this House and is a strong proof of the above statement. The *kadkhudā* (lord of the geniture) which is Saturn and is in exaltation, and his companion Jupiter having come into this House, give to the holy life the influences of two *kadkhudā*(s). Mars is the third (*kadkhudā*) so that the Native will exceed the natural period of life, *viz.*, 120 years.[2] The Moon's being paramount over this House is another corroboration of the well-groundedness of this blessing.

---

[1] Perhaps Saturn is meant; Libra is his House of exaltation. If so, the word *ṭāli'* must be taken not to mean *ascendant* but the whole of the horoscope. It may also be the Moon, as she is described as being paramount over the Second House.

[2] 120 years was considered by astrologers and doctors the natural period of a man's life. See Ibn Khaldūn's *Prolegomena*, (*Notices et Extraits.*) XIX, 347. "Selon les médicins et les astrologues, la vie naturelle de l'homme est de cent vingt ans, de l'espèce que ceux-ci nomment grandes années humaines." Similarly A. F. says, (Blochmann 121) "The elephant, like man, lives to an age of one hundred and twenty years." A. F. seems actually to have hoped that Akbar would outlive 120 years and that he himself might have the honour of recording the events of that period. (Jarrett III. 416.) *Kishwarkhudā*, 'world's lord,' (Jarrett II, 258, 1.3) seems to mean Akbar himself and not his dynasty. *Varāha Mihira* says (*Bṛhat Jātaka* I. ver. 63) that 120 years and 5 days is the maximum of the life of men and elephants. Badāonī tells us (Lowe 335) that the *Jogīs* promised Akbar he would live three or four times as long as ordinary men. No doubt they referred to the three *kadkhudā*(s) spoken of by A. F. (See also Albīrūnī on the length of human life. Chronicle of Ancient Nations, 90.) The three *kadkhudā*(s) might give a total of nearly a thousand

### Judgments of the Third House.

As the lord of the Ascendant (the Sun) is in the Third House, this signifies perfect mildness, sedateness, constancy and reverence and the succouring of kinsmen. But this tribe, out of short-sightedness, will not be single-minded. However as that centre (*markaz*) where the lord of the Ascendant (Scorpio) is, is the House of Mars and also his triplicity, term, decanate, *ādarjān* and *darījān*, and as he himself is in the Fifth House which is his House of exaltation[1] and his *gaudium* (*faraḥ*) and is the triplicity and face of Jupiter, and the *ādarjān* of the lord of the Ascendant,—the improper thoughts of this faction will become a cause of increased glory and enhanced dominion to the Native. And as the beginnings of the Third House which have to do with brethren, are a station[2] of the Sun's majesty, this signifies that brethren will be of no account alongside the glory of the holy being (Akbar) and that they will quaff the cup of anguish to the dregs. The middle and last portions of the Third House, which signify allies and helpers[3] are, according to Ptolemy, the Part of Fortune and they are also the face of the Sun and he is co-partner with the *kadkhudā* (Saturn). This signifies that friends and loyalists will be on the carpet of union (lit: *one colour*) and devotion, and be steadfast in respect, and will be advanced by the Native to prosperity and wealth. And as this place of the Third House has connection with Mars who is in his exaltation, and that House is the *gaudium* and House of Saturn who

---

years, according to Badāonī, one of the periods mentioned by the *Jogīs*, for it appears from the *Libellus Isagogicus* of Alchabitius, that the maximum of Saturn's years, (*Fridaria*) is 465, of Jupiter's 264, and of Mars', the same; 465+264+264=993. 120 was the maximum of the *Fridaria* bestowed by the Sun. As a matter of fact, Akbar did not reach even the Scriptural three-score and ten,—dying on 13th October, 1605, (Elphinstone), in his climacteric (63 years,) just before the anniversary of his birth 15th October, 1542.

[1] *Viz.*, that of Capricornus into which the Fifth House of the figure extends.

[2] *Maurid-i-saṭwat-i-naiyir-i-a'ẓam.* The Third House begins at 28° 1' Libra, but the allusion is probably to the Sun's being in the first degree, 0° 45′ 57″ Scorpio; for the entry of a planet into a new Sign is a time of special power and auspiciousness. See *Akbarnāma* I, 55, l.2 fr. foot, in the account of Enoch.

[3] The Text and all authorities read اخوان *ikhwān*, 'brothers,' but the editors propose to read *a'wān*, 'allies or helpers,' and no doubt this is the true reading. See *Akbarnāma*

is a foremost *kadkhudā* and who is also in his exaltation,—friends will always be in honour and glory. And as Saturn who is a *kadkhudā* and is in exaltation, is paramount in the House, this is a convincing proof of these things. And the lord (Mars) of the Third House being in the Fifth, is a proof of the establishment of noble children, and also signifies that there will be travelling and short[1] excursions[2] which will be provocative of joy.

One of the wonderful things is that the part of the other world, according to all, and the Part of Fortune, according to Ptolemy and Muḥyī'u-d-dīn Maghribī, are in one[3] place; to wit, 18° Scorpio in the Third House. This rarely occurs in horoscopes, and forcibly indicates that good fortune upon good fortune will come in succession from the other world, and is also strong evidence for information about hidden matters, so that the enlightened mind of the Native will be a rendezvous of mysteries.

38 JUDGMENTS OF THE FOURTH HOUSE.

As Mars is lord of the cusp (*markaz*) of this House, and he is in his exaltation,[4] face, and his own *trigon* (*muṣallaṣa*) and is dominant

26 11.3 and 17 and 'Abdu-l-ḥamīd's *Bādshāhnāma* 25 and 27.

'Abdu-l-ḥamīd of Lāhor is said to have been a pupil of Abu-l-faẓl (See Rieu's Catalogue I. 260, quoting Ṣāliḥ), and certainly has done his best to imitate A. F.'s turgidities. He himself tells us that he was chosen by Shāh Jahān to be his Court historian on account of his being a proficient in the style of Abu-l-faẓl. It goes without saying that writing under Shāh Jahān, he is a much straiter Musulmān than his master. The lengthy account of Shāh Jahān's horoscope which he gives, was drawn up by Mullā 'Alā'u-l-mulk of Tun in Khurāsān who afterwards got the title of Fāẓil Khān. (*Badshāhnāma* 13). Apparently the conjunction of planets which led to Shāh Jahān's receiving the title of Second Lord of conjunction (the first being Tīmūr) took place in 991 (1585), nine years before Shāh Jahān's birth. Great importance was attached to Shāh Jahān's having been born in the thousandth year of the Hijra. He was born under Libra the sign under which the Prophet was born.

[1] *Naql* means also 'zest to wine,' etc.

[2] See Shāh Jahān's horoscope for a similar expression. *Bādshāhnāma* 20 1.5.

[3] This does not seem quite accurate. In the previous account of the Houses, we are told that the Part of the other world is 17° 50′ Scorpio and that of Fortune, according to Ptolemy and Muḥyī'u-d-dīn is 18° 9′ Scorpio.

[4] We are told above that Mars is posited in 10° 48′ 23″ Capricorn which is his House of exaltation. The Fourth House begins at 27° 21′ Scorpio which is Mars' mansion.

over this House and it is the term of Jupiter, what is signified is that in the beginning of his (the Native's) career territory will come into possession through the exertions of military officers. And as this House is a Fixed Sign, and its lord (Mars) is in exaltation and has a beneficent[1] aspect, territory will continually be coming into the possession of the King's[2] servants and whatever so comes will remain there permanently.

As the 8th and 4th[3] of the degrees which belong to the beginning of Scorpio are Gemini (*Jauzā'*) whose lord (Mercury) is occulted by the Sun's rays, this signifies that when the Native shall arrive at years of discretion, the might of his intellect will become displayed,

---

1 Apparently the meaning is that Mars is in the Fifth House, in Capricorn, and so has the beneficent trine aspect to the First House, that is, the House of the Native's life.

2 *Auliyā-i-daulat.* This seems an honorific circumlocution for the king himself, but may mean that Akbar was then a minor, and that conquests were made by his regent, Bairām Khān.

3 This is a difficult passage, and I am uncertain of the meaning. Perhaps the text is corrupt, but all the MSS. I have examined give the same reading with the apparently unimportant difference that some omit the conjunction *u* between *hashtum* and *cahārum*. The difficulty lies in understanding how the constellation Gemini comes in here. *Jauzā'* means Orion as well as Gemini, but the latter seems intended here, for A.F., goes on to speak of its lord being occulted by the Sun and this can only refer to Mercury who is the lord of Gemini. It is possible that the meaning is that Gemini is the Eighth and Fourth House from the beginning of Scorpio, *i.e.*, is Eight Houses apart on one side of the Third House, to which the first degrees of Scorpio belong, and Four Houses apart on the other. It is also possible that A.F. has confounded *Jauzā'*, Orion, with *Jauzā'*, Gemini. But I rather think that by *Jauzā'* may be meant the "lesser Twins," *viz.*, the stars $\beta$ and $\delta$ *Scorpionis*. See Sayce's "Higher Criticism and the Monuments," p. 69n. where Professor Hommel is quoted as stating that there are three sets of Twins, *viz.*, Castor and Pollux in Gemini, the lesser Twins in Scorpio and the lesser Twins in Aries. Mercury is in 25° 24′ Libra of the horoscope, and so is occulted or immersed in the rays of the Sun which is posited in the first degrees of Scorpio. But I do not see why the first degrees of Scorpio are referred to by A.F., in his description of the Fourth House, for that begins near the end of Scorpio. Perhaps *awwal* is a mistake for *ākhir*. The Fourth House is that of the father and so may deal with his death. It is also that of lords and states.

and that his honoured[1] father will at this time, have his face turned towards the hidden and inner world and will depart to the eternal city. As most of this House belongs to Sagittarius and the lord of the term (Jupiter) is in the Second House of the horoscope, the Native will be affectionate and grateful to his father and will receive an appanage[2] from his dominions.

### Judgments of the Fifth House

As the lord of most of the Third House which is connected with lovers and sincere friends and helpers, to wit, Mars, is in the Fifth and in exaltation, this signifies the glorious condition of the sons of the Native and their sincerity and affection. And as Saturn is paramount over this House, is in exaltation and in his own triplicity and is a *kadkhudā*,—and as Jupiter is in his face and triplicity and is associated with the *kadkhudā* (Saturn) and is lord of the cusp of this House,—this signifies that the sons of the Native will be fortunate and be defenders of the State and that they will not remove the head of respect from the plane of well-pleasing. Aquila, who is of the constitution of Mars, and Jupiter and Cygnus, who is of the constitution of Jupiter and Venus, are in this House and forcibly indicate an abundant catch (*ṣaid*) of pleasure and auspiciousness.

### Judgments of the Sixth House.

As the master (Saturn) of this House (Capricorn) is in his exaltation, and the Dragon's Head is in this House, they signify the lasting sovereignty of the Native and the acquisition of abundant

---

[1] Humāyūn was killed by an accident when Akbar was little over thirteen. I suppose the meaning is that when Akbar was born his intellect, represented by Mercury, was subject to his father, but that when he came to the age of puberty, it emerged.

[2] This refers to the fact that Jalālābād was assigned by Humāyūn for Akbar's maintenance. See quotation from the *Mirāt Āftābnāma* of Shāh Nawāz Khān in Kanī Lāl Dās' paper *J. A. S. B.* for 1886, p. 83. See also, what is more to the point, *Akbarnāma* I, 315, where we are told that the servants and properties of his deceased uncle Hindāl, including Ghaznī, &c., were made over to Akbar when he was ten years old. Jalālābād used to be called Jūī Shāhī and was named after Akbar (Jalālu-d-din). See *Akbarnāma* I. 200 l.8 from foot.

wealth and property, and permanence of elemental health, and equability of disposition. Should a little sickness affect the hem of his holy constitution, it will speedily terminate in perfect health. And as Mars is paramount over this House, in co-partnership with Saturn, and both are in exaltation, there will be numerous auspicious servants[1] and attendants.

### Judgments of the Seventh House.

As the lord of the cusp of the Seventh[2] House is Saturn[3] and he is in exaltation, the Native will in his first youth, marry[4] chaste veiled ones from the ruling families of India. And as Saturn is in the Second House,[5] this may indicate that those chaste, curtained and holy ones will belong to his tributary and wealth-increasing princes. And as the Part of friendship and love is this House, this signifies increasing relish of friendship and love, especially as the Part of affection is in Pisces which is the House of Jupiter and the exaltation of Venus.

### Judgments of the Eighth House.

As the cusp of this House belongs to Pisces and its lord, Jupiter, is in the Second, in his own term and triplicity and the Part[6] of excellence is in this House, and as Venus is paramount over this House in co-partnership with Mars who is in exaltation,—this signifies the absence of fear[7] and danger, and the being rendered safe by the protection and defence of God.

### Judgments of the Ninth House. 39

As the cusp of this House is in the Sign of Aries and its lord, Mars, is in his exaltation and gaudium (*faraḥ*) and is dominant over

---

[1] The Sixth House is that of servants.

[2] The Seventh is the House of marriage.

[3] Saturn rules India.

[4] In 969 (1562) *i.e.*, when Akbar was in his twentieth year, he married Bihārī Mal's daughter. We do not hear of any other marriages in early youth with Indian ladies, but Badāonī (Lowe 211) tells us that Akbar said he had on coming of age, married many wives, both freeborn and slaves, and had not restricted himself to the legal number of four.

[5] The Second is the House of wealth.

[6] Perhaps this is the *pars nobilitatis* of Guido Bonatus and which appears to be 19° Aries *i.e.*, the Sun's exaltation.

[7] The Eighth House is a House of misfortunes, death, etc.

this House, the Native will reap benefit from travel,[1] and the journies which take place, will be accompanied by acquisition of territory.

### Judgments of the Tenth House.

As the cusp of this House belongs to Taurus, which is the House of Venus, and she is dominant over it and is in the Ascendant, this signifies perfect felicity and general superiority, which is an expression for a great kingship; also that this sublime dignity will long be in the possession of the Native, especially as this House is the exaltation of the Moon. And the Moon is in an aspect[2] towards this House and towards the Ascendant which is one of entire friendship. And as the Part of Fortune is, by the opinion of the majority, in this House, this signifies perfect fortune and increase of State, and that the Native will spend most of his days in managing and arranging the affairs of Church and State. And as the Part of reason and speech is in this House, it signifies that his reason and speech will be king of reasons and at the head of utterances. Much too of the specialties of Venus, who is lord of pleasure and joy, will be bestowed on him.

### Judgments of the Eleventh House.

As the cusp of this House belongs to Gemini and its regent (Mercury) is in the Second House, which is that of wealth, this signifies that the hopes which he forms with regard to fortune and territory will be realized to his heart's desire. It also proves that he will have sincere friends and that the masters of wisdom and knowledge will arrive at high rank in his service. And as the Part of the conclusions of actions is in this House, this signifies that his hopes[3] and desires will have a happy termination.

### Judgment of the Twelfth House.

As the cusp of this House belongs to Cancer and its lord, the Moon, is in detriment[4] and gaudium (*faraḥ*), this proves that the

---

[1] The Ninth is a House of travels.

[2] The Moon is in the Fifth House *viz.*, 19° 48′ 14″ Capricorn and so she is in trine to the First and Tenth Houses.

[3] The Eleventh House is that of hopes.

[4] The Moon is in the Fifth House in 19° 48′ 14″ Capricorn and so is in detriment as being in the Sign opposite to her Mansion, *viz.*, Cancer. The Twelfth is the House of private enemies and a House of misfortune. Had the Moon been in it, this would

enemies of the State will be constantly in adversity and distress to whatever extent may be agreeable to the Native. And the fact of the Dragon's Tail[1] (*Katabibazon* or *Z̲anab*) being there in the first degree, is strong evidence of this. And as the Part of knowledge and clemency is in this House, it signifies that the Native will, together with his insight (into character), be clement and forgiving to the short-sighted and cross-grained ones. And patience, breadth of view and general benevolence will be among his necessary attributes.

May Almighty God prolong the life of the Lord of Fortune for generations and cycles, since the attributes of greatness,—which are the root and flower of universal sovereignity and world-adornment, and are a cause of capturing the hearts of friends and foes, and attract souls and knit together the thoughts of high and low,—are revealed in all their perfection and (as it were) on an open highway (Praise be to the gracious God for it) in the aggregation of refined qualities of this Doctor of the High School of Unity; and have made him by his idiosyncracy and fundamental nature, sole owner of sublime dignity and peculiar grace. And of a certainty, all those admirable qualities and dispositions have, without effort or vaunting, become the blissful possession of this celestial Being, so that from this fountain-head of justice, they are distributed by the garden-channel of the lords[2] of liberality.

*Verse.*

For ever, and so long as there are stars in the firmament,
For ever, and so long as there are bodies with souls,
May there be no revolution of the spheres without thy pleasure,
No movement of the heavenly bodies except according to thy will.

---

have been a bad omen. I do not understand how the Moon is said to be in *faraḥ*, *i.e.*, joy; but apparently the author draws from this the inference that the enemies will be distressed and the Native will be gladdened. Possibly it refers to the Moon's being in the Fifth House and so in trine to the Ascendant. Perhaps the word is a mistake for فرغ *farg͟h*, emptiness or disengagement.

[1] The Dragon's Tail is a cause of misfortune and increases evil influences. Apparently *awwal* 'first,' must be a mistake for *āk͟hir*, 'last,' for the Dragon's Tail is in the last degree of the Twelfth House *viz.*, 27° 29′ 13″ Leo. (See *supra*.)

[2] ارباب *arbāb*. Blochmann says (563n.) that this word, which is the plural of *rabb*, is used in Persian as a singular to mean a *headman* or *magis-*

40 This is a sketch of the judgments of the auspicious horoscopes; but if the gifts of the stars, the blessings of the aspects, and the significations of the Houses, were fully set forth, registers would be compiled and books composed.

*Verse.*[1]

His exquisite exaltations cannot be reckoned up,
Star-gazing mathematicians can but adumbrate them.

---

*trate.* Perhaps then the expression *arbāb-i-istifāẓa* refers to Akbar himself. Otherwise, it refers to his ministers.

[1] The couplet is Faiẓī's and occurs with slight variation in the preface to his Līlāvatī. Calcutta 1828 p. 2.1.4.

## CHAPTER VII.

### DIAGRAM OF THE HOLY HOROSCOPE, CAST BY MAULĀNĀ ALYĀS OF ARDABĪL,[1] IN ACCORDANCE WITH THE ĪLKHĀNĪ TABLES.

At the time of writing these pages which are a record of auspiciousness, a horoscope came under my view which had been drawn by the very erudite Maulānā Alyās of Ardabīl who held high rank among mathematicians and was one of his Majesty Jahānbānī Jannat-āshiyānī's courtiers.

This horoscope also has been copied in sketch[2] but without details of the influences of the Houses and the Judgments. It has been copied partly in consideration of the repute of the drawer,[3] and partly because, unlike the others, it is based on the Īlkhānī Tables.

---

[1] A town in Persia, west of the Caspian. It was the capital of the province of Āzarbāijān. (See Meynard's *Yāqūt*, Paris, 1861, 21 and Jarrett III, 81). Maulānā Alyās would naturally follow the Īlkhānī Tables, for he belonged to the country of Tabrīz or Marāgha where Naṣīru-d-dīn Ṭūsī had his observatory.

[2] بجنس *bajins* apparently means *in genere* or in gross, *i.e.*, without details.

[3] مستخرج *mustakhrij*, lit. 'extractor.'

FIGURE IV.

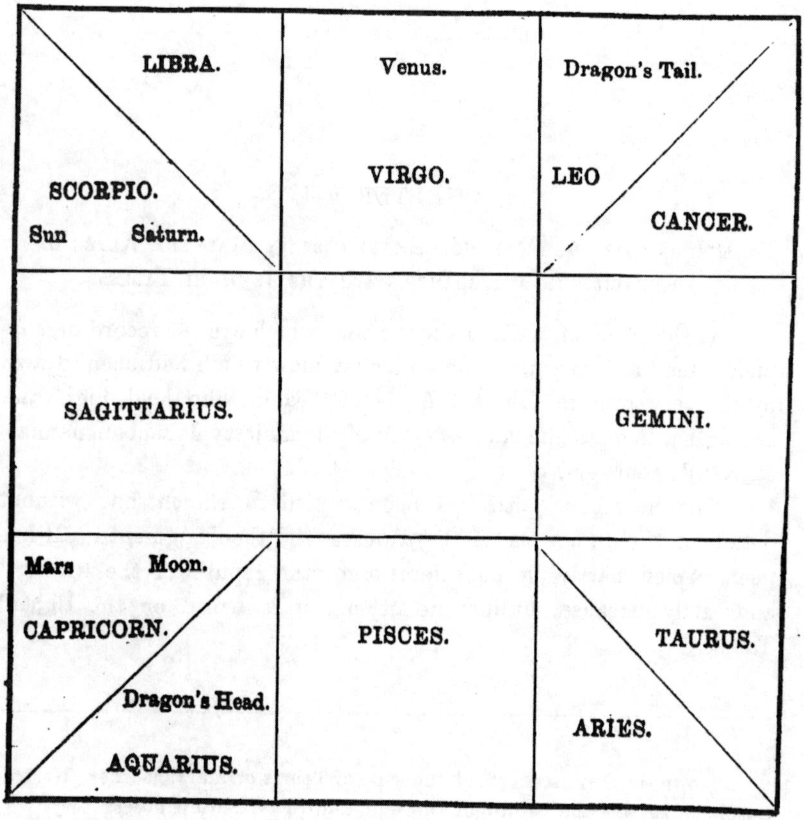
LIBRA.
Venus.
Dragon's Tail.
SCORPIO.
Sun
Saturn.
VIRGO.
LEO
CANCER.
SAGITTARIUS.
GEMINI.
Mars
Moon.
CAPRICORN.
Dragon's Head.
AQUARIUS.
PISCES.
TAURUS.
ARIES.

# CHAPTER VIII.

## ACCOUNT OF THE DESIGN OF PROVIDENCE (*Ḥikmat*) IN THE DIFFERENCE 41
## BETWEEN THE GREEK PHILOSOPHERS AND THE INDIAN ASTROLOGERS IN THE MATTER OF HIS MAJESTY'S AUSPICIOUS HOROSCOPE.

Some scientific men used to think that the disagreement between the Indian and Greek astronomers,—the former placing the horoscope in Leo and the latter in Virgo, was due to a difference of opinion among philosophers about the movement of the Zodiacal Heaven. A crowd[1] of ancient philosophers, including Aristotle, were agreed that, the Eighth[2] Heaven had no motion. The philosopher Hipparchus contended that it did move, but he did not ascertain the rate of progression. Ptolemy said the motion was one degree in a century and that the revolution was completed in 36,000 years. Most philosophers hold that the rate is one degree in seventy years and that the revolution is completed in 25,200 years. Another school say that a degree is traversed in sixty-three[3] years and that the revolution is completed in 22,680 years. The cause of such

---

[1] This passage is substantially repeated in the *Āīn* (III, 11; Jarrett III, 20.)

[2] This is the Heaven of the Fixed Stars. In the *Āīn* (III, 34; Jarrett III, 33) this is numbered as the Second Heaven,—the Eighth being that of Mercury. Here the author counts them in reverse order, beginning with the lowest, *viz.*, that of the Moon,—and by thus counting upwards, the Heaven of the Fixed Stars becomes the Eighth. It will be remembered that the ancients attributed motion to the Fixed Stars or at least to the sphere in which they were supposed to be placed. "The Ptolemaic astronomy attributes motion and a regular course to those stars which we now call Fixed but which the Greeks merely called ἀπλανεῖς undeviating." (Ashmand 4n.)

[3] I do not know what school is referred to here. In the *Āīn* (II, 11 1.7 fr. foot) Ibn A' (A'lam) (cir. 985 A.D.) and Naṣīru-d-dīn Ṭūsī (cir. 1272 A.D.) are mentioned as holding that the rate is one degree in sixty solar years. Perhaps the sixty-three are lunar but these are equal to more than 60 solar years,—for at the rate of eleven days a year, we get only 660 days or not quite two years.

According to Sédillot (Notes et Éclaircissements. *Prolegomena.* 289)

discrepancies is a difference in the equipment and instruments of the observatories and difference in the profundity and subtlety[1] of the observations.

The fact is, the earliest philosophers did not suspect the motion of the Fixed Stars, on account of its exceeding slowness. For this reason, they did not get sufficient time to observe it.[2]

At the time when the Signs of the Zodiac were determined, the figure Leo which was regarded as a constellation of several fixed stars, was opposite to and in front of a (certain) part of the Heaven of Heavens,[3] and now, owing to the movement of the Zodiacal Heaven,[4] it has moved from that part and is in the station where

---

Naṣīru-d-dīn as well as Ulugh Beg held seventy years to be the time. But he refers to his *Matériaux* (481) as showing that Arzachil knew of a movement as correct as that of our modern Tables. Arago, in his lectures, says that the movement is 50″·103 a year, and that the revolution is completed in 25, 867 years.

In the *Astronomica quaedam ex traditione* Shāh Cholgīl published by Greaves (Gravius) about the middle of the 17th century, we are told that according to observations made in the time of the Khalīf Al-Māmūn (813–34 A.D.) a degree was passed in 66 years and 8 months. Perhaps these were lunar, and if so, they would correspond nearly to the 63 (solar) mentioned in the Text. Muḥammad Shāh Quljī wrote a commentary on the Tables of Naṣīru-d-dīn Ṭūsī in 866 (1461). A. F. perhaps copied from him, for the passage in the beginning of the *Āīn* (Jarrett 6) about the explanation of the term *zīj*, etc., is very similar to one on Muḥammad Shāh Quljī, as given by Greaves and also it appears, by Sédillot. But Oriental writers copy so much from one another that it is difficult to know who was the original source. Shāh Quljī also gives seventy years as the rate of precession according to the Marāgha Tables; and says that the annual rate was 51″ 26.‴

[1] The text reads وقت time, but MS. 564 has دقت which I have adopted.

[2] I suppose the meaning is that the motion being less than a minute a year, it could not become perceptible unless after a lifetime of observations or unless the observations were continued for generations.

[3] *i.e.*, the Ninth or Crystalline Heaven.

[4] The Penny Cyclopaedia (Art. Astrology) says: "The astrologers never made any allowance for the precession of the equinoxes. Thus though the constellation Aries is now in Taurus and the influences of its stars ought to have moved with them, we find that the astronomical Aries or first 30° of the ecliptic, is used for the constellation. Under the circumstances, this is of little consequence, but such a practice would be fatal to astronomy."

Virgo then was. Similarly Virgo has moved to the station of Libra, Libra to Scorpio and so on, up to the last Sign. Now the calculation of Indian astrologers[1] is in accord with the observations of the ancient philosophers which were based on the notion that the Fixed Stars did not move. The calculation of the new observations[2] is founded on the movement of the Zodiacal Heaven which has caused the constellation Leo to move to the House

---

Ashmand (Preface and p. 32) defends astrologers against this charge and says, "We should rather say that the stars have changed places than that the parts of heaven in which they once were situated have done so."

[1] The author does not mean that the Indian astronomers were ignorant of the movement of the stars, *i.e.*, of the precession of the equinoxes. The account in the *Āīn* (Jarrett III. 19) shows that they held the movement to be 54 a year. But they thought that the (westward) movement only extended to 27° Aries and that then the stars retrograded to 27° Pisces and afterwards recommenced. In other words they held that the stars librated between 27° Aries and 27° Pisces.

[2] By the "new observations" those of Ulugh Beg are commonly meant, and it must be those which are referred to here, for A. F. is dealing with the horoscope of Maulānā Cand which, we are told, was founded on the Gurgānī Tables, *i.e.*, those of Ulugh Beg. According to Bābar (Erskine 51) the tables used by the Indian astronomers were those of Vikramāditya and he says that 1584 years had elapsed from the building of Vikramāditya's observatory. Apparently Bābar was writing this in 1527-28, =1584 Vikramāditya Era (which began B.C. 57.) But his statement in no way coincides with A. F.'s for Ulugh Beg's Tables were drawn up in 1434 and published in 1437 and if we deduct 1190 from 1434, we get 244 A.D. as the date of the Indian Tables.

(Sédillot gives the epoch of Ulugh Beg's Tables as 841 H.=1437 A.D.)

Nor can we reconcile the statements by supposing that the "new observations" mean those of Naṣīru-d-dīn Ṭūsī which were made at Marāgha in the latter part of the 13th century. According to the *Āīn* (Jarrett 4) Naṣīru-d-dīn's observatory was built 362 years and Ulugh Beg's 156 before A. F. wrote his book. Now the *Āīn* was composed in the 40th year of Akbar, *i.e.*, 1596, so that 1234 would be the date of the Marāgha observations and 1434 those of Samarqand (Ulugh Beg's). The date 1234 is, however, certainly wrong, as it is nearly a quarter of a century before the destruction of Baghdād (1258) and we know that it was after this that Hulāgū Khān installed Naṣīru-d-dīn at Marāgha. According to D'Herbelot, Naṣīru-d-dīn was established at Marāgha in 657 (1259) and published his Tables in 668 (1270). Perhaps شصت *shast*, sixty, is a

of Virgo. The difference between the two calculations is 17°,[1] each Sign having moved 17° from its place. From this it may be known that 1190 years have elapsed from the observations of the Indian philosophers to the new ones, assuming that a degree is traversed every seventy years, and most philosophers are agreed that we should multiply 17 by 70. On the view of Ptolemy that the movement is one degree a century, the interval between the two sets of observations is 1700 years.

Keen-sighted inquirers after truth and subtle perceivers of the secrets of the skies fell into the valley of perturbation on account of these discrepancies. Now that the pattern of the philosophers of the Age, 'Aẓdu-l-daulah Amīr Fatḥu-l-lāh of Shīrāz, has shewn by the Greek Canon and the Persian rules that his Majesty's auspi-
42 cious horoscope is in Leo as has been stated above, it clearly appears that the explanation of the disagreement is not, as was commonly supposed, that the Indian philosophers deny the existence of the spheres, as has been set forth in the Second Volume.[2] Rather it was the Divine wisdom (*ḥikmat-i-ilāhī*) and the Divine jealousy which demanded that the description of this cavalier[3] of the plain of majesty

---

copyist's error for بیست *bīst*, twenty which would yield the date 1274. A. F., however, with all his industry, is not to be trusted about dates as Silvestre de Sacy has shewn with reference to a statement in the *Āyār-i-Dānish* about the poet Rūdagī. Even if we deduct the 1190 years from 1272, the date of the Marāgha observations, we do not get back to Vikramāditya's era, though we get very near that of Sālivāhana, *viz.*, 78 A.D.

The most probable explanation is that Bābar was mistaken in supposing that the Vikramāditya of the Tables was the Vikramāditya of the Era. The Indian Tables were probably composed in the time of the second Vikramāditya and in that of Varāha Mihira, though this date is also inconsistent with A. F.'s calculation.

[1] It would seem (Text III. 440 1.5 fr. foot) that the exact difference was a little more than 17°, for we are told that Bānū Ārām, Akbar's daughter, was born under 19° Sagittarius or 1° 54′ according to Hindū calculation.

[2] The Lucknow ed. has "last volume," and this is probably correct, the reference apparently being to the concluding volume of the *Āīn*, *viz.*, III. 8. (Jarrett III. 13.)

[3] فارس *fāris*. It also means a lion and so there may be an allusion to the constellation Leo. Akbar is called (*Āīn* I. 139) *shāhsuwār-i-'arṣa-i-iqbāl*, 'the royal rider of the plain of fortune.'

and confidant of the sublime cabinet, should remain hidden from the gaze of keen-sighted, penetrating, minute inquirers, as well as from the eyes of the evil-disposed and inwardly blind.

It was from this cause, that his Majesty Jahānbānī Jannat-āshiyānī, who in astrolabic investigations and studies of astronomical Tables and observations, was at the head of the enthroned[1] ones of acute knowledge and was a second Alexander,—in spite of his perfect labours and exertions in the matter of the horoscope of the Lord of the Age, did not attain to the truth (did not reveal the whole truth). And likewise all those others who were versed in the secrets of astrology, remained within the curtain of contradiction and did not arrive at a perfect knowledge of the mystery. And notwithstanding the identity of the canons of calculation and the inquiries of right-thinkers,—for natural philosophers do not materially disagree in these matters,—owing to the jealousy of God, the truth of the holy nativity remained under the veil of concealment and was hidden behind the curtain of contradiction. But on the whole, if each of the horoscopes be looked at with the eye of judgment—and a sketch of each has been given,—it becomes plain that in the matter of power, dignity and sublimity, external and internal, there is nothing equal to them. Though the horoscopes are discrepant, they agree in external and internal splendour and congratulate the Native as supreme over the visible and invisible worlds. And those intimate friends of his Majesty Jahānbānī Jannat-āshiyānī, whose outward and inward beings were clothed with truth and righteousness, have been heard to tell that when his Majesty had the auspicious horoscope shewn to him and had considered it, it happened several times that when in his private chamber and with the doors all closed, he fell a'dancing, and from excess of exultation, revolved with a circular motion. Why indeed should not sitters in the front ranks of the pavilion of true glory, and tasters of the trays of eternal knowledge—who have partaken of the sweets of ecstacy and the knowledge of God, indulge in transports of joy at the sweets of this revelation, and why should they not chaunt strains of rapture? For these perfections are steps or

---

1 The author seems to refer to the fact of eminent astrologers, having been princes, *e.g.*, Alexander, Alphonso of Castile and Ulugh Beg.

stages of exaltation and are the essence of Divine knowledge. And his Majesty Jahānbānī Jannat-āshiyānī was by the perfection of his personality, enlightened by flashes of forthcoming events and glimpses into the future, and his senses were warmed by the auspicious advent of his Majesty, the King of Kings. And all these lights were seen, before realization in the ranks of actions, in the mirror of the wondrous horoscope. And he many times said to those who were privileged to converse with him, that the horoscope of this Light of Fortune was superior, in several respects and by sundry degrees, to that of his Majesty, the Lord of Conjunction[1] (Tīmūr)
43 as indeed clearly appears to the scrutinizing students of the prognostications. And when these two auspicious documents are compared, and the gifts of the planets and the blessings of the heavens[2] are weighed in the balance of reflection, it will be seen what are the communications of the horoscope of the Lord of Conjunction, and what are those of the holy horoscope. Praise be to God! notwithstanding the remoteness of the horoscopists in time, place and condition, and the discrepancy of their canons, every one of the glorious schemes agrees—as has been shewn—in this, that the Native will attain lofty, spiritual and temporal rank, and that his holy personality will be a collection of inward and outward excellencies and will be possessed of various perfections and will have sway over the visible and invisible world. He will have various kinds of sovereignties and various degrees of rule, and will attain lofty rank in worship of the Truth and in theology. He will befriend the poor and humble, and will have long life and soundness of body and an equable disposition and will be praised by high and low and thanked by great and small. He will have perfect knowledge of the world, and will rule countries and guard the paths of righteousness,

---

1 The horoscope of Tīmūr is given in the *Zafarnāma* but without much detail. There is also one, as noticed by Gibbon, in Hyde's *Syntagma* (Dissert: II. 466) which was cast by Ashmole.

2 علويات *'alwīyāt*. Perhaps this word has a technical meaning here, *viz.*, the superior planets, Mars, Jupiter and Saturn, which were so-called because their orbits were supposed to be higher than that of the Sun. See *Mafātīḥu-l-'ulūm*, 229, top line. Mercury and Venus and the Moon are called *kawākabu-s-siflīya*, inferior planets.

and will perform the duties of government and of the administration of the world.

It is a remarkable circumstance that all those qualities which astrologers have come to know by toil and meditation, are read by simple-minded persons who know nothing of the diagrams of stellar mysteries, by dint of their own insight, on the forehead-page[1] of his Majesty's career, though they have humbly to acknowledge the inability of language to expound them.

*Verse.*

Thy attributes have made tongues incoherent,
Thy glorious personality has changed certainty into conjecture.

## NOTE ON THE HOROSCOPES OF AKBAR.

Abu-l-faẓl gives four horoscopes. The first and fourth however appear to be substantially the same. Both were made by Muḥammadan servants of Humāyūn,—the first by Maulānā Cānd and the fourth by Maulānā Alyās of Ardabīl. Maulānā Cānd's was drawn up according to the "New Tables," *i.e.*, those of Ulugh Beg Mīrzā who was Tīmūr's grandson. These were calculated for 1437. Maulānā Ilyās' horoscope was cast according to the Ilkhānī or Imperial Tables, *i.e.*, those made by Naṣīru-d-dīn Ṭūsī at Marāgha—about 50 miles S. by W. of Tabrīz—in the reign of Hulāgū Khān cir. 1272.

Abu-l-faẓl, writing in the 40th year of Akbar, (1596) says (Jarrett II, 4.) that 3(.. years had elapsed since Naṣīru-d-dīn built his observatory and 156 since Ulugh Beg built his at Samarqand. This gives a date of 1440 for Ulugh Beg's Tables and of 1234 for Naṣīru-d-dīn's, but the latter is certainly wrong, and probably there is some clerical error in the text. If Hulāgū Khān first established him in Marāgha, it is assuredly wrong, but A. F. evidently thinks he was there earlier. (*Āīn* II, 11.)

The second horoscope was made by Jotik Rai, Akbar's astrologer. We do not know its exact date but it was, of course, drawn many years after Akbar's birth and after the construction, by Humāyūn's orders, of the first and fourth horoscopes.

The third was made by Fatḥu-l-lāh of Shīrāz and could not have been drawn earlier than 991 (1583), for this astronomer did not come to Akbar's Court till that year. Indeed A. F. tells us that it was in the first year of Fatḥu-l-lāh's service that he asked him to compare the horoscopes and reconcile their discrepancies.

---

[1] The meaning is, that the actual facts of Akbar's life exhibit all those wonderful qualities which astrologers have found by painful investigation of his horoscope.

Both Maulānā Cānd and Maulānā Alyās put the birth under Virgo and there is no doubt this is correct,—if correctness can be predicated of such matters. The Indian astrologers probably put the birth in Leo because that Sign is the House of the Sun, between whom and Akbar there was supposed to be a mysterious connection. Possibly however, the earlier date of their Tables warranted them in putting the birth under Leo, as A. F. has explained in his chapter on the discrepancies. But granting that this was so, we are not told why their Tables should be preferred to those of Naṣīru-d-dīn and Ulugh Beg. And indeed Abu-l-fazl does not prefer them. He tells us that Indian Tables agree with the observations of those philosophers who are not aware that there was a movement of the Fixed Stars. In other words, he admits that they are wrong.

If the precession of the equinoxes account for the difference between the Tables, why stop short at the Hindū observations? A. F. calculates that these were made 1190 years before Ulugh Beg's, *i.e.*, about 1336 before Fatḥu-l-lāh cast Akbar's horoscope. According to Bābar (Erskine 51.) the Hindū Tables were made at Ujjain in the time of Vikramāditya, *i.e.*, cir. 57 B.C. According to Tod, (Rājpūtānā) Hindū astronomers now follow the Tables of Jai Singh which were made in 1728. (See Dr. Hunter's paper, Asiatic Researches V, 177.) But why did not he or Fatḥu-l-lāh carry the calculation further back and ascertain the position of the constellations of the Zodiac at the time, say, of the birth of Adam or at least, of Enoch or Idris who, according to Muḥammadans, is the father of astronomy? Some astrologers professed to know the position of the stars at the time of the Creation and held that Adam was born under 1° Capricorn (See *infra* for A. F.'s account of Adam). And at all events A. F., who seems to have accepted the chronology according to which Adam was born about 7000 before his own time, could have had no difficulty in calculating the position of the constellations at that period, allowing one degree for every seventy years.

According to A. F. the difference between the Indian astrologers and Maulānā Cānd amounts to 17°. But apparently Fatḥu-l-lāh did not adopt the Indian calculations, which indeed he probably could not read. (He was a Persian and we are told in the *Āīn* (Blochmann 104) that he superintended the translation of part of Ulugh Beg's Tables, though, if as has been supposed, these were originally written in Persian, one does not see what necessity there was for translating them. There is however a doubt on the point and A. F.'s remark implies that Ulugh Beg's Tables were written in a foreign language, *e.g.*, Arabic or Turkish. According to D'Herbelot, they were first written in Arabic but Sédillot has no doubt that Persian was their original language). Fatḥu-l-lāh, we are told, based his calculations on the Greek and Persian Tables, not on the Indian, and found the cusp of the Ascendant to be 28° 36′ Leo.

Leo is the Sign immediately preceding Virgo, and if the difference of the Hindū and Persian calculations be 17°, the cusp according to the former, should apparently be 20° Leo, for Maulānā Cānd's horoscope brought out the cusp of the Ascendant as 7° Virgo. We are not told what Tables Fatḥu-l-lāh used and are left in the dark as to his *modus operandi*. The difference between his calculations and those of Maulānā Cānd was apparently, about 8½° *viz*., from 28° 36′ Leo to 7° Virgo. If, as A. F. does, we take the rate of precession to be one degree in 70 years, Fatḥu-l-lāh must have used Tables made about 600 years before Ulugh Beg's. This would give a date of about 830 A.D., which approximates to the Baghdād observations of the Khalīf Māmūn referred to in the *Āīn* (Jarrett II. 3.)

If we take the more correct rate of precession, *viz*., one degree in 72 years, we get a still closer approximation for 8½° = 612 years and this, deducted from 1434 = 822 A.D.

I regret that I have not been able to translate the four horoscope chapters in a satisfactory manner. They are difficult, for several words of frequent use in them, are not to be found in our dictionaries, at least not with their astronomical meaning. Dozy's Supplement is of little or no use for astrological terms, and Lane appears to ignore them altogether. Unfortunately with all his amplitude of detail, A. F. fails us at the very pinch of the case. That is, he gives no explanation of Fatḥu-l-lāh's *modus operandi* and does not tell us how he managed to bring the horoscope into Leo.

It is probable that in places, the text is corrupt.

Books on astrology are very numerous. One of the best of the old treatises is *De Judiciis Astrorum* by 'Alī Abu-l-ḥasan (Albohazan Haly Aben Rajal). He, it appears, was born in Spain, for he is styled Ash-Shaibānī and Ash-Shabīlī (Hispaliensis) and his full name is Abu-l-ḥasan 'Alī Ibn Abi-r-rajālu-sh-shaibānī.

In Hammer-Purgstall's History of Arabian Literature, (6436) he is styled 'Alī Ibn Rajāl and we are told that Europeans called him Aben-Ragel and that he was born at Cordova and lived in the beginning of the 5th century of the Hijra.

His work on astrology, "*Opus magnum de astrologia, octo partibus comprehensum*," was first translated from Arabic into Spanish by order of Alphonso, the king of Castile, and afterwards from Spanish into Latin. He appears also to have been a poet, for a poem of his on astrology is mentioned in Casiri's catalogue of the Escurial Library I, 128 and 344. The best edition of Haly's work appears to be that by Anthony Stupa, Basle, 1551. There is a copy of this in the British Museum and bound up with it, is an elaborate treatise on astrology by Guido Bonatus and also a commentary on the *Tetrabiblos*.

Guido Bonatus, also called Guido Bonatti and Bonati, was a noted astrologer of the 13th century. He was a native of Florence, but is commonly called *Forolivienais* or *De Foro Livii*, the modern Forli, a town on the eastern side of the Appenines and not far from Ravenna. He is said by his astrological skill to have saved Forli from a siege. Eventually he became a monk and died in 1296.

Lilly quotes Abu-l-ḥasan under the name of Haly and Sir Walter Scott makes Guy Mannering refer both to him and to Guido Bonatus. Délambre says, in his History of astronomy in the Middle Ages, that Abu-l-ḥasan's book "est l'un des plus clairs, des plus méthodiques, and des plus complétes que nous ayons. C'est une compilation de tout ce que les sages de différents pays et de différents siécles avaient écrit sur ce sujet futile." It appears that Haly was a Christian. There is a MS. copy of his work in the British Museum written in beautifully clear Arabic characters. It is numbered 23,399. See Codices Arabici 623*b*. It is to be hoped that some day an Arabic scholar will print and edit it.

Lilly's Christian Astrology and the works of Zadkiel are useful and so also are Wilson's Dictionary of Astrology (London, 1819), and a work by E. Sibley in two quarto volumes and published in 1817. For Hindū astrology, I can recommend two Bengali books kindly sent me by Dr. Grierson, *viz.*, the *Jyōtiṣa Prakāça* (Beni Madhab De & Co., Calcutta, 1882, Sak. 1804) and the *Varāha Mihira* of Kali Prosanna Chattarji (1891, Fasli 1300). I have also found the notes of Muḥammad Ṣādiq 'Alī the Lucknow editor of the *Akbarnāma* very useful and I have obtained some light from the two elaborate horoscopes of Shāh Jahān,—one of his birth and the other of his accession,—which are given in 'Abdu-l-ḥamīd's *Bādshāhnāma*.

Mr. Rehatsek's Catalogue of the Mullā Fīrōz Library in Bombay shews that it is very rich in Persian works on astrology.

To the useful books on Astrology may be added the treatise of Julius Firmicus Maternus, a Latin writer of the 4th century A.D. A good and cheap edition of this work is in course of publication at Leipsic under the editorship of Charles Sittl. Firmicus describes the *Dodecatemoria*, p. 48, the *Decani*, p. 41, and has a chapter, p. 233, on empty and full degrees, the full being degrees where the *Decani* are found, and the empty where their influence does not operate.

# CHAPTER IX.

## STATEMENT OF THE HONOURED NAMES OF THE BLISSFUL NURSES AND SPIRITUALLY-MOULDED CHERISHERS[1] (*qawābil-i-rūḥānī-qawālib*) OF HIS MAJESTY, THE KING OF KINGS.

When the lightsome day of his creation arrived, at once was Heaven envious of Earth for his passing,[2] and Earth exultant o'er Heaven for his august advent. The status of knowledge and insight became exalted, and with rites which are the glory of the ministers of outward show, was that holy essence and pure pearl —already washed and cleansed at the fountain-head of Divine Light and in the ocean of infinite knowledge (*ma'rifat*)—bathed and composed by the hands of shade-loving, radiance-darting, chaste, rose-bodied nymphs. Even-tempered, spiritually-minded nurses swathed the divine form and heavenly body in auspicious swaddling-bands, purer than angelic veils, and laid him with respect and reverence in the sacred arms and bosoms of pure-dispositioned ones. And then his honied[3] lips being brought in contact with the benign breasts, his mouth was sweetened by the life-giving fluid.

---

1 قوابل pl. of قابلة. The word seems properly to mean a midwife, but, as it comes after *dāya* and as no midwife is mentioned by name—unless *Dāya Bhāwal* be one,—I have rendered it cherisher. The word داية means both a midwife and a wet-nurse.

2 *Farr-i-wilādat*. There is a play here on the two meanings of *farr*. *Farr* in Arabic means flight, and is here used in the sense of departure or passing, being contrasted with *maqdam*, advent or coming. The birth or vital principle of Akbar left Heaven and came upon Earth, thereby making Heaven envious and Earth leap for pride. But *farr* or *far* means in Persian, light or splendour, being etymologically the same word as the Greek πῦρ and the English fire and so, *farr-i-wilādat* also means the light or splendour of the birth. *Farr* is often used by A. F. to mean the sacred light which belongs to a king. Thus at the beginning of the *Āīn*, he speaks of kingship as a light emanating from God, which light modern language calls the *farr-i-īzadī* or Divine light and which in ancient times was called the sublime halo. (*Kīyān-khura.*) (Blochmann iii.)

3 The word in the Text is not honied but only sweet. However there is perhaps an allusion to the

*Verse.*

He drew forth milk by the bounty of his lips,
Milk and sugar were commingled.
It was not milk he drank from the breast of hope,
'Twas water from the Sun's fountain that he imbibed.

44 As the nobly-born Shamsu-d-dīn Muhammad of Ghaznī had done a good service at Kanauj,[1] his Majesty Jahānbānī Jannat-āshyānī, shortly before the rising of this light of fortune, (Akbar) in magnificent recompense of his deed, made him hopeful of eternal bliss by promising him the majestic boon, that his high-souled, chaste-natured consort—who has now the lofty title of Jījī[2] Anaga—should be clothed with the glorious head-dress (*mi'jar*) and mantle of distinction, by obtaining the auspicious service of nursing this new fruit of the spring-tide of sovereignty and fortune, and should have the blissful charge[3] of the nosegay of the house-garden of greatness and glory.

Accordingly her Majesty, Maryam-makānī, Qadasī-arkānī (Pillar of Purity) having sent for that adorner of Heaven's table (*i.e.*, celestial caterer) placed in an auspicious moment, the child-treasure in her hopeful bosom. But as the period of pregnancy[4] of this purely-framed nurse was not yet fulfilled, her Majesty ordered that receptacle of chastity, Dāya Bhāwal—a special servant of his Majesty Jahānbānī, and distinguished for virtue and purity—to suckle the infant. It appears that first of all, he accepted the milk of his royal mother. Then Fakhr-i-nisā,[5] wife of Nadīm Koka was honoured by the charge, then Bhāwal Anaga, then the wife of Khwāja Ghāzī,[6]

practice of putting honey into the mouths of the newly-born.

[1] Spelled here Qanauj. Shamsu-d-dīn helped Humāyūn up the steep bank of the Ganges, after he had swum across on an elephant when defeated by Shēr Shāh. (Blochmann 321.)

[2] According to Meninski (1698) Jījī, in Turkish, means a child's plaything. It also, in Turkish, means handsome.

[3] حضانت *hiẓānat*, the technical word for the charge of a child. (Baillie's Mu. Law, 429.)

[4] The child to whom she afterwards gave birth was 'Azīz Koka, the later Khān A'ẓam. He was thus only slightly younger than Akbar who used to say that a channel of milk connected them together. (*Ma'āsir* I. 675). Jījī is said to have died in 1008 (1599). See l.c. 685 where she is called Bīca Jiū.

[5] Gulbadan (26) speaks of Fakhr-i-nisā Anaga as the mother of Nadīm Koka and wife of Mīrzā Qulī.

[6] There is an account of him in Text (I. 222) and he is mentioned in Bāyazīd Sulṭān's list of the officers

then Ḥakīma. After these, the chaste Jījī Anaga, in accordance with her wish, obtained external and internal felicity. After her, Kokī Anaga, wife of Tōgh Begi[1] and after her, Bībī Rūpā[2] had their turn of this auspicious service. Then Khāldār (*i.e.*, the mole-marked) Anaga, mother of Sa'ādat Yār Koka,[3] was selected for this great boon. And at last, that chaste matron, Pīja Jān Anaga,[4] mother of Zain Khān Koka, acquired a stock of everlasting greatness by obtaining her wish for this great blessing. Many other fortunate cupolas of chastity were exalted by the excellence of this service. It was as if there were Divine wisdom in thus implanting varied temperaments[5] by this series of developments (*i.e.*, the wet-nurses) so that the pure entity,[6] advancing by gradations, might become familiar with the divers methods of Divine manifestation. Or it

---

who came to India with Humāyūn. A. F. calls him Khwāja Ghāzī Tabrīzī and says that he was distinguished for his knowledge of accounts and made a *dīwān* by Humāyūn, and was subsequently, for a long time, excluded from Court and only returned at the end of his life to the Court of Akbar and when his intellect was enfeebled by age. Bāyazīd calls him Khwāja Ghāzī Shīrāzī and says Humāyūn made him a *dīwān* when he was in the Takht-i-sulaimān country. The fact of his long exclusion from Court and of his not being entered in the Grandees of the *Āīn* or of the *Ṭabaqāt*, might explain, supposing him Māham Anaga's husband, (see note at end of chapter) why no mention is made of him in that relation.

1 Mentioned in Bāyazīd's Catalogue as Toq Begī Sāqī, *i.e.*, page or cupbearer.

2 Apparently a Hindūstānī and possibly a Hindū.

3 Sa'ādat Yār Koka is mentioned three times in the *Akbarnāma*, in the third volume, *viz.*: (192) where he is one of those sent on pilgrimage to Mecca; (579) where we are told, his brother's daughter was given in marriage by the Emperor to A. F.'s son 'Abdu-r-raḥmān (see Blochmann, Life of A. F. XXXV.) and lastly (656) where we are told of Sa'ādat Yār's death in the 39th year (Āzar 1003, November 1595), from excessive drinking and of the Emperor's sorrow for this and of his paying a visit of consolation to the house of his sister, Ḥājī Koka.

4 Called by the *Ma'āṣir* and Blochmann, Pīcah Jān Anaga. She was the wife of Khwāja Maqṣūd of Herāt.

5 *Mashārib*, dispositions, but also beverages, and *ṭabaqāt*, dishes or trays as well as stages or degrees, so that apparently one of the intended meanings is "divers beverages in divers vessels," signifying the varied nature of the nurses' milk.

6 The text has *wuḥūd*, unity, but I presume this is a mistake for *wujūd*, which occurs in No. 564.

might be designed that the acute and discerning should perceive that this nursling of fortune belonged to the limpid streams of Divine bounty and was not such as to make spiritual progress by outward nutriment, for as to the spiritual nature of this company (of nurses),[1] it is evident to all of what kind that was, as also are the lofty degrees of the holy stages of this chosen one.

Among other wondrous indications there was this, that contrary to the way of other infants, his Majesty, the king of kings, at his birth and at the first opening of his eyes on the visible world, rejoiced the hearts of the wise by a sweet smile.[2] Penetrating physiognomists recognized the smile as the herald-augury of the smiles of the spring of dominion and fortune and saw in it, the opening bud of hope and peace.

After that (*i.e.*, the suckling), in a cradle lighter than a phantom
(which the carpenters of the throne of sovereignty had framed of
sandal-wood and lign-aloes, and where they had, as it were, comminglـ
45 ed civet[3] and rose-leaves, and on whose corners and sides they had
hung rubies and pearls of price) was laid with gentlest movement
that unique Pearl of nine mothers o'pearl,[4] and then they softly
swayed and rocked him. For cheer and soothing, they chaunted
with musical (*mūsīqī*) rhythm the name—auspicious to begin with and
fitting as a close—of the Creator, the Lord of Glory and Bounty. The
inmates[5] of holy hermitages and those who live in the throng of

---

[1] This seems rather ungracious, especially after such complimentary expressions about them.

[2] This is a trait mentioned of Zoroaster. (See *Dabistān* trans: I. 218). Only he is said to have laughed aloud when he was born. Anquetil du Perron (Life of Zoroaster 13*n.*) quotes Pliny who, in his Natural History, says, "Risisse eodem die quo genitus esset, unum hominem accepimus Zoroastrum." The account of Solomon in the Apocrypha is more touching. "When I was "born, I drew in the common air "and fell upon the earth which is of "like nature, and the first voice "which I uttered, was crying, as all "others do."

[3] The Lucknow ed. says that this means the Nine Heavens. *Ṣadaf* means the oyster-shell and also the vault of heaven. It is also a name given apparently to the two constellations of Ursa Major and Minor. See *Burhān-i-qāti'*.

[4] شاخ *Shākh*, also called *sabād*, whence civet. (Blochmann 79.)

[5] *'ākifān-i-ṣawāmi'*. This phrase occurs in one of Faiẓī's odes (*Āīn* I. 240) and is translated by Blochmann (559) "those who constantly worship

men who are the stewards of time and the terrene and hold together the spheres of the universe, attained their desires and thus were benefits bestowed on the world and on mankind. They sang this gratulatory strain to the darling[1] of the skies.

*Verse.*

Hail to thee to whom is committed reason's exaltation.[2]
The kingly revolution of the universe is for thee.
Like thee, the earth has no garden;
Like thee, heaven's vault no lamp.
Creative ocean rolled many a wave
Till it cast ashore a pearl like thee.
Fate's pencil drew many a sketch
Till she made a portrait like thee.
The world's book is but an allusion[3] to thee,
Heaven's volúme but an analysis[4] of thee.

---

in cloisters." The next expression *sākinān-i-majāmi'-i-ins* may mean "dwellers in mosques" as the note to this passage in No. 564 seems to hold, but I am inclined to think that here it means laymen or those who carry on the affairs of the world, in opposition to the solitaries and ascetic. What A. F. intends to say is, I think, that by Akbar's birth, everybody attained their desires, that is both the lonely ascetic and the worldling, and thus the whole universe was benefited. It may however be that the two classes of holy men are, intended *viz.*, anchorites and men who live in monasteries or congregations of saints. I admit too, that this interpretation seems to agree better with what follows, *viz.*, the description of such persons "preserving the stars from wrong." But see Text (87) where we are told that the preparations for the revelation of the unique Pearl (Akbar) were completed, as now the stages of solitude and society had been traversed.

[1] *Jigargosha* lit: liver-lobe.

[2] *Sharaf*, an astrological term signifying the exaltation of a planet or star. This first couplet is adapted from Faizī. (*Akbarnāma* III, 678.)

[3] تلميح "*Talmīḥ*" says Gladwin (Dissertations on Persian Rhetoric 53.) "literally signifies using something savoury and is employed "when the author alludes to some "popular story or verse, *e.g.*, 'O light "'of my eyes! when the garden of "'my condition is deprived of the "'rose of thy countenance, my state "'becomes like Jacob in the house "'of mourning.'"

[4] تشريح *tashrīḥ*. This is from *sharḥ* and seems primarily to mean dissection. (Dict: of T. Ts. 735.)

## MĀHAM ANAGA.

It is singular that this name does not occur in the list of Akbar's nurses. This may be due to *Māham Anaga's* being a title and not a proper nāme, and it is possible that the lady who was afterwards thus designated, is mentioned in the list under some other appellation. She may, for instance, be the nurse described as the wife of Khwāja Ghāzī and whose own name is not given. But even if the title were not bestowed till a later period, one would have expected A. F. to have added it to his description, just as he mentions Shamsu-d-dīn's wife by her title of Jījī Anaga. The true explanation of the omission probably is that Māham Anaga means Head or Superintendent of the nurses rather than chief nurse and that the Māham Anaga of the *Akbarnāma* was not a wet-nurse. She certainly was not the chief nurse in the sense that the child Akbar drew most of his nourishment from her, for we are told that Jījī Anaga was chief in this respect, so much so that the other nurses accused her of practising witchcraft in order to prevent the infant prince from accepting any breast but her own.

Though *Anaga* seems primarily to mean a wet-nurse, it has not always this meaning. Pavet de Courteille says (Turkish Dictionary, 57) "اناکا et اناکه, nourrice, sage-femme, gouvernante; on donne aussi à la mère du Khān le titre de قل نکه." We find also that the mother of Cingīz Khān had this title, her name being given in the *Akbarnāma* (I. 72, top line) as "Olun Anaga" though Erdmann spells it *Eke*. Apparently the Turkish pronunciation is *Enge*. See Redhouse *s. v.* He states that it means a sister-in-law, the wife of an elder brother or lady-relative of a bridegroom who is sent to fetch the bride home. A. F. sometimes calls Māham Anaga, Māham Bega and Māham Āgha, and it is generally by the title of *Bega* that Bāyazīd Sultān speaks of her in the so-called *Tārīkh-i-humāyūn*. (I. O. Ms. No. 216). He calls her (15) Māham Bega and adds the explanation *ke āgha anaga Nawāb-i-ishān būd*, *i.e.*, who was head of the Prince's nurses. And then follows the statement that she was accompanied by Jījī Anaga, wife of Shamsu-d-dīn Mu. Ghaznawī who was the Prince's nurse (*anaga*). (Unless indeed the word is *atgah* and refers to Shamsu-d-dīn.)

In the *Akbarnāma* (II. 55) we are told that Māham Anaga had served the prince from his cradle, but it does not follow that she first did so in the capacity of wet-nurse. It may be remarked too that the fact of our not hearing that she had a husband or a child of about Akbar's age militates against the notion that she was his wet-nurse. Though her son, Adham Khān was a young man at the time of his death, he was probably several years older than Akbar as otherwise Bāyazīd would hardly have named him in the list of servants in Akbar's train at the time when Humāyūn marched to India.

# CHAPTER X.[1]

ACCOUNT OF THE ARRIVAL OF HIS MAJESTY AT THE WORLD-TRAVERSING CAMP[2] OF HIS MAJESTY JAHĀNBĀNĪ JANNAT-ĀSHYĀNĪ, FROM THE FORT OF AMARKOṬ AND OF THE AUSPICIOUS[3] CONJUNCTION.

As the world-seeing eye and auspicious glance of his Majesty Jahānbānī Jannat-āshyānī was looking for the glorious vision of the king of kings, a gracious order was issued that he should be brought to the curtain[4] of honour and encampment of fortune, in charge of her Majesty Maryam-makānī. Khwāja Mu'azzam,[5] Nadīm Kūkal-tāsh and Shamsu-d-dīn Mu. of Ghaznī were sent to be in attendance on the auspicious litter. Accordingly his Majesty left Amarkoṭ, on the 11th Sha'bān[6] in a fortunate hour, under the care and in the arms of her Highness Maryam-makānī and departed in a travelling litter.[7]

---

1 The heading of this chapter is omitted in the text and the account of Akbar's visit to his father is made part of Chapter IX. But the heading is given in No. 564 and other MSS. and is clearly required. The Persian is as follows;

ذکر قدوم حضرت شاهنشاهي بموکب
گيتي نورد حضرت جهانباني جنت آشياني
از حصار امرکوٹ و قران سعدين -

In the Lucknow ed. بموجب *bamūjib* is, apparently by mistake, substituted for بموکب *bamaukib*.

2 According to Niẓāmu-d-dīn, the meeting-place was in *pargana* Jūn. A. F. also states that it was in Jūn. (I. 184.)

3 قران سعدين, a phrase applied to the conjunction of the two Fortunes, Jupiter and Venus. It is the title of a famous poem by Amīr Khusrau on the meeting of Kaiqūbād and his father Naṣīru-d-dīn. (Stewart's Bengal 78).

4 سرادق عزت *surādiq-i-'izzat*. Dozy says (647*b*) "Dais (au-dessus d'un trône.) Ce qu'on nomme en persan سراچه (dont سرادق est peutêtre une altération) ou سراپرده c. à. d. l'énorme enceinte de toile que dans les pays musalmans, entoure la vaste tente du souverain."

5 Apparently he had previously left his sister and joined Humāyūn's camp.

6 20th November, 1542 O. S., According to Jauhar (trans. 45) the day was 10th *Ramaẓān*.

7 *Takht-i-rawān*. See Ives' voyage to India (278) for a representation of this conveyance. It is usually carried on mules.

*Verse.*

Ere the cradle had fulfilled its season,
His exalted fortune (*bakht*) sat on a throne, (*takht*)[1]
Eye unopened, but with the eye of the mind,
He looked to the ordering of religion and realm;
Hand unopened, but his heart desiring
To put the world 'neath his signet-ring,
Of his thousand roses, not one in bloom,
Yet the world was culling flowers from the garden of his fortune.

When the travelling litter of his Majesty, the king of kings, the ambulatory treasury of Divine knowledge, had nearly arrived and but two stages remained, a world-obeyed order was issued that the chief officers[2] and pillars of the State and the general public, small and great, should turn towards the altar of fortune and go to meet the *ka'ba* of hopes. Avant-couriers of good tidings were arriving every minute and bringing, from time to time, the news of the appropinquating of the glorious advent.

*Verse.*

The cavalcade approaches with the king of both worlds in its wake,[3]
46 The caravan of joy goes forth to meet him.

And on the last day of Sha'bān which was the day for the glorious alighting, and when the camp of good fortune was only one stage distant, his Majesty (Humāyūn) was pleased to observe "Assuredly the child is compact of auspiciousness, of potent horoscope and has the good fortune of the two worlds enfolded in him, for, as he draws nigh, there is another[4] assemblage of spectators in the upper world who exhibit a virgin joy." What marvel is it that the pure soul and illumined intellect of his Majesty Jahānbānī Jannat

---

1 Meaning the *takht-i-rawān* (travelling-litter.)

2 *Lit.*: eyes of the Sultānat. There is a play on the original meaning. The eyes were to be turned towards the *qibla, etc.*

3 دنبال *dambāl.* From *Āīn* IV. 438 (Jarrett IV. 393) we learn that Akbar objected to the use of the word *dambāl* in poetry as being prosaic. It literally means tail.

4 Meaning that there was a second assemblage, *viz.*, one in addition to that upon earth.

-āshyānī should be cognizant of the Divine secrets and be aware of the truths hidden in celestial treasuries ? Or how is it strange that there should be an epiphany on the apparition of his Majesty, the king of kings, the shadow of God, the archetype of the strange frontispieces of the universe, and collection of the catalogues of the perfections of the sons of Adam ? And in an hour which held the auspicious influences of the conjunctions of the two Fortunes[1] and of the two luminaries (the Sun and Moon), his Majesty (Akbar) alighted with felicity and dominion at the majestic and glorious enclosure, and became fortunate by arriving at the station of light and took repose under the shadow of the phoenix (*humā*) of eternal prosperity. The blessed crown (*tārak, i.e.*, crown of the head) of his Majesty, the king of kings, was made fortunate by touching the throne-brushing feet of his Majesty Jahānbānī and by becoming united to a perfect saint (*pīr*). The latter took him lovingly in his arms and kissed him on the luminous brow, the tablet of the fortunes of the two worlds and title-page of happiness everlasting.

*Verse.*

Whiles he held him to his lip, whiles to his heart, and whiles to his head.

After gazing on this holy light, the inspired tongue engaged in returning thanks to the Lord God, Most High and Most Glorious, and the pole-star-like[2] head was lowered in supplicating prostration at the portals of the All-sufficient One.

*Verse.*[3]

Not only was the head ever bowed,
Each hair of his body also bent in adoration.

The guardians of the Divine bounty and the treasurers of infinite auspiciousness delivered that deposit of eternities—past and

---

[1] Jupiter and Venus ; but perhaps this is only a rhetorical way of describing the meeting between Akbar and his father or his arrival in his mother's company. The time being the end of the month would be that of the conjunction of the Sun and Moon.

[2] فرقد *farqad*, a bright star near the Pole. The word is often written فرقدين and applied to two bright stars, $\beta$ and $\gamma$, in the Little Bear. (Lane 2387*a*.)

[3] These lines are Faiẓī's.

future—into the king's gracious bosom and warbled, sweet and low, this strain of thanksgiving.

*Verse.*

This is the Divine deposit.
Ask of this treasury whatever thou desirest,
This is he in whose heart they placed
Essential substance, verity absolute.
This is he whose threshold's *ka'ba*[1]
Is seized upon by kings as their altar (*qibla*).
This is he who hath the foot of dominion,
Enlightener of the throne royal.

Readers of the page of the human countenance beheld him with the eye of meditation and reflection and physiognomists perused him with the glance of consideration and contemplation.

*Verse.*

What did they see? A picture such as never
Did they see in Creation's tables.
From astonishment naught did they say, save
Hail, Light of Wisdom, Eye of Insight, hail.

47 Kingly lights shone from his lustrous brow. The letters "Shadow of God" were apparent in the lines of his palm. The witnesses of Reason were visible in the composite of his substance. The notes of Theosophy were manifest in his whole being. Justice was demonstrated in the evenness of his temperament. Proofs of beneficence were revealed in the essence of his nature. The characters of a Lord of Conjunction shone out from the fair schedules of his ephemeris. Knowledge of occult sciences was evidenced in the illumined records of his constitution. Remote mysteries were revealed by his keen sight. Far-reaching thoughts streamed out from his lofty glance.

---

[1] The allusion probably is to the threshold of the Caliph's palace at Baghdād which contained a piece of the famous black stone of Mecca. See Richardson's Dict. *s. v. dar* and D'Herbélot art. *Bāb*.

# CHAPTER XI.

## ACCOUNT OF SOME OF THE WONDERFUL ETEOSTICS ON THE AUSPICIOUS BIRTH OF HIS MAJESTY, THE KING OF KINGS.

Ingenious men made eteostics in prose and verse on the noble nativity and composed gratulatory odes. They tendered them for acceptance at the Court of his Majesty Jahānbānī which was the assay-room of human jewels, and received glorious gifts.

Among them, this chronogram by Maulānā Nūru-d-dīn Tarkhān[1] received the palm of applause and approbation.

*Quatrain.*

When the fateful pen of destiny wrote the record,
It added a comment to the immortal verse
And wrote, "From the birth-boon of the world's king of kings
"The date is Shāhinshāh Jahāngīr."[2] (World-seizing king of kings.)

And this wonderfully apposite chronogram was discovered by one of the learned of the Age.

*Verse.*

Laus Deo! there has come into being
He who is the world's epitome,
A king greater[3] than the kings of the Earth,

---

[1] For an account of him, see Blochmann No. 55, (541) and Badāonī III. 157 and especially 197. He ended his days as guardian of Humāyūn's tomb.

[2] These words make 949 as follows.

sh=300
h= 5
n= 50
sh=300
h= 5
j= 3
h= 5
ā= 1
n= 50
g= 20
ī= 10
r=200

Total ... 949

[3] *Akbar*, comparative of *Kabīr*.

Akbar his name, Jalāl (Glorious) his title.
The year, the month, nycthemeron of birth
Are "Sunday night, five Rajab."[1] (949 H.)

---

[1] شب يكشنبهٔ پنج رجب *shab-yak-shambih, panj rajab.* The text has an *ū* and the editors remark that this makes the number of years six too much, *viz.*: 955, but that if the *ū* be excluded as in one of their MSS. the letters give the correct date, 949. I find that the Lucknow ed. and No. 564 omit the *ū*. The letters give 949 thus :—

| | | | |
|---|---|---|---|
| sh=300 | sh = 300 | p= 2 | r=200 |
| b= 2 | n = 50 | n= 50 | j= 3 |
| ī= 10 | b = 2 | j= 3 | b= 2 |
| k= 20 | h = 5 | | |
| | | Total ... | 949 |

According to Mu. calculation Akbar was born on Sunday night, for they count the night first and then the day, beginning at sunset, but according to ordinary parlance, he was born on Saturday night, *i.e.*, early on Sunday morning.

# CHAPTER XII.

THANKSGIVING OF ABŪ'L-FAẒL, THE AUTHOR OF THIS NOBLE VOLUME, FOR HAVING BEHELD THE TIME OF THIS SOVEREIGNTY AND FOR HAVING LONG SERVED HIS MAJESTY THE KING OF KINGS.

Although it be a heavy sorrow that, at the rising of the Luminary of Fortune, the author of this noble volume was in the abode of non-existence,[1] without being or the adornment of Divine worship, yet how can he discharge his debt of thanks for the grand mercy of his having witnessed the era of the subjectively and objectively Great One, the ruler of the visible and the invisible ? and of having been one on whom has fallen the glance of his favour and guidance ? And hundreds more of thanks for this, that, ere he had seen the holy horoscope, or its noble secrets and wondrous glories had been revealed to him, he had understood that perfection of sanctity and sovereignty which is beyond the reach of the astrologer's science, and was a slave of the Divine power.[2] And praise upon praise be to God that I am not, like Imāmu-l-kalām, Ḥassānu-l-'ajam, Lisānu-l-ḥaqīqat, Ḥakīm Khāqānī,[3] sighing for the Lord of the Age who is indispensable for the control of the visible and invisible worlds. For instance he has written thus :—

---

[1] Abū'l-faẓl was born 14th Jan., 1551, so that he was 8 years and 3 months younger than Akbar.

[2] The author is referring, in part, to the supposed fact that the true horoscope of Akbar was not known until 1583.

[3] Khaqānī is a famous Persian poet who died at Tabrīz in 580 (1185), according to one account and in 595 (1199) according to another. The lines quoted by A. F. are to be found in Khaqānī's Quatrains, (St. Petersburg ed. 1875) p. 26, Rubā'ī 145 and p. 18, Rubā'ī 101. See also J. A. S. B. New Series xxxvi. Oct., 1841, 156. For account of Khaqānī, see M. Khanykov's *Mémoir, Journal Asiatique*, Sixth Series, 1864, iv, 137 *et seq.* and 1865, v, 298.

*Quatrain.*

They say that every thousand years of the world
There comes into existence a true man.
He came before this, ere we[1] were born from nothingness,
He will come after this when we have departed in sorrow.

Elsewhere he says,

Every now[2] and then, the world is saturated with wretches,
Then a shining soul comes down out of the sky.
Khāqānī ! seek not in this Age for such a thing,
Sit not by the way for the caravan will come late

By auspicious good fortune, I obtained the service of this issuer of universal orders and explicator of the ways, and by the favour of his patronage and exalted kindness, comfort was brought to my soul,—perturbed by the deceptions of the day and dumb-founded in a wilderness of wants,—and no connexion with the world nor anxiety remained save to acquire his favour which indeed is tantamount to the pleasing of God. And my mind being freed from the bondage of secularity and the restraints of the world, was neither agitated[3] by regret for the past nor longing for the future. Hereafter[4] there will be given in its proper place, an account of my obtaining the blessing of his service, of my reaching the shade of favour and kindness, and of my being exalted above the *apices* of honour and eminence to the Seventh[5] Heaven of cognition (*ma'rifat*).

---

[1] I adopt the reading of the St. Petersburg MS. and No. 564, of ما *mā* instead of the یا *yā* of the Text.

[2] See text, p. 51, l.5 fr. foot, for the word *har-yak-chandī*.

[3] The allusion is to Khaqānī's quatrain. A. F. means that having, like Raphael in Hypatia, found the true man, he neither sighs for a past appearance nor longs for a future advent. Cf. Wordsworth's "The past unsighed for and the future sure."

[4] See Text III. 83ff. A. F. was introduced to Akbar in the 19th year, 981 (1574).

[5] *Gharfat*, paradise. It means first an upper chamber and hence is used to denote the Seventh Heaven or highest place in Paradise. (Lane 2249c.) A. F. means that, by acquiring Akbar's intimacy, he has risen higher than if he had had high office and distinguished outward rank. Blochmann remarks (xxviii) that A. F. "never *accepted* a title." But this is rather a question-begging phrase. He is No. 71 in the list of *Manṣabdārs*, being a Commander of Four Thousand and he had the title of 'Allāmī. Bāyazīd calls him Nawāb.

# CHAPTER XIII.

## Arrangement of the lofty-titled line and list of the noble names of the eminent ancestors of his Majesty, the King of Kings.

The following list gives the excellent appellations of the heaven-descended forefathers of his Majesty, who are linked to celestial[1] ancestors by degrees of exaltation and gradations of greatness, and all of whom came as kings, kings of kings, kingdom-bestowers and king-makers, and governed the world by God-given wisdom and true insight, such as justice and equity require, so that they have left behind them on this earth the reverberation of a good name, which is a second life, or rather, is life eternal.

*List.*[2]

1. Adam. Peace be upon him.
2. Seth. (Text, Shīs̤.)
3. Enosh.
4. Kenan.
5. Mahalalil. (Text, Mahalāīl.)
6. Jared. (Text, Yarid.)
7. Enoch. (Ikhnūkh, Text.)
8. Methusalah.
9. Lamech.
10. Noah.
11. Japheth. (Text, Yāfis̤.)
12. Turk.

---

[1] آباى علوي *ābāī 'alwī*, sublime fathers, *i.e.*, the seven planets.

[2] The original gives the list in an ascending order, beginning with Akbar. I have taken the names of the patriarchs from the revised version of the Old Testament.

13. Alinja[1] Khān.
14. Dīb Bāqūī.
15. Kayūk Khān. (Text, Gayūk.)
16. Alinja Khān.
17. Mughal Khān.
18. Qarā Khān.
19. Aghuz Khān. (Text, Aghur.)
20. Kun Khān.[2]
21. Āī Khān.
22. Yaldūz Khān.
23. Mangalī Khān. (Text, Mankalī.)
24. Tingīz Khān.
25. Īl Khān.
26. Qīyān.

(Here there is a break.)

Of the descendants of Qīyān are;—

27. Tīmūr Tāsh.
28. Mangalī Khwāja.[3]
29. Yaldūz.
30. Jū'īna Bahādur.
31. Ālanqū'ā, daughter of the preceding.
32. Būzanjar Qā'ān,[4] son of the preceding.
33. Buqā Qā'ān.
34. Zūtamīn Khān.[5] (Also Dūtamīn.)
35. Qāydū Khān.

---

[1] Major Raverty (*Ṭabaqāt-i-nāṣirī*, 873*n*) prefers Alminja. Sir H. Howorth has Iltchi. Apparently Alinja is the grandson and not the son of Turk, his father's name having been Tutak. Probably "Alinja" is wrong for we find this name a little lower in the list. Col. Miles (Genealogical Tree of the Turks) has Obluchi.

[2] Major Raverty (880) says that Kun means the Sun, Āi the Moon, and Yaldūz a star, and that the three were brothers. A. F. in his account of Oghuz Khān makes them brothers and also mentions Tingīz (*i.e.*, the sea) as one. (Text, 60 l.2 fr. foot.)

[3] It appears from D'Herbélot that this is the Turkish form of Michael, hence its frequent recurrence.

[4] *Qāān*, Khākān, *i.e.*, Great Khān.

[5] Variously written in the text. In one place it is Dumanīn. Howorth has, after Erdmann, Dutūm Menen. (I. 39.)

36. Bāysanghar Khān.
37. Tumana Khān.
38. Qāculī Bahādur.[1]
39. Iradam-cī Barlās.
40. Sūghuj-cī.[2]
41. Qarācār Nuyān.[3]
42. Ical Nuyān.
43. Alankīr Bahādur. (Var. *infra*, Ailanyar Khān.)
44. Amīr Barkal.
45. Amīr Ṭarāghāī.
46. Ṣāḥib Qarān Quṭbu-d-dunyā wa-d-dīn, Amīr Tīmūr Gūrgān.
47. Mīrān Shāh.[4]
48. Sulṭān Muḥammad Mīrzā.
49. Sulṭān Abū Sa'īd Mīrzā.
50. 'Umar Shaikh Mīrzā.
51. Ẓahīru-d-dīn Muḥammad Bābar Pādshāh.[5]
52. Naṣīru-d-dīn Muḥammad Humāyūn Pādshāh.
53. Abū'l-Muẓaffar[6] Jalālu-d-dīn Muḥammad Akbar Pādshāh.

---

[1] Here, for some time, the list ceases to record the names of kings. Qācūlī is also spelled Qājūlī. He was twin-brother of Qabal Khān, the ancestor of Cingīz Khān. In accordance with his father, Tumana's interpretation of his dream, he became Commander-in-Chief. (See his biography *infra*.)

[2] Spelled also Sūghu-jijan. It means wise, according to Raverty (898).

[3] Spelled also Nu-yīn. The word is explained as meaning, in Mongolian, king's son or prince and also a chief or general. See Jarrett III. 344n. where it is transliterated Novian. See also *Farhang-i-Rashīdī* II. 277. Quatremère (*Rashīdu-d-dīn*, Trans. 76.) says, "Le mot *noian* نويان ou *noin* qui appartient à la langue mongole, désignait le chef d'un *toman*, c'est à dire d'un corps de dix mille hommes."

[4] Blochmann (Genealogical Table) calls him Jalālu-d-dīn Mīrān Shāh and A. F. does so too. (Text 81.)

[5] Gulbadan mentions that Bābar took the title of Pādshāh after the birth of Humāyūn. Pādshāh was changed to Bādshāh in India because, says Blochmann, Pād means *crepitus ventris*.

[6] In the preface of the Persian translation of the *Mahābhārat*, (B.M. No. 5638, p.8.) A. F. calls him Abū'l-fatḥ and this is the name given in the document drawn up by A.F.'s father, Mubārak, and others and preserved by Badāonī. (Blochmann 185 and Lowe 279.) There too he is styled Ghāzī. A.F. also uses the title Abū-l-fatḥ in the introductory verses of the *Tafsīr-i-Akbarī* or Great

49 Let it not be concealed that the auspicious record of these high-born ones is implanted and contained in the breast-pages[1] of the transmitters of words, and recorded and expressed by the conserving tongues of the writings of epochs, as far as Yaldūz who is the 25th[2] (*i.e.*, counting upwards) in ascent from his Majesty and that for the period from Mangalī Khwāja to Īl Khān[3] which may be reckoned as 2,000[4] years, nothing has come to light. The cause of this will be explained hereafter.

From Īl Khān to Adam there are 24[5] persons. These have

---

Commentary which he presented to Akbar on his second introduction to him in 982 (1574). (The *abjad* value of the words *Tafsīr-i-Akbarī* is 983, but the introduction took place in 982 H. See *Inshā*, III.) The full name of the Emperor as there given is Abū'l-fatḥ Jalālu-d-dīn Muḥammad Akbar Shāh Al-Ghāzī, and it would seem that the Commentary which A.F. then presented was on the opening of the Ṣūratu-l-fatḥ, in allusion to Akbar's name and also to his recent victories in Bengal. On the other hand, Faiẓī (*Nal ū Daman* Calcutta ed. 1831. 24.) calls Akbar, Abū'l-muẓaffar Jamālu-d-daula ū Jalālu-d-dīn Muḥammad Akbar. Perhaps Muẓaffar was the original name and was changed to Fatḥ, after the victories in Bengal and to assimilate it to the name of Akbar's favourite residence, Fatḥpūr Sīkrī. The words Muẓaffar and Fatḥ are nearly synonymous, one meaning a victory or victorious, and the other victory.

This seems a fitting place, for noting that the first letter of the word Akbar is short and the Emperor's name should not be pronounced Ākbar but Ăkbar. Hence the word used to be written in English Ukbar or Ukber. The word *Akbarnāma* has a double meaning; it may signify the History of Akbar and also the Great or Supreme Book. It is perhaps rather significant that both A.F. and his brother should omit the title of *Ghāzī* which was given to the young Akbar after the defeat of Hēmū.

1 *Or*, pages issuing from.

2 That is counting Akbar as No. I. According to the series given by the author, Yaldūz (it is Yaldūz, No. 2, and the No. 29 of the English list), is the 24th. *jadd* or ancestor of Akbar. Either on this account or because he found *four* in his MS. Chalmers has *24th* ancestor.

3 Apparently this should be Qīyān Khān for he is described as the son and not merely as the descendant of Īl Khān. For a similar reason, it should be Tīmūr Tāsh and not Mangalī Khwāja.

4 It will be pointed out hereafter that A.F. has greatly overstated the time during which the Mughals were in Irgānaqūn. Other historians give the time as between 400 and 500 years.

5 Chalmers makes this 25, and this is correct, unless one exclude Īl Khān himself.

been described by historians, and a brief account of them will be given.

Far-sighted philosophers who with ripe judgment and God-given wisdom, have investigated the records of the past, and who have made the recognition of truth a sacred trust, and who exhibit research in the weighing of facts, are aware that the hearsay reports and traditions about man's origin occurring 7,000 years ago is a thing not to be accepted by sages who contemplate the rise[1] and decay of the world and (can appreciate all the tones) of the seven climes.

In these matters, right-thinking and far-seeing Reason, after true and just investigation, sometimes answers in the negative, and sometimes, out of caution—that baiting place of tranquillity and station of wisdom—delays either to admit or to deny.

By help of Reason—the glory of the world,—and the assistance of trustworthy records and reliable statements about the world, such as the ancient books of India and Cathay (K̲h̲iṭā), *etc.*, which have been preserved from the agitations of accidents and with which agree the principles of astronomy and the conclusions of astronomical observations, (and such things yield trustworthy evidence) and also from the successive series of the biographies of the sages of those countries and the *catena* of opinions of this disciplined body (philosophers), it appears that the beginning of the world and of mortals and the source of the manifestations of the Divine attributes has not been discovered. Either it is eternal, as was the opinion of many ancient philosophers, or of such antiquity as to approximate to 50
eternity.

The sect of Siūrhā[2] (Jains) who are preëminent in all the countries of India for austerity, asceticism and science, divide time—

[1] *Lit.* observe the spring and autumn of the four-fold garden (*i.e.*, the world) and know the gamut of the seven assemblages from the highest the lowest notes—*anjuman*, which I presumes here means climes and not the planets.

[2] Colebrooke says (As. Res. IX. 291.) "In Hindustan, the Jains are usually called Syauras but distinguish themselves into Srāvacas and Yatis." The name does not seem to be in use now. I do not know its origin unless it be a corruption of Çvētāmbara. (*See* Jarrett IV, 210*n*.)

The name Syaurā was evidently in common use in Sūrat in the middle of the last century for Anquetil du Perron refers to it and

called *kāl* in the Indian language—into two parts. One is *Avasarpiṇī* (descending cycle), *i.e.*, the period whose beginning is joyful and end grievous, and the other is *Utsarpiṇī* (ascending cycle), *i.e.*, the opposite of the first. Each of these periods is divided into six parts, called *āras*.[1] Each *āra* has a distinct name in accordance with its speciality.

The first *āra* of the *Avasarpiṇī* is called *Sukhmān-sukhmān*, the meaning of the reduplication being that this portion brings joy upon joy and happiness upon happiness. The length of this happy time is four *kōrākōr-sāgar*. The name of the second *āra* is *Sukhmān*, *i.e.*, a time of felicity and joy. Its duration is three *kōrākōr-sāgar*. The name of the third *āra* is *Sukhām* (*Sukhmān*) *Dukhmān*, *i.e.*, sorrow and misfortune crop up in the time of joy. Its duration is two *kōrākōr-sāgar*. The fourth *āra* is called *Dukhmān-sukhmān*, *i.e.*, joy and freedom from care rise up in the time of grief and sorrow. Its duration is less than one *kōrākōr* by 42,000[2] years.

The fifth *āra* is *Dukhmān* being the opposite of the second which was *Sukhmān*. The duration of this *āra* is 21,000 years. The sixth *āra* is *Dukhmān-dukhmān* being the opposite of the first. Its length is likewise 21,000 years. The names of the *āras* of the second period (*Utsarpiṇī*) are the same but the first of them corresponds to the sixth *āra* of the first period, the second to the fifth, the third to the fourth, and the fourth to the third, the fifth to the second, and the sixth to the first of the first period. Their opinion is that at the

---

says, (*Discours Préliminaire*, 365), that the two leading classes of Hindūs at Sūrat are the Brāhmans and the Sciouras. He calls these, Hindū priests, and says that they also go by the name of Djettis (*Yatis*). They seldom marry, he says, dress in white and have the head uncovered and wear their hair short, "like the *Abbés* in France." They carry a "*ballett*" (brush) to clean the places where they sit down, lest they should crush an insect. In a note, he says that the Sciouras call the first man Rikaba Deva and his mother, Maru Devi, and that they say these beings were created by God in Aiodha, *i.e.*, the north of Delhi (Oudh?). Probably, however, Aiodha is a misprint for Agroha or Agaroa. (*See* Tieffenthaler I. 135, where Saraug is probably a mistake for Scioura). Perhaps this is why they compared (*See* Text) the hair of *yugala* infants with that of Delhi children.

[1] Sanskrit आर *āra*, a spoke in time's wheel.

[2] So also As. Res. IX. 258. Major Mackenzie's account of the Jains.

present day, two thousand and odd years of the fifth *āra* of the first period have elapsed.

Be it known[1] that the arithmeticians of India call 100,000 a *lak;* ten *laks* a *prayūt,* ten *prayūts* a *krōr,* one hundred *krōrs* an *arb,* ten *arbs* a *kharba,* ten *kharbs* a *nikharb,* ten *nikharbs* a *mahāsarūj* or *padm,* ten *padms* a *sankha,* and ten *sankhas* a *samudr* or *kōrākōr.*

Be it known also that their opinion is that in a former period, in a particular place, a son and a daughter were born at each birth, a notion also prevalent amongst ourselves.[2]

This sect thinks also that the hair of the infants of the district of Delhi is 4096 times coarser than the hair of those beings whom they call *juglī*[3] (*yugala*).

---

[1] As to these numbers, *see* Jarrett III. 111 and Faizī's *Līlavatī,* Cal. 1828, 7 and 8. The statement in the text may be put into tabular form as follows:—

100,000 = *lak.*
1,000,000 = *prayūt.*
10,000,000 = *krōr.*
100,000,000 = *arb.*
1,000,000,000 = *kharb.*
10,000,000,000 = *nikharb.*
100,000,000,000 = *mahāsarūj.* or *padm.*
1,000,000,000,000 = *sankha.*
10,000,000,000,000, = *samudr* or *kōrākōr.*

In Text it is stated that 100 *krōrs, i.e.,* 1000 millions = an *arb* but this is probably a mistake for 10 *krōrs.* (See the scale in *Āīn,* Jarrett III, 111.) Cf. मवासरोजा – *Mahāsarūj* Great Lake-born, *i.e.,* the lotus, Monier Williams (Dictionary 761*a*), says it is equal to *mahāmbuja, i.e.,* a billion.

[2] A.F. is apparently referring to the Mu. tradition that Eve produced twins at every birth, *viz.,* a boy and a girl. He may also be referring to the views of the Gerbanites as given by Abraham Ecchellensis (Principles of Geology, Lyell, Chap. II). In that case, the words son and daughter should be translated male and female.

[3] (Jarrett IV. 196 and 200.) Sansc. *yugala,* a pair. I do not know why the number 4096 has been selected; 4696 is given in the *Āīn* as the period that had elapsed from the reign of Yudhiṣṭhira to 40th Akbar (Jarrett II. 15) and also as that from the Deluge to the time of writing the *Āīn, i.e.,* 40th Akbar (1596 A.D.). Perhaps 4096 is a mistake for 4696.

The passage (about the hair) occurs also at *Āīn* II. 104 (Jarrett III. 200) but there seems an error in the *Āīn* (Text) inasmuch as it represents the hair of a *yugala* child as 4096 times thicker than that of a Delhi child. The point, however, clearly is that the chopped hair (*See* Text *infra*) used for filling the cavity, be excessively fine, to wit, that of a *yugala*

51 And they say that if the hair of a seven days old *juglī* infant, which is excessively fine, be subdivided to the uttermost and an abyss (*lit.*, a well) ten miles[1] in depth, breadth and length, be filled with such particles and after a lapse of a hundred[2] years, one segment be taken out, the time in which, at this rate, the abyss will be emptied is a *palūpam* ( ? पल्य *palya*). And when ten *samudr*,—an explanation of which term has already been given,—of *palūpam*(s) have elapsed, the period is a *sāgar*. The durations of the aforesaid cycles transcend, in their opinion, the power of calculation or description. Their opinion also is that for the management of the visible and invisible world, twenty-four venerable men (*ādam*) come forth from the hidden universe into the apparent one, every six *āras* and then pass[3] away. The name of the first of these is Ādināth and they call him also Raghunāth. The sway of this chosen one of God lasts fifty *krōrs* of *laks* of *sāgaras*. The name of the last is Mahāvīra.[4] His sway lasts for 20,000 years, of which 2,000 have elapsed at the present day. And the belief of this sect is that these twenty-four have come into existence many times and will come again many times.

---

child, which is 4096 times finer than that of a Delhi child and that of a seven days' *yugala* child being still finer. Colebrooke (As. Res. l. c. 313) quotes Hēmacandra's Vocabulary, and says, "I do no find that he "anywhere explains the space of "time denominated *sāgara* or ocean. "But I understand it to be an extra-"vagant estimate of the time which "would elapse before a vast cavity, "filled with chopped hairs, could be "emptied at the rate of one piece of "hair in a century; the time required "to empty such a cavity measured by "*yojanas* every way is a *palya* and "this repeated ten *cotis* of *cotis* times "is a *sāgara* 1,000,000,000,000,000 *pal-*"*yas* = one *sāgara* or *sāgaropama*."

1 Four *kōs*, but the Indian word is *yōjana*.

2 The *Āīn* has 100 years and this seems the correct reading here for B.M. MSS. Nos. 5610 and 1709 have *har ṣad sāl*, every hundred years. In the text is *ṣad hazār*, a hundred thousand.

3 This is, apparently, differently stated in the *Āīn* (Jarrett III, 192), but perhaps the meaning of the *Āīn* (Text) is only that 24 demiurges appear in each *āra* and live for three or four *āras*.

4 The text has Mahādēō, but this is clearly a clerical error. (See *Āīn* II. 99, 1.4), where the spelling is given. The error is apparently repeated at II. 106, 1.3 fr. foot.

## Opinions of the Brāhma.

The Brāhma of India whose teachings and practices are observed by the majority of Indians, are agreed that the revolutions of the world consist of four Ages. The first, the period of which is 1,728,000 years, they call the *Sat Yug*. In this Age every single action of mankind is right, and high and low, rich and poor, great and small make truth and uprightness their rule, and show a walk and conversation pleasing to God. The natural life of man in this Age is 100,000 years.

The second Age is called *Trētā* and lasts 1,296,000 years. In it, three-fourths of mankind follow ways well-pleasing to God, and the natural duration of life is 10,000 years.

The third Age is called the *Dwāpar* and lasts 864,000 years. In it, one-half of mankind speak and act rightly, and the natural life is 1,000 years.

The fourth Age is the *Kal Yug*. Its period is 432,000[1] years. During it, three-fourths of mortals follow ways of falsehood and unrighteousness, and the natural life is 100 years.

This school firmly believes that every now and then the Life-Giver of mankind and producer of beings, brings an ascetic and sage[2] from the veil of concealment and non-existence to the palace of manifestation and existence and makes him the instrument for the creation of the world. This mighty one is called Brahmā. Their belief is that a Brahmā lives 100 years, each consisting of 360 days[3] and every day[3]

---

[1] Anquetil du Perron remarks (Tieffenthaler II. XXI), that the fourth Age has served to form the first three by adding successively 432,000.

[2] *Tajarrud-nihād ū danish-nizhād.*

[3] The word day is used here in two senses, first as the nycthemeron or day of 24 hours and then in its ordinary sense, as opposed to night. There seems to be an error in the Text هزارو *hazār ū*, "a thousand and" being a mistake for هزاروي *hazārwī*, a thousandfold. The meaning is "equal to a thousand of four Ages, *i.e.*, *Mahāyug*(s)." The "1,000 *Mahāyug*(s)" is apparently a statement in round numbers, the more exact figures being 980, for each Manu existed for 70 *kalpas* (71 according to another account) or *Mahāyug*(s) and as there are 14 successive Manus in a day of Brahmā, the length of it is $70 \times 14 = 980$. Firishta has copied A.F. (he acknowledges this, stating that he is epitomizing A.F.'s translation of the *Mahābhārat*), but he has gone to A.F.'s preface rather than to the *Akbarnāma*. See his Introduction

52 and every night is equal to a thousand times four Ages (*Mahāyug.*) In their opinion, the number of Brahmās who have come into existence cannot be known by the human intellect, but they say that according to what has been received from authorities[1] on the subject of Brahmā, the present Brahmā is the thousand and first, and that fifty years and half[2] a day of the life of this wondrous being have elapsed at the present time.

The writer of this divine masterpiece has written the account of these two doctrines according to the translation of learned and pious Indians[3] from their venerated books. Also in the writings of Shaikh Ibn 'Arabī[4]

---

(Elliot-Dowson's trans. VI. 532 E. n. E.) A.F.'s preface to the Persian translation of the *Mahābhārat* is to be found in the B.M. Add. No. 5638. It was written in the 32nd Akbar and contains an account of the four Ages corresponding to that in the Text. (See l. c. 12*a*).

I find in the *Çāntiparvan*—(Twelfth Book of the *Mahābhārat*)—(II, 237, Pratab Chandra Rai's tran.) that the four *Yugs* (Ages) contain 12,000 years of the gods, *i.e.*, 432,000 ÷ 360; and that this period is called a *Dēvayug*. "A thousand such *Yugas* (*i.e.*, *Dēvayugas* or *Mahāyugas*) compose a single day of Brahmā. The same is the duration of Brahmā's night."

1 ثقات *ṣiqāt*, "trusty friends or confidants." For use of this word, see Text 121 1.12, A.F. probably means here Manu or the Manus. Firishta has copied the expression and Professor Dowson (Elliot VI. 563) translates, "I have heard from my Brāhman *friends*, etc."

2 It would seem from the *Āīn* (Jarrett II, 15) that the half day has not fully expired, for we are told that 14 Manus appear in each of Brahmā's days. When A.F. was writing, 50 years had elapsed, and consequently 360 × 14 = 5,040 Manus had appeared. But instead of 7 Manus of the first day of the 51st year's having appeared, *i.e.*, the number that appear in half a day, we are told that only 6 Manus had appeared and departed, and that only a portion of the time of the 7th, *viz.*, 27 *kalpas*, 3 *yugas* and 4,700 years of the 4th *Yug* had elapsed. If this be correct, the 7th Manu had then more than half his time to run, *viz.*, 43 *kalpas* out of his 70.

3 See Jarrett III, 210 where A.F. speaks of having got his information about the Jains from learned men of the *Çvētāmbara* order, and says that he could not get exact information about the tenets of the *Digambaras* (sky-clad.)

4 Apparently the writer referred to is Muḥyī'u-d-dīn Ibnu-l-'Arabī, author of the *Fuṣūṣu-l-ḥikam* (Hājī Khalfa IV. 424). *See* Rieu's Cat. II. 831*b*, item III. and 832*b*, Item XVII. and Ar. Cat. No. 233. He was also the author of the *Futūḥāt-i-makkīyah* (*see* Rieu II, 874*b*) and of a number of definitions appended to Jor

and Shaikh Sa'du-d-dīn[1] Ḥamūī who were great saints and masters of exposition and ecstacy, it is stated in the explanation of Divine (*Ilāhī*) days and of *Rabbānī*[2] days that each *Rabbānī* day is made up of 1,000 years and every Divine day of 50,000. And the author of *Nafā'isu-l-funūn*[3] has related that in the histories of Cathay, it

---

jānī in Flügel's ed. The latter gives the name as "Mohjied-dīn Mohammed b. Ali Hatimi Tajī vulgo Ibn Arabi dictus," and says. he died in 638-1240. A.F. refers to Muḥyī'ū-d-dīn in the *Āīn* (II. 221 and Jarrett III. 373.) *See* also Badāonī, Lowe, 265.

[1] Apparently Sa'du-d-dīn Mu. B. al-Mu'ayyad Ḥamūī who died 650 H. (Rieu 755*a* and 1095*a*.) He is referred to in the *Āīn* (Jarrett III. 390), and there is a short notice of him in Prince Dārā Shikōh's *Sajīnatu-l-auliyā'* where it is stated that he died in Khurāsān 650 H. (1252 A.D.)

[2] ربانی *rabbānī*. Lane defines this as meaning one who devotes himself to religious services or exercises, or applies himself to excess of devotion. He does not give the meaning of "a period of time," but states that *rabbī*, the sing. of *rubūb*, means thousand, and that some say it means 10,000. Richardson gives *ribbī* as meaning thousands, a myriad. In the second Epistle of St. Peter ii. 8, we have the expression (as pointed out, I believe by Sale) "One day is with the Lord as a thousand years and a thousand years as one day." *See* also Psalm xc. 4. In the preface to the *Mahābhārat*, A.F. refers to the views of Ibn 'Arabī and Imām Ja'far Ṣādiq.

[3] See Rieu II. 435*a* for an account of this work. It is an encyclopædia written by Mu. B. Maḥmūdu-l-āmulī. I have not in B. M. MS. No. 16827, been able to find the passage referred to by A. F., but the volume is thick and has no index. *See* Jarrett II. 19, where we aret old that 8,884 *wans* 60 years, have elapsed up to the date, of the *Āīn*. These figures seem inconsistent with those of the Text, and apparently both are wrong. D'Herbélot (art. *Van.*) states that the Mughals reckon that 874 H. corresponds to the 8863rd. *van* of 10,000 years each, and then adds that 874 H. corresponds to 1443 A.D. In the end, the figures will come out nearly as A.F.'s if we substitute a six for an eight in the *Āīn* figures, making them 8864 and insert an eight in our text so as to read 8863 instead of 863.

Here we are told that 863 *wans*, 9,800 years, had elapsed from the time c Adam to 735 H.=1334 A.D. Consequently, 1003 H., 1594 A.D. the 40th Akbar and the date of the *Āīn* would correspond with 864 *wans*, 60 years, for 1594—1334=260 years.

874 H. is 88,639,860 years from the Creation. 8 7 H.=1443 A.D., so that this calculation agrees pretty nearly with that quoted by A.F. for 1334 A.D., *viz.*, 8863 *wans* 9800 years, the difference being 109-60=49 years. Sédillot refers to a passage of

is written that from the time of Adam Abū-l-bas͟har (Father of mankind) till now (*i.e.*, the date when the author of the *Nafā'is* was writing) which is 735 H., (1334 A.D.) 8863 *wans*[1] (Text, 863) 9,800 years have elapsed.

A *wan* with them is 10,000 years. Such is the wide expanse of God's kingdom that it is not improbable that these tales and traditions may be true. There may have been many Adams. Indeed it is stated by Imām Ja'far Ṣādiq, (Peace be on him!) that there have been thousands upon thousands of Adams before the Adam who was our father. And S͟haik͟h Ibn 'Arabī says it is not improbable that after a Divine (*Rabbānī*) week, which is 7,000 years and the period of the cycle[2] of the sovereignty of the seven planets, one race is terminated and another Adam puts on the robe of existence.

And now, giving truce to length of words and littleness of matter, I proceed to sketch in this glorious record, without converting[3] it into extensive histories, the blissful biography of those fifty-two persons who extend[4] from Adam down to his Majesty, the king of kings, so that it may be a cause of increase of knowledge. As I know that this exposition of grandeur will be a complement to the account of his Majesty, the king of kings, I shall treat it with the concision which is the adornment of an author.

---

D'Herbélot which, he says, is derived from Greaves. Sédillot considers that the true figures are 8863 *wans*, 9860 years; or 9820 according to one MS. This last figure agrees best with A.F., for in the *Āīn* (Jarrett II. 19) he says that according to the *Khaṭāī* Era, 8884 *wans* 60 years have elapsed up to the date of his writing, *i.e.*, 40th Akbar=1596 A.D. 1596-1443 =158, and this does not differ materially from 9864 *wans* 60 years —8863 *wans* 9820 years = 140.

[1] The Text has *har* before *wan* which seems a mistake.

[2] There is probably some mistake here. The cycle of the planets was generally reckoned as much longer than 7,000 years. See amongst other places, Principles of Geology, Lyell, Cap. II. Quotation from Abraham Ecchellensis. Perhaps A. F. means that each *Rabbānī* day is 7,000 years long and that thus a *Rabbānī* week is 49,000 years. If so, the trs. should be "After a week of *Rabbānī* days."

[3] Perhaps "not being satisfied with big books." The Persian is *iktifa'* for use of which see Text 10, l.2 fr. foot. A.F. may mean that certain voluminous histories do not give the facts properly.

[4] A.F. tells us later that these 52 persons do not fill the gap between Adam and Akbar. There is no record of some 25 generations.

# CHAPTER XIV.

## Account of Adam (Peace be upon him!)

It is well-known that he came into existence about 7,000[1] years ago through the perfect power of God, without the intervention of a father's loins or a mother's womb and that he was equably compounded of the four elements. His soul emanated from the fountain of bounty in perfection proportionate to his body. He was entitled man (*insān*) and received the name of Adam.

At that time the first degree of Capricorn[2] coincided with the eastern horizon, and Saturn was in that Sign, while Jupiter was in Pisces, Mars in Aries, the Moon in Leo, the Sun and Mercury in Virgo, and Venus in Libra. Some have said that at that time, all the planets were in their degrees of exaltation, but clearly this does not accord with astronomy for there is a difficulty about Mercury,—the Sun's exaltation being in Aries and Mercury's in Virgo. But Mercury can never be more than 27° distant from the Sun, how then can he be in exaltation when the Sun is in exaltation, or how can the Sun be in exaltation when Mercury is so? And reflecting on the astrological principle that Mercury takes the nature of whatever planet he be associated with, it has occurred to me that Mercury may have been in the condition of *applying*[3] to some other planet which was in exaltation.

---

1 The Era of Adam is described in the *Āīn*. (Jarrett II, 2.) All the periods given there are under 7,000 years. The "7,000 years" of A.F.'s authorities are probably lunar and about 211 have to be deducted to convert them into solar. Many dates of the Creation, etc., are given in the *Ḥabību-s-siyar*.

2 Capricorn is Saturn's nocturnal mansion; Pisces the nocturnal mansion of Jupiter, and Aries the diurnal house of Mars. There does not seem to be any special connection between the Moon and Leo but perhaps she is there as Vizier or deputy for the Sun, who is in Virgo,—the nocturnal house of Mercury,—but whose mansion is Leo. Libra is the diurnal house of Venus.

3 *Ittiṣāl*. This is the technical meaning of the term but A.F. may only intend that Mercury was near some other planet.

Adam was of lofty stature, of a wheaten colour, had curling hair and a handsome countenance. There are different accounts of the stature of this patriarch, but most agree that he was sixty cubits high. Almighty God produced Eve from his left side and gave her in marriage to him, and by her he begat children. Historians have told many strange and wondrous things about this hero and though there be no difficulty about the extent of God's power, yet experienced and practical men of the world, on looking to the course of nature, rather hesitate about accepting them. It is said that at the time of his death, he had 40,000 descendants, and that his immediate children were 41, *viz.*, 21 boys and 20[1] girls, but some say there were 19 girls. Seth was the most eminent of them all.

Some have said that Adam wrote about elixirs[2] (?) (*ta'fīnāt*) and

---

1 The Muḥammadan tradition is that Eve, at every parturition produced twins except at Seth's birth. He was born alone,—hence the numbers 21 males and 20 females. See account of Seth, *infra*.

2 The Text and No. 564 have تعفينات *ta'fīnāt*. Ordinarily this seems to mean evil smells or putridities, but Steingass gives also the meaning tincture—" ( تعفين *ta'fīn* v. n. 2 of عفن tincture)." If this be taken in the sense of elixirs or efficacious drugs, it may be that *ta'fīnāt* is right and it agrees with the statement in the *Ḥabību-s-siyar* that Adam's book dealt, among other subjects, with the properties of medicines. Yet A.F. would hardly class medicine among the occult sciences. In the sense of tincture, possibly *ta'fīnāt* has reference here to the tradition mentioned in the *Prolegomena* to the *Ẓafarnāma*, that when Adam was cast out of Paradise, he fell upon the mountains of Ceylon, and spent 100 years there in prayer and penitence. During this time, he wept so much that plants grew up out of the pools of his tears, and all of these were medicinal or aromatic like cloves, cinnamon, etc.

In B.M. No. MCCCVI, (p. 19) (Rieu, Ar. Cat. 601,602) which is the Ar. Text of Shahrazūrī's *Tārīkh-i-ḥukamā*, the word is not *ta'fīnāt* but apparently, *alba'qīnāt*, which does not seem to have any meaning. The passage is بعضی کتب فی البعقینات *ba'ẓī kutub fi-l-ba'qīnāt*. Perhaps the word should be اليقينيات *alyaqīnīyāt*, "certainties" such as articles of religion. In I.O. No. 1579, (Per. trs. of Shahrazūrī by one Maqṣūd 'Alī of Tabrīz) we find (16*a*) that unfortunately the *alba'qīnāt* or *alyaqīnīyāt* of Shahrazūrī's Text is represented by a word without diacritical marks. The passage is *ū dīdam man ba'ẓī az kutubhā-ī-ōrā dar* معععات *ẓāhir imām*. Taking the illegible word to be *ta'ṣībat* fr. *ta'ṣīb*, the appointing a man as chief and

other occult sciences. For example the very learned Shahrazūrī[1] has so stated in his "Lives of Philosophers." It is said Adam died

---

which with *ẓāhir*, may mean the external marks or indications of such a person, this may be rendered, "And I saw various books about the marks (or notes) of an *Imām*" (? *anām*, mankind.) Some countenance is given to this view by finding that Seth, a son of Adam, laid down 16 rules or marks of a true believer (*mu'min*) as if the father had laid down those of an *Imām* (apostle) and the son, those of a disciple.

Another suggestion which has occurred to me is that the word is البينات *al-bayyināt*, demonstrations," and which has also the technical sense of "cabalistic interpretations of the meanings of letters." This word occurs in Ḥājī Khalfa's account of the *Sifr-i-ādam* (Book of Adam) (Fluegel's ed. III. 599,600.) Here we are told that Adam's book was written on 21 olive leaves of Paradise and its gates (?) and dealt with the properties of letters, etc.

One more suggestion remains, *viz.*, that A.F.'s word is *taflīnāt*, *i.e.*, Heb. *tephillim*, "amulets or phylacteries." The variants in the notes to our Text do not seem of value, and MSS. which I have consulted, throw no light on the point. Evidently the word is used in an unusual sense and the copyists have been unable to understand it.

The *n* of *ta'fīnāt* does not, I think, occur in the MSS. I have consulted. In the beautiful MS. of Halhed (No. 5610, 31 1.3 fr. foot) the word appears to be تعفيات *ta'fiyāt*, "obliterations, amendments." In R.A.S. No. 116 it is clearly written تعقليات *ta'qliyāt*, and this might yield a good sense for *ta'qliyāt* (fr. *'aql*) seems to mean abstruse points in philosophy. (Lane 2114 *a* and *b*.) R.A.S. No. 117 has تعفيات *ta'fiyāt*.

[1] This is the Imām Shāmsu-d-dīn Muḥammad Shahrazūrī referred to by Āmir Khwānd (Khondamīr) in his *Khalāṣatu-l-akhbār*. (Persian *Munshī*, Gladwin, 1801, Part II. 265,266.) The *Rauẓatu-ṣ-ṣafā* (Rehatsek II. Part I.) states that he was the author both of the *Tārīkh-i-ḥukamā* and the *Nazhatu-l-qulūb* (Hearts' Delight), but if so, the latter is apparently not the work described by Rieu (I. 418*a*.) Shamsu-d-dīn is also mentioned in B.M. Ar. Cat. 209, 601, 602. The book there described is anonymous and entitled *Nazhatu-l-arwāḥ ū Rauẓat-l-afrāḥ*, "Delights of Souls and Gardens of Joy, *Oblectamen Spirituum et Viridarium Gaudiorum*," but Dr. Rieu observes that it agrees almost entirely with the work of Shamsu-d-dīn ash-Shahrazūrī described by Ḥājī Khalfa (Fluegel VI. 321.) It is in two parts, the first, an account of ancient philosophers, the second, of those subsequent to Muḥammad, and it contains 108 Lives (that described by Ḥājī Khalfa had 111.) Apparently *Tārīkh-i-ḥukamā* is the secondary title. It seems to have been written at Baṣra in 995 (1587). Its author wrote a commentary on Shahrawardī, a philosopher who was

in India and was buried on a mountain in Ceylon[1] (an island) which lies towards the south and which is now known by the name of *Qadamgāh-i-ādam* (Adam's footprint, *i.e.*, Adam's Peak.) He was ill 21 days and Eve died, according to one account, a year, according to another, seven years and according to a third, three days after him. Seth, his successor and administrator, buried her by Adam's side, and it is reported that Noah brought their coffin on board the Ark at the time of the Deluge, and afterwards buried them on *Abū qubais.*[2] According to another account, they were buried in Jerusalem, and according to a third tradition, in Najf-Kūfa.[3]

## SETH—PEACE BE UPON HIM

Was the most excellent of Adam's immediate descendants, and was born after the catastrophe of Abel. It is said that whenever Eve became pregnant, she gave birth to a son and a daughter, but that Seth was born alone. Iqlīmīyā,[4] the (twin) sister of Cain was

put to death at Aleppo by Saladin in 587 (1191). (D'Herbélot *s.v.* Scheher-verdi.) There is a Per. trs. (T.O. No. 1579) of the *Tārīkh-i-ḥukamā* by Maqṣūd 'Alī of Tabrīz, begun under the orders of Akbar and completed under Jahāngīr. The translator calls the author that pattern of writers Shamsu-l-mulka wa-d-dīn Maulānā Shamsu-d-dīn Muḥammad Shahrazūrī. A.F. seems to have made considerable use of the *Tārīkh-i-ḥukamā*; his account of the three Hermes in the notice of Enoch agrees closely with the Persian of Maqṣūd 'Alī.

Shahrazūr is a town in the hill-country of Persia and apparently near the battle-field of Arbela. (Jarrett III. 80,81.) A.F. gives Shahrazūr as the name of a district also. (Meynard's *Yāqūt,* 356.) The name is said to mean the city of Zūr,—the son of Ẓoḥāq a Persian king and founder of the town.

[1] A.F. includes Ceylon in India (Hindūstān.) The Arabs call the mountain on which Adam was buried, Rāhūn.

[2] Richardson spells Abū Kais, after D'Herbélot, and says it is 3 m. from Mecca. (D'H. *s.v.* Abu Cais Mecca.) Abū qubais is a mountain n. of Mecca. Abraham is said to have proclaimed from it, the institution of pilgrimage.

[3] Nedjif about 1½ m. (2 *kil.*) w. of Kūfa. (Réclus IX. 458) (Kūfah. Jarret III. 64.) Najf means high land and tumulus. A.F.'s account of Adam's burial-place is perhaps taken from the *Nafā'isu-l-funūn,* (B.M. No. 16,259*a* 827.)

[4] Much of A.F.'s account of the Patriarchs seems taken from the *Rauẓatu-ṣ-ṣafā* of Mīr Khwānd (Mīrkhond) and the *Ḥabību-s-siyar* of his grandson, Khwānd Amīr (Khondamīr) or from their sources. The *Rauẓatu-ṣ-ṣafā* has been translated

given in marriage to him (Seth.) When Adam reached the age of a thousand, he made Seth his successor, and enjoined all to submit to him. In succession to Adam, he carried on, by his weighty intellect, the administration of the temporal and spiritual worlds. He always 54
conducted himself with outward composure and inward efficiency, and his were the only descendants who survived Noah's Flood. He is called the first *Uria*,[1] a word which in Syriac means teacher. He occupied himself with the medical,[2] mathematical and theological sciences, and spent most of his life in Syria. Many of his descendants abandoned secular affairs and practised asceticism in hermitages. He left the world when he was 912 years old. Some say that he was Adam's grandson and that his father was Sulha,[3] but this tale is without foundation.

---

in part by Mr. Rehatsek, and his translation published by the Or. Trs. Fund. This work may advantageously be consulted in connection with A.F. See also Persian Ṭabarī, Zotenberg's trs.

The story of Iqlīmīyā is given in Ṭabarī, (Cap. XXX.) and in the *Rauẓatu-ṣ-ṣafā*. According to one tradition, Cain murdered Abel on her account, as he was not willing that she should marry Abel. Her name is variously written Iqlīmīyā, Iqlīmā (*Burhān-i-qāṭi' s. v.*) and by Bayle, Calmana. Iqlīmīyā means litharge, foam of silver. After Abel's death, Iqlīmīyā was married to Seth.

[1] Muḥammadans spell this name like that of Bathsheba's husband, but there is no connection between the two persons. Uriah means "Light of Heaven." (Ox. "Helps to the Bible.") D'Herbelot, Art. Uriai says: "Les Arabes se servent de ce mot, qui est tiré du Chaldaïque et du Syriaque *Ouraïa* et *Ouroïo*, pour signifier un Maître ou Docteur de la première classe, tels qu'ont été, Edris, Khedher, Hermes, qui portent les titres de premier, sécond et troisième Maîtres ou Docteurs de l'Univers." Chwolsohn in his work on the Sabæans, gives the variants, *Arānī* and *Arāfī* and comes to the conclusion that the word is not Syriac but merely a corruption of *Orpheus*. See I, 782 and 800 where he says, "sammt und sonders corruptionen aus Orpheus." But may it not be connected with *Ūr*, *i.e.*, the Ūr of the Chaldees or with the *ūr* which means light? The form *Arānī* is given by Mas'ūdī (Book of Indication and Counsel, deSacy IX. 342 n.)

[2] This is the Muḥammadan division of the sciences. (Blochmann 279 n.) It is derived from Aristotle.

[3] The *Rauẓatu-ṣ-ṣafā* (Trs.) has *Ṣupha*, but is unlikely that Mr. Rehatsek spelt an Ar. word with a *p*.

## Enosh.

Enosh was born when Seth was 600 years old. A number of writers say that his mother was an immaculately-born[1] one who, like Adam, was clothed with the garment of life without the instrumentality of father or mother. He succeeded his father in accordance with a testament, and was the first who in this cycle, laid the foundations of sovereignty.[2] They say he reigned 600 years. According to Jewish and Christian[3] traditions, he lived 965 years,—according to Ibn Jauzī,[4] 950,—and according to Qāẓī Baiẓāwī,[5] 600. He had many children.

## Kenan.[6]

Kenan was the most enlightened, fortunate and sagacious of the sons of Enosh. After his father's death, this hero, in accordance with a testamentary disposition, swayed the affairs of mankind and walked in the ways of his illustrious ancestors. He erected the buildings of Babylon and founded the city of Sūs.[7] They ascribe to him the first establishment of houses and gardens.

The numbers of mankind greatly increased during his time. By his wisdom, he distributed them (over the earth), and himself

1 The *Rauẓatu-ṣ-ṣafā* says his mother was a houri. (Rehatsek I. 67.)

2 *i.e.*, he was the first monarch. He is also said to have first planted palms.

3 According to Genesis, Enosh. lived 905 years.

4 The Abū'l-farāj of the *Āīn*. (Jarrett 83.) His full name is Abū'l-farāj 'Abdu-l-raḥmān b. 'Alī Ibnu-l-jauzī'l-bakrī. He died 597 (1200). His work is called the *Muntaẓam*. (Rieu, Ar. Cat. No. 460.) Quatremère speaks of Ibn Jauzī as author of the *Mirātu-z-zamān*, but it appears that this was written by Ibn Jauzī's grandson, Abū'l-muẓaffar Yūsuf b. Kizughlī who died 654 (1256). (Rieu l. c. No. 465.)

5 Qāẓī Naṣīru-d-dīn 'Abdu-l-lāh b. 'Umaru-l-baiẓāwī. (Jarrett II. 36n. and Rieu II. 823*b*.) His work is called the *Niẓāmu-t-tawārikh*, and is a general history from Adam to 674 (1275). He is best known as a commentator on the Koran.

6 Text, *Qainān*.

7 A town in Khūzistān, anciently the capital of Persia;—the Susa of Herodotus and Shusan of Scripture. According to the Persians, it was founded by Hūshang, grandson of Kaiūmarṣ (Gayomars). Mīr Khwānd ascribes the building of it to Kenan's son, Mahalalil and says that before the latter's time, men lived in caves.

settled with the descendants of Seth in Babylonia. He lived 926 years, but some say he drank the water of life, (*i.e.*, lived) 640 years, and one school says that he consoled the sorrows of the world, (*i.e.*, reigned) for about a century.

### MAHALALIL.

Mahalalil was the best of Kenan's sons. Kenan placed him on
the throne when he himself had attained the age of 900. He ruled 55
for 300 years. He lived either 928 or 840 or 895 years.

### JARED (TEXT, *Ĭrad.*)

Jared was the most right-minded of the sons of Mahalalil and by his honoured father's orders, he administered the affairs of the world. He made canals and conduits, and attained the age of 962 or, according to some, of 967 years.

All these magnates of the household of fortune came into existence during Adam's lifetime.

### ENOCH (TEXT, *Ikhnūkh.*)

Enoch is generally known as Idrīs, and was the distinguished son of Jared and born after Adam's death. Though the last-born of Jared's sons, he was, in wisdom and intelligence, older than all of them, and was before them all in felicity and understanding. He is the first lawgiver since the time of Seth. Some say that Idris was 100 years old at the time of Adam's death and some that he was 360 years. He was unrivalled in his knowledge of the science of government and the refinements of contrivance. Though some assign all sciences and arts to Adam, yet, according to most, astronomy, writing,[1] spinning, weaving and sewing were introduced by Enoch. He learned wisdom from Agathodæmon[2] of Egypt whom they call *Uria* the Second.

**Among his lofty titles is that of Harmasu-l-harāmasa[3] (Hermes of Hermeses or Trismegistus) and he is also called the third *Uria*. He**

---

[1] Blochmann (99) mentions Idrīs as the inventor of the Hebrew alphabet.

[2] Text, *Aghāzīmūn*. See Al-bīrūnī's India and Chwolsohn on the Sabæans. Seth is the first *Uria*.

[3] *Āīn* II. 49 l.4 fr. ft. Jarrett III. 109 n.

attained high rank in theology and summoned[1] mankind to worship in seventy-two languages. He founded 100[2] cities, of which Madīna-i-roha[3] was the least. It was a city of Mesopotamia (Jazā'ir) though some place it in the Ḥijāz (Petrœa Arabia). It was inhabited up to the time of Hulākū Khān who, it is said, destroyed it for the sake of the honour of the country and the well-being of the people.[4]

He (Idrīs) instructed every tribe and every rank of mankind by a special procedure in accordance with their capacities. They say that he guided men to the reverence of the Great Light (the Sun) for most of them, before his time, were without his abounding wisdom and did not give thanks for that light of lights. He regarded it as the stock of visible and invisible fortune, and prescribed a great festival at the time of its passing[5] from one Sign to another which is a special time of glory, and above all when it enters Aries.

---

[1] The phrase for "summoned" is *da'wat farmūd.* The *Tārīkh-i-ḥukamā* (Per. trs. 17*b*, foot) has *ū khalā'iq-i-rab'-maskūn bahaftād ū dū zabān da'wat numūd ū 'ilm ū adab āmōkht.* Mr. Rehatsek remarks that 72 is a common number in Muḥammadan theology, etc., and that David is spoken of as having 72 notes in his voice. Mas'ūdī says (Meynard, 78) that after the Deluge, the 72 languages were divided as follows:—Shem 19, Ham 17, Japhet 36; total 72.

[2] The *Tārīkh-i-ḥukamā* has 108. (17*b* foot.) Abū'l-farāj (Pococke) ed. 1663, p. 6 has 180.

[3] Text, *Zoha,* but there is a var. *Roha* which I adopt, for the city meant is probably Edessa, the Roha of the Arabs and the modern Orfa. It is in Asiatic Turkey, east of the Euphrates. (Réclus IX. 445 and Lectures on the Jewish Church, Stanley, 6.) If, however, A.F. means Edessa, there must be some mistake on his part, for Edessa was not, I believe, taken by Hulākū Khān and it certainly was not destroyed, for it still exists. See Quatremère's Rashīdu-d-dīn (334) for a note (128) on a Roha mentioned by Rashīdu-d-dīn as having been taken by Hulākū Khān. In the Persian it is spelt روح and Quatremère translates "Houlagou en personne se dirigea vers Rouhah dont il se rendit maître." The note says "J' ignore quelle est la ville que notre historien a voulu indiquer, et si le nom est correctement écrit." Possibly the town is Riha or Riah S.W. of Aleppo. (Réclus IX. 765 and 772 n.)

[4] A.F. here refers to the destruction of the Ismailians by Hulākū, the grandson of Cingiz Khān, in the middle of the 13th century. Cf. Gibbon's remark that the extirpation of the Assassins or Ismailians of Persia by Hulākū may be considered a service to mankind.

[5] Lit. alighting of glory and renovation of felicity,—*nuzūl-i-ijlāl ū taḥwīl-i-iqbāl.*

And whenever the planets, who are fed from the bounteous table of 56
its rays, entered their own Houses or attained their *exaltation*, he regarded them as of special dignity, and gave thanks for the wonders of creation. Such seasons he looked upon as stations and manifestations of the favour of God, and he spent all his days in the service of holy spirits and pure forms.

He also built the pyramids of Egypt which are known as the Domes of Haramān (*Gumbaz̤-i-haramān*). And in those lofty buildings, all the arts and their tools have been depicted, so that if the knowledge of them be lost, it may be recovered. It is recorded that he deputed one of his nobles to lay the foundations of these pyramids whilst he himself traversed the entire world, eventually returning to Egypt.

Abū Ma'shar[1] of Balkh relates that there have been many Hermes but that three were preëminent;—(1). Harmasi-harāmasa (Hermes of Hermeses) or Idrīs whom the Persians call the grandson of Kayūmars̤.[2] (2). Hermes of Babylon who built Babylon after the Deluge. Pythagoras was one of his disciples. By the exertions of this Hermes of Babylon, the sciences which had been lost in Noah's Flood were resuscitated. His home was in the city of the Chaldeans (Kaldānīn)[3] which is called the city of the philosophers (wise men) of the East (Madīna-i-filāsafa-i-mashriq). (3) The Hermes of Egypt who was the teacher of Esculapius (Asqlīnus).[4] He too excelled in all sciences, especially in medicine and chemistry and spent much time in travel.

The birth-place of Harmasu-l-harāmasa (Idrīs) was Manīf (Memphis) now known by the name of Manūf,[5] in the land of Egypt. Before the founding of Alexandria, it was called the city of philo-

[1] (Jarrett II. 10. No. 43.) He was known in the Middle Ages as Albumaser. This passage closely resembles the *Tārīkh-i-ḥukamā* (166-ft. ff.)

[2] This is Hūshang. (Ṭabarī Zotenburg, I. 100.)

[3] Mas'ūdī, de Saçy. Paris 1877, IX.' 324 n. Their city was Kalwādha.

[4] The author of the Tārīkh-i-ḥukamā distinguishes between Esculapius, who he says is the son of Āmūr, and Asqlīnus.

[5] منوف Manūf, but the ū seems wrong; the *Āīn* gives Manf or Minf. (Jarrett III. 75.) It is the Noph of the Bible. The Text here agrees closely with the *Tārīkh-i-ḥukamā*.

sophers, but when Alexander built that city,[1] he brought the philosophers of Memphis and other places to Alexandria.

Among the sayings of Enoch is this, "The three[2] most excellent things are truth when angry, bounty when poor and mercy when strong." Wonderful stories are told in histories about his departure from this world, which wise men hesitate about accepting. One tradition is that he was then 865, another that he was 405 and a third that he was 365.

### METHUSALAH.

Methusalah was the son of Enoch. He had many children, so that it is difficult to enumerate them. After his father, he was the head of his tribe and called men to Divine worship. When he was 900, he had a son whom he called Lamech. After that he lived 290 years.

### 57 LAMECH.

Lamech was the unique of his time for lofty character and exalted virtue. After his father, he became firmly seated on the throne. The period of his life was 780 years. And some call him Lamkān, Lāmak, and Lāmakh.

### NOAH (NŪH).

Noah, the son of Lamech, was born under the Sign of Leo, 126 years after Adam's death. He was strong in the ways of religion and firmly based on the foundation of justice. The story of his calling[3] mankind to the worship of God, the disobedience of his people and the event of the Flood, etc., are well-known.

Historians have mentioned three floods. First, a flood which

---

[1] The *Āīn* gives this name to Athens. (Jarrett III. 78.)

[2] This passage occurs in the *Tārīkh-i-ḥukamā*. (Mīr Khwānd, Rehatsek I. 72.) The first of these three things receives explanation from another remark of Enoch (Mīr Khwānd, Rehatsek, II. Part I.) to the effect that a man should beware of uttering in the time of anger, words which will be a cause of disgrace to him. It may be noted here that Mīr Khwānd's account of some of the patriarchs is to be found in two places,—at the beginning of his work and again among the biographies of the philosophers.

[3] Koran, Sura 71. Noah is said to have invented the *nāqūs* ناقوس = wooden gong.

occurred before our Adam came into existence. Thus[1] the very learned Shahrazūrī says, "Adam belongs to the first cycle which commenced after the world had been devastated by the first flood." The second flood was in the time of Noah and began at Kūfa, in the oven[2] of Noah's house. It lasted six months, and there were eighty persons in the Ark (*kishtī*). On this account the place where they disembarked and settled was called the Eighty-Market[3] (*Sūqu-s-samānīn*). The third[4] flood was in the time of Moses and was confined to the Egyptians. Although romancing historians,[5] in treating of the floods, make the last two also extend over the whole world, it is evident that this was not so, for in India,[6] where they have books many thousand years old, there is not even a trace of these two floods. To be brief, in a short space of time, all the eighty occupants of the Ark died except seven, *viz.*, Noah, his three sons, Japheth, Shem and Ham, and their wives. Noah assigned Syria, Mesopotamia, 'Irāq and Khurāsān to Shem; the western countries, and Abyssinia, Indian, Scinde and the Sūdān[7]

1 This passage occurs in the *Tārīkhi-ḥukamā* (Maqṣūd 'Alī).

2 This is the Muḥammadan tradition. (Ṭabarī, Zotenberg, I, 108 and Koran, Sale, Cap. XI). "And "the oven poured forth water, or, "as the original literally signifies, "boiled over, which is consonant to "what the Rabbins say, that the "water was boiling hot." (*Rauẓatu-ṣ-ṣafā*, Rehatsek I, 90).

3 Ar. *Sūqu-s-samānīn*. It was at the foot of the mountain Al Jūdī, *i.e.*, Mount Ararat. (D'Herbelot art. *Thamanin*). D'H. states that it is called also Jazīra Banī 'Umar (in Mesopotamia). Mas'ūdī says (Meynard, 74) that Al-Jūdi is in the country of Baṣra and in Jazīra ibn 'Umar, that the eighty persons were 40 men and 40 women and that Ṣamānīn existed in his day, 332 H.

4 Referring apparently to the hailstorm—the seventh plague of Egypt, or perhaps to the overflowing of the Red Sea.

5 Shahrazūrī describes Noah's Deluge as universal (17*b*).

6 It is curious that A.F. should assert there was no trace of Noah's Flood in the Indian annals for Satyavrata and his Flood have often been identified with Noah and the Deluge. Probably A.F. identified Satyavrata's Flood with that which occurred before the birth of Adam, for Satyavrata belongs to the beginning of the *Satya Yuga* and apparently A. F. assigned Noah's Flood to the commencement of the *Kali Yuga* and the beginning of the reign of Yudhiṣṭhira, for he gives 4696 years as the interval between these events and the 40th Akbar. (Jarrett II-15 and 22).

7 Or, "country of the blacks." (Jarrett III, 108 and 109. Apparently A. F. includes the Arabs among the descendants of Ham.

to Ham; and China, Sclavonia[1] and Turkistān to Japheth. And in the opinion of historians, the aboriginal inhabitants of those countries at the present day, are descended from these three, and the lineage of mankind from the days of the Flood is derived from them. Noah died when he was either 1600 or 1300 years old. There are other stories too about his age, such as that he lived for 250 or 350 years after the Flood and that he was born either 126 years after Adam's death or in Adam's last days, and that he sat upon the throne of
58 guidance, (*i.e.*, became a prophet) when he was 50, or 150, or 250, or 350 years old, and that he was a guide to mortals for 950 years.

Ham[2] had nine sons, *viz.*, Hind, Sind, Zanj (Zanzibar), Nūba, Canaan, Kush, Qabṭ (copt),[3] Berber, Ḥabsh (Abyssinia), and some have written that Ham had six sons. They omit Sind and Canaan and make Nūba the son of Ḥabsh.

Shem also had nine sons, *viz.*, (1) Arfakhshad,[4] (2) Kayūmarṣ who is the progenitor of the kings of Persia, (3) Asūd[5] who founded Madā'in[6] (the twin-cities of Seleucia and Ctesiphon), etc., Ahwāz[7] and Pahlū (? Peleg) are his sons and Fārs is the son of Pahlū, (4) Ighan[8] the father of Shām (Syria) and Rūm (Asia Minor), (5) Būraj,[9] of whom historians tell nothing except the name, (6) Lāūẕ (? Lud) from whom the Pharoahs of Egypt are descended, (7) Elam who built the cities of Khuzistān; Khurāsān and Tambāl[10] are his sons,

---

1 صقلاب *Ṣaqlāb*,—the original Sclavonia, between the Oxus and the Dnieper, (Jarrett III, 104.) In the *Āīn* (Text) Ṣaqlāb is described as a city of Rūm which must be a mistake for Rūs. It seems that Ṣaqlāb and Chalybes are the same word.

2 Jarrett III, 327. There A.F. apparently repudiates the idea that the Hindus are descended from Ham.

3 Corresponds to Mizraim of the Bible.

4 Arpachshad of Genesis 10, 22.

5 Ashur.

6 *Āīn*, Madā'in of Chosroes. (Jarrett III, 65 and 96. Also III, 326.)

7 Ahwāz, a town in Khūzistān (Persia) on the Karun, (Jarrett III, 65) famous for its weir. (Réclus IX, 287 and Curzon Pro. G. S. 1890.)

8 Var. Ifan and Iqīn and (*Ḥabību-s-siyar*) Iqan. Probably the last is correct for the name seems connected with Iconium (Koniah) and to be that of the eponymous hero of the city.

9 So too *Ḥabību-s-siyar* but it calls him Nūraj.

10 Tubal. Miles calls him Hakyal. Perhaps the same as Tūmbel. (Jarrett II, 245 and 250.) Tambol appears as a person's name in the *Tārīkh-i-Rashīdī* and Bābar's Me-

and 'Irāq is the son of Khurāsān, and Kirmān (Carmania) and Makrān[1] are sons of Tambāl, (8) Aram from whom the tribe of 'Ād is descended, (9) Būzar whose sons are Āzarbaijān, Arān, Arman and Farghān.

Some say that Shem too had only six sons and omit Kayūmarṣ, Būraj and Lāüz. In short, there is much discrepancy about the descendants of those two (Shem and Ham).

JAPHETH. (YĀFIṢ.)

Japheth was the most just of Noah's sons. The lofty line of his Majesty, the king of kings, is linked with him, and the Khāns of the eastern cities and of Turkistān all derive from him. He is called the Father of Turk (*Abū-l-turk*), and some historians call him Alūnja Khān. When Japheth left Sūqu-ṣ-ṣamānīn with his wife and family, to go to the eastern and northern countries which had been assigned to him, he begged his father to teach him a prayer by which he might have rain whenever he wanted it. Noah gave him a stone which had the property of bringing rain, and indicated that he had pronounced over it the Ineffable Name[2] (*lit.* Great Name) with the design that the foolish should not comprehend the matter and transgress his precepts, or perhaps he really recited the Ineffable Name over it. And at present there are many of these stones among the Turks which they call *yedatāsh*. The Persians call them *sang-i-yada*[3] and the Arabs *hajaru-l-maṭar*, (rain-stone). And Japheth, on

moirs. *Tembal-khāna* was also a name for Farghāna, Bābar, 196.

[1] D'Herbelot art. Macran. Mekrān here appears to be the well-known maritime province of Baluchistan.

[2] The passage is obscure and perhaps there is an error in the Text. Maulavī 'Abdu-l-ḥaqq 'Abīd, to whom I referred the passage, writes: "The meaning is not clear. There may be some misprint in the Text. As the passage stands, it may be translated, 'I have uttered over it the Great Name, in order that the simple, not getting clue to it, may not depart from his (your) command (or counsel), or he actually uttered the Great Name over it." The usual account is that Noah engraved the Great Name on the stone, and possibly we should read كند "engraved," for خواند "uttered," in the last clause. A friend has referred me to the passage in Revelations II, 17, "I will give him a white stone, and upon the stone a new name written, which no one knoweth saving he that receiveth it."

[3] Bābar, Erskine xlvii. Rashīdu-d-dīn, Quatremère's elaborate note, 428, and Vullers II, 334a.

going to those regions, became a dweller in deserts, and whenever he wished, the cloud of God's bounty, came down in rain through the virtue of that stone. In course of time, children were born to Japheth and he established excellent laws among them, which were at once comforting to the short-thoughted and joy-increasing to lofty minds. He left eleven sons, *viz.*, 1, Turk, 2, Cīn, 3, Ṣaqlāb, 4, Mansaj,[1] also called Mansak, 5, Kamārī,[2] also called Kaimāl,
59 6, Khalaj, 7, Khazan, 8, Rūs, 9, Sadsān, 10, Ghaz,[3] 11, Yāraj.[4] Some books mention only eight sons, omitting Khalaj, Sadsān and Ghaz.

## Turk.

Turk was the eldest son of Japheth, and the Turks call him Yāfiṣ Ōghlān.[5] He excelled all his brothers in wisdom, management and care for his subjects. On his father's death, he sat upon the throne of sovereignty and dispensed gentleness, manliness and relief of the oppressed. He settled in a place which the Turks call Sīl-ūk[6] or Salīkāī and which had hot and cold springs and delightful meadows. He made dwellings of grass and wood and constructed tents, and made clothes by sewing together the skins (and furs) of beasts of burden and of prey. Salt[7] was discovered in his time. One of his laws was that the son should inherit naught but a sword and that whatever was wanted should go to the daughter. They say he was contemporary with Kayūmarṣ, and that as the latter was the first king of Persia, so Turk was the first sultan of Turkistān. He lived to the age of 240.

---

[1] The reputed father of Gog and Magog and, apparently, the Scriptural Mishesh.

[2] Gomer of Genesis. Probably the Text *k* is the MS *g*.

[3] Guz in Vullers II, 609*a*. Gozz in Mas'ūdī I, 212. The supposed ancestor of the Turkomāns.

[4] D'Herbelot calls him Taraga and the ninth son, Isan.

[5] A note to Text states that Ōghlān means son in Turkish.

[6] ? Issigh-kul. Text, *Sīlūl*. Perhaps the river Selenga, but the description better applies to the lake of Issik-kul (Hot Water) which is said to be ten times the size of Lake Geneva. Réclus VI, 350. It lies N. of Yarkand. Its waters do not freeze. The *Shajaratu-l-atrāk* calls it Jaeelgan. (Miles 25).

[7] The discovery is said to have been made accidentally by his son Tūnag or Tūtak.

### Alinja Khān.[1]

Alinja Khān was the best of Turk's sons. When the measure of Turk's years was fulfilled, Alinja Khān was placed on the throne by the will of the chiefs. He made far-sighted wisdom his rule, and spent his days in the administration of justice. When he became old, he went into retirement (*i.e.*, became a hermit).

### Dīb Bāqūī.[2]

Dīb Bāqūī became king on his father's retirement and in accordance with his appointment.

### Kīyūk Khān.

Kīyūk was the worthy son of Dīb Bāqūi. When the father bade adieu to the world, he made over the throne of the Khānate to Kiyūk who, knowing the duties of sove eignty, acted up to them.

### Alinja Khān.

Alinja Khān was the son of Kīyūk and became heir-apparent in the end of his father's days. He was extravagant in his liberalities, and in his reign the Turks became intoxicated[3] by the world and
strayed from the path of wisdom. After a long time, twin-sons were 60
born to him. One was named Mughul and the other Tātār. When they came to years of discretion, he divided his kingdom into two portions and gave one half to Mughul and one half to Tātār. When their illustrious father died, each of the two sons reigned in his own territory, in harmony with one other.

As this lofty line (Akbar's) has no connection with Tātār and his eightfold[4] branches (*i.e.*, generations) I pass them over and proceed to relate the history of Mughul and his noble descendants.

### Mughul Khān.

Mughul Khān was a wise prince. He so conducted himself that the hearts of his subjects were attached and obedient to him and

[1] *Shajratu-l-atrāk*, Abluchi Khān.

[2] D'Herbélot, "Great Dignity."

[3] This refers to their becoming idolaters. (Khāfī Khān I, 3).

[4] *I.e.*, eight in all, Tātār being one. (*Shajratu-l-atrāk*, Miles 29). According to D'Herbélot (Art. Tatar) Alinja Khān, the father, is required to make up the eight.

all tried to serve him properly. The generations of the Mug͟huls are nine in number, beginning with Mug͟hul K͟hān and ending with Īl[1] K͟hān. The Mug͟huls have taken the usage of *Tuqūz*[2] (nine) from this, and they consider this number most excellent in all matters. The Creator bestowed on Mug͟hul K͟hān four sons, Qarā K͟hān, Āzar K͟hān, Kar K͟hān and Ūz K͟hān.

## Qarā K͟hān.[3]

Qarā K͟hān was both the eldest son and preëminent in justice and the art of government. He sate upon the throne in succession to his illustrious father and made his summer (*ailāq*) and winter (*qis͟hlāq*) quarters in Qarāqūm[4] near two mountains called Irtāq[5] and Kirtāq.

---

[1] Vullers 481b. The generations are said to end with Īl K͟hān because, in his time, the Mug͟hul race was all but extirpated. If the statement of the Turks, mentioned below, that this catastrophe occurred 1000 years after Ag͟hūz's death, be correct, it is evident that far more than nine generations must have intervened between Mug͟hul and Īl K͟hān.

[2] Steingass *s.v.* "Nine, hence present, gift, such being offered to kings, *etc.*, by nines, as a sacred number."

[3] *I.e.*, the Black Prince. A.F. omits to mention that he was put to death by his own son, Ag͟hūz. (K͟hāfī K͟hān I, 5.)

[4] *I.e.*, black sand or dust. The Text wrongly has قرا قرم *Qarāqaram.* The *Āīn* mentions the place as belonging to the Sixth Climate. (Jarrett III, 102). The *Āīn* (Text II, 46), describes it as a mountain in Turkistān (not Kohistān as Jarrett has it) and the editor says (l.c.n.) that many MSS. read قرا قوم *Qarāqūm.* This is the correct reading. (Vullers *s.v.* II, 717b, and D'Herbélot art: Caracum.) In Gladwin's *Āīn* the lat. and long. of Qarāqūm and of K͟hānbālīg͟h which immediately follows, are given; the long. for Qarāqūm being 115° and for K͟hānbālīg͟h 124°.

*N.B.* K͟hānbālīg͟h is described in Text as the capital of Cathay, not of China.

[5] Erdmann, اورتاق و گزتاق Urtāq and Gaztāq. D'Herbélot calls them Artak and Ghertak, and says they are part of Mount Imaus (Paradise Lost III, 431), and that the city of Caracum lies between them, Artak being N. and Ghertak S. He gives the long. as 116° which agrees very well with Gladwin. Of course both longs. are calculated from the Fortunate Isles. Greenwich long. is between 72° and 80.° The lat. of the Karakoram Pass (Imperial Gazeteer, Hunter), is 35° 33″ or about 11° less than that given in the *Āīn*. (46 N.). This would imply that Qarāqūm and Qarāqaram are totally different names and places,

## Aghūz[1] Khān.

Aghūz Khān was the worthy son of Qarā Khān, and was born of his chief wife during the time of his rule. Romancing story-tellers relate things about his naming himself and about his progress in the path of piety, which a just-judging intellect is not disposed to credit. He was admittedly an enlightened, pious and just ruler and framed excellent institutions[2] and laws whereby the varied world was composed and the contrarieties of the Age conciliated. Among Turki kings, he was like Jamshīd among the kings of Persia. By his ripe wisdom, lofty genius, felicity and native courage, he brought under his sway the countries of Īrān (Persia) Tūrān,[3] Rūm[4] (Asia Minor), Egypt, Syria, Europe (Afranj),[5] and other lands. Many nations came within the shadow of his benevolence, and he established titles among the Turks suitable to their ranks and which

---

but on the other hand, D'Herbélot gives the lat. of Caracum as 36° 36″. There is an account of the city of Karacum (Caracorum) in Gibbon who (Cap. 64) makes it about 600 m. N.W. Pekin. It was also called Holin.

1 Text, Aghūr. For account of him see Khāfī Khān I, 4 and 5, D'Herbélot *s.v.* Ogouz Khān, *Shajratu-l-atrāk* (Miles) 30. The story is that Aghūz refused immediately after birth to take the breast, and that his mother had a dream in which he told her that he would not permit her to suckle him until she became a believer in Islām. Accordingly she secretly embraced that faith. Also, when he was a twelvemonth old, he told the conclave assembled to decide upon his name, that it was Aghuz (Khāfī Khān l.c.). These things occurred long before the birth of Muḥammad, but the latter was only the Seal (last) of the Prophets, and the religion of Islām is considered to have existed from all time. Hence the Mu. formula of "Peace be upon him" is applied to Adam and others of the patriarchs.

2 یاسا *yāsā*. Text, *bāyistahāī* which is an error. The best known *yāsā* are those of Cingiz Khān. (Miles l. c. 90 and Gibbon and D'Herbélot art. Jassa).

3 Turkistān or Transoxiana. It is said to have been named after Tūr, the son of Farīdūn (D'H. art. Mogal), but if so, A.F.'s use of it here is an anachronism, for he describes Tūr as nearly exterminating the Mughuls about a thousand years after Aghūz Khān's death.

4 This may mean the whole Greek Empire or only Asia Minor (Roumelia).

5 Afranj is properly the name of a people, *viz.*, the Franks. *Rauẓatu-ṣ-ṣafā*, V, gives a similar list.

are on men's tongues to the present day, such as Aīghūr,[1] Qanighlī, Qibcāq, (Kipcāk), Qārligh, Khalaj, etc. He had six sons, *viz.*, Kūn (sun), Āī (moon), Yūlduz (star), Kōk (or Gōk) (sky), Tāgh (mountain), and Tangīz (sea). The three elders were called Buzmaq[2] and the
61 three others *Ujūk*. His sons and sons' sons became 24 branches, and all the Turks are descended from these magnates. The term Turkomān did not exist in old times, but when their posterity came to Persia (Īrān) and propagated there, their features came to resemble the Tājīks. But as they were not Tājīks, the latter called them Turkomāns, *i.e.*, Turk-like. But some say that the Turkomāns are a distinct tribe and not related to the Turks. It is said that after Aghūz Khān had conquered the world, he returned to his own settlement (*yūrat*), and seating himself on the throne of dominion, held a Khusrū-like feast and conferred royal gifts on each of his fortunate sons, faithful officers and other servants, and promulgated lofty ordinances and excellent canons as guides for the perpetuation of prosperity. He laid it down that the right wing, which Turkomāns call *Burānghār*, and the succession should appertain to the eldest son and his descendants, and the left wing, *i.e.*, the *Jarānghār* and the executive (*wakālat*) to the younger sons. And he decreed that this law should always be observed, generation after generation;—hence at the present day, one half of the twenty-four branches is associated with the right wing and one half with the left. He ruled for 72 or 73 years and then bade adieu to the world.

## Kun Khān.

Kun Khān took his father's place, in accordance with his testament and acted in administration and government by his own acute

[1] The meanings of this and following terms are given by Mīr Khwānd and Miles. Erdmann, the authority often quoted by Howorth, writes قارلوک *qārlūk*, and says it means snow-lord. Qipcāk is said to mean a hollow tree.

[2] Said to mean "Broken" and "Three arrows." The legend of origin is given by Miles. Text, Bājuq for Ujūq. *Uq* is an arrow, and *uc* means three. The etymologies are also given in Abū-l-ghāzī Des Maison 24. The name *Buzmaq or* "Broken" was given to the three elder sons because they brought in three pieces of a golden bow. The three younger brought in three golden arrows.

understanding, and[1] the sage counsels of Qabal[2] Khwāja who had been Vizier to Aghūz Khān. He so arranged about his brothers, his children and his nephews—who were 24 in number, for each of the six brothers had four sons—that each recognized his position and assisted in the management of the State. Having reigned for 70 years, he appointed Āī Khān his successor and departed.

### Āī[3] Khān.

Āī Khān observed the laws of his illustrious father, adorned justice with amicability, and combined wisdom with good actions.

### Yuldūz Khān.

Yuldūz Khān was the eldest[4] son and successor of Āī Khān. He attained high rank in world-sway and in the dispensing justice.

### Mangalī Khān (Michael).[5]

Mangalī Khān was the beloved son of Yuldūz Khān and sate 62
upon the throne in succession to him. He was distinguished for devotion to God, and for praising the pious.

### Tangīz Khān.

Tangīz Khān conducted the affairs of sovereignty after his honoured father's death and wore the crown of dominion in Mughulistān for 110 years.

### Īl Khān.

Īl Khān was his noble son. When the father became old and weak, he gave Īl Khān the management of affairs, and alleging the number of his years as an excuse, went into solitary retirement.

### Qiyān.[6]

Qiyān was the son of Īl Khān and, by the mysterious ordinances of Divine wisdom, he became a resting-place (*maurid*) of adversities.

---

1 The conjunction *ū* has dropped out of the Text, but occurs in the Lucknow ed. and in No. 564.

2 Text, *Irqīl*, but admittedly this is against all the MSS.

3 Apparently he is Kun's brother, and the "illustrious father" must be Aghūz.

4 According to another account, he was Āī Khān's brother.

5 *Mangala* may also mean sun, or the forehead, (Tar. Rash 7n.)

6 Though this name is the heading of the Text, the narrative is in part that of Īl Khān's reign.

When the God of wisdom desires to bring a jewel of humanity to perfection, He first manifests sundry[1] favours under the cover of disfavours of misfortune, and grants him the robe of existence after having made some great and pure-hearted ones his ransom and sacrifice (*fidā*). There is an instance of this in the story of Īl Khān who, after the turn of sovereignty came to him, was passing his life according to a code which provided for the control of the outer world and the contemplation of the world of reality, and was binding up the hearts of the distressed, until that Tūr, the son of Farīdūn, obtained sway over Turkistān, and Transoxiana (*Mā-wārāu n-nahr*) and in conjunction with Sunij Khān, the king of the Tātārs and Aighūrs, made a great war upon Īl Khān. The Mughul army, under the excellent dispositions of Īl Khān, made a desperate struggle, and many of the Turks, Tātārs and Aighūrs were slain. In the combat, Tūr and the Tātārs were unable to resist and fled. They took refuge in stratagems and vulpine tricks and dispersed. After going a little way, they hid in a defile, and then at the end of the night, suddenly made an onslaught on Īl Khān's army. Such a massacre took place that of Īl Khān's men not one escaped except his son Qiyān, his cousin Takūz[2] and their two wives[3] who had hidden themselves among the slain. At night, these four withdrew to the mountains and with many troubles and difficulties, traversed the valleys and ravines, and came to a meadow which had salubrious springs and fruits in abundance. In their helpless state, they regarded this pleasant spot as a godsend and settled in it. The Turks call it Irganaqūn and say that the terrible calamity happened 1000 years after the death of Aghūz Khān.

The sage knows that in this wondrous destiny there lay the
63 plan for the production of that all-jewel, his Majesty, the king of kings, so that the status of sacrifice might be attained and also that the ascents of banishment, seclusion, and hardship might, in this strange fashion, be brought together to the end that the unique pearl,

---

1 There is perhaps a play on the words *mirād* and *murād;* the first meaning a precious stone possessed of wondrous qualities, the second success.

2 Probably Naqūz is more correct.

3 The Text does not distinctly say that the women were wives, the word used being *ḥaram*. One account says sisters.

his Majesty, the king of kings,—who is the final cause of the creation of the glorious series (*ṭabaqa*) and also the material for this record of Divine praise,—might become the aggregate of all the stages of existence and be acquainted with the grades of humanity, which might thus arise,—and should achieve spiritual and temporal success, and that in this way there be no defective round (*girdī*) on the periphery of his holiness.

In fine, after Qiyān and his companions had settled in that place, they begat children and grew into tribes. Those who sprang from Qiyān were called Qiyāt and those who descended from Takūz were called Darlgīn. No account is forthcoming of the descendants of Qiyān while they were in Irganaqūn—a period of about 2,000 years. Presumably in that place and age reading and writing were not practised. After the lapse of about 2000 years and in the last period of Nū<u>sh</u>īrwān's[1] reign, the Qiyāt and Darlgīn desired to leave the place, as it was not large enough for them. A mountain which was a mine of iron barred their way at the beginning. Able minds devised deer-skin bellows (*gawazn*, perhaps elk) and with these they melted that iron mountain and made a way. Then they rescued their country from the hands of the Tātārs and others, by the sword, and contriving vigour, and became firmly seated on the throne of success and world-rule. From the circumstance that in four[2] thousand years previous to this event, (*i.e.*, the emigration from Irganaqūn) there

[1] Nūshīrwān, a king of Persia, celebrated for his justice, reigned 531-579 A.D. Muḥammad congratulated himself on having been born (578 A.D.) in his reign.

[2] I do not understand the principle of this calculation. Yuldūz <u>Kh</u>ān, under whom the Mu<u>gh</u>uls emigrated from Irganaqūn, is the 29th ancestor, reckoning from Adam, and the total of 28 must be made up of 25 who lived previous to the flight to Irganaqūn *plus* three, *viz.*, Qiyān, Tīmūr Tā<u>sh</u> and Mangalī, who are the only three denizens of that settlement whose names have been preserved. The period after the exodus (cir. 579 A.D.) up to the date of A.F.'s writing, was about 1,000 years, and in it there were 25 rulers including Akbar. But how do calculators reckon, upon these data, that the number of ancestors who lived in Irganaqūn for 2,000 years, was 25? One would rather expect the figure 50. But perhaps the calculation is based on lives twice as long as later ones. (Gibbon Cap. 42n.) Apparently it is roughly based on a progressive diminution of the period of human life. A.F. reckons that 7,000 years more or less,

were twenty-eight lofty ancestors and twenty-five in the millenium after it, sagacious calculators conjecture that during these two thousand years (spent in Irganaqūn) there were twenty-five ancestors.

Be[1] it remembered that Mughulistān is to the eastward and far from civilization. Its circuit is seven or eight months' journey. On the east, its boundary extends to Cathay (Khiṭā) and on the west, to the country of the Aīghūrs; on the north, it touches Qargaz and Salīkā (? Kirghiz and Selenga) and on the south, it adjoins Tibet. The food of its people is the produce of hunting and fishing and their clothing the skins and fur of wild and tame animals.

### Tīmūr Tāsh.

Tīmūr Tāsh is of the auspicious stock of Qiyān. He was exalted by sovereignty and command.

---

elapsed from the birth of Adam to 40th Akbar (1596). From Adam to the death of Īl Khān, 4,000 years are counted, and in this period, were 25 generations. (A.F. speaks of 28, but this is inclusive of Īl Khān's son, Qiyān and Tīmūr Tāsh and Mangalī Khwāja, *viz.*, the grandfather and father of the Yuldūz who came out from Irgānaqūn). In the thousand years between the emigration and 40th Akbar, there were also 25 generations, and so, apparently, it was calculated that for the intervening 2,000 years (required to make up the 7,000) there must have been 25 generations. In other words, there were 4,000 years in which the length of a generation was 160 years, 2,000 in which it was 80 and 1,000 in which it was 40. I do not, however, know what authority A.F. had for his 2,000 years. "The tradition of the Mughuls," says Gibbon (Cap. 42n.) "of "the 450 years which they passed in "the mountains, agrees with the "Chinese periods of the History of "the Huns and Turks. "(De Guignes ".Tom. I, Par. II, 376), and of the 20 "generations from their restoration to Gingis." (Cingīz Khān). Howorth (I, 35) puts the period at 400 years. Rashīdu-d-dīn mentions a period of 2,000 years, but this is the interval from the destruction of Īl Khān and the Mughuls by the Tātārs up to the date of Rashīdu-d-din's writing, consequently the former event occurred about 700 B.C. D'Ohsson says (I, Cap. II, 21) that according to Mughul traditions, their defeat by the Tātārs occurred 2,000 years before the birth of Cingīz Khān. (Jan. 1155 A.D.) D'Herbélot (art. Genghiz Khān) says that the Mughuls remained in Irganaqūn for several generations, and that the period was over 1,000 years. None of these statements supports A.F.'s chronology. Possibly he wrote one and not two thousand.

[1] This description is taken from *Ẓafarnāma, Prolegomena.*

### Mangalī Khwāja.

Mangalī Khwāja is the worthy son of Tīmūr Tāsh. He exalted the crown of dominion and auspiciousness and possessed the dīvān of power and justice.

### Yuldūz Khān.

Yuldūz Khān was the high-thoughted successor of Mangalī
Khwāja who at the coming out of the Qiyāt and Darlgīn was the 64
chief and leader. From the time of Qiyān, his (Qiyān's) descendants had reigned generation after generation in Irganaqūn. Yuldūz Khān, by the help of the fortunate star of his dominion, gradually emerged from the horizon and civilized the tribes of the Mughuls. He was powerful and magnanimous and among the Mughul families, he is counted of good blood and fashion who can trace his origin up to Yuldūz Khān.

### Jūīna[1] Bahādur.

Jūīna Bahādur was the worthy son of Yūldūz Khān and when the cup of his father's years was full, sate on the throne of world-government.

---

[1] Also spelled Jūbīna and Cūbīna. For further information regarding the Muḥammadan accounts of the descendants of Japheth, I beg to refer the reader to the full and interesting note of Major Raverty which begins at p. 869 of his translation of the *Ṭabaqāt-i-nāṣirī*.

## CHAPTER XV.

### HER MAJESTY ĀLANQUWĀ, THE CUPOLA OF CHASTITY AND VEIL OF PURITY.

Whatever, God, the wondrous Creator, brings forth from the hidden places of secrecy to the light of manifestation, is attended by extraordinary circumstances. But the sons of men fail to perceive these, from the heedlessness which has its props and foundation in fulness of life and the wrappage of worldliness. Were it not so, man would be ever standing at gaze and not applying himself to action. Hence the world-adorning Initiator hides most of the wonders of His power from the sight of mortals, but lest they should be entirely shut out from the extraordinary spectacle of the Divine decrees, He raises this veil from before a few of the holy hiding places of His secrets. And again, after much seeing, a heedlessness which fate has made a constituent of their natures, causes this very sight to become a screen against perception. And again[1] after that, the universal benevolence of the Deity, for a thousand diverse purposes—one being the instruction of the minds of negligent mortals,—brings forth a new creation, and raising the veils and curtains somewhat, displays a wondrous picture.

The extraordinary story of her Majesty is a case in point. She was the happy-starred daughter (*dukhtar-i-qudsī-akhtar*) of Jūīna Bahādur of the Qiyāt tribe and Barlās[3] family. Her physical and

[1] The passage is obscure, but I think the sense is that men get accustomed to the wonderful and so their very seeing becomes blindness. The B.M. No. 5610 (Halhed's) omits the *az* after *bisyār*, thus making *ghaflatī* (heedlessness) the nominative. I have adopted this reading as I think it makes the better sense.

[2] Khāfī Khān Bib. Ind. I, 7*n*. According to one copy of the *Ẓafarnāma—Prolegomena*, Jūbīna was a woman and a daughter of Yuldūz Khān.

[3] Erdmann says she belonged to the tribe of Qūrulas قورلس. See also *Tārīkh-i-rashīdī*, Ney Elias and Ross 51, where the author states that she

mental beauty went on increasing from her earliest years, until by loftiness of thought and sublimity of genius, she became the Unique of the Age, and by acknowledgment of friends and foes, relatives and strangers, was magnanimous, pious, and a lover of wisdom. The lights of theosophy shone from her countenance, the Divine secrets were manifested on her forehead. She sat secluded behind the screen of chastity and abode in the privy chamber of meditation on the Unity, was a theatre of holy epiphanies and an alighting-stage of Divine emanations. When she arrived at maturity, she was, according to the custom of princes and the practice of great ones of Church and State, given in marriage to Z̤ūbūn Bīyān, king of Mug͟hulistān and her own cousin and (thus) they joined that unique pearl of purity with a temporal ruler. As he was not her match, he
hastened to annihilation and her Majesty Ālanquwā who was the repose 65
(*āsāyis͟h*) of the spiritual world, became likewise the ornament (*ārāyis͟h*) of the temporal world and, applying herself of necessity to outward acts, she became the sovereign of her tribe (*alūs*).

One night this divinely radiant one was reposing on her bed, when suddenly a glorious[1] light cast a ray into the tent and entered the mouth and throat of that fount of spiritual knowledge and glory. The cupola of chastity became pregnant by that light in the same way as did her Majesty (*Ḥaẓrat*) Miryam[2] (Mary) the daughter of 'Imrān (Amram).

Praised be the God who maintained holy human souls from Adam down to this child of light, in prosperity and adversity, abundance and want, victory and defeat, pleasure and pain, and other contrasted conditions, one after another, and made them partakers of emanations of the holy light. Before this holy light made its fortunate alighting from high heaven, Qiyān was withdrawn from the associations of climates and cities and supported in a solitary wilderness, and many ancestors were given to her (Ālanquwā), generation after

---

was a Kurkluk (?). In B.M. No. 7628 of Ras͟hīdu-d-dīn's great work, 456*b*, the name of the tribe is written قورولس Qūrūlas. Barlās then must be a copyist's error.

[1] Cf. K͟hāfī K͟hān I, 8. He says the light was like the sun's disk, and that it entered Ālanquwā's mouth which was open (from astonishment apparently, at the spectacle).

[2] The Virgin Mary whom Muḥammad calls the daughter of 'Amrān, apparently because he confounded her with the sister of Moses.

generation, for two thousand years in these Highlands (*kōhistān*), thereby purifying her and familiarizing her with the land of holiness and converting the human element into a collection of all degrees, Divine and earthly. When the spiritual preparation was complete, Yuldūz Khān was brought—for the ends of Divine wisdom—from the mountains to the city, and seated on a throne, till the turn of the holy series reached her Majesty Ālanquwā and that divine light, after passing without human instrumentality, through many eminent saints and sovereigns, displayed itself gloriously in the external world. That day[1] (*viz.*, of Ālanquwā's conception) was the beginning of the manifestation of his Majesty, the king of kings, who after passing through divers stages was revealed to the world from the holy womb of her Majesty Miryam-makānī for the accomplishment of things visible and invisible.

It needs a Plato of abstract thought to comprehend the saying "The Lord[2] of Time (*zamān*) remains behind the veil whilst Time's products (*zamāniyān*), *i.e.*, mortals, rend it with outward sorrow and inward anguish."

---

[1] I should have been inclined to read *nūr*, light here, instead of *rōz*, day, but all the MSS. seem to have *rōz*.

[2] I do not fully understand this passage. It seems to be a quotation, a sort of Sybilline utterance, and is naturally dark, since we are told that it needs the utmost meditation of a Plato to understand it. The Lucknow editor says the meaning is that a master of wisdom should study with might and main how the veil may be rent for suffering humanity, but I do not see that this sense can be got out of the words. The translation which I have given is the result of a good deal of reflection and of a consultation with my friend Mr. Beames. Mr. Beames has given me the following note. "Though the construction "of the sentence is somewhat harsh "and irregular, yet the general mean- "ing of the passage seems clear from "the context." "A.F. starts (Luck- "now ed. 52 1, 2) by the amazing "assertion that the beginning of "the manifestation of Akbar, dated "from the day of Ālanquwā's "miraculous conception by the Sun "and continued through many gene- "rations till he ultimately saw the "light from the womb of Miryam- "makānī."

"Then it evidently occurs to him "that this is rather a hard saying "and that some one might object. "'How could Akbar be conceived in "'the womb of Ālanquwā, seeing "'that she lived so many centuries "'before him?' To this he replies "that only a sage who devotes him- "self to profound thought and medi-

But now returning to the beginning of the story, I repeat that the holy abode of that cupola of chastity was continually at auspicious times and seasons, made resplendent by the brilliance of that

---

"tation can understand this mystical "saying, *viz.*, that while ordinary "mortals rend the veil (*parda-dar*), "*i.e.*, are born, in due course, Akbar "was miraculously held back from "being born, he remained behind "the veil or, in courtier-like phrase, "adorning the veil (*parda-ārāī*)—for "many ages till his full time arrived. "The passage may therefore be "translated as follows:—

"It requires a Plato of deep meditation to accept this statement "with the ear of his understanding, "that the Prince of the Age is in "the condition of adorning the veil, "while (ordinary) mortals rend the "veil with visible pain and inward "groaning."

"The grammatical awkwardness "lies in A.F.'s putting *ast* after "*parda-dar* instead of *and* (they are) "which would agree better with the "plural subject *zamāniyān*; and in "leaving out *ast* after *ārai*. But "this kind of construction is not "unusual. The substitution of the "uncouth phrase *dar parda-ārāī* 'in "veil adorning-ness' for the simpler "*parda-ārā*, 'veil adorning' is per-"haps due to a desire to play upon "the two meanings of *dar* (1), in "and (2) tearing; contrasting the "lot of Akbar who remained for "some generations miraculously re-"served behind the veil, *i.e.*, in the "womb of successive females, with "the lot of ordinary mortals who "when they are conceived and de-"veloped, rend the veil, *i.e.*, are born; "a contrast which, as he justly "observes, it takes a Plato, at least, "to grasp."

I have adopted Mr. Beames' note with some modifications. My idea is that A.F. means to say it is so extraordinary that the Lord of Time or Prince of the Age should remain behind the veil (*i.e.*, continue unborn), while wretched mortals come into existence to their own loss as well as to the detriment of the epoch, that only a Plato can comprehend the mystery or final cause thereof. Perhaps A.F.'s thought is illustrated by the words of St. Paul, "For we know the whole Creation groaneth and travaileth in pain together until now." See also Cap. XI where A.F. speaks of <u>Kh</u>āqānī, a poet of a former age, vainly longing for the appearance of a *Ṣāḥib-i-waqt*, a Lord of the Age or Time.

I think too that he, as usual, has a double meaning, and that he plays upon the double sense of *parda-dar* which means both to rend a veil and to be dissolute, thus corresponding to the double meaning of the Latin *profanus*. I have consulted a number of MSS. for variants but without success. Several *e.g.*, I, O. 564 and Add. B.M. No. 4944 have *parda-dōst*, veil-loving (? loving blindness). But this seems no improvement. *Parda-dar* is probably right as enabling A.F. to take advantage of the two words *dar* fr. *darīdan*, to tear, and *dar*, within, and to contrast *dar parda-ārāī* with *parda-dar*.

light and from time to time, her moral and material nature brightened by its effulgence. Those who by a soaring flight on the wings of genius, have passed beyond the worship of materiality and can behold the Causer, do not think occurrences like this strange or wonderful in the wide domain of Divine power, and the incredulity of worshippers of routine and superficiality is of no weight in their esteem. As for those who have remained among secondary causes and have not advanced their foot further and cannot, by auspicious guidance, forego superficial computations, they too do not abide by their first principles, (*i.e.*, are not consistent). For instance they admit there was a child without father or mother, *viz.*, the first man or Adam, and they accept a child without a mother, whom they call Eve. Why then not admit a child without a father? Especially when they are fully assured of such an occurrence in the case of Jesus and Mary.

*Verse.*

If you listen to the tale of Mary,
Believe the same of Ālanquwā.

66 But the world-fashioning Creator who from their inception brings all his works to their final accomplishment, effects His purposes by means of the contradictions and oppositions of His beautiful and His terrible Attributes (*asmā, lit.* names). Accordingly there is a section of mankind of lofty intelligence, right judgment, exalted thought, sublime power and correct thinking, whom He hath placed apart and whose condition He advances day by day. So also there is a multitude of human shapes, purblind, feeble of apprehension, crooked in thought and of evil imaginations, void of usefulness, whom He hath marked out and whom He keeps in a state of perturbation. And although the cup of His designs may be filled in either of these ways, yet there are many contrivances involved in the combination. Accordingly darkness is united with light, bad fortune with good, adversity with prosperity and the wicked and black-hearted are always putting forward stones of stumbling. But soon they are disgraced spiritually and temporarily and depart to the street of annihilation.

This brilliant event is an illustration of the above, for when such a wondrous thing occurred, evil thoughts arose in the hearts of the short-sighted dullards and worshippers of externals who had no share in real merit and were alien from the grace of Divine knowledge. That enthroned vestal (Ālanquwā), out of her perfect benevolence, did not desire that these blind wretches should remain caught in the slough of this thought and so apprized her nobles of the matter. She intimated that "if any dullard or simpleton, unaware of the wondrous power of God and the forms of Divine decrees, fall into the misfortune of evil thoughts and sully his mind's mirror with the rust of wicked imagination, he will for ever and ever abide in distress and loss. It is better then that I clear the courts of their intellect of such confusion. For this purpose, it is necessary that awakened-hearted truth-knowers and trusty persons of sincerity watch by night around the tent, so that the darkness of suspicion and doubt caused by the blackness of their hearts may by the light of Divine events and the beholding of hidden radiances, be changed into illumination and that evil thoughts may pass from their turbid minds."

Accordingly several wakeful and prudent, keen-sighted watchers were placed around the tent and like night-burning stars, they closed not their eyes. Suddenly in the middle of the night,—which is the time for the descent of Divine mercies,—a shining light, like bright moonlight,—just as the lady, the curtain of chastity, had said,—came down from on high and entered the tent. A cry was raised by the watchers. For a little while, people were stunned and then their vain thoughts and evil imaginations were exorcised.

When the period of pregnancy was fulfilled, Ālanquwā bore three noble sons. The first was Būqūn Qanqī from whom the Qanqīn tribe is descended; the second was Yūsuqī Sāljī from whom the Sāljīūts are sprung. The third was Būzanjar Qāān. The descendants 67
of these nobly-born ones are called Nairūn, *i.e.*, light-produced and are considered to be the noblest class among the Mug͟huls.

### Būzanjar Qāān.

Būzanjar Qāān is the ninth ancestor of Cingīz K͟hān and Qarācār Nūyān, the fourteenth of his Majesty, the Lord of Conjunction, and the twenty-second[1] of his Majesty, the king of kings. When he came to years of discretion, he adorned the sovereignty of Tūrān,

---

[1] So Text, but apparently it should be twenty-first.

and the chiefs of the Tâtâr and Turk tribes, etc., who were like satraps (*Mulūk-i-ṭawā'if, i.e.,* the Arsacidæ) bound the girdle of service on their waists. He composed the distractions of the time by the vigour of his administration, distributed justice and benevolence and, for a prolonged period, soothed and adorned the world by his nobility and wisdom. He was contemporary with Abū Muslim Marwazī.[1] When his existence closed, there remained two sons, Būqâ and Tūqabâ (? Tūqtā).

### Būqā Khān.

Būqā Khān was the eldest son of Būzanjar Qāān and the eighth ancestor of Cingīz Khān and Qarācār Nūyān. He ascended the throne in accordance with his father's testament and adorned the royal dīvān by justice and equity. He devised new regulations for world-ruling and world-subduing and framed the code of the Khāqâns of the world. He so carried himself towards his subjects that one and all were rendered happy by him.

### Dūtamīn Khān.

Zūtamīn[2] Khān was the upright son of Būqā Khān. When the father perceived his own life passing away, he appointed him his heir and successor. Zūtamīn exerted himself in controlling the administration and in increasing the prosperity of the kingdom. He had nine sons, and on his death, their mother Manūlūn who was unique in wisdom and management, went into retirement and devoted herself to their upbringing. One day, the Jalāirs who belong to the Darlgīn tribe, laid an ambush[3] and killed Manūlūn and eight of her sons. Qāidū Khān, the ninth son, had gone off to China (Mācīn) in order to become his cousin's[4] son-in-law and so escaped. With the

[1] Abū Muslim 'Abdu-r-raḥmān, son of Muḥammad and called the missionary of the 'Abbasides, *i.e.*, *Ṣāḥib-i-da'wat* or author of the call of the 'Abbasides, (Gibbon cap. 52.) and also called جریان Jaryān. He was a general of the 'Abbasides and the origin of their power but was put to death 136 H. 753 by Khalīf Manṣūr. (Mas'ūdī, Meynard. VI, 58, 176, *etc.*) Merv was one of the four chief cities of Khurāsān and its inhabitants were called Marwazī. (D'Herbélot art. Merou.)

[2] The Text follows the MSS. which spell the name in two ways.

[3] The *Shajratu-l-atrāk* has a long story as to the cause of these murders.

[4] The *Shajrat* makes Mācīn his grand-uncle's son, *viz.*, son of Tūqtā or Tūqabā the brother of Būqā who was Qāidū's grandfather.

help of Macīn, the Jalāirs were brought to rue their folly and induced to put to death seventy men who had been engaged in the murder of Manūlūn and her children. They also bound their wives and children and sent them to Qāidū Khān who marked their foreheads with the token of servitude. Their descendants remained for a lengthened period in the prison of slavery.

### Qāidū Khān.

Qāidū Khān after many adventures, sat upon the thone of sovereignty and supervised the world's civilization.[1] He founded 68
cities and had a following of many clans. He warred with the Jalāirs and firmly established his power. When he passed away, he left three sons.

### Bāyasanghar Khān.

Bāyasanghar Khān was the eldest son and the unique of his Age for administrative capacity and for the management of subjects and soldiers. He sat upon the throne agreeably to his father's testament.

### Tūmana Khān.

Tūmana was the worthy son of Bāyasanghar Khān. When his father was departing from this world, he made over the kingdom to him. The dīvān of sovereignty and world-rule gained lustre during his reign. He graced it by his courage and wisdom, and augmented the glory of the Age by his magnanimity and bearing of burdens. By strength of arm and vigour of mind, he increased his hereditary kingdom by adding to it, much of Mongolia (Mughulistān) and Turkistān. There was not his like for might and prestige in all Turkistān. He had two wives by one of whom he had seven sons and by the other twins. One of the twins was named Qabal and was the great-grandfather[2] of Cingīz Khān and the other was named Qācūlī.

---

1 The *Shajrat* says he dug a canal.

2 Though he was only the third in ascent from Cingīz Khān, the latter was fourth in succession for Qūbila, the son of Qabal was succeeded by his brother Bartān Bahādur and he by his son Yasūkā the father of Cingīz. This accounts for Cingīz being the fourth star which emerged from Qabal's bosom. (See *infra*).

## QĀCŪLĪ BAHĀDUR.

Qācūlī Bahādur is the eighth ancestor of his Majesty the Lord of Conjunction (Tīmūr). He was a theatre of the lights of dominion and a station of the impressions of auspiciousness. The refulgence of greatness radiated from his countenance and the glory of fortune shone from his brow. One night he beheld in a dream [1] a shining star emerging from Qabal Khān's breast. It rose to the zenith and then was extinguished. This happened thrice. The fourth time, a wondrous bright star arose from his (Qabal's) breast and took the horizons with its light. The rays thereof reached and enkindled other stars, and each of them lighted up a region, so that when the globe of light disappeared, the world still remained illuminated. He awoke from his vision, and loosed the bird of thought that he might interpret the strange augury. Suddenly sleep again [2] overcame him and he saw seven stars rise in succession from his own breast and disappear The eighth time, a mighty star appeared and lighted up the whole world. Then some small stars branched off from it so that every corner of the universe was illuminated. When the great star became invisible, these other stars shone forth and the universe remained bright as before. At daybreak, Qācūlī Bahādur reported the occurrence to his honoured father Tūmana Khān. The latter
69 gave the interpretation that from Qabal Khān there would come three princes who should sit on the throne of the Khānāte and be lords of lands. But the fourth time, a king would come after these, who should bring most of the earth under his sway and should have children, each of whom would govern a region. From Qācūlī would come seven dominant descendants, bearing on their brows the dia-

---

[1] Khāfī Khān (I, 9) makes each brother have a dream but says that the stars seen by Qācūlī were less bright than those beheld by the elder brother Qabal. Apparently he either rejects the application to Timur or holds that he was descended from the elder brother (through Cingīz Khān). D'Herbélot has a full account of the dream. (Art. Toumanah Khān). See also Sharafu-d-dīn's *Zafarnāma*, (*Prolegomena*), and Bābar and Humāyūn, Erskine I, 70 and *Shajratu-l-atrāk* (Miles). There is a good deal about the dream and the covenant between the brothers in the so-called Memoirs of Timur.

[2] There is a play on the word *bās*, the other meaning being "the hawk "(*bās*) of his sleep snatched at" the bird of thought.

dem of primacy and the crown of rule. The eighth time a descendant would arise who should exhibit world-wide sovereignty and exercise sway and chiefship over all mankind. From him would come descendants who should each rule a division of the earth.

When Tūmana Khān had made an end of his interpretation, the two brothers, in accordance with his orders, made a mutual league and covenant to the effect that the throne of the Khān should be committed to Qabal Khān and that Qācūlī should be Commander-in-Chief and Prime Minister. And it was established that the descendants of each should, generation after generation, observe this arrangement. They drew up a solemn compact (*'ahd-nāma*) to this effect in Uighūr (Turkish) characters and each brother put his seal to it and it was styled the "*Āltamgha* of Tūmana Khān." The illustrious ancestors of his Majesty, the king of kings,—who is the final cause of the series having been set in motion—were, from Adam to Tūmana Khān, distinguished by absolute sovereignty and by independent sway, and so established the throne of justice. Some members of the glorious company also attained to the spiritual world and so were, both outwardly and inwardly, plenipotent, as hath been set forth in ancient chronicles.

The Divine strategy—in providing for the apparition of the consummation of all degrees, spiritual and temporal, by the intervention of so many rulers of the visible and invisible worlds,—was awaiting the birth-time of his Majesty, the king of kings,—for, as being the quintessence of humanity, his robe must be gorgeously embroidered,—and so was day by day accomplishing the preparations. Hence in order to completeness and to cause appreciation of the glory of service and the sweets of management, Qācūlī Bahādur was arrayed in the disguise of vicegerency (*wakālat*) so that the grades of this status too might come within the purview of this glorious company and a provision of every stage of development be accumulated for his Majesty, the king of kings. Thus, notwithstanding the guiding power, dexterity, greatness and high-mindedness of Qācūlī Bahādur, Qabal Khān became the heir. Though in the external point of age,—which is not regarded by the wise,—he was greater, yet in reality, the controlling power of the Divine wisdom was engaged in completing the work (of preparation for Akbar). When Tūmana Khān's star set in the west, Qabal Khān became established on the throne of rule and Qācūlī Bahādur, in accordance with that fidelity to his promise which is the material of eternal bliss, undertook with concord and singleness of aim, the management of the State in conformity with the rules of loving-mindedness and king-making.

And when Qabal Khān went from this world of troubled existence to the peaceful home of nothingness, Qūbila[1] Khān who out of six sons was the one worthy of the throne and crown, obtained the
70 sovereignty, and Qācūlī Bahādur remained engaged in the same high office of Commander-in-Chief, observed his compact and, by help of wisdom and courage, carried on the affairs of the State. Qūbila Khān with the support of such a grandee, who was possessed both of God-given wisdom and a world-conquering sword, took vengeance for his brother from Āltān Khān (*i.e.*, the Golden Khān) the ruler of Cathay and having made great wars which were masterpieces of men of might, inflicted a heavy defeat on the army of Cathay.

The abstract of this affair is as follows :—The rulers of Cathay always were in dread of this noble race and always kept on friendly terms with it. When Āltān Khān was confirmed on the throne of Cathay, he became much alarmed at hearing of the bravery and ability of Qabal Khān. By means of skilful embassies, he established concord between them to such an extent that he invited Qabal Khān to Cathay. The Khān with the sincerity and honesty which are the characteristics of this family, made over the care of the kingdom to Qācūlī Bahādur and went to Cathay. His reception was very friendly and after indulging in pleasure and enjoyment,[2] he set his face homewards. Some of Āltān Khān's grandees of base and ignoble nature, disturbed his mind with improper words so that he repented having said adieu to Qabal Khān and sent a message to recall him. Qabal Khān saw through the plot and replied that as he had left in an auspicious hour, it would not be proper to return.[3] This enraged Āltān Khān who sent troops with orders to bring him back by hook or by crook. Qabal Khān caused the officer in command to alight

[1] Text, Qūīla, but a note says that the *Ẓafarnāma* (*Prolegomena*) has Qūbila and this appears the correct reading.

[2] The *Prolegomena* l.c. and the *Shajrat* say that Qabal got drunk and insulted Āltān.

[3] *Prolegomena* l.c. has *Shagūn na mīdānam* "I do not regard it as of good omen (to return)."

at the house of a friend of his named Sāljūqī who had his dwelling by the way-side, and agreed to turn back. Sāljūqī secretly told him that to return was not advisable and that he had a swift and enduring horse which no one could come up with and that the proper[1] thing for Qabal Khān was to mount this horse and get away as quickly as possible from this dangerous neighbourhood.

Qabal Khān acted on this advice and getting on the horse, proceeded to his own camp (*yurt*). When the Cathay messengers heard this, they pursued him with all rapidity but did not come up with him till he was in his own camp. Qabal Khān seized these wicked people and put them to death. Meanwhile his eldest child Ūqīn[2] Barqāq who was matchless for beauty, was keeping company with the gazelles on the borders of the wilderness when a party of Tātārs surprised him and took him to Āltān Khān. The Khān put this delicate fawn[3] to death[4] in satisfaction for those dog-souled wolves.

When Qūbila Khān who was the second son, came to the throne, he collected an army and marched against Āltān Khān to revenge his brother's[5] death. A great battle ensued and the Cathāians suffered
a sore defeat and were plundered of their property. 71

When the onset of the army of death fell upon Qūbila Khān, his honoured brother Bartān Bahādur, was established on the throne, agreeably to the counsels of the nobles. He preserved the institutions (*yāsāq, i. e. yāsā*) of his father and brother and as in his time, he

---

1 The meaning apparently is that when Qabal was on his way back with Āltān's officer he got the latter to halt at the house of a friend by the wayside. The *Prolegomena* (l.c.), tells the story somewhat differently, stating that Qabal evaded his pursuers by entering the house of a friend but was inclined to give himself up and return with them, *etc.*

2 The *izāfat* of the Text after *kalān* is wrong. See D'Herbélot art. Kil Khān and *Prolegomena* l.c.

3 *Ghazāl-i-shīrnizhād*, "a milk-born gazelle." Cf. Dryden's milk-white hind.

4 It is said that Āltān nailed or sewed him to a wooden ass in revenge for the death of his messengers. One account says he was hunting but A.F.'s words seem to imply that he was too young for this, that he was, as it were, a fawn himself and so, sporting with the gazelles. The *Prolegomena* seems to say that the child had strayed into the plain.

5 The word *birādar* is loosely used and for the sake of assonance with *bahādur*. Qācūlī was really uncle of Bartān.

had no rival who could contend with him in war, the title Khān was marked in people's mouths by that of Bahādur and they stamped the coin of his courage with this awe-augmenting appellative. At this period, Qācūlī Bahādur who was at once a life-sacrificing brother and a Commander-in-Chief Bahādur, departed to the eternal world.

### Īradam-cī Barlās.

Īradam-cī Barlās was the upright son of Qācūlī Bahādur and was distinguished for his wisdom and military talent. On his father's death, the patent (*tughrā*) of the Commander-in-Chiefship was exalted by the entry of his name and he managed affairs according to the rules which his father had made illustrious. He was the first who bore the title of Barlās, the meaning of which fine word is brave and of noble lineage. The whole Barlās clan traces its origin[1] from him.

When Bartān Bahādur died, Yesugai[2] Bahādur, the third of his four sons, and father of Cingīz Khān, and who was adorned with the cuirass of wisdom and the helmet of courage, placed the crown of the Khānate on his head and graced the throne of world-sway. At this time Īradam-cī Barlās died, leaving twenty-nine sons.

### Sūghū Cīcan (The Wise).

Sūghū Cīcan was distinguished among the noble sons of Īradam-cī Barlās for courage, wisdom and administrative ability. He was also the eldest son. He took the place of his honoured father; ostensibly he was Commander-in-Chief, in reality he was sovereign. Yesugai Bahādur, by the world-adorning advice of Sūghū Cīcan marched against the Tātārs and trod under-foot their glory and their grandeur. When he had, by God's help and the might of good

---

[1] If so, it seems an anachronism to speak of Ālanquwā as belonging to the Barlās family in the way A.F., (according to the MSS.,) has done in his account of that lady. And indeed there seems no doubt that Barlās is a clerical error for Qārūlās which is the word in *Rashīdu-d-dīn.* The Text has *lafẓ-i-mu'allā* "lofty word," but Quatremère (*Rashīdu-d-dīn* 250n.) thinks that *mu'allā* is a clerical error for *mughalī* and translates "un homme brave et d'une naissance illustre;" and adds "le mot *barlās* dans la langue des Mongoles désignait un homme brave et d'une naissance illustre."

[2] Text, Bīsūkā, but a note states that many MSS. have Yasūkā. It is Yasūkā in the *Prolegomena* l.c., Yesugai or Jesugai seems to be the correct form.

fortune, overcome the Tātārs, he set out for Dīlūn[1] Būldaq. When he arrived there, his chief wife (Khātūn) Ūlūn Anaga[2] whom he had 72
left pregnant, gave birth to a noble son on 20th *zī-l-qa'da* 549[3] (26th Jan., 1155), in the cycle-year of the Hog (*Tankūz*). Yesugai Bahādur called him Temūcīn.[4] Sūghū Cīcan, who possessed lofty intelligence and exalted understanding, told Yesugai Bahādur that by the secrets of calculation and the favourable aspects of the heavens, it was clear that this was the very star which had emerged the fourth time from Qabal Khān's breast.

## Cingīz[5] Khān.

Though in the noble line of his Majesty, the king of kings, which in this book of Divine praise is the starting-point[6] of utterance, it is unnecessary to mention Temūcīn who is a branch of the holy tree, yet as he was a ray of the divine light of Ālanquwā, a brief account of him is indispensable. The horoscope of Temūcīn was Libra and the seven planets[7] were in it. The Dragon's

---

[1] Text, Dīlūn Yuldaq. Howorth (I, 47) says the place is called Doligun Buldagha, near the Onon by Ssanang Ssetzen and that it is still known by the same name, *viz.*, Delūn Boldaq. It is in northern Mongolia, near the Russian frontier and on the right bank of the Onon. D'Herbélot art. Genghiz Khān calls it Diloun Joloun.

[2] Called by Hammer Ūlūn Ike and by Erdmann Ulun Egeh. Apparently the Turkish pronunciation of *anaga* is *enegeh*. The *a* is not long.

[3] Chinese historians put his birth seven years later, *viz.*, 1162 A.D. for they say he died in 1227 at the age of 66 and not of 72, as Muhammadans state. D'Herbélot, Supplément (Visdelou) art. Genghiz Khān. Hammer-Purgstall (56) prefers the date 1155.

[4] Howorth, Temudjin and Temujin. The word is said to mean "finest iron." It may be noted here that the best biography of Cingīz appears to be Prof. Franz von Erdmann's Temudschin der Unerschütterliche. (Leipsic, 1862.) There is a Chinese Life of Cingīz trs. by Prof. R. R. Douglas, Lond., 1877.

[5] Gibbon, Zingis; Howorth, Jingis.

[6] Meaning, I suppose, that the book is called the *Akbarnāma*.

[7] *i.e.*, the five known to the ancients *plus* the Sun and Moon. Their conjunction is supposed to indicate a cataclysm. (D'Herbélot art. Keran). According to the *Habību-s-siyar*, the seven planets were in conjunction in Cancer—the horoscope of the world—at the time of the Deluge. See History of the Golden Horde, Hammer-Purgstall, 75 *n.*, for statement of position of five of the planets on 6th Jan., 1155, *i.e.*, shortly before Temūcīn's birth.

Head[1] was in the Third House and the Dragon's Tail[1] in the Ninth. But some say that in 581[2] (1185), when he became head of the Nairūn tribe and family, the seven planets were in conjunction in Libra.

## Qarācār Nūyān.

Qarācār Nūyān was the noble son of Sūg͟hū Cījan and was of kingly mind and princely[3] bearing. In the year of the Hog 562 (1167), Yesugai Bahādur died and in the same year, Temūcīn became thirteen and Sūg͟hū Cījan, the centre of the sovereignty and administration and leader of the armies, marched nearly contemporaneously with this, to the camp of annihilation. Qarācār[4] Nūyān was then of tender age. The Nairūn tribe left Temūcīn and joined the Tāījīuts[5] so that Temūcīn was in difficulties and entangled in misfortunes. At length, by heaven's aid, he was rescued from those whirlpools and terrible dangers and waged war with the Jāmūqa, Tāījūt, Qanqarāt, Jalāīr and other tribes. When he was over thirty, he became head of his own clan and family (the Nairūn). On account of the opposition of various rulers of Turkistān, he went in his fortieth year, by the advice of Qarācār Nūyān to Āvang[6] K͟hān, the chief of the Kerāyat tribe and who had an old friendship with Yesugai Bahādur. Temūcīn did good service for him and displayed pre-eminent excellence. His favour and intimacy with him and the loftiness of his rank came

---

[1] Anabibazon and Katabibazon. They are evil influences. The Third House is that of brethren and short journeys. D'Herbélot says that Libra which is regarded by us as the Sign of Justice, is considered by Orientals to be that of winds and tempests.

[2] I do not find this date in any of the lives of Cingīz K͟hān. He assumed the name of Cingīz, which apparently means the Powerful or Unshakeable, in 599 (1202). The period 581 seems again referred to a little lower where we are told that Cingīz became head of his tribe when over thirty. A.F.'s date does not differ greatly from the 1187 given by Marco Polo as that of Cingīz', recognition nor from the 1189 given by Ssanan Ssetzen.

[3] *S͟hahryār-nis͟hān.* Qu. kingmaker.

[4] If A.F.'s other dates are right, Qarācār must have been an infant at this time for,—if he died in 652 at the age of 98,—he must have been some 12 years younger than Cingīz.

[5] Text, Tāljūt and another form is Tānjūt. It seems a different word from Tangūt.

[6] Or Wang,—the Prester John of mediæval writers and travellers D'Herbélot art. *Krit* and Supplement (Vīsdelou) 279. Hammer-Purgstall says Tog͟hril was the proper name of Āvang or Owang.

# NOTE

on page 180, line 4, from bottom of text.

---

The Society's MS. No. D. 29, in Maulavī Ashraf 'Alī's Catalogue, omits the *wāw* between *zamān wa-zamāniyān* of the printed editions, and this appears to me preferable. The passage accordingly runs thus :—

خدیو زمان در پردهآرائی زمانیـــان با درد چشـــم و زحیر باطن پرده در است

the translation would be : "The Lord of Time, for the advancement of timely beings, is in the habit of rending the curtain (*i.e.*, he is born again and again) with pain of the eyes and dolour of the heart."

The Lord of Time is Akbar, or rather the Divine Light conceived by Alanquwā, which had to go through a successive course of births, before it appeared in its final perfection in the person of His Majesty, King Akbar. This was done by him for the benefit of men, for the purpose of improving their condition (*parda-ārāī*). To the act of child-bearing the word *zaḥīr lit.* "pains" directly refers. The pun hardly can be translated. It lies in the fact that Akbar "rends the curtain for the purpose of mending it," both expressions being used in a metaphorical sense.

T. BLOCH,
*Hon. Philol. Sec., A. S. B.*

to such a point that the sweet savour of his sincerity was made fragrant by the pastile of friendship[1] so that the great officers and relatives (of Āvang Khān) became jealous.

Jāmūqa, chief of the Jājarāt tribe, joined with Sankū,[2] the son of Āvang Khān, to speak evil of him and they devised falsehoods against him whereby the heart of Āvang Khān was drawn away from the right path and he began to entertain evil thoughts. Temūcīn became alarmed and escaped from that danger by the counsels and assistance of Qarācār Nūyān. Twice were great battles fought be- 73
tween them in which Temūcīn was victorious.

When in his 49th, or as some say, his 50th year, he, in *Ramaẓān* 599 (May–June 1203), attained the rank of a sovereign and ruler of the world. When three years of his reign and rule had passed But Tengri,[3] a seer of the invisible world and herald of the Divine Court, was inspired to give Temūcīn the title of Cingīz Khān or king of kings. Day by day, the star of his fortune rose higher and higher and year by year, the lightning of his majesty became more vivid. He acquired sway over all Cathay, Khotan, Northern and Southern China (*Cīn ū Mācīn*), the desert of Qibcāq, Saqsīn,[4]

---

[1] According to one account, noticed by D'Herbélot, Cingīz married a daughter of Āvang.

[2] Also Shankū and Shakūn.

[3] Text, Tab Tengri; but I adopt the variant of But Tengri, given also in No. 564. Hammer-Purgstall (65) calls him Buttanri, the son of Itschke and says he was step-brother of Cingīz, being son of Cingīz's mother by her second husband.

[4] Text, سفين Safīn, but the notes give variants, Saqīn and Sabaqīn and the Āīn (Jarrett III. 100, where see note) Saqsīn. It is the Sacassīn mentioned in D'Ohsson. (I. 346 *n.*) "Sacassīn, dit le géographe de Bacu, était une grande ville du pays des Khazares. Sacassīn est à présent submergée." As D'Ohsson remarks it seems connected with the Sakae or Scythians. Apparently it was a place or country near the Caspian and is used by A.F. to indicate the extent of Cingīz' conquests in the West. The *Ẓafarnāma Prolegomena* says, in reference to Cingīz' conquests, that they extended *az ibtidā'i Bulghār ū Saqīn tā intihā'i Cīn ū Saqsīn (?) ū Mācīn* where apparently Saqsīn denotes an eastern country. Vullers *s.v.* Saqsīn, says "*nom. regionis ignotae*" and refers to the *Burhān-i-qāṭi'* and the *Farhang-i-Rashīdī*. The latter says it is a country of Turkistān and quotes a line of Niẓāmī which contains the expression "from Saqsīn to Samarkand."

In 1652 Greaves published two Geographical Tables one by Naṣīru-d-dīn Ṭūsī and the other by Ulugh Bēg. These are in great measure

Bulgaria,[1] Ās,[2] Russia, Ālān,[3] etc. He had four sons, Jūjī, Caghatāī, Ōkadāī, Tūlī. He placed with Jūjī the management of feasts and hunting. Judiciary matters (*yārghū*) and the carrying out of punishment, in which administrative government is involved, were committed to the wisdom of Caghatāī. Government and political matters were assigned to Ōkadāī. The management of military affairs and the protection of the camp were made over to Tūlī.

In the months of 615 (1218), he marched to Transoxiana against Sulṭān Muhammad, king of Khwārizm[4] and the people of that country received the chastisement of capital punishment.

When he had finished the affairs of Transoxiana, he crossed the Amu (Oxus) and turned his world-opening reins towards Bālkh. He despatched Tūlī Khān with a large army to Khurāsān and after conquering Īrān and Tūrān, he came from Bālkh to Ṭāliqān.[5] From thence he went off to put an end to Jalālu-d-dīn Mangbarnī[6] and in

---

identical and perhaps the repetitions in Āīn (Jarrett III. 47 *et seq*), are due to indiscriminate copying from both. In Greaves' Tables, Saqsīn is given in Long. 86° 36′ and Lat. 43° and as belonging to the 5th climate; Bolgar, Long. 90° and Lat. 49° and as belonging to the 7th climate.

Quatremère (Hist. des Mongoles) states that Klaproth has treated at great length of the subject of Saqsīn.

[1] Bular, *i.e.* Bulghār, (Āīn. Jarrett, etc.) III. 103) a town on the Caspian. This is therefore not the European Bulgaria to the west of the Black Sea but Great Bulgaria on the Volga.

[2] Vullers (34*a*) gives Ās as a town in Qibcāk from which the Osseti took their name. But the Ās of the Text appears to be the Crimea or its neighbourhood. See Jarrett III. 102 where it is spelled Aṣ a form not given by Vullers. Quatremère (Hist. des Mongoles, Pref. 70*n*. 87), says "Le mot Ās ou آس désigne les Alains qui portent encore aujour d'hui le nom de *Ossets*."

[3] See Vullers and D'Herb. Ālān is said to be a town in Turkīstān but apparently the Ālān of the Text is the Allan of D'Herbélot which was in the Caucasus and the home of the tribe known as the Alānī, and which occupied country between the Caspian and Black Seas.

[4] The modern Khiva. The citizens were all massacred.

[5] Ṭāliqān, a town in Khurāsān, E. of Bālkh. (Jarrett III, 87). The Khurāsān and Badakhshān Ṭāliqāns seem to be identical. See Howorth's map.

[6] Text, Mankīrnī, but Āīn (II. 204 and Jarrett III. 343) has Mangbarnī or Mankbardī, Jarrett observes that Hammer-Purgstall says it should be written Mankbarnī but that on Jalālu-d-dīn's coins it is Mankbarīn. If as Hammer states, (74) the term means short or flat-nosed (*stumpf-*

c-

*Ramazān*[1] 624 (Aug. 1227), defeated him up to the banks of the Indus. From thence he went to Transoxiana towards his permanent encampment (Karakoram). He died in the year of the Hog which was also that of his birth and accession, on 4th *Ṣafar*[2] 624, in the borders of the country of Tangūt.[3]

Before his death, he directed that when the inevitable event occurred, they should keep it secret until the affair of the people of Tangūt was completed and that there might be no commotion in distant countries. His sons and officers carried out his instructions and took steps to conceal the event till the people of Tangūt had come out[4] and been made the forage of the sword. Then they marched off bearing the body (of Cingīz) in a chest, putting to death every-

---

*näsig*) we should hardly expect to find such a nickname on coins. Vambéry (Hist. of Bukhara, 1342) says the word is Mengberdi, (heaven-sent); Raverty (*Ṭabaqāt-i-naṣīrī*, 285) that it means having a mole on the side of the nose. (See also 299*n.*) *Mang* is given as meaning a mole in Shaw's Vocabulary of Eastern Turkish. The epithet would thus be equivalent to *Khāldar*, and,—a mole being regarded as a beauty,—the sobriquet is honorific.

For an account of the gallant Jalālu-d-dīn see Gibbon Cap. 64 and D'Herbélot art. *Jelaleddin* and Āīn l.c.

[1] This date is wrong as perhaps the copyists might have inferred from the fact that just below Cingīz is described as dying in *Ṣafar*, the 2nd month of 624, whereas *Ramazān* is the ninth. Jalālu-d-dīn's defeat really occurred in *Rajab* 618 (Aug.-Sep. 1221). It was therefore the time of the rains which enhances the splendour of Jalālu-d-dīn's feat in swimming his horse over the Indus.

[2] D'Herbélot, 4th *Ramazān*. This agrees with Howorth and Hammer-Purgstall who also give the corresponding European date as 18th Aug. Apparently A.F. had inadvertently written the date of death as that of the defeat of Jalālu-d-dīn. 4th *Ṣafar* is 24th Jan. (1227). Ṣafar is given in one place by Rashīdu-d-dīn whom A.F. copies. (See Hammer-Purgstall, G. Horde 92 *n.* 4.) But see Erdmann l.c., p. 573.

[3] Text, Tankaqūt. It seems to be the Tunkah of the Āīn (Jarrett III. 98) in 5th climate and belonging to Tashkand. See D'Herbélot art. *Tangat* where it is stated that the Arabs call the town Tanghikunt a form which approaches that in Text. The country is also called Hia. (See Howorth I. 4 on Hia or Tangut). It lies north-west of China and west of the Yellow River. On some modern maps the country is marked as that of the Tangūts. See Supplement (Visdelou, 302), for remarks on Scheidercou and Tamghoul.

[4] They came out under their king Shīdaqū (called by Minhāj, Tingū Khān) to treat with Cingīz who had

body whom they met, so that the news might not be quickly conveyed to the different countries. On 14th *Ramaẓān* of the same year, they brought the body to the great camp and proclaimed the death. They buried Cingīz at the foot of a tree which he had, one day when
74 hunting, approved as a site for his grave. In a short space of time, the branches became so thick that the tomb was hidden by them and no one could ascertain the spot. There is a strange mystery in this which cannot be understood, except by the wisdom of the wise and far-seeing, to wit, that as in life he was under God's protection, so also in death did he come under God's supervision, in order that the short-sighted might not put forth hands of disrespect against the place. Though to take much thought about a tomb is to make one self ridiculous to mankind, yet as rulers have to deal chiefly with the superficial-minded, this providential guarding (of Cingīz' tomb) is a great blessing. And why should not the Divine protection watch over one who was so great that an universe abode in the shade of his guardianship?

Though this great man be in the eyes of the vulgar and even to the *élite,*[1] at first glance, a leading exponent of Divine wrath, yet to the far-reading view of the wise, *élite* of the *élite,* he is an emanation of Divine blessings. For in the kingdom of Divine justice of which human government is a ray, there can be no injustice or oppression, and everything which comes into existence in the world of evil is based on certain spiritual principles, the real nature of which the superficial cannot perceive and which cannot be comprehended save by the intellects of the far-seeing and awakened-hearted.

His years were seventy-two complete and most of the seventy-third had also elapsed. Of them, twenty-five were spent in reigning and conquering. If we look to the dates[2] of his birth and his death,

---

promised them safety, but as he was dead, his heirs, I suppose, did not think themselves bound by his promise and put them all to death. Apparently it was to give a loophole for this that Cingīz bade the fact of his death to be concealed. (*Ṭabaqāt-i-naṣīrī*, Raverty 1087*n*.)

[1] Minhāj always calls Cingīz the accursed.

[2] i.e., reckoning the death as in *Ṣafar*. If *Ramaẓān* be taken, the age would be 74, there being 10 solar months in a lunar year.

as stated in histories, his age comes to seventy-four years and three months. Apparently the discrepancy is due to the difference between lunar and solar months and years, or it may be owing to some cause other than the ostensible one. During this period, the high matters of government and administration were made illustrious by the world-adorning counsels of Qarācār Nūyān. Why should not a potentate who hath such a kinsman (*birādar*) in blood and in spirit by his side as his director to dominion and fortune, brush with the head of majesty the highest zenith of conquest and rule?

*Verse.*

Qarācār and Cingīz are cousins (*ibn-i-'am and*).
In conquest too, they are allied (*qarīn-i-ham and*).

When the drum of death was beat, the Khānship was made over to Ōkadāī. The gist of this distressful occurrence is that when on the China expedition, he (Cingīz) had one night an intimation by a vision, that the time of leaving this mirage-like world was at hand. He called his sons, Qarācār Nūyān, the Commander-in-Chief, and the other nobles and pillars of his empire and after imparting to them counsels which might dominate mankind, he appointed Ōkadāī as Khān. He sent to the treasury for the covenant which had been executed by Qācūlī and Qabal Khān and which was the Āltamgha of Tūmana Khān and which his high-souled predecessors had successively signed, and had it read before the noble assembly. He observed, "I swore to this deed together with Qarācār Nūyān, do you also fulfil its conditions." He also had another deed drawn up 75
between Ōkadāī and his other sons and his kinsmen and made it over to Ōkadāī.

Transoxiana, Turkistān, the borders of Khwārizm, the cities of the Uighūrs, Kāshghar, Badakhshān, Bālkh and Ghaznih as far as the Indus, he assigned to Caghatāī Khān. He also made over the covenant of Qabal Khān and Qācūlī Bahādur to Caghatāī and said to him, "Depart not from the counsels of Qarācār Nūyān and regard him as your partner in rule and realm." He also established between them the bond of fatherhood[1] and sonship. In this way the noble line

[1] According to a MS. of Tīmūr's Memoirs Cingīz did this by marrying Qarācār to a daughter of Caghatāī. If so, Qarācār must surely

(Akbar's) came to be called Caghatāī;[1] otherwise the relationship of Caghatāī and his ancestors with his Majesty, the king of kings, is one of glory and superiority not of propinquity and similarity.

The Princes and Nūyāns acted according to the testament. Good God! could there be such a breach[2] of covenant by an eminently wise man like Cingīz Khān! The covenant which had been adorned by the seal-royal (Āltamgha) of Tūmana Khān should have been given to Ōkadāī Qā'ān and he should have been made over to be educated and succoured by the weighty counsels of Qarācār Nūyān so that the provisions of the compact might be carried into effect; or did they not produce[3] that covenant till he (Cingīz) was carried

have been many years younger than Cingīz and hardly fitted to be his counsellor. The passage in the Memoirs is *dukhtar-i-Caghatāī Khānrā bā Qarācār Nūyān 'aqd kard ū bar āō Gurkān nām nihād.* But A.F.'s view and that commonly accepted is that Qarācār acted as a father to Caghatāī. (*Shajratu-l-atrāk,* Miles 344.)

1 This does not seem quite correct. Bābar's mother was a Caghatāī being a daughter of Yūnus Khān, a descendant of Cingīz,—a fact which A.F. notices later on in his account of Bābar.

2 A.F. holds that Cingīz broke the compact by not attaching Qarācār to the Khāqān (Great Khan). But Caghatāī was the elder son though passed over in favour of the younger, Ōkadāī and thus; in one sense, the assigning of Qarācār to him was right.

The *Prolegomena l.c.* states that Cingīz made the arrangement because Transoxiana had been assigned to Caghatāī and as Jalālu-d-dīn Mangbarnī was still alive, it was necessary to have Caghatāī supported by an experienced general like Qarācār.

Tīmūr does not seem to have thought there was a breach of agreement for he tells us that when Taghlāq Tīmūr shewed him the agreement—which had been written on a steel plate and signed by Qābal and Qācūlī,—he acquiesced and accepted the Commander-in-Chiefship. (Tīmūr's Memoirs, Stewart 12.) See too page 22 (Stewart) where Tīmūr's father tells him that he had been *Sipāh-sālār*. Apparently if there were a breach of compact, it occurred when Tīmūr's grandfather, Amīr Barkal gave up his duties as *Sipāh-sālār* and retired into private life.

3 I am not sure of the meaning of this passage. My friend Mr. Beames thinks it is that the courtiers should not have produced the deed before Cingīz so that posterity might have ascribed his conduct to ignorance and not to a deliberate design of breaking the compact. But Cingīz had asked for the deed, so that they could not well have evaded its production, and it is difficult to see how an intentional omission to consult the deed could make Cingīz's conduct or that of his courtiers any better. Apparently the words "*ḥāẓir nami-*

away by the inbred forgetfulness[1] of human nature, and thus the mark of censure in the book of his knowledge was obliterated by the line of obliviousness. It is strange too that old writers while treating of this subject with verbiage, cavilling and equivocation have not come to a right determination about it. It appears as if the world-adorning Deity desired to remove from the frame of this lofty lineage, the disguise of the Commander-in-Chiefship which Tūmana Khān had imposed but which had really been fashioned by the Divine artificers while completing the evolution of his Majesty, the king of kings, (and that so) a forgetfulness ensued which surpassed in excellence thousands of good designs. Inasmuch as the Divine protection was ever guarding this lofty line, no failure in the compact and agreement occurred on the part of Qācūlī Bahādur's descendants so that when the turn of sovereignty, which was due to their innate and acquired power of direction, arrived and they attained the divan-adorning Caliphate, there could be no reproach brought against them by the wise. Likewise this was the beginning[2] of the rise of that

---

*sākhtand*" must refer to the officers and not to Cingīz for they are commonly used of the act of inferiors in bringing something before their superior. I am inclined then to think that A.F. means to suggest as an excuse for Cingīz, that he was at death's door and incapable of recollecting the contents of the deed. Or it may be that the important word is *ān* (that) and that A.F. means to suggest that possibly the courtiers did not produce *that* deed, *i.e.*, the real deed, but some other.

The *Shajrat* (344) remarks that Cingīz exceeded in recommending Qāracār to Caghatāī. Probably this remark is based on A.F. and indicates that the *Shajrat* was written after the *Akbarnāma*.

[1] Alluding to the Arabic proverb (Abū'l-ghāzī, Désmaisons, Preface) *awwalu' n-nāsi awwalu' n-nās*, "the first forgetter was the first man." This again, I believe, refers to the tradition that Adam surrendered 40 years of life in favour of his descendant, King Ḍavid but repudiated or forgot having done so when the Angel of Death came to him at the close of his 960th year. In consequence of this forgetfulness by Adam, it was laid down in the book which Seth received from heaven, that all promises or agreements should be ratified by the presence of two witnesses.

[2] Tīmūr is regarded as a lineal descendant of Qarācār Nūyān, though according to Vambéry, the claim is without foundation. It seems that Rashīdu-d-dīn says nothing about Qarācār's being Caghatāī's generalissimo. (D'Ohsson II. 109 *n.*) But he is mentioned in the *Ṭabaqāt-i-naṣīrī* by Minhāj who was

light of fortune, his Majesty, the Lord of Conjunction (Tīmūr) whose holy existence was the forerunner of the perpetual dominion of his Majesty, the king of kings.

After his father's decease, Caghatāī Khān made Pēshbālīgh[1] his capital and having made over the control of the army and of the subjects to Amīr Qarācār Nūyān, he spent most of his time in the service of Ōkadāī Qā'ān. Though Ōkadāī was younger than himself, he shewed no slackness in performing his duties and in the *minutiæ* of obedience and heartily observed the conditions of the will.

When Caghatāī Khān arrived at his life's term, he appointed Amīr Qarācān Nūyān administrator of the kingdom and made over
76 his children to him. He died seven months before Ōkadāī Khān,[2] in the year of the Ox, *Zī-l-qa'da* 638 (May-June 1241). Qarācār Nūyān, in accordance with his promise, took charge of the management of the kingdom and after some time, made over to Qarā Hulāgū Khān, son of Mawātkān,[3] son of Caghatāī, the government of his grandfather's dominions.

After some years, when Giyūk Khān, son of Ōkadāī became Khān (*i.e.*, Khāqān) Qarācār Nūyān deposed[4] Qarā Hulāgū Khān, and appointed Īsū Mangū, son of Caghatāī in his room. Let it not be concealed that Ōkadāī Qā'ān had, during his sovereignty, nominated his eldest[5] son, Kūcū as his heir, but Kūcū died during his father's lifetime. He then made his (Kūcū's) son Shīrāmūn who was his favourite, his heir. When the Qā'ān (Ōkadāī) died, Giyūk Khān was in Russia, Circassia and Bulgaria (*i.e.*, Great Bulgaria) and came to the great camp[6] (*i.e.*, the capital) three or four years afterwards

---

born 60 years, before Rashīdu-d-dīn. (Bib. Ind. ed. 365, 1.3 and Raverty, 1063.) In these the name is written Nūyān Qarācār but there can be no doubt that Qarācār is meant. There is also a great deal about him in the *Prolegomena* which was written in 822 (1419).

[1] D'Herbélot, Bishbalīgh (Pentapolis) and this is no doubt right. It is described in Ney Elias' introduction to the *Tārīkh-i-Rashīdī* (62) but it is stated (l.c. 32 and 364) hat Caghatāī's capital was at Almālīgh.

[2] Ōkadāī died 11th Dec., 1241.

[3] Blochmann 429. (Howorth I. 158. D'Ohsson, II. 87.)

[4] The *Shajratu-l-atrāk* (Miles 355) states that Qarā Hulākū was deposed at the instance of Giyūk who represented that a grandson could not succeed before his uncle (Īsū Mangū).

[5] Third, Howorth, I, 160. Kiyūk or Giyūk was the eldest.

[6] Karakoram, the Cambalu of Chaucer and Milton.

He established justice and the cherishing of subjects. When Īsū Mangū was covered with the veil of annihilation, Qarācār Nūyān again appointed Qarā Hulāgū to the government of the country and died during his reign in 652 (1254),[1] full of honours and success, at the age of 89.

## Aijal Nūyān.

Aijal Nūyān was the most distinguished for wisdom and godliness of Qarācār Nūyān's ten[2] children. During the reign of Qarā Hulāgū he took, on account of his wisdom and vigour, the place of his father (Qarācār). In 662 (1264) he was confirmed on the divan of dominion. The Caghatāī tribe (*alūs*) was prosperous in his time, but as there was much opposition and strife among the descendants of Caghatāī Khān, he got disgusted with affairs and settled in his ancestral city of Kesh until the time when Mangū Qā'ān, son of Tūlī Khān, son of Cingīz Khān, sent his brother Hulāgū to Persia (Īrān) and attached to him officers and men from each of the four tribes (*alūs*) of Jūjī, Caghatāī, Ōkatāī (Ōkadāī) and Tūlī. By universal request, Aijal Nūyān was selected from the Caghatāī tribe and appointed as companion[3] to Hulāgū Khān. That Khān treated him with great respect and assigned Marāgha-Tabrīz[4] to him.

---

[1] D'Ohsson (II. 109*n.*) quotes Mīr Khwānd as saying that Qarācār died at the age of 79 but the lithographed ed. of the *Rauzatu-s-safā* (Part V. 69) gives 89 as the age and Mīr Khwānd's source, the *Zafarnāma, Prolegomena*, gives also 89. He died in the year of the Hare in the Turkish cycle.

[2] Five, *Prolegomena l.c.* gives their names.

[3] Text, *bi-rasm-i-sālbūrī* *Sālbūr* does not occur in the dictionary and is perhaps *sālār-i-bār*, (*princeps aulae regiae*)—for which, see Vullers *s.v.* *sālār*. Possibly the true reading is ساوری *sāwarī*, a present. For an account of this word, see Quatremère, *Notices*, etc., XIV. 27*n*. The meaning would then be "He was sent as a *nazr* or present to Hulākū." I observe, however, that *sālbūrī* occurs as a title in the *Zafarnāma*. (See extract therefrom, *Tārīkh-i-rashīdī*, 26, where we have Khwāja Sālibarī.) A MS. however of the *Zafarnāma* gives the word as Salbarī. So too, Bib. Ind. ed. I. 88 and II. 23 l.5 fr. ft.). *Sālbar* occurs in the *Burhān-i-qāti'* but only with the meaning of a tree which bears every second year.

[4] Jarrett III. 81*n*.

### Amir Ailangar Khān.

Amīr Ailangar Khān was the most distinguished son of Aijal Nūyān. When Aijal departed from Tūrān with Hulāgū Khān to
77 Īrān, Ailangar was made his father's representative in the Caghatāī tribe and when Aījal left this deceitful world in Īrān, Davā Khān, son of Barāq Khān, son of Bīsūtavā, son of Mawātkān, son of Caghatāī Khān, son of Cingīz Khān who had become Sulṭān [1] made him *Amīru-l-umarā* [2] and gave him his father's rank and assigned to him powers of binding and loosing. And being full of wisdom and insight, he undertook the management of the affairs of the kingdom. He embraced the glorious Muhammadan religion.

### Amīr Barkal.[3]

Amīr Barkal was very high-minded and when his noble father, Amīr Ailangar Nūyān left this comfortless world, in the time of Tarmashīrīn Khān, son of Davā Khān, he was the only surviving son. As he was always occupied with the care of his own soul, he had no leisure for other things and so, abstaining from the companionship of Khāns, he transferred the paternal avocations to his cousins and remained independent in Kesh. He was assiduous in seeking God's favour and in acquiring virtues. He spent his life in that neighbourhood and provided for his daily sustenance from the various estates and villages which belonged to his old possessions and was content therewith till he went to the holy kingdom and the eternal country.

### Amīr Ṭarāghāī.

Amīr Ṭarāghāī was the distinguished son of Amīr Barkal and is the father of the Lord of Conjunction (Tīmūr). From early years and the flower of youth, the lights of dominion and fortune shone from the court of his nature and the notes of greatness and glory illuminated the antechamber of his ways. That noble-minded man had a younger brother, Haibat [4] by name, who was a perfect paragon

---

1 R. A. S. MS. No. 114 has *ki saltanat* before *ba ō rasīda būd* and they seem needed.

2 This is regarded as the third renewal of the compact between Qabal and Qācūlī. (Miles 381).

3 Aḥmad b. 'Arab Shāh gives Abghai as the name of Tīmūr's grandfather.

4 In the *Prolegomena l.c.* the name seems to be Salbitā or Malbitā, and in the *Khulāṣatu-t-tawārīkh* to be Bīta

of truth and truth-seeking. But the lot of spiritual and temporal eminence had fallen on the elder brother. Like his honoured father (Barkal) he always kept his face on the threshold of the lords of holiness and was favoured by the associates of the portals of eternity. Especially that pattern of the masters of ecstacy, Shaikh Shamsu-d-dīn Kalāl,[1] greatly honoured and respected the Amīr and by his spiritual insight apprized him of the advent of the star of the Lord of Conjunction.

---

I do not find his name in Tīmūr's Memoirs. An uncle, Ḥājī Barlās and another, Aidku, are spoken of, but they were probably his maternal uncles. They were unfriendly to him (Stewart's Tīmūr, 55).

[1] The *Prolegomena l.c.* and *Khulāṣat* call him Shamsu-d-dīn Kalār, and the former describes him as a successor of Shaikh Shihābu-d-dīn Shahrawardī (perhaps the famous Shahrawardī of Baghdād). The *Prolegomena* states also that in 775 (1374), Tīmūr removed his father's body to near Shamsu-d-dīn's shrine beside the chief mosque. Probably Kalār is right for the Amīr Kalāl whom Tīmūr often mentions seems a different person. (Price and Davey (Tīmūr's Institutes) call him Gulāl, a word which signifies red powder, *i.e., abīr*).

An Amīr Kalāl is described in the *Safīnatu-l-auliyā* also. D'Herbéiot mentions a Shamsu-d-dīn al-Fakhaur-who lived in Kesh and was consulted by Tīmūr, but Tīmūr's special *Pīr* seems to have been Quṭbu-l-aqṭāb Shaikh Zainu-d-dīn Ābū Bakr. (Davey and White's Tīmūr 4*n*.) Apparently Aḥmad b. 'Arab Shāh is the authority for this, who in the beginning of his Life of Tīmūr, speaks of a Shaikh called Shamsu-d-dīn Al Fakhuri whom Tīmūr consulted.

A.F.'s reference to Shamsu-d-dīn's foretelling the greatness of Tīmūr to his father is interesting because it seems to be an allusion to Tīmūr's Memoirs where the story is told. If this is so, it goes to support the genuineness of the Memoirs by showing that they were in existence before, at least the reign of Shāh Jahān. The story, however, about Shamsu-d-dīn's prophecy also appears in the *Ḥabību-s-siyar*.

The Āīn (Jarrett III, 358) mentions an Amīr Kalāl who was a saint of the Naqshbandī order.

# CHAPTER XVI.

## The Lord of Great Conjunctions, Third Pole[1] of the Universe, Pole of Realm and Religion, Amīr Timur Gūrgān.[2]

The eternal decree and unchanging will of God hath adorned the world by assigning thousands of designs to everything. Thus the Almighty, by implanting in the fifty-two persons who form the
78 lofty line of the king of kings and who are the instruction of the wise,—command, wisdom, sovereignty, guidance, favour, bounty and other glorious graces and illustrious qualities, fashioned and finished the unique pearl of the Imperial Vicegerency (*Khilāfat*). And from and after Qācūlī Bahādur, He caused seven heroes of the sacred line to descend from the position of visible sovereignty and awarded them the status of Commander-in-Chief and king-making (*shāhinshāhī*) so that by experiencing the stage of subjection in the garb of obedience, they might in an admirable manner, set forth to the apparatus of the universal laboratory. And as for the exalted ancestors who spent their days in Īrganaqūn, albeit we have no record

---

1 *Ṣāliṣu-l-quṭbīn.* Probably this means that he is a Pole supplemental to the two Poles, making with them a Trinity. But it may mean umpire or arbitrator between the two Poles, or that he was three kinds of Pole, *viz.*, *quṭbu-l-millat* (religion), *quṭbu-d-dunyā* (the world) *quṭbu-d-dīn* (faith), as Tīmūr is styled in the *Prolegomena* (*Ẓafarnāma*). Ruy Gonzales de Clavigo (Clements R. Markham trs. 124) says, "The arms of Timur Beg were three circles like "o"s drawn in this manner °₀° and this is to signify that he is lord of three parts of the world." He adds that Tīmūr ordered this device to be stamped on his coins and on everything that he had and that he ordered his tributaries to use it on their coins. Possibly the epithet in the Text alludes to this device.

2 Tīmūr, we are told, never took any title higher than that of Amīr (officer) which is an allusion to the Commander-in-Chiefship held by his branch and was accordingly a title hereditary in his family. The title *Gūrgān* (son-in-law) refers apparently to his ancestor Qarācār Nūyān's marriage with a daughter of Caghatāī, son of Cingīz. But it may also refer to his own marriage with princesses.

of them, yet they too, generation after generation, were seized of greatness. Though the name of sovereignty was not, they possessed the reality and shewed it forth by preserving their honour while shut out from the haunts of men. And now that the stages of solitude and society had been fulfilled and a complete preparation had been made for the coming forth of the unique pearl of his Majesty, the king of kings, God, the Creator of the world, stripped off the disguise of dependency which had seemingly been imported into the line by the counsels of Tūmana Khān, and displayed a hero fit for and capable of a great sovereignty. Such was the appearance of his Majesty, the Lord of Conjunction, Adorner of the Seven Climes, Exalter of Throne and Diadem, Amīr Tīmūr Gūrgān. This great one came forth and planted his foot in existence in the environs of Kesh,[1] commonly known as the *Shahr-i-sabz* (Green City) and one of the towns of Īrān,[2] on the night of Tuesday, 25th *Sha'bān*, 736[3] (9th April, 1336) in the Mouse Year (First of the Turkish cycle) under the Sign of Capricorn, from the fair womb and pure veil of her Majesty, the perfection of modesty and blessedness, glory of choiceness and purity, guardian of realm and religion, Tagīna[4] Khātūn. This axis of the sphere of the great vicegerency and ocean-centre of sublime sovereignty is the star of fortune which arose eighth from out the bosom of Qācūlī Bahādur.

According to the view of one historian,[5] the true vision of Qācūlī Bahādur was fulfilled thereby but, as has already been indicated, this

---

[1] About 40 miles S. by E. of Samarqand. It was called the Green City on account of the verdure of its gardens. (*Zafarnāma* I. 301.) It has been described by Bābar (Erskine, 54) P. de Courteille (I. 106) and E. Schuyler. It is also mentioned in the *Āīn* (Jarrett, III. 97) as in the 5th climate and in Badakhshān (!). It is generally reckoned a day's journey from Samarqand.

[2] One MS. has Tūrān and so has Abdu-l-ḥamīd (*Bādshāhnāma*, Bib. Ind. I. 43) Īrān is perhaps right, for the word is vaguely used. (D'Herbelot *s. v.*). Kesh is in what is usually called Transoxiana and a variant gives *Māwarā'u-n-nahr* (Transoxiana) instead of Īrān.

[3] Gibbon quoting Hyde says 1336, 9th April, 11-57 P.M., lat. 36.

[4] Sometimes Nagīna, *e. g.*, in Khāfī Khān.

[5] Sharafu-d-dīn 'Alī Yazdī (*Zafarnāma*). The *Ḥabību-s-siyar* says the same thing. A.F. has already censured Sharafu-d-dīn (Cap. I. near the end) for identifying the seven stars which emerged from Qācūlī's bosom, with the seven descendants

day was, according to the profound investigations of the wise and far-seeing,[1] only the beginning of the ascent of the constellation and the flashing of the first star.

In the fortunate Age in which the Lord of Conjunction was born, Tarmas͟hīrīn[2] K͟hān, son of Davā K͟hān, son of Barāq K͟hān, son of

who intervened between Qācūlī and Tīmūr. A.F. says it is wrong to take for stars, men who did not rule, and holds that Tīmūr was the first of the eight stars and not the last. But his interpretation is liable to the same objection. It is true that Akbar was the eighth in descent from Tīmūr, but this was through a younger son of the latter, *viz.*, the third, Mīrān S͟hāh, and neither Mīrān nor his son, Muḥammad Mīrzā (who also was not an eldest son) were ever kings. Certainly they were never what A.F. calls world-adorners and cannot for instance, be compared for kingly qualities, extent of dominion and duration of reign with S͟hāhruk͟h Mīrzā (Tīmūr's fourth son) or for intellectual eminence with S͟hāhruk͟h's illustrious son Ulug͟h Bēg. Indeed of the six who intervened between Tīmūr and Akbar, only three were kings, *viz.*, Abū Sa'īd, Bābar and Humāyūn.

1 This is singular and perhaps refers to Amīr Fatḥu-l-lāh of S͟hīrāz.

2 This seems a mistake. Tarmas͟hīrīn was killed in 1330 according to D'Ohsson (IV. Table II.), and Mr. Oliver (R. A. S. J. XX. New Ser.) thinks he died in 1334. It would seem that he was living in 1333, for Ibn Baṭūṭa apparently visited him in that year and Mr. Oliver (J. A. S. B. 1891, II. eleven) gives one of his coins dated 733 (1333). Both D'Herbélot and Miles speak of Amīr Kazgān as ruling in Transoxiana at the time of Tīmūr's birth but Amīr Kazgān was only a rebellious subject. According to S͟harafu-d-dīn—who ought to be a good authority and whom Mas'ūdī servilely copies,—Sulṭān Qazān was the nominal ruler when Tīmūr was born and his reign lasted from 733-747 (1332-1346) but the real authority was possessed by Amīr Qazān. (Bib. Ind. ed.. has Qarān Sulṭān K͟hān and *Prolegomena* (A. S. B. MS. *Oa*, 26, p. 69*a*) Qarā Sulṭān K͟hān. Pétis de la Croix has Cazan. See also Miles 374. S͟harafu-d-dīn dilates in the *Prolegomena*, on the birth of Tīmūr in this reign).

Later on, (I. 43) S͟harafu-d-dīn states that Tug͟hlaq Tīmūr, a grandson of Davā and nephew of Tarmas͟hīrīn, came to Transoxiana in *Rabī'u-s-sānī* 761 (February 1360) and that in the 33 years previous, dating from the death of Tarmas͟hīrīn, there had reigned eight kings of the Cag͟hatāī line. This would fix Tarmas͟hīrīn's death in 728 (1328). This is also the date expressly stated in the *Prolegomena* (A. S. B. MS. *Oa*, 26, p. 68*b*) as that when Tarmas͟hīrīn was put to death by his cousin Purān.

The evidence of Ibn Baṭūṭa against this is perhaps not of overwhelming

Bīsūtawā, son of Bīsūkān, son of Caghatāī Khān was ruling in Transoxiana. In Īrān four months had passed since the death of Sulṭān Abū Sa'īd [1] and there was on that account universal confusion in that country.

Amīr Ṣāḥib Qarān from his earliest years up to the flower of his 79
youth, was occupied in practising the art of hunting [2] and the methods of war and battles. In the Mouse Year 762 [3] (1361) Amīr Ṭarāghāī departed from this world. He had four sons and two daughters, *viz.*, Ṣāḥib Qarānī, 'Ālam Shaikh, Siyūrghtamsh, Jūkī, Qutlagh [4] Tarkān Āghā and Shīrīn Bēgī Āghā.

---

weight for he is always confused and vague about dates and he seemingly never clearly states when he saw Tarmashīrīn. But the evidence of the coin is more difficult to get over. It is not however quite conclusive for apart from the fact that posthumous coins are not unknown, we have the fact that there was an apparently fictitious claimant to the title of Tarmashīrīn and the coin of 733 might have been struck by him.

Mr. Oliver's opinion is that Jinkshī or Jinikishai was reigning in 736 and he doubts that Buzūn ever reigned. This is the statement in the R. A. S. J., but in the subsequent list in J. A. S. B., Buzūn is put down as having reigned from 742–44. On the other hand, Mr. Stanley Lane Poole, as quoted by Mr. Ney Elias, gives Buzūn as reigning in Transoxiana at Tīmūr's birth (*Tārīkh-i-rashīdī*, Intr. 49.)

1 The Abū Sa'īd "b. Algiaptou (*i.e.*, son of Oljaitu)" of D'Herbélot who gives a long account of him and states that he was the last prince of the house of Cingīz whom the Mughals recognized. He was descended from Hulāgū Khān. The *Shajratu-l-atrāk* (Miles 309) says he died at the age of 32, childless, on 13 *Rabī'u-l-ākhar* 736 (D'Ohsson and Beale, 30 Nov., 1335; Gladwin 1 Dec.). It was Abū Sa'īd who put to death the famous historian and minister Rashīdu-d-dīn. D'Herbélot mentions that as the year 736 was full of calamities, it was designated لوز *lauẓ*. This word both gives by *abjad* the figure 736 (*viz.*, *l*=30, *w*=6, and *ẓ*=700), and also indicates by its meaning of "taking refuge," the necessity for a protector of the Age, *viz.*, Tīmūr.

2 This is from the *Ẓafarnāma* (15) which states that Tīmūr practised hunting and the art of war from 10 years of age.

3 Apparently he died in 761 or very early in 762, otherwise the corresponding cycle-year must have been that of the Ox. The *Ẓafarnāma* too, although not explicit, seems to say that Tīmūr's father died in 761,—the year in which Tughlaq Tīmūr invaded Transoxiana and Tīmūr's uncle, Ḥājī Barlās fled to Khurāsān. However the *Tārīkh-i-Jahāngīr* (the *Prolegomena*, of the *Ẓafarnāma*) gives (near the end) the date of Ṭarāghāī's death, 762.

4 She died 785 (*Ẓafarnāma* 355).

When Ṣāḥib Qarānī arrived at the age of 34[1] solar years, he with auspicious horoscope and lofty fortune and by the counselling of his God-given wisdom which is a station of Divine inspiration, placed on his head on Wednesday, 12 *Ramaẓān*, 771 (9, April,[2] 1870), corresponding to the year of the Dog (Īt) the diadem of rule and the crown of world-conquest and made lofty the throne of sovereignty and world-government. And for 36[3] years which was the time of his supremacy and world-adornment, he brought under his control and into his permanent possession, the countries of Transoxiana, K͟hwārizm, Turkistān, K͟hurāsān, the two 'Irāqs,[4] Āẕarbāījān, Persia, Māzindarān, Kirmān, Dīyārbakr, K͟hūzistān, Egypt, Syria, Asia Minor (Rūm), *etc.*, by means of his world-conquering courage and his capacious intellect, and uplifted the banners of authority and sovereignty in the four quarters of the world and in the seven climes.

Whosoever was befriended[5] of Salvation, came forward to meet him with the foot of obedience and for such an one, the rose of auspiciousness bloomed on Fortune's pinnacle. Whoever had misfortune and eventual destruction enfolded in his skirt, and disengaged his head from the collar of submission, arrived with tearing of hair[6] at the Judgment-seat of the Dispenser (*Qahramān*) of Justice and beheld in his own bosom the thorn-brake offspring of his acts.

On Monday of Ẕī-l-qa'da[7] 789, he massacred the inhabitants of

---

[1] Abū-l-ḥamīd (*Bādshāhnāma*, 43), gives Tīmūr's age then as 35 yrs. 17 dys.

[2] Apparently on his birthday.

[3] Abū-l-ḥamīd says for 35 yrs. 11 ms. 5 dys.

[4] This might mean either Media and Babylonia or the cities of Kufa and Basra but here it is the former for Abū-l-ḥamīd who copies A.F. says (43) the 'Irāqs of Arabia and Persia.

[5] *Lit.* to whomsoever Salvation was the friend of his fortune's day. Four MSS. have *daulatash* instead of *daulat* as in Text.

[6] *Mūī-kashān lit.* hair-dragging but here perhaps "dragged by the hair."

[7] It was 6 Ẕī-l-qa'da (6th November, 1387), according to Price (Retrospect III. 72.) The inhabitants rose against Tīmūr while negociations for the surrender of the city were going on and killed many of his soldiers. Tīmūr thus alludes to the affair (Institutes, White and Davy, 119) "And I conquered the city of Iṣpahān. And I trusted the people of Iṣpahān and I delivered the castle into their hands. And they rebelled and the *Darogha* whom I had placed over them, they slew with 300 of the soldiers. And I also commanded that a general slaughter should be made of the people of Iṣpahān."

Iṣpahān on account of their sedition and rebellion. Thence he turned the reins of resolution towards the capital (Shīrāz) of Persia (Fārs) where the Muẓaffar[1] family (Āl-i-muẓaffar) became his servants. When news came of the opposition of Tūqtamish[2] Khān the ruler of Dasht Qipcāk[3] (the desert of Qipcāk, *i.e.*, the Khirgiz Steppe) and one of those who had been supported[4] by his Majesty (Tīmūr), he twice led his army against him and having exalted the banners of victory, he returned. He traversed Dasht Qipcāk which is a thousand leagues (*farsangs*) long and six hundred wide and cleared it of the rubbish of strife.[5] A second time he marched against Īrān in 795 (1393) and brought death to Shāh Manṣūr[6] who had cocked[7] the bonnet of frowardness, and he extirpated the Muẓaffar race.

And in that country, he performed feats which obliterated those of Rustam[8] and Afrāsiāb[9] and for the sake of the repose of the ministers[10] of his victorious dominion, converted the country of Persia into a thornless garden (*gulzār-i-bīkhār*). After[11] that he conquered Baghdād by the strength of his dominion and fortune. He went several times into Georgia and brought there as his companions, victory and conquest. In 12 Muḥarram, 801 (23rd September, 1398),

---

1 D'Herbélot art. Madhaffar, and Rieu's Cat. I. 82 and 168*a*. The dynasty was known by the name of Āl-i-muẓaffar. It began in 718 (1318) and was overthrown by Tīmūr in 795 (1393). It ruled over Kirmān.

2 D'Herbélot art. Toctamish.

3 Jarrett III. 102.

4 Tūqtamish at one time owed his kingdom to Tīmūr. He was a descendant of Cingīz through his son Jūjī.

5 *Khas ū khāshāk* "weeds and briars."

6 D'Herbélot art. Mansor; Ẓafarnāma Bib. Ind. I. 608, and Gibbon Cap. 65. Manṣūr was killed by Shāhrukh and Gibbon says Tīmūr declared his esteem of the valour of his foe by extirpating all the males of so intrepid a race.

7 *Cf.* Macaulay's account of Sir John Fenwick cocking his hat in Queen Mary's face.

8 Alluding apparently to the taking of the famous White Fort (*Qil'a-i-safīd*) 45 miles N.W. of Shīrāz and which was taken by Rustam also. (Hist. of Persia, Malcolm I. 27 and 46.)

9 Afrāsīāb, *i.e.*, conqueror of Persia. He was afterwards killed by Zāl and his son Rustam.

10 *Auliyā-i-daulat*, but this phrase is often only a respectful way of mentioning the king himself.

11 This was the first taking of Baghdād, in Sep. 1393. It was taken again 20th June, 1401.

he made a noble[1] bridge over the Indus and by dominion and fortune conquered Hindūstān.[2] In 803 (October 1400) he made an expedition against Syria,[3] and then raised the morning-breeze of fortune.
80 The lights of celestial victories illumined that world-conqueror. On that occasion Aleppo was taken and then the army went to Damascus and shed the blood of the rulers of Syria who were confined in the wretchedness[4] of prison.

Next year he raised his standards for the purpose of subduing Rūm and on Friday, 19[5] Ẕī-l-ḥijja, 804 (20th July, 1402), having arrayed his army and adorned the flag of contest with the crescent of victory,

---

1 The bridge was of boats and rafts and made in two days and hardly entitled to be styled a *jasr-i-'ālī* Tīmūr crossed where Jalālu-d-dīn Mangbarnī swam the river.

2 A.F. has a short notice of this expedition in the Āīn, under the heading "Comers into India." See Jarrett 349, where instead of "the booty obtained was not considerable" we should read "they did not value it" (the conquest of India). Sir A. Cunningham (Indian Eras) gives the date of the capture of Delhi as Wed. 18th Dec., 1398.

3 The reference appears to be to the slaughter of prisoners from Aleppo, etc., after the first battle before Damascus (*Ẕafarnāmu* II. 314). Among them were S͟hadūn, governor of Damascus and apparently many other rulers of Syrian cities. These had all assembled at Aleppo under the orders of the king of Egypt (l.c. II. 287.) Aḥmad 'Arab S͟hāh tells how a number of the chief men of Damascus surrendered themselves to Tīmūr after the Sulṭān of Egypt had deserted the city and that many of these were afterwards put to death (Manger, II. Cap. VI and XIII). Tīmūr killed them and also the prisoners taken in the battle, apparently because the king of Egypt had tried to have him assassinated and because he (the king) had put one of his ambassadors to death and imprisoned Altams͟h Qujīn (l.c. II. 275). But the Text may also refer to Tīmūr's severities against the principal men of Damascus after he had taken the city. He was incensed against them because they were Sunnīs and belonged to the house of Yazīd, the slayer of Ḥusain, and because they had neglected the tomb of the Prophet's widows.

4 I am not sure of the meaning of *ẓall-i-qaid*. Several MSS. write it without the *iẓāfat* and as if it were the name of a place. There is a town and fortress of Zillah in Asia Minor (near to which Cæsar gained his *Veni, Vidi, Vici* victory) but I cannot find that the Syrian Amīrs were confined there or that Tīmūr was ever there. Possibly *ẓall* is a variant for *ẓill*, shadow.

5 Aḥmad 'Arab S͟hāh, Thursday, 27 Zī-l-ḥijja.(*Thamuz*). (Manger, II. 255.)

he fought near Angora (Ancyra), a glorious battle with Īlderim (Thunderbolt), the Cæsar of Rūm, and by the secret aids which rode[1] always beside this royal cavalier of the plain of supremacy, the assembled armies of victory and conquest became his stirrup-holders, and the proclamation[2] of success was issued in the name of that world-subduing lord. Īlderim Bāyazīd (Bajazet) was made prisoner and when they produced him at the foot of the lofty throne, he was, out of perfect kindness and chivalry, given a seat above the princes.[3]

From thence[4] Tīmūr went to Āẕarbāījān and spent there eighteen months in the administration of justice. Kings and kings' sons from

---

[1] *Ham-'inān, lit.* equal-reined.

[2] Referring to announcements of victory sent to Persia, Tartary, etc. (*Ẓafarnāma* II. 447).

[3] Text, *zīr-i-dast-i-s̲h̲āhzāda* but most MSS. have *s̲h̲āhzādahā* and no doubt this is the true reading. I am also convinced that *zīr* is a mistake for *zabar* which I have found in one A.S.B.MS. See Vullers *s.v. zabardast* where the meaning *prior locus in consessu* is given and also the phrase *zabardast nis̲h̲astan, locum altiorem, i.e., magis honoratum occupare,* together with a very apposite Persian couplet.

I do not know whether A.F. was justified by his authorities for the statement in the Text. The *Ẓafarnāma* merely says Tīmūr gave Bāyazīd a seat near himself and the *Rauẓatu-ṣ-ṣafā* that Bāyazīd was given an honourable seat (*s̲h̲araf-i-julūs*).

A.F. knows nothing or says nothing about Bāyazīd's subsequent confinement in an iron cage (Gibbon). The story is, however, now regarded as disproved. The *Rauẓat* states that according to the testimony of an eye-witness Tīmūr at first spoke roughly to Bāyazīd and reproached him for his obstinacy and folly. The *Ẓafarnāma* admits this but represents the reproaches as given after the removal of his chains.

Bāyazīd was restored to his kingdom and allowed the place of a subject or vassal prince (*Ẓafarnāma* II. 461). According to Hammer, the "cage" was a woman's litter. But a recent writer in the Z. D. M. G. has refuted Hammer and has, apparently unconsciously, vindicated the acumen of Gibbon.

[4] This statement is misplaced. Tīmūr went to Āẕarbāījān before the battle of Angora and the "18 months" referred to seems the interval between the taking of Damascus in January, 1401 and the battle of Angora in July, 1402. A.F. says nothing of the capture of Smyrna from the Knights of St. John which occurred after the battle of Angora in 805 (December, 1402) and was one of Tīmūr's greatest achievements. The whole of A.F.'s account of Tīmūr is very poor and bears marks of haste.

various countries came and did homage. The ruler of Egypt coined much red and white money in his name and sent it to the world-protecting Court. Other rulers of the surrounding countries raised the flag of well-wishing on the plain of obedience. And from the pulpits of Mecca, Medina and other holy places, the *khuṭba* was read in his name. In Ẕi-l-qa‘da, 806 (May, 1404), he marched against Fīrūza-kūh[1] and having won victory there that very day, he, without delay, turned towards Khurāsān. In the beginning of Muḥarram 807 (9th-10th July, 1404) he went by Nīshāpūr to Transoxiana and there in his native country inaugurated a great feast[2] such as astonished the lords of greatness and splendour.

After gratifying mankind with largesses and favours, he set forth to subdue the territories of China (*Khiṭā*).

On the night of Wednesday, 17 Sha‘bān, 807 (18th February, 1405) in the village (*mauẓa‘*) of Utrār[3] which is 76 leagues (*farsakh*) from Samarqand, he, by the irresistible order of God turned his face towards the eternal city and rode the steed of life into the spacious abode of the everlasting world. They brought his sublime corse to Samarqand with the respect due to so great a man. The following lines record the years of the events of this world-adorner.

*Quatrain.*

Sulṭān Tīmūr is he to whom no king was like;
In 736, he came into existence;
In 771, he ascended the throne,
In 807, he bade the world adieu.

---

[1] A town in Māzindarān, on the Caspian. It takes its name from a neighbouring mountain which yields turquoise or according to another derivation, is :. "Hill of Victory." (D'Herbélot art. *Firouzcouh* and Réclus 242.) It was seen by Clavigo who calls it Berescote, when on his way to visit Tīmūr (Markham, 101).

[2] The Diet and entertainment described by Clavigo and Gibbon and at which six marriages of Tīmūr's grandchildren were celebrated. It took place September, 1404, at Samarqand.

[3] Lat. 44 N. Long. 67 E. and about 300 miles N. by E. of Samarqand on right bank of the Sīhūn (Jaxartes). Bābar (Erskine I. 11*n.*) says it was called also Yenghi. Hence it is the Yenghi-kent (New Town) of Turkistān mentioned in the *Āīn* (Jarrett III. 101).

This auspicious Lord of Conjunction had four sons. (1) Ghiyāṣu-d-dīn Jahāngīr Mīrzā. He died in Samarqand in 776[1] (1375) in the early part of his father's reign. He left two sons, Muḥammad Sulṭān 81
whom Tīmūr made his heir but who died after the conquest of Asia Minor (Rūm) on 17 Sha'bān, 805, at Sūrī[2] a fort of Rūm; and Pīr Muḥammad who was made his heir after his brother's death and in whose favour his Majesty Ṣāḥib Qarānī made a will at the end of his life. At that time he (Pīr Muḥammad) was ruler of Ghaznīn and the borders of India. But he was martyred on 14 Ramaẓān, 809 (22nd February, 1407), by Pīr 'Alī Tāz,[3] one of his officers and thus the stain of an eternal curse was affixed to the brow of that disloyal one.

The second son of his Majesty Ṣāḥib Qarānī is Mīrzā 'Umar Shaikh who ruled over Persia. He too died in his father's life-time in Rabī'u-l-awwal, 796 (January, 1394), below the fortress of Kharmātū.[4]

---

1 Tīmūr's Memoirs and *Ẓafarnāma*, 777. See *Ẓafarnāma* I. 271 where it is said that 777 corresponds with the Crocodile Year. The death was in the beginning of 777 and so about June 1375.

2 I do not know the authority for this statement. Sūrī Ḥiṣār is mentioned in the *Ẓafarnāma* (II. 448) and Pétis de la Croix says it is a fortress between Angora and Kutaya (Cotyaeum). See also Retrospect, Price, III. 397. In Réclus' map it is Sivri Hissar.

But the *Ẓafarnāma* does not say Muḥammad Sulṭān died there. What it says is (II. 492) that he died three stages from Qarā Ḥiṣār (Black Fort) while his father was having him conveyed in a travelling-litter,—apparently from Qarā Ḥiṣār for change of air. (See for account of his illness and death, *Ẓafarnāma* II. 490. Also Price l.c. III. 424.) The *Ẓafarnāma* gives date of death 18 Sha'bān, (11th March, 1403), and thus about a fortnight after Bāyazīd's; according to Hammer, four days only—he putting Bāyazīd's death 14 Sha'bān, 803 (8th March, 1403). According to Aḥmad 'Arab Shāh (Manger, I. 147) Muḥammad Sulṭān died in Āq Shahr where died also Bāyazīd.

One MS. (B.M. Add. 27, 247) has *dar sawārī* for *dar sūrī* and possibly this is the true reading, for apparently Muḥammad Sulṭān died in his travelling-litter.

3 D'Herbélot and several MSS., *Yār*. Tāz appears right. For account of the murder (which was committed near Shibarghan, W. of Balkh) see Hist. of Bukhārā, Vambéry 215 and 'Abdu-r-razzāk, Quatremère, *Notices et Extraits* XIV. 101. Pīr 'Alī was afterwards put to death by Shāhrukh.

4 Also Kharmānū. It is a petty fort in Kurdistān. The prince had been sent for by his father from Persia and was on his way to join

The third son was Jalālu-d-dīn Mīrān Shāh Mīrzā of whom a short account will be given as he belongs to this noble series.

The fourth son was Mīrzā Shāhrukh who governed Khurāsān and who attended his father's stirrup in many battles. Shortly after his father's death, he became confirmed in sovereignty; and Īrān, Tūrān and such other countries as had been under his father's control, were under his successful sway for 43 years. He was born on Thursday 14th Rabī'u-l-ākhar, 779 (21st August, 1377), and died on New Year's Day (Pers. Era) Sunday morning, 25th Zī-l-ḥijja, 850 (13th March, 1447).

## Jalālu-d-dīn Mīrān Shāh.

Jalālu-d-dīn Mīrān Shāh is the sixth ancestor of the king of kings. His noble birth was in 769 and in his father's lifetime he governed the Arabian[1] and Persian 'Irāqs, Āzarbāījān, Diyārbakr (Mesopotamia) and Syria.

When his Majesty Ṣāḥib Qarānī marched against India, all these countries[2] were placed under his (Jalālu-d-dīn's) management so that not for a moment, was there intermission of justice and sovereignty.

One day while hunting roebuck,[3] his horse shied (or perhaps took fright) in galloping and he was thrown from the point of the

---

him in Diyārbakr. He was killed by an arrow from the fort while reconnoitering it. (*Rauẓatu-ṣ-ṣafā* B.M. Add. 27, 236, 107*b*, and lith. ed. VI. 69; also Retrospect, Price, III. 172).

1 Text *wa*, after 'Irāq, is wrong.

2 Syria can hardly have been among these for it was not conquered until after the Indian expedition.

3 Text سر قوچ *sar-i-qūc*, but *Ẓafarnāma*, *qūc* which Vullers translates *aries bellicosus*. But *sar-i-qūc* also means roe-deer and Pétis de la Croix translates it *chevreuil* (Book V. Cap. I. 189). The *Ḥabību-s-siyar* calls the animal a *qūc-kuhi*, qu. ibex. *Sar-i-qūc* does not occur in the Dictionaries and is perhaps a mistake for *sāī-qūc*, a desert-antelope. Shaw's voc. gives *Sāī-kūk*, for an antelope.

For an account of the accident which occurred in the autumn of 798 (1396) and thus some two yrs. before the Indian expedition, see *Ẓafarnāma* II. 200; Retrospect, Price, III. 292 and *Rauẓatu-ṣ-ṣafā* Book VI. 98 lith. ed. where further details are given such as that Mīrān Shāh took up the deer on his saddle bow and that it fell off and so startled the horse. The accident was near Tabrīz where there were not likely to have been wild sheep.

saddle to the ground and sustained grave injuries to his head and face.[1] Able physicians and surgeons applied remedies and restored him to physical health but his mind remained clouded (*lit.* a mist encircled the centre of his mind's equability) from the accident. After Tīmūr's death, Mīrān S͟hāh's eldest son Abābakr Mīrzā read the *k͟hutba* and struck coins in his father's name. His Highness the Prince (Mīrān S͟hāh) lived principally in Tabrīz[2] and all affairs of 82
sovereignty were carried on by Mīrzā Abābakr. On 24th Z̤ī-l-qa'da, 810 (21st April, 1408), he was killed[3] in a battle with Qarā Yūsuf Turkmān in the environs of Tabrīz. He had eight sons,[4] Abābakr, Alankar Mīrzā, 'Us̤mān Calbī Mīrzā, 'Umar K͟halīl, Sulṭān Muḥammad Mīrzā, Ījil Mīrzā, Siyūrg͟htamis͟h.

## Sulṭān Muḥammad Mīrzā.

Sulṭān Muḥammad Mīrzā is the dominion[5]-holding son of Mīrān S͟hāh. His noble mother was Mihr Nūsh[6] and of the tribe of Fūlād

---

[1] *Z̤afarnāma*, head and face.

[2] Clavigo (Markham 95) saw Mīrān S͟hāh at Sultania and describes him as 40 yrs. of age and a large, corpulent and gouty man. He describes his misconduct and why he had been deprived of power by his father.

[3] *Notices et Extraits*, Quatremère XIV, 135 and *Rauz̤atu-ṣ-ṣafā* lith. ed. VI. 168 and Price l.c. IV. 504. The last two give date 26 Z̤ī-l-qa'da 810.

[4] See Blochmann's *Āīn*, Genealogical Table.

[5] This is said merely for the jingle *farzand-i-daulat-paiwand*. In fact Sulṭān Muḥammad never reigned. It seems (*Z̤afarnāma* II. 735) that he died before his father and grandfather, *i.e.*, before 807, for he is not named in the *Z̤afarnāma*, among Tīmūr's surviving 36 sons and grandsons. This may account for Clavigo's not mentioning him and it also shows how confused and unreliable A.F.'s account is. A.F. would lead us to suppose Sulṭān Muḥammad living when K͟halīl was sent by his uncle S͟hāhruk͟h (Price l.c. IV. 521) in 812 (March, 1410), to Rhey or Rey (Rhages) where he died in Rajab 814 (2nd November, 1411). If as is most probable, Sulṭān Muḥammad Mīrzā died so early—before even his father had acceded to power—A.F.'s representing him as a *Jahān-ārāī wālā-qadr* (powerful world-adorner) and as typified by one of the seven stars of Qacūlī's dream, becomes doubly ridiculous.

[6] Perhaps the lady called K͟hānzāda by S͟harafu-d-dīn (205), Clavigo, etc., who went off to Samarqand and reported her husband's insanity to Tīmūr. Clavigo says she was the mother of K͟halīl and it seems probable from their living together that K͟halīl and Sulṭān Muḥammad were

Qīyā. The Mīrzā always lived with his brother Mīrzā Khalil in Samarqand and when the latter proceeded to 'Irāq, Mīrzā Shāhrukh told Mīrzā Ulugh Bēg (his son) what he knew of Muḥammad Mīrzā's good qualities and praised his noble character; and the Prince (Ulugh Bēg) always shewed him brotherly (*i.e.*, cousinly) kindness. Muḥammad Mīrzā had two sons, Sulṭān Abū Sa'īd Mīrzā and Manūcihr Mīrzā. When he was ill and about to die, Mīrzā Ulugh Bēg came to inquire after him and the latter strongly recommended his son Abū Sa'īd to Mīrzā Ulugh Bēg. Accordingly Abū Sa'īd was brought up with all enjoyment under the care of Ulugh Bēg and daily moved upwards on the steps of dominior and fortune under his guidance. One day,[1] one of Ulugh Bēg's intimates observed to him "Your cousin (Abū Sa'īd) is serving you very zealously," to which the Mīrzā replied, "He is not serving us but is learning the arts of conquest and victory from our companionship." And in this the Mīrzā was speaking from his perfect insight and perception.

## Sulṭān Abū Sa'īd Mīrzā.

Sulṭān Abū Sa'īd Mīrzā's auspicious birth was in 830 (1427) and he became Sulṭān when he was 25. For 18 years he ruled Turkistān, Transoxiana, Badakhshān, Kābul, Ghaznīn, Qandahār and the borders of Hindūstān and in the end of his reign, 'Irāq too came into his possession. And with this prosperity and extent of territory which might become a thousand-fold source of intoxication, he was discreet and open-minded and sought for enlightenment from dervishes and ascetics. In 872 (1468) Mīrzā Jahān Shāh, son of Qarā Yūsuf, the ruler of Āzarbāījān, had marched to put down Āzūn Ḥasan Āqquyanlu[2] but owing to his great carelessness and complete want of

---

full brothers. Clavigo (147) calls her Hansada. He says "She was of the lineage of the old emperors and for this reason, Timur Beg treats her with great respect." This points to her identity with Mihr Nūsh to whose lofty lineage A.F. refers. Qīyā seems the same as Qiyāt mentioned by A.F. in the account of Irganaqūn but I do not know the tribe Fūlād (steel).

[1] Bābar, Erskine, Introduction LIV.

[2] White sheep. (Price l.c. III. 608). The proper spelling appears to be *Āq-quyūn-lū*. The Black sheep are the Qarāquyanlū. Āzūn Ḥasan, *i.e.*, Ḥasan the Long, was maternal grandfather of Shāh Ismā'īl Ṣafavī, king of Persia.

management, was killed by him.[1] The Sulṭān (Abū Sa'īd) led an 83
army against him (Āẕūn Ḥasan). Though Āẕūn Ḥasan proferred peace, it was not accepted and being driven to extremity, he cut off the supplies of corn. Consequently a great famine arose in the camp (of Abū Sa'īd) so that for 14 days the royal horses had no barley and as a result of the famine, the soldiers dispersed. Āẕūn Ḥasan gained the victory and on 22 Rajab, 873 (4th February, 1469), the Sulṭān fell by fate into the hands of Āẕūn Ḥasan's men. Three days afterwards he was made over to Yādgār Muḥammad Mīrzā, son of Sulṭān Muḥammad Mīrzā, son of Bāysanghar Mīrzā, son of Shāhrukh Mīrzā who was an ally of Āẕūn Ḥasan. This worthless inauspicious one slew that powerful king on the pretext[2] of the murder of Gauhar Shād Bēgum who was the wife of Shāhrukh Mīrzā. The words *Maqtal-i-Sulṭān Abū Sa'īd* (the slaughter-spot of Sulṭān Abū Sa'īd) give the date (873 = 1469).

## 'Umar Shaikh Mīrzā.

'Umar Shaikh Mīrzā was the fourth[3] son of Abū Sa'īd Mīrzā, being

---

[1] This is the occurrence referred to by Herbélot in his notice of Abū Sa'īd. He says that in 861 (1457), Abū Sa'īd was in a bad humour owing to having failed to capture the citadel of Herāt and that at this time, some evil-disposed persons told him that Sulṭān Ibrāhīm Mīrzā (a grandson of Bāysanghar and great-grandson of Shāhrukh) had sent messengers to Sulṭāna Gauhar Shād and that he had a secret understanding with her. In consequence, Abū Sa'īd hastily ordered her to be put to death. She was the widow of Shāhrukh, the great-grandfather of Yādgār and had been living in Herāt which had been her husband's capital and where he had died in 850 (1447). Abū Sa'īd had taken the town but had failed to get possession of the citadel.

[2] Gauhar Shād (Jewel of Delight) seems to have been Shāhrukh's favourite wife, and Vambéry states (Hist. of Bukhārā, 236) that some of his verses about her are still remembered by the people of Herāt. Bābar speaks of visiting her tomb. She must have been an elderly woman when put to death, and the vengeance taken by her descendant was not excessive and was in accordance with the Muḥammadan law of retaliation. She was put to death on 10 Ramaẕān, 861 (31st July, 1457. Price l.c. IV, 598.) See inscription on her tomb in Cap. Yates "Notes on the City of Herāt." (J.A.S.B. 1887. Vol. 56, p. 98.) She is there called Gauhar Shād Āghā and the date of her death is given only as the middle of Ramaẕān, 861. Yādgār was only a boy at the time, for Bābar (88) speaks of him as an inexperienced lad of 17 or 18 when he was killed at Herāt in the following year, 1470.

[3] A. F.'s list of Abū Sa'īd's sons

younger than Sulṭān Aḥmad Mīrzā, Sulṭān Muḥammad and Sulṭān Maḥmūd Mīrzā and older than Sulṭān Murād Mīrzā, Sulṭān Walad Mīrzā, Ulugh Bēg Mīrzā, Abū Bakr Mīrzā, Sulṭān Khalīl Mīrzā and Shāhrukh Mīrzā. He was born in Samarqand in 860 (1455). Sulṭān Abū Sa'īd Mīrzā at first gave Kābul to the Prince and sent him off under the guardianship of Bābā Kābulī, but he recalled him from Dara-gaz [1] for the purpose of a festival.[2]

After it was over, he gave him the country of Andijān and the Takhtī-Ōzjand [3] and after providing him with officers, sent him to that country under the guardianship [4] of Tīmūr Tāsh [5] Bēg. The reason for giving this country to the best of his sons was an exceeding desire to preserve his ancestral territory and as his Majesty Ṣāḥib Qarānī gave it to his son 'Umar Shaikh Mīrzā who was of singular ability, so did Abū Sa'īd on account of the sameness of name, gave it to his son 'Umar Shaikh. Ṣāḥib Qarānī is reported to have repeatedly remarked, "We conquered the world by the might of 'Umar Shaikh Mīrzā's "sword, by his staying in Andijān and being a strong barrier between "our territory and the desert of Qipcāk and by his guarding the "passes, the people of Qipcāk were not able to rebel or be turbulent "and we could in security brace ourselves up for the conquest of the "world."

And this wise ruler ('Umar Shaikh the Second) also took extreme precautions that no hostile army should be able to cross this territory

---

does not agree with Khwāndamīr and is incorrect. S. Maḥmūd was the second, and S. Muḥammad the third son. Abū Sa'īd left eleven sons, and it would appear in spite of Bābar's own statements, that his father was the 6th and not the fourth son, the 5th being Ulugh Bēg. The 11th son was apparently a Sulṭān 'Umar, who was distinct from 'Umar Shaikh.

1 "The valley of Gez or Manna which lies on the Dihas or Balkhab, south of Balkh." (Erskine l. c. 7n.) According to Sir H. Rawlinson, (R. G. S. Pro. 1876, 170n.) Daragaz means valley of the tamarisk. As Abū Sa'īd had sent 'Umar Shaikh from Samarqand, the latter would pass Dara-gaz on his way to Afghānistān.

2 Abū Sa'īd's famous six months' festival which he celebrated at Merv, in 1465 and in honour of the circumcision of his sons.

3 Apparently Ōzkand in Eastern Farghāna.

4 'Umar Shaikh was then only ten years old. Much of this is from Bābar's Memoirs.

5 His full name is Khudābandī Tīmūr Tāsh. (Bābar, Erskine 8 and 14.)

which was the boundary of Mongolia. And though Yūnus[1] (Jonas) Khān tried, he could not get possession of it and not the slightest injury happened to its tranquillity. That fortunate and lofty-starred 84
Prince was one who weighed his words and was eloquent; he had a great liking for poets and could recite poetry. He had a poetical temperament but was not solicitous of writing verses and spent most of his time in reading books, historical and poetical. The *Shāhnāma* was often recited before him and he was an excellent companion; of open brow and good disposition and fond of quoting good poetry. A lofty genius warmed his soul and the beauty of fortune was manifest on his brow. He had no equal among his contemporaries for administrative ability, care of his subjects and dispensing of justice. His courage and generosity were on an equal footing and his genius was companioned by his energy. He adorned the throne of sovereignty.[2]

For example, once a caravan from China (Khiṭā) had come to the hill-country east of Andijān. There was a heavy snow-storm and the caravan was overwhelmed so that only two persons escaped. When this just man heard of the catastrophe, in spite of his necessities at the time, he did not touch any of the goods but appointed trustworthy persons and attached the property until the heirs were collected from their native country to receive the goods, the rights of each being ascertained.[3]

This king was always of a dervish mind and inclined to the society of religious persons and asked for wisdom at the doors of the hearts of the God-knowing. Especially the holy Nāṣiru-d-dīn[4] Khwāja ʿAbīdu-l-lāh, known by the name of Khwāja Aḥrār.

---

[1] This is hardly a fair description of Yūnus Khān's proceedings. ʿUmar Shaikh made over his capital Akhsī to Yūnus and then repented and made war on him. He was defeated and taken prisoner and owed his life to Yūnus' generosity. (*Tār. Rashīdī*, 96.)

[2] All this is from Bābar. (Erskine 8 and also Pavét de Courteille.) But the Turkish seems more concise than the Persian. A.F. probably used the latter for his account is in closer accord with Erskine than with De Courteille.

[3] This story is told in Bābar's Memoirs (8). The stress laid on this simple act of honesty by Bābar and A.F. is rather significant of the morals of the time. Probably ʿUmar Shaikh's self-denial on this occasion inspired his son Bābar to similar action towards the Hindustānī merchants at Kilāt-i-ghilzāī. (Memoirs 225.)

[4] For references to this saint, see

In succession to his father, he ruled in Andijān, the capital of Farghāna and also Tāshkand, Shāhrukhīya and Sīrām were in his possession. He several times led an army against Samarqand and he several times brought to his help Yūnus Khān who possessed the dominions of Caghatāī Khān and was Khān of the Mughals and was nearly related to him. Whenever he brought him, he assigned some province to him and then as occasion served, Yūnus Khān would go back to Mughalistān. On the last occasion 'Umar Mīrzā gave him Tāshkand and up to 908 (1502-3) this and Shāhrukhīya were in the possession of the Caghatāī rulers. At this last date the Khanship of the Mughal tribes belonged to Maḥmūd Khān, eldest son of Yūnus Khān. This Maḥmūd Khān and Sulṭān Aḥmad Mīrzā brother of 'Umar Shaikh ruler of Samarqand, having concluded an alliance, marched their forces against the Mīrza ('Umar Shaikh). Sulṭān Aḥmad Mīrzā proceeded from the south of the Khajand river and Sulṭān Maḥmūd Khān from the north of it. Just at this crisis an
85 extraordinary thing happened to the Mīrzā. The brief account of it is as follows.

Akhsīkat which is known as Akhsī, is one of the seven towns of Farghāna. Mīrzā 'Umar Shaikh had made it his capital. The town was on a precipitous ravine and all the buildings were on its edge.[1] As fate would have it, on Monday 4th Ramaẓān, 899 (9th June, 1494), he was sitting near his pigeon house which was one of these buildings, watching the motions of his birds, when an attendant reported that the precipice was breaking away. The Mīrzā at once got up and had put one foot into its slipper but had not had time to put in the other, when the whole precipice gave way and the terrace fell down. The Mīrzā's outward form fell to the bottom but in reality, he ascended to the zenith. He was then 39 years old, having been born in 860, at Samarqand. (This last fact has been mentioned already.)

Be it known that Farghāna belongs to the fifth climate and is on

---

*Tār. Rashīdī* 97, etc., and *Nafaḥātu-l-uns*, Lees, 465. He lived in Samarqand. Dr. Rieu gives the date of his death as 29th Rabī' I. 895 (2nd March, 1490), (Pers. Cat. III, 1086*a*). See also Blochmann 423.

[1] Apparently only the fort was on the edge of the ravine and the town some distance off. The fort looked down on the Sīhūn and 'Umar Shaikh had increased the steepness of the precipice by scarping the rock of the ravine. Perhaps this partly caused the accident.

the borders of the civilized world. East of it is Kāshghar and west, Samarqand; south, the mountains on the borders of Badakhshān. To the north, although formerly there were cities such as Almālīgh, Almātū, Yāngī, known as Utrār, but at present no traces or ruins even of them remain. In the west where are Samarqand and Khajand, there are no mountains. Except in this direction, there is no entry for foreigners. The river Sīhūn, known as the Āb-i-khajand, coming from the north-east flows west. It then runs on the north of Khajand and south of Fināk at which is known as Shāhrukhīya. Then inclining to the north, it flows towards Turkistān and meeting no other river in its course, it disappears beyond Turkistān in the sands. In this country there are seven towns, (*qaṣba*) five to the south of the Sīhūn and two to the north. The southern towns are Andijān, Ūsh, Marghīnān,[1] Asfara (var. Isfaraj) and Khajand. The northern are Akhsī and Kasān.

This unique pearl of sovereignty had three sons and five daughters, the eldest son being his Majesty Firdūs-makānī Ẓahīru-d-dīn Muḥammad Bābar Pādshāh. Jahāngīr Mīrza was the next and younger by two years and was the son of Fāṭima Sulṭān who belonged to the Tōmān officers (*i.e.*, chiefs of 10,000 men) of the Mughals. The third was Nāṣir Mīrzā younger than Jahāngīr by two years. His chaste mother was from Andijān and was a concubine named Ummed. The eldest daughter was Khānzāda Bēgum, full sister of his Majesty Gītī-sitānī Firdūs-makānī and older than he by five years. When Shāh Isma'īl Ṣafawī defeated the Uzbēgs (Shaibānī) at Merv, that chaste 86
one was in Merv and Shāh Isma'īl sent her with all respect to his Majesty Gītī-sitānī Firdūs-makānī at Qunduz.[2]

After a lapse of ten years, an interview took place between them, and his Majesty Gītī-sitānī Firdūs-makānī says, "When they "came I and Maḥmūdī Kōkultāsh (foster-brother) went to meet them "but the Bēgum and her attendants did not recognize us, although "we made ourselves known. After a while they recognized us."[3]

---

[1] The modern name is Marghīlān (Erskine l.c. 3n.) It is west of Andijān.

[2] A town north, of Kābul and east of Balkh. Sometimes spelled Khunduz. (*Tārīkh-i-rashīdī*, 239.)

[3] Perhaps the meaning is that she could not distinguish Bābar from his foster-brother. (See Erskine, 10 and P. de Courteille, 17). The non-recognition of her brother is curious considering that she was about 24

The next daughter was Mihr Bānū Bēgum, full sister of Nāṣir Mīrzā and eight years younger than Firdūs-makānī. The next was Yādgār Sulṭān Bēgum. Her mother was a concubine named Āghā Sulṭān. The next was Raẓīya Sulṭān Bēgum. Her mother was Makhdūma Sulṭān Bēgum known as the Qarā-gūz (Black-eyed) Bēgum. Then two daughters were born after 'Umar Shaikh's death. There was also a daughter born of Anūsh Āghā, daughter of Khwāja Ḥusain who died young.[1]

---

when separated from him and also that Ḥaidar Mīrzā says (Ney Elias 239) that Shaibānī divorced her on account of his suspecting her attachment to her brother. When Bābar left her she became the wife of Shaibānī and had a son by him. The *Shaibānī-nāma* says her marriage with Shaibānī was a love-match and it seems probable that Bābar has not mentioned the whole of the circumstances and that her being left behind was a part of Bābar's agreement with Shaibānī. Ḥaidar Mīrzā, Bābar's cousin, distinctly states (*Tārīkh-i-rashīdī*, Ney Elias, 175, 196 and 239) that Bābar gave his sister to Shaibānī. Bābar's own daughter Gulbadan mentions the arrangement in her Memoirs, so that there can be no doubt as to the fact. When Shaibānī divorced Khānzāda, he gave her in marriage to a Sayyid, but he as well as Shaibānī, was killed in the battle of Merv.

1 A.F.'s account of 'Umar Shaikh's family as well as of Farghāna (Khōkand) is taken almost *verbatim* from Bābar, Memoirs. He omits the name of Bābar's third daughter, Shahrbānū Bēgum, from the list, nor can she be the nameless daughter mentioned at the end of his account by A.F. for her mother was Anūsh Āghā whereas Shahrbānū was full sister of Nāṣir Mīrzā son of a concubine named Ummēd. In fact A.F. has confused Mihrbānū and Shahrbānū. The former was two years older than Bābar and it was Shahrbānū, misnamed Mihrbānū by A.F., who was eight years younger than Bābar. Bābar gives the youngest daughter's name as Ruqīya and not Raẓīya as in A.F.

The Turkish version of Bābar's Memoirs gives, apparently wrongly, Qarā-gūz as a sobriquet of Bābar's sister instead of his step-mother. The nameless daughter mentioned by A.F. is referred to later by Bābar (Erskine 14 and P. de Courteille 25) so that in fact 'Umar Shaikh had six daughters. The wife whom the text calls Anūsh Āghā is called by Bābar, Ūlūs Āghā and a note to the text states that this name appears in many MSS. She was removed from the harem a few months after she had given birth to a daughter.

With reference to A.F.'s omission of the name of the third daughter Shahrbānū, it is curious to note that a similar omission occurs in two MSS. of the Persian translation of Bābar's Memoirs, B. M. Add. 24, 416 and 26,200, though No. 26,200 has a marginal correction giving her name.

# CHAPTER XVII.

## His Majesty Gītī-sitānī Firdūs-makānī Ẓahīru-d-dīn Muḥammad Bābar Pādshāh Ghāzī.[1]

King of the four quarters,[2] and of the seven heavens; celestial sovereign; diadem of the sublime throne; great of genius and greatness-conferring; fortune-increaser; of excellent horoscope; heaven in comprehensiveness; earth in stability; lion-hearted; clime-capturer; lofty in splendour; of active brain; searcher after knowledge; rank-breaking lion rampant; exalter of dominion; ocean-hearted; of illustrious origin; a saintly sovereign; enthroned in the kingdom of reality and spirituality, Ẓahīru-d-dīn Muḥammad Bābar Pādshāh Ghāzī. His pearl-like nature was a station for the marks of greatness and sublimity; freedom and detachment together with lofty restraint and majestic power flashed forth in his nature; in asceticism and absorption (*faqr ū fanā*[3]) a Junīd[4] and Bāyazīd; while the magni-

---

[1] World-gripper, Paradise-inhabiting, Defender of the Faith, Muḥammad Bābar (Lion), the holy warrior-king. Bābar is commonly said to mean lion or tiger, but this seems to me a little doubtful, for the word for lion is *babr*, not *bābar*. Besides why should the Turks use a Persian word? May it not be connected with the Caghatāī word *bābari* or *bayarī* old or primitive. See P. de Courteille, Turc Dict. 155.

[2] *Cār bālish-i-haft manẓar*, lit. four cushions or elements, seven scenes or theatres. The four cushions mean four thrones and so four quarters of the world.

[3] Another favourite expression is *fanā ū baqā* for which see *Notices et Extraits*, S. de Sacy, XII., 327n. *Fanā* is used by mystics for the Ṣūfī's relation to externals, *viz.* his dying to them and *baqā* for his relation to God.

[4] Usually Junaid but here Junīd, unless Bāyazīd be written Bāyazaid. Junaid was a famous ascetic known as Al-Baghdādī and is said to have performed the pilgrimage to Mecca thirty times, on foot and alone. (Beale art. Junaid). He died about 909 A.D. See *Nafaḥātu-l-uns*, Lees, 89, No. 81 and Jarrett III. 352, where however A. F.'s account is only an abridgement of Jāmī. S. de Sacy has translated Jāmī's life of Junaid. (*Notices et Extraits* XII, 366 *et seq.*)

Bāyazīd is Bāyazīd Bisṭāmī, also known as Ṭayfūr b. 'Īsā. He, as well as Junaid, belonged to the Naqsh-

ficence and genius of an Alexander and of a Farīdūn shone from his brow. The holy birth of this majestic one was on 6 Muḥarram 888 (14th February 1483) from the holy womb and pure veil of the gloriously chaste and nobly-born, Qutlaq Nigār Khānum. That jewel of fortune's ocean and sparkling star (*durrī*) of the heaven of glory arose from a happy quarter. She, the coiffure of purity and scarf of chastity, was the second daughter of Yūnus (Jonah) Khān and elder sister of Sulṭān Maḥmūd Khān. Her lineage is as follows:—daughter of Yūnus Khān b. Vais Khān, b. Shīr 'Alī Ōghlān, b. Muḥammad Khān, b. Khiẓr Khwāja Khān, b. Tughlaq Tīmūr Khān, b. Isān Bughā Khān, b. Davā Khān, b. Barāq Khān, b. Īsūn Tava,[1] b. Mutakan, b. Caghatāī Khān, b. Cingīz Khān. Maulānā Ḥisāmī[2] Qarākūlī recorded the date of the noble birth as follows.

*Verse.*

Since on 6 Muḥarram was born that bounteous king,
His birth's chronogram is also 6 Muḥarram (*shash-i-Muḥarram.*[3])

87 Though the chronogram be of marvellous coincidence and unfathomable in its significance, there is something stranger yet, *viz.*, the chronogram is in six letters which are reckoned by the masters of

---

bandī order and he was Junaid's his predecessor and teacher. According to the *Khazīnatu-l-auliyā* (I, 519) Junaid said, "Bāyazīd among us is like Gabriel among the angels." Bāyazīd was descended from a family of fire-worshippers and was a native of Bisṭām in Persia. (S.S.E. of the Caspian and 3 m. N.E. of Shāhrūd.) He died 261 A.H. (874 A.D.) and is buried in Bisṭām. See Meynard's Yāqūt 104, Jarrett III., 352 and 359 and Curzon's Persia I.,283 who spells the name of the town Bostam and notices the saint's tomb.

[1] Text, Bīsun Tava.

[2] T. R. 173, calls the author of the chronogram Munīr Marghīnānī and describes him as having been one of the *'ulamā* of Ulugh Beg. The Luck. ed. calls him Jāmī Qarākūlī. I have consulted the B. M. MSS. of T. R., the name is not clear, it may be Munīr or Mushīr. Erskine (MS. trs. Add. No. 26, 612) calls him merely Maulānā Marghīnānī. Munīr means illustrious in Arabic and may here be descriptive, so that the difference between the two names may be only as to that of origin, *viz.*, Marghīnān or Qarākūl.

Qarākūl (Black Lake) is about 28 miles S. W. of Bukhārā. (Bābar, Ers. 54.)

[3] Bābar, Ers. Intro. LXI.

computation as a lucky number[1] and also the phrase (*lafz*) *shash ḥarf* and the pips (*naqsh*) *'adad-i-khair* both indicate the date. Another wonderful thing is that the units, tens and hundreds of the date are all the same (8-8-8), thus pointing to equability of dispositions. His life corresponded to these mysteries of birth. That exemplar of high saints, Khwāja Aḥrār himself with his own bounty-shedding tongue gave him—the auspicious one—the names of Ẓahīru-d-dīn Muḥammad, but as this weighty appellation with its majesty and sublimity, was not readily pronounceable or current on the tongues of the Turks, the name of Bābar was also given to him.

His Majesty was the eldest and straightest of the sons of 'Umar Shaikh Mīrzā. In his twelfth year, on Tuesday, 5 Ramaẓān, 899 (10th June, 1494), he sate upon the throne in Andijān. Few kings have encountered such difficulties as he, and the courage, self-reliance and endurance which he displayed in the battle-field and in danger were superhuman. When the inevitable accident of 'Umar Shaikh Mīrzā occurred in Akhsī, his Majesty Gītī-sitānī Firdūs-makānī was in the Cārbāgh (Palace) of Andijān. Next day, *viz.*, Tuesday, 5 Ramaẓān, the news was brought to Andijān. In a moment he mounted his horse and proceeded to the fort of Andijān. As he was alighting at the gate,[2] Shīram[3] Ṭaghāī seized his bridle and carried him towards the namāzgāh (place of prayer) in order to take him to Ōzkand and the foot of the hills. His idea was that, as Sulṭān Aḥmad Mirzā was coming with great power, the treacherous officers might make over the country to him; if out of disloyalty, they did so, his Majesty's sacred person might be saved from this danger and be conveyed to his maternal uncles Ilanja[4] Khān or Sulṭān Maḥmūd

[1] Referring to throws at dice, I suppose. *Shash-ḥarf* and *'adad-i-khair* both yield 888, *viz.*, 2*sh*=600, *ḥ*=8, *r*=200 and *f*=80, total 888. Again, *a*=70, 2*d*=8, *kh*=600, *i*=10, *r*=200, total 888. The great standard was called *shash tughjī*. (*T. R.* l. c. 93.) The chronogram is in six letters, *viz.*, sh, sh, m, ḥ, r, m.

[2] Bābar, Ers., Mīrzā's Gate.

[3] Apparently the Shīrun Ṭaghāī mentioned in *T. R.* l. c. 228, as maternal uncle of Bābar and as a pillar of the State. See too Bābar, Ers. 59 and 94. Apparently he was Bābar's grand-uncle, being his mother's uncle. (Erskine, B. and H. I, 334) Ṭaghāī or ṭaqāī means maternal uncle in Caghatāī and Firishta calls him the taghāī of 'Umar Shaikh Mīrzā.

[4] P. de C. (I. 32), Alaja and Bābar.

Khān. The officers, on becoming aware of this intention, sent Khwāja Muḥammad Darzī to dispel anxieties that had arisen in his mind. The *cortège* had reached the *namāzgāh* when Khwaja Muḥammad came up with it. He calmed his Majesty and induced him to
88 return. When he (Bābar) alighted at the citadel of Andijān, all the officers came to wait upon him and received marks of favour from him. It has already been mentioned that Sulṭān Aḥmad Mīrzā and Sulṭān Maḥmūd Khān had united and come against 'Umar Shaikh Mīrzā. Now that by the decree of fate, an inevitable accident had occurred, all the officers, small and great, united to defend the fort. Sulṭān Aḥmad Mīrzā had taken possession of Ūrātippa, Khajand and Marghīnān which are districts of Farghāna, and had encamped within four *kos* of Andijān. Though they sent ambassadors and knocked at the door of peace, he did not listen but continued to advance. But as secret aids were always in attendance on this family, on account of the strength of the fort and the unanimity of the officers and of a pestilence which broke out in the camp and of the deaths of the horses,[1] Sulṭān Aḥmad got into difficulties and came to despair of his former designs. He therefore came to terms and returned without effecting anything. Coming from the north side of the river of Khajand, Sulṭān Maḥmūd Khān invested Akhsī. Jahāngīr Mīrzā, brother of his Majesty, and a large number of loyal officers were there. The Khān made several assaults, the officers made a spirited resistance, and so the Khān also did not effect his purpose, and being attacked by a sickness, had to give up his vain enterprise and turn his reins towards his own country. For eleven[2] years, his Majesty waged great wars in Transoxiana against the Caghatāī princes and the Uzbēgs. Thrice he conquered Samarqand, *viz.*, once in 903 (end of November 1497) when coming[3] from Andijān, he took it from

(Ers. 18) Ilcheh. His real name was Sulṭān Aḥmad Khān and Ilcheh is a sobriquet meaning slayer. (Ers. l. c. 13). He was a son of Yūnus Khān and half-brother of Bābar's mother.

[1] Many horses were drowned in crossing the Kaba and many died of disease.

[2] Apparently a clerical error for 18, *viz.*, for the period from 899 to 917. Some MSS. seem to have 15 (which is easily confounded with 11) and Price has 15. (Ret. IV, 666.)

[3] The Text reads as if it were Bāyasaughar who came from Andijān but Bābar's Mem. show what is meant.

Bāyasanghar Mīrzā, son of Sultān Maḥmud Mīrzā; secondly, from Shaibak (Shaibānī) Khān in 906 (autumn of 1500); and thirdly, after Shaibak Khān had been killed in 917 (October 1511). As God's plan was the revealing of that unique pearl, his Majesty the king of kings, and designed that the country of Hindustān should be acquired and that his Majesty should proceed to a strange land and there arrive at greatness and felicity,—he caused the gates of trouble to be opened in his own native land which is the meeting place of faithful servants, so that in no way could that be fit for him. He was compelled to proceed with a small force towards Badakhshān and Kābul. When he reached Badakhshān, all the people of Khusrū Shāh who was ruler there, accepted his service. And the ruler himself was compelled to do so, though this wretch was ring-leader of the unjust ones and had martyred[1] Bāyasanghar and blinded Sultān Mas'ūd 89
Mīrzā, which two princes were his Majesty's cousins. He (Khusrū) also showed signs of pitilessness and inhumanity when at a time of calamity,[2] his Majesty's army was passing into Badakhshān.

Now when he beheld the face of his deeds in the mirror of recompense, and fortune had turned away her countenance from his worthless self, his Majesty from perfect humanity and excessive generosity, did not exercise retaliation,[3] but gave orders that he should carry away as much of his property as he desired and go off to Khurāsān. So he took five or six strings[4] of mules and camels, laden

---

[1] (Bābar, Ers. 73.) Bāyasanghar, who was a poet, was second son of Sultān Muḥammad Mīrzā of Herāt, the second son of Abū Sa'īd. He was put to death on 17th August, 1499. (Bābar, Ers. 72.) Mas'ūd was his brother. See account of his being blinded l. c. 63. It was in 1497 that Bābar drove Bāyasanghar out of Samarqand.

[2] Text *ṣāḥibqarānī* which does not make sense. Luck. ed. and several MSS., *qarānī*, calamity or crisis. قيران *qairān* seems to be Turkish for breaking. This passage must refer to Khusrū Shāh's treatment of Bābar when he came to Ḥiṣār (Ḥiṣār-i-shādmān) on his flight from Samarqand in 907. Bābar says, (Ers. 126), "Twice did my course "lie through the country of this "Khusrū Shāh, so famed for his "liberal conduct and generosity, "and that humanity which he dis"played to the meanest of men, he "never showed to me." See also T. R. 175. See Ers.'s remarks on Bābar's behaviour to Khusrū Shāh (125).

[3] Bābar, Ers. 131 and 132. *T. R.* 176.

Leyden states that seven mules

with jewelry and gold ornaments and went off to Khurāsān. And his Majesty Gītī-sitānī Firdūs-makānī having put Badakhshān into order, went to Kābul.

At that time Muḥammad Muqīm, son of Ẕū-n-nūn Arghūn had taken Kābul from ʿAbdu-razzāq Mīrzā, son of Ulugh Beg Mīrzā, son of Sulṭān Abū Saʿīd Mīrzā, who was his Majesty's cousin. On hearing the noise of the coming of the victorious standards, he fortified himself, but after some days he sought for peace and obtained permission to go to his brother Shāh Bēg in Qandahār with his property. Kābul fell into the hands of his Majesty's servants in the end of Rabīʿu-l-awwal 910 (beginning of October 1504). After that his Majesty proceeded in 911 to capture Qandahār, and Qilūt (Khelat) which is a dependency of Qandahār was conquered. After that, for reasons of state policy, he abandoned the taking of Qandahār and went south and having attacked the Afghān tribes of Sawāsang and Alātāgh,[1] returned to Kābul.

In the beginning[2] of this year there was a great earthquake in Kābul and its environs. The ramparts of the fort and many buildings in the citadel and city fell down. All the houses in the village of Pemghan[3] fell down and there were three-and-thirty shocks in one day and for a month the earth shook two or three times day and night. Many persons lost their lives, and between Pemghān and Baktub a piece of ground a stone's throw[4] in breadth separated itself and

go to a string (qaṭār), (Bābar 132) but A. F. (Blochmann 152) gives five as the number.

[1] Bābar, Ers. 171n.

[2] The year 905 began 4th June but the earthquake must have been in July. From Bābar's Memoirs, it appears that it occurred about 40 days after his mother's death which was in the beginning of the year.

[3] Also Pemghān. Bābar, Ers. 146. It is S. or S. W. of Kābul.

[4] Text, *yak kata bāsh andāz* which is unintelligible. I have examined the two B. M. Persian MSS. of Bābar's Memoirs. In both, the passage is the same but in the margin of Add. No. 26, 200—the copy used by Erskine—we have *bir kata tāsh andāz*. No doubt *tāsh* (Turk. stone) is correct. *Kata* is Turkish for large but its use here in that sense is not apparent unless we take *tāshandās* as one word and say "a great" or "long stone-throw." Neither Erskine nor P. de Courteille translates *kata* by great. I should be inclined to regard it as the Hindūstānī *kitta* and as pleonastic; *yak kitta tāsh* might then mean merely a stone. The passages in the B. M. MSS. are p. 135*b* of No. 24,416 and p. 141*a* of No. 26,200.

descended the length of a bowshot and springs burst out from the breach. From Istirghac [1] to Maidān,[2] a distance of six *farsangs*, (cir. 24 m.) the ground was so contorted that part of it rose as high as an elephant. In the beginning of the earthquake, clouds of dust rose from the tops of the mountains. In the same year there was a great earthquake in India.[3]

One of the occurrences of this time was that Shaibak (Shaibānī) Khān collected an army and proceeded towards Khurāsān. Sulṭān Ḥusain Mīrzā assembled all his sons and marched to oppose him. He also sent Sayyid Afẓal, the son of Mīr Sultān 'Alī Khwāb-bīn (vision-seer) to urge on the advance of his Majesty Firdūs-makānī. Accordingly he proceeded towards Khurāsān in Muḥarram 912 (end 90
of May 1506). On the way he received at Kāhmard [4] the news of Sulṭān Ḥusain's death. His Majesty Firdūs-makānī, thinking it still more necessary [5] to advance, went on towards Khurāsān contrary to the calculations of politicians. Before his army reached Khurāsān, short-sighted [6] and inexperienced men had placed jointly on the throne the Mīrzā's sons, Badī'u-z-zamān and Muẓaffar Ḥusain Mīrzās.

On Monday, 8th Jumāda-l-ākhar his Majesty met the Mīrzās at the Murghāb and at their request came on to Herāt. But as

---

[1] Now Sirghac. Bābar, Ers. 146n.

[2] Ers. (Bābar, 170) has "to the plain" (*maidān*) but P. de C. (I, 349) seems correct in taking it as the name of a place, Maidān. His trs. completes the description by saying there were holes large enough for a man to hide in.

[3] Ers. (B. and H. I, 229) notes that there was an earthquake at Āgra on 5th July, 1505. Elliot (V, 99) gives Sunday, 3rd *Ṣafar* (6th July).

[4] P. de C., Kāhmard. Wood (Journey to Source of the Oxus, 132), Kamrūd. It is in Afghanistān, N.-W. of Kābul and according to Bābar (Ers. 199) in a valley not far from the Dandān-shikan (tooth-breaking) Pass.

[5] Bābar (Ers. 200) says that he went on "from a regard to the reputation of our family though I also "had other motives," apparently to try conclusions once more with Shaibānī.

[6] The folly consisted in the dual appointment for A.F. and his school held that kingship, being the shadow of Godhead, must be single. Bābar, referring to the joint appointment, says, (199) "This was a strange "arrangement. A joint kingship "was never before heard of. The "well-known words of Shaikh Sa'dī "in the *Gulistān* (I, 3) are very appli- "cable to it. Ten dervishes sleep "in one coverlet (*galīm*) but two "kings have not room in one clime "(*iqlīm*)." See also *T. R.* 196.

he did not perceive in them signs of guidance and dominion, he set out on his return to Kābul on 8th Sha'bān (24th Dec., 1506). While in the Hazāra Hills, news arrived that Muḥammad Ḥusain Mīrzā Daghlāt [1] and Sulṭān Sanjar Barlās had drawn over to their side all the Mughals left in Kābul and had raised up Khān Mīrzā[2] and were besieging Kābul. They also spread among the commonalty a report that the sons of Sulṭān Ḥusain Mīrzā were meditating[3] treachery against his Majesty Firdūs-makānī. Mullā Bābāī[4] Bashāghari, Amīr[5] Muḥibb 'Alī Khalīfa, Amīr Muḥammad Qāsim Kōhbar[6] Aḥmad Yūsuf and Aḥmad Qāsim to whom the protection of Kābul had been entrusted, were looking after the defence of the fort. As[7] soon as he heard this news, he made over the baggage to Jahāngīr Mīrzā who was somewhat ill,[8] and accompanied by a few men crossed the passes of the Hindū Kōh which were full of snow, under great difficulty, and descended one morning early upon Kābul. The rebels all crept into concealment at the news of his Majesty's approach. He first went to his step-grandmother (mother's step-mother) Shāh[9] Bēgum, who

1 Text, wrongly, *wafāt kard ōghlat* (Bābar, Ers. 214). This Muḥammad Ḥusain was the father of Bābar's cousin Ḥaidar, author of the *T. R.*

2 Bābar's cousin; being son of Sulṭān Muḥammad Mīrzā, third son of Sulṭān Abū Sa'īd and Sulṭān Nigār Khānum, daughter of Yūnus Khān and Shāh Bēgum. He was thus doubly Bābar's cousin, being son of Bābar's father's elder brother and of his mother's half-sister. Mīrzā Khān's proper name was Sulṭān Vais Mīrzā. Khusrū Shāh killed his brother Bāyasanghar and blinded his brother Mas'ūd. He afterwards became king of Badakhshān.

3 The report was that they had imprisoned Bābar in the Eagle Castle, near Herāt. (Mem. 214).

4 *T. R.* l. c. 356. Both Bābāī and Muḥammad Aḥmad Kōhbar afterwards rebelled against Bābar.

5 Bābar, Ers. 214, Khalīfa Muḥibb 'Alī Qurca.

6 Price (Ret. IV, 67) renders this, mountain-piercer, but it probably comes from the town Kōhbar, in Sind, mentioned by Jarrett, (II, 337). Kōhbar appears also to be the name of a Caghatāī tribe (Blochmann 613n.) Mr. Blochmann quotes the name of Muḥammad Qāsim Kōhbar as that of a poet; perhaps this is the Kōhbar of the Text.

7 Taken from *T. R.* l. c. 200.

8 Apparently from excessive drinking.

9 Daughter of the king of Badakhshān and widow of Yūnus, Bābar's maternal grandfather. Bābar's own grandmother was Ais or Isān Daulat Bēgum. (Memoirs, Ers. 12.)

had been the cause of the putting forward of Khān Mīrzā, and addressed her after kneeling down before her. Knowing well what her state of mind was, he spoke to her with modesty and magnanimity, and with soothing words observed to her, "If a mother have special "affection for one child, why should another child be aggrieved?, "there is no limit to her authority." Then he said, "I have been "up long and have come a long way," and laying his head on her lap, he went to sleep. Thus in order to reassure the Bēgum who was very uneasy, he behaved in a very kind manner[1] to her. Ere he had fully fallen asleep, his aunt, Mihr[2] Nigār Khānum, came in and his

[1] Ers. B. and H. I, 253 and *T. R.* 200. The Text is not quite clear.

[2] Eldest daughter of Yūnus Khān. She was first married to Sulṭān Aḥmad Mīrzā, uncle of Bābar, and on his death, to Shaibānī. (*T. R.* 96 and 196). Bābar, in order that he might escape from Samarqand, gave his sister Khānzāda in marriage to Shaibānī and as she was niece of Mihr Nigār, Shaibānī divorced the latter "as it was unlawful for both to be married to the same man." Mihr Nigār died childless. (*T. R.* 155).

A.F. has apparently taken his account from the Tārīkh-i-rashīdī but has altered its language. Erskine who, I believe, had not read the *T. R.* when editing Leyden's Bābar, makes some mistakes here. (Bābar, 217 and 218). It is clear that the Khānum was Mihr Nigār, Bābar's maternal aunt. She was probably called Khānum because she was the eldest daughter and indeed eldest child of Yūnus Khān, by his chief wife, Isān Daulat Bēgum. (*T. R.* 86). She was also the only surviving daughter of that marriage, for her younger sister, Bābar's mother, had lately died. The Khānum was certainly not Khūb Nigār for she had died some years earlier. (Bābar, Ers. 99 and *T. R.* 157 where we are told that Khūb Nigār died a year and a half before 907=1500 or 1501). Nor is it correct to say that A.F. speaks of Mīrzā Khān's being brought by his mother Sulṭān Nigār. His mother was the daughter of Yūnus Khān by Shāh Bēgum but, as Erskine correctly states, she does not appear to have been at Kābul at the time. (It should, however, here be said that Gulbadan, in her Memoirs, describes Khān Mīrzā as having been brought before Bābar by his mother, Sulṭān Nigār. This must be a mistake, I think). She was first married to Sulṭān Maḥmūd, son of Sulṭān Abū Sa'īd, and had by him one son, *viz.*, the Mīrzā Khān or Sulṭān Vais of the Text and afterwards king of Badakhshān. Sulṭān Maḥmūd died in January, 1495, and some years later (Bābar 13) she was married to 'Ādil Sulṭān (Ers., Uzbak Sulṭān) and when 'Ādil died, to his brother, Qāsim Khān (the famous ruler of the Kirghises who defeated Shaibānī's troops, *T. R.*

Majesty hastily arose and saluted her (*īshān-rā daryāftand*). They arrested Muḥammad Ḥusain Mīrzā and brought him in. His Majesty being a mine of kindness, gave him his life and gave him permission to go to Khurāsān. After that the Khānum (Mihr Nigār) brought in Khān Mīrzā and said, "O life of your mother! I have brought

373). Ḥaidar Mīrzā's account, from which A.F. has copied, may be seen in Ney Elias and Ross' trs. (200) but the word grandson is there a mistake for nephew. The MS. of Ḥaidar's Text has apparently not *nabīra* but *yugan* or "*yezneh*," nephew, as Erskine has written in the margin of his MS. trs. of *T. R.* B. M. Add. No. 26,162. Erskine has apparently written *yezneh* but the right word seems to be یگان *yugan* which like the Latin *nepos*, means both a nephew and a grandchild. Perhaps *nabīra* has a similar double meaning. یزنه the *yezneh* of Erskine is given by P. de Courteille as brother-in-law or son-in-law. A.F. calls Mihr Nigār the Khālazāda, *i.e.*, cousin of Bābar and the same word appears in the *T. R.* Erskine in a marginal note (B. M. Add. No. 26, 612, 192) observes that this word which signifies cousin, seems an error. I am not sure that the original word is not *khālazāid* which perhaps might be held to mean a birth-aunt or full-aunt. Or perhaps it is *khānazāda*, home-born in allusion to her being his mother's full sister.

The discrepancies in the three accounts, *viz.*, Bābar's (Ers. 217, etc.) Ḥaidar's and A.F.'s, are curious. Bābar is presumably most correct. for Ḥaidar was but a child at the time, but Ḥaidar's account, derived presumably from his father, is the most graphic. He says that just after Bābar had laid his head in his grandmother's lap, the aunt Mihr Nigār Khānum came in. He saluted her and then she bade him go to the castle and see his family and that she would come there after him. He went and she followed, bringing with her, her nephew (Mīrzā Khān) and Ḥaidar's father, Muḥammad Ḥusain. Bābar advanced to meet her and she said, "O life of your "(dead) mother, I have brought your "guilty nephew and your unfor-"tunate cousin." (*Ai jān-i-mādar yezneh* (or *yugan*)*-i-gunāhgār ū birādar-i-nāsāzkār bar āwurdam.*) "What do you say to them?" A. F. has altered the words which Bābar used to his grandmother. Shāh Bēgum and Mihr Sulṭān afterwards went towards Badakhshān with Khān Mīrzā but the ladies were caught on the road by Abū Bakr and taken to Kāshghar where they were imprisoned and eventually perished miserably. Evidently Mihr Nigār was strongly attached to her stepmother and her nephew and perhaps she was displeased with Bābar for having contributed to her divorce. Bābar expresses himself as vexed at her leaving him for Badakhshān. "It would have been better and more becoming for her to have remained with me." (Ers. 232).

"your guilty cousin (*birādar*), what is your pleasure?" His Majesty took him in his arms and spoke kindly to him. After that he left 91
it to his option to go or stay. The Khān Mīrzā was so ashamed that he could not make up his mind to remain. He took leave and went to Qandahār.[1] This happened in the same year.

Next year he (Bābar) proceeded to Qandahār[2] and fought a great battle with Shāh Bēg, son of Ẕū-n-nūn Arghūn and Muḥammad Muqīm his younger brother. The Khān did good service here. His Majesty presented Qandahār to Nāṣir Mīrzā, the younger brother[3] of Jahāngīr Mīrzā and returned to Kābul. He permitted Shāh Bēgum and Khān Mīrza to proceed to Badakhshān. After many adventures Khān Mīrzā put Zabīr Raghī[4] to death and became confirmed in the dominion of Badakhshān. He always retained his loyalty (to Bābar).

In 916 (early in December 1510) an express[5] brought the news that Shaibānī Khān was killed and that it was proper for Bābar to move in that direction. Accordingly in Shawwāl, he proceeded[6] there and fought great battles with the Uzbēgs. He was ever victorious and took Samarqand for the third time, in 917 (Oct. 1511). He ruled there for eight months but in Ṣafar 918 (April 1512) he had a great battle at Kūl Malik with 'Ubaidu-l-lāh Khān. Though he had won the victory, suddenly by the jugglery of the heavens, he sustained a defeat and proceeded to Ḥiṣār.

---

[1] This is in accordance with *T. R.* 201, but Bābar says he got leave to go to Khurāsān. It would seem from *T. R.* that both Mīrzā Khān and Maḥmūd Ḥasan got leave to go to Qandahār but that the latter went as far then, while Mīrzā Khān stayed. Ḥaidar says his father went on because he wished to go to Mecca. He, however, accepted an invitation from Shaibānī and was killed by him.

[2] *T. R.* 357, Bābar besieged Qandahār for 5 years and 5 months.

[3] Half-brother only of Jahāngīr and Bābar, his mother being a concubine. (Bābar, Ers. 10).

[4] Probably Rāgh a hill-district in N.-W. Badakhshān and not the Rāg which is the Rhages of Tobit and lies south of Teheran. See *T. R* 203*n*.

[5] The express was sent by Mīrzā Khān from Badakhshān. The courier had traversed the Hindū Kush in the snow and got frost-bitten. He arrived early in *Ramaẓān* which in that year began 3rd December. Ers. B. and H. I, 306 and *T. R.* 237).

[6] Lit. turned the reins of his world-traversing steed. Ers. B. and H. I, 322 and *T. R.* 260 for account of battle. 'Ubaidu-l-lāh, called also Sulṭān, married Mīrzā Ḥaidar's sister and became king of Bukhārā He was Shaibānī's nephew.

On another occasion,[1] he along with Najm Bēg, had a great battle below Fort Ghajdiwān with the Uzbēgs. Najm Bēg was killed and his Majesty went towards Kābul.[2] Moreover by secret inspiration, he was led to lay aside marching to Transoxiana and to press forward to the conquest of Hindustān. Four times did he turn towards this enterprise and as often did he, from stress of circumstances, retrace his steps. The first[3] time was in Sha'bān 910 (Jan. 1505) when he went by Bādām Cashma[4] (Almond Spring) and Jagdalīk, passed through the Khaibar and halted at Jam (Jamrūd). In the *Wāqi'āt-i-bābari*, a Turkī book written by his Majesty himself, it is stated that when in six marches, he went from Kābul to Ādīnapūr,[6] he had never before seen the *Garmsīr*[7] (warm regions) nor the country of Hindustān. "Immediately on "reaching them, I beheld a new world. The grass was different, the "trees different, the wild animals of a different sort, the birds of a "different plumage, the manners and customs of the people (ایل والوس[5] "*ail ū ālūs*) of a different kind. I was struck with astonishment, and "indeed there was room for wonder."[8] Nāṣir Mīrzā came to this stage from Ghaznīn to pay his respects. He (Bābar) halted at Jam-

[1] Ers. B. and H. I, 325 and *T. R.* 261. Ghajdiwān is north of Bukhārā. The battle was apparently fought on 3 *Ramaẓān* 918 (12th November, 1512). *Najm* means star and the real name of the general was Yār Muḥammad. He is said to have been Finance Minister. He seems to have been put to death in cold blood and in revenge for the massacre of Karshī.

[2] He did not go direct to Kābul but first to Ḥiṣār and was there nearly murdered by the mutinous Mughals. Thence to Kunduz and "at last, despairing altogether of "recovering Ḥiṣār, he returned to "Kābul." The date of his return does not seem known but probably it was in 920, (1514). Ers. B. and H. I, 329*n*.

[3] Bābar, Ers. 156. Bābar (309) seems to reckon the expedition of 925 as the first of the five, and Firishta and Khāfī Khān take the same view. Ers. B. and H. I, 417*n*.

[4] Jarrett II, 399 and Bābar, Ers. 141*n*. Bādām Cashma is a pass S. of the Kābul River and between Little Kābul and Barīk-āl.

[5] From Jamrūd, Bābar rode out to Bikram (Peshawar).

[6] Now Jalālābād. Ers. (B. and H. I, 233. Jarrett II, 405). But Ādānīapūr lay about a mile south of the modern Jalālābād.

[7] *Āīn* V. Jarrett II, 394.

[8] The change here described occurs at Gandamak. Bābar's Mem. 157 and Erskine's note.

rūd and consulted about crossing the river Indus known as the Nīlāb. 92
Owing to the avarice of Bāqī [1] Caghanā'īānī the crossing of the Indus was postponed and he proceeded against Kohāt. After taking Kohāt, they attacked Bangash and Naghz.[2] Then they went to the country of the 'Isā Khail and halted in the environs of Tarbīla[3] which is a village on the Indus and in the country of Multān. Then he made several marches down the river. From thence he came to the borders of Dūki[4] and after some days to Ghaznīn. In the month Zī-ḥajja (May 1505) he returned to Kābul.

The second[5] time, the illustrious army proceeded in the month of Jumāda-l-awwal 913 (Sep. 1507) by way of Little Kābul (Khurd Kābul) to the conquest of Hindustān. They went first from Mandraur[6] by 'Atar and Shiweh and then returned owing to differences of opinion among the officers. They crossed by Kūner[3] and Nūrgil[7] and from Kūner he (Bābar) came on a raft (*jāla*)[8] to the camp and then by way of Bādīj[9] to Kābul. By order of his Majesty, the date

---

[1] Text, "some Caghatāīs." The Luck. ed. is right. (Bābar Ers. 156 and 256). The "avarice" refers to Bāqī's love of plunder. He was younger brother of Khusrū Shāh, Bābar's Memoirs, 128, Caghānīān was in Transoxiana. *T. R.* 177*n*.

[2] Text, Newar. Jarrett II. 389, 399 *n*. 6.

[3] The Belah of Ers. p. 163. Apparently the Darbēlah of the *Āīn* Jarrett II, 334. Caghānīān is a name given to Ḥiṣār. Bābar. Ers. Intro. XXXV.

[4] Jarrett, II, 397. Dukī means a hill or hill-country. Text, Kī. Luck. ed. دكي. See Bābar 164*n*. and 149 where the expedition is described.

[5] Bābar, Ers., 232.

[6] Jarrett II, 406.

[7] Bābar, Ers., 143. The two places are on opposite sides of the river of Caghānserāī or Kameh, Jarrett II, 392*n*.

[8] Also ژاله *zhāla*. (*Farhang-i-rashīdī s. v.*). The *Burhān-i-qāṭi'* describes a raft as a thing made of wood and grass on (? under) which inflated *massaks* are laid and which is used for crossing deep streams. Probably Bābar used one only for crossing the river. Raverty (Notes, 34) quotes a description of a raft from Jahāngīr's Memoirs. This kind of raft is still in use. "From Jalālābād we embarked on rafts of inflated skins and dropped down with the stream to Peshawur." (Journey to the source of the Oxus. Wood, 280). See too "At the Court of the Amīr," Gray, 12.

[9] This name does not seem known now. Ers. (Bābar, 142*n*.) suggests Bādpāsh. Price remarks (173*n*.) that he has not been able to find in the maps any of the places mentioned in this expedition. I have altered the names of the Text so as to accord with Erskine.

of his crossing was engraved on a stone above Bādīj. This wondrous[1] writing still exists. Till this time, the noble descendants of the Lord of Conjunction were called Mīrzās. His Majesty ordered that in this inscription,[2] he should be styled Pādshāh.

On Tuesday, 4 Z̤ī-l-qa'da of this auspicious year (6th March, 1508), occurred, in the citadel of Kābul, the fortunate birth of his Majesty Jahānbānī Jannat-āshīyānī (Humāyūn). Of this an account will be given hereafter.

The third time, on Monday,[3] 1 Muḥarram 925 (3rd Jan., 1519), while the army was marching against Bajaur, there was a great earthquake which lasted for half a sidereal hour. Sulṭān 'Alā'u-d-dīn Siwādī (of Swat) arrived as an envoy on the part of Sulṭān Vais Siwādī. In a short time, the fort of Bajaur was captured and was presented to Khwāja[4] Kilān Bēg, son of Maulānā Muḥammad Ṣadr, who had been one of the great officers under Mīrzā 'Umar Shaikh. This Khwāja was related to his Majesty in a singular manner for his six brothers had given their lives in his service. He himself was a special *protegé* of his Majesty on account of his wisdom and sagacity. When his Majesty was contemplating the Siwād (Swat) expedition and the conquest of the Yūsufzāīs, Ṭāūs Khān, the younger brother

---

[1] One MS. has "This writing has not yet disappeared."

The pass was east of Kābul and near the Lamghan (Laghman) district. (Bābar, Ers., 142). According to Raverty, (Notes, 100) the proper spelling is بادپج Bādpaj ;—*bād* meaning wind and *paj* or *fajj* Ar. for pass. "Thus Bādpaj means the Windy Pass, the name being given on account of the strong wind generally blowing there and which at times, renders its passage impracticable." Probably then this is the pass described by a friend (? Alexander Burnes, Erskine Hist. I, 517) of Mr. Erskine as Bādpāsh. (Bābar, Ers., 142*n*.) "Bādpāsh is a steep *kotal* (pass) half a day's journey to the north of Andrūr on the Kābul River and about 16 or 18 miles west of Targarī where the streams of Alingār and Alishang join." (l. c. 142*n*.)

[2] Bābar merely says that the change took place at this period but, by the word *tārīkh*, A.F. seems to mean that the title was adopted in the inscription. It would be interesting to know if it still exists. Bābar complains that it was not well cut.

[3] Text, Saturday but Monday, MSS. and Bābar's Memoirs? de Courteille II. 36 note.

[4] *T. R.*, 468. According to Bābar's Mem. Bajaur was taken before Sulṭān 'Alā'u-d-dīn's arrival and not after, as A. F.'s account implies.

of Shāh Manṣūr, who was chieftain of the Yūsufzāī tribe, brought the latter's daughter[1] and uttered words of humility and submission. There was also a difficulty about supplies of corn in that country of wild beasts. His (Bābar's) fixed determination too was to undertake the expedition to Hindustān. He turned his rein from Siwād. Although the preparations for the march to India had not been made and the officers were not in favour of it, he lighted the torch of courage and set forth for the tenebrous regions[2] of Hindustān. On the morning of Thursday, 16 Muḥarram, he crossed the river (Indus) with horses, camels and baggage,[3] while the camp (*urdū*) bāzār was floated across on rafts. They encamped at Kacākōt.

Seven kos from Bhīra,[4] towards the north, there is a mountain, 93
called in the *Ẓafarnāma* and other books, the hill of Jūd and there they encamped. His Majesty writes in his Memoirs (Erskine, 254), "At first I was ignorant of the origin of its name, but afterwards "discovered that in this hill there were two races of men descended "of the same father. One tribe is called Jūd, the other Jenjūheh." He sent 'Abdu-r-raḥīm Shaghāwāl to Bhīra in order to reassure the people and prevent anyone from committing violence. At the end of the day, he halted east of Bhīra, on the bank of the river Bihat

---

[1] Bābar married her. (Ers., 250*n*.) Her name was Bībī Mubārak according to Raverty. (Notes, 234). Erskine, Bābar's Memoirs, 251*n*. calls her Bībī Macherikah.

[2] Siwād means also blackness.

[3] Text, *partāl* but the word is Hindūstānī and spelt *partal*.

[4] Perhaps there are two Bhīras. (Bābar, Ers., 253*n*.) Bābar speaks (253) of Jūd as 7 *kos* from Bhīra and (255) of the middle of Jūd's being 10 *kos* from Bhīra. Jūd evidently belonged to the Salt Range. Erskine remarks that Bābar's account of it is not very exact and that he considered all the rough and mountainous country between the Khaibar and Salt Ranges to be one hill. Erskine or rather Leyden (for the latter's translation comes down to this point) says (254) "This hill got the name of Jūd from a supposed resemblance to the celebrated hill of Jūd (Ararat)." This makes Bābar and A.F. more intelligible but the passage is not in the Turkish (P. de C. II, 54) and has the air of being a marginal note which has slipped into the text. Moreover Ararat is Jūdī or Jūda and not Jūd. Nor does it seem likely that there is any resemblance between the lofty isolated Ararat and a spur of the Salt Range. *Jūd* is probably Sanscrit *yuddha* 'war.' The reference to the Kūh-i-Jūd in the *Ẓafarnāma* is at II, 48, l. 1.

(Jhelam, the ancient Hydaspes). He levied 400,000 *shāhrukhīs*[1] from Bhīra as the price of protection, and presented the country to Hindū Bēg, assigning the revenues of it to him as a maintenance. Khushāb he made over to Shāh Ḥasan[2] and arranged that he should assist Hindū Bēg. He sent Mullā Murshid[3] on an embassy to Sulṭān Ibrāhīm, son of Sulṭān Sikandar Lōdī, who had succeeded his father five or six months previously[4] in the kingdom of Hindustān, in order to convey to him salutary counsels. Daulat Khān, the governor of Lāhōr, detained the ambassador and with utter folly, sent him back without having fulfilled his mission. On Friday, 2 Rabī'u-l-awwal (4th March, 1519), the news came of the birth of an auspicious son. As the expedition against Hindustān was then in progress, he was by secret inspiration and augury, named Hindāl.[5] On Monday,[6] 5 Rabī'u-l-awwal the administration of Bhīra was given to Hindū Bēg and he

[1] About ten or eleven pence each, (Bābar, Ers., 254*n.* and 335) so that the sum levied was some £20,000. The Text might read that this money was given to Hindū Bēg and has been so understood by Price (Ret. IV, 674), but if so, A.F. seems to have mistaken his authority (Bābar, 256, 258 and 309) where Bābar says he divided the money among his troops. P. de C. (II, 64) does not mention the sum 400,000 *shs.* but represents Bābar as stating that he assembled the headmen of Bhīra and fixed their ransom at a thousand *shāhrukhīs* apiece. A.F.'s Text has *cahār sad shāhrukhī māl* and which is unintelligible. The MSS. give the correct *māl-i-amān*, price of peace.

[2] Incorrect. Bābar says (Ers., 260) that he bestowed Khushāb on Lenger Khān who was the prime cause and adviser of the expedition and that he left him behind to support Hindū Bēg. Khushāb is on the right bank of the Jhelam while Bhīra is on the left.

[3] P. de C. II, 62 gives Thursday 1 Rabī'u-l-awwal (3rd March, 1519). Apparently the ambassador was sent partly to claim some portions of the Panjāb which had been held by the Turks from the days of Tīmūr.

[4] Erskine considers the date of Sikandar's death uncertain but would put it in 1518 (B. and H. I, 407*n.*) but there does not seem sufficient reason for doubting Firishta's statement that he died in November 1517. Bābar's statement (Ers., 257) is too loosely expressed to be relied on.

[5] The affix *āl* is Turkish and means 'to take,' so that Hindāl would mean "taken of India." According to Bābar, P. de Courteille II, 46 (the passage is not in Erskine) the name was given by Māhim the wife of Bābar and adopting mother of Hindāl.

[6] Text. Sunday, 15th, but *vide* Bābar, 259. One MS. has 11 (eleventh) which is the right day of the month for Sunday.

(Bābar) for state reasons, proceeded to return to Kābul. On Thursday, the last day of Rabī'u-l-awwal (31st March) he arrived at Kābul. On 25 Rabī'u-l-ākhar (April 25th) Hindū Bēg who, out of carelessness,[1] had left Bhīra, came to Kābul.

The date of the setting out of the fourth expedition has not come to light but it appears that he (Bābar) returned after the taking of Lāhōr and from the chronogram[2] of the taking of Dīpālpūr, which will be stated hereafter, it appears that the expedition was in 930 (1524). As every event has its special time, this splendid project (of conquering India) was postponed. The ostensible cause of this was the sluggishness of the officers and the non-co-operation of his brothers. At last, on the fifth time, by the guidance of God and the leadership of Fortune, on Friday, 1st Ṣafar 932 (17th Nov., 1525), when the Sun was in Sagittarius, the standards of light were unfurled, such as might disperse the darkness of an universe, and placing the foot of resolve in the stirrup of reliance on God and of abstention from sin,[3] he proceeded towards the conquest of India. Mīrzā Kāmrān was left in Qandahār and the care of Kābul was also entrusted to him. When this expedition was made, victory followed on victory and fortune upon fortune. Lāhōr and some other large cities of India were taken and on 17 Ṣafar (3rd Dec.) his Majesty Jahānbānī, Jannat-āshīyānī, Naṣīru-d-dīn Muḥammad Humāyūn arrived from Ba- 94
dakhshān with his army, at the camp which was in the Bāgh-i-wafā[4]

---

1 Bābar does not blame him but says he was left without sufficient means. (267).

2 This is explained by Bābar (Ers., 368) where *Wāsiṭ shahr Rabī'u-l-awwal* is given as the chronogram of the taking of Dīpālpūr. These words yield "Middle of Rabī'u-l-awwal 930" and so the conquest occurred about 22nd Jan., 1524. See *Akbarnāma* I, 110 where the reading is *Wasaṭ*. This seems the more correct as *Wāsiṭ* would yield 931. Bābar thus alludes to this expedition (Ers., 141). "In the year in which I defeated Bahar Khān and conquered Lāhōr and Dībālpūr, I brought plantains and planted them here," (in the Bāgh-i-wafā, near Jalālābād). Dīpālpūr is in the Montgomery District, Panjāb, and formerly on the Beas. It is now in a state of decay owing to its distance from the river. Text, Dībālpūr and according to Raverty, this is correct. (J.A.S.B. 1892, Part I. 375*n*. 380) Khāfī Khān (I, 47) has a good deal to say about this expedition.

3 For Bābar's vows of penitence, see Memoirs, Ers., 292.

4 Bābar made this garden in 914, (1508). It was opposite Ādīnapūr which was south of the Kābul River

(Garden of Fidelity). K͟hwāja Kilān Bēg also came at this time from G͟haznīn.

On 1st Rabīʿu-l-awwal (16th Dec.) he crossed the Indus near Kacakōt[1] and held a muster[2] of the army. Twelve thousand[3] cavalry, Turks, Tājīks, merchants,[4] *etc.*, were reckoned up. Then they crossed the Bihạt (Jhelam) above[5] Jīlum (Jhelam). Near Buhlūlpūr they crossed the Cīnāb and encamped.

On Friday, 14 Rabīʿu-l-awwal (29th Dec.) they encamped at Sīālkōt and his Majesty formed the plan of transferring its population to Buhlūlpūr. At this time news came that the enemy was assembling and when his Majesty reached Kalānūr, Muḥammad Sulṭān Mīrzā, ʿĀdil Sulṭān and the other officers who had been appointed to defend Lāhōr, arrived and paid their respects.

On Saturday, 22 (Text 24) Rabīʿu-l-awwal, the fort of Milwat[6] was taken. Booty was obtained and the books of G͟hāzī K͟hān which were in the fort were got possession of. Some of them were given to his Majesty Jahānbānī and some were sent as a present to Kāmrān in Qandahār. As it was reported that Ḥamīd K͟hān, governor[7] of Ḥiṣār-fīrūza[8] had advanced two or three stages, on Sunday, 13 Jumāda-l-awwal the army marched from Ambāla and halted on the bank of a tank (*kūl*) and Humāyūn was sent against him (Ḥamīd K͟hān). Amīr K͟hwāja Kilān Bēg, Amīr Sulṭān Muḥammad Dūldāī, Amīr Walī K͟hāzin, Amīr ʿAbdu-l-ʿazīz, Amīr Muḥibb ʿAlī, K͟hwāja K͟halīfa and some of the officers who had stayed in Hindustān such as Hindū Bēg, ʿAbdu-l-ʿazīz, Muḥammad ʿAlī Jang-jang were appointed to accompany

---

and about a mile south of Jalālābād. (Bābar, Ers., 141 and 278 and Raverty, Notes, 49).—Eleven years later, he made the Bāg͟h-i-ṣafā at the lake of Keldeh-Kehār, in the Salt Range. (Ers., 255).

1 Bābar (293) says they crossed the river of Kacākōṭ, *i.e.*, the Haroh (Jarrett, II. 324).

2 Text *k͟hān* but I prefer the variant *sān*, *viz.*, a review or counting of an army. It would seem from P. de C.'s version (II, 36) and from Erskine (Bābar, 293) that advantage was taken of the crossing to count the troops while they were embarking or disembarking.

3 "Great and small, good and bad, servants and no servants, they amounted to 12,000 persons." (Bābar, 293).

4 *Saudāgar*. So too, Bābar (Ers., 310) but the meaning here seems doubtful, perhaps mercenaries.

5 Bābar, below.

6 The Malot of the Imp. Gaz.

7 Text, *ḥākim*. Bābar, *s͟hikdār*.

8 (Ḥiṣār, Jarrett II, 105, 293).

him. Baban, who was one of the nobles of Hindūstān, came in on this day and did homage. His Majesty Jahānbānī gained an easy victory.

On Monday, the 21st of the same month, he returned to the camp. His Majesty bestowed on him, Ḥiṣār-fīrūza with its dependencies and subordinate districts (*lawāḥiq*) which were worth a *kror* and also a *kror* in money as a guerdon for this victory which was the first of countless ones. The army continued its march. News repeatedly came that Sulṭān Ibrāhīm was advancing with 100,000 cavalry and 1,000 elephants. The army encamped near Sirsāwah (Sirsa). Here Ḥaidar Qulī (Text, 'Alī) a servant of Khwāja Kilān Bēg who had been sent to procure information brought the news that Dāūd Khān and Ḥaitim Khān (Text, Ḥātim) had advanced in front of Sulṭān Ibrāhīm's camp with five or six thousand horse. Accordingly on Sunday, 18 Jumāda-l-ākhar (1st April) Cīn Tīmūr Sulṭān, Muḥam- 95
mad Sulṭān Mīrzā, Mahdī Khwāja, 'Ādil Sulṭān, with the whole left wing commanded by Sulṭān Junaid, Shāh Mīr Ḥusain and Qutlaq Qadam, as well as part of the centre under Yūnus 'Alī, 'Abdu-l-lāh Aḥmadī, Kita Bēg and others, were appointed to operate against this body. And these heroes proceeding swiftly to the field of battle, were victorious over the enemy and slew a great number of them with the lightning of the sword and the rain of the arrow. Ḥaitim Khān with 70 others were made prisoners and sent alive to the exalted camp where they suffered capital punishment. Orders [1] were issued that wheeled carriages should be collected and Ustād 'Alī Qulī was directed to yoke them together in the Ottoman[2] (Rūm) manner with chains[3] and cow-hides of which they made ropes. Between every two car-

---

[1] The corresponding passage about collection of carts, is not in Erskine (Bābar, 304, l. 1) but in P. de Courteille, (II, 161) we read, "I ordered all "the soldiers to bring carriages, each "according to his means. They col- "lected in this manner 700."

[2] Elliot (VI, 468) observes that the reference is doubtless to the victory obtained by Sulṭān Salīm the Grim (*Yāwas*) over Shāh Isma'īl in 1514, in which this method had been found very effective. The battle was fought on 23rd Aug. at Caldīrān near Tabrīz. (His. of Persia, Malcolm I, 504 and Hist. of Ottoman Empire, Hammer-Purgstall II, 412). Probably Ustād 'Ālī had been present in it.

[3] A.F.'s rendering does not seem quite correct. The twisted cow-hides were in lieu of chains.

riages there were placed six or seven gabions[1] so that the matchlock men might fire their pieces from behind them in security. In a few days these arrangements were completed.

At length on Thursday, the last day of Jumāda-l-ākhar (12th April) the phœnix (humā) of victory made a shade with his wings at the city of Pānīpat. The ranks of the army were arranged in an excellent manner. The right wing rested on the city and environs, and the carriages and gabions were placed in front of the centre. The left wing was defended by trees and ditches. Sulṭān Ibrāhīm, with a large army was drawn up six *kōs* from the city and for a week the young men and the veterans daily engaged numerous bodies of the enemy on the borders of the hostile camp and were always victorious. At length on Friday, 8 Rajab (20th April) Sulṭān Ibrāhīm marched against the camp with a mighty army and an array of elephants. His Majesty Gītī-sitānī also drew up his forces and adorned the battle-field in the following manner.[2]

### Battle between his Majesty Gītī-sitānī Firdūs-makānī and Sulṭān Ibrāhīm and account of the array.

As the Protector and Doer desired to repair old defeats and to convert past afflictions into felicities, He arranged the preliminaries for this, and set things in order. Among such arrangements were the advancing of Sulṭān Ibrā hīm for the purpose of giving battle and the drawing up of the army of his Majesty Gītī-sitānī. As the Divine aid was accompanying the latter, and ever-increasing fortune was in his van, he, in spite of a plenitude of difficulties and a paucity of favouring circumstances, had recourse with a tranquil mind and firm soul to the inalterable Arbiter and addressed himself to the marshalling of his troops.

The centre was adorned by the presence of his Majesty in person. In the right centre which the Turks call *ūnk-ghūl*,[3] Tīmūr Sulṭān,
96 Sulaimān Mīrzā, Amīr Muḥammadī Kōkultāsh, Amīr Shāh Manṣūr Barlās, Amīr Yūnus 'Alī, Amīr Darwesh Muḥammad Sārbān, Amīr

---

1 *Turā*, (Vullers s. v. and Quatremère, Hist. of the Mongols, 337*n*. 130). The latter quotes the passage from the *Akbarnāma*.

2 Text, اورنچیان which may be intended for cuirasses but the true word seems *āncunān*, as follows.

3 Text, *ūn*. Erskine *ung*. See Bābar, Ers., 227 where this and other terms are explained.

'Abdu-l-lāh Kitābdār were stationed. On the left centre which the Turks call *sūl-ghūl*, Amīr Khalīfa, Khwāja Mīr Mīrān Ṣadr, Amīr Aḥmadī Parwāncī, Amīr Tardī Bēg, brother of Kūc Bēg, Muḥibb 'Alī Khalīfa, Mīrzā Bēg Tarkhān were stationed. The right wing was in charge of his Majesty Jahānbānī Jannat-āshīyānī; Amīr Khwāja Kalān Bēg, Sulṭān Muḥammad Duldāī, Amīr Hindū Bēg, Walī Khāzin, Pīr Qulī Sīstānī were in attendance on him. On the left wing were stationed Muḥammad Sulṭān Mīrzā, Sayyid Mahdī Khwāja, 'Ādil Sulṭān, Sulṭān Junaid Barlās, Khwāja Shāh, Mīr Ḥusain, Amīr Qutlaq Qadam, Amīr Jān (text, Khān) Bēg, Amīr Muḥammad Bakhshī and other heroes. In the vanguard were Khusrū Kōkultāsh and Muḥammad 'Alī Jang-jang;[1] Amīr 'Abdu-l-'azīz had charge of the reserve. At the flank of the right wing, Walī Kazil,[2] Malik Qāsim, Bābā Qashqa with their Mughals, were appointed as a flanking-party (*tūlghāma*). At the extremity of the left wing, were stationed Qarāqūzī, Abū-l-Muḥammad Nīzabāz (lance-player), Shaikh 'Alī, Shaikh Jamāl, Tengrī Qulī Mughal, as a flanking-party. Accordingly the brave swordsmen stood with firm foot on the battle-field and with life-taking arrows (*sahām*) and blood-drinking scimitars (*ṣamṣām*) displayed bravery and daring.

*Verse.*

The brave stood with firm foot,
Trees learned from them how to stand.

At length after great contest, the heavenly aids accompanied the centre and wings of the army and by the Divine aid, there ensued victory and the defeat of the enemy. A great victory for the servants always taking refuge in God became manifest. Sulṭān Ibrāhīm was slain unrecognised and in a corner, and numerous Afghāns were the harvest of the royal sword, and the caravans of the city of destruction were conducted to the rest-house of annihilation by the escort of victorious soldiers and the flambeaux of world-opening swords. Near the body of Sulṭān Ibrāhīm, there lay

[1] (Ers. 305) states that this officer was wounded on the day before and unable to take his place in the battle. But in S. Zain's recension we are told that though wounded he contrived to take part in the great battle.

[2] Text, Sharmal.

on the spot five or six thousand dead. The sun had mounted spear-high when the onset of battle began and at noon there blew the breeze of victory, and the north wind of vernal conquest.

How can this great victory, which was the masterpiece of fortune, be explained? And how can language describe what is beyond the bounds of comprehension? When Sulṭān Maḥmūd[1] Ghaznavī came to Hindūstān, he was in possession of Khurāsān; the kings of Samarqand and Dāru-l-Marz[2] and of Khwārizm were subject to him and he
97 had an army of over 100,000 men. Nor was Hindūstān subject to one monarch. Rāīs and Rājas were stationed here and there and were not on terms with one another. Sulṭān Shihābu-d-dīn[3] Ghōrī came to the conquest of India with 120,000 cuirassiers, mounted on mail-clad[4] horses. Then too, there was no ruler in all that vast territory. And though his brother Ghiyāṣu-d-dīn held Khurāsān, yet he was not outside his influence. His Majesty,[5] the Lord of Conjunction (Tīmūr), at the time of his conquest of Hindūstān, gave orders for a muster of his troops in the plain of Samānah,[6] and Maulānā Sharafu-d-dīn 'Alī Yazdī states (*Ẓafarnāma* II, 83) that the line of the army (*ṭūl-i-yesāl*) occupied a space of six *farsakhs* in length, and persons experienced in military matters have calculated that a *farsakh* represents 12,000 horse, consequently, exclusive of the servants of servants (*naukar-i-naukar*[7]) there were 72,000 horsemen. The servants of servants occupied two *kos*.[8] His opponent, Mallū

---

1 Jarrett, III, 340. A.F. bewails there Sulṭān Maḥmūd's bigotry but was it worse than Bābar's?

2 *Lit.*, Land of the marches. Redhouse, Turkish Dict. explains that it means the whole country under the chain of the Persian Caucasus, bordering on the Caspian Sea.

3 Called also Mui'zzu-i-dīn. Jarrett, III, 342 and Bābar, Ers., 148.

4 "Cataphract horse" (Bābar, Ers., 310). Minhāju-d-dīn is the authority referred to by Bābar. See his *Ṭabaqāt-i-nāṣirī*. Raverty, 465.

5 It is singular that Bābar (Ers., 309) takes no account of the conquest of India or at least, of Delhi, by his ancestor Tīmūr. He mentions the expeditions of Maḥmūd of Ghaznih, Shihābu-d-dīn and then says his own was the third. Evidently he did not count Tīmūr's because it was not followed by any permanent settlement in the country. He has a reference to Tīmūr's expedition at p. 255.

6 W. of Thaneswar and cir. lat. 29·55 and lat. 76·6. (Bābar, Ers., 301*n*. See also Jarrett, II, 296).

7 The Text is incorrect here.

8 Sharafu-d-dīn says 2 miles (*mīl*). A.F.'s description is not clear neither is Sharafu-d-dīn's account (*Ẓafar-*

Khān, had 10,000[1] horse and 120 elephants. Yet with all this, many of those in the Lord of Conjunction's camp were frightened and his Majesty observed the alarm of his soldiers and heard improper remarks from them. And in order to reassure them, he commanded that a palisade should be made of branches of trees, in front of his troops, and that in front of this, a ditch should be dug and that behind that bullocks and buffaloes should be placed opposite each other, and fastened by their necks and feet with leathern thongs. Also many triangular (caltrops) iron prongs[2] were made and it was arranged that foot soldiers should take these and throw them in the way at the time of the onset and when the elephants came on. His Majesty Gītī-sitānī Firdūs-makānī who was the fourth world-soother (*gītī-nawāz*) of India, in that great victory, which was one of the glorious gifts of God, had not with him more that 12,000 men, both soldiers and others. More astonishing still, his territories consisted of Badakhshān, Qandahār and Kābul. Nor did he get assistance from these countries for his armies; on the contrary, the expenditure, in order to protect some of the borders from the enemy and for other state purposes, was such as to exceed the receipts. And the contest was with Sulṭān Ibrāhīm who had nearly 100,000 cavalry and 1,000 war-elephants and who ruled from Bhīra to Bihār without an opponent. It was solely by the Divine aid and the assistance of heaven that that glorious work was

---

*nāma* II, 83) from which A.F.'s is taken, easy, to understand. Apparently the length of the line of the army was 20 *kos* or 6 *farsakhs* (about 40 miles) (*Sic* Sharafu-d-dīn but according to A.F. (Jarrett II, 415), 6 *farsakhs* would be 18 *kos*.) Perhaps, however, A.F. is justified in regarding a *mīl* which he says was the third of a *farsakh*, as equal to one *kos*. (Jarrett II, 415 and 417). The breadth according to Sharafu-d-dīn was two miles (*dū mīl*) and not two *kos* as A.F. puts it.

The cavalry are called *naukar* and their servants *naukar-i-naukar*. The latter would probably be on foot. See trs. of these passages in Retr., Price, III, 250 and IV, 681. Major Price considers that the horse were arranged two deep.

Gibbon, quoting the Institutes, says Tīmūr had 92 squadrons of each 1,000, corresponding to the 92 names of Muḥammad.

[1] Text, two, but MSS. and Retr., Price, show this a mistake. 10,000 also is named in *Ẓafarnāma* (II, 100). Mallū Khān was Prime Minister of Maḥmūd Tughlaq, the young king of India.

[2] *Ẓafarnāma* II, 102.

accomplished. Men of judgment and experience feel powerless to panegyrize properly this masterpiece of the Ages. Hail, Holy One, carrier of the world illuminating light of his Majesty, the king of kings, what marvel if such feats were wrought by Thee! In
98 short, his Majesty Gītī-sitānī Firdūs-makānī, on the rising of the lights of victory glorified his forehead-mirror with the dust of thanksgiving prostration. He proclaimed presents to all mankind and sent his servants to all countries and regions.

But a deed fit to surpass the lofty designs of those world-opening princes who conquered Hindūstān, was the victory of his Majesty Jahānbānī Jannat-ās͟hīyānī which by the blessing of the existence of his Majesty, the king of kings (Akbar) took place in the plain of Siḥrind.[1] Accordingly an account will hereafter be given of how with 3,000 men, he delivered India from Sikandar Sūr who had more than 80,000 men. Still stranger is the masterpiece of fortune of the Shadow of God (Akbar) who by the Divine aid so rescued India with a few men from the hands of many rebellious[2] chiefs that the tongue of the Age becomes dumb before it. An abridged account will be given in its proper place.

*Verse.*

Should Fortune grant me hope,
Heaven, leisure and opportunity,
By the kindling society of the truthful,
I shall embroider tale upon tale.[3]
On this tablet of immortals,
I'll draw a picture for posterity's behoof.

On the very day of the victory, his Majesty Jahānbānī Jannat-ās͟hīyānī, Amīr K͟hwāja Kalān Beg, Amīr Muḥammad Kōkultās͟h, Amīr Yūnus 'Alī, Amīr S͟hāh Manṣūr Barlās, Amīr 'Abdul-l-lāh Kitābdār, Amīr 'Alī K͟hāzin were by orders of the king sent with a force to Agra, the capital, the seat of Sulṭān Ibrāhīm's government, to take possession of the treasure. They gave confidence to the inhabitants—

[1] 22nd June, 1555. (B. and H. Ers. II, 518).

[2] Referring apparently to the rebellion of 'Alī Qulī and others against Akbar which is known as the Rebellion of Jaunpūr. (Emperor Akbar, Von Noer, A. S. Beveridge, I, 106 *et seq*).

[3] Text *dāstān dāstān*. One MS. has *dāstān darastān*.

who are trusts from God—by diffusing the lights of justice. Sayyid Mahdī Khwāja, Muhammad Sultān Mīrzā, 'Ādil Sultān, Amīr Junaid Barlās, Amīr Qatlaq Qadam were sent to Delhi, to preserve the treasures and secret stores of that place and to acquaint the subjects and inhabitants with the royal graciousness. On the same day proclamations of victory were written and sent by couriers to Kābul, Badakhshān and Qandahār. And he himself, on Wednesday, 12 Rajab, (25th April, 1526), alighted at Delhi. On Friday, 21[1] (4th May) he unfolded the umbrella of fortune in Agra and dispelled the darkness of the land.

Everyone,[2] small and great, in Hindūstān experienced the royal kindness and balminess. Out of his comprehensive kindness, the mother, children and dependants of Sultān Ibrāhīm were made partakers of his bounty and special stipends were assigned to them. An 99
allowance of a property worth seven *lakhs* of *tankas* was made to Ibrāhīm's mother. Similarly pensions were bestowed on his other relatives. The distracted world was soothed. His Majesty Jahānbānī Jannat-ashiyānī who had previously arrived at Agra, presented a diamond eight *misqāls*[3] in weight and which was valued by jewellers at one-half of the daily expenditure of the inhabited world. They said that this diamond had belonged to the treasury of Sultān 'Alā'u-d-dīn (Khiljī). He[4] (Humāyūn) got it from the family of

---

[1] Bābar, 22, but if Wed., 12 Rajab, be right, Friday was the 21st.

[2] Mīrzā Haidar remarks that all the world, from Turkey to China, benefited by the expedition, for the treasures obtained by the army, enabled them to buy the goods of these countries. An interesting allusion to the effects of commerce!

[3] 320 *ratīs*=279$\frac{9}{16}$ carats. (Bābar, Ers., 308) Erskine (B. and H. I, 438) inclines to identify this diamond with the one shewn by Aurangzēb to Tavernier and valued by him at £888,000. By some it is regarded as identical with the Kōh-i-nūr. For full discussion of the question, see Tavernier's Travels trs. Valentine Ball, II, 431 *et seq.*

I have treated of this subject in the *Calcutta Review*, &c., and my conclusion is that the Bābar diamond is the Kōh-i-nūr. Humāyūn carried the diamond away with him and gave it to Shāh Tahmāsp who sent it to the king of Ahmadnagar.

[4] The text seems to say that 'Alā'u-d-dīn got it from Vikramāditya's heirs and has been so understood by Price. But both Ers. and P. de C. make it Bābar's statement that Humāyūn got it from Vikramāditya's heirs. How 'Alā'u-d-dīn got it is not explained. Khāfī Khān says 'Alā'u-d-dīn got it in the Deccan.

Bikramājīt, the Rāja of Gwaliār. His Majesty, from the nobility of his nature, first accepted it and then returned it to him (Humāyūn) as a present.

On Saturday,[1] 29th Rajab, he began to examine and distribute the treasures and hoards, the collections of many kings. He gave his Majesty Jahānbānī, 70 *lakhs* of Sikandarī *tankas* and a treasure-house of which no account or inventory had been taken. To the Amīrs, he gave in accordance with their rank from five to ten *lakhs* of *tankas* and to every soldier and servant he gave presents superior to their position. All the man of learning, small and great, were made happy by gifts. No one, either in the camp or the cantonment (*urdū-bazār*) went without a share in the good fortune. The scions[2] of the royal family in Badakhshān, Kābul and Qandahār also received presents, *viz.*, Kāmrān Mīrzā, 17 *lakhs* of *tankas ;* Muḥammad Zamān[3] according to their rank 15 *lakhs* and similarly ʿAskarī Mīrzā, Hindāl Mīrzā and all the ladies of the *harem* and shining stars[4] of the *Khilāfat* and all the officers and servants who were absent from the dais received in accordance with their degree, jewels and rich varieties and also gold and silver money. Also to all the relatives and dependants, of his Majesty in Samarqand, Khurāsān, Kāshghar and ʿIrāq, there were sent valuable gifts. Presents too were despatched to the holy sepulchres (*mashāhid*) and blessed shrines in Khurāsān, Samarqand, *etc.* And an order was issued that to every inhabitant of Kābul, Ṣaddara,[5] Warask, Khūst, and Badakhshān, male and female,

[1] Saturday, Erskine (Bābar, 334) says the date is wrong, for 29th Rajab was a Friday and suggests that the distribution of treasure on a Friday might have interfered with Bābar's religious duties. P. de C., Monday, 29th *Rajab.* Price, "30th of the month."

[2] *Lit.* trees of the garden of success. The reference is to the presents sent to Kāmrān and others. (Bābar, Ers. 335).

[3] Son of Badīʻu-z-zamān Mīrzā, son of Sulṭān Ḥusain Mīrzā of Herāt, but the gift was probably made to him as being the emperor's son-in-law. He served under Bābar and Humāyūn and was drowned in the Ganges at Causa in 1539. (Elliot, V. 203).

[4] *Darrārī*, pl. of Ar. *durrī*, a sparkling star or gem.

[5] There are some unintelligible words here. P. de C. (II, 233) has "Dans toute la circonscription de "versek et la principauté de Kābul, "il n'y eut pas une âme vivante, "maitre ou dame, esclave ou homme "libre, adulte ou non adulte qui ne "reçut un *bâberi* de gratification,"

small and great, a *shāhrukhī* should be sent. Thus all and sundry, the *élite* as well as the commonalty, were fed from the table of his Majesty's bounty.

---

and adds in a note to "circonscrip- "tion," "Le mot que je traduis ainsi "par conjecture est *sada* que la "version persane se contente de "réproduire sans l'intrepréter." To "bâberi," he has the note, "Un "*chahrokhi* suivant la version per- "sane et la traduction anglaise." Erskine (Bābar, 335) seems to have considered that *ṣada ū rasak* should be read *ba sadur rashk*, (for producing emulation), for he translates, "To the country of Kābul, as an "incentive to emulation, to every "soul, man and woman, slave or free, "of age or not, I sent one *shahrukhī* "as a gift!" I have examined the passage in the two B.M. MSS. Add. Per. of Bābar's Memoirs, *viz.*, No. 24,416, p. 269*b*, and No. 26,200, p. 285*a*. The latter was used by Erskine and the passage is as follows:—

بولایت کابل و صدهٔ و ارسک براهر
جان داري از مرد وزن از بنده و ازاد بالغ
و نا بالغ یکم شاروخي انعام شد *

There is nothing in either MS. about Badakhshān or Khūst.

The explanation of their mention in the A.N. however seems to be that A.F. used Shaikh Zain's trs. of Bābar's Memoirs. This was made much earlier than 'Abdu-r-raḥīm's for Shaikh Zain was one of Bābar's courtiers and wrote for him the pompous *firmāns* given by Bābar. (Ers., 355 and 359). He is also mentioned in the *Akbarnāma* (I, 119) as Shaikh Zain, the *Ṣadr* and grandson of Shaikh Zainu-d-dīn Khwāfī (Blochmann, 592*n*). There are two fragments of this translation in the B.M., *viz.*, Add. No. 26,202 (Rieu, I, 246) and Or. No. 1999 (l. c. III, 926) Shaikh Zain's version is written in an ornate and rhetorical style and in the third person. Both fragments contain the transactions of 932 and both speak of Khūst or Khwāst Badakhshān in describing the sending of the *shāhrukhīs*. The passage in Add. No. 26,202 occurs at 70*a*, and in Or. No. 1999 at 70*b*. It runs thus,

و فرمان صدور یافت که تمامي متوطنان
دار الملک و ساکنان صده درسک و از
خوست بدخشان که اهالي آن بزهد و
واخ امتیاز تمام دارد هر مرد را از مرد
و زن —

"And an order was passed that all "the inhabitants of the capital (? Kābul) and the dwellers in Ṣada Darask (or Warask) and Khust Badakhshān, who were distinguished for religion and piety, should each get a *shāhrūkhī*." Apparently then, Ṣada Darask is some hamlet of Khūst in Badakhshān. All the other B.M. MSS. of 'Abdu-r-raḥīm's trs. agree with the two already named in omitting any mention of Badakhshān.

The Ṣaddara of the Text might mean the hundred valleys and according to Steingass *Dara* is a district in Badakhshān. Ṣada is given by Vullers, on the authority of *Notices et Extraits*, (XIV, 771) as meaning a company of 100 men and possibly it may be the title of a divi-

*Verse.*

From the showering of the jewel-shedding hand,
Joy burst out afresh in the world.
Pleasant is the gift that cometh from afar,
As the Moon sheds light on earth from her sphere.

---

sion of a country, *e.g.*, the English hundred. I can find no such district as Warsak or Versak but possibly Wakhsh or Vakhsh is meant. (T. R. N. E. & R. 263, and Bābar, Ers. Intro. XXX).

"Khūst or Khost is a district on the northern slope of the Hindū Kūsh, between south and south-east of Kunduz and lies very near the hill tracts known on our time as Kāfiristān." T. R., trs. 103n.). Khūst is given in Raverty's Pushtū Dictionary, as a province in Afghānistān. (See Bābar, Ers. 151, 268 and 270.) It lay in the west of Badakhshān. Mr. Ney Elias' map marks it as north of Cārīkār and west-north-west of Citrāl.

On the whole it appears that Erskine's rendering "to excite emulation" cannot be correct though he adheres to it in his Bābar and Humāyūn (I, 440) adding that perhaps Bābar's object was to assist in recruiting his army, but Mr. Erskine had not then probably examined Shaikh Zain's translation. It appears to me that Bābar's motive was rather to enable the people of Afghānistān to defend themselves against the Uzbēgs and to strengthen their loyalty. It is probably to these presents that he alludes when he says (Ers. 310) that Badakhshān, Kunduz, Kābul and Qandahār were dependent on him, but that instead of being a help, he had to send extensive supplies to some of them, on account of their being near the enemy. This enemy can only mean the Uzbēgs. I should note that the last *ū* of the Text, *viz.* that between Khūst, and Badakhshān does not occur in all the MSS. Price (Retr. IV, 684) has "at Kābul and the neighbourhood." Firishta too has nothing about Badakhshān and merely speaks of the inhabitants of the city of Kābul, adding that Bābar received, on account of his improvidence, the title of Qalandar. Nor does Khāfī Khān (Bib. Ind. I, 53) speak of Badakhshān. Bābar sought afterwards to recoup his extravagance by adding 30 per cent. to the taxes (Memoirs, 387).

There is still another trs. of Bābar's Memoirs, that by Mīrzā Pāyanda Ḥasan Ghaznavī and Muḥd. Qulī Mughal Ḥiṣārī. Rieu, II, 799*b*.

Since writing the above note I have seen Wood's Journey to the Source of the Oxus (Lond. 1872) and am now inclined to think that Ṣada is a mistake for the Arabic سده *sadda*, a gate or pass. Ṣad or Ṣadda seems a common name of places in Badakhshān and in one of Wood's maps (p. XC) there is a pass marked Sad-Ishtragh or Ishtrākh which may be the Ṣada or Ṣaddara rasak of the Text. It is north of Citrāl and perhaps recent expeditions to that neighbourhood, have thrown or will throw light on the locality mentioned in the Text. *Ṣad* seems to be used in Badakhshān as equivalent to *dara*.

It is a fixed law that when the world-adorning Creator designs 100
to reveal a unique jewel from its casings, he brings strange things to pass so that a man being tried in such ways by word and deed may become glorious in the minds of all for firmness and foreseeing. Among these, there was this strange circumstance that with all this victory and largesse, there was a defect of similitude (*qillat-i-mujānasat*) which worked a want of intimacy (*'illat-i-'adam-i-muwānasat*) with the people of India.

The soldiery and the peasantry (of India) abstained from intercourse (with the invaders). Although Delhi and Agra had come into possession, opponents held the country. Many of the neighbouring forts were held by rebels. Qāsim Sanbalī held Sanbal (Rohilkhand) and in the fort of Biāna (Bhartpūr) Niẓām Khān was beating the drum of opposition. Ḥasan Khān Mewātī had established himself in Mewāt (south of Delhi) and raised the standard of revolt. Muḥammad Zaitūn had established himself in Dhōlpūr (Rājpūtānā) and was breathing opposition. Tātār Khān Sārangkhānī (Firishta, son of Sārang Khān) was holding Gwāliār; Ḥusain Khān Lōḥānī, Rāprī (on the Jumna); Quṭb Khān, Etāwa, 'Alām Khān, Kālpī. Marghūb, a slave of Sulṭān Ibrāhīm, held Mahāwan (Mathurā) which is near Agra. Qanauj and the other cities beyond the Ganges, were in the hands of the Afghāns, under the headship of Nāṣir Khān Lōḥānī and Ma'rūf Farmulī who had contended also with Sulṭān Ibrāhīm. After his death, they had acquired many other countries and having advanced some stages, had made Bahār Khān, son of Daryā Khān, king and styled him Sulṭān Muḥammad.[1]

During this year, while his Majesty had his head-quarters in Agra, the hot winds were very oppressive. An impure *samūm* and sickness were added to the pusillanimity of the camp. A large number absconded out of senseless imaginations. Owing to the rebels, the inclement weather, the impassableness of the roads, the delay of coming by merchants, there was distress for food and a want of necessary articles. The condition of the people became bad. Many officers resolved to leave Hindūstān for Kābul and its neighbourhood, and many soldiers deserted. Though many old officers and veteran soldiers used improper language in the Presence, and also secretly

---

1 B. and H., Ers. I, 412.

used language disagreeable to his Majesty, yet his Majesty Gītī-sitānī who was unique for far-seeing and endurance, did not heed this but set about the administration of the country. At length on the part of the *élite* and those who had been trained by his Majesty and from whom different things were to be looked for, there were stale movements of old times.[1] Especially was this the case with Aḥmadī Parwāncī and Walī Khāzin. Still more astonish-
101 ing, Khwāja Kalān Bēg,—who in all the battle fields and occasions, especially in the expedition to Hindūstān, had always spoken gallantly and given such opinions as befitted a brave man—now changed his views and was the foremost in advocating the abandonment of the country, both openly and by covert hints. At length his Majesty summoned his officers and spoke wise words of counsel to them, unveiling their secret imaginings (*makhṭūrāt*) and forbidden (*maḥẓūrāt*) ideas. He announced his firm determination, saying, "We have "won this fine country by labour and hardship, to give it up for a "little fatigue and contrariety, is neither the way of world-conquerors "nor method of wise men. Joy and sorrow, comfort and distress are "linked together. Now that all those labours and troubles have "been brought to their end, assuredly rest and smoothness will ap-"pear in like degree. You must lay firm hold on the strong cable "of reliance on God and not utter any more vain and factious words. "Whoever has a mind to depart to Kābul (*Wilāyat*) and to exhibit "his own worthlessness, it matters not, let him go. But we, relying "on the lofty courage which rests on the Divine help, have fixed "India in our heart." At last all the officers, after consideration and meditation, agreed and confessed that what his Majesty said was true and that "the king's word was the word-king." With heart and soul they placed the head of submission on the ground of command and bound themselves to remain. Khwāja Kalān who was keener than the others about leaving for Kābul (*Wilāyat*) received permission to depart and the presents for the princes and others were sent with him.[2] Ghaznīn, Gardēz,[3] and the Sulṭān Mas'ūdī

[1] The meaning is not clear, but I think A.F. is sneering at the presumptuous ways of old servants, Cf. text 133, seven lines from foot.

[2] He received money also for repairing a reservoir at Ghaznīn. (149).

[3] *Cir.* 65 *m.* south-east of Kābul. Jarrett II, 407. Bābar, Ers., 150).

Hazārca[1] were given to him in fief. In Hindūstān too the *pargana* of Ghurām[2] was given to him. Mīr Mīrān also got leave to go to Kābul.

The Khwāja got leave to depart (to Kābul) on Thursday,[3] 20 *Zī-ḥijja* (28th August). It is manifest that every right-minded, fortunate one who conducts business with subtle prudence, is more and more successful in proportion as he arrives at high positions. A mirror of this is the grand story of his Majesty Gītī-sitānī Firdūs-makānī who in such a commotion of the soldiery and in presence of much opposition, had recourse to world-conquering courage, and who, relying on the Divine protection, set his face to accomplish his work and achieve his desires and made the city of Agra, which is the centre of Hindūstān, his fixed residence and with strength of counsel and courage and abundant liberality and justice, composed the distractions of the country. Accordingly many of the officers of Hindūstān and rulers of the country gradually entered his service. Among them was Shaikh Ghūran[4] who brought with him as many as 3,000 men of mark.[5] Everyone of them received favours above his 102
condition.

There were also Fīrūz Khān, Shaikh Bāyazīd, Maḥmūd Khān Lōḥāṇī, Qāẓī Jīā, who were amongst the famous *sirdārs*, and who entered the service and obtained their desires. Fīrūz Khān received a *jāgīr* from Jaunpūr of one *kror* odd[6] of *tankas*. Shaikh Bāyazīd one *kror*[7] from Oudh; Maḥmūd Khān 90[8] *lakhs* from Ghāzīpūr. Qāzī Jīā had an assignment of 20 *lakhs* from Jaunpūr. In a short time, there was peace and comfort and joy and pleasure and such prosperity as belongs to a permanent government. Some[9] days

---

[1] Bābar, Ers., 151 and 156. Jarrett, 401*n*.

[2] Guhrām, Jarrett II, 296. As my friend Mr. Beames has pointed out to me, this is Ghurām in Sihrind. It is now in the native State of Patiala and on the Ghaghar (the old and famous Saraswatī), about 25 miles south-west of Ambāla and 24 miles due west of Shāhābād.

[3] Bābar, Ers., 341.

[4] Ers. and P. de C., Kūren. Badāonī I, 337, Khūran. Badāonī speaks of him as unrivalled in his knowledge of music.

[5] Bābar calls them bowmen (*tarkashband*) from the Dūāb.

[6] I kr., 46 lakhs, 5,000, P. de C.

[7] I kr., 48 lakhs, 50,000, P. de C.

[8] 90 lakhs, 35,000 P. de C. See also Ers. B. and H. I. 446*n*., correcting trs. of Mem.

[9] About 11th July, 1526.

after the 'Id of Shawwāl, there was a great feast at Agra, in the palace of Sulṭān Ibrāhīm when a treasury of gifts was showered into the lap of the public. Sambal was assigned to Jahānbānī, in addition to Sarkār Ḥiṣār-fīrūza which formerly had been given him as the reward of valour. Amīr Hindū Bēg was appointed as his deputy to preside over that district. As Bīban had besieged the fort of Sambal, the aforesaid Amīr, Kita Bēg, Malik Qāsim, Bābā Qashqa with his brothers and Mallā Āpāq, Shaikh Ghūran and his soldiers from the middle Dūāb were rapidly sent there. Biban engaged them and was defeated and as that seditious and disloyal one (*ḥarām-nimak*) after having experienced the sweets of service, had out of evil nature turned his back, never again did he behold fortune's face.

---

# CHAPTER XVIII.[1]

## DELIBERATIONS OF HIS MAJESTY GĪTĪ-SITĀNĪ (BĀBAR) AND UNDERTAKING BY HUMĀYŪN OF THE EXPEDITION TO THE EASTWARD.

As his Majesty Gītī-sitānī Firdūs-makānī was now victoriously established in Agra, the capital of the kingdom, and as the rainy season,—which is the spring of India and the period of freshness and verdure, of enjoyment with one's friends, and of garden delights,—had passed away and the time for expeditions had arrived, he consulted with his ministers as to whether he should proceed to the east to quell the Lōḥānīs who had advanced with nearly 50,000 cavalry beyond Qanauj and were meditating hostilities, or should march westward against Rānā Sāngā[2] and subdue him, as he was very strong and had recently got possession of the fort of Khandār[3] and was cocking the cap of disobedience. After consultation, it was decided that as Rānā Sāngā had repeatedly sent representations to Kābul and had made protestations of loyalty, the facts of his not having done so since and of his having taken the fort of Khandār 103
from Ḥasan, the son of Makan, who had not yet done homage,—were not sufficient evidence of disloyalty, and that it was not adviaable to proceed against him at present. The proper course was to send capable men to ascertain his dispositions and that until the truth about him was known, the first thing was to march eastwards and put down the Lōḥānīs. The Emperor intimated that he would attend to this matter in person, but meantime his Highness Jahānbānī,—the plant of whose greatness had grown tall in the garden of hope,—represented that if this weighty affair were committed to him, he would by the help of the royal fortune, bring it to a successful ter-

---

[1] Chalmers resumes his translation here after missing out from p. 112, p. 102 of the text.

[2] According to Tod, Sāngā is a contraction of Sangrām Singh, "the lion of battle."

[3] Kandār is a strong hill-fort a few miles east of Rantanbhur. Bābur, Ers., 389. Text and Jarrett II, 275, Khandār.

mination. The Emperor greatly approved of this request and gladly accepted the offer, and his Highness Jahānbānī girded himself for the task with energy and good fortune. Orders were issued that there should join themselves to Humāyūn, 'Ādil Sulṭān, Muḥammad Kōkultāsh, Amīr Shāh Manṣūr Barlās, Amīr Qatlaq Qadam, Amīr 'Abdu-l-lāh, Amīr Walī, Amīr Jān Bēg, Pīr Qulī, Amīr Shāh Ḥusain,—who had been deputed to take Dhōlpūr and its neighbourhood from Muḥammad Zaitūn and to make it over to Sulṭān Junaid Barlās and then to march against Biānā. For this purpose Kābulī Aḥmad Qāsim was despatched in all haste to direct these officers to meet Humāyūn at Candwār. Sayyid Mahdī Khwāja, the *jāgīrdār* (fief-holder) of Etāwa, Muḥammad Sulṭān Mīrzā, Sulṭān Muḥammad Dūldī, Muḥammad 'Alī Jang Jang and 'Abdu-l-'azīz,[1] Master of the Horse, with the rest of the army which had been sent to subdue Quṭb Khān Afghān who had raised the standard of revolt in Etāwa,—were also appointed to serve his Highness (Humāyūn). On Thursday, 13 Ẕilq'ada (21st August, 1526) he came out from Agra at an auspicious moment and encamped at a distance of three *kos* from the city. He marched on from there, accompanied by the breeze of victory. Naṣīr Khān who had collected an army in Jājamū', fled while Humāyūn was 15 *kos* distant, and crossing the Ganges went to the territory of Kharīd.[2] Humāyūn also went in that direction, and having brought that region into order, partly by severity and partly by gentle measures, turned the reins of enterprise towards Jaunpūr. Having reduced Jaunpūr to order by justice and equity, he administered the country with the wisdom of age and the energy of youth. When near Dalmau, Fatḥ Khān Sarwānī, who was one of the great nobles of India and whose father had received from Sulṭān Ibrāhīm the title of A'ẓam Humāyūnī,
104 came and did homage to his Highness Jahānbānī. He (Jahānbānī) sent him to the imperial Court under the charge of Sayyid Mahdī Khwāja and Muḥammad Sulṭān Mīrzā. There he was royally[3] treated and received a robe of honour. He received the allowances of his father and also a *kror* and six *lakhs* in addition. Though out of sim-

---

1 Text, 'Alī, but this is wrong as Bābar's Mem. and A.S.B. MS. C. 27 and Text 107 and 108 show.

2 Mentioned also in Bābar's *firmān*. Ers., 360. It is a large *pargana* in the district of Balia, N.-W. P. Jarrett II, 163.

3 Cf. Bābar, Ers., 344. The total amount of the allowances is there stated as one *kror* and 60 *lakhs*.

plicity he wished for the title which his father had possessed, he received that of Khān Jahān and was dismissed to his estates. His son Maḥmūd Khān was exalted by obtaining permanent service. His Majesty Gītī-sitānī was both in appearance and in reality successful and munificent in the capital.

In Muḥarram 933 (Oct. 1526) the joyful news came from Kābul that Māham Bēgam, the mother of his Highness Jahānbānī, had given birth to a son. His Majesty Gītī-sitānī named him Muḥammad Fārūq. His birth occurred on 23 Shawwāl, 932 (2nd Aug., 1526), and he died in 934 before his father had ever seen him.

Description of various auspicious events in this year (933), of the news of the rebellion of Rānā Sāngā and of the meeting of his Highness Jahānbānī with his Majesty Gītī-sitānī.

On Wednesday, 24 Safar[1] (30th Nov., 1526), orders were issued to his Highness Jahānbānī that he should make over Jaunpūr to some officers and himself return with all speed, as Rānā Sāngā was advancing with a large army of Hindūs and Muhammadans. The conveyance of this message was given to Muhammad 'Ali, son of Mihtar Ḥaidar Rikābdār.

In this year Niẓām Khān, the governor of Biāna, did homage through the instrumentality of that fountain of blessings Rafī'u-d-dīn Ṣafavī,[2] and made over the fortress of Biāna to the imperial officers. Tātār Khān also tendered Gwālīār and kissed the threshold; and Muḥammad Zaitūn made over Dhōlpūr and submitted himself. Everyone received royal favours corresponding to his sincerity and loyalty and was secured against calamities.

On 16 Rabī'u-l-awwal (21st Dec.) of this year, the mother of Sulṭān Ibrāhīm formed a plot[3] by the means of the cooks which had a happy[4] issue,—the crude imaginings of evil-disposed persons coming to nothing and they themselves meeting with punishment.

---

[1] 24 Muḥarram, Ers. and P. de C. This is probably correct. A.F. has probably written Ṣafar because that month appears in a preceding entry in Bābar's Mem. 24 Muḥarram=31st October.

[2] A native of Ij near the Persian Gulf. He was a teacher of A.F.'s father and was buried opposite Agra. Blochmann, Preface ii and 523 and Jarrett II, 180 and III, 423.

[3] She attempted to have Bābar poisoned. Bābar, Ers., 347.

[4] *Bakhair guzasht*, qu. turned out

When the orders were received by his Highness Jahānbānī, he appointed Shāh Mīr Ḥusain and Amīr Sulṭān Junaid Barlās to the command of Jaunpūr, and leaving Qāẓī Jīā who was one of those trained up by his Majesty Gīti-sitānī, to assist these two officers, he set out for the capital. He also appointed Shaikh Bāyazīd to Oudh and as 'Ālam Khān held Kālpī and it was necessary to dispose of him, either peaceably or by force, he led his victorious army thither. By working on his hopes and fears, he brought him into the path of
105 obedience, and taking him in his train, presented him at the world-protecting Court. On Sunday, 3rd Rabī'u-s-sānī, he arrived at the Cārbāgh,[1] known later as the Hasht Bihisht (Eight Paradises) and which was by its verdure the spring of power and fortune, and presented himself before his Majesty Gīti-sitānī. On the same day Khwāja Dōst Khāwand arrived from Kābul, and was received with honour.

At this time representations were continually arriving from Mahdī Khwāja who was in Biāna, about the rebellion of Rānā Sāngā and his war-like preparations.

well. Price (IV. 691) seems to have read *bukhīr guzasht*, went into darkness, i.e., was killed. But it would seem from the Memoirs that she was only put into confinement. See too Firishta.

[1] Now called Rāmbāgh; A. F.'s birthplace and opposite Agra. Blochmann, ii and Jarrett II, 180 and 423.

# CHAPTER XIX.

## OF HIS MAJESTY GĪTĪ-SITĀNĪ FIRDŪS-MAKĀNĪ'S DRAWING UP HIS FORCES AGAINST RĀNĀ SĀNGĀ, AND UPREARING THE STANDARDS OF VICTORY.

Whene'er a design takes root in the bosom of an auspicious one, on whose honoured head God, the world-arranger, hath placed the diadem of true sovereignty, and whose lofty intellect is set on obeying the behests of the Lord of Lords, his action rises above the petty views of the vulgar, and he achieves success in realm and religion (*dīn ū dunyā*). The wondrous deeds of his Majesty Gītī-sitānī Firdūs-makānī are an instance of this, for as his felicity increased so also did his wisdom, and in proportion as the causes of dizziness augmented, so also did his prudence become enhanced. He ever took refuge in the Divine Unity, and in the administration of justice and the management of State affairs, never deviated a hair's breadth from the highway of reason. And at this time when Rānā Sāngā, in the pride of his numbers and courage and with his brains full of boastful madness, began to act presumptuously, and to remove his foot from the circle of equanimity, and was drawing nigh with the stride of boldness, he (Bābar) made the favour of God his stronghold, and gave no admission to the attacks of dismay but proceeded to quell that ill-fated disturber of the Age.

On Monday, 9 Jumāda-l-awwal (11th February, 1527), he marched out from Agra to extirpate this sedition, and pitched his camp in the neighbourhood of the city. Reports were continually arriving that the ill-fated one (Rānā Sāngā) had attacked Bīāna with a large army, and that the troops who had come out of that town, had not been able to withstand him and had turned back. Sankar Khān Janjūha was killed on that occasion, and Amīr Kita Bēg[1] wounded. Having halted four days, he (Bābar) marched on the fifth and encamped in the plain of Mandhākar[2] which lies between Agra

1 *T.R.* 313ff. He was brother of Mīr Aḥmad Qāsim Kohbar.

2 Perhaps the Mandāwar of the Āīn. Jarrett II, 182.

and Sikrī. It occurred to him that there was no water-supply for the troops except in Sikrī—(which after returning thanks for his victory, his Majesty Gītī-sitānī, by giving diacritical points, named Shukrī (thanksgiving) and which is now by the auspicious felicity of
106 the king of kings, known as Fatḥpūr, from its giving victory to hearts)—and it might happen that the hostile army by using despatch, would get possession of this. In consequence of this just thought, he proceeded next day towards Fatḥpūr and sent Amīr Darvēsh Muḥammad Sārbān in advance in order that he might find a proper ground for encampment. The said Amīr fixed on an eligible spot in the neighbourhood of Fatḥpūr Lake (*Kūl*) which is a broad sheet of water and an ocean-like reservoir, and that was made the pleasant ground of encampment. From thence messengers went to summon Mahdī Khwāja and the other officers who were in Bīāna. Bēg Mīrak[1] who was a servant of Jahānbānī and a number of the Emperor's special attendants were sent to collect information. In the morning intelligence was brought that the opposing army had advanced one *kos* beyond Bisāwar and were eighteen *kos* distant. On the same day Mahdī Khwāja,[2] Muḥammad[3] Sulṭān Mīrzā and the other officers who had been in Bīāna, arrived and did homage. During this time, daily skirmishes took place between the outposts in which gallant soldiers distinguished themselves and received the royal approbation.

At length on Saturday, 13 Jumāda-l-ākhar 933 (16th March, 1527), Rānā Sāngā advanced with a large army to a hill near the village of Khānwa[4] in the Sarkār of Bīāna and about two *kos* from the imperial camp.

His Majesty states in his Memoirs that according to the Indian calculation by which territory yielding one *lakh* of revenue furnishes 100 horse, and one of a *kror* of revenue, 10,000 horse, the dominions

---

[1] Possibly the grandfather of Niẓāmu-d-dīn Aḥmad, the author of the *Ṭabaqāt*.

[2] Bābar's brother-in-law. The statement that he was a son-in-law is a mistake of Erskine. Khwāndamīr tells us near the end of the Ḥabību-s-siyar that Mahdī Khwāja was married to Bābar's sister Khānzāda.

[3] A grandson of Sulṭān Ḥusain of Herāt. Bābar made him governor of Kanauj, Mem. 181.

[4] 37 miles west of Agra, in the Bhartpur State.

of Rānā Sāngā, as yielding ten *krors* of revenue, furnished 100,000 horse. Many chiefs also, who had never served under him before, gave in their allegiance and increased his army. Thus Silāhu-d-dīn,[1] the ruler of Rāisīn and Sārangpūr, etc., supplied 30,000 horse; Rāwal Ūdī Singh of Nagaur, 12,000; Ḥasan Khān Mewātī, ruler of Mewāt, 12,000; Bihārī[2] Mal Īdarī,[3] 4,000; Nirpat Hādā, 7,000; Sitarvī Kacī (of Cutch), 6,000; Dharan[4] Deo, ruler of Mīrtha, 4,000; Narsingh Deo Cūhān,[5] 4,000; Maḥmūd Khān, son of Sikandar Sulṭān, though he had no territory, yet[6] in hope of regaining his ancestral throne, brought with him 10,000 horse; so that the whole force amounted to two *lakhs* and 1,000 horse.

When his Majesty heard of the arrival of the enemy, he set about arranging his forces. The royal station was in the centre. Cīn Tīmūr[7] Sulṭān, Mīrzā[8] Sulaimān, Khwāja Dōst Khāwand, Yūnus 'Alī, 107
Shāh Manṣūr Barlās, Darvēsh Muḥammad Sārbān,[9] 'Abdu-l-lāh Kitābdār, Dōst Īshak Āqā and others of the great officers were stationed in the right. On the left were 'Alā'u-d-din,[10] son of Sulṭān Buhlūl Lōdī; Shaikh Zain Khwāfī, Amīr Muḥibb 'Alī, son of Niẓāmu-d-dīn 'Alī Khalīfa; Tardī Bēg, brother of Qūc Bēg; Shīrāfgan, son of Qūc Bēg; Āraish Khān, Khwāja Ḥusain and many other servants of the Sulṭānate and pillars of the State.

The right wing was adorned by the fortunate presence of his

---

[1] Text, Silhadī. See Erskine's B. & H. I, 471*n*.

[2] Erskine, *Bārmal* (360).

[3] Īdar or Edar in Kāthiāwar, Gujrāt.

[4] Text, Parm and also in fragment of Bābar's Mem. trs. by P. de C. II, 445.

[5] This passage occurs in the report of the victory drawn up by Shaikh Zainu-d-dīn (Bābar, Ers., 360). There is some discrepancy about the proper names and I have corrected some of those in the Text.

[6] Copied from Bābar (Ers., 360), but the meaning there is that 10,000 horsemen followed him because they hoped that he would recover his ancestral possessions.

[7] The eighth son of Sulṭān Aḥmad Khān and grandson of Yūnus Khān, so he was Bābar's cousin, *i.e.*, his mother's nephew. He died of dysentery at Agra. (*T.R.* N. & R., 161).

[8] Son of Mīrzā Khān and afterwards ruler of Badakhshān.

[9] A disciple of Khwāja Aḥrār.

[10] Brother of Sulṭān Sikandar and uncle of Ibrāhīm Sulṭān who was killed at Pānīpat. Ers. B. & H. I, 423 and 421*n*. According to another account, 'Alā'u-d-dīn was Ibrāhīm's brother. He was generally known as 'Ālam Khān.

Highness Jahānbānī and on his right were Qāsim Ḥusain Sulṭān, Aḥmad Yūsuf Ōghlāqū, Hindū Bēg Qūcīn, Khusrū Kōkultāsh, Qawām Bēg, Urdū-shān, Walī Khāzin, Qarāqūzī, Pīr Qūli Sīstānī, Khwāja Pahlwān Badakhshī, 'Abdu-l-shakūr and many other gallant men. On the victorious left of his Highness Jahānbānī, were Mīr Hama, Muḥammadī Kōkultāsh, and Khwājagī Asad Jāmdār.

And on the right wing there were nobles of India such as the Khān-khānān, Dilāwar Khān, Mulkdād Karāranī and Shaikh Ghūran.

On the left wing were Sayyid Mahdī Khwāja, Muḥammad Sulṭān Mīrzā, 'Ādil Sulṭān, son of Mahdī Sulṭān, 'Abdu-l-'azīz Mīr Akhūr, Muḥammad 'Alī Jang Jang, Qatlaq Qadam Qarāwal, Shāh Ḥusain Bārbēgī, Jān Bēg Atka. And of the nobles of India there were Jalāl Khān and Kamāl Khān, sons of Sulṭān 'Alā'u-d-dīn, 'Alī Khān Shaikhzāda Farmulī, Niẓām Khān of Biāna and many other brave warriors who girt the waist of service with perfect loyalty. And as a flanking party, there were Tardī Īkka, Mulk Qāsim, brother of Bābā Qushqa and many Mughals on the right wing. Mūman Atka and Rustam Turkamān with many of the Emperor's special dependants were stationed on the left wing.

For the sake of protection, the practise of the holy warriors of Rūm was followed and a line of carts was arranged and connected by chains so that there might be cover for the matchlock-men and cannoniers, who were in front of the soldiers,—and Niẓāmu-d-dīn 'Alī Khalīfa was appointed to command this line. Sulṭān Muḥammad Bakhshī, after arranging the commanders and officers in their posts, stood near the Emperor to hear his commands which were allied to Divine inspiration,—and despatched adjutants (*tawācīān*) and couriers to all sides who conveyed the orders to the officers. When the pillars of
108 the army had been arranged in this excellent manner, a command was issued that no one should stir without orders from his position, nor without permission advance his foot into the battle. A watch of the day had passed[1] when the fire of war was kindled.

*Verse.*

The soldiers bestirred themselves on each side,
Day and night were commingled,

[1] About 9 A. M.

On each side arose a war-cry,
Two seas of hate foamed at the lips,
The steel-shod hoofs of the chargers
Reddened the ground with the blood of the brave.
The world-holder mid his glorious camp
Moved exultant on his prancing steed.

Such a battle raged on the right and left wings that the earth quaked and the universe resounded with the clangour. The left wing of the enemy moved against the imperial right and fell upon Khusrū Kōkultāsh, Mulk Qāsim and Bābā Qushqa. Cīn Tīmūr Sulṭān was ordered to go to their assistance and by his intrepid aid he drove the enemy nearly to the rear [1] of their centre. A noble reward was assigned to him for this. Muṣṭafā Rūmī brought forward the carts from the centre of his Highness Jahānbānī's division and by his matchlocks and culverins (*ẓarbzan*) so broke up the ranks of the enemy that the rust was scoured off from the mirror-hearts of the brave combatants, and many of the enemy were laid level with the earth and were annihilated. And, as from time to time, the hostile troops advanced, so did his Majesty Gītī-sitānī send on picked men to succour his victorious soldiers.

At one time orders were given to Qāsim Ḥusain Sulṭān, Aḥmad Yūsuf and Qawām Bēg; at another to Hindū Bēg Qūcīn; at another to Muḥammad Kōkultāsh and Khwājagī Asad. After that Yūnus 'Alī, Shāh Manṣūr Barlās and 'Abdul-l-lāh Kitābdār received orders. Then Dōst Ishak Āqa, Muḥammad Khalīl Ākhta Bēgī were sent to assist. The enemy's right wing repeatedly attacked the left wing of the victorious army but every time the loyal souled Ghāzīs affixed some of them to the ground by a rain of calamitous arrows, and slew many of them with the lightning of daggers and scimitars. Mūman Atka and Rustam Turkamān acting according to orders, attacked the benighted bands from the rear, and Mullā Maḥmūd and 'Alī Atka Bāshlīq who were servants of Khwāja Khalīfa went to their assistance. Muḥammad Sulṭān Mīrzā, 'Adil Sulṭān, 'Abdu-l-'azīz Mīr Akhūr, Qatlaq Qadam Qarāwal, Muḥammad 'Alī Jang Jang, Shāh Ḥusain Bārbēgī and Mughal Ghānjī engaged in action and maintained a firm position. Khwāja Ḥusain went with a body of the household troops

[1] Bābar, nearly to their centre.

109 (*dīwāniān*) to their assistance and all the victorious warriors,—who with jeopardy of their lives devoted themselves to service,—made lofty the standards of toil by taking vengeance on the enemy, and choked the springs of the enemy's hope with the dust of failure.

*Verse.*

The hands[1] of the javelin-throwers were knot upon knot (*girih bar girih*),
The backs of the brazen-bodied ones were cuirass upon cuirass (*zirih bar zirih*).
On each side, the rock-piercing spears
Closed with thorns the path of safety.
The shining of caerulean scimitars
Deprived eyes of sight by their gleaming.
The dust of the earth put a cap on the Moon
And stopped the breath in the throat.

As the engagement was long, owing to the numbers of the enemy, orders were issued to the household troops, who were behind the carts like chained tigers,—to emerge from the right and left centre and after leaving a space in the middle for the musketeers, to charge from both sides. In accordance with the noble call the gallant youths and valiant warriors, like tigers breaking from their chains and gaining their liberty, dashed forward. The clashing (*cakācāk*) of swords and the whizzing (*shipāshāp*) of arrows reached the heavens, and that rare one of the Age, 'Alī Qūli,[2] stood with his following in front of the centre and performed wonders in discharging stones[3] and in firing of culverins and muskets. Just then orders were issued for moving forward the carriages of the centre and his Majesty himself moved against the foe. When this was perceived by the glorious army, they became agitated like a billowy sea and all at once made an assault on the hostile ranks. At the end of the day the flame of conflict so blazed up that the right and left of the victorious army forced and drove the enfeebled left and right of the

[1] The meaning seems to be that the opposing soldiers were locked together in flight. The phrase brazen-bodied was an epithet of Isfandiyār, a Persian hero killed by Rustam.

[2] Ustād 'Alī Qūlī the cannonier.

[3] *Sang*. It may also mean cannon-balls.

enemy into one mass with their centre, and so beat upon that wretched body that all those ill-fated ones washed their hands of life and rushed upon the right and left centre of the imperialists. They approached very near but the high-minded G͟hāzīs stood firm and quitted themselves like men. By heaven's help, the opponents were unable to abide the contest and those ill-fated, wretched ones were compelled to loose the rein of firmness from the palm of contrivance and to take flight and to regard as meritorious their escaping half-dead from such a courage-testing contest. The breezes of victory and success blew on the grove of fortunate standards, and the buds of strength and
help blossomed on the branches of faith and exertion. Many of the 11
hostile troops became the food of the blood-drinking sword and of the hawking arrow. And many wounded, the remains of the sword, turned the dust-stained cheek of courage, and the besom of dismay swept away the rubbish of their presence from the field of battle, quivering like moving sands, they became a Sahara of wretchedness. Ḥasan K͟hān Mēwātī was killed by a bullet and Rāwal Uday Singh,[1] Mānik Cand Cūhān, Rāī Candrabhān Dilpat Rāī, Gangū, Kram Singh, Rao Nagarsī[2](?) and many of their great chiefs were slain. Many thousand wounded were destroyed by the hands and 'neath the swift foot of the victorious army. Muḥammadī-Kōkultās͟h, 'Abdu-l-'azīz Mīr Āk͟hūr, 'Alī K͟hān and some others were sent to pursue Rānā Sāngā.

His Majesty Gītī-sitānī Firdūs-makānī having become victorious returned thanks for this great victory and sublime blessing to Almighty God, Glory be to His Name, (who arranges the series of fates by re-setting the openings and shuttings of things visible and invisible), and pursued the enemy for one *kos* from the field of bottle, till at length night fell; that day was black for foes and that night joyful for friends. Then he recalled his lofty spirit from the enemy and beating high the drum of success, turned and reached his camp some hours after night-fall. As it was not ordained of God that that abandoned one (Rānā Sāngā) should be taken, the men who were sent in pursuit of him, did not manage well. His Majesty observes thereon, "The time was critical, I should have gone myself and not have trust-

1 Tod, "of Dangarpūr."

2 Text, Ḍūngarsī. Erskine, Rao Bikersī with the variant Nagarsī. P. de C., Rao Niguersī.

ed to others." Shaikh Zain the Ṣadr who was possessed of distinguished qualities, found the date of this great victory in the words *Fatḥ-i-Bādshāh-i-Islām* [1] and Mīr Gēsū sent the same chronogram from Kābul. His Majesty writes in his Memoirs that there was a similar coincidence in the chronograms of the former victory of Dīpālpūr when two persons found the date *Wasaṭ-i-shahr-i-Rabī'u-l-awwal.* [2]

When so great a victory had been gained, the pursuit of Rānā Sāngā and the attack on his country were postponed and preference was given to the conquest of Mēwāt. Muḥammad 'Alī Jang Jang,
111 Shaikh Ghūran and 'Abdu-l-Mulūk Qūrcī were sent with a large force against Ilyās Khān who had raised the head of sedition in Kōil [3] in the Dūāb and had imprisoned Kacak 'Alī the governor of that place. When the victorious army approached, he was unable to resist them and retired. After the victorious army had reached Agra, that rebel was produced before the royal Court and met with capital [4] punishment.

As the conquest of Mēwāt had been determined upon by the world-adorning soul (of Bābar), he proceeded to that province. On Wednesday, 6 Rajab (7th April, 1527), he arrived at Alwar which is the capital of Mēwāt. The treasures of Alwar were bestowed on his Highness Jahānbānī. And when this territory had been annexed, he returned to the capital in order to undertake the reduction of the eastern territories.

## Departure of his Highness Jahānbānī for Kābul and Badakhshān, and the march of the royal army to Agra.

As it was necessary to arrange for the administration of Kābul and Badakhshān, and as the time was exigent, and as Badakhshān had been committed to Humāyūn since 917 [5] (1511) when Mīrzā Khān

[1] The letters make 933.

[2] The letters make 930. See supra. Bābar (Ers., 368) says that it was the same persons, Shaikh Zain and Mīr Gēsū, who found out the Dīpālpūr chronogram.

[3] Jarrett II. 188. Text, Kōl. It is in 'Alīgarh.

[4] He was flayed alive. Ers., Bābar, 368 and P. de Courteille II. 310.

[5] As pointed out by Ers. (B. & H., I. 341) and Blochmann (311*n.*) and Mr. Ney Elias (T. R. 373*n.*), this date which is also given by Ḥaidar Mīrzā, must be wrong and is perhaps a mistake for 927 (1521). In 917, Humāyūn was only three or four years old, and in the T. R. (353) we have an account of Mīrzā Khān as reigning in Badakhshān in 924.

had died, and as many servants were employed there, his Highness Jahānbānī, ornament of world-subduing, jewel of the sword of fortune, forehead of glory, frontispiece of splendour and glory, preamble of an incomparable model, pupil of the eyes of sovereignty and the *Khilāfat*, the father of victory (*abū-n-naṣr*), Naṣīru-d-dīn Muḥammad Humāyūn was, on 9th Rajab of this auspicious (*humāyūn-fāl*) year (11th April, 1527), at 3 *kos* from Alwar despatched to that country. At the same time, the Emperor swiftly applied himself to the reduction of Biban Afghān who during the Rānā's disturbance had besieged Lakhnaw and taken possession of it. Qāsim Ḥusain Sulṭān, Malik Qāsim Bāba Qashqa, Abū'l-Muḥammad Nīzabāz, Ḥusain Khān, and —from among the Amīrs of India,—'Alī Khān Farmulī, Mulkdād Kararānī, Tātār Khān and Khān Jahān were sent along with Muḥammad Sulṭān Mīrzā against him. That luckless one, on hearing of the approach of the glorious army, left all his goods behind him, and fled with naught but the coin of life in his palm. His Majesty at the end of this year, visited Fatḥpūr (Sīkrī) and Bārī[1] and then proceeded to Agra. In 934 he visited Koil and went from thence to Sambal[2]
to hunt, and after viewing these delightful Highlands, returned to 11
the capital. On 28th Ṣafar (23rd Nov.) Fakhrjahān Bēgam[3] and

According to P. de C.'s fragment of Bābar's Mems. (II. 452) Mīrzā Khān did not die till 934. This must be wrong, for Bābar speaks of Badakhshān as belonging to himself at the time (932) of his conquest of India, and it is plain that Mīrzā Khān was not alive after 927. (Bābar, Ers. 286 and note.) Most probably he died in 926, as Firishta says and as is in accordance with Ḥaidar Mīrzā's statement (Elias & Ross 387) that Humāyūn's reign in Badakhshān began in 926. The events of this year, with the exception of those of the first month, are not recorded in Bābar's Memoirs which are blank for the six years from Ṣafar 926 to 932. Gulbadan does not give any precise date for the death but says that ambassadors from Badakhshān brought the news about the time of the Bajaur campaign. Apparently they brought Sulaimān, Mīrzā Khān's young son, with them. Gulbadan says that thereupon, Bābar sent Humāyūn to Badakhshān and she adds the interesting circumstance that Bābar and Māham (Humāyūn's mother) followed him there and stayed a few days.

[1] In Dhōlpūr, Rājpūtānā and 44 miles south-west of Agra.

[2] Or Sambhal. See Jarrett II, 281, where A. F. states that the rhinoceros is found in Sambhal.

[3] Bābar's paternal aunts; they seem to have made a short stay only with him and then to have returned

Khadīja Sulṭān Bēgam arrived from Kābul, and his Majesty embarked on a boat and went to meet them and behaved with liberality towards them.

As news was frequently brought that Medini Rāī, the ruler of Canderī[1] was collecting troops and that the Rānā also was preparing war and putting together the materials of his own destruction, the Emperor marched in a fortunate hour against Canderī and also sent 6,000 or 7,000 gallant men from Kālpī under Cīn Tīmūr Sulṭān to Canderī. On the morning of Wednesday, 7th Jumāda'l-awwal (29th Jan., 1528), a splendid victory was gained at Canderī. *Fatḥ-i-dāru-l-ḥarb* (Conquest of the hostile country, *i.e.*, of the country of the infidels = 934) is the chronogram of this Divine aid. After this Canderī was made over to Aḥmad Shāh, grandson of Sulṭān Naṣīru-d-dīn and then the Emperor returned on Sunday, 11th Jumāda'l-awwal (2nd Feb.).

It has been stated by trustworthy annalists that the Rānā (Sānga) had meditated revolt and been collecting an army before the Emperor marched against Canderī, and that when the former came to Īrij,[2] Āfāq,[3] a servant of his Majesty Gītī-sitānī Firdūs-makānī, had put it into a condition of defence. That black-fated one came and besieged the place, but one night he beheld in a dream an ancestor of his under a dreadful appearance. He awoke in terror and horror and began to tremble in all his limbs. After this he immediately set about his return and on the way, the forces of death attacked him and he died. The victorious army crossed the river of Burhānpūr and it came to the ears of the Emperor that Ma'rūf, Biban and Bāyazīd had gathered their forces and that the imperial servants had abandoned Kanauj and come to Rāberī and that the enemy had taken the fort of Shamsābād from Abū'l-muḥammad Nīzabāz. Accordingly the reins of resolution were turned to that quarter and a number of heroes were sent on in advance. Merely on seeing the soldiers, the son of Ma'rūf became dumbfounded and fled from Kanauj; and Biban, Bāyazīd and Ma'rūf having heard of the royal army, crossed the Ganges and re-

---

to Kābul. (Bābar, Ers. 382 and 387.) Gulbadan says there were seven of them, all daughters of Abū Sa'īd and she gives some of their names.

1 Jarrett II, 196. It is in Gwālyār.

2 Jarrett II, 187.

3 Bābar, Ers. 387, Mullā Āfāq.

mained on the east side, opposite Kanauj, with a view to dispute the passage. The royal army continued to advance and on Friday, 3rd Muḥarram, 935 (18th Sept., 1528), Mīrzā 'Askarī who had been sent for from Kābul before the Candērī disturbance, to advise (with the Emperor) on the affairs of Multān, arrived and entered upon auspicious service. On Friday next, the *'Ās͟hūrā*, (10th Muḥarram) his Majesty halted at Gwālyār and next morning surveyed the palaces of Bikramājīt and Mān Singh and then proceeded towards the capital. 113
He arrived there on Thursday, 25th Muḥarram.

On Monday, 10th Rabī'u-l-awwal, couriers arrived from his Highness Jahānbānī in Badak͟hs͟hān and brought several pieces of good news. It was written that a son had been born to his Highness Jahānbānī by the chaste daughter of Yādgār Ṭag͟hāī and that he had received the name of Al-amān.[1] As this name was equivocal and had an improper meaning among the generality, it was not approved of. It was not acceptable also because it had not received the assent of his (Bābar's) holy heart. The pleasing of the father, especially such a father and such a king, is fruitful of blessings, visible and invisible, and the displeasing of him is the cause of a hundred evils, external and internal. What marvel then if men of experience regard the rapid disappearance of this first fruits of sovereignty as a mark of this displeasure.

When his Majesty had been settled in the capital, he convened the Turkī and Indian nobles and had a splendid feast and held a consultation about the settlement of the eastern districts and the extinguishing of the flame of rebellion. After much discussion it was agreed, that before his Majesty took the field, Mīrzā 'Askarī should be sent to the east with a large force and that when the trans-Gangetic Amīrs had joined him with their forces, some great expedition might be undertaken. In accordance with this determination, Mīrzā

---

[1] *Al-amān*, in Arabic, means peace or protection; also the protected one, the trusty. But Bābar did not like the name because people in general pronounce it *alaman* or *ilaman*, and these words in Turkī have bad meanings, *viz.*, *alaman* is a plunderer or runner, and *ilaman*, "I do not feel." (P. de C. II, 363*n*. See also Dicts. *s. v.*) Bābar's objections to the name are given in his letter to Humāyūn (Ers., 391). Besides the ambiguity mentioned above, he objected because it was unusual to place the article *al* thus before a name.

'Askarī departed on Monday, 7th Rabī'u-l-ākhar, while the Emperor himself went for a visit and for hunting towards Dhōlpūr.

On 3rd Jumāda'l-awwal news came that Maḥmūd,[1] the son of Iskandar, had taken Bihār and was raising the head of rebellion. His Majesty returned from hunting to Agra and it was settled that he should proceed in person to the eastern districts.

At this time, couriers came from Badakhshān with the intelligence that his Highness Jahanbānī had collected the troops of those provinces and accompanied by Sulṭān Wais,[2] had set out with 40 or 50 thousand men on an expedition against Samarkand. It was also reported that there was talk of a peace. In an auspicious moment a message was sent that, if the time for negociations had not passed, he should make peace until the affairs of India had been cleared off. The letter also summoned Hindāl Mīrzā and mentioned that Kābul was to be a royal domain. He (Bābar) also wrote "God willing, "when the affairs of Hindūstān which are near settlement, shall be "finished, we shall leave these faithful servants and ourselves visit "our hereditary kingdoms. It is proper[3] that all the servants of "these countries should make preparations for the expedition and "await the arrival of the imperial army." (Bābar's)

114 On Thursday, the 17th of the said month, he crossed the Jumna and went towards the eastern districts.

In these days the ambassadors of Nuṣrat Shāh,[4] the ruler of Bengal, brought valuable presents and did homage.

---

[1] Brother of the Ibrāhīm slain at Pānīpat.

[2] Ers., B. & H., I. 509. He was an Amīr of Khatlān (T.R. 21*n.*) and is often called Sulṭān Awais or Uwais. He was Sulaimān's father-in-law. (Blochmann, 311.) Bābar refers to him in a letter to Humāyūn (392). Apparently he was at one time king of Swāt. (Bābar, Ers., 249).

[3] In this and other passages of this chapter, describing the events of 935, A.F.'s abstract agrees with P. de C.'s trs. (Vol. II.) rather than with Ers. The meaning is not clear in the text, but seems to be that the army to be awaited is Bābar's. The corresponding passage occurs in a letter to Humāyūn (P. de C. II, 456) and refers to Bābar's desire that all his subjects should assist Humāyūn in his projected expedition against the Uzbēgs. P. de C. has, "En attendant, il est nécessaire que tous nos sujets se joignent à Humaiun dans cette éxpedition et le servent avec fidélité."

[4] Son of 'Alā'u-d-dīn Ḥusain Shāh. Bābar has a short notice of him (Ers., 311). He was also called Naṣīb and apparently reigned 1518–1532.

On Monday, 19th Jumāda'l-ākhar, Mīrzā 'Askarī arrived on the banks of the Ganges and tendered his duty. He was ordered to march with his army down the opposite bank of the river. Near Karra[1] news came of the defeat of Maḥmūd Khān, the son of Sulṭān Sikandar. Having advanced near the borders of Ghāzīpūr, he stopped at Bhōjpūr[2] and Bihīya.[2] In that place Bihār was bestowed on Mīrzā Muḥammad Zamān.[3] On Monday, 5th Ramaẓān,[4] being set at ease with regard to Bengal and Bihār, he proceeded to Sirwār[5] to put down Biban and Bāyazīd. The enemy engaged with the victorious army and was defeated. After visiting Kharīd[6] and Sikandarpūr and being satisfied with the state of things there, he rode post[7] towards Agra which he reached in a short space of time.

His Highness Jahānbānī Jannat-āshiyānī had spent one year pleasurably in Badakhshān. Suddenly a desire for the society of his Majesty Gītī-sitānī,—who was a world of internal and external perfections,—took possession of him and being unable to restrain himself, he made over Badakhshān to Sulṭān Wais, the father-in-law of Mīrzā Sulaimān, and proceeded towards the *Qibla* of fortune and *Ka'ba* of hopes. Thus in one day he arrived at Kābul. Mīrzā Kāmrān had come there from Qandahār. They met in the 'Īdgāh[8] and

---

1 42 miles north-west of Allāhābād and in Allāhābād district. Jarrett II, 167.

2 Towns in Shāhābād.

3 The Mems. say (418), that the government of Jaunpūr was conferred on Muḥammad Zamān but he also held Bihār (409 and 410).

4 Should be 15th (24th May). (Ers., 419).

5 So in Text, but in Mems. (Ers., 419) instead of Sirwār, we have the river Sarjū or Gogra mentioned and are told that Bābar marched from his station on its banks to put down the rebels. But A.F. is nearly in accord with P. de C. II, 456, where Bābar says that on Thursday, 7th Ramaẓān, he marched towards Sirwār to repulse Biban and Bāyazīd. Sirwār is also mentioned in Mem. (Ers. 420) and appears in the list of Bābar's provinces. (Ers., B. & H., I. 541). See Blochmann, 381*n*. where it is stated that Sirwār got its name from the river Sarwa.

6 In Jaunpūr. Jarrett II, 163 and 164.

7 Probably because his family had just arrived from Kābul. He met Māham, his favourite wife and Humāyūn's mother at midnight on Sunday, 27th June, 1529.

8 P. de C. (II, 457) has "lors des céremonies du Bairām." Probably Kāmrān came there for this festival. There are two Bairāms (Vullers *s. v.*), one on 1st Shawwāl and one on

Kāmrān being surprised to see him, asked him the cause of his journey. Humāyūn replied it was a desire to see his sovereign, and that though he was always seeing him with his mind's eye, yet this was not equal to a personal interview. He ordered Mīrzā Hindāl to proceed from Kābul for the protection of Badakhshān and putting the foot of purpose in the stirrup of courage, and urging along the charger of joy on the highway of determination, he in a short time reached Agra and was rewarded by tendering his service.

A wonderful thing was that his Majesty Gītī-sitānī was sitting at table and talking with his (Jahānbānī's) mother about him when suddenly[1] the shining star emerged from the ascension-point of Badakhshān. Their hearts were rejoiced and their eyes brightened. Each day of princes is a feast but that day, by the advent of his Highness Jahānbānī, was made a fēast such as cannot be described.

Mīrzā Ḥaidar writes[2] in his Tārīkh-i-rashīdī that his Highness Jahānbānī came to Hindūstān in 935 (1528–29) at the summons of his Majesty Gītī-sitānī and that he left Faqr 'Alī in Badakhshān.

At this time the darling (lit. eye-pupil) of the Sulṭānate, Mīrzā

---

10th Zī-l-ḥijja. Probably the latter is meant. On the other hand Bābar (Ers., 428) seems to imply that Humāyūn was at Agra on 8th July, 1529. If so the Bairām referred to must have been that of 1st Shawwāl (June 8th) and Humāyūn must have reached Agra at about the same time as his mother. This too would harmonize with A.F.'s story that he appeared all of a sudden when his father and mother were talking of him. It agrees better too with Ḥaidar's statement that Sa'īd Khān left Kāshghar for Badakhshān in the beginning of Muḥarram 936 (Sept. 1529). If Humāyūn only left Badakhshān in the middle of August, there was hardly time for the Badakhshīs to send to Sa'īd Khān for help and for him to get his army together by the beginning of September. According to P. de C. (II, 457*n.*) and Ers., (Bābar, 426) Humāyūn did not leave Badakhshān till 936 (1530).

[1] We are not told the date of his arrival but as he was at Kābul during the Bairām and reached Agra in a few days (Bābar, P. de C. II, 457) he probably arrived at end of August, 1529. His mother had come about two months before, for Bābar met her on Sunday night, 27th June. She had been six months on the journey.

[2] T.R., E. & R., 387. Ers. (B. & H., I. 508) has given good reason for doubting the statement. Very probably Humāyūn gave out that his father had sent for him and Ḥaidar, who was in Badakhshān shortly afterwards, may have recorded what he heard then.

Anwar[1] had just died and his Majesty was deeply grieved on that account. The coming of his Highness Jahānbānī was therefore a great comfort to his heart. His Highness Jahānbānī remained for a while in attendance on him and the Emperor many times declared that Humāyūn was an incomparable companion. In fact the name of *Insān-i-kāmil* (Perfection of Humanity) might well be applied to that majestic one. When he left Badakhshān for India, Sulṭān Sa'īd Khān, who was the Khān of Kāshghar and was related[2] to his Majesty and who, moreover, had been in his service and had received favours and instruction from him,—being stimulated to crude imaginations by messages from Sulṭān Vais and other Amīrs of Badakhshān, left Rashīd Khān (his son) in Yārkand and marched against Badakhshān. Before he arrived there Mīrzā Hindal had reached Badakhshān and established himself in Qil'a Ẓafar.[3] Sa'īd Khān besieged the

1 Gulbadan calls him Alūr or Alwar Mīrzā and he appears in her list as the youngest child of her own mother, Dildār Bēgam. He must have been quite a child when he died in 1529, for his elder sister Gulbadan was only eight when Bābar died in December 1530. She describes Alūr's illness and death. He was born at Kābul. Bābar says (Ers. 250) that several children were born to him in 925 (1519) but none of them lived. See in P. de C. (II. 45) a paragraph on this subject which is not in Ers. Its language causes confusion about the birth of Hindāl for it would appear from Bābar (Ers. 250 and P. de C. II. 45) that he was born in 925. But if so, how could Bābar make over the infant to his mother (P. de C., II. 46) who had died in 911. The explanation is that there is a mistake in P. de C.'s trs., and that the child was made over to Māham, Bābar's wife, and not to his mother and thus became at once a son to Bābar and a brother to Humāyūn.

2 Bābar's cousin, being the son of Sulṭān Aḥmad, the brother of Bābar's mother. He was indebted to Bābar for hospitality at Kābul and for the government of Farghāna (Mems., Ers. 217). It was Bābar who suggested to Sa'īd Khān that he should call his son 'Abdu-r-rashīd. (T. R., E. & R., 140). The account of Sa'īd's raid into Badakhshān is given in the T. R., 387. It began at the commencement of 936 (about 5th September 1529; l. c. 388).

3 The old capital of Badakhshān. It was on the Kōkca and was built by one Mubārak Shāh about the beginning of the 16th century. He called it Qil'a-ẓafar on account of a victory which he gained there over the Uzbēgs and because he belonged to the Muẓaffar tribe (qu. the Ahl-i-muẓaffar of Tīmūr's day?) The ruins of the fort still exist but the modern capital is Faiẓābād. (T. R. 220 and n.) The old name of Qil'a-ẓafar was Shāf-tiwār, (Bābar, Ers. 167).

fort for three months and then returned, *re infectâ* to Kāshghar. His Majesty Gītī-sitānī heard that the Kāshgharīs had taken possession of Badakhshān and he directed Khwāja Khalīfa to go and put the affairs of that country in order. But the Khwāja in his folly delayed to obey. Then his Majesty asked Jahānbānī who by his fortune had come to reside with his Majesty,—what he thought about going there himself. He represented in reply, that he had suffered affliction by being debarred from the blessing of his Majesty's presence, and had vowed that he would never again voluntarily exile himself but that there was no help for it, if he were ordered to go.

Accordingly Mīrzā Sulaimān was despatched to Badakhshān and a letter written to Sulṭān Sa'īd saying, "Considering[1] my numerous "claims on your consideration, this affair seems strange; I have "recalled Hindāl Mīrzā and have sent Sulaimān. If you have any "regard for hereditary rights, you will be kind to Sulaiman and "leave him in possession of Badakhshān, for he is as a son to us "both. This would be well. Otherwise I, having given up my
116 "responsibility, will place the inheritance in the hands of the heir. "The rest you know."[2]

[1] Bābar says (Ers. 217) "Sulṭān "Sa'īd Khān, the Khān of Kāsh-"ghar" (he was not so then which shows that Bābar did not write his Memoirs year by year) "came to me "with five or six naked followers on "foot. I received them like my own "brothers and gave him the *Tumān* "of Mandrāur."

[2] I have substituted Mr. Ross' trs. (T.R., 389) for A.F.'s abstract. The meaning of the last sentence in the letter, is more clearly brought out by Ers.' paraphrase (B. & H. I. 512) "If not," (*i.e.*, if Sulṭān Sa'īd did not yield), "the Emperor, having "resigned to him (Sulaimān) his own "claims, would know how to sup-"port him against the pretensions of "others." It seems evident that Ers. is right (508) in rejecting Ḥaidar Mīrzā's statement that Humāyūn left Badakhshān in obedience to his father's commands. Perhaps he is confounding 935 with 932, when Bābar summoned Humāyūn to help him in the conquest of India. It is clear that Humāyūn's abrupt departure in 935, deranged Bābar's project of reconquering his ancestral kingdom and also that it led to disasters in Badakhshān. But Bābar was probably too near his end and too fond of Humāyūn to quarrel with him for leaving his post and coming to Agra. As Ers. remarks, the visit was probably arranged between Humāyūn and his mother. See P. de C. II. 457, for the passage which A.F. must have had before him.

Before Mīrzā Sulaimān had reached Kābul,[1] Badakhshān had been freed from the oppression of evil-thoughted men and been made an abode of peace, as has been already stated. When he arrived at Badakhshān, Hindāl in accordance with orders (from Bābar) made over the country to him and proceeded to India.

After some time spent in attendance, his Majesty sent his Highness Jahānbānī to Sambal[2] which was his fief (*jāgīr*). He remained happily there for six months and then was suddenly attacked by fever. The malady gradually increased and his Majesty Gītī-sitānī Firdūs-makānī, growing disturbed at the alarming news, ordered, in his affection for him, that he be brought to Delhi and thence by water to Agra, in order that he might be treated by skilful physicians under the Emperor's own eyes. A large number of learned doctors who were always in attendance at the royal Court, were directed to employ their talents in effecting a cure. In a short space of time, he was conveyed by boat. Though physicians used their skill and exhibited Messiah-like science, he did not get better. As the sickness was prolonged, the Emperor one day was seated with the wise men of the Age by the Jumna and considering about remedies. Mīr Abū Baqā[3] who was one of the most distinguished saints of the Age, represented that it had been received from the ancient sages, that in a case like this, when physicians were at a loss, the remedy was to give in alms the most valuable thing one had and to seek cure from God. His Majesty Gītī-sitānī said, "I am the most valuable thing that "Humāyūn possesses; than me he has no better thing; I shall make "myself a sacrifice for him. May God the Creator accept it."

Khwāja Khalīfa and the other courtiers represented that Humāyūn would, by the grace of God, recover and attain to the limit of his

---

1 Meaning that Sa'īd Khān had already retreated. Mr. Ney Elias (389*n*) supposes that Kābul is a mistake in the T.R. for Badakhshān, but no correction seems needed, for Sulaimān would go by Kābul from India to Badakhshān. (Price IV. 715) Sulaimān was then 16, having been born in 920 (1514). In the passage already referred to, (P. de C. II. 457) "Sulaimān" must be a mistake for Sulṭān Wais and the meaning be that the latter was Sulaimān's father-in-law.

2 In the Muradābād district; north of Agra and east of Delhi. It was given to Humāyūn in fief in 1526 (Bābar, Ers., 338).

3 T.R. (E. & R.) 478. He was apparently related to Khwāja Khwānd Maḥmūd also called Khwāja Nūra.

natural life under the shadow of his Majesty's fortune. Why had such an expression come from his tongue? The meaning of the saying of the great men of old was that the most valuable article of property should be given in charity, consequently the priceless diamond which had in a mysterious way been obtained in the war with Ibrāhīm and had been presented to Humāyūn, should be sacrificed. He replied, "What value has worldly wealth? and how can "it be a redemption for Humāyūn? I myself shall be his sacrifice. "He is in extremity and I have lost the power (*ṭāqat*) to behold his
117 "powerlessness (*bī-ṭāqatī*), but I can endure all his pain." Thereafter he retired to his oratory and having performed such special rites as befitted the occasion, he thrice walked round his Highness Jahānbānī Jannat-āshiyānī. When his prayer had been heard by God,—Glory be to His name!—he felt a strange effect on himself and cried out, "We have borne it away. We have borne it away." Immediately a strange heat of fever surged upon his Majesty and there was a sudden diminution of it in the person of his Highness Jahānbānī. Thus in a short time he entirely recovered, while Gītīsitānī Firdūs-makānī gradually grew worse and the marks of dissolution and death became apparent.

Then out of his active mind and truth-seeking soul, he summoned his officers and nobles and making them place the hands of homage[1] to the empire (*Khilāfat*) in the hands of Humāyūn, appointed him his heir and successor, placing him on the throne of sovereignty, while he himself remained bed-ridden (*ṣāḥib-i-farāsh*) at the foot of the throne. Khwāja Khalīfa, Qambar 'Alī Bēg,[2] Tardī Bēg, Hindū Bēg, and all the others were in attendance. Lofty counsels and weighty mandates, such as might form a stock of lasting fortune and eternal auspiciousness,—were imparted. Advice was given about munificence and justice, about acquiring the favour of God, cherishing subjects, pro-

1 بيعت—This Arabic word is derived from بيع a contract or sale. In swearing allegiance it was usual, says Lane, for the person making the covenant to place his hand in that of the prince in confirmation of the covenant, as is done by the seller and buyer.

2 T. R. (E. & R.) 307, 357, 422. He belonged to a family of Bārkī and was a son of Mīr Kāka also called, apparently, Amīr Qāsim Kucīn. Perhaps he is the Qambar 'Alī Mughal of Bābar's Mem. (Ers., 17).

tecting mankind, the accepting of apologies of those who had failed in duty and the pardoning of transgressors; about the honouring of those who did good service and the casting down of the rebellious and the oppressors. And he exclaimed "The cream of our testament-"ary directions is this, 'Do naught against your brothers even "'though they may deserve it.'" In truth it was owing to his observing the mandates of the Emperor that his Majesty Jahānbānī Jannat-āshiyānī suffered so many injuries from his brothers without avenging himself, as will clearly appear from this history.

When his Majesty Gītī-sitānī Firdūs-makānī was at the height of his disorder, Mīr Khalīfa took a short-sighted view — as is the nature of mankind — and from a suspicion that he entertained about his Highness Jahānbānī wished to place Mahdī Khwāja on the throne.[1] The Khwāja too, from his evil disposition and wickedness and folly, gave way to vain thoughts and coming every day to the *Darbār*, made a disturbance. At last by the intervention of right-speaking, far-sighted men, Mīr Khalīfa was brought to the true path and passing from such thoughts, forbade the Khwāja to appear at the *Darbār*, and also prohibited anyone from visiting him. Thus, by the Divine aid, things came to their own place, and Right was fixed in its own centre.

He (Bābar) left this world on 6th Jūmāda'l-awwal,[2] 937, in the 118
Cahārbāgh, on the banks of the Jumna in Agra. The eloquent of the Age composed chronograms and elegies about his Majesty. Among them was this chronogram by Maulānā Shihāb Mu'ammā'ī (the Enigmatist).

*Verse.*

Humāyūn becomes his kingdom's heir.[3]

It would be impossible even if volumes were employed to detail the perfections of this Holy One. Among them he possessed

[1] For an account of this intrigue see Ers. (B. & H., I. 515 and Elliot, V. 187). Mahdī Khwāja was Bābar's brother-in-law. Perhaps Mīr Khalīfa was afraid of Humāyūn's addiction to opium (T. R. E. & R. 469). Humāyūn's sudden leaving his post in Badakhshān must have given the old man a bad opinion of him.

[2] Firishta, Monday, 5th Jumāda'l-awwal (21st December, 1530). Erskine B. & H., I. 517.

[3] *Humāyūn buwad wāris-i-mulk-i-wai.*

the eight essentials of empire, *viz.* (1) high fortune; (2) great designs; (3) conquering power; (4) administrative capacity; (5) civilizing faculty; (6) devotion to the welfare of God's servants; (7) the cherishing of the army; (8) the restraining it from evil.

And in acquired accomplishments, he was at the head of his Age. He held high rank as a poet and a prose-writer, and especially in Turkī poetry. The Turkī *dīwān* [1] (*dīwān-i-turkī*) of his Majesty is of great eloquence and purity, and its contents are charming. His book of *Masnawī* which has the name of *Mubīn* [2] (clear) is a famous composition and is mentioned with great applause by critics. He versified the *Risāla-i-wālidiya* [3] of Khwāja Aḥrār which is a pearl from the ocean of knowledge, and very excellent it was. He also wrote his Acts (*Wāqi'āt*) from the beginning of his reign to the time of departure with fidelity and in a lucid and eloquent style. It is an Institute for all earthly sovereigns and a manual for teaching right thoughts and proper ideas. This Institute of dominion and fortune was, by the world-obeyed commands of the king of kings, translated into Persian by Mīrzā Khān Khān-khānān, son of Bairam Khān, in the 34th year of the Divine Era, at the time of the return of the standards of glory from the roseate vernal abode of Kashmīr and Kābul, so that its exquisite bounties might moisten the lips of all the

[1] Probably A. F. could not read Turkī and has copied Ḥaidar Mīrzā's panegyric (T. R. E. & R. 173) for he seems only to use the Persian trs. of the Memoirs.

[2] Perhaps, *Mubayyan*. It was in Persian and Erskine says he has never met with it. According to Badāonī (I. 343) it was a versified treatise on Muḥammadan law or Theology according to the Ḥanafī school and Shaikh Zain wrote a commentary on it which he called *Mubīn*. See also Dr. Ranking's translation, 450. There are two excellent articles on Bābar and Abū'l-fazl by Dr. Tempel in the Z. D. M. G. In one he mentions that a poem by Bābar has been published by Ilminsky.

[3] Bābar, Ers., 388 and P. de C., II. 358. The *Wālidīya* or *Walidīya* was a treatise in honour of Khwāja Aḥrār's parents. Bābar put it into verse about two years before his death, in hopes that the Khwāja (then dead) would cure him of his fever, in the same way as the author of a *Qaṣīda* had been cured of his paralysis. The trss. differ here. P. de C. says it was Sharafu-d-dīn al-Būṣīrī, the author of the Borda, who was cured. He wrote an Arabic poem in praise of Muḥammad and died in 694 (1294-5). But if the cure was effected by the Khwāja, it must have been for another Sharafu-d-dīn, possibly of Bukhārā.

thirsty and that its hidden treasures might be beheld by those whose hands were empty of learning.

His Majesty was also eminently skilled in music and composed charming verses in Persian. Among them the following quatrain is a product of his bounteous muse.

*Verse.*[1]

Though I be not related to dervishes,
Yet am I their follower in heart and soul.
Say not a king is far from a dervish;
I am a king but yet the slave of dervishes.

The following two *Maṭla'* are also sparkles from his enlightened mind.

*Maṭla' I.* 119

Parting from thee were perdition,
Else could I depart from this world.

*Maṭla' II.*

Whilst my heart is bound with her cypress locks,
I am free from the griefs of the world.

His Majesty was also famous for treatises on prosody, and among them is a book called *Mufaṣṣal* which is a commentary on the science.

His Majesty left four sons and three daughters :—(1) His Majesty Jahānbānī Naṣīru-d-dīn Muḥammad Humāyūn Pādshāh, (2) Kāmrān Mīrzā, (3) 'Askarī Mīrzā, (4) Hindāl Mīrzā.

The daughters were :—Gulrang Bēgam ; Gulcihra Bēgam ; Gulbadan Bēgam, all three by one mother.[2]

---

[1] I have in part copied Ers.' trs. (Bābar, 431).

[2] Dildār Bēgam who was also Hindāl's mother. A. F.'s list of Bābar's children is very imperfect. According to Gulbadan, her father had eighteen children, all of whom were born at Kābul except two daughters, born at Khōst. Apparently she does not reckon the Fakhru-n-nisā, who was born at Samarqand and lived only some 40 days. Her list is as follow :

I. Māham Bēgam's children :—Humāyūn, Bārbūl, Mihr Jahān, Ishān Daulat, Fārūq.

II. Gulrukh's children : Kāmrān, 'Askarī, Sulṭān Aḥmad, Gul'azār.

III. Dildār's children : Gulrang, Gulcihra, Hindāl, Gulbadan, Ālar.

Among the illustrious men, courtiers and companions who attained to felicity in the field of honour of his Majesty Firdūs-makānī, there were:—

(1). Mīr Abū-l-baqā[1] who was of lofty rank in learning and wisdom.

(2). Shaikh Zain Ṣadr, grandson of Shaikh Zainu-d-dīn Khwāfī.[2] He had acquired practical sciences (*'ulūm-i-muta'ārifa*[3]) and had distinguished abilities. He was skilled in prose and the art of letter-writing. He was distinguished by his long association with his Majesty. He[4] was also noted in the time of his Majesty Jahānbānī Jannat-āshiyānī.

(3). Shaikh Abū-l-wajd Fārighī,[5] paternal uncle of Shaikh Zain. He was a pleasant companion and of good disposition. He wrote poetry.

(4). Sulṭān Muḥammad Kūsa (beardless.) A pleasant man and a critic of poetry. He was a companion of Mīr 'Alī Shīr[6] and lived in the glorious society of his Majesty.

(5). Maulānā Shihāb Mu'ammāī[7] (the Enigmatist) whose poetical name was Ḥaqīrī.[8] He had an abundant share of learning, eloquence and poetry.

(6). Maulānā Yūsufī the physician. He was sent for from Khu-

---

IV. Ma'ṣūma's child, Ma'ṣūma.

These do not bring up the number to eighteen for Mihr Jān and Gulrang were the daughters born at Khōst; perhaps 18 is a mistake for 16. Gulbadan says the taking of Kābul was clearly a good omen, for Bābar, then 23 and without a son, had many children born thereafter and she gives it as a reason for his liking Kābul that it was their birthplace. His attachment to it is also proved by his choosing it as his place of burial.

[1] T. R. E. & R. 478 and A. N. I. 128. The learning (*'ilm*) meant is probably religious learning. He was a brother of Khwāja Dōst.

[2] Blochmann, 592*n*.

[3] Perhaps, the science of exposition and arrangement. Dict. of T. T., 1066.

[4] He was the first to translate or rather to paraphrase Bābar's Memoirs into Persian. Badāōnī, I. 341, 471, and Elliot, IV. 288.

[5] *Waḥīd*, in corresponding passage of P. de C. (II. 463). He made chronograms (Bābar, Ers. 389).

[6] Bābar, Ers. 184 and Elliot, IV. App. 527.

[7] He came from Herāt with Khwānd Amīr in 1528. Bābar, Ers. 382.

[8] P. de C., Faqīrī.

rāsān. He was distinguished for good qualities, for dexterity as an operator [1] and for assiduity.

(7). Surkh Widā'ī. An old and inartificial poet. He wrote in Persian and Turkī.

(8). Mullā Baqāī. He had a correct taste (*salīqa-i-darast*) in poetry. He composed *maṣnawī* in the metre of the *makhzan*,[2] in the name of his Majesty.

(9). Khwāja Niẓāmu-d-dīn 'Alī Khalīfa.[3] On account of his long service, trustworthiness, soundness of understanding and steadfastness of counsel, he held high rank under his Majesty. He possessed various qualities and excellences and in particular was a successful physician.

(10). Mīr Darwīsh Muḥammad Sārbān,[4] a favourite pupil of 120
Nāṣiru-d-dīn Khwāja Aḥrār. He was distinguished for learning and social qualities and was much relied upon at Court.

(11). Khwānd Mīr,[5] the historian. He was learned and an agreeable companion. His writings are well known, *e.g.*, the *Ḥabību-s-siyar*, *Khulāṣatu-l-akhbār*,[6] *Dastūru-l-wuzarā*,[7] *etc.*

(12). Khwāja Kilān Bēg, one of the great officers and who was allowed the honour of a seat.[8] Distinguished for gravity of manners and discretion. His brother Kīcak Khwāja[9] was keeper of the seals and was especially trusted and was allowed a seat.[8]

---

1 "Trés habile dans l'art de tâter "le pouls et de faire le diagnostic "des maladies." (P. de C. l. c. 463.) He is Yūsuf bin Muḥammad Harātī and the author of several medical works. Rieu, Pers. Cat. II. 475*b*. and Browne, Cat. Pers. MSS. Camb. 278.

2 The *Makhzanu-l-asrār* of Niẓāmu-d-dīn.

3 Commonly known as Mīr Khalīfa.

4 Bābar, Ers. 273. Honourably distinguished for temperance.

5 Joined Bābar only two years before the death of the latter. See account of meeting, Elliot, IV. 143, 155.

6 Text, *akhyār*.

7 Contains the biographies of famous ministers. Elliot, IV. 148.

8 *Ahl-i-nishast.* This epithet is generally applied to hermits, but I think it means here that Khwāja Kilān and his brother were allowed to sit in Bābar's presence. Khwāja Kilān was a poet and composed an elegy upon Bābar's death. Badāonī, I. 341.

9 A Kūcak Bēg, an elder brother of Khwāja Kilān, is mentioned in the Mems. (Ers., 171) but he was killed in 911. Apparently there were seven brothers and all were killed in Bābar's service except Khwāja

(13). Sulṯān Muḥammad Dūldāī, one of the great officers and of excellent morals.

I refrain from mentioning others as the design of this glorious work is to describe the lofty lineage of his Majesty, the king of kings, and I proceed to the holy traits of his Majesty Jahānbānī Jannatāshiyānī. And in completing the accounts of those ancestors (*buzurgān*) I prepare myself for the description of the great one of realm and religion and lord of the visible and invisible.

---

Kilān (248*n.*) There is a Kūcak Khwāja mentioned in Bābar, Ers., 420. Possibly A.F. means Khwāja Mullā, also an elder brother of Khwāja Kilān. He was a *Ṣadr* (Chief Judge), and Bābar's father made him keeper of the seals. He was killed by an arrow in 902. (Bābar, Ers. 43.)

# CHAPTER XX.

## His Majesty Jahānbānī Jannat-Āshiyānī Naṣīru-d-dīn Muḥammad Humāyūn Pādshāh-i-Ghāzī.

Theatre of great gifts; source of lofty inspirations; exalter of the throne of the Khilāfat of greatness; planter of the standard of sublime rule; kingdom-bestowing conqueror of countries; auspicious sitter upon the throne; founder of the canons of justice and equity; arranger of the demonstrations of greatness and sovereignty; spring of the fountains of glory and beneficence; water-gate for the rivers of learning; brimming rain-cloud of choiceness and purity; billowy sea of liberality and loyalty; choosing the right, recognizing the truth; sole foundation[1] of many laws; both a king of dervish-race[2] and a dervish with a king's title; parterre-adorning arranger of realm and religion; garland-twiner of spiritual and temporal blossoms; throne of the sphere of eternal mysteries; *alidad*[3] of the

---

1 Perhaps codifier or reducer into unity.

2 Alluding to the circumstance that Humāyūn, as well as his wife, was said to be descended from the famous saint Aḥmad-i-jām.

3 عضادة *'uẓāda.* The *alidad* or *alhidada* of English dictionaries is a corruption of this word with the prefix of the Arabic article. It meant the index or fiduciary of an astrolabe. In Murray's English Dictionary, we are told that the *alidad* is the revolving radius of a graduated circle and that in the astrolabe, it revolved at the back and was called by Chaucer, the Rule. The statement, however, that it revolved at the back, seems not quite correct. In the astrolabes that I have seen, the index—it has two limbs—is on the face of the instrument. Perhaps the explanation is that the astrolabe had two limbs or indices attached to it, one called the Rule and attached to the back of the instrument and another in front and called the Label. (See Prof. Skeat's Chaucer, III and the plates there given.) According to Moxon's Dict. it is the Label which is the *alidad.* Whitney (Century Dict.) quotes in part an interesting passage from the Ency. Brit. (X. 181, col. 2). The whole of it is as follows: "The astrolabe (used by Vasco de Gama) was a metal circle graduated round the edge with a limb called the *alhidada,* fixed to a pin in the centre and working round the graduated circle. The instrument had two sights fitted upon it, one at each end and was

astrolabe of theory and practice; in austerities of asceticism and spiritual transports, a Grecian Plato [1] *(Aflāṭūn-i-Yūnānī)*; in executive energy and the paths of enterprise, a second Alexander *(Iskandar-i-s̤ānī)*; pearl of the seven oceans and glory of the four elements; ascension-point of Suns and dawn of Jupiter; phœnix (*Humā*) towering to the heights of heaven,—Naṣīru-d-dīn Muḥammad Humāyūn Pādshāh-i-Ghāzī,—May God sanctify his soul! [2]

Great God! 'twas as if the veil of humanity and the elemental screen had been cast over a holy spirit and a sacred light. The open plain of language narrows in the quest of his praises, and the parade-ground of indication remains league upon league distant from the city of his virtues. God be praised that the time is nigh when I may withdraw my hand from lofty genealogy and plunge it in the
121 skirt of my real intent. I now essay an abridged account of the astonishing actions of his Majesty Jahānbānī Jannat-āshiyānī for this is at once a preliminary nigh to my far-seen goal and a commentary forming part of the history of my saint and sovereign (*Pīr ū Pādshāh*). By unveiling the reflected godhead [3] of the divine lord, I shall satisfy the thirsty-lipped [4] with the sweet waters of knowledge and bring my own parched heart near the shore of the sea of the com-

suspended by a ring so as to hang vertically on one hand, while the *alhidada* was worked up and down until the Sun could be seen through both sights. It then gave the Zenith distance." (See Littré, *s.v.* Alidada, Lane, *s.v.* and Dict. of T. Ts., I. 291 and II. 952.) According to the last named book, the *alidad* was at the back of the instrument as stated in Murray's Dict. A.F. applies the term to Humāyūn on account of his attainments, real or alleged, in mathematics.

[1] Orientals seem to have regarded Plato as a great ascetic. See account of him in Gladwin's Persian Munshī (87) where we are told that he spent much time in the mountains and deserts.

[2] *Anāra-llāhu burhānahu*, lit. "May God illuminate his proof" or "God taught him his proof." Lane, 2865*a*.

[3] A. F. means apparently that Humāyūn is the reflected or derivative glory of his son but the exact force of his blasphemous language is hard to discover. Certainly he carried his adulation higher than any other Muḥammadan writer. Had A.F. been a good Musalman, he would have been a better man, for then he never would have confounded the Creator and the creature as he so often does.

[4] Several MSS. have *dilān*, hearts, and this is probably the correct reading as being in antithesis to *tishna-jigar*, lit. thirsty-liver in the next clause.

prehension of the holy virtues of the exquisitely perfect one. Avaunt! Avaunt! How may the praise of the perfections of this unique pearl come from one like me? It behoves his panegyrist to be like himself but alas, alas! where is anyone like that unique pearl of the ocean of knowledge? I confer a lustre on my own words and I compass an achievement for myself inasmuch as I make my heart familiar with sacred knowledge and give unto my tongue the glory of spirituality.

O searcher[1] after the knowledge of events, arouse thyself, and receive the announcement that the auspicious birth of his Majesty Jahānbānī Jannat-āshiyānī occurred on the night of Tuesday, 4th Zī-qa'da, 913 (6th March, 1508) in the citadel of Kābul and from the holy womb of her chaste Majesty Māham Bēgam.[2]

That pure one was of a noble family of Khurāsān and related to Sulṭān Ḥusain Mīrzā. And I have heard from some reliable persons that just as the honoured mother of his Majesty, the king of kings, was descended from his Holiness Shaikh (Aḥmad) Jām, so also was Māham Bēgam connected with him. His Majesty Gītī-sitānī Firdūs-makānī married her when he was residing in Herāt to condole with the sons of Sulṭān Ḥusain Mīrzā. Maulānā Masnadī found the date of his Majesty's birth to be *Sulṭān Humāyūn Khān*; and *Shāh-i-fīrūz-qadr* (Victorious Prince) and *Pādshāh-i-ṣaf-shikan* (Rank-breaking king) and also the saying "*Khush bād*" (May he be happy) give the date of this fortunate epoch, as discovered by the learned of the Age.[3] Khwāja Kilān Sāmānī[4] has said:—

*Verse.*

It is the year of his fortunate birth,
May God increase his glory.
I've taken *one alif* from his date,
That I may blind *two* evil eyes.

---

[1] Here A.F. addresses his readers.

[2] Māham is evidently not her full name. Erskine asks if Māham be not a term of endearment used by Bābar and signifying "My Moon."

[3] The first, second and fourth chronograms yield 913, the true date, but the third, 853 only. If we read *pādshāh-i-ṣaf-shikan-īn* (īn = he) the chronogram will be correct.

[4] Apparently meaning that he was of the race of the Sāmānidæ, ancient princes of Transoxiana. His chronogram is enigmatic. The

The accession of his Majesty took place in Agra on 9th Jumāda'l-awwal, 937 (29th December, 1530), and *Khairu-l-mulūk* (Best of kings)[1] is the chronogram. A few days later, he made an excursion upon the river and placing the barks of pleasure in the stream of joy, gave away on that day, a boat full[2] of gold, and by the largesse
122 laid a golden foundation of dominion. Bravo! the first grace bestowed on him upon whom is conferred the sovereignty of the world, is munificence and liberality.

*Verse.*

Not every man is exalted.
He becomes head who is kind to men.
The lion became king of all beasts
Because he was hospitable in the chase.

And one of the learned found the date of this wave of giving in the words *kishtī-i-zar* (boat or tray of gold = 937).

From the commencement of his career till his accession when he had arrived at the age of 24,[3] the notes of success and fortune were conspicuous on his destiny's forehead and the lights of glory and empire streamed forth from the tablets of his greatness and glory. How should not his lustrous temples radiate greatness and magnanimity when he was carrying the light of the king of kings and was the custodian of the granary of Divine knowledge? It was the same light which was shewn forth in the victories of his Majesty Gītī-sitānī Firdūs-makānī and that gloriously appeared in the dawnings

---

words of the second line, *Zādaka-llāhu ta'ālā qadran* yield 914 which is one too much. So the composer says, he takes away an *alif* which represents the figure one and also, from its shape, resembles a bodkin or the fine pencil (*mīl*) used for blinding. Or it may perhaps be better to take *burda am* to mean "I have added," *e.g.*, that he has added the *alif* at the end of *qadran* but in that case, the preposition *az* constitutes a difficulty. I should state that the word *Allāh* in the chronogram is reckoned as 66, being considered to contain three *l*s, only two of which however are counted.

[1] Badāonī (I. 344) gives the couplet ending in the chronogram. See Dr. Ranking's trs. 451.

[2] *Kishti* means both a boat and a tray but here A.F. seems to mean the former. But see Elliot V. 188 and Badāonī, Ranking, 451.

[3] Gregorian Calendar, 22 years, 10 m. only.

of the world-conquering rays of his Majesty Ṣāḥib Qarānī. And it was this same light which from the time of the ocean pearl-shell Alanqūā, displayed itself from the royal shells and pearls under the veils of women in travail. It was the same light by whose splendour Ug͟haz K͟hān was made glorious, and it was the same light which was preparing and increasing from Adam till Noah. The secrets of the revelation of this light, and the strange notes of its manifestation are beyond the circle of restraint and limitation, nor is everyone capable of recognizing this secret substance or of understanding its subtleties. To sum up; His Majesty Jahānbānī was illuminating the world with the power of this Divine light, which through so many cycles and epochs had been concealed under various garbs, and the time of its apparition was now at hand. Accordingly the glory of spiritual and temporal greatness was radiating from the arch of his Majesty's shining forehead. Perfect modesty and exceeding courage were conjoined in his holy nature, and all his lofty energy was devoted to fulfilling the desires of his great father; and the excellence of intrepidity being united with consummate majesty and dignity, out of his magnanimity and high-thoughtedness, he paid no regard to self and held himself of no account. Consequently he was glorious for right-mindedness and lofty courage in every enterprise that he engaged in and every service that he undertook. In the whole of his auspicious life, he adorned the world by joining knowledge with power, and power with compassion and clemency. In many sciences and especially in mathematics, he had no rival or colleague. His noble nature was marked by the combination of the energy of Alexander and the learning of Aristotle. He displayed great justice 123
in carrying out the provisions of the will for the distribution of territories and exhibited thorough equity or rather exceeding kindness and beneficence therein. But superiority in spiritual perfections (which is real sovereignty), that was his own by God's grace; none of his brothers shared in the dainties of that table of inheritance.

Everyone connected with the Court received offices and pensions. Mīrzā Kāmrān obtained Kābul and Qandahār as his fief: Mīrzā 'Askarī, Sambal; Mīrzā Hindāl, Sarkār Alwar. Badak͟hs͟hān was made over and confirmed to Mīrzā Sulaimān; and the nobles and great officers and the whole of the victorious army were brought into obedience by proper measures. Everyone who breathed disaffection, *e.g.*, Muḥammad Zamān Mīrzā, son of Badī'u-z-zamān Mīrzā, son of Sulṭān Ḥusain Mīrzā (who had been in the service of his Majesty Gītī-sitānī Firdūs-makānī and been distinguished by being made his son-in-law,[1] but who had from short-sightedness and deficiency of judgment opened the sleeve of contumacy), bound the cincture of service on the waist of obedience. His Majesty, after five or six months, turned his attention to the conquest of Kālinjar[2] and besieged that fort for about a month. When the people within became distressed, the governor submitted and sent twelve *mans*[3] of gold with other presents. His Majesty had regard to his supplications and entreaties and forgave him. From thence he proceeded towards Cunār and besieged it.

Let it not be concealed that this sky-based fortress was in the possession of Sulṭān Ibrāhīm and was held for him by Jamāl K͟hān K͟hāṣṣa K͟hail Sārangk͟hānī.[4] After the catastrophe of Sulṭān Ibrāhīm, Jamāl K͟hān's life came to an end from the evil design[5] of a worthless son, and S͟hēr K͟hān sought the widow (who was called Lāḍ Mulk, and was adorned with beauty and charm) for his wife and by this contrivance got possession of the fortress. When S͟hēr K͟hān heard of the approach of the conquering army, he left his son, Jalāl K͟hān[6] with a number of trusty persons, in the fort, and came out himself. He sent clever ambassadors and wove crafty speeches. His Majesty, recognizing the circumstances of the time, accepted his proposals and S͟hēr K͟hān sent his son, 'Abdu-r-ras͟hīd[7] to serve his Majesty Jahānbānī so that he might himself remain guarded from the blows of the imperial armies and might arrange the materials of pride and
124 presumption. This son was for a long time in the service, but when his Majesty came to Mālwa, to subdue Sulṭān Bahādur, that worth-

---

[1] He married Bābar's daughter Ma'ṣūma whose mother (also called Ma'ṣūma) died in childbed. Ers. B. & H. I. 525 and 526 *n.*

[2] In Bundelkhand.

[3] Akbar's *man* was apparently 34¾ lbs. (Wilson's Glossary) but Price (Retrospect, IV. 713) estimates it at 28 lbs.

[4] Tārīk͟h-i-S͟hēr S͟hāhī, Tāj K͟hān. Elliot, IV. 343. See also Bābar's Mem., 406. Bābar visited Cunār.

[5] See the story in Elliot, l. c. and Ers. B. & H. II. 132.

[6] Also called Islām K͟hān and his father's successor on the throne of India.

[7] Also called Quṭb K͟hān. Ers. l. c. II. 12 *n.*

less one fled from the imperial army. In 939, when Biban and Bāyazīd the Afghāns rose in rebellion, his Majesty proceeded to the eastward. Bāyazīd was killed in battle against the warlike heroes and this rubbish was cleared away, and Jaunpūr and the neighbouring territories, having been given to Sulṭān Junaid Barlās, his Majesty returned to the capital.

As the echo of his Majesty's victories and conquests was high-sounding in various kingdoms, Sulṭān Bahādur, the ruler of Gujrāt, sent, in 940, experienced ambassadors bearing valuable presents to him and set in motion the processes of friendship. His Majesty received his overtures with imperial kindness and set his heart at rest by sending him diplomas of amity. In the same year, a city was founded on the banks of the Jumna, near Delhi, which received the name of Dīnpanāh.[1] One of the learned of the Age found the chronogram *Shahr-i-pādshāh-i-dīnpanāh* (City of the King, Defender of the Faith=940). After that, Muḥammad Zamān Mīrzā and Muḥammad Sulṭān Mīrzā with his son, Ulugh Mīrzā, took the path of hostility and rebellion. His Majesty turned the reins of resolution against them and encamped on the Ganges near Bhūjpūr. Yādgār Nāṣir Mīrzā was sent across the river with a large force against the rebels, and by Divine help, he gained a victory. Muḥammad Zamān Mīrzā, Muḥammad Sulṭān Mīrzā and Walī Khūb Mīrzā were made prisoners. Muḥammad Zamān was sent to Biāna and the other two were blinded and thereby cast down from the pillar of respect. Muḥammad Zamān Mīrzā did not recognize the kindness with which he had been treated, but got out of prison by presenting a forged order.[2] He then fled to Gujrāt to Sulṭān Bahādur.

Many of the delightful countries of India which had not been conquered in the time of his Majesty Gītī-sitānī Firdūs-makānī on account of want of leisure and shortness of time were subdued by his (Humāyūn's) arm of dominion and strength of fortune.

---

[1] See Khwānd Mīr's account of the founding of this city. Elliot, V. 124. It was Shihābu-d-dīn who discovered the chronogram.

[2] According to Ers. (II. 18 and 42) he won over his custodian Yādgār Taghāī who was governor of Biāna Fort and, I presume, Humāyūn's father-in-law. (*Vide supra*).

## CHAPTER XXI.[1]

### Account of Mīrzā Kāmrān's coming to the Panjāb.

When Mīrzā Kāmrān heard of the demise of his Majesty Gītī-sitānī Firdūs-makānī, he, out of an inordinate spirit, made over Qandahār to Mīrzā 'Askarī and proceeded to India in hope that some
125 advantage might accrue to himself. But whene'er felicity's diadem hath exalted the head of a fortunate one and the Divine protection is watching over him, what save evil (*tabāhī*) can happen to the evil-disposed (*tabāh*)? It is stated that at that time Mīr Yūnus[2] 'Alī was, in accordance with the orders of Gītī-sitānī Firdūs-makānī, Governor of Lāhōr. Having laid his plans, Mīrzā Kāmrān one night pretended to be enraged with Qarāca Bēg[3] and used violent language towards him. Next night Qarāca Bēg fled with his soldiers from the Mīrzā's camp to Lāhōr. Mīr Yūnus 'Alī regarded his coming as of much importance and received him with great kindness and frequently invited him to his own quarters. They were on friendly terms but Qarāca was watching his opportunity, till at length on one night when there was a convivial party, and Yūnus 'Alī's best soldiers were away at their quarters,[4] he seized him and, putting him in prison, placed his own men in charge of the Fort gates. He then hurried off a message to Mīrzā Kāmrān. The Mīrzā (who was in expectation of this), came post to Lāhor and took possession of the city. He released Mīr Yūnus 'Alī, apologized to him and said that if he would remain, he

[1] This chapter is a parenthesis and should apparently have been inserted by A. F. before the latter part of the preceding one. It relates to the years 938-939 (1532-33).

[2] Mentioned several times in Bābar's Mem., *e.g.*, 365, near top and 382 where he is said to be a friend of Khwānd Amīr, the historian. He died in 952 (1545-6). A. N. I. 245.

[3] Killed by a musket ball near Kābul in 958 (1551-2) when leading a charge of cavalry against Humāyūn. (Jauhar, Stewart 101 and A. N. I. 304).

[4] *Jāīgīr*, perhaps should be *Jāīgāh*. B. M. No. 4944 has *Jāīdīgar* elsewhere. I do not think it can mean estates. Ers. II. 7 translates it as quarters.

might continue to be Governor of Lāhōr. Mīr Yūnus 'Alī did not consent to serve him and taking leave, went off to his Majesty Jahānbānī Jannat-āshiyānī. Mīrzā Kāmrān appointed his own creatures to the *parganās* of the Sirkār [1] of the Panjāb and took possession up to the Satlaj (which is known as the Water of Lūdhiyāna). Then he craftily sent skilful ambassadors with protestations of loyalty and sincerity and begged that he might be confirmed in the province. His Majesty Jahānbānī, partly because the sea of his liberality had been set in motion, and partly from a desire to observe the precepts of his Majesty Gītī-sitānī Firdūs-makānī, made over the province to him and issued a decree appointing him to the charge of Kābul, Qandahār and the Panjāb. The Mīrzā returned thanks for this unexpected favour and sent presents to the Court. He followed this up by opening the gates of correspondence and by sending eulogiums of his Majesty Jahānbānī. Among them was the following ode :—

*Ode.*

May thy beauty increase each moment ;
May thy star be splendid and fortunate ;
May every mist which rises on thy way,
Be the dimming of the light of my own eyes.
Should dust arise [2] on Laila's path,
May its place [3] be Majnūn's eyes.
Whoe'er moves not round thee like the limb of a compass, 126
May he be ejected from this sphere.
Be victorious [4] while this world endures,
May Humāyūn be the Cyrus (Khusrū) of epochs.

And in truth his prayer was heard, for by reason of his disloyalty, he was ejected from the sphere of respect or rather from the sphere of existence, as will be stated in its own place. In short,

1 More generally, *Ṣūba* Lāhōr.

2 Price (IV. 717) seems to have read the words *gird kān, i.e.*, should dust, as *gar dukan*, if moss (or touchwood) ; for he translates, "Does the moss and the thistle overgrow the path of Laila."

3 No. 4944 seems to have *jāfī*, injurious.

4 *Kāmrān.* There is a play on the author's name and the words may also be rendered, "O Kāmrān."

his Majesty out of his magnanimity, looked to his outward loyalty and made him the recipient of princely favours and from exceeding kindness, rewarded him for the ode by bestowing upon him Ḥiṣār Fīrūza (Hissar). The Mīrzā always kept up appearances and continued in obedience and became the receptacle of many favours. In 939,[1] (1532–33), Mīrzā Kāmrān made over the government of Qandahār to Khwāja Kilān Bēg. The cause of this was that when Mīrzā 'Askarī was coming to Kābul he encountered the Hazāras on the way and was defeated by them. Mīrzā Kāmrān was displeased by this and took away Qandahār from him.

---

[1] The Text and several MSS. have 933 which must be wrong. No. 4944 B. M. has 939 which is no doubt correct and which Price must have found in his MS. (*Vide* IV. 718).

# CHAPTER XXII.

## March of the army of His Majesty Jahānbānī Jannat-Āshiyānī for the subjugation of Bengal, abandonment of the design, and return to the Capital.

When the mind of his Majesty Jahānbānī was at leisure from the affairs of his dominions, he, in 941 (1534), turned the rein of intent towards the eastern quarter and the conquest of Bengal. The standards of felicity had reached the town of Kānār,[1] within the limits of Kālpī, when it came to the royal hearing that Sulṭān Bahādur, under the pretext of besieging Citōr, had gathered a large body of men under Tātār Khān, son of Sulṭān 'Alā'u-d-dīn, and that he was entertaining wild projects. His Majesty after an enlightened consultation, despatched, in Jumāda'l-awwal 941 (November-December, 1534,) a force to quell the enemy, and himself beat high the drum of return.

It is not unknown to the circumspect that Sulṭān Bahādur was ever engaged in high-flying imaginings, and was always holding in his palate the bruised thorn[2] of evil wishes. But as, before he became the ruler of Gujrāt and was but a private individual, he had seen with the eye of warning a specimen of his Majesty Gītī-sitānī Firdūs-makānī's way of fighting in the campaign against Sulṭān Ibrāhīm; he could not bring himself for any consideration to resolve on encountering the victorious soldiers of that illustrious family. And this view he repeatedly expressed to his confidants. When Tātār Khān

---

1 Kinār of Erskine, II. 16. See Jarrett, II. 184 and Bābar's Memoirs, Ers. 374, 375 and 379. It is mentioned there as a ford on the Jumna, two or three miles below the junction of the Cambal. It is described in Atkinson's Gazetteer, N.-W. P., I. 217 as an old pargana in Jalaun. The town, on the west bank of the Jumna, is now in ruins. Elliot, Supp. Glossary, 315.

2 Cf. Spenser's description of envy:

"And still did chaw
Between his cankered teeth a venomous toad
That all the poison ran about his jaw."

came and waited upon him, he was continually filling his mind with vain propositions and was representing that it was easy for him
127 to advance beyond the sacred ground of respect. For a time Sulṭān Bahādur was not caught, but at length he one day laid bare the truth, and said to Tātār Khān: "I have been a witness[1] of the superiority of those splendid soldiers; the Gujrāt army is no match for them, so I shall by craft and contrivance win over his (Humāyūn's) army to myself." Accordingly he opened the doors of his treasuries and lavished gold and thereby gained over as many as 10,000 men, who had the skill[2] to appear as soldiers without being in reality such. During this time Muḥammad Zamān Mīrzā escaped from confinement by the connivance of his custodians,[3] the servants of Yādgār Bēg Ṭaghāī,[4] and came to Gujrāt. The lord of that country, on account of the crude plans that he was concocting, regarded the arrival of the Mīrzā as a gain and treated him with great consideration. His Majesty Jahānbānī wrote to Sulṭān Bahādur that treaties and engagements required that all who had turned obligations (*ḥuqūq*) of service into disobligations (*'uqūq*) and had fled to his (Bahādur's) dominions, should be sent back or at least be driven out from his presence, so that their unanimity (his own and Bahādur's) might be evidenced to the world. Sulṭān Bahādur, either from inexperience or the intoxication of the world, wrote in reply "Should a high-born man take refuge with us and be treated with consideration, there could not be in this any breach of good feeling or of sincerity, nor any detriment to treaties. For instance, in the days of Sikandar Lōdī, there was perfect friendship betwixt him and Sulṭān Muẓaffar (Bahādur's father), yet his brother Sulṭān 'Alā'u-d-dīn and many Sulṭāns' sons came upon occasions from Agra and Dehli to Gujrāt and

[1] Bābar's Mems. Ers. 343. Bahādur had quarrelled with his father and taken refuge with Ibrāhīm, and was with him at about the time of the battle of Pānīpat, though apparently he left before the battle. Bābar calls him a bloodthirsty and ungovernable young man.

[2] This, I presume, is the meaning of the phrase *ki ḥukm-i-numūd-i-bībūd dāsht*, *i.e.*, had they been real soldiers they would not have deserted.

[3] Erskine, II. 42, speaks of his escaping along with his keeper Yādgār Ṭaghāī. According to the *Sikandarnāma*, Bayley's Gujrāt, 374, Muḥammad Zamān was under the charge of Bayazīd Khān Afghān.

[4] Humāyūn's father-in-law? Bābar's Memoirs, 388.

were received with kindness. Never did this cause a breach of friendship!" His Majesty Jahānbānī sent a suitable missive in reply, to this purport, "The note of steadfastness in the path of observance of treaties is simply this, that any act which can shake the pillars of loyalty be utterly eschewed so that the cheek of concord be not scratched by the nail of enmity." He also enclosed these two couplets in the rescript.

*Verse I.*

O Thou who vauntest a loving heart
Hurrah a million times, if heart and tongue accord.

*Verse II.*[1]

Plant the tree of friendship that the heart's desire may bear fruit,
Uproot the sapling of enmity that yields countless ills.

"Beware, a hundred thousand times beware; listen to my advice with the ear of understanding and send that abandoned one (*makhzūl*) to the foot of the throne, or withdraw the hand of favour from him and let him not abide in thy dominions. Else how can reliance be put on thy friendship? Strange it is that you liken this matter to those
of 'Alā'u-d-dīn and others like him. What analogy is there between the 128
cases? That affair was one thing, and this is another. Mayhap you have learnt from books of history that in spite of the refractoriness of Ildarīm Bayāzīd, his Majesty Ṣāḥib Qarānī (Tīmūr) was constitutionally indisposed to invade Rūm, inasmuch as Bayāzīd was engaged in a war with the Franks. But as Qarā Yūsuf Turkmān and Sulṭān Aḥmad Jalāīr had fled to him, his Majesty by sundry good counsels forbade him to entertain them. When Bayāzīd refused to accede to this, his Majesty showed what his might was."[2]

---

[1] According to Firishta (see his account of Bābar's reign) this couplet was sent by Shāh Ismā'īl to Shaibānī to warn him against attacking Persia.

[2] Two of the letters which passed between Humāyūn and Bahādur are given at greater length in the *Mirāt-i-Sikandarī*, B.M. Add. 26,277, 1330. See also Bayley's Gujrāt; the letters are also given, as Sir E. C. Bayley has pointed out in the collection of letters B.M. Add. 7688; Rieu I. 390*b*. Tīmūr's letter to Bayāzīd is given in the *Ẓafarnāma*, II. 256, and the reasons why he made war on him are stated at 389 l. c., Bib. Ind. ed. But, as Bayley has pointed out, Tīmūr only

Sulṭān Bahādur out of a weak head and foolishness did not write a sensible reply. Meanwhile Tātār Khān kept saying vain things[1] to Sulṭān Bahādur calculated to deceive narrow intellects, and kept urging that he himself might be sent towards the imperial dominions, representing that the royal army had grown pampered and comfort-loving, and was no longer such as the Sulṭān had seen. In consequence of the misrepresentations of strife-mongers, Sulṭan Bahādur made preparations for despatching Tātār Khān and sent to the fort of Ranthanbhūr twenty *krors* of the old coinage of Gujrāt[2]—equal to forty *krors* of the current Dehlī coinage—to be used under Tātār Khān's instructions for the hiring of new soldiers. He also sent Sulṭān 'Alā'u-d-dīn, father of Tātār Khān, with a large force towards Kalinjar, to stir up a disturbance in that quarter. Likewise he deputed Burhānu-l-mulk Banyānī[3] and a body of Gujrātīs to proceed to Nāgōr and make an attempt on the Panjāb, dividing his forces with the idea that the imperial army would thereby be thrown into confusion. Though able and experienced men told him that his forces

speaks of Qarā Yūsuf Turkmān Aḥmad Khān Jalāīr was the Sulṭān of Baghdād and was driven out by Tīmūr. He was a friend of Qarā Yūsuf, but afterwards behaved treacherously to him and was defeated and put to death by Qarā Yūsuf in 1410. Apparently Sulṭān Aḥmad took refuge with the king of Egypt, and not with Bayāzīd. There is a long account of him in D'Herbelot, under the head, Avis Aḥmad Ben Avis or Virs. According to the *Mirāt-i-Sikandarī* Bahādur did not know how to read and write, and so depended on a Munshī who had deserted from Humāyūn and took the opportunity of revenging himself by writing disrespectfully to his old master.

[1] *Tangsharābī*, *lit.* easily becoming drunk.

[2] *Zar*, gold; but apparently silver coinage is meant. Erskine in his MS. translation of the *Akbarnāma* (in the British Museum,) seems to regard the money as silver, but in his History, II. 44, speaks of it as gold, and says A.F. estimates the Gujrāt gold coins as double that of his own time. But surely A. F. would never admit that the Gujrāt gold coins were as fine as or finer than Akbar's! See *Āīn* Blochmann, 18 and 31. In Firishta's account of Bahādur Shāh, (History of Gujrāt,) the amount is spoken of as thirty *krors* of *muzaffarīs*, though Briggs seems to have had three and not thirty in his MS. Niẓāmu-d-dīn, from whom Firishta probably borrowed his figures, has thirty in his account of Gujrāt.

[3] *Multānī* Text, but it is clear from the *Mirāt-i-Sikandarī* that Banyānī, given in the Bib. Ind. as a variant, is the true reading.

should march in one direction, they were not successful, and though both by hints and plain speech they delineated on the board of manifestation the inauspiciousness of treaty breaking, it was of no avail. He gave way to the vain thought that as the Lūdiyān party claimed the sovereignty of Hindūstān, the supporting of them (*talāsh-i-īshān*) did not interfere with his promises, and that the consequences of a violation of engagements would not recoil upon himself. He sent Tātār Khān on a bootless quest towards Dihlī and, keeping both aloof from and in touch with him, addressed himself to the siege of Cītōr[1] so that he might both capture the fortress and be an intermediary for helping the Lūdiyāns when occasion offered. Be it known that Sulṭān 'Alā'u-d-dīn bore the name of 'Ālam Khān. He was brother of Sikandar Lōdī and paternal uncle of Sulṭān Ibrāhīm. After Sulṭān Sikandar's death he contended with Sulṭān Ibrāhīm, and in the territory of Sihrind set up a claim to the sovereignty and giving himself the title of Sulṭān 'Alā'u-d-dīn, marched towards Agra with a force of double-faced Afghāns. Sulṭān Ibrāhīm came 129
out to fight, and the two factions met near Hōdal.[2] Sulṭān 'Alā'u-d-dīn not finding himself strong enough to engage in a pitched battle made a night attack, but was unsuccessful and had to return with loss. Fraudulently and with evil intent he went to Kābul,[3] and in the war with Ibrāhīm he was with the victorious army. After the conquest of India his Majesty Gītī-sitānī Firdaus-makānī became cognisant of his hidden motives and sent him to Badakhshān.[4] With

[1] This must be the second siege of Cītōr by Bahādur. On the first occasion the Rānā bought off the attack. It is to Bahādur's wars with the Hindūs and Portuguese that Humāyūn refers when speaking of Tīmūr's abstention from invasion whilst Bayāzīd was making war on Constantinople.

[2] In Sarkār Sahār, Ṣūbah of Agra, Jarrett II, 96 and 195. In the Persian text of the *Āīn* I, 357 and 455, it is spelt Hōṛal هورل, and Tiefenthaler I, 169 and 207, spells it Horel and says it has many brick houses, and lies on the road from Mathurā to Dihlī. It is about 80 miles south of Dihlī. Hunter, I. G., has Hodāl and describes it as in the Gurgāōn district, Panjāb.

[3] This is a mistake. 'Alā'u-d-dīn went to Kābul before his defeat and after it he met Bābar in India near Pelhūr. Bābar's Mem., 297.

[4] Qil'a Ẓafar seems to have been used by Bābar as a state-prison. He sent Shāh Bēg, the son of Ẓu-n-nūn, there before the final capture of Qandahār, but Shāh Bēg managed to escape by the help of a slave, Sumbul

the help of Afghān traders he escaped from Qil'a Ẓafar and came to Afghānistān, and from thence to Balūcistān, and finally reached Gujrāt.

In short, when the armies set out Tātār Khān laid hold of the treasure and set about recruiting soldiers. Nearly 40,000 cavalry, Afghāns and others, gathered round him, and he came to Bīāna and took it. When this news was brought to his Majesty Jahānbānī, who had marched to subdue the eastern countries, he turned the reins of attention, and with the greatest rapidity arrived at Agra, the capital. He despatched Mīrzā 'Askarī, Mīrzā Hindāl, Yādgār Nāṣir Mīrzā,[1] Qāsim Ḥusain Sulṭān, Mīr Faqīr 'Alī,[2] Zāhid Bēg and Dōst Bēg with 18,000 horse to put down this disturbance. His Majesty remarked that the putting down of this large army, which was approaching Dihlī with evil designs, would be in reality the extirpating of the other armies; it was therefore best to address one's efforts to the subduing of it. When the victorious army drew near the opposing force, fear fell on the latter and there were daily desertions, so that it gradually decreased and in brief space dwindled down to 3,000 horse. As Tātār Khān had obtained his army by

---

Mihtar. The story is told in the Tārīkh-i-sind. Bābar does not mention it, but with an evident reference to Sumbul's subsequent achievement he speaks with regret (p. 230), of Sumbul effecting his escape after Qandahār was taken.

As pointed out by Erskine II, 58, and 44*n*., there were two 'Ālam Khāns, (Bayley 276*n*., says there were three), and there is considerable confusion between them. The one who called himself 'Alā'u-d-dīn, and was the brother of Sikandar, had a command at the battle of Khānwā in 1527 (Bābar 363), and his son or sons were there also, l. c. 364. He was put to death in Gujrāt in 950 (1543). Bird, 260, 261. See Dorn's Hist. of the Afghāns and Bābar's Memoirs, 295, for accounts of his defeat by Ibrāhīm (his nephew). Erskine, Hist. I, 422*n*. remarks on the great age of 'Alāū'd-dīn as shown by the statement in Firishta. He is apparently the man whom the Portuguese saw at Diu in 1535. See Rehatsek, Calcutta Review, 1882, No. 147, p. 73, where it is said that one of those present was a brother of the Emperor of Dihlī and apparently seventy years old. He is also probably the 'Ālam Khān of the same article, pp. 960 and 99. The other 'Ālam Khān appears to have been a nephew of Ibrāhīm, and consequently a grand-nephew of the 'Ālam Khān who was 'Alā'u-d-dīn.

[1] Humāyūn's cousin.

[2] Later on, the name is spelt Faqr. Possibly it should be Fakhr, and it is so spelt in Badāonī I, 352.

great importunity and had spent vast sums of money on it, he neither could make up his mind (*rāī*) to retire, nor could he make head (*rūī*) in war. At last he washed his hands of life, and came to an engagement at Mandrāil.[1] After having for a while struggled hand and foot, he became handless and footless and was made the target of fatal arrows, and the harvest of blood-shedding heroes. On the dispersal of this army what the inspired mind had foreseen came to pass, for the two other forces broke up of themselves on the report of the victory and felicity of the conquering army.

---

[1] Apparently this is the Manḍlāēr of the *Āīn*, Jarrett II, 190, and the Mandalayan or Madrael of Tiefenthaler I, 174. It is in Sarkār Manḍlāēr, and is, according to Tiefenthaler, two miles west of the Cambal. He describes it as 12 miles S.S.E. of Karaulī in which Rājpūtānā State it seems to be situated. It lies south of Agra and apparently not far from Bīānạ. According to Niẓāmu-d-dīn and Firishta, Tātār Khan's force was reduced to 2,000 men, and he perished with 300 of his officers after a very gallant fight. The author of the *Mirāt-i-Sikandarī* gives an account of his struggle.

## CHAPTER XXIII.

### Account of the expedition of His Majesty Jahānbānī Jannat-Āshiyānī for the subjugation of Gujrāt, of the defeat of Sulṭān Bahādur, and the conquest of that country.

130 Though the world-conquering heart (of Humāyūn) was void of the thought of the conquest of Gujrāt so long as its ruler trod the path of harmony and sincerity, yet when the Creator wills to adorn a country with the splendour (*far*) of a lawgiver's advent, He inevitably prepareth the means therefor. The actions of the ruler of Gujrāt are a proof of this, for he, out of native arrogance, the assaults of flatterers, abundance of intoxication and intoxicated men, poverty of prudence and of the prudent, broke without object, treaties and visible ties, and became author of many improper acts. Thus it grew imperative for the lofty spirit (of Humāyūn) to march his army towards Gujrāt. Accordingly in the beginning of Jumāda-l-awwal, 941, (8th November, 1534), the foot of determination was placed, in a happy hour, in the stirrup of felicity, and the reins of prowess were directed to the subjugation of Gujrāt. When the army approached the fortress of Rāisīn,[1] the garrison submitted entreaties together with rich presents, representing that the fort was his Majesty's, and themselves his Majesty's slaves, and that as soon as the affair of Sulṭān Bahādur was settled, of what use would the fort be? In fact, as the object in view was the conquest of Gujrāt, the army did not delay here, but marched on towards Mālwā. When the army had encamped at Sārangpūr[2] the news of its arrival reached Sulṭān Bahādur who was then besieging Cītōr. He awoke from the sleep of carelessness and sought the advice of his followers.

---

1 Fort in Bhōpāl, I. G. and Jarrett II, 199. It was taken by Shēr Shāh in 1545.

2 On the Kālī Sind, Dewās State of the Central Indian Agency, 80 miles from Indore, I. G., Jarrett II, 203, and Tiefenthaler I, 351, who describes it as ruined.

Most were of opinion that as the matter of Cītōr could be settled at any time and the garrison was not giving any annoyance at present, the proper course was to put off the reduction of the fort and to march against the royal army. But Ṣadr Khān, who was prominent for knowledge and eloquence, and who ranked high in the congress (*jirga*) of soldiers and was renowned for wisdom and counsel, said that the proper thing was to finish the matter of the fortress, already nearly accomplished, and that as they had come out against infidels, the King of Islām would not come against them. Should he do so, they would then be excused if they abandoned a holy war (*ghazā*) and attacked him. This view commended itself to Sulṭān Bahādur, so he went on with the siege, and on 3rd Ramaẓān, 941, (8th March, 1535), subdued the fort of Cītōr. Thereupon he marched against the illustrious army which was then encamped at Ujjain.[1] When the news of Sulṭān Bahādur's audacity reached the royal hearing, his Majesty also accelerated his movements, and the two armies encamped in the territory of Mandasōr,[2] belonging to Mālwā, on the opposite banks of a lake which for greatness and breadth was a sea. An engagement took place between the van 131
of his Majesty Jahānbānī's army commanded by Bacaka Bahādur, and Sulṭān Bahādur's van under Sayyid 'Alī Khān and Mīrzā Muqīm, who had the title of Khurāsān Khān, in which the latter was worsted. Sulṭān Bahādur too was worsted (*shikasta*) in his heart. Tāj Khān and Ṣadr Khān said to him "Our army is flushed with the victory of Cītōr and has not yet greatly felt the force of the royal army; it will address itself to battle with a stout heart. We

---

1 In text without *tashdīd*, but see *Āīn* Bib. Ind. I, 457.

2 Now in Gwālīār. In Jarrett II, 208, spelt Manōsōr. It is about 80 miles north-west of Ujjain and on the north bank of the Seū, a tributary of the Cambal. There is a plan of the British encampment near Mandasūr in Blacker's Mahratta War, London 1821, but no lake or tank is shown there. Possibly the lake has dried up since A.F.'s time as had happened with the Kānkaria reservoir near Aḥmadābād, Tiefenthaler I, 378; or perhaps A.F. means Lake Debār which is not very far off and lies between Cītōr and Ujjain. See the Rājpūtānā Gazetteer III, 12. It is true this lake is said to have been only made in the end of the 17th century, but it may have existed before this. Neither Firishta, Niẓāmu-d-dīn nor the *Mir'āt-i-Sikandarī* refers to any lake.

should without delay go forth to fight." Rūmī Khān[1] who commanded the artillery, and all the others, said to the Sulṭān "We have a grand park of artillery; when we have such a force of firearms, what sense is there in swordplay? The proper course is to make a bulwark of gun carriages (*arāba* lit. carts) and then having put a moat round this, let us first use those arms of long range so that the enemy may be diminished day by day, and be dispersed. Fighting with arrows and swords has its own proper place."

In the end this plan was adopted. There were constant encounters and the Gujrātīs were always defeated.[2]

The following was one of the fortunate occurrences. One day a number of heroes and choice spirits were banqueting and became heated with wine. Everyone was exhilarated and talked of his exploits. One of them, who was further gone than the others, fell to saying, "How long shall we boast of the past! To-day the enemy is before us. Let us up and at them and so give a specimen of our valour." Ere the reflecting portion of the army could know their design, those wine-flown revellers, about 200 in number, accoutred themselves and set out for the hostile camp. When they approached, a Gujrātī noble, with about 4,000 men who were on guard outside the camp, advanced, and then ensued such an engagement as beggars description. The Gujrātīs gave way and retired to the camp discomfited, whilst the battle-lovers returned in triumph. The report of this daring robbed Sulṭān Bahādur's army of repose and after it they seldom came outside their fortification of gun-carriages. The

---

1 This is Rūmī Khān Khudāwand Khān and not the Rūmī Khān Ṣafar who built the fort of Surat. Erskine II, 82*n*. Yet though there were certainly two distinct Rūmī Khāns, Niẓāmu-d-dīn gives the name of Khudāwand Khān to the builder of the fort. Elliot V, 347.

2 The *Mir'āt-i-Sikandarī* ascribes this advice to treachery but probably only because Rūmī Khān afterwards deserted Bahādur, being disgusted, it is said, because the Sulṭān did not fulfil his promise of making him governor of Cītōr. Bahādur seems to have been misled by his experience in the war between Bābar and Ibrāhīm. He imitated Bābar's plan of entrenching himself, but Humāyūn (perhaps because he had read his father's Memoirs) was more cautious than Ibrāhīm, and instead of dashing himself to pieces against the entrenched camp, destroyed Bahādur's army by cutting off the supplies. Had Ibrāhīm acted with like prudence, the Mughals might never have reigned in India.

victorious soldiers went everywhere, hindering the transport of corn, so that there arose great scarcity in the Gujrātī camp.

On the 'Īd of Ramazān, (4th April, 1535), Muḥammad Zamān Mīrzā advanced with 500 or 600 men, and the other side also came forward to fight. After making two or three discharges of arrows the Gujrātīs dispersed, and by this stratagem brought the victorious army within 132
the range of the guns. All at once they opened fire, and on that day some of the king's men were destroyed. After 17 days, when the auspicious hour had arrived, his Majesty Jahānbānī resolved that an attack should be made on the camp of Sulṭān Bahādur. Meanwhile the fear and distress of the Gujrātīs increased daily, and the conditions of misfortune became more marked. At length by the Divine favour, on the night of Sunday,[1] 21st Shawwāl, (25th April), Sulṭān Bahādur grew distracted, and ordered that his cannon and great mortars[2] should be crammed full of powder and set fire to so that they should burst. When evening came, Sulṭān Bahādur got out by a slit in the enclosure (*sarā-parda*), accompanied by Mīrān Muḥammad Shāh[3] and a few others of his intimates and set off for Māndū, taking first the road to Agra in order to throw out pursuers.[4] Ṣadr Khān and 'Imādu-l-mulk Khāṣakhail took, with 20,000 horse, the direct road to Māndū.[5] Muḥammad Zamān Mīrzā went off towards Lāhōr with a body of men in order to stir up a commotion there. That day there was a strange uproar and confusion in the Gujrātī army, nor was the real state of matters known in the royal camp. His Majesty Jahānbānī remained under arms with 30,000 men from evening till morning and awaited the good news of a mysterious victory. At length after one watch (*i.e.*, three hours) of the day it became known that Sulṭān Bahādur had fled to Māndū. The heroes

---

1 Probably Saturday night is meant.

2 The *Mir'āt-i-Sikandarī* speaks of two large mortars known as Laila and Majnūn, Bayley's Gujrāt, 385. See also Jauhar, Stewart, p. 4.

3 Prince of Khāndēsh, sister's son and short-lived successor of Bahādur. Ers. II, 53 and 97.

4 Badāonī I, 346 and Nizmud-dīn, Elliot V, 192, give an apt chronogram for Bahādur's shameful flight, *viz.*, "Zall-i-Bahādur," "Bahādur's disgrace," but it seems to be out by one year, yielding 942 instead of 941. It may however be taken as referring to the flight from Māndū.

5 It is Mandū in text, but Māndū is the more correct spelling.

of the victorious army came to the camp of Sulṭān Bahādur and set about plundering it. A quantity of spoil, including many elephants, and horses fell into their hands. K͟hudāwand K͟hān [1] who had been both preceptor (*ustād*) and finance-minister (*wazīr*) of Sulṭān Muẓaffar was made prisoner and was treated by his Majesty with great favour and made one of his servants. Yādgār Nāṣir Mīrzā, Qāsim Sulṭān, and Mīr Hindū Bēg were despatched with a large force to pursue the routed army.

Verily, whoever consorts with men of darkened understanding, become darkened. Especially shall an evil day come upon the man who violates treaties and engagements, and comes forward as a juggler, and plays the game of deception against such a world-lord who is the cynosure of sincerity and rectitude. In fine, after Ṣadr K͟hān and ʿImādu-l-mulk had departed, his Majesty's army went straight to the fort of Māndū. His Majesty followed in the wake of his troops, and halted at Naʿlca,[2] and drew his camp round the
133 fort. Rūmī K͟hān[3] deserted the hostile army and entered his Majesty's service and received a robe of honour. On the 14th day[4] Sulṭān Bahādur after passing by circuitous routes entered the fort of Māndū by the Cūlī Mahesar[5] Gate. A talk of an agreement took place, according to which Gujrāt and the recently acquired Cītōr should remain with the Sulṭān, while Māndū and its territory should belong to his Majesty Jahānbānī. Maulānā Muḥammad Parg͟hālī[6] on his

1 This was an old man, and quite different from the two Rūmī K͟hāns. His proper name was apparently Ḥājī Muḥammad; Bayley, 312.

2 The text has G͟halca, but this is corrected in the *Errata*. It is mentioned, (Jarrett II, 112 and 207) as a *maḥal* in Sarkār Māndū and is described in Dr. Campbell's account of Māndū, Journal Bomb. R. A. S. XIX, 154 for 1896. He spells it Naālcha and describes it as three miles north of the Dihlī Gate of Māndū.

3 It will be seen from this that K͟hudāwand K͟hān, the *wazīr*, and Rūmī K͟hān are different persons. According to the *Mir'āt-i-Sikandarī* (Bayley's Gujrāt, 386), Rūmī deserted at Mandasōr. The author tells an amusing story, on the authority of his father, about Rūmī K͟hān's being abused by Bahādur's parrot.

4 The month is not given, but it must be Ẕī-l-qaʿda, so the date corresponds to 19th May, 1535. Possibly however what is meant is the 14th day after Humāyūn invested the fort.

5 Mentioned as a *mehāl* of Māndū, Jarrett II, 206.

6 Text Pīr ʿAlī.

Majesty's side and Ṣadr Khān on behalf of Sulṭān Bahādur sat down together in the Nīlī Sabīl[1] to make arrangements. At the end of the night the sentinels of the fort left off pacing to and fro, and about 200 soldiers of the victorious army entered at the back, some by placing ladders and some by ropes. Then throwing themselves down from the wall, they opened the fort gate there and brought in their horses and mounted them. Other soldiers entered by the gate. The news was brought to the officer in charge of the works,[2] Mallū Khān of Māndū, who had the title of Qādir Shāh. He got on horseback and galloped to the Sulṭān who was still asleep. He (Bahādur) was awakened by Qādir Shāh's cries and, between sleeping and waking, took to flight, and rushed out with three or four others. On the way Bhūpat Rāī,[3] son of Silhadī, who was one of his companions, came up from behind and joined him with about twenty horsemen. When they got to the gate opening on the esplanade, about 200 horsemen of the victorious army came forward to intercept them. The Sulṭān was the first to attack them and he was seconded by some others. At last he and Mallū Khān and one other follower cut their way through and reached the fort of Sungad.[4] Bahādur lowered down horses from there by ropes, and then letting himself down he after a thousand troubles took the road to Gujrāt. Qāsim Ḥusain Khān was standing near the Fort. An Uzbak named Būrī who had deserted from the Sulṭān's service and become the servant of Qāsim

[1] Blue road. Perhaps this is the Nīlkanth celebrated by Jahāngīr and which was visited by Akbar. See Dr. Campbell's article already cited. I do not however find the name Nīlkanth in the Tūzak. See p. 181 of Sayyid Aḥmad's ed.

[2] *mūrcal,* battery or earthwork. Niẓāmu-d-dīn in his history of Gujrāt calls it the battery of 700 steps.

[3] According to the *Mir'āt-i-Sikandarī,* lithog. ed. 279 and Bayley, 388, Bhūpat betrayed Māndū to the enemy in revenge for his father who had been killed in 938 (1532), when fighting against Bahādur. Silhadī or Ṣulḥu-d-dīn, his father, was a Hindū and prince of Mālwā. He fought against Bābar at the battle of Khānwā. Bahādur attacked him and deprived him of Rāīsīn, &c., because he kept Musalmān women in his harem. He was induced to turn Muḥammadan and his name was altered to Ṣulḥu-d-dīn. But he recanted and died a Rājpūt's death, a circumstance which may remind us of Cranmer's end. See Bayley, 364.

[4] It is the inner part or citadel of Māndū. See Dr. Campbell's article. In text it is written Sūnkar.

Ḥusain Khān, recognised the Sulṭān and informed the Khān. But the latter, owing to his length of service,[1] treated what he heard as unheard and so Bahādur carried off half-a-life into safety, and was joined by 1,500 men by the time he had reached Cāmpānīr. When he got there, he sent as much of his treasures and valuables as he could to the port of Diu.[2]

Now that the narrative has come so far, we cannot avoid giving some account of the beginning of this auspicious victory. As the victorious heroes were so rapid in getting into the fort of Māndū and in performing prodigies of valour there, no authentic news of their success emerged in the early morning. When two hours of day had
134 elapsed his Majesty Jahānbānī heard of the entry, &c., and mounting his horse proceeded towards the fort and entered by the Dihlī gate.[3]

Ṣadr Khān and his men were meanwhile fighting at the entrance to his house, and though he was wounded he continued firm. At last, the nobles seized his rein and conducted him to Sungad. Many people went with him and took refuge there, and among them was Sulṭān 'Ālam. The victorious soldiers plundered the houses of the enemy for three days, and then an order was issued for restraining the spoilers. Reliable persons were sent to Ṣadr Khān and Sulṭān 'Ālam, who inspired them with confidence. After long parleys of little moment, they gave the besieged quarter and brought them out, but as Sulṭān Ālam had several times committed sedition and rebellion, he was hamstrung[4] and let go. To Ṣadr Khān royal favours were shown. Three days after this victory, his Majesty came down from the fort and proceeded by forced marches to Gujrāt, accompanied

[1] *Viz., kuhna-'amalagī.* This is a sneer at old servants whom A. F., being himself a new man, did not like. See a similar use of *kuhna-'amala* at 157 l. 9, and also see 139, l. 3.

[2] Text, Dīp dīn but spelt Dīū in *Mir'āt-i-Sikandarī.*

[3] The northern gate.

[4] *Pai kardą.* See *Mir'āt-i-Sikandarī*, 258, for account of this man, and also Bayley, 366*n*. Apparently he was Sulṭān Ibrāhīm's nephew and consequently grand-nephew of the 'Ālam Khān who called himself Sulṭān 'Āla'u-d-dīn. He was the son of Jalāl Khān, and at one time was governor of Kālpī. Perhaps Humāyūn was incensed against him because he had proved ungrateful for Humāyūn's kindness in introducing him to Bābar. Bābar's Mem. 349, 375. According to Bayley 388, he was put to death at Māndu

by 30,000 chosen horsemen, while the camp was ordered to follow stage by stage.

When the victorious troops came near Cāmpānīr they halted, and drew up by the side of the Piplī Gate near the tank of 'Imādu-l-mulk which is three *kōs* in circumference. When Sulṭān Bahādur heard of this, he strengthened the fort and went out by another gate, on the side of the Shukr tank, and fled to Cambay. By his instructions the town (Cāmpānīr) was set on fire, but when his Majesty Jahānbānī arrived, he directed the flames to be extinguished. Leaving Mīr Hindū Bēg and the rest in Cāmpānīr he took about a thousand horse and set off rapidly in pursuit of Sulṭān Bahādur. As soon as the Sulṭān came to Cambay he hastened to Diu, after setting fire to a hundred warships (*Gharāb*), which he had prepared against the Portuguese, lest the soldiers of the sublime army should embark on them and pursue him. On the same day that he left for Diu, his Majesty Jahānbānī reached Cambay and encamped by the seaside. From thence he despatched a force in pursuit of Sulṭān Bahādur. When the Sulṭān reached Diu, the victorious soldiers returned from its neighbourhood with abundance of booty. By the favours of heaven were 135
Māndū and Gujrāt conquered in 942 (1535). Whoever is stayed upon God and whose standard is a good intention, will assuredly have his desire placed within his bosom.[1]

In the beginning of Sh'abān of this year, (25th January, 1536), Mīrzā Kāmrān marched from Lāhōr to Kābul, and after a great battle won a victory over Sām Mīrzā,[2] the brother of Shāh Ṭahmāsp Ṣafavī. The short account of this is as follows. Sām Mīrzā came to Qandahār with a large body of Qizilbāshīs (*Persians*). Khwāja Kilān Beg had strengthened Qandahār and defended it for eight months. Meanwhile Mīrzā Kāmrān marched from Lāhōr with a full equipment. A great battle took place between him and Sām Mīrzā. Aghzīwār Khān, one of the great officers of the Qizilbāshīs and Sām Mīrzā's tutor, was taken prisoner and put to death, and many of the Qizilbāshīs perished.[3] Mīrzā Kāmrān returned victorious to Lāhōr,

---

[1] Cf. the line in preface of Anwār-i-Suhailī' "No seeker leaves that door without obtaining his desire."

[2] Then about 20 years of age. He afterwards wrote biographies of Persian poets. Rieu's Cat. I, 367*b*.

[3] There is an account of this victory in the *Tār. Rash*. Ross & Elias, 468. Ḥaidar attributes the victory to Khwāja Kilān.

and the disturbance caused by Mīrzā Muḥammad Zamān was put down. The explanation of this is briefly this. It has been already mentioned that after the defeat of Sulṭān Bahādur, M. Muḥammad Zamān marched against Lāhōr with the idea of stirring up strife there. When he came to the borders of Sind, Shāh Ḥusain, the son of Shāh Bēg Arghūn and the ruler of Sind, did not give him a place in his own territory, but pointed out Lāhōr to him as M. Kāmrān had gone towards Qandahār, and suggested that as such a rich country was unprotected he should go there. The ill-fated Mīrzā came to Lāhōr, thinking he had got an open field, and besieged it. Meanwhile M. Kāmrān arrived near Lāhōr and beat the drum of superiority. M. Muḥammad Zamān was disconcerted, and saw no resource except to return to Gujrāt. Driven out and abandoned, he went there. In this year Mīrzā Ḥaidar Gūrgān came from Kāshghar[1] *viâ* Badakhshān and joined M. Kāmrān in Lāhōr. Next spring Shāh Ṭahmāsp came in person to the district of Qandahār, and Khwāja Kilān Bēg put all the wardrobes, pantries and other offices in order and sent the keys of the store-houses and of the fort to the Shāh, saying that he had no means of holding the fort and was unable to give battle, and that it was inconsistent with loyalty and his duties as a servant to his master that he should come and do homage to the Shāh. Hence he thought it proper to set his houses in order and to make them over to his guest and for himself to withdraw. He then went by way of Tatta and Ucc[2] to Lāhōr. M. Kāmrān for a month would not allow him to
136 pay his respects, saying "Why could you not have waited till I arrived?" After various transactions M. Kāmrān made his preparations and marched against Qandahār for the second time, leaving M. Ḥaidar in charge of Lāhōr. Before this Shāh Ṭahmāsp had put Bidāgh Khān Qajār,[3] one of the great officers, in charge of Qandahār

[1] *Tar. Rash.*, 467. He came from Tibet and Badakhshān.

[2] In Bahāwalpūr, Panjāb, 10 miles S. S. W. Multān. Spelt Āch in text but corrected in *errata*.

[3] Qacār in text, but with variant Qajār. It is the present royal family of Persia. It is curious that Ṭahmāsp should have, apparently, employed the same Bidāgh Khān again and sent him with his infant son to accompany Humāyūn. Ḥaidar Mīrza, (*Tar. Rash.*, 405), remarks on the curious readiness with which Bidāgh Khān surrendered to Kāmrān, and he does not seem to have been more efficient when attacked by Humāyūn.

and had departed. M. Kāmrān arrived and laid siege to Qandahār, and Bidāgh Khān capitulated and retreated. The Mīrzā got possession of Qandahār, and after putting it into a condition of defence returned to Lāhōr.

Whither have my words strayed? It is certainly better that I withdraw my hand from these affairs and attach myself to the thread of my design.

When his Majesty Jahānbānī was encamped at Cambay with a small force Malik Aḥmad Lāḍ and Rukn Dāūd who were officers of Sulṭān Bahādur, and leading men in Kōlīwāra, arranged with the Kōlīs and Gawārs[1] of that country that as there were few men with his Majesty Jahānbānī there was a suitable opportunity for making a night attack. They accordingly made preparations. By good fortune an old woman who had heard of this came to the royal enclosure and told one of the attendants that she had urgent business and wished to have a personal interview. As she was very importunate and appeared to be honest she was admitted to the presence, and communicated the plot of the night attack. His Majesty said "Whence comes this well-wishing of yours." She replied "My son has been confined by one of your servants and I want him released as a reward for this well-wishing. If I have spoken falsely, punish both me and my son." In accordance with orders, her son was produced, and a guard placed over them both. As a measure of precaution the troops were got into readiness and drawn off. Near dawn 5 or 6,000 Bhīls and Gawārs fell upon the royal enclosures, his Majesty Jahānbānī and the troops having retired to a rising ground. The Gawāns came and proceeded to plunder, and many rare books, which were real companions and were always kept in his Majesty's personal possession, were lost. Among these was the Tīmūr-nāma,[2] trans-

---

[1] Text *Kawārān*, but corrected in *errata*.

[2] Ers. II. 62*n*. supposes that this was the *Ẓafarnāma* of Sharafu-d-dīn. This may be so but *Tīmūr-nāma* is properly the title of a poem by Hātifī, *i.e.*, 'Abdu-l-lāh, the sister's son of Jāmī. See Rieu II, 652 and Bābar's Memoirs, 196. Ers. takes A.F. to mean that the very copy that was lost was recovered, but A.F. does not clearly say so, and the words "having been recovered" quoted by Ers. do not occur in the text. Probably all that A.F. means is that there is now a *Tīmūr-nāma* in the imperial library. It is rather grotesque that A.F. should

cribed by Mullâ Sulṭân ʿAlī and illustrated by Ustād Bihzād, and which is now in the Shāhinshāh's library. To sum up in a short space of time the breeze of salvation's morn breathed from fortune's ascension, and the brave warriors turned upon that mob and discomfited and scattered those hapless wretches by discharges [1] of arrows. That old woman's face was brightened, and she gained her desire. The majesty of the royal wrath, and the onslaught of o'ermastering rage boiled over and an order was issued for plundering and burning
137 Cambay.[2] After that the pursuit of Sulṭān Bahādur was abandoned, and the army returned to Campānīr. The fortress [3] was besieged for four months. Ikhtiyār Khān, who was sprung from a family of Qāẓis in Narīād [4] which is a town in that country, and who was, for his justice and ability one of the Sulṭān's, confidants brought great exertions to bear on the defence of the fort.[5] In addition to all these

---

call books Humāyūn's companions just at the time when he left them behind to be plundered. In Blochmann, 108, mention is made of an illustrated *Ẓafarnāma,* but this was one executed in Akbar's reign, and from the remark on the preceding page that Akbar had pictures worthy of Bihzād, it would appear that he had not any by Bihzād himself. Bihzād was a famous painter of Sulṭān Ḥusain Herātī's Court. See Bābar, 197, who criticises his style of pourtraying youthful beauty. Blochmann, 1072, says that Bihzād lived at the Court of Shāh Ismaīl Ṣūfī, and he may have done so subsequently. Sulṭān ʿAlī Mashhadī was, according to Bābar, 197, the best writer of the nastālīq character. See also Blochmann, 101. It seems probable that Humāyūn inherited this book from his father, for he had not yet been to Persia himself. The Timūrnāma of Hātifī, it may be remarked, is a poem in imitation of one of Niẓāmī's and more likely to be illustrated that the somewhat ponderous and prosaic *Ẓafarnāma.*

[1] *Shība,* unnecessarily corrected in Errata to *shapa, i.e.,* whizzing. See Richardson l.c. 559*a* and Vullers 490*a*.

[2] See Elliot V, 193 and Erskine II. 62*n*. Ṣadr Khān was killed in the attack by the Gawārs.

[3] See description of fort by Col. Miles, Bom. L. S. Transactions I. 150 (reprint of 1877). He spells the name Champaneer.

[4] Nirbād in text, but corrected in Errata. It was a district in Aḥmadābād Sarkar, Jarrett II, 253, and is now a station on the Aḥmadābād railway. Also a place on the sea-shore in the Surat Sirkār, Jarrett, l. c., 257.

Erskine understands A.F. as meaning that this arrangement about drawing up provisions was made by Ikhtiyār Khān. But I doubt if this is correct. A.F. seems to mean that in addition to all protections and precautions it happened that from time to time sundry mountaineering (*kūh-naward*) woodcutters entered by ravines, which from the density of trees and jungle were difficult for foot passengers to traverse, and of course impracticable for traffic, and for the sake of gain brought corn and ghee to the foot of the fort in order to sell them at a high price, while men in the fort let down money by ropes and drew up the goods.

As the siege was long drawn out his Majesty Jahānbānī would sometimes visit the different sides of the fort and search for a possible entrance for his army. On one occasion he went forward from the side of Hālul, which is a garden, and fell in with the people who were coming out of the jungle after selling their corn and butter. An order was given to find out what their business was. They said they were woodcutters, but as they had no axes or hatchets with them, their story was not accepted. They were told that they would not escape punishment unless they told the truth. Being helpless they confessed the truth. Upon this they were bidden to go forward and to point out the place. When his Majesty saw it he recognised that it was 60 or 70 yards [1] high and very smooth,[2] so that it would be very difficult to climb. By his Majesty's orders 70 or 80 iron nails were brought, and driven into the precipice right and left at distances of one yard. The young heroes were bid climb these degrees of daring (*mi'rāj-i-mardānagī*). Thirty-nine had ascended when his Majesty himself wished to climb. Bairām Khān begged him to delay till the men ahead had got higher up. Saying this he himself stepped up, his Majesty Jahānbānī followed him and was the 41st. Standing[3]

---

Ikhtiyār's plans there was this favourable circumstance that the garrison were supplied by the Kōlīs. Both Firishta and the Mir'āt-i-Sikandarī, Bayley, 391, represent that there was plenty of food in the fort, and the former evidently takes the view that the fort was captured owing to the greed of the Kōlīs in selling provisions to the garrison and which led to Humāyun's exploit, A.F. is favourable to Ikhtiyār Khān, perhaps on account of his literary abilities, but Bahādur is said to have had a very low opinion of him, Bayley, 391.

[1] *Gaz.* The exact length does not seem known, but probably was about 33 inches, Jarrett II, 58, and Wilson's Glossary.

[2] *Hamwārī.* The Brit. Mus. MSS. have the opposite of this, *viz.*, *nāhamwārī*, but *hamwārī* is probably right.

[3] *i.e.*, about 300 in all, not 341, see what follows.

there he had about 300 men drawn up by this iron ladder. An order was given that the victorious army, which was stationed at
138 the batteries, should attack the fort. The garrison were thrown off their guard, and addressed themselves to repel the men from without and were looking down from the battlements when suddenly the 300 braves came from behind, and overwhelmed the garrison with showers of arrows. And when they realised the fact that his Majesty Jahānbānī in person had ascended the stairs of victory, the bewildered foe crept into hiding-places. The drum of victory beat high, and Ikhtiyār Khān went off to a higher point called Mūlīya[1] and there took refuge. Next day they gave him quarter and sent for him. Together with his practical knowledge (*dānish*) and his management of state affairs he was fully possessed of sciences, especially mathematics and astronomy. He was also skilled as a poet and composer of enigmas. He was honoured by being allowed to sit in the assembly of the learned, and was distinguished by princely favours, and was admitted among the intimates of the threshold of sovereignty. One of the eloquent found the date of this victory "*Awwal hafta-i-Māh-i-Ṣafar,*"[2] *i.e.*, first week of Ṣafar (943) = 19th–26th July, 1536.

As the country of Gujrāt was in the possession of the servants of the empire up to the Mahindrī,[3] and as no one was appointed to administer the territory on the other side (the West), the peasantry wrote to Sultān Bahādur and announced that the collections were ready and that a collector of these was necessary; if one were appointed, they would discharge their obligations. All the officers to whom the Sulṭān spoke on the subject remained silent. 'Imādu-l-Mulk however had the courage to come forward, and he agreed to accept the office on condition that there should be no questioning afterwards

---

[1] In Jarrett II, 256, the upper fort is called Pāwah, but according to Miles Bom. L. S. T. I. 152 (reprint) the proper spelling is Pavanagaḍa, wind-fort.

[2] The text has mah, but unless we read māh the abjad seems to be incorrect, being 942 instead of 943. Erskine VI, 64. Badāonī, Brit. Ind. I, 347, has another chronogram "*Nuh Shahr-i-Ṣafar būd*" according to which the fort was taken on 9 Ṣafar, 942, or 9th August, 1535. But Ṣafar is only the second month of the Muḥammadan year, and the operations at Cambay, and the length of the siege seem to require 943.

[3] Also called the Mahī I. G. T. V.

as to any land or authority that he should give to any one in order to execute the work of the collection. He proceeded with 200 horse towards Aḥmadābād. On the way he gave written grants,[1] of land to those whom he knew. When he arrived at Aḥmadābād he had collected 10,000 cavalry. He gave everyone who possessed two horses a *lak* of *gujrātīs*. In a short time he had gathered 30,000 cavalry. Mujāhid Khān, Governor of Jūnagaḍh joined him with 10,000 horse.

At this time his Majesty Jahānbānī on account of the conquest of the fort of Cāmpānīr and of the falling of abundant treasure into his hands was holding magnificent banquets and was constantly arranging royal entertainments on the banks of the Dū Rūya tank. One of the paramount conditions of authority is that special servants and those in near attendance should have certain fixed rules to abide by, and that in every section of them there should be some discreet and prudent person appointed who may continually look after their rising and sitting, their going and coming, and take precautions against evil companionship, which is the father and mother of wrong ideas. Especially is this required at a time when details are veiled from a Lord of the Age by the multiplicity of business. It is fitting 139
that in such circumstances he should appoint right-speaking, right-acting intelligencers who may always bring him correct information of the real state and of the gist of the doings of this body of men. Otherwise many of the narrow-minded become from length of service less susceptible of the prestige of royalty, and the wine of familiarity carries them out of their senses, and leads them into the stumbling of eternal ruin. And great seditions emerge from this intoxication. Accordingly they became apparent on this occasion. The story of this is that on the night of the rejoicing and banquetings on account of the marvellous victories, some feeble souls who were fated to be admitted to the verge of the sublime assemblage, *viz.*, book-bearers, armour-bearers, ink-horn-bearers and the like, happened to have gone to the gardens of Halūl,[2] the scent of whose flowers might cure the melancholy, and whose heart-expanding breeze might give motion to congealed[3] blood, and to have started a

[1] *Mawājib* fiefs. For this use of the word see text 154 l. 15.

[2] Four m. from the modern city, Miles.

[3] Produce a ferment in sleeping blood or perhaps, blood of a murdered and unregarded man. See Vullers I. 759.

winefeast. In this state of exultation which had put to flight sense and reason, they took up the Zafarnāma and read of the beginnings of the victorious career of his Majesty Ṣāḥib Qirānī (Tīmūr)—how that prince had with him, in the vernal prime of his glory, forty chosen companions, and how one day he took from each a couple of arrows and after tying them all together, gave them to each companion to break. Though each put the bundle across his knee and exerted all his strength, it was of no use. But when he opened the bundle, and gave each two arrows every one broke them. His Majesty had then observed "we are forty persons, if we are united like this bundle of arrows victory will attend us wherever we go." In accordance with this right thought and lofty idea they girt up their loins of courage and went forth to conquer.[1]

Those ignorant fools when they heard this story did not reflect that each one of the forty was a heaven-aided host. They thought merely of the external circumstances and so fell into ruinous imaginings. When they reckoned themselves up they found they were four hundred, and in their madness and folly they conceived that unanimity among 400 persons must be exceeding wrong, and formed the notion of conquering the Deccan. Under this hallucination they proceeded to tread the broad and downward path to destruction. Next day though search was made for those near yet so far (*nazdīkān-i-dūr*), no trace of them could be found. At last an intimation of their wild idea was obtained, and a thousand men were sent to seize them. They soon brought to Court those fortune-buffeted and doomed men, bound neck and hand. It was Tuesday,[2] a day when his Majesty wore the red vesture of Mars and sate on the throne of wrath and vengeance. The crowd of criminals were brought forward,
140 section by section, and each of them received sentences fitting

[1] I have not found this story in Sharafu-d-dīn though at I. 75, Bibl. Ind. ed. there is an allusion to Tīmūr's having forty followers. The same story is told of Cangiz Khān who when on his deathbed used the illustration of weapons tied together and separate, to teach the necessity of union to his sons. See Petit de la Croix's life, quoted by Erdmann 639, and 442.

[2] Humāyūn assigned particular days of the week to certain duties. Thus Monday being Mars-day, was one of that assigned to the administration of Criminal Justice. See extract from Khwānd Amīr in Elliot V. 121 and A. F.'s text I. 358 and 361

their destiny, and the requirements of complete justice. Some they bound and made trodden under the feet of mountain-like elephants. Many who had carried their heads beyond the line of respect received distinction by the removal of the burden of their heads from their bodies. A number who, not distinguishing between their feet and their hands, had clapped their hands at seditious thoughts were made handless and footless. A set of them who from arrogance (*khud-bīnī* lit. self-contemplation) had not kept their ears for the royal commands found ears and nose gone from their places, others who had laid the fingertip of intent on the edge of misfeasance saw no more the figure of a finger in their hand.[1]

After executing these judgments and orders the time of evening prayer arrived. The Imām, who was not void of obtuseness, at the first genuflection recited the Sūra '*A-lam tara kaifa*' "Hast thou not seen how." After the conclusion of the service the order of vengeance[2] was issued that the Imām be thrown under the foot of an elephant because he had designedly and allusively recited the chapter of the elephant, and had degraded justice to tyranny, and had uttered an evil presage.[3] Maulānā Muḥammad Parghālī[4] represented that the Imām did not know the meaning of the Qurān. But as the fire of wrath was darting tongues of flame he got no reply except abusive

1 Erskine justly remarks that these details are very disgusting, and exhibit the wretched punning propensity of our James I., but on an occasion when it is not ridiculous but revolting. The sentences pronounced depend on idiomatic Persian phrases, hardly translatable. A. F.'s poor wit may be paralleled by a too-famous passage in Paradise Lost, B. VI, but at least it may be said that Milton puts his jests into the mouths of devils.

2 *Ḥukm-i-gardūn-intiqām, lit.*, the order of the sphere of vengeance. Vullers *s. v.* quotes the Bahār-i-'Ajam as giving *gardūn* the meaning of executioners.

3 Apparently the *fāl-i-bad* was that Humāyūn would be destroyed like the impious king of Yaman. Is it possible that Humāyūn thought the Imām was playing on the word *kaifa*, which in Persian means intoxication, and was suggesting that he was drunk? As Erskine remarks, the Sūra does not seem to contain much matter of offence. Probably however the reference to the elephant was enough.

4 It is pleasant to find this man, of whom Ḥaidar Mīrzā speaks so ill, Tar. Rash. 398, acting properly and courageously. He was afterwards drowned at Causa.

epithets. After a time when the light of the Imām's simplicity shone on the marge of his holy heart and the conflagration of the flames of wrath was stayed, he expressed much regret and spent the whole night in sorrow and weeping.[1]

After the completion of this affair Tardī Bēg Khān was left in Cāmpānīr, and the royal standards proceeded towards Aḥmadābād, and encamped on the bank of the Mahindrī.[2] 'Imādu-l-Mulk had the courage to advance, and to make a march for each one that the royal army made. Between Nariād and Maḥmūdābād[3] he encountered Mīrzā 'Askarī who was in the van and several stages ahead (of the main body). A great battle ensued, and the Mīrzā was worsted until Yādgār Nāṣir Mīrzā, Qāsim Ḥusain Khān and Hindū Bēg arrived with a large body of men and unfurling the flag of fortune proclaimed to the enemy the approach of the imperial ensigns with a "Lo, the sublime army has arrived." The utterance of this word, and its sound reaching the ears of the enemy were simultaneous with Yādgār Nāṣir Mīrzā's victory and the defeat of the foe. As Yādgār Nāṣir Mīrzā was ahead of all, the brunt of the battle fell upon him. On the side of the enemy 'Ālam Khān Lōdī[4] and some others offered opposition till 'Imādu-l-mulk retired half dead. Darwēsh Muḥammad Qarāshīr, father of Shujā'at Khān,[5] obtained martyrdom in this engagement. Meanwhile the flashing of the royal standards appeared and victory upon victory disclosed itself. After the arrival of the
141 sublime army 3 to 4,000 of the enemy were slain. His Majesty

[1] A.F. does not clearly say that the order to trample the Imam to death was carried out, but Erskine says it was, and A. F.'s silence implies this. Had Humāyūn repented in time, we should have had a flourish of trumpets about the imperial clemency.

[2] Or Mahī. Cāmpānīr is upwards of 60 miles E. S. E. Aḥmadābād, but is visible from the minaret of the Jāma' Masjid, Miles.

[3] Jarrett II. 241, now a station on the Bomb. Baroda and Central I. Ry. It lies south-east of Aḥmadābād and is, as A.F. states, nearly half-way between Nariād (spelt Nadiad in time-tables) being 11 miles from Nariād and 10 from Aḥmadābād.

[4] It does not appear who this 'Ālam Khān is. He can hardly be the man who was mutilated at Cāmpānīr and yet possibly he is. If he was the No. III of Bayley then his real name was Ṣafdar Khān and he was perhaps not a Lōdī at all. See p. 329.

[5] Also called Muqīm-i-'Arab, Blochmann, 371.

asked Khudāwand Khān[1] if there was likelihood of another battle, and he replied that if that leprous slave, meaning 'Imādu-l-mulk, had been personally in the fight, it was over, and if he had not been there was likelihood of another bloody bout. Men were appointed to inquire into this matter, and from two wounded men, who were lying half dead among the dead, it was ascertained that 'Imādu-l-mulk had commanded in person. Next day the grand army marched on and then halted, M. 'Askarī going on as before in front. When the army had encamped on this side of the Kankārīyā[2] tank M. 'Askarī represented that if the whole camp entered the city, the inhabitants would be harassed. An order was given that provost-marshals (*yasāwalān*) be stationed at every gate of the city and that they should admit no one except M. 'Askarī and his men.

The army encamped on the delightful spot of Sarkāj, and on the third day his Majesty, attended by many of his courtiers, came to the city. After that he gave his attention to the affairs of Gujrāt and settled them in a proper manner. Hindū Bēg was stationed there with a large force in order that he might go wherever he was required. Pattan was given to Mīrzā Yādgar Nāṣir; Broach, Nansārī and the port of Surat to Qāsim Ḥusain Sulṭān;[3] Cambay, and Baroda to Dōst Bēg Ishak Āqā; and Maḥmūdābad to Mīr Būcaka.

When the affairs of Gujrāt had been settled his Majesty proceeded towards the port of Dīu. When the army was leaving Dandūqa, which is 30 *kōs* (W. S. W.) from Aḥmadābād, representations came from Agra, the capital, to the effect that as his Majesty was far from the seat of Government rebellious men had raised the head of disaffection, and extended the arm of strife. Couriers too

[1] This is probably the Wazīr and not Rūmī Khān. The expression used by him about 'Imādu-l-mulk may refer to his being a Circasisan (according to Firishta) and to his grandfather's having been a slave. Bayley 233, 235. Firishta says he was the son of a Cangiz Khān.

[2] See Tiefenthaler I. 378, who states that in his time the tank was nearly dried up. It was cleared out by Mr. Borrodaile in 1872. Bom. Gaz. IV. 17 and Hope's Aḥmadābād. It lies north of Aḥmadābād. In text the name is wrongly spelt Kangareyā. It means the limestone or pebble tank. It is also called the Ḥauẓ-i-Quṭ and was made in 1451. It covers 72 acres.

[3] A grandson of Sulṭān Ḥusain of Herāt. Bābar's Mem. 353.

arrived from Mālwā and reported that Sikandar Khān[1] and Mallū Khān had sallied forth and fallen upon Mihtar Zambūr the Jagīrdār of Hindiā[2] and that he had taken his property with him and came to Ujjain, and that all the soldiers who were stationed here and there in that province had collected there, that the authors of strife had assembled in great numbers and were besieging the city, and that
142 Darwēsh 'Alī Kitābdār (librarian) had received a gunshot wound and had died, and that the rest of the besieged had asked for quarter and had submitted. His Majesty thereupon determined to return and to make Māndū his capital for a time, so that Mālwā might be cleared of rebels, and also that the newly conquered Gujrāt might be brought into order, and also that the flames of disaffection which had blazed forth in the settled portion of the empire might be extinguished. Accordingly having made over Gujrāt to M. 'Askarī and a number of officers he turned his rein and halted at Cambay. From thence he went to Baroda and Broach and from thence to Surat, and from thence to Āsīr[3] and Burhānpūr. He stopped seven days in Burhānpūr and then marched on and passing under the fort of Āsīr established himself at Māndū. As soon as the disaffected heard the sound of the return of the royal standards, they were troubled and crept into corners. His Majesty found the climate of Mālwa agreeable to his constitution and made many of his servants jāgīrdārs thereof. And the gates of success and satisfaction of desires were thrown open to the world.

[1] Apparently the Governor of Sīwās who was afterwards killed with Bahādur at Diu, Bayley 349, &c.

[2] In Hōshangābād, Central Prov. I. G., S. V. Handīa and Jarrett II. 207 where it is spelt Hindīah.

[3] Āsīrgārh in Nimār, Central Provinces.

# CHAPTER XXIV.

## MĪRZĀ 'ASKARĪ LEAVES GUJRĀT WITH REBELLIOUS DESIGNS.

Of a surety, a grandee who does not recognise the force of kindness and prestige, and takes the road of ingratitude, smites his own foot with a hatchet,[1] and of his own act falls into the hell of ruin. The story of the doings of Mīrzā 'Askarī and the officers of Gujrāt is a proof of this, for owing to the smallness of their capacities a little success made them give way to rebellious thoughts. From immoderate living there arose the beginnings of mutual strife and their actions were darkened by the mist of dissimulation. Accordingly after about three months the enemy stirred up commotion. Khān Jahān of Shīrāz and Rūmī Khān, who had the name of Ṣafar and who is the builder of the fort of Surat, united and took possession of Nausārī which was held by 'Abdullāh Khān, a relative of Qāsim Ḥusain Khān Ūzbēg. 'Abdullāh Khān left that quarter and came to Broach. About this time they also took the port of Surat. Khān Jahān marched by land to Broach, while Rūmī Khān came there by sea with warships carrying guns and muskets. Qāsim Ḥusain Khān lost his head (lit. lost hands and feet), and hurried to Cāmpānīr, and then from there went on to Aḥmadābād to Mīrzā 'Askarī
and Hindū Bēg in search of help. Sayyid Isḥāq who had received 143
from Sulṭān Bahādur the title of Shitāb Khān (the swift Khān) took possession of Cambay, and Yādgār Nāṣir Mīrzā went off from Pattan to Aḥmadābād at the summons of 'Askarī Mīrza. Daryā Khān and Muḥāfiẓ Khān set out from Rāīsīn and were going towards the Sulṭān at Diu, when finding Pattan empty (*i.e.*, undefended), they took possession of it. From want of union and want of counsel things came to such a pass that one Ghaẓanfar[2] (the lion), a

---

[1] A proverbial expression. See Roebuck's Oriental Proverbs, Part I. No. 103.

[2] Blochmann, 348 and Elliot, V 197. He was brother of Mahdī Qāsim Khān and foster-brother of 'Askarī.

servant of Yādgār Nāṣir Mīrzā deserted with 300 horse and joined Sulṭān Bahādur. He invited the Sultān to come (to Aḥmadābād) and letters of loyalists followed in succession, so that Sulṭān Bahādur marched towards Aḥmadābād, and soon halted near Sarkēj. 'Askarī Mīrzā, Yādgār Nāṣir Mīrzā, Hindū Bēg, and Qāsim Ḥusain Khān proceeded with nearly 20,000 horse and confronted the Sulṭān in the rear of Asāwal. They faced him for three days and nights, and then, as they were neither loyal to his Majesty Jahānbānī nor clear-headed they, out of a darkened understanding and evil thoughts, went off without fighting to Cāmpānīr. Much mischief ensued.

'Tis evident how far they carried the eating of the salt and the breaking the salt-cellar on the table-top[1] and how in the domain of thanksgiving they trod the arena of crime and the field of little service. Good God, I understand their lack of fidelity, which is a priceless jewel and of rare occurrence in this wicked world, but why should they drop from their hands the coin of common sense which is negotiable every where? In fine, Sulṭān Bahādur who had been in a thousand anxieties, grew bold and pursued them. Sayyid Mubārak of Bukhārā was at the head of the vanguard and came near the imperial army. Yādgar Nāṣir Mīrzā who commanded in the rear turned and fought bravely with the result that many of the Sulṭān's vanguard were killed, while the Mīrzā was wounded in the arm. The enemy halted at Maḥmūdābād, and the Mīrzā joined the main army. As M. 'Askarī had lost heart he incontinently crossed the Mahindrī which was in front of him, and many of the soldiers lost their lives in its floods. The Sulṭān arrived at the edge of the river and the Mīrzā went on to Cāmpānīr. Tardī Bēg Khān made arrangements for their entertainment, and then went back to his post.

Next day the Mīrzās sent a treacherous message to Tardī Bēg Khān to the effect that they were in distress, and their army in evil case, and begged that he would send them by way of assistance a portion of the fort treasures in order that they might give it to their soldiers. When they had refreshed themselves, they would use
144 diligence to attack the enemy. They were reporting to Māndū, where the imperial camp was, but it would take a courier six days to

[1] A proverbial expression. Cf. Roebuck, l. c. p. 377, No. 2023 and p. 392, No. 2129 and Vullers, s. v. *namak* 1351*a*.

get there. Tardī Bēg Khān did not consent to this, and the Mīrzās plotted to seize him so that they might get hold of the whole of the treasure, and establish the sovereignty in the name of M. 'Askarī. If they defeated Sulṭān Bahādur so much the better, but if not, as his Majesty Jahānbānī liked the Mālwā climate, and the territory of Agra, the capital, was undefended, they would go there. Tardī Bēg Khān came down from the fort and was going to wait upon the Mīrzās when he got wind of this plot. He hastened back to the fort and sent word to the Mīrzās that it was not fitting for them to remain there. They sent back a message that they were leaving, but asked him to come that they might discuss sundry matters with him and bid him farewell. He knew their design and returned a suitable answer, and next morning opened fire on them. The Mīrzās went off with evil intentions and proceeded by Ghāt Karjī[1] towards Agra. So long as the victorious (?) army was in the neighbourhood of Cāmpānīr the Sulṭān did not cross the Mahindrī which is 15 *kōs* from Cāmpānīr. But when news came that the Mīrzās had retreated and gone off towards Agra with evil designs, the Sulṭān crossed the river and came to attack Cāmpānīr. Tardī Bēg Khān, in spite of the strength of the fort, and the store of preparations there abandoned the fort and took the road of safety. He reached Māndū and had the honour of paying his respects. He made known to his Majesty the Mīrzās' evil intentions and his Majesty on being apprized thereof hastened by way of Cītōr so that the Mīrzās might not get to Agra before him. By good fortune he came up with them on the way, near Cītōr. The helpless Mīrzās submitted to his Majesty and he out of innate kindness and clemency did not regard their offences and made universal forgiveness, the intercessor for their faults. He made liberality to supplement forgiveness and distinguished them by princely gifts.

One of the evils of the time which were the cause[2] of his Majesty's returning from this country to Agra was that Muḥammad Sulṭān Mīrzā and his son Ulugh Mīrzā, who had deviated from the

---

[1] I have not found this place.

[2] Khāfī Khān, Bib. Ind. I, 80, and Ferishta give the real reason of the disastrous change in Humāyūn's affairs, *viz.*, that he had been living at Māndū or Shādīābād (abode of joy) as it was called, and had been enslaved by opium.

highway of obedience and become rebellious, as has been already mentioned, emerged at this time, owing to their constitutional worthlessness, from the corner of contempt and raised the head of molestation. Thus did those who had been appointed to blind him receive a
145 lessou.[1] They now attacked pargana Bilgrām[2] and then proceeded to Qanauj. The sons of Khusrau Kōkaltāsh,[3] who were there asked quarter and yielded up Qanauj to them. M. Hindāl who was in Agra, went forth to quell this disturbance, and the two armies met after he had crossed the Ganges at Bilgrām. A battle ensued, and as the vogue of rebels and strife mongers is like a grass-fire the flames were extinguished in a moment by the blowing of Fortune's gale. The north[4] wind of victory blew and the victorious army pursued and came to Oudh.[5] There Ulugh Bēg M. and his sons had gathered an army and again offered battle. Meanwhile the news came of the arrival of the victorious army from Gujrāt to Agra. The wretched enemy again fought and were again defeated. Mīrzā Hindāl returned victorious and kissed the sublime threshold. When the grand army of his Majesty Jahānbānī arrived at Agra Bhūpāl Rāī, governor of Bījāgaḍa (in Nimār), finding the fort of Māndū undefended boldly entered it, and Qādir Shāh returned to Māndū, and also Mīrān Muḥammad Fārūqī came there from Burhānpūr. Sulṭān Bahādur after staying about two weeks in Cāmpānīr returned to Diu. When his Majesty Jahānbānī and the invincible fortune of his family had turned away from Bahādur with glories of power and majesty, an event[6] which he thought to be to his advantage became the cause of his ruin. For after being routed by the victorious army, and after

1 At p. 124 of text A.F. says that M. Sulṭān was blinded, but here he seems to imply that the operation was not effectual. See Erskine II, 14. M. Sulṭān is a different person from M. Zamān though both were grandsons of Sulṭān Ḥasan of Herāt. M. Sulṭān was a daughter's son, Blochmann, 462.

2 In Hardoi, a district of Oudh, Jarrett 173, 178 and 145 and I. G. II, 455.

3 Bābar's Mem. 363 and 364.

4 It appears from Jauhar, Stewart 8, that A.F. is here referring to the fact that a North-Wester blowing in the face of the rebels was the cause of their discomfiture. See also Erskine II, 90.

5 Qr. the town of Ayōdhyā.

6 Apparently the meaning is that Humāyūn's departure which Bahādur might think an advantage eventually turned out to be his destruction by leading to his death at the hands of the Portuguese.

beholding the impact of the majestic troops he sent persons with presents to the Feringhī Viceroy [1] who was the Warden of the Ports, and invited him to come to him. At the time when M. 'Askarī went off from Gujrāt and the Sulṭān had come to Diu, the Viceroy arrived there by sea with ships and soldiers. When he learned the state of affairs he grew apprehensive, lest now that the Sulṭān was independent of his help he would act perfidiously after an interview. He therefore feigned illness and sent messengers to the Sulṭān to say that he had come in compliance with his request and would wait upon him as soon as he was better. The Sultān left the highway of caution and on 3 Ramaẓān 943 (13th February, 1537), at the close of the day, went by boat to inquire after the Viceroy's health. As soon as he arrived he saw that the illness was feigned, and reporting that he had come he immediately proceeded to return. The Feringhīs thought that "when such a prey has come into our grasp it will be well if we get some harbours out of him." The Viceroy intercepted him and requested him to stay till some presents should be brought before him. The Sulṭān said "send them afterwards," and saying this he hastily went towards his own vessel. The Feringhī Qāẓī [2] stopped him and bade him wait and the Sultan impatiently drew his sword and clove him to the waist. He then jumped from their vessel on to his own. The
Portuguese boats which were round about closed in upon her and a 146
fight began. The Sultān and Rūmī Khān [3] flung themselves into the sea. A Feringhī acquaintance of Rūmī Khān drew him out, but the Sulṭān was drowned, [4] and his attendants also perished. The chrono-

---

[1] وزری representing the Portuguese Viserei. His name was Nuno da Cunha.

[2] Apparently Manuel de Sousa, Governor of Diu. Qāẓī seems used here for Magistrate or Governor.

[3] This Rūmī Khān was himself an European, which may account for his being saved by a Portuguese. Barros says he was the son of an Albanian father and an Italian mother and was born at Brindisi, and first came to the east on the fleet of the corsair Sulaimān in 1516 (Conti says his birthplace was Otranto). He built the fort of Surat, apparently in 947 and not in 930, as stated by Anquetil du Perron. See Blochmann, 354. The Portuguese called him Khwāja Ṣafar and Ṣafar Āghā. Hē was killed at the siege of Diu in 1546.

[4] The accounts of Bahādur's death are very conflicting, and it is difficult to decide how he came by his death. My friend Mr. Whiteway has refer-

gram is *Faringiyān-i-Bahādur-kush*[1] (943=1531). And some used to say that he (Bahādur) came to the surface and reached the shore in safety. And subsequently there were reports in Gujrāt and the Deccan of his having been seen by people. For instance, on one occasion a person appeared in the Deccan whom the Niẓāmu-l-Mulk acknowledged, and played *Caugān* (polo) with. A crowd gathered round him, and the Niẓām perceiving this resolved to put him to death. On that same night he disappeared from his tent, and people concluded that the Niẓām had destroyed him. One day Mīr Abū Turab[2] who is one of the Gujrāt grandees, related that Mullā Quṭbu-d-dīn of Shīrāz, who was Sulṭān Bahādur's preceptor, was at that time in the Deccan and that he took an oath that the man was certainly Sulṭān Bahādur, and that he had spoken to him of certain matters only known to themselves, and had received intelligent replies. It cannot be said that in the wide kingdom of God's power such things are impossible.

In fine, when Sultān Bahādur had thus disappeared in the sea, and his officers were sitting in the dust (*i.e.*, were in mourning),

---

red me to a long and interesting account by Correa. Naturally this man puts the blame on Bahādur. It would be more satisfactory if we could get the official report on the occurrence which must surely be somewhere in the Portuguese archives. No doubt the responsibility of explaining Bahādur's death rests on the Portuguese for he was their guest or at least visitor, and was killed among their ships. There is a long account of the affair in the Mirāt-i-Sikandarī, p. 28 *et seq.* See also Bayley's Gujrāt. There is this to be said for the Muḥammadan chroniclers that they do not represent Bahādur as guiltless in the matter. They represent him as trying to outwit the Portuguese and anxious to get the viceroy into his power. They are therefore more honest than the Portuguese who try to make out that Bahādur went on board to kill the viceroy and that the Portuguese were altogether blameless. Probably the truth is that Bahādur went on board in order to induce the viceroy to return with him, that the viceroy on the other hand wanted to detain him, and that then a scuffle arose in which Bahādur was slain. It is curious that the Mirāt-i-Sikandari does not mention Ṣafar Āghā in his list of Bahādur's companions, and that he says they all likewise perished.

[1] "Feringis, slayers of Bahādur" (or "of heroes"). A more poetical chronogram was devised by Ikhtiyār Khān, *viz.*, *Sulṭānu-l-bar—Shahīdu-l-bahr*: "Monarch ashore, Martyr asea" This also makes 943.

[2] Blochmann, 506.

Muḥammad Zamān Mīrzā put on blue clothes as mourning for the Sulṭān, and by hypocritical means got a portion of the treasures of Gujrāt into his possession, while another portion fell into the hands of the Feringhīs, and some was plundered. He also called himself the son [1] of Sulṭān Bahādur's mother, and sometimes demanded from the Feringhīs satisfaction for the murder, and sometimes secretly sent them large sums of money in order that they might use their influence in having him acknowledged as sovereign (lit. recite the *Khuṭba* in his name). So that for some days they read the *Khuṭba* in his name in the Ṣafā [2] Mosque. And he for some time went about as an adventurer till at last 'Imādu-l-mulk brought an army against him and defeated him. From thence he being helpless and ashamed cast a glance of hope towards kissing the threshold of his Majesty Jahānbānī, as will be hereafter related in its proper place. But leaving such matters, to speak of which is to indulge in amplifications and rhetoric, I proceed to my proper subject.

When his Majesty Jahānbānī Jannat-āshiyānī arrived at the capital the audacious spirits of that neighbourhood who had raised the head of refractoriness, and extended the neck of dispute came into subjection and obedience, and made tribute the material of their 147
own peace and safety. The dominions became adorned with repose and steadfastness.

---

[1] See Mirāt-i-Sikandarī 293.

[2] I do not know where this is. The Mirāt-i-Sikandarī lith. ed., p. 293, says that M. Zamān was near Ūnah which is 3 kos from Diu, and that he there set himself up as Sulṭān. Ūnah is referred to in Jarrett II, 244 and 247 and 258. See also I. G. art. Una. The Mirāt says 'Imādu-l-mulk defeated M. Zamān-at-Zamār in Surat (*Kāthiāwār*) near Ūnah. Probably the mosque in question is in Diu for Mr. Whiteway tells me that the Portuguese authorities say that the *Khuṭba* was read for a time in M. Zamān's name in Diu.

## CHAPTER XXV.

### March of His Majesty Jahānbānī Jannat-Āshiyānī to subdue Bengal; his conquest of that country and return to the Capital, and what happened in the meanwhile.

When the world-adorning mind had finished the affairs of those regions, (*i.e.*, Agra and the territories referred to at end of last chapter) his princely genius addressed itself to the arrangements for an expedition to Gujrāt, so that he might again turn the reins of his intent towards that province and might, contrary to former dispositions, make over its management to men whose behaviour should show steadiness in administration, and whose proceedings should not be characterised by mutability and confusion. He purposed that when his mind was at ease with regard to the settlement of the province, he would return to the capital. Meanwhile news came of the emergence of Shēr Khān and of his commotions in the eastern provinces. Hence the design of subduing Bengal, which had entered his Majesty's heart before the affairs of Gujrāt and had been put off on account of the latter now revived, and orders were issued to make preparations for an expedition to Bengal. It was decided that Shēr Khān should be put down and the territories of Bengal subdued.

### Account of Shēr Khān.[1]

This Shēr Khān belonged to the Afghān tribe of Sūr. His old name was Farīd, and he was the son of Ḥasan, the son of Ibrāhīm Shērakhail. Ibrāhīm was a horse-dealer, nor had he any distinction among the crowd of tradesmen. His native country was the village

---

[1] A. F's. account is inferior to Niẓāmu-d-dīn's (copied by Firishta) and to Khāfī Khān's. See also Dorn's History of the Afghāns, p. 80 *et seq*, and Garçin de Tassy's translation of the Chronicle of Shēr Shāh.

of Shamla[1] in the territory of Nārnūl.[2] His son Ḥasan developed some nobleness[3] and from trading took to soldiering. For a long time he was in the service of Rāīmal, the grandfather of Rāīsāl Darbārī,[4] who is at present honoured by being in the service of his Majesty the Shāhinshāh. From there he went to Caund[5] in the territory of Sahasrām and became a servant of Naṣīr Khān Lūḥānī who was an officer of Sikandar Lōdī. By service and ability he surpassed his fellows, and when Naṣīr Khān died, he entered the service of his brother Daulat Khān. After that he was enrolled among the followers of Baban who was one of the grandees of Sulṭān Sikandar Lōdī, and achieved a certain amount of distinction. Many things' 148
were accomplished by his management. His son Farīd pained his own father by his arrogance and evil disposition, and separated from him. For a time he was in the service of Tāj Khān Lōdī and for a while he was in Oudh in the service of Qāsim Ḥusain Uzbak. For a long time he was servant of Sulṭān Junaid Barlās.[6] One day Sulṭān Junaid Barlās had taken occasion to introduce him and two other Afghans who were in his service to his Majesty Gītī-sitānī Firdaus-makānī. As soon as the farseeing glance of his Majesty fell upon him he remarked "Sulṭān Barlās, the eyes of this Afghān, (pointing to Farīd) indicate turbulence and strife-mongering, he ought to be confined." He received the other two favourably. Farīd got apprehensive on seeing his Majesty Gītī-sitānī's look, and fled before Sulṭān (Junaid) could make him over to his men. Meanwhile his father died and his property fell into his hands. In the territory of Sahasrām, and in the jungles of Caund, which is a pargana of Rohtās, he began to give trouble by practising theft,[7]

---

1 Or Simla, according to some. A pencil note to Chalmers' MS. translation has Shamly 55 miles N. of Dihli.

2 In the district of Agra. Jarrett, II, 193.

3 *Ba qadr rashdī paidā karda.*

4 Blochmann, 419.

5 The text has Jāna. Caund or Cānd is correct. See Beames J.A.S.B. for 1895, p. 81. It was in Sarkār Rohtās.

6 He was governor of Kara Mānikpūr (in Allāhābād) under Bābar and was younger brother of Bābar's Vizier Niẓāmu-d-dīn. Dorn l.c. 92. He died in 943, (1536-37). See Firishta.

7 These charges may be exaggerated, but they are corroborated by Shēr Shāh's alleged confession to Mallū Khān. Elliot IV, 393n.

robbery and murder. In a short space of time he by craft and unrighteousness surpassed the rebels of the age. Accordingly Sulṭān Bahādur of Gujrāt sent him a subsidy by the hands of merchants and summoned him to his side. Farīd made the money into capital for sedition, and sent excuses for not going. He occupied himself in usurpations, attacks and in plundering towns and villages In a short time many rascals and vagabonds gathered round him. Meanwhile the governor[1] of Bihār who was one of the Lūḥānī nobles, departed this life, and there was no one left to take up the thread of his duties. Shēr Khān and his vagabonds made a raid and got hold of much property. Then he returned to his own place, and suddenly attacked Ulugh Mīrzā, who was near Sirwa (Sirū). By craft he got the better of him. From there he turned and attacked Benares, and when he had acquired troops and property he went to Patna and took possession of that country. He fought a battle at Sūrajgaṛh[2] which is the boundary of the territories of the ruler of Bengal, and won a victory. That country also came into his hands. For a year he carried on war against Nuṣrat Shāh,[3] the ruler of Bengal, and for a long while he besieged Gaur.[4]

One remarkable circumstance was that Shēr Khān came to hear of an eminent astrologer in the service of the Rājā of Orissa. As he had vain and rebellious thoughts he sent for this astrologer to get information about his success. The Rājā would not let him go, but the astrologer wrote to Shēr Khān that he would not prevail over Bengal till the lapse of a year, and that he would prevail on a particular day, on which the Ganges would be fordable for an hour.
149 By fate, what was written came to pass.[5]

1 This is Sulṭān Muḥammad, son of Daryā Lūḥānī. Stewart's Bengal 131. Khāfī Khān calls him Bahādur Khān Lūḥānī; Bib. Ind. ed. I, 89. In Dorn's History and in Stewart he is called Pīrkhān.

2 In Monghyr and at the east end of that district. But apparently this is a slip of the author for Tēlīagaṛhī in the Sonthal Parganas. See Jarrett II, 116 and note.

3 Text, *naṣīb* but this is wrong. See Jarrett II, 147*n*. and *Riyāzu-s-salāṭīn*, Bib. Ind. text 139.

4 The text has Gōrakhpūr, but a note says that many MSS. have Gaur. The context and history show that Gaur is right. See Stewart's Bengal, 120. Gaur capitulated in 1537 to Shēr Shāh's son.

5 See Erskine's note on this prediction II, 135*n*. Apparently the pre-

*Verse.*

I heard from a sage that wisdom is plentiful,
But that it is scattered about among mankind.

During the time that the royal standards were engaged in conquering Mālwā and Gujrāt, Shēr Khān seized his opportunity and made great progress. The above is a sketch of the beginning of his career. The remainder of his story, the last of his actions, and his wretched end will be narrated in a parenthesis of the account of his Majesty Jahānbānī, so that the authors of strife and contention may take warning therefrom.[1]

In fine, as the idea of an expedition to the eastern provinces had become fixed in the mind of his Majesty Jahānbānī, Mīr Faqr 'Alī, who had been one of the great officers of his Majesty Fīrdaus-makānī Gītī-sitānī was appointed to the charge of Dihlī while Agra was entrusted to Mīr Muḥammad Bakhshī, who was one of the trusted servants of the State. Yādgār Nāṣir Mīrzā, his Majesty's cousin, was sent to Kālpī which was his *jāīgīr* in order to manage that quarter. Nūru-d-dīn Muḥammad Mīrzā[2] who was married to his Majesty's sister Gulrang Bēgam and was the progenitor of Salīma Sulṭān Bēgam, was appointed to the charge of Qanauj. His Majesty having in this manner arranged the officers of his kingdom went off to the eastward by boat, along with his chaste and veiled

diction must refer to something that occurred at the siege of Gaur, which was situated on an old channel of the Ganges, for we do not hear that the real Ganges became fordable on the days of Causā and Qanauj.

[1] A.F's moralising is rather misplaced. Was Shēr Khān's death when engaged in a holy war and in the hour of victory, as pitiable as the slip on a stair which ended Humāyūn's days?

[2] The *Ma'āṣir-i-raḥīmī* (MS. A. S. B. 194*a*) says that Nūru-d-dīn was the son of Mīrzā 'Alā'u-d-daula who was related to Khwāja Ḥasan 'Aṭṭār who again was son of Khwājā 'Alā'u-d-dīn who was the first Khalīfa of the Naqshbandī order. The Gulrang Bēgam whom Nūru-d-dīn married was Humāyūn's half-sister, being a daughter of Dildār Bēgam and full-sister of Hindāl and Gulbadan Bēgam. Her daughter Salīma was first married to Bairām and afterwards to Akbar. Bairām received Salīma in marriage as a reward for his helping Humāyūn to conquer India, and also perhaps because they were related. Salīma's great-grandmother, Pāshā Bēgam being a daughter of Bairām's ancestor 'Alī Shukr who belonged to the Turkomāns of the Black Sheep.

consorts. Mīrzā 'Askarī and Mīrzā Hindāl accompanied him, while among the officers were Ibrāhīm Bēg Cābūq,[1] Jahāngīr Qulī Bēg, Khusrau Bēg Kōkaltāsh, Tardī Bēg Khān, Qūc Bēg,[2] Tardī Bēg of Etāwā, Bairām Khān, Qāsim Ḥusain Khān Uzbak, Būcakā Bēg, Zāhid Bēg, Dōst Bēg, Bēg Mīrak, Ḥājī Muḥammad (son of) Bābā Qushqa,[3] Yā'qūb Bēg, Nihāl Bēg, Rōshan Bēg, Mughul Bēg and a large number of other distinguished men. The army proceeded by land and by water whilst his Majesty, sometimes sitting in a boat and sometimes riding on horse-back, deliberated on the affairs of state and proceeded towards the fort of Cunār where was Shēr Khān. When the army drew nigh to Cunār, M. Muḥammad Zamān came from Gujrāt with the dust of confusion on his forehead and the drops of shame on his cheek, and had the happiness to be permitted to kiss the lofty threshold. The brief account of this occurrence is as fol-
150 lows. His Majesty's dear sister Ma'ṣūma Sulṭān Bēgam,[4] the Mīrzā's wife, had in Agra petitioned about the Mīrza's guilt and had received an order of reconciliation. His Majesty from his innate goodness, drew the line of forgiveness over his offences and directed that he should be sent for. When the Mīrzā arrived near the grand army, a number of high officers were sent to meet him, and when he was a day's journey off, M. 'Askarī and M. Hindāl went out in accordance with the lofty commands and embraced him. M. 'Askarī saluting him by raising his hand up to his breast, while M. Hindāl saluted[5] by putting his hand on his head. They brought the Mīrzā with respect to the camp and that day the Mīrzā, in accordance with the king's command, was conveyed to his own tent. Next day he was brought to the lofty pavilion and having done homage, was treated with royal favours. Twice was he exalted in one assemblage by a special *khil'at*, a belt, a sword and a horse. Bravo! At the

---

1 Blochmann 332, who writes Jābūq Probably *cābuk* 'celer,' is the correct reading. Perhaps he is the Ibrāhīm Bēgcik of the *Tar. Rash.* Elias and Ross, 470, and described there as father of Jahāngīr Qulī.

2 Blochmann 455, Bābar 95 and 363.

3 Qushqa is a Turkish word meaning the star on a horse's forehead. Bāba Qushqa was a servant of Bābar, 364.

4 Half-sister of Humāyūn, being the daughter of Ma'ṣūma, the daughter of Sulṭan Aḥmad and who married her cousin Bābar. Bābar 208.

5 See Blochmann 158 for A.F.'s account of the *taslīm*. 'Askarī being the elder brother did not salute so humbly as Hindāl.

gate of God's elect, sins are requited (*lit.* bought) by benefits, and wickednesses are reckoned as virtues. There is such plenty in the store-house of divine grace that His peculiar mercies are co-ordinate with offenders; in proportion as they increase their crimes and sins do they obtain increase of grace and forgiveness. This attribute is the more appropriate to princes in that they are the shadows of God, so that by passing over offences no harm is done to the breadth of their mercy and the amplitude of their power; and the wretch who is ashamed of his evil deeds, obtains an order of release from the pit of torture. In short his Majesty Jahānbānī Jannat Āshyānī, in spite of rebellion so great that (even) to pardon it were improper, became an expounder of the Divine ethics and returned good for evil. God be praised! His Majesty, the Shāhinshāh of the Age, (Akbar) hath these noble qualities and weighty ethics; they are part of his nature and of the essence of his holy soul, and in the meting out of punishment he practises a consideration and hesitation such as no other king has been adorned with from the cycle of Adam until now. In this book a few instances will be given out of many. May God Almighty increase daily this family and may He, in reward of this generous nature bestow plenteous blessings on his Majesty's life and dominion!

In short when Shēr Khān was apprized of the uprearing of the victorious standards, he left his son Quṭb Khān and many others in Cunār, and after strengthening the fort, departed to Bengal. He conquered that country in war and obtained much booty. When the world-conquering army of his Majesty Jahānbānī Jannat-āshi- 151
yānī encamped near Cunār, he applied himself to the taking of the fortress. Rūmī Khān who was the paragon of the age for overcoming grand forts and sky-high castles, and who had left Sulṭān Bahādur after the victory of Mandasōr, and been enrolled as one of his Majesty's servants, and exalted by the office of *Mīr Ātash* (Director of Ordnance) constructed a covered way (*sābāṭ*) upon boats and arranged such a roof (*saṭha*) with strong partitions (?) on the top of a platform of planks that the ingenious and skilful bit the finger of astonishment in admiration of the workmanship.[1] And

[1] See Niẓāmu-d-dīn's account, Elliot V, 200. It is more detailed and more intelligible than A.F.'s. Apparently Rūmī Khān built a wooden tower so lofty that when placed on boats and conveyed across the river

he carried such mines under the walls that when they were fired, Time and the Terrene (*zamīn ū zamān*) were shaken. Quṭb Khān fled, and the remainder of the garrison asked for quarter and came out. The fort fell into the possession of the king's servants. As for those admitted to quarter, they were about 2,000 in number, though his Majesty Jahānbānī had ratified Rūmī Khān's promise and had pardoned (?) them, yet Mu'ayyid Bēg Dūldai,[1] who was one of the confidential officers, added to the order that their hands should be cut off, and represented that this was the king's command; such was the usurpation[2] of authority that he displayed! His Majesty Jahānbānī censured him for this. Rūmī Khān received royal favours, and his influence and renown were increased. In return for his services the fort was made over to him, but in a few days he became by destiny an object of envy to the world and passed away, poisoned.

When his mind was free of this affair, the expedition to Bengal presented itself before him. Naṣīb Shāh,[3] the ruler of Bengal, came

---

to the foot of the hill, it enabled the assailants to get to the wall under cover. See also Jauhar, Stewart 10, and Tiefenthaler's plate I, 450, No. XXIX which shows a wall coming down to the water's edge.

1 Dorn's History of the Afghans, p. 112, calls him the son of Sultān Maḥmūd, and the Chronicle of Shēr Shāh says the same thing but adds the epithet Dūldai. Garcin de Tassy, p. 84.- Dūldai is a division of the Barlās tribe. Blochmann 388*n*. Niẓāmu-d-dīn says that only the artillerymen had their hands cut off, and that this was done by Humāyūn's orders. It is impossible that 2,000 men could have their hands cut off without Humāyūn's becoming acquainted with the fact while the brutality was going on. Jauhar, (Stewart 10), who is perhaps the most to be trusted, as he was with Humāyūn at the time, says that Rūmī Khān caused the hands of the artillerymen to be cut off, and that Humāyūn was very angry with him on this account. The same authority says that Rūmī Khān's floating battery, &c., did little execution. Bayāzīd 21*b*. tells us that Mu'ayyid died in Kābul shortly after the first taking of it, to the universal joy of the army, who regarded him as a Satan and as the cause of the loss of India, &c.

2 I am not sure of the meaning but think that *taḥakkum* is used in the sense of fancied or slf-assumed authority. B. M. MS. has a *ki* at the end of the words which perhaps is an improvement, the meaning then being that M. Bēg so far usurped authority that Humāyūn had to rebuke him.

3 Naṣīb is apparently intended for Nuṣrat, but both names appear to be wrong. Nuṣrat died in 943

wounded to the world-protecting Court, and implored help against Shēr Khān. This was an additional reason for conquering Bengal, and another call to him to proceed there. His Majesty comforted him by his princely sympathy, and distinguished him by royal favours. As the expedition had now been determined upon, Jaunpūr and its territory was made over to Mīr Hindū Bēg who was one of the great officers, while Cunār was given to Mīrak Bēg. Preparations having been made, the army proceeded by land and water. When Patna became the camping ground, the loyal servants of the Court represented that the rainy season had arrived, and that if his Majesty delayed the Bengal expedition until this season had passed over, this would be consonant with the rules of conquest, since the passage of cavalry into Bengal at this season was very difficult, and would be productive of destruction to the soldiers. The ruler of Bengal looked to his own interests and represented that Shēr Khān had not yet confirmed himself in Bengal, and that to
march speedily against him would be a means of extirpating him 152
with ease. His Majesty out of consideration for this oppressed one, and from the plausibility of his statements, gave orders for the advance. In Bhāgalpūr he divided the army, sending M. Hindāl across the river with 5000 or 6000 men to march along its banks on that side. When the army had encamped at Monghyr, news came that Jalāl Khān, the son of Shēr Khān, who after his father's death took the name of Salīm Khān,[1] with Khawāṣṣ Khān, Barmazīd,[2] Sarmast Khān,[3] Haibat Khān Niyāzī,[4] and Bahār Khān[5] with about 15,000 men had come to Gaṛhī which is, as it were, the gate of Bengal, and that having strengthened it they were meditating strife and sedition.

---

A.H., or earlier, and the King of Bengal who fled, wounded, to Humāyūn, was Maḥmūd or Sulṭān Maḥmūd Shāh, another of the 18 sons of the famous Ḥusain Shāh. No Naṣīb appears in the list of kings of Bengal, but probably there was such a name for there is a quarter of the town of Murshidābād called Naṣībpūr.

[1] Elsewhere A. F. calls him Islām Khān.

[2] Barmazīd Goor, Dorn, 128.

[3] An Afghān tribe, Jarrett II. 403.

[4] This according to Dorn, 93, was a title given by Shēr Khān to Ḥabīb Khān Kakar.

[5] Or Pahār.

The account of this affair is as follows: When Shēr Khān heard of the approach of the imperial army he could not bring himself to fight but went off by way of Jhārkhand,[1] so that when the grand army came into Bengal, he might go to Bihār and stir up commotion in that province, and also that he might place the spoils of Bengal in safety. He left Jalāl Khān and a large body of men near Garhī and arranged that when the conquering army approached and he himself had got to Shērpūr,[2] they should make haste to join him, and should avoid fighting. His Majesty deputed from Bhāgalpūr Ibrāhīm Bēg Cābūq, Jahāngīr Qulī Bēg, Bairām Bēg, Nahāl Bēg, Rōshan Bēg, Gurg 'Alī Bēg, Bacaka Bahādur, and a large force consisting of about 5000 or 6000 men. When the imperial army arrived in the neighbourhood of Garhī, Jalāl Khān departed from his father's instructions, got together his army and attacked the camp. The men of it had not put themselves in order for fighting so as to combat properly. They were not properly drawn up, and the enemy was numerous. Nor were the former ready for battle. Bairām Khān turned several times and attacked the enemy, and dispersed them. He made gallant efforts but from want of management he was not properly supported, and things did not go satisfactorily. 'Alī Khān Mahāwanī,[3] Ḥaidar Bakhshī and several other officers attained the glory of martyrdom. When this news came to the hearing of his Majesty, he rapidly proceeded to the spot. On the way the sea-adorning boat which was his special barge, was sunk at Colgong. When the royal army came near the black-fated Afghāns, the wretches fled. Mīrza Hindāl, who had been appointed to Tirhut
153 and Purnīyā was, at his own request, permitted to depart to his new

1 Jhārkhand is sometimes identified with Chūtia Nāgpūr. It also represents the jungle *mahals* of Midnapūr. It seems to me not improbable that the name here is a mistake for Bharkūnda in Bīrbhūm. See Beames's Notes on Akbar's *Sarkārs* J., R. A. S., January, 1896, p. 97 and Jarrett II, 139. Bharkūnda was in *sarkār* Sharīfābād. Dorn p. 107, speaks of Shēr Khān's retreating to the mountains of Bercund, and Garcin de Tassy's Chronicle of Shēr Shāh (76) is to the same effect. If the Shērpūr mentioned later be Shērpūr Aṭāī, Bharkūnda is more likely to be right than Jhārkhand.

2 There are several Shērpūrs, but Shērpūr Aṭāī is probably the one meant. Blochmann 341, Jarrett II, 140, and text Āīn I, 407.

3 Possibly the name is Mahāwatī.

fief, so that he should come from thence with a proper equipment to Bengal. His Majesty Jahānbānī proceeded from there, march by march, to Bengal, and by the Divine aid conquered it in 945.[1] Shēr Khān and the other Afghāns having taken the choicest treasures of Bengal[2] went off by Jhārkhand towards Rohtās, and got possession of it by means of stratagem.

### Shēr Khān's taking of Fort Rohtās.

The short account of this is as follows: When Shēr Khān arrived in the neighbourhood of Rohtās, which is a very strong fort, he sent messengers to Rājā Cintāman,[3] a *brahman*, the owner of the fort, reminding him of past favours, and after making a foundation of friendship, he represented to him that he was in a difficulty, and begged him to treat him with humanity and to receive his family and dependants into the fort, and thus make him (Shēr Khān) pledged to be his benefactor. By a hundred flatteries and deceptions the simple-minded Rājā was persuaded by the tricks of that juggler. He, a stranger to friendship's realm, prepared six hundred litters, and placed in each two armed youths, while maidservants were placed on every side of the litters. By this stratagem[4] he introduced his soldiers and took the fort. Having placed his family and soldiers there, he extended the arm of sedition and blocked the road to Bengal.

### History of Humāyūn (resumed).

His Majesty Jahānbānī found the climate of Bengal agreeable and sat down to enjoy himself. The army finding a plentiful country gathered the materials of insouciance. At this time too M. Hindāl was led by evil companions and authors of strife to entertain wicked designs, and went off in the height of the rains and without permission, towards Agra. Though admonitory mandates were

---

[1] 30th May, 1538, to 18th May, 1539. Apparently Gaur was taken during the rains and probably in June, 1538.

[2] Bangāla. Probably here and elsewhere Gaur, and not the province, is meant.

[3] Nizāmu-d-dīn and Khāfī Khān call him Har Kishan. Dorn, 93, speaks of the Rājā of Rohtās' having a *brahman* named Churāman who had much influence with him and who was won over by Shēr Khān.

[4] According to Dorn, 110, the story of the litters is false.

sent to him they were without effect. After some days he arrived at the capital and arranged his seditious plans. In the inner-chamber of his brain, which was void of the divine halo, he concocted the desire of sovereignty. Shēr Khān, seeing the propitiousness of the time, extended his strife and sedition. He came and besieged Benares; he soon took it and put to death Mīr Faẓlī the governor. From there he went to Jaunpūr which was held by Bābā Bēg Jalāir, the father of Shāham Khān, he having been appointed after the death of Hindū Bēg. Bābā Bēg brought Jaunpūr under discipline and sedulously strengthened it. Yūsuf Bēg, son of Ibrāhīm Bēg Cābūq, was marching from Oudh to Bengal. He joined Bābā Bēg, but was always scouring the country with an advanced
154 guard and was ever in quest of an engagement. Jalāl Khān got news of this, and made a rapid march with 2,000 or 3,000 men. Yūsuf Bēg saw the dust of the army and was eager to fight. Though his comrades pointed out to him the largeness of the enemy and the smallness of his own force, it was of no avail, and he bravely drank the last draught in the neighbourhood of Jaunpūr. Next day the enemy invested Jaunpūr. Bābā Khān Jalāir gave proof of courage and skill in defending it, and sent off reports to the Mīrzās and officers. He also made repeated representations to the Court (at Gaur). Mīr Faqr ʻAlī came from Dihlī to Agra, and proffered sound advice to M. Hindāl. After much discussion he brought away the Mīrzā from Agra to the other side of the river. He also appointed Muḥammad Bakhshī to give what help the time allowed of, in despatching Mīrzā Hindāl quickly to Jaunpūr. Mīr Faqr ʻAlī then went off from there to Kālpī to get Yādgār Nāṣir Mīrzā equipped for the army, and to arrange for a meeting of the Mīrzās in the territory of Karra,[1] and for a march onwards from there. At this time Khusrau Bēg Kōkaltāsh, Ḥājī Muḥammad (son of) Bābā Qushqa, Zāhid Bēg, Mīrzā Naẓar and many others, out of crookedness and strife-mongering absconded from Bengal and came to M. Nūru-d-dīn Muḥammad who had been left in Kanauj. The Mīrzā reported their arrival to M. Hindāl, and requested that they should be personally

1 Agra in text, but Lucknow ed. and Price have Karra (4 miles W.N.W. Allāhābād) and this is clearly right. Tiefenthaler I, 235 has a plan of Karra.

received. M. Hindāl sent friendly letters to them by Muḥammad Ghāzī Tūghbāī,[1] who was one of the Mīrzā's confidants. He also wrote explanations of their arrival to Yādgār Nāṣir Mīrzā and Mīr Faqr 'Alī. The officers who were with M. Nūru-d-din Muḥammad, did not wait for an answer but came on to Kūl ('Alīgarh) which was in Zāhid Bēg's fief. Hindāl's messenger heard of this on his way and hastened to join them. These short-sighted disloyalists opened their raving mouths and plainly said, " Henceforth we do not serve the king; if you, as you have already purposed, will have the *khuṭba* read in your own name, we will enter into your service and render you faithful allegiance; otherwise we shall go to Mīrzā Kāmrān where happiness and a welcome are waiting for us (*lit.* are in our bosom)." Muḥammad Ghāzī Tūghbāī returned and secretly delivered the officers' message and said, that one of two things was inevitable. Either Hindāl must have the *khuṭba* read in his own name and send for and caress the officers, or they must be laid hold of by stratagem and be confined. M. Hindāl, whose head was always itching after folly, looked upon this opinion as a valuable find, and with promises of kind treatment sent for those irreflecting traitors and spoke soothingly to them, and confirmed them in their evil imaginings.

When the alienation of Benares and Jaunpūr was reported to his Majesty Jahānbānī and the deceitful designs of M. Hindāl became known to him, he despatched Shaikh Buhlūl who was one of the great Shaikhs of India and the recipient of royal favours, 155
from Bengal that he might proceed quickly to the capital, and by sage advice restrain the Mīrzā from evil thoughts and induce him to act with one accord in extirpating the Afghāns. The Shaikh arrived post-haste, just when the officers were propounding their wicked schemes and were near drawing M. Hindāl away from the straight path. M. Hindāl went out to welcome him and brought him with honour and respect to his own house. The Shaikh's weighty words strengthened M. Hindāl in the intention of serving with which he had gone forth. Next day Muḥammad Bakhshī was brought in order that all the preparations for the army—gold, camels, horses, accoutrements—might be made. Muḥammad Bakhshī represented that there was no money for the soldiers, but that there

[1] Or Tūqbāī. It is the name of an Afghān tribe. Jarrett II, 403.

was abundance of materials and stores, and that he would carry out everything as was desired. Four or five days had not passed since this conversation when M. Nūru-d-dīn came in haste from Qanauj. And apparently all that the officers had plotted together was strengthened by his coming. Muḥammad Ghāzī Tūghbāī was sent a second time to the officers and they reiterated what they had said before, and made this condition, that, as an indication that their proposals had been accepted, Shaikh Buhlūl, who was the king's envoy and was confounding their schemes, should be publicly put to death, so that everyone might be assured that M. Hindāl had separated himself from the king, and that they (the officers) might serve him with minds at ease. The Shaikh was engaged in arranging for the march of the army, and was looking after the ordering of the accoutrements, when the messenger[1] returned. In accord with M. Nūru-d-dīn Muḥammad the unbecoming proposal was ratified, and M. Nūru-d-dīn Muḥammad seized the Shaikh, by M. Hindāl's orders, in his house and taking him across the river, ordered him to be beheaded[2] in a sandy spot near the Royal Garden. The abandoned officers came and did homage to the Mīrzā, and in an inauspicious hour and in a time of confusion the *khuṭba* was read in M. Hindāl's name. The troops then marched[3] on. Though the chaste Dildār Āghāca Bēgam, M. Hindāl's venerable mother, and the other Bēgams counselled him, it was absolutely of no avail. The tongue of his actions uttered this verse.

"Advice of man is wind in mine ear,
But 'tis a wind that fans my fire."

---

[1] *i.e.*, Tūghbāī. He had gone to 'Alīgarh where the officers still were, being afraid to come on until Hindāl had proved his adhesion to their schemes.

[2] Badāonī describes this occurrence and gives the chronogram "Assuredly he died a martyr," *faqad māta shahīdan*=945 (1538). Shaikh Buhlūl or Pūl was one of the great saints of India and elder brother of Muḥammad Ghaus of Gwālyār. Badāonī I. 4. M. Ḥaidar speaks disparagingly of him as merely a sorcerer, (p. 398,) but apparently never saw him, and was prejudiced against him because Humāyūn's attachment to Buhlūl had made him neglect Khwāja Nūra, Ḥaidar's patron saint.

[3] Presumably towards Dihlī.

When M. Hindāl had the *khuṭba* read in his name and came before his mother, that cupola of chastity had a blue [1] cloth over her breast. The Mirzā said, "What kind of dress is that you have donned at such a time of rejoicing?" That cupola of chastity replied, out of her foresight, "Why do you regard me? I am wearing mourning for you; you are young (he was only 19) and have, from the 156
instigation of irreflecting sedition-mongers, lost the true way; you have girded your loins for your own destruction." Muḥammad Bakhshī [2] came and said, "You have killed the Shaikh; why do you delay about me?" The Mīrzā treated him kindly and took him with him. When Yādgār Nāṣir Mīrzā and Mīr Faqr 'Alī heard of this bad business they made a rapid march from Kālpī *viâ* Gwālyār, and coming to Dihlī took measures to strengthen the city and to provide for the fort. The Mīrzā had reached Ḥamīdpūr, near Fīrōzābād [3] when the news came that Yādgār Nāṣir Mīrzā and Mīr Faqr 'Alī had arrived at Dihlī. The Mīrzā and the officers consulted together and proceeded to invest Dihlī. Many of the petty *jāgīrdārs* round about came and did homage to the Mīrzā, and he made march after march and besieged Dihlī. Yādgār Nāṣir Mīrzā and Mīr Faqr 'Alī exerted themselves in holding the fort, and sent an account of affairs to M. Kāmrān and begged him to come and quell the sedition. He set out from Lāhor and when he came near Sōnpat, [4] M. Hindāl hurried off to the province of Agra without having accomplished his purpose. When M. Kāmrān approached Dihlī Mīr Faqr 'Alī came and had an interview with him, while Yādgār Nāṣir Mīrzā continued to hold the fort as before. Mīr Faqr 'Alī induced M. Kāmrān to proceed to Agra, and M. Hindāl not having the resolution to remain there went off to Alwar. M. Kāmrān, after he came to Agra, desired that cupola of chastity, Dildār Āghāca Bēgam to soothe M. Hindāl and to

---

1 *kabūd* the sign of mourning.

2 Also called Sulṭān Muḥammad, (A.N., I. 259,) and perhaps the Bakhshī called Sulṭān Muḥammad of Badakhshān. Blochmann 528. He was a servant of Bābar. (348 and 364.)

3 24 miles east of Agra. A pencil note to Chalmer's MS. suggests either Umīdpūr 8 miles W. by N. Fīrōzābād, or Muḥammadīpūr, 8 miles S. E. Fīrōzābād. Y. Nāṣir Mīrzā and Faqr 'Alī went by the West of Dihlī and Hindāl by the East, but he must have been very remiss to let them get from Kālpī to Dihlī before him.

4 I. G. 28 miles N. N. W. Dihlī. Jarrett II, 287, where it is spelt Sōnīpat.

recall him to obedience. That matron (*kadbānū*), the pavilion of chastity, brought M. Hindāl from Alwar and introduced him to M. Kāmrān with his shroud (*fūṭa*) round his neck. The Mīrzā (Kāmrān) behaved with propriety, and next day he forgave the seditious officers and held a levee for them. The Mīrzās and officers joined together and crossed the Jumna in order to put down the rebellion of S͟hēr K͟hān. But as auspiciousness did not guide those highborn ones they did not obtain the blessing of such a glorious service.

In fact when by celestial aid the country of Bengal had come into possession of the imperial servants, and its capital had become the headquarters of the army, and the great officers had obtained large territories in fief, they gathered the materials of enjoyment and pleasure and opened the gates of negligence in the front of their lives. The pillars of sovereignty paid less attention to administration, and strife-mongers, of which wretches this wide world is never free, raised the head of discord and sedition. The time was at hand when slumbering strife should lift up her downcast eyelashes. Fissures found their way into the foundation of circumspection.
157 Information such as could be depended upon did not come to headquarters, or if one thing out of many became known to any of the confidants, he had not the courage to communicate it, for the arrangement then was that no particle of unpleasantness should be bruited in the august assemblage. When by degrees the truth about the rebellion in Hindūstān was conveyed by real well-wishers, who, in disregard of their own advantage, represented the true facts, his Majesty Jahānbānī called together the pillars of the state and determined on the return of the Grand Army. Though from excessive rain the country was under water, and the rivers were tempestuous, and it was not the season for campaigning, yet on account of the emergency it was considered that a return was necessary for the preservation of the empire. The charge of Bengal was ordered to be entrusted to Zāhid Bēg,[1] but that worthless one took up the presumptuous ways of an old servant, and having given

[1] He was married to a sister of Humāyūn's favourite wife Bēg͟ha Bēgam otherwise Ḥājī Bēgam and presumed thereupon. Jauhar, 13. Some years afterwards he was governor of G͟haznīn and was put to death by Kāmrān.

way to evil desires, absconded and joined Mīrzā Hindāl. His Majesty made over Bengal to Jahāngīr Qulī Bēg and left a large force to support him. He then in the height [1] of the rains turned his bridle and set out for the capital (Agra).

When Shēr Khān heard of the returning of the royal army, and of the departure of the Mīrzās from Agra he withdrew from Jaunpūr and proceeded towards Rohtās. His plan was that if the sublime standards should come against him, he should avoid a battle and return by the Jhārkhand route, by which he had come, and aim at Bengal, (qr. Gaur the capital). And if this should not happen (that Humāyūn's army should follow him) and if the imperial army should proceed towards Agra and an opportunity offered itself, he would follow in its wake and attempt a night attack. When the sublime army of his Majesty Jahānbānī arrived at Tirhut,[2] Shēr Khān came to know the smallness of the force and the disorganization of the royal camp, and waxed audacious (*shīrak*) [3] and advanced with a large and fully equipped army.

He got under his control all the country round about the army, and no one was able to procure information about the enemy's manoeuvres. Ibn 'Alī Qarāwalbēgī (chief scout) went and brought authentic news which were communicated to his Majesty through

---

[1] This is not very intelligible. The rains of 946, (1539,) cannot be meant, for the battle of Causa did not take place till 27th June, 1539, and after Humāyūn had been encamped in the neighbourhood for 2 or 3 months. I suppose Humāyūn must have left Gaur in the end of the rains of 1538, *i.e.*, in September or October, and before the country was sufficiently dried up. But if so, he must have marched very slowly indeed not to get to Causa till March or April. The Hindūstānī chronicler of Shēr Shāh, Garcin de Tassy, says Humāyūn left Bengal when the sun was entering the sign of the Bull (*i.e.*, in April). The same phrase *'ain-i-bārān*, height of the rains, has been already used at p. 151, with reference to Hindāl's departure, though that must have taken place a considerable time before Humāyūn left Gaur.

[2] There is the variant Narhan, but neither form seems correct, both being too far east. Price has Purtuh which he conceives may be Patna, and a pencil note to Chalmer's suggests Pūrnīyā. This last seems most likely. Humāyūn does not seem to have advanced on the N. bank of the Ganges beyond over against Monghir.

[3] A pun, *shīrak* meaning a little *shēr* tiger.

M. Muḥammad Zamān. Though the grand army had crossed the Ganges, and was marching to the capital, yet when news was brought of Sh̲ēr K̲h̲ān's arrival and of his being close by, the flames of the royal wrath were kindled, and out of his perfect majesty and dominion he turned his reins towards him. Though it was represented to him that at such a time, when the army was in the highest degree without equipment—it having travelled such a distance through
158 mud—it was improper to march against the foe and to hasten to the field of battle and that what was proper was to halt somewhere and recruit the army and then to undertake the crushing of the enemy,—such views were not acceptable to his Majesty and so he crossed the Ganges and marched against the foe.

It behoves us to know that it is an ancient canon and fixed principle that, when the stewards of the kingdom of Divine destiny assign to an individual an article of price, they open beforehand the gates of failure and cast him into a tumult of anguish, so that felicity may not remove the unique pearl from its place, and that by this experience sorrow may be fulfilled and things brought to an equilibrium. Accordingly,—as the apparition of the light-increasing star of mortals, which by showing itself in dreamland from out of Qācūlī Bahādur's bosom had exalted the vigilant by the blessing of expectation, was drawing nigh,—the countenances of the thoughts of the meditative and farseeing are not scarred if before this there appeared some misfortunes. Thus did such things happen at the hands of sundry black-hearted, unwashed Afg̲h̲āns, to a force which might have conquered the universe. Thus was it that, contrary to the advice of ministers, the army marched against the Afg̲h̲āns, and came face to face with Sh̲ēr K̲h̲ān at the village of Bihīya[1] which is a dependency of Bhōjpūr.[2] There a black[3] river called the Karmnāsā (Text, Kanbās) flowed between the two armies. The royal army made a bridge over it and crossed. Though the royal army was small and many were without equipments, it was victorious in every skirmish, and the Afg̲h̲āns were slaughtered on every side. But the period of encountering and slaying was pro-

[1] Fatḥpūr Bihia. Beames J.A.S.B., 1885, 6. Jarrett II. 157.

[2] In Sh̲āhābād.

[3] An allusion to the evil reputation of the Karmnāsā, or Destroyer of merit, among the Hindūs. See Bābar, 408.

longed, and the great brethren, (Humāyūn's brothers), each of whom could have conquered a clime, placed, out of shortsightedness, a stumbling block in the way of their own fortune, and did not act harmoniously. The blessedness of learning what service was at such a crisis did not help their destiny. Though admonitory rescripts were sent to them, the impressions on these inspired tablets took no form in the minds of those iron-hearts. Shēr Khān, out of craft, sometimes sent influential persons to the sublime porte to knock at the door of peace, and sometimes cherished wicked thoughts of war. At length he deceitfully and fraudulently left a body of infantry and inefficient men, together with his artillery, in face while he himself marched two stages to the rear and then encamped. The royal army, which had all along been victorious, did not understand the craft of that trickster, so they followed and encamped. When
an event is going to happen in accordance with destiny, carelessness 159
on the part of the sagacious comes in to help. In this way great remissness ensued in keeping watch. At length Muhammad Zamān Mīrzā showed utter negligence on a night when it was his watch. That fox (Shēr Khān) who was waiting for an opportunity, made a night march and in the morning presented himself at the rear of the camp. His army was divided into three bands (*tōp*), one led by himself, one by Jalāl Khān, and one by Khawāṣṣ Khān. The royal troops had not time to buckle their saddles or to close their cuirasses. His Majesty Jahānbānī when he became apprized of the army's negligence, was confounded by this specimen of fate's workshop, and the thread of resource dropped from his hand. As he was mounting, Bābā Jalāir and Qūc Bēg[1] arrived, and he bade them go quickly and bring away the noble lady Ḥājī Bēgam.[2] Those two faithful and zealous servants drank the wholesome sherbet of martyrdom at the door of honour's enclosure. Mīr Pahlwān Badakhshī also and many others obtained the blessing of offering up their lives around the enclosure of chastity. The time was very brief; her Highness could not come out, but as the Divine protection and defence was her surety and safe-

---

1 See Errata, but according to some MSS. Tardī Bēg Qūc Bēg is one man's name.

2 Daughter of Yādgār Taghāī, uncle of Humāyūn's mother. She was, in her youth, his chief wife, and was greatly revered by Akbar.

guard, the boisterous blasts of the evil-minded could not impinge on the sanctuary of the harem of chastity, nor the mists of black-hearted men touch the hem of the curtain of the illustrious recluses. Divine[1] spirits from the glorious sanctuary of sublimity defended the veiled ones of the chamber of chastity with the wands of the door-keepers of[2] jealousy; wicked thoughts did not find their way into the hearts of those wretches, and Shēr Khān sent[3] off with all honour that cupola of chastity in perfect security and observance of seclusion.

In fine, when his Majesty came to the bridge, he found it broken. There being no other resource he plunged with his steed into the water like a river-traversing crocodile. By fate he got separated from his horse. Just then, as Providence was watching over his Majesty, a water-carrier became the Elijah[4] of his course, and by the help of his (the water-carrier's) swimming, he emerged from that whirlpool to the shore of safety. On the way his Majesty asked him his name. He answered, "Niẓām." His Majesty replied, "A very Niẓām Auliyā."[5] He showed him kindness and favour and promised that when he safely sate upon the throne, he would give him royalty for half a day. This anguish-fraught affair (*qiṣṣa-i-pur-ghuṣṣa*) occurred on 9th Ṣafar, 946, (7th June, 1539), on the bank of the Ganges at the Causa[6] ferry. M. Muḥammad Zamān, Maulānā Muḥammad Parghalī,[7]
160 Maulānā Qāsim 'Alī Ṣadr, Maulānā Jalāl of Tatta and many officers and (learned) learned men sank in the waters of annihilation. His Majesty in company with M. 'Askarī and a few others rapidly proceeded to Agra. M. Kāmrān was exalted by kissing the threshold, and after some days, M. Hindāl was brought from Alwar by the intervention of M. Kāmrān and his (Hindāl's) mother, and did homage

---

1 *Nufūs-i-nāmūs-i-ilāhī.*

2 This recals the expression *shiḥna-i-ghairat*, p. 2 of text.

3 Sher Khān eventually sent her to Humāyūn in Afghānistān, when the latter returned from Persia.

4 Khiẓr or Elijah is said to have discovered the water of life. A. F. however distinguishes between Khiẓr and Elias. Jarrett III, 375 and 377. It is mentioned in Roebach's Oriental Proverbs, Part II, Sec. I, 91, that Khwāja Khiẓr is considered in India to be the guide of those who have lost their way.

5 A famous Dihlī saint.

6 In Shāhābād. Beames, J. A. S. B. l.c.

7 See *Tār. Rash.* 398 and 469 for some severe remarks on this man.

with shame and downcast looks. His Majesty from his innate clemency forgave his offences and made many inquiries about his welfare. When from causes beyond control a destined event suddenly made its appearance, he at once sought to remedy it. He engaged himself in collecting arms and in retrieving the position. Officers and soldiers came from the provinces and had the honour of performing their obeisances. At this time the honest water-carrier[1] presented himself at the foot of the throne in reliance on the great promise. His Majesty Jahānbānī, who was the crown-giver and throne-conferrer of the land of generosity and urbanity, when he saw the friendless water-carrier afar off, immediately gave his Cyrus (*k͟husrau*)-covenant a place on the throne of fulfilment, and having vacated the seat of sovereignty in favour of the Elijah of the path, he set the water-carrier, in accordance with his promise, upon the throne for half a day, thereby equalling him to the monarch of midday. Having excepted sundry kingly powers and functions which his capacity could not have comprehended, he exalted him by conferring on him the dignity of command, and wiped away, with the swelling sea of munificence, the dust of want from the countenance of his condition and of that of his tribe. Every order which during that incumbency on the kingly throne, issued from the water-carrier, was executed forthwith. M. Kāmrān on beholding such loftiness of soul displayed the wrinkle of cavil on the forehead of criticism, and a pretext (for displeasure) was furnished to his trouble-seeking heart.

After this affair of deceit (that of Causa) S͟hēr K͟hān made an attack on Bengal. He came to the extremity of Bihār, and then halted there and sent Jalāl K͟hān with a force of troublers against Bengal. In a short time there was a battle with Jahāngīr Qulī K͟hān who bravely maintained the contest. Inasmuch however, as the design of Providence was otherwise, the Bengal officers did not act harmoniously in putting down the rebellion, but sought their own comfort and did not combine in this war. After struggles and trials Jahāngīr Qulī was unable to keep the field, and had to retreat and take refuge with the landholders (*zamīndārān*). He came forth thence on a false

[1] The Persians call the sun *Pādshāh-i-Nīmrūz*, and A. F. seems to pun upon this and also on the circumstance that Nīmrūz is a name for Sīstān and Mekrān.

treaty and engagement and was despatched, along with many others, to the plains of annihilation. S͟hēr K͟hān being at ease about Bengal
161 went towards Jaunpūr. This he subdued and made long the arm of strife. He sent his younger son, Quṭb K͟hān, with a large body of vagabonds against Kālpī and Etāwa. When news of this reached the august ears, Yādgār Nāṣir, M. Qāsim Ḥusain K͟hān Uzbak, who held these parts in fief, and Iskandar[1] Sulṭān, who had charge for M. Kāmrān of some estates in Kālpī, were sent against Quṭb K͟hān. These lions of bravery's field encountered the foxy tricksters and fought a great battle. By the Divine aid, they gained the victory and Quṭb K͟hān was slain.

His Majesty Jahānbānī stayed for a while in Agra, the capital, arranging his troops, and conciliating his brothers and relatives and amending their secret dispositions. Though he washed the dust-stained cheek of Kāmrān with the limpid waters of counsel, he could in no wise cleanse it, and however much he scoured the rust of contrariety with the burnisher of advice, the brightness of concord could by no means be developed in the mirror of his fortune. And in such a crisis, when, even if there were internal dissension, outward concord was necessary to safeguard his own fortunes, and at such a time, when together with other resources he had 20,000 tried soldiers with him, and when by the abounding and beneficent favours and prestige of his Majesty Jahānbānī, territory from Kābul to Dāwar Zamīn[2] in the north, and to Samāna[3] in the south was in his possession, he, being contentious and wanting in his duty to so eminent a king, elder brother and benefactor, alleged illness and with abundance of carelessness and absence of circumspection, held himself aloof from such important service. Almighty God returned to him in this workshop of recompenses (this world), the fruit of his deeds and in the forefront of life he beheld by his own[4] eyes the punishment of his actions. Some of these results will be briefly described with the pen of manifestation in their proper place.

---

1 Probably the son of Sa'īd K͟hān referred to in the *Tār. Rash.*, 340, 467, &c.

2 Dāwar Zamīn, or Zamīn Dāwar is in Afg͟hānistān, N.-W. Qandahār.

3 In Sihrind, Panjāb. Jarrett II. 296.

4 Alluding to Kāmrān's being blinded by Humāyūn.

*Hemistich.*

When his fortune was departed, the omen came true.

He had some chronic diseases, and instead of being aroused by those secret monitions, he out of perversity, grew stubborn[1] in the path of discontent against his benefactor, and in the displeasing of his superior. First he sent Khwāja Kalān Bēg with a large force to Lahor, and then turning away from the *qibla* of fortune, himself followed him. He became an author and architect of destruction and detriment, drawing[2] evil on friends and attracting good to foes. Though his Majesty Jahānbānī said, "Prince, if you may not give the blessing of companionship and must throw away such an opportunity, make your men join me," the Mīrzā in direct oppo-
sition to his Majesty's desire perverted even the king's men and took 162
them with him. Mīrzā Ḥaidar, son of M. Ḥusain Gūrgān,[3] who was the cousin[4] of his Majesty Gītī-sitānī Firdaus-makānī, had come with M. Kāmrān to Agra, and had enjoyed the privilege of serving his Majesty Jahānbānī, and had been treated with abundant favours. Mīrzā Kāmrān made his own ailment an excuse and laboured to induce him (Ḥaidar) to accompany him. The Mīrzā showed himself favourably inclined towards M. Kāmrān and proceeded to excuse himself (to Humāyūn), and out of want of consideration brought forward the matter of leave. His Majesty observed, "If kindred be the point for consideration, you are equally related to us both; if loyalty and truth be regarded, the tie to me is closer. If glory and manliness be sought, you should accompany me for I am marching against the foe. As to what M. Kāmrān is representing about his illness, you are not a physician nor a druggist, that you should go with him. What the Mīrzā imagines about Lāhor's being a place of safety, is idle for, if anything is clear as the result of his holding back from this expedition, it is that he will not find a corner of safety in India. Your action cannot be divested of two difficulties. Should I succeed, what face can you put on the matter or what

1 Kāmrān persuaded himself that Humāyūn had tried to poison him.

2 Cf. *Tār. Rash.*, 474; "giving strength to the enemy, and preparing defeat for his friends."

3 Or Kūrkān, *i.e.* son-in-law. See *Tār. Rash.*, 278 and Mr. Elias's note.

4 *Khālazāda*, maternal aunt's son. His mother was younger sister of Bābar's mother.

respect will you have? You will not from shame be able to lift your head from the ground, so that death will be preferable to life. If, which God forbid, the result be otherwise, it will be impossible for you to remain in Lāhor. Whoever has suggested such a thing to M. Kāmrān is either wrong in his brain, or he is treacherous and has concealed the truth and entered on the path of flattering."[1] In fine, M. Ḥaidar happily found the path of good counsel and gloriously associated himself with the army of honour. M. Kāmrān out of his abundant forces contributed 3,000 men under the command (*bāshlīqī*) of M. 'Abdu-l-lāh Mughul, and did not himself obtain the blessing of service.

[1] This account is abridged from the *Tār. Rash*. See Elias & Ross, 472 *et seq*.

# CHAPTER XXVI.

## MARCH OF HIS MAJESTY JAHĀNBĀNĪ JANNAT-ĀSHIYĀNĪ'S ARMY FROM AGRA, THE CAPITAL, TO THE EASTERN PROVINCES FOR SUPPRESSING SHĒR KHĀN'S REBELLION; THE RETURN AFTER CONTESTS, AND THE ADMONITORY EVENTS WHICH FOLLOWED.

As the wondrous artists of fate's picture gallery pursue divers methods of painting and decoration, it is matter for thanksgiving and not for complaint if their workmanship on this occasion be not in accordance with desires. Hence God the world-artificer removed concord from the illustrious brotherhood and converted combination
into separation. His Majesty went with few forces against many 163
enemies, and out of a stout heart and native courage heeded not the paucity of friends and the plurality of foes.

When the sublime army reached Bhōjpūr,[1] Shēr Khān came with a numerous force to the other side of the Ganges and encamped. His Majesty determined to cross the river with his small army, and in a short time a bridge was put together at the Bhōjpūr ferry. About 150 heroes made themselves ready for the fray and plunged into the river like sea-lions, heedless of the waves and whirlpools. Like river-traversing crocodiles they rushed into the treacherous deep and crossing over, routed the numerous enemy. After giving proof of their courage and accomplishing their object, they were returning to the camp, and when they came near the bridge the Afghāns brought forward the elephant Girdbāz,[2] which had remained with the enemy at the battle of Causa, to break down the bridge. That enormous elephant approached the head of the bridge and broke

---

1 This is the Bhōjpūr in Sarkār Qanauj. Jarrett II, 184. It is in the Farukhābād District, 8 miles south-east of Farukhābād and 31 miles north-west (upstream) of Qanauj.

2 Chalmers' MS. has Girdbād.

its supports. Just then a cannon ball from the royal camp amputated[1] the legs of the elephant Girdbāz, and the enemy which was pressing on, was put to flight. The gallant men who had signified their devotion returned in safety.[2] The plan of campaign was that the army should march along the river bank to Qanauj. They proceeded warily and slowly, march by march. On the way the enemy's boats came in sight. A gun was fired from the royal artillery, and a large boat of the foe was broken to pieces, and was shivered by the dashing of the waves of vengeance. For more than a month the armies confronted one another near Qanauj. At length Muḥammad Sulṭān Mīrzā and his sons[3] Ulugh Mīrzā and Shāh Mīrzā—who traced their genealogy up to Ṣahib Qirānī, and were daughter's[4] grandsons of Sulṭān Ḥusain Mīrzā and had been exalted by serving Gītī-sitānī Firdaus-makānī, and who, after his death, had set themselves in opposition to his Majesty Jahānbānī Jannat-āshiyānī, (as has already been alluded to)—finding neither glory nor profit in vain strife, and that strife-mongering against their benefactor was unsuccessful, returned to the threshold of his Majesty Jahānbānī and proffered the prostration of obedience. His Majesty from his perfect kindness and liberality regarded their committed offences as uncommitted, forgave them and treated them with royal favours. But as they were radically bad and ungrateful, they again out of worthlessness and inaptitude took to flight at such a crisis and withdrew their feet from the sphere of
164 constancy and patience. They also pointed the way of desertion to other wretches, so that many took the path of disloyalty and withdrew themselves. To his Majesty Jahānbānī it appeared the proper course to cross the river and to engage at any cost, so that any form which was to emerge from the screen of secrecy might show its full face. If they delayed, things might take another (*i. e.* adverse) turn and a large number might desert. With the view then of putting an obstacle in the way of desertion, a bridge was made and a crossing

---

[1] Chalmers is probably right in translating this "deprived the elephant of one of its legs."

[2] It would seem however that Humāyūn did not succeed in crossing the river with his main army, though presumably that was the reason for making this bridge.

[3] See *Errata* to text.

[4] Sulṭāna Bēgam, the eldest daughter of Sulṭān Ḥusain of Herāt. Sulṭān Muḥammad Mīrzā was her grandson, Bābar 181 and *Tār. Rash.* 474.

ordered. A trench was dug in front of the army, and the artillery carriages were put into position and redoubts (*mūrcalhā*) constructed. Opposite to this, Shēr Khān drew up a crowd of rebels and encamped after digging a trench. Every day the young men on each side came out and engaged. Meanwhile the sun entered Cancer,[1] and the rainy season began. The clouds gathered with tumult, like rutting[2] elephants, and distilled moisture. The encampment became flooded, and they were compelled to seek for high ground which should be free from water and mud, and where the tents, the artillery-park, &c. might be placed. It was arranged that the army should be drawn out on the morning of the 'Āshūr day, (10th Muḥarram) and that if the enemy should come out of his trenches and advance, they would fight, and if he remained stationary, they would encamp in the selected spot. With this view they mounted their horses on 10th Muḥarram 947 (17th May, 1540), and drew up their lines. Muḥammad Khān Rūmī and the sons[3] of Ustad 'Alī Qulī and Ustād Aḥmad Rūmī, and Ḥasan Khalfāt, who were the directors of the artillery, arranged the gun-carriages and mortars, and stretched chains according to rule. The centre was dignified by the presence of his Majesty; M. Hindāl had the fore-centre; M. 'Askarī the right wing, and Yādgār Nāṣir Mīrzā the left.

M. Ḥaidar writes[4] in his *Tārīkh-i-rashīdī* "His Majesty on that day stationed me on his left so that my right was close to his left, and from me up to the end of the left centre there were twenty-seven bannerets.[5] Shēr Khān arranged his forces in five divisions, two, which were the largest, stood in front of the trench, and then advanced. Jalāl Khān, Sarmath Khān, and all the Niyāzīs faced in front of M. Hindāl. Mubāraz Khān, Bahādur Khān, Rāī Ḥusain Jalwānī and

---

1 This is a mistake. The sun does not enter Cancer till after the middle of June, and the battle was fought on 17th May. It is true this is old style, but even then the ordinary beginning of the rains had not arrived. Perhaps it was only a May storm.

2 A. F. here alludes apparently to the moisture which exudes from elephant's foreheads when they are in heat. Blochmann, 120.

3 Apparently it should be M. K. Rūmī, son of Ustād 'Alī Qulī. Ustād 'Alī Qulī was Bābar's artilleryman.

4 The quotation is not exact. See *Tār. Rash.* 475 *et seq.* and Erskine's Hist. II, 187.

5 *Lit.* Tūgh-bearing Amīrs.

all the Kararānī faced Yādgār Nāṣir Mīrzā and Qāsim Ḥusain Khān. Khawāṣṣ Khān, Barmazīd and many others came opposite M. 'Askarī.
165 The first encounter was between M. Hindāl and Jalāl Khān. A wondrous hand to hand fight occurred and Jalāl Khān fell from his horse. The royal left wing[1] drove back the enemy to their centre. When Shēr Khān saw this, he made an onset in person with a large force, while Khawāṣṣ Khān and his companions fell upon M. 'Askarī. As soon as the Afghāns attacked, many officers did not stand their ground but gave way. His Majesty twice attacked the foe and threw them into confusion. Though it is not reckoned that the king himself should share in a fray, yet at that time of testing manhood, how could rules be adhered to? Hence two lances were broken in his Majesty's hands on that occasion and the claims of endeavour and courage were satisfied. But the brothers did not show brotherhood, and the captains did not keep the foot of fortitude in the circle of steadfastness, but from superfluity of naughtiness were negligent, and brought disaster on their lord. It would seem as though when this externally and internally great man, who saw with the eyes of truth and was capable of contemplating mysteries, went on this expedition with such a small army, full of hypocrisy, empty of sincerity, it had crossed his lofty mind that it was many degrees better to hasten to the city of annihilation on the steed of valour and to urge on the horse of his life to the goal of nothingness, than to be courteous to friendship-affecting enemies, to league oneself in hypocrisy with them, and to play the game (*nard*) of altercation (*radd ū badl*) with unfair gamesters. Better a mirage (*sarāb*) than a river (*ābī*) which must be drunk[2] in company with those wretches (*ābrūyān*)! Such to men of the world clearly appeared to be the case from his method of personal onset. Some of the loyal and single-hearted smote the hand of intercession and solicitude on the stirrup of dominion and forcibly withdrew him. This I say looking to the processes of the world of secondary causes. But in the world of reality, it was God, the world adorner, who withdrew him! Inasmuch as the ascension of the

---

1 Text, *Jarānghār* probably for *Jawānghār*. Apparently however the word should be *varānghar* for it was the right wing under Hindāl which was successful. Jauhar 21.

2 *Khurda* in text, but see *Errata*, Cf. with this about the mirage, text, p. 182, top line.

birth-star and the glorious celebration of the apparition of his Majesty, the king of kings (Akbar), were drawing nigh, the wondrous Creator manifested such strange marvels! One school of sages considers that such events are intended to quicken the attention and to arouse the noble-minded, and are not of the nature of recompense for actions. Accordingly it was held by ancient philosophers that worldly calamities were a process of polishing for the elect, and of rusting for the crowd. A number of the enlightened and pure-hearted are of opinion that such occurrences are a process of education. When the stewards of fate's workshop are advancing a chosen vessel to a lofty rank, they first make him compact of all worldly states, of joy and sorrow, health and sickness, ease and labour, expansion and contrac- 106
tion, so that he may be fitted for the lofty rank of sovereignty. And many of the swift traversers of the fields of contemplation are agreed that the reason of such trials is because it is God's will that whenever the boon of greatness is to be bestowed on an auspicious one and the time of attaining that blessing be close at hand, there should be in that period's antechamber a station of labours, and a vent of trials; and that the dust of blemish should mark the skirts of his grandeur and glory so that when he hath ascended to the perfect stage and the most distant height, this mole-stain may prove his charm[1] against the fatal[2] eye. To speak more clearly; as the times of the appearances of the Holy Light in mortal manifesters and human ascension-points—such as was the holy office of her Majesty Alanquā—were made resplendent in mysterious withdrawals and apparitions of divers individuals, and so planted themselves in the visible[3] world, and were acquiring, under God's special supervision, the acmé of development, so,—now that the period of the showing forth of the final cause of that Light, to wit, the holy incarnation of his Majesty, the king of kings, was at hand,—untoward occurrences were made the prophylactic charm of this great blessing.

---

[1] *Sipand*, wild rue. Blochmann 139*n*. and 577*n* and Cf. Jarrett III, 425 and note. Herklots in his Glossary says Ispand is the seeds of the Mehndi or Lawsonia inermis, generally thrown into the fire along with benzoin and mustard seed.

[2] *'Ainu-l-kamāl*, the perfect eye, or an eye capable of killing by its glance. Lane 2211*a* and 2423*a*.

[3] The text has *'ālam-i-mulk-i-sha-hādat* but 3 B. M. M. S. have *mulk ū shahādat*.

Such was the beauteous fashioning of Creation's workshop! And now I return from the unveiling of mysteries to the thread of my narrative.

In fine, when defeat (*s̲h̲ikastī*), which was to lay the foundation of the righting (*durustī*) of the world, made its appearance, the officers fled without fighting to the bank of the Ganges, which was about four miles (a *farsak̲h̲*) distant, and as the requital of their disloyalty and ingratitude, sank in the whirlpool of disappointment, giving the vessels of their lives to the boisterous waters of annihilation in recompense of their unrighteousness. His Majesty Jahānbānī mounted with firm foot on an elephant and proceeded across the river. He descended from the elephant at the water's edge and was looking around for an exit. As the bank was high, no way out presented itself. One of the soldiers who had been saved out of the whirlpool came there and seizing his Majesty's sacred hand drew him up. In truth he then, by help of heaven's favouring hand, drew to himself fortune and power. His Majesty asked him his name and birthplace. He made answer "My name is S̲h̲amsu-d-dīn Muḥammad, my birthplace is G̲h̲aznī, and I am a servant of M. Kāmrān." His Majesty made him hopeful of princely favours. Just then Muqaddam Bēg,[1] one of M. Kāmrān's officers, recognised his Majesty and enrolled[2] himself among those who had received the gospel of good fortune. Acting upon this, he brought forward his horse, and obtained the news of distinction from royal promises. His Majesty proceeded from there towards Agra, and was joined on the way by the Mīrzās. When they came to the environs of Bhangāpūr[3] the villagers closed the market against the king's men, and behaved in an
167 unruly manner, attacking every one who fell into their hands. When the august mind was informed of this, M. 'Askarī, Yādgār Nāṣir M. and M. Hindāl were ordered to attack the villains and to chastise them. Nearly 3,000 horse and foot of the insolent knaves had gathered together. When the royal order arrived, M. 'Askarī delayed

---

[1] Apparently all that is meant is that he entered Humāyūn's service.

[2] Probably the man mentioned in Bābar's Mem. 400 and 401 as a servant of K̲h̲wāja Kalān.

[3] See Erskine, Hist. II, 192*n*. The place meant is Bhangāōn in the Mainpūrī district, and on the Grand Trunk Road. Jarrett II, 184, where it is spelt Bhūgāōn (note by Mr. Irvine.)

to proceed and Yādgār Nāṣir Mīrzā gave him some strokes with his whip, saying that it was from his discord that things had come to such a pass. Still he did not take warning, and Yādgār Nāṣir Mīrzā and M. Hindāl obeyed and went against the crowd. A great fight ensued, and a large number of the ill-fated villagers (*gūwārān*) were killed. The Mīrzās after giving them a lesson returned, and M. 'Askarī who had come to complain, was reprehended. His Majesty Jahānbānī hastened on to Agra. The provinces were in confusion and sedition raised its head on every side. Next morning his Majesty proceeded to the dwelling of that great exemplar, Mīr Rafī',[1] who was sprung from the Ṣafavī Sayyids, and was incomparable for knowledge and wisdom, and was the choice favourite of princes. He took counsel with him, and the final conclusion of his Majesty was that he should go towards the Panjāb. If M. Kāmrān were helped by the sovereignty of reason and auspiciousness, and should bind on himself the girdle of good service and come actively forward to help, the rift of strife might still be closed. With this right intention he proceeded to Lāhor. M. 'Askarī went to Sambal and M. Hindāl to Alwar. On 18th Muḥarram (26th May, 1540) Qāsim Ḥusain Sulṭān joined the king near Dihlī through the influence of Bēg Mīrak, and a large body of men collected for the king's service. On the 20th he again set out, and on the 22nd M. Hindāl and M. Ḥaidar joined him in Rohtak.[2] On the 23rd his Majesty halted there. The garrison shut the gate of the city in his face, thereby opening the doors of disgrace for themselves. His Majesty addressed himself to the attack and in a short space of time chastised the garrison. On 17th Ṣafar the army arrived at Sihrind and on the 20th Mīr Faqr 'Alī closed life's litter while on the march. When the army approached Lāhor and were near Daulat Khān's *sarāī*, M. Kāmrān came forward to meet him and did homage. His Majesty alighted in the garden of Khwāja Dōst Munshī which is the most charming spot

[1] A. F.'s mother belonged to this family. Cf. Jarrett III. 423, where Mīr Rafī' is called Mīr Rafī'u-d-dīn Ṣafavī of Ij (Shīraz). See also Bābar's Mem. 345, 349. A. F. speaks in the *Āīn* of his being one of the Hasan and Ḥusainī Sayyids. He died in 954. Jarrett l.c. Rafī' was one of the doctors who encouraged Sher Shāh to break his word to Purān Mall and the garrison of Raisīn.

[2] In the Panjāb, 42 miles northwest of Dihlī.

168 in Lāhor, while M. Hindāl took up his quarters in the garden of Khwāja Ghāzī, who was then M. Kāmrān's *dīwān*. After that M. 'Askarī came from Sambal and settled himself in the house of Amīr Walī Bēg. At this time the fortunate Shamsu-d-dīn Muḥammad who had given his hand at the river-bank, arrived and was exalted by princely favours. On the 1st[1] Rabī'u-l-awwal, 947, all the noble brothers and Amīrs and other servants collected but in spite of so many lessons and celestial warnings, these fine fellows (*'azīzān*) were not taught and did not bind the girdle of sincerity on the waist of resolve. Several times they gathered together on his Majesty's service, and deliberated and made vows and promises of unity and concord, and took the great and godly as their witnesses. Khwāja Khāwand[2] Maḥmūd, brother of Khwāja 'Abdu-l-ḥaqq and Mīr Abu-l-baqā frequently took part in the deliberations. At length one day all the Mīrzās, nobles and grandees having been assembled, wrote out a deed (*tazkira*) of concord and unanimity, and to this auspicious minute all the officers gave their signatures.

When this record of confidence had been executed, the deliberations began. His Majesty gave lofty counsels and uttered excellent words. With his pearling tongue he said,[3] "The miserable end of those who deviate from the straight highway of concord is known to all. Especially since not long ago when Sulṭān Ḥusain Mīrzā beat the drum of death in Khurāsān, he left eighteen[4] capable and fortune-favoured sons and yet, in spite of all their array of wealth, in consequence of fraternal discord, the kingdom of Khurāsān (which for so many years had been a centre of peace), became in a short space a centre of calamities and was transferred to Shāhī Bēg. No trace remained of any of the sons except of Badī'u-z-zamān who went[5] to Turkey, and all the sons of the Mīrzā had been reviled and reprobated by

---

1 Three days after this Humāyūn had a vision in which the coming birth of Akbar was announced. A. N. 13. Cf. Gulbadan's account, f. 39*b*.

2 See *Tār. Rash.*, 395, where he is called Ḥazrat Makhdūmī Nūra. Abdu-l-ḥaqq was his younger brother.

3 An exaggeration, which occurs also in the *Tār. Rash.* (B. M. Ms. Or. 157, 348*b*) Sl. Ḥusain had fourteen sons and of these, seven (according to Khwānd Amīr) died before their father.

4 A. F. gives Humāyūn the credit of this speech, but the *Tār. Rash.*, from which he no doubt copied it, ascribes it to Ḥaidar. See p. 478.

5 He too, it seems, went there as

high and low. With what difficulty had his Majesty Gītī-sitānī-Firdaus-makānī conquered a Hindūstān—so vast a country! If through your disunion it pass from our possession into the hands of nobodies (*nākasān*) what will the wise say of you? Now is the time to sink the head into the bosom of good counsel and to exsert it from jealousy's collar, so that you may attain headship among mankind, and be a means of gaining the favour of God."

Every one of the authors of compact and of the lords of confederacy forgot the recent agreements, and each declaimed according to his own good pleasure. M. Kāmrān said, "What occurs to me is that the king and all the Mīrzās should spend some days unencumbered in the mountains while I take their families to Kābul. When I have put them into safety, I shall return and join you." M. Hindāl and 169
Yādgār Naṣir Mīrzā said, "At present we cannot fight the Afghāns The thing to do now is to go to Bhakkar and to subdue that country. By its means we shall conquer Gujrāt, and when these two kingdoms have fallen into our hands and we have brought the business to an end, the deliverance of this country (India) will be effected in an admirable manner." M. Ḥaidar said, "It is proper that all the Mīrzās should settle down after securing the slopes from the mountains of Sihrind to those of Sārang.[1] I engage that with a small force I will in two months get possession of Kashmīr. When that news comes, let every man send his belongings to Kashmīr, for there is no safer place. It will take Shēr Khān four months to arrive and he will not be able to bring into the hill country the gun-carriages and

---

a prisoner, having been taken by Sultān Salīm. He died many years before this speech was made, of plague, in 926. Possibly the reference was to his son Muḥammad. Zamān, who served Bābar and survived till the battle of Causa in 1539.

[1] See *Tār. Rash.*, 479*n.* Mr. Elias is no doubt right in considering that Sārang is not a place-name. There is an Afghān tribe in the Salt Range called the Sārangzāī, (Temple, J. A. S. B., 1880, pp. 101 and 106), and perhaps Ḥaidar M. referred to them rather than to an individual. His idea was that the Mughuls should occupy the lower ranges between the Indus and Kashmīr, *i. e.*, from Sihrind in the S. E. to Rāwalpindī on the N. W. For Sultān Sārang, see Blochmann 456; and Delmerick, J. A. S. B. 1871, p. 87. He was Sultān Ādam's brother and must have died in Shēr Shāh's time, for it was Sultān Ādam who delivered up Kāmrān to Humāyūn.

cannon which are the support[1] of his warfare. In a short time the Afghān army will be ruined."

As their words and their hearts were not in unison, the meeting ended without any conclusive speech. Whatever proposals were brought forward, and whatever sound advice his Majesty communicated in the hope that perchance the lamp of wisdom might be lighted for M. Kāmrān and that he would turn away from his dark ideas and come to the abode of candour, the Mīrzā did not alter what he had said. All his endeavour was that every one should be ruined, and he counted it a gain that he himself might go to Kābul and secure a corner for his own enjoyment. He was perpetually occupied with evil thoughts, and fortune-conferring words did not arouse him. Ostensibly he breathed unanimity and would say, "I shall come forth in some fortunate hour and shall gird on the belt of courage and fight the foe with singleness of heart." But secretly he was strengthening the foundations of opposition, and this to such an extent that out of wickedness and blindness, he privately sent Qāẓī 'Abdu-l-lāh his *ṣadr* to Shēr Khān, that he might establish friendly relations with him, and made a contract of affection with him. He sought the fulfilment of his desires from the help of enemies, and he wrote a letter to the effect that if the Panjāb were secured to him as formerly, he would soon bring affairs to a successful issue!

After these occurrences Shēr Khān came to Dihlī, but did not advance further. He saw that what had happened was due to his good fortune, and was apprehensive lest if he went on further, his affairs would retrograde. He was extremely frightened about the combination which he heard was making progress in Lāhor. Meanwhile the seditious *ṣadr* (*ṣadr-i-pur-ghadar*) who added vile malice to natural baseness, arrived. Shēr Khān whose centre was pivoted in
170 craft, warmly embraced him, and was a thousand times emboldened[2] by the good news of disunion. He gave him an answer in accordance with the Mīrzā's requests. That wretch (the *ṣadr*) instigated him to make a hostile advance, and held out prospects of desertion. Shēr Khān sent a crafty fellow along with him to ascertain the real state of affairs and then return. M. Kāmrān received Shēr Khān's am-

[1] Babar's Mem, 416, mentions that the Bengalis, *i.e.*, the Afghāns, are famous for their skill in artillery.

[2] *Lit.* one heart became a thousand.

bassador in the garden at Lāhor, and held a feast on that day. He also by entreaties induced his Majesty Jahānbānī to come there. That crude, short-sighted Mīrzā again sent the same wretch (his *ṣadr*) to Shēr Khān. On this occasion the betrayer of his salt came to the bank of the Sulṭānpūr river, and brought forward disloyal proposals and encouraged Shēr Khān to cross the river. Thereupon Muẓaffar Turkmān, who was stationed on outpost duty near the Sulṭānpūr river, came and reported to his Majesty that the enemy had crossed the river (the Bīās) and killed his brother's son Junaid Bēg, who from his qualities of mind and body was a *persona grata* at Court.

In the end of Jumāda-l-ākhir his Majesty Jahānbānī and the Mīrzās crossed the Lāhor river (the Rāvī), which was fordable, and marched stage by stage to the Cināb. As his Majesty Jahānbānī was resolved to attempt Kashmīr, he sent a body of troops in advance with M. Ḥaidar to that province. For, when M. Kāmrān made a rapid march to Qandahār to contend with Sām Mīrzā, he left M. Ḥaidar in charge of Lāhor. Khwāja Ḥājī, 'Abdu-l-mākrī,[1] Zangī Cak, and many of the nobles were opposed to the ruler of Kashmīr and came to Lāhor in order that by their intimacy with M. Ḥaidar they might obtain an army from M. Kāmrān and so get possession of Kashmīr. Though M. Ḥaidar exerted himself, their wish was not fulfilled. When M. Hindāl raised a disturbance by having the *khuṭba* read in his own name, and M. Kāmrān marched from Lāhor to Agra, M. Ḥaidar by great exertions contrived to raise an army and to despatch it from the capital[2] under the charge of Bābā Jūjak[3] who was one of Kāmrān's superior officers. His design was that this force should proceed to Kashmīr under the guidance of the Kashmīrī nobles aforesaid, and take possession thereof. Bābā Jūjak was negligent in setting out and meanwhile the disaster of Causa ferry, which was a blow to eternal dominion, came to be known. He gave

---

[1] Text, Bākrī, but the variant Mākrī is right. Zangī is Rumkī in text.

[2] Agra. See *Tār. Rash.* 482.

[3] *Tār. Rash.*, Cūcak Ḥaidar does not say he was an officer of Kāmrān and apparently he was a Kashmīrī. It appears from Niẓāmu-d-dīn and from Jarrett II, 390, that there was an expedition before this from the Panjāb and that Kāmrān sent one, Muḥammad Bēg into Kashmīr but that after plundering he had to return. Apparently this was not long after Humāyūn's accession.

up the expedition, and the Kashmīrī nobles tarried in Naushahr,[1] Rajaurī and the hollows of the hills in the expectation of some event.
171 But they were continually writing letters to M. Ḥaidar full of the advantages of conquering Kashmīr, and the Mīrzā used to bring these to his Majesty Jahānbānī's notice. His holy heart grew daily more and more eager to visit the charming country of Kashmīr, and meanwhile he gave permission to the Mīrzā to proceed in the first place to Naushahr with a body of troops. If the Kashmīrī nobles, who were always urging the expedition, should come forward, Sikandar Tūpcī, who was a fief-holder in that neighbourhood, was to join him with his troops. When he got to the passes, Amīr Khwāja Kalān, who was one of the high officers of his Majesty Gītī-sitānī Firdaus-makānī, and of whom some account has already been given, was to come and help. As soon as the news of Khwāja Kalān Bēg's arrival should reach his Majesty Jahānbānī he would proceed in person towards that province. His Majesty was on the bank (the right or west bank) of the Cīnāb when M. Kāmrān and 'Askarī Mīrzā went off to Kabul with Khwāja 'Abdu-l-ḥaqq and Khwāja Khāwand Maḥmūd. Muḥammad Sulṭān Mīrzā, Ulugh Bēg Mīrzā and Shāh Mīrzā on hearing, in the territory of Multān, about the separation, joined M. Kāmrān on the bank of the Indus. In the beginning of Rajab, 947, M. Hindāl, Yādgār Nāṣir Mīrzā and Qāsim Ḥusain Sulṭān succeeded by importunity in taking his Majesty Jahānbānī off to Sind, though his intention had been to march to Kashmīr. Khwāja Kalān Bēg, who had promised to accompany his Majesty Jahānbānī Jannat-āshiyānī, went off from Siyālkūt and joined M. Kāmrān. Sikandar Tūpcī withdrew to the Sārang hills. In the same Rajab, after his Majesty Jahānbānī had gone towards Sind at the Mīrzā's instigation they, after going some stages, left him out of thoughtlessness and the suggestions of Bēg Mīrak, who had abandoned his service and joined them. Meanwhile Qāẓī 'Abdu-l-lāh arrived with some Afghāns. M. Hindāl's scouts seized them and brought them before him. The ill-fated Afghāns were put to death, but the wretch 'Abdu-l-lāh having still some breaths of his life remaining, escaped punishment at the intercession of Mīr Bābā[2]

---

1 In the Peshawar district.

2 I believe this to be the father of Ḥamīda, Akbar's mother. See Gulbadan who calls Ḥamīda's father Mīr Bābā Dōst. As he was a teacher in Hindāl's service he might naturally intercede for a learned man.

Dost. For twenty days the Mīrzās wandered in the desert of astonishment. They had no idea what to do or where to go. They were severed from fortune and auspiciousness, and having left dominion's fellowship, they had lost their object. As they had not followed the path of purpose, they were astonished and confounded. His Majesty Jahānbānī had gone by way of the desert towards Bhakkar, and was wending his way according to guess and conjecture. They found no water, and there was no grain, but went on under the guidance of endurance and with the rations (*zād*) of reliance upon God. At length one day they heard the sound of a kettle-drum. On inquiry, it was found that M. Hindāl and Yādgār Nāṣir Mīrzā were three *kōs* 172
away and were pacing the valley of search. His Majesty Jahānbānī sent Mīr Abū'l-baqā, who had left the society of M. Kāmrān, and become a companion of the sublime army, to the Mīrzās to give them information about the camping ground, and to speak wise words and advise them to come and kiss the sublime threshold. The Mīr in accordance with these instructions counselled the Mīrzās and acted as their guide to the blessing of service. They proceeded in harmony towards Bhakkar. Khawāṣṣ Khān and a large army of Afghāns was coming up in the rear, but though the imperial army was very small, the former had not the courage to give battle. In the end of Sha'bān (last days of 1540) when the camp reached Ūc[1] the Amīr Sayyid Muḥammad Bāqir Ḥusainī, who was the frontispiece of Sayyids and of the 'Ulamā of the age, expired and was buried there. His Majesty grieved much for his death, but as this evil earth is a scene of departure and dismissal (*guzashtanī u guzāshtanī*), he displayed that resignation to the Divine command which is the ornament of those whose regard is fixed on the station of submission (*maqām-i-taslīm*). When they had encamped near the residence of Bakhshūī Langā one of the landholders and grandees of that part, an order of grace and a mandate of favour was sent together with a glorious *khil'at* by Bēg Muḥammad *Bakāwal*, and Kacak Bēg, and hopes were held out that he should receive the title of Khān Jahān, a flag and a kettle-drum, and he was invited to do loyal service and to send corn to the camp. He came forth to meet the envoys, saluted them, and behaved with

[1] That is, arrived opposite Ūc for they were travelling down the west side of the Cināb and between it and the Indus.

respect. Though he had not the good fortune to come and kiss the threshold, yet with regard to what was ordered, he showed obedience and alacrity, and also sent a proper present. Likewise he arranged for traders to bring articles for sale at the royal camp, and he provided many boats for crossing the river on the way to Bhakkar. Yādgār Nāṣir Mīrzā went on with the advance guard, and on 28th Ramaẓān (26th January, 1541), the army reached the neighbourhood of Bhakkar. Two days before this Qāẓī G͟hiyāṣu-d-dīn of Jām, who was connected with the illustrious family,[1] and was adorned with gifts and graces, was raised to the office of *ṣadr*.

When by God's help they had passed through so many perils on the way and had reached the territory of Bhakkar, they pitched their tents at Lūhrī (Rūhrī) which is on the river bank[2] and opposite Bhakkar. His Majesty took up his quarters in a garden on the
173 environs which was unequalled for pleasantness and delight. Charming houses had been erected there and were made illustrious by his presence. The other gardens and houses were divided among his followers. M. Hindāl went four or five *kōs* and encamped, and some days afterwards made his station on the other side of the river. Yādgār Nāṣir Mīrzā also settled afterwards on that side. Sulṭān Maḥmūd of Bhakkar, who was a servant of Mīrzā S͟hāh Ḥusain Bēg Arg͟hūn, laid waste the Bhakkar territory and strengthened the fort. He also took away the boats from this (the east) side of the river, and anchored them under the fort. This S͟hāh Ḥusain Bēg was the son of the Mīrzā S͟hāh Bēg Arg͟hūn who, when his Majesty Gītī-sitānī Firdaus-makānī took Qandahār from him came to Tatta and Bhakkar and brought all that country into his subjection.

When the majestic army established the light (*far*) of its rendezvous at Lūhrī, a lofty mandate was sent to Sulṭān Maḥmūd calling upon him to pay his respects and to deliver up the fort to the royal servants. He represented in reply that he was the servant of Mīrzā S͟hāh Ḥusain, and that so long as the latter did not come, it would not be consistent with loyalty for him to present himself, nor could

[1] Humāyūn's mother was connected with Aḥmad Jām, and so was his wife, the mother of Akbar. G͟hiyāṣu-d-dīn wrote a *Mauladnāma*, or account of Akbar's birth. Blochmann 382, and Maāṣir III. 231 in account of Mīr 'Alī Akbar. G͟hiyāṣu-d-dīn afterwards deserted Humāyūn.

[2] On the east bank.

he make over the fort without Shāh Ḥusain's permission. Such and such like were the expressions of inability that he used. His Majesty accepted his excuses, and sent Amīr Ṭāhir *ṣadr* and Mīr Samandar, two of his confidential servants, to M. Shāh Ḥusain at Tatta, and dignified him by promises of favour. M. Shāh Ḥusain received the envoys with respect, and sent Shaikh Mīrak, the flower of the descendants of Shaikh Purān whom all the Arghūns reverence and rely upon from old times, as a messenger, and with a suitable present, to accompany the royal ambassadors to the Court. He represented that the district of Bhakkar yielded little, while that of Ḥājkān[1] was rich and populous and possessed much corn; that it was fitting that his Majesty should turn his reins towards it and take it into his possession, and that in that way the army would be comfortable, and also he (Shāh Ḥusain) would be at hand with his service. It was a fortunate and auspicious circumstance for him that his Majesty should now come to those parts, and that in course of time his fears and apprehensions would disappear and he would do himself the honour of paying his respects. He also represented that after he had had the gratification of paying his respects, his Majesty would, with a little exertion, be able to bring Gujrāt into his possession, when the other torritories of Hindūstān would fall into his hands. That sordid 174
one converted duties (*ḥuqūq*) into disobediences (*'uqūq*) and coming forth by the door of deceit and dissimulation, made a display of false though fair-seeming expressions. His Majesty appointed M. Hindāl to Pātar[2] and its territory, and himself spent five or six months in the

[1] Jarrett II. 340.

[2] In Sarkār Sīwastān (Schwān) and lower down the Indus then Bhakkar. Jarrett II. 340, where it is spelt Bātar, but with the variant Pātar. Niẓāmu-d-dīn says it is 50 *kos* from Lūhrī. Jauhar, 30, says it is 20 miles west of the Indus. It is perhaps the Pīr Patta of Burnes's journey to Kabul, p. 10. The best account of it is in Major-General Haig's Indus Delta (1894), p. 91, note. He says "The ruins of the town of Pāṭ, where in August, 1541, Humāyūn married Ḥamīda, and where some time later (since 1545) his brother Kāmrān married the daughter of Shāh Huseyn lies a little to the east of the present village of that name in the Kakar Pargana, and bears the name of Pāṭ-kuhna (old Pāṭ). On the west side of the old site, and separating it from the new village, is an old channel, now containing standing water. In this channel, says a local chronicle relating to that part of the country, the river ran at the time of

pleasant spot of Lūhrī in the hope that the ruler of Tatta would enter on the right path. During this interval he honoured M. Hindāl by visiting him in his camp at Pātar.

As the period of the appearance of the light of fortune and the rise of the star of glory and grandour,—which should give grace to spiritual and physical beauty and be the perfect beautifier of this world and the next,—were approaching, so did the apparatus for the attainment of this grand blessing and the notes of the existence of this supreme gift become more and more prepared. The waiting eyes of the heavenly saints of many thousands of years were brightened by the bounteous advent of that nursling of light, and the dim evening of earthly hopes assumed the beauty of the morning from the glory of the coming light of that great pearl of the Caliphate's diadem. For it was on this expedition and in a most excellent season and point of time, that in the year 948[1] he brought Her Highness Maryam-makānī, the sacred and noble lady, the glory of whose chastity and purity and the light of whose sovereignty and sainthood, show forth from her lustrous brow, into the bond of matrimony, with lordly ceremonies and royal rites. A festival of fortune was arranged, and coins from the treasury of gifts were showered on the head of the world, and hearts were rejoiced by blissful favours. Khwāja Hijrī[2] of Jām rendered good service in this auspicious affair. Thereafter the yoke-fellows of blessing and fortune proceeded towards the camp. For a time the territory of Bhakkar was their place of residence. Gradually, owing to the disloyalty of the landholders, orn became dear

Humāyūn's visit, so that coming from Babarlo (a little to the south of Rōhrī) by Bhētānī in Kandhīārā and Darbelo, he had no water to cross. The river now runs (or did a few years ago) 5 or 6 miles east, and also 3 miles south of Pāṭ. The place gave its name to an extensive and very fertile tract of country in former times."

[1] A. F. does not give the month and day. Gulbadan says, p. 43b, that the marriage took place at midday on a Monday in the beginning of Jumāda'l-awwal, 948, and that Humāyūn himself took the astrolabe and calculated the auspicious moment.

[2] See Badāōnī III. 386. Hajrī was a religious poet, and apparently the meaning is that he celebrated the marriage in verse. He was a descendant of Aḥmad Jām. He called himself Ḥasan Hijrī, the last being an assumed name and signifying apparently that he was one who lived apart.

and the country was made desolate. Imbecile apprehensions and improper schemes passed into the minds of the Mīrzās who were his Majesty's companions,—such thoughts as might be entertained and impressed on the minds of the insincere—till at length M. Hindāl, at the instigation of Yādgār Nāṣir Mīrzā who was always secretly in opposition, and by the stirring up of Qarāca Khān who held the government of Qandahār on M. Kāmrān's behalf, set off and went to Qandahār. He also sent a man to Yādgār Nāṣir Mīrzā to tell him of his own departure, and to call upon him to do likewise.

When his Majesty heard of this he went on Tuesday, 18th Jumāda'l-awwal, 948 (September,[1] 1541), to the quarters of Mīr Abū'l-baqā and held a conference with him. He then sent him, under the most 175
respectful circumstances, as an envoy to Yādgār Nāṣir Mīrzā, that he might bring him from the danger-spot of error to the straight path of rectitude. The Mīr went and by judicious counsels brought the Mīrzā back from the path of opposition to the highway of concord, and by his faithful and truthful utterances withheld him from improper schemes. He settled that the Mīrzā should cross the river and acknowledge service, and should henceforth remain steadily in the fore-court of submission and devotion. The conditions were that when Hindūstān should be conquered, the Mīrzā should get one-third, and that when they arrived at Kābul, he should have Ghaznī, Carkh and Lōhghar,[2] which his Majesty Gītī-sitānī, Firdaus-makānī had given to the Mīrzā's mother.[3] On Wednesday the Mīr proceeded to return after fulfilling his mission. The men of the fort of Bhakkar got news of his departure and sent a force against his boat, and discharged a shower of arrows on the Mīr. He received several dangerous wounds, and died next day. His Majesty Jahānbānī was exceedingly grieved at this, and said with his truth-speaking tongue, that the oppositions and contumacies of brothers, the ingratitude of those whom his salt had nourished, and the helplessness of comrades and friends whereby the kingdom of India had been lost and many troubles had appeared, were all but one side to (i.e.,

[1] 18th Jumāda'l-awwal would apparently be 11th September, 1541, but then the 18th was a Saturday, not a Tuesday. Perhaps A. F. wrote 13th.

[2] Bābar's Mems. 148, Jarrett II. 406.

[3] Bābar's sister-in-law, widow of his youngest brother Nāṣir Mīrzā.

were all equalled or balanced by) the loss of the Mīr; nay, those calamities did not equal this one. And in truth the Mīr's eminence was such as he in his appreciation declared it to be.[1] But inasmuch as passing wisdom and right-thinking were rooted in his Majesty Jahānbānī's sacred person and were supreme there, an event like this, which might have been a place of stumbling to the saints of faith and might, made him draw nigh to perfect wisdom and swayed him to submission and resignation. Even in such a wisdom-robbing catastrophe, which might have displaced many a man's foot of patience, this wise and God-fearing one took counsel with God-given reason and submitted to the Divine will. Or if by reason of the onsets of circumstance, and the constraining power of his temperament, he could not attain to this blissful retreat, he put aside sighing and crying, as is the manner of those whose hearts are tied and bound to outer things, and was contented with the narrow pass (*tangnāī*) of long-suffering patience. Praise be to God that though his Majesty was at first, owing to his humanity, somewhat overcome by cares and afflictions, yet under the guidance of right reason he became cheerful under worldly troubles and recognised good in the Divine decrees, according to the fashion of the pious and steady of eye who bind nosegays and gather fruit in the rose-garden of submission and resignation, and who come to contemplate with truth-
176 discerning eyes the flowers of such gardens. Five or six days after this presaging disaster, Yādgār Nāṣir Mīrzā crossed the river and had the good fortune to do homage to his Majesty Jahānbānī, who gave him a gracious reception. Meantime Shaikh Mīrak, the ambassador from Tatta, received his *congé* and a rescript was sent to the ruler of Tatta, to the effect that his representations were accepted on condition that he faithfully came and did homage. The ruler of Tatta for a time gave out that he was coming. As his words were unillumined by sincerity's lamp, they did not attain the glory of performance. At length his Majesty Jahānbānī granted Bhakkar and its territory to Yādgār Nāṣir Mīrzā and in the beginning of Jumāda'l-ākhir, 948,

[1] It was the Mīr who made the remark which led to Bābar's devoting himself for Humāyūn's recovery from sickness, so Humāyūn may have thought he was indebted to him for his life. The Mīr is mentioned in the *Tār. Rash.* 478. It was he also who arranged about the marriage of Humāyūn and Ḥamīda See Gulbadan's Mems. p. 43*b*.

(latter half (of September, 1541), marched against Tatta. Having given to the Mīrzā that bad country which by the benediction of kingly justice had turned its face towards civilization and became rich in corn and vegetables, he moved forward. Near the castle of Sehwān, Fazīl Bēg the brother of Mun'im Khān, Tarash Bēg, elder brother of Shāham Khān, and others, to the number of about twenty were proceeding by boat when a party came out from the castle and attacked them. They disembarked and assaulted the foe who fled into the castle. Some of these tigers of valour's forest went up to the fort, but as they were not supported, they withdrew and joined the camp. On 17th Rajab his Majesty Jahānbānī reached Sehwān and invested the castle. Previous to this, the garrison had laid waste the buildings and gardens in the environs. During the siege the ruler of Tatta advanced, and blocking the way, prevented corn from reaching the camp. Owing to the protracted siege and the scanty supplies of corn, the base and dishonest began to desert and even the feet of great men, whose notions of rectitude had departed, came to slide from their places. For instance, Mīr Ṭāhir *ṣadr*, Khwāja Ghiyāṣu-d-dīn of Jām, and Maulānā 'Abdu-l-baqī went off to the ruler of Tatta's camp, while Mīr Barka, Mīrzā Ḥasan, Ẓafar 'Alī, son of Faqr 'Alī Bēg, and Khwāja Muḥibb 'Alī *Bakhshī* hastened off to Yādgār Nāṣir Mīrzā. At this time it came to his Majesty's ears that Mun'im Khān, Fazīl Bēg and many others had joined together and were intending to withdraw. His Majesty as a precautionary measure
imprisoned Mun'im Khān, their ringleader. I shall now stop this 177
part of the narrative, and give some account of Yādgār Nāṣir Mīrzā.

### *Account of Yādgār Nāṣir Mīrzā.*

He made Lūhrī his residence when his Majesty left him at Bhakkar. Twice did the garrison attack him by surprise, and, willing or unwilling, the Mīrzā showed courage in these engagements. Muḥammad 'Alī *Qābūcī* (*i.e.*, door-keeper) and Shēr-dil, both of them related to Mun'im Khān, bravely drained the wholesome cup of martyrdom. On a third occasion, they (the enemy) had the daring to leave their boats and draw up their forces on the sands. On this occasion the Mīrzā's men showed such superiority that nearly 300 or 400 of the enemy were killed, and the hot sand was saturated with the evil blood of those victims. Such fear fell upon the enemy that they did not again venture to come out. Mīrzā Shāh Ḥusain increased his craft and led the Mīrzā out of the straight path. He sent his seal-bearer, Bābar Qulī, to him, representing that he was old and had no sympathiser,[1] that he would give him his daughter in marriage and make over his treasures to him, that he did not wish to spend uselessly the few remaining days of his borrowed life, and that they two together might conquer Gujrāt. In fine he deceived that simpleton by lying promises,[2] and the latter being void of understanding and crooked in thought, stained his forehead with disloyalty. If he had had a particle of magnanimity or a glimmering of discernment, he would never even for valid promises have planted his foot in the circle of disloyalty, nor have hearkened to the interested representations of the perfidious, but would have practised honesty and kept his head erect!

When his Majesty Jahānbānī saw the straits to which the army was reduced, he sent a messenger to Yādgār Nāṣir Mīrzā requesting him to fall quickly upon the ruler of Tatta, who was blocking up the way, so that the army might emerge from the strait of difficulty into ample space. Though the Mīrzā had in his heart became alienated, yet he preserved appearances a little by sending out an advance-camp. But with the same crudity of thought, he delayed and loitered in marching out. Thereupon his Majesty Jahānbānī sent Shaikh 'Abdu-l-ghafūr, who was sprung from the Shaikhs of Turkistān, and whom his Majesty had made one of his intimates,[3] to contrive that

---

[1] Shāh Ḥusain never had more than two wives, and from the first he soon passed. He never had a son.

[2] "The lying promises of 'Urqūb." See Lane, 2032*n*.

[3] *Yakī az muqarrabān-i-khud sākhta būdand.* There are three variants, from *muqarrabān*: *Mulāzimān*, *Mīr Mālān* and *Mīr Pālān*. Apparently Mīr Mālān is right for Erskine has it in his MS. trs. B.M. Add. 26,607, and Niẓāmu-d-dīn describes 'Abdu-l-ghafūr as Humāyūn's *Mīr-i-māl*, *i. e.*, (according to Blochmann VI), keeper of the privy purse. See also D'Herbelot *s. v.* *Mirimal.* 'Abdu-l-ghafūr is perhaps the man mentioned in Blochmann 538, and whom Niẓāmu-d-dīn also names in the list of learned men and of whom he says that he for a long time taught in *pargana* 'Aẓīmpūr. See also Badāonī III. 42. Evidently his language was unbecoming because he frightened Yādgār by giving him a bad account of Humāyūn's position. Niẓāmu-d-dīn says that 'Abdu-l-ghafūr gave such a description of the Emperor's difficulties that Yādgār and his men thought it best to await the takin of Bhukkar.

the Mīrzā should advance quickly. But that worthless fellow walked crookedly and as the saying is,—

*Verse.*[1]

This very road on which you are going leads (also) to Turkistān.

He perverted his mission and by his improper language so affected 178
the short-sighted Mīrzā that he even neglected appearances and recalled his advance-camp. When his Majesty Jahānbānī perceived that the times were so unpropitious, and that the army's difficulties were beyond conception, he saw that it was useless to remain longer near the fort (Sehwān), and proceeded on 17th Ẕī'l-qa'da (23rd February, 1542), towards Bhakkar and Lūhrī. At this juncture one of Yādgār Nāṣir Mīrzā's censurable acts was, that at the instigation of the ruler of Tatta, he seized and sent to him Gandam[2] and Hāla, who were loyal zamīndārs, and had shown their loyalty by collecting boats, &c. That[3] unrighteous one put them to death in punishment for the meritorious act of this service. His Majesty passed over this vile act and a hundred like it and was always for conciliation, thinking that perchance he (the Mīrzā) would write words of regret on the page of his actions and come into the house of amendment. When the sublime standards reached the borders of Lūhrī, Yādgār Nāṣir Mīrzā came out with a body of men to attack the camp. His Majesty on hearing

---

[1] *Gulistān* Book II, Story 6. The whole verse is—

" O Arab, I fear you'll never reach the *Ka'ba*,
The road you're on leads (also ?) to Turkistān."

The meaning is not very clear, but I think it is, that all depends on how the face is set. The road leads to the *Ka'ba*, but also to Turkistān, *i.e.*, in the opposite direction. I do not know if A. F. means to charge 'Abdu-l-ghafūr with treachery, or only with awkwardness. Probably the latter is meant, the envoy having by his bad driving, made the Mīrza go back instead of forward. Perhaps there is a point in the envoy's belonging to Turkistān.

[2] This story is told at greater length by Niẓāmu-d-dīn. Elliot V. 210. Hāla is the name of a division in Sind (Ḥughes' Gazetteer, 185) and perhaps Gandam is a place name also. The Zamīndārs' offence was that they enabled Humāyūn to cross the river from Bhakkar by raising some sunken boats. *Gandam* means wheat and Price so renders it, but here it seems to be a person's name.

[3] The clause begins with *tā* and perhaps what is meant is that they were sent in order to be put to death and not that this actually occurred.

this immediately got on horseback. Hāshim Bēg, who was one of the Mīrzā's right-thinking confidants, on hearing of this shameful proceeding, went quickly to him and violently seizing his rein, turned him back. He chided and reproved him, and speaking bitterly and harshly, said "Apparently gentlemanly feeling, shame, respect and reverence have left the world. In what religion and by what canons of reason and sense, is it allowable to exhibit such levity and to set oneself up against one's benefactor?"

*Verse.*

Good was that commander's saying,
Watch the measure of thy work,
Plant thy foot on the pedestal of thy ability,
So that thou make thyself a place on the sky-top.
Whoever does not quit his own affairs,
Eats the fruit of whate'er he sows in this world.

By such wise counsels he brought the Mīrzā back to Bandar[1] Laharī. Meanwhile many, such as Qāsim Ḥusain Sulṭān, followed the path of error, and separated from his Majesty, and came over to Yādgār Nāṣir Mīrzā's side.

*Return to the main narrative.*

When by the requirements of the mysteries of Divine wisdom and by the subtleties of eternal counsel, which arrange within the cover of every failure (*nāmurādī*) many materials of success (*asbāb-i-murād*), there was no form of success in Sind and when the decisive test for
179 man's unmanliness had been applied, and the disloyalty of the army, the unhelpfulness of brothers, the folly of kindred and the unfavourableness of fortune had been revealed, his Majesty desired to don the dress of the recluse and the ascetic and to strike with the foot of longing into the desert path of the travellers on God's way, and to take up the circumambulation[2] (*ḥalqa*) of the *ka'ba* of purpose and

[1] This is either a mistake, or an unusual expression. Bandar Laharī is not Lāhrī or Rūhrī on the Indus, but a seaport at the mouth of the river and in *sarkār* Tatta. Jarrett II. 339. Bhakkar is placed by A. F. in Multān. Jarrett. 327.

[2] *Ḥalqa-i-ka'ba-i-murād.* *Ḥalqa* means a ring and also a doorknocker but I suppose the meaning here is that Humāyūn thought of going to Mecca and making a devotional circuit round the *ka'ba*.

the thread of the skirt of resolution, or to retire into a hermitage, preferring the cell of ease to the beholding of his contemporaries, and wishing to be far removed from this world full of care (*āsīb*) and worldlings full of craft (*farīb*). All his right-thinking comrades who in weal and woe had waited on his stirrup and kept close to the reins of his society, besought him to abandon this idea and represented that the thing to be done now was to cast the shadow of fortune's *Humā* [1] on the country of Māldēō and there to recruit his spirits, for Māldēō had repeatedly sent representations of devotion and made protestations of loyalty; that he had an army and an arsenal; that evidently he regarded this as a favourable opportunity and that when he was at the stirrup of good fortune, he would become a spring of good service, and that by degrees, the secret hopes and wishes of his Majesty's well-wishers would be fulfilled. His Majesty from a regard to the ideas of these faithful ones ordered a march towards that country. He sent a gracious rescript, together with salutary counsels, by Ibrāhīm Bēg Ishak Āqā to Yādgār Nāṣir Mīrzā, for perchance he might become conscious of his base acts and come to tread the path of repentance, and might depart from villany and display the grace of propriety. The following verse was endorsed on the letter:

*Verse.*

O thou moon-cheeked one, others' eye and lamp,
I burn! How long wilt thou plaster others' scars?

As the slumbrous-witted Mīrzā did not possess an awakening spirit, the expostulation made no impression on him. With the same old vain hopes he took the road of disloyalty and stayed behind in Lūhrī. His Majesty Jahānbānī proceeded to Ūc on 21st Muḥarram 949, and from thence went towards Māldēō on 18th [2] Rabī'u-l-awwal; and on the 14th idem halted at the foot of Dilāwār.[3] On the 20th

---

[1] Cf. *Tar. Rash.* 399, where Khwāja Nūr bids Humāyūn not to throw his shadow in a country where the parrot was rarer than the kite. Probably by this the saint meant Gaur where Humāyūn was wasting his time. The saying is a common one, and is to be found in the *Anwār-i-suhailī*.

[2] A note to text suggests that 18 is a mistake for 13. Possibly the dates 18 and 14 have been transposed.

[3] In Bahāwalpūr, Panjāb. I. G. Text, Dīwarāwal. See Jarrett II. 331, where it is spelt Dīwar-i-awwal. See Raverty J.A.S.B. 1892, p. 184, note 74, and id. Extra No. 1897, 428, and note 463.

he encamped at Ḥasalpūr,[1] and on 17th Rabī'u-l-ākhir he encamped twelve *kōs* from Bikānīr. On the way the far-seeing members of his retinue became apprehensive of the deceit and perfidy of Māldēō and represented this to his Majesty. They continually suggested that cautious action which is the illuminated border of fortune's rescript. At length Mīr Samandar, who was at the head of men of sense, was
180 sent on rapidly to Māldēō. He returned when he had penetrated the secrets of his heart, and represented that though Māldēō was making protestations of sincerity, it was evident that he did not possess the true light. When the standards of fortune approached his territory, Sankāī (or Sangāī) of Nāgōr, who was one of Māldēō's confidants, came to the camp under pretext of trade and sought to purchase a valuable[2] diamond. As his demeanour did not savour of rectitude, his Majesty Jahānbānī bade them impress on this (would-be) buyer that such jewels were not to be obtained by purchase. They either fell by the shimmer of the flashing sword into the hands of him for whom Providence destined them, or were obtained by the favour of great monarchs. In fine, his Majesty was rendered even more cautious by the arrival of this cheat, and applauded the acuteness of Samandar. Again acting on vigilance and prudence which are the net with which princes work, especially in times of trouble and difficulty, he sent Rāī Mal Sūnī with instructions to go quickly to where Māldēō was and to report what he discovered. If unable to write, he was to communicate by means of a pre-arranged signal. That is, the signal of Māldēō's faithfulness was to be the messenger's clasping all his five fingers, and that of opposition and hypocrisy was to be the clasping of his little finger. The camp moved on two or three stages from Phalūdī[3] which is thirty *kōs*

---

[1] Text, Wāṣilpūr, but see Errata. It is however Wāṣilpūr in three B. M. MSS.

[2] This seems to be an allusion to the stone known as Bābar's Diamond but which should be rather known as Humāyūn's. Humāyūn carried it with him in his wanderings, and presented it to Shāh Ṭahmāsp. In Humāyūn's remarks there is a play on the word *jauhar* which means both a jewel and the wave-markings or lustre of a sword. Jauhar *Aftūbcī*, p. 38, mentions that two of Humāyūn's attendants told Māldēō that Humāyūn had valuable jewels, and instigated him to demand them.

[3] Jarrett II. 276. "Phalodi, a salt marsh in the north-west corner of the State, near the Jesalmīr frontier," Rājpūtānā Gazetteer II. 224, also

from Jōdhpūr, the abode of Māldēō, and stopped at the Kūl-i-jōgī (the recluse's pond). Rāī Mal Sūnī's courier arrived there, and clasped his little finger. This signal explained the state of matters, and afterwards it clearly appeared that the thoughts of this black-fated scoundrel were deceit and perfidy, and that he had an evil intention in sending a large body of men under pretence of setting off the welcome. His Majesty turned his reins towards Phalūdī. Yet many people are of opinion that Māldēō was in the first instance well-intentioned, and desirous of doing service, and that afterwards he was diverted from the right path either by learning the distressed condition of the troops and their small numbers, or by the false promises of Shēr Khān and by perceiving his ascendency. Or he was withheld from help and service by his (Shēr Khān's) threats. In any case he abandoned the path of counsel and auspiciousness and *turned the page* of loyalty. The general opinion, however, is that from beginning to end his protestations of service and his sending petitions of obedience were all based upon hypocrisy and hostility.[1]

In short, as at that time the adorners of the pinakothek of 181
fate were engaged in decoration of another sort, nothing that his Majesty undertook came to any result, and trouble and wickedness appeared in every place when there was a prospect of good and of welfare. When the gilding of those counterfeit troops[2] was subjected to the test, and the perfidy of Māldēō's unrighteous thoughts had been revealed in the ante-chamber of his Majesty's sacred heart, he ordered Tardī Bēg Khān, Mun'im Khān and a number of his other servants to go out and stop the advance of the evil-minded ones and prevent them from putting foot in the sublime camp. After thus keeping them in check, they were to return but if an opportunity offered, they should defeat them. His Majesty marched on with a few devoted followers and with his veiled ladies. Among the soldiers were Shaikh 'Alī Bēg Jalāir, Tarsūn Bēg, son of Bābā

"Phalodi is a large town to the north-west of Mārwār near the borders of Bekanir and Jesalmir," *l. c.*, p. 263.

[1] A. F. probably expatiates on the subject of Māldēō, because he had heard a good deal about it from his father who was then at Nāgōr.

[2] Probably the troops who were ostensibly sent to welcome him.

Jalāir, Fazīl Bēg and others, the total number being about twenty. There were also some domestic slaves and some faithful menials. Of learned [1] men there were present Mullā Tāju-d-dīn and Maulānā Cānd the astrologer.[2]

When the camp had left Phalūdī and arrived at Sātalmīr,[3] Māldēō's army appeared in sight, whilst the officers who had been despatched to check them, had lost their way and gone off in another direction, so that there was a passage for the enemy to the royal standards. His Majesty, who was a rock of power and a world of courage, placed the foot of steadfastness on the skirt of resolution and dignity, and turned against them with God-given reason and innate understanding. Many of the ladies were dismounted and their horses given to fighting men, and the troops having been distributed into three [4] bands, were sent against the foe. Shaikh 'Alī Bēg with three or four trusty brethren advanced and attacked the enemy, who were huddled together in a defile. To attack them and to put them to flight was one and the same thing. A large number of them were killed, and by the Divine aid the king's servants obtained the victory. His Majesty Jahānbānī after returning thanks to God proceeded towards Jesalmīr, where he encamped in the beginning of Jumāda'l-awwal. At this stage the officers who had lost their way and whose minds had been distressed by agitations [5] experienced the blessing of service, and made the dust of the royal camp the collyrium of fortune's eye. The Rāī of Jesalmīr, who was

---

1 *Ahl-i-sa'ādat*, good or auspicious men. See Humāyūn's classification of the people, Elliot V. 120 and text, *infra* I. 357. At p. 9 of text the phrase *arbāb-i-sa'ādat* has a similar meaning and should have been so translated by me. A. F. there represents himself as the last or humblest of the learned men who adorned Akbar's Court.

2 He afterwards cast Akbar's horoscope. Mullā Tāju-d-dīn is perhaps the Tāju-d-dīn of Dihlī mentioned by Badāonī, Blochmann 181. But more probably he is the Shaikh Tāju-d-dīn Lahrī whose death at Jūn is recorded soon afterwards. Text, p. 185.

3 Jarrett II. 276. "Sātalmīr was built by Satal, the eldest son of Rao Jodha (after whom Jodhpur is named) on the top of a low ridge of hills, there is nothing left but the ruins of an old Jain temple."

4 The three seems doubtful. In two B. M. MSS. the word is more like *sar* and the correct reading is perhaps *sar-i-fauj*.

5 *Anājīr*, perhaps false reports of disaster.

called Rāī Lōnkaran,[1] took up, out of wickedness, the position of hostility and set guards over the water-pond, so that the royal army
which had experienced the toils of the desert and had come from a 182
wilderness of mirages to this evil halting-place, was put to trouble from want of water. The tigers of fidelity's forest advanced and showing their superiority, defeated that vile crew. From thence they proceeded on towards the bounty-encompassed fort (*ḥiṣār-i-faiz-inḥiṣār*) of Amarkōṭ on 10th Jumāda'l-awwal (23rd August, 1542). After difficulties from hunger and thirst, the glory of arriving at that guarded fort (*haṣn-i-haṣīn*), which is the ascension-point of glory and storehouse of fortune's jewel, was conferred upon them. The ruler of the fort, who was called Rānā Parsād, regarded the sublime advent as a glorious adornment and tendered acceptable service.

One of the marvels (*barakāt*) resulting from the sacred existence of his Majesty, the king of kings, which moved the wonder of the acute of the time, was that in that propitious period when her Majesty Maryam-makānī was pregnant with that Unique of creation's workshop, she one day when she had been rapidly traversing the desert, had a longing for a pomegranate. In that waterless and grainless Sahara where it was difficult to find any trace of corn, the caterers for the holy court were in despair, when suddenly a man brought a bag (*anbān*) full of millet (*jawār*) for sale. When they took him into the tent and were emptying his bag, suddenly a large, juicy pomegranate emerged. 'Twas a cause of joy and gladness, and an astonished world ascribed it to a miracle.

Some[2] days were spent in that delightful spot, and it was there that Tardī Bēg Khān and many others who had accumulated goods and wealth—all of it acquired by the abiding good fortune (of the royal house)—grudged giving it in such a time of distress and difficulty, even when his Majesty asked for it! By the help of the Rāī of Amarkōṭ his Majesty got possession[3] of the goods, and out of his perfect kindness, liberality and justice, distributed a portion among his followers for their expenses, but returned the bulk of it to

[1] The Noonkarn of Todd. A Rāja Lōnkaran is mentioned in Niẓāmu-d-dīn as one of Akbar's nobles. Blochmann, 531.

[2] About six weeks.

[3] *Cf.* Jauhar, 43.

those low-minded, narrow-souled ones. God be praised! How have the necks of contemporaries—from the blessing of his Majesty the king of kings and shadow of God's holy essence—come into the noose of zeal and loyalty, so that whilst in that past age great officers and those holding high trusts did not ascend to even a low stage of loyalty, and were at such a crisis niggardly of wealth which they had gathered by the blessing of their master's favour, at the present day the despised and they who stand a great way off from devotion's court, have with respect to self-sacrifice, a delight in climbing to the loftiest stages of perfect loyalty, even though they be in the position
183 of being abused and reproached! How much more then they who are the *élite* of the court and bystanders of the pedestal of the sublime throne! May Almighty God hold aloft, for epochs and cycles, this chosen one from eternity on the *masnad* of bounty, and on the throne of the *khilāfat*, that he may conduct the affairs of the world and of mankind.

As[1] his Majesty Jahānbānī had in his mind the firm intention of marching forwards and as the time of the appearance of the Lord of Time and the Terrene was at hand, he, having ascertained the propitious hour, committed, on 1st Rajab, 949 (11th October, 1542), the litter of her Majesty Maryam-makānī and some faithful followers to the world-upholding Creator, and with fortune and prestige set out on his expedition.

1 According to the text this sentence closes the chapter, but I think it would have been better to end with the preceding paragraph. The headings are probably not by the authors and are often arbitrary. The Lucknow edition has not a new chapter here.

# CHAPTER XXVII.

## RECEIPT OF THE NEWS OF THE AUSPICIOUS BIRTH OF HIS MAJESTY THE KING OF KINGS, BY HIS MAJESTY JAHĀNBĀNĪ JANNAT-ĀSHYĀNĪ, AND OTHER DETAILS.[1]

At this time, when the hoping eyes of the watchers of the night of expectation were opened and the door of hopelessness was closed for the world, the exaltation-point (*sharaf*) of the birth of his Majesty, the king of kings and shadow of God, displayed its countenance. As has already been stated, that nursling of Divine light emerged from the womb of concealment into the world of manifestation on the night of Sunday,[2] 5th Rajab, 949 (15th October, 1542), in order that all the sorrows of mortals might end in everlasting joy; that the sorrow-pelted heart of his Majesty Jahānbānī might receive the balm of assuagement; that the perturbed outer world might assume *kosmos* and the rent-spiritual world be composed; that the spectators of Divine power (*i.e.*, the angels) might rejoice over the spectacle of the accomplished fact and the expectants of the spiritual and temporal world have their desire satisfied; that to Wisdom there should come a master, to Justice a gracious father, to Perception a wise friend, to Law a righteous king, to Love an acute appreciator; that universal peace might have a wise daysman; that an adorner of the outward and a shewer-forth of the inward might appear. God be praised that in adequate correspondence with hope, there shone a dawn of union after a dark night of distraction, and that a morning of joy succeeded an evening of gloom. The desire of celestials was accomplished, the glory of terrestrials revealed. When this darkness-destroying refulgence and universe-lighting flash came from holy heaven and unveiled itself in that land

---

[1] A better sub-heading would be, "Some account of Bairām Khān."

[2] Saturday, according to our reckoning, the birth being early on Sunday morning.

of roses,[1] swift-messengers hastened to convey the good news. While they were yet on the way, the heart of his Majesty Jahānbānī,—for his far-seeing eye was on the watch on account of the secret intimation,—became a thousand hearts from the life-giving good news. He prostrated himself in thanksgiving to Providence who had made fortune's rose bloom in the thorn-brake of misfortune, and had in the emptiness of failure, cast thousands of fruitions into his bosom. Within and without, there was a feast of joy, and all addressed themselves to enjoyment. The noble and the humble, the rich and poor, the small and great, opened the hand of rejoicing,
184 and beat the feet of delight in that feast of fortune, and secured endless favours. An account of this sublime feast, which was the celestial *'Īd* and the world's New Year, and of the arrival of the honoured cradle of his Majesty, the king of kings, at his Majesty Jahānbānī's sublime camp, and of other occurrences which are the adorning frontispiece of this auspicious rescript and the illuminated border of this mandate of fortune, has been incorporated in the beginning of this lofty-titled volume; for this real Pinacothek,[2] wherein are depicted the wondrous events, noble deeds and glorious victories of his Majesty, the king of kings, is fashioned in accord with the initiative of the exaltation-point (*sharaf*) of the holy nativity, and whatever else has been traced by the pen of supplication is but ancillary to this and but a diluent[3] or vehicle of the

---

[1] *Gul-zamīn*. Perhaps Maryam-makānī's bosom is meant.

[2] *Artang* or *Arshang*, the house of the painter Mānī and also his album. D'Herbelot *s. v.* Ertenk & Jarrett III. 336, 337. Mānī is the supposed founder of Manicheism.

[3] *Sīrābī-i-sukhan, lit.* irrigation of words. A. F. here explains why he began his work with the horoscopes of Akbar and the details of his birth although this causes some repetition in his account of Humāyūn's reign. It may be worth while noting that A. F. divided his history according to *qarans* or periods of thirty years, of his hero's life. Thus his first volume embraced the first thirty years of Akbar's life, *viz.*, from his birth to the end of the seventeenth year of his reign, for Akbar ascended the throne when he was 13. The next book was to contain the history of the reign up to the end of the 47th year, but was not completed because A. F. was killed in that year. Apparently he had carried on the history till the end of the 46th year. His hope, as he tells us in the *Āīn*, Jarrett III. 416, was that he might write four volumes, *i. e.*, the history of four

discourse, and has a real connection with that subject. God be praised! The imposing record of this ever-during progression has been accomplished even from Adam, down to this period (Akbar's birth), generation after generation. That it may go on, the veil is being withdrawn from the countenance of narration.

In short, as his Majesty Jahānbānī Jannat-ashyānī was a world of urbanity and generosity, he had stayed his desire of retirement for the sake of his loyal companions, and with his far-seeing eyes had set about the ordering of the world of interdependencies, as is the special purpose of the existence of princes, and had proceeded towards Māldēō's country. Māldēō that ravening demon (*dēv-maāl-i-dad-sīrat*) did not comprehend the magnitude of the blessing—such as he could not see even in a dream, and behaved in an unworthy manner. Of necessity and at the request of his devoted followers, his Majesty proceeded back to Sind on the chance that the rulers of that country might awake from the slumber of negligence, and amend the past. Though the world-adorning mind did not approve of this, still in accordance with fate he agreed to return. When the sublime army came near the boundary, it became known that the Arghūniāns were assembled in Jūn and were prepared to fight. His Majesty Jahānbānī sent forward Shaikh 'Alī Beg Jalāīr, whose ancestors were of hereditary devotion and loyalty from the time of the uprearing of the standards of glory of his Majesty *Ṣāḥib-qirānī* (Tīmūr), together with a body of brave men. He himself followed. As Shaikh 'Alī had at his back the victorious

---

*qarans* (120 years). The third volume which he refers to in the passage mentioned above is the *Āīn*, which was finished, in a manner, in the 42nd year, *i. e.*, 1597-98. No doubt, however, he intended to add to it from time to time according as new regulations were issued by Akbar, and new territories added to his kingdom. The *Āīn* is generally called the third book of the *Akbarnāma*, but it should be remembered that it is not a continuation of the first two, and that it was completed (in a manner) before the historical part of his work was finished. It is in reality an *excursus* or side-piece to his history. A. F.'s division of his work has not been preserved in the *Bib. Ind.* edition which is in three volumes, the first ending with Akbar's accession and not with his 17th year as A. F. designed. The expression *sīrābī-i-sukhan* above referred to is used again by A. F. at p. 195 of text when he digresses into accounts of Sher Khān, Ḥaidar Mīrzā and others.

army, he went forward bravely with a few men and soon scattered the foe. The breeze of victory's morn blew from the orient of the sword and the horizon of the bow, and the sun of fortune burnt up the darkness of that field of nemesis. The army encamped near Jūn.[1] To that town of lofty threshold (*qaṣba-i-rafī'-'ataba*) there came from Amarkot, the birth-place, the honourable litter of her Majesty Maryam-makānī and the sublime cradle of his Majesty, the
185 king of kings, attended by fortune and happy augury. Accordingly a detail of the circumstance has been made an adornment to the Introduction. As this spot was on the banks of the Indus and was eminent among the cities of Sind for its many gardens, streams, pleasant fruits and amenities, the army stayed there for some time. There were continual fights with the Arghūniāns who were always defeated. Shaikh Tāju-d-dīn Lārī,[2] who was one of his Majesty Jahānbānī's favourites, became a martyr here.[3] One day Shaikh 'Alī Beg Jalāīr, Tardī Beg Khān, and a body of men were despatched to attack the neighbouring district. Sulṭān Maḥmūd of Bhakkar and a large number of people fell upon them. Tardī Bēg was remiss in fighting, but Sher 'Alī Bēg stood firm and in that battle-field (*razm*) which is the banquet-table (*bisāṭ-i-bazm*) of the brave, quaffed with unaltered mien the sherbet of martyrdom. The heart of his Majesty Jahānbānī was grievously wounded by the fate of so faithful a follower, and some other untoward circumstances having occurred, his heart cooled towards the country of Bhakkar and he determined to go to Qandahār. Just then, on 7th Muḥarram 950 (13th April, 1543) Bairām Khān arrived alone from Gujrāt and laid a balm on the wounded spirit of his Majesty, and was a cause of cheerfulness and joy. One of the wonderful things was that as

---

[1] As Stewart remarks, Jūn is not marked on the maps. A. F. puts it in Hājkān. Jarrett II. 340. Apparently it was on the east bank, between Tattah and Sehwān. General Haig. (l. c., p. 92) says "Jūn, the chief town of a fertile and populous district, was situated on the left bank of the Rēn. It is 75 miles south-west of Umarkote and 50 miles north-east of Tattah." A note adds that the ruins of Jūn are to be seen two miles south-east of the present Tando Ghulām Ḥaidar.

[2] Lār or Lāristān is a maritime province of Persia. D'Herbelot s. v. Lār.

[3] Perhaps all that is meant is that he died a natural death.

he was coming to the camp, he had first to pass over a battle-field. Before he could make his obeisance or reveal himself, he had to prepare for war and to fight bravely. The victorious soldiers were amazed, and thought "he comes from the secret army (of God)." When it transpired that he was Bairām Khān, a shout was raised by those standing in battle-array, and the heart of his Majesty Jahānbānī rejoiced. On account of this arrival, they continued for some [1] days to halt in that land of roses (*gulzamīn*).

*Account of Bairām Khān.*

The brief account of Bairām Khān is as follows. After exposing his life in the unfortunate affair of Qanauj, he went to Sambal. There he took refuge with Rāja Mitter Sen, one of the great landholders of that country, in the town of Lakhnūr [2] and for a while remained there under protection. When Sher Khān heard of this, he sent a messenger for him, and the Rāja being helpless, sent the Khān. They met on the road [3] to Mālwa. At the beginning of the interview, Sher Khān rose up to receive him and in order to attract him, spoke crafty words to him. Among his remarks was this, "Who- 188
ever keeps his loyalty, stumbleth not." "Yea," replied Bairām Khān, "whoever keeps his loyalty, shall not stumble." He contrived, after a thousand difficulties, to escape from near Burhānpūr in company with Abū'l-qāsim, the governor of Gwāliyār, and set out for Gujrāt. While they were on their way, Sher Khān's ambassador who was coming from Gujrāt, got information about them and sent people who arrested Abū'l-qāsim,—who was remarkable for the beauty of his person. Bairām Khān out of nobleness and generosity stoutly asseverated that he was Bairām Khān, while Abū'l-qāsim heroically said, "This is my servant; he would sacrifice himself for me, beware and withdraw your hand from him." Thus it was the case of

---

[1] Three months according to A. F.'s own chronology, for they did not leave Jūn till 11th July. It is more probable that it was Bairām's arrival and energy which made Humāyūn take such a decided step as that of leaving Sind.

[2] Jarrett II. 298. There is a fuller account of Bairām's visit to Sambhal in 'Abbās' chronicle.

[3] At Ujjain, according to the chronicle of Sher Shāh.

*Verse.*[1]

"Leave me, seize the hand of my friend."

In this way Bairām Khān escaped and went to Sulṭān Maḥmūd in Gujrāt. Abū'l-qāsim was taken before Sher Khān, and from failure[2] to appreciate him, that mine of magnanimity was martyred. Sher Khān used frequently to remark that "as soon as Bairām Khān said in the assembly 'Whoever keeps his loyalty shall not[3] stumble,' we gathered that he would not come to terms with us." Sulṭān Maḥmūd of Gujrāt too, though he tried to induce him to stay with him, could not succeed. He (Bairām) got leave to go on pilgrimage and came to Sūrat. Thence he hurried off to the country of Hardwār[4]

---

[1] Gulistān V. 20.

[2] *Az nā-shināsī*; this cannot mean, owing to his not being recognised, for Sher Khān had seen the real Bairām.

[3] I adopt the variant *na khwāhad*.

[4] Corrected in the Errata to Mārwār, but apparently on the authority of one MS. only and I suspect that Mārwār is merely a guess devised to get rid of the improbability of Bairām's having gone to such a distant place as Hardwār. The *Ma'āṣir-i-umarā* has Hardwār and so has the *Ma'āṣir-i-raḥīmī*. It does not agree very well with A. F.'s statement that Bairām joined Humāyūn from Gujrāt, but then neither does Mārwār. Though Hardwār be very far it is not impossible that Bairām who was trying to hide, went the distance in order to escape Sher Khān and Sulṭān Maḥmūd. He may have done so in disguise and in company with Hindū pilgrims. Possibly too he went there because it was not far from his old refuge of Sambhal. At first I was inclined to accept Mārwār and to suppose that A. F. wrote it in the form Marūwār or Marūwar (مرووار or مروور) which according to Tod, is the original word and which might easily enough be read by a copyist as Hardwār. It might also have been supposed that Bairām went to Mārwār, *i.e.*, Jodhpūr, in pursuit of Humāyūn of whose expedition into Māldeō's country he may have heard. A pencil note in Chalmers' Ms. suggests Dwārkā (in Gujrāt) which would do very well if we had any evidence that Dwārkā was ever called Hardwār. On the whole I think that we must hold that A. F. wrote Hardwār. The *Ma'āṣir-i-raḥīmī* has a biography of Bairām taken apparently from a work called the *Tārīkh-i-akbarī* by Muḥammad 'Ārif Qandahārī who had been Bairām's steward. It uses the word Hardwār twice apparently without any suspicion of mistake. It describes Bairām's parentage, his birth in Qil'a Ẓafar in Badakhshān, the death of his father, Saif 'Alī at Ghaznīn, his entering Humāyūn's service, and becoming his *muhrdār* (chancellor), and finally, with refer-

and from there he came to the feet of his own master (*ṣāḥib*) and the benefactor of mankind in the village of Jūn.

---

ence perhaps to A. F.'s remarks on the thousand difficulties which Bairām experienced in making his escape to Gujrāt,—it tells us how he in the course of his wanderings, fell in with a party of Gūwārās who were drinking and dancing, and how they constrained him to take part in their merry-making.

## CHAPTER XXVIII.

### SINGULAR MANIFESTATION BY HIS MAJESTY, THE KING OF KINGS, IN THE EIGHTH MONTH FROM HIS NATIVITY'S EXALTATION-POINT (*sharaf*), BEING THE ILLUMINATED BORDER OF MIRACLES (*karāmāt*), AND PRESAGE OF HIS CAREER (*maqāmāt, lit. stages or stations*).

In the pages of Divine knowledge, which are "the guarded tablets"[1] from and for eternity, it is laid down that when the diadem of distinction is set on the marvellous head of a world-adorning creature in the temporal and spiritual enthroning-room, there are emitted, from the auspicious birth-hour of that glorious one, flashings and wonders (*bawāriq-i-ḥālāt-ū-khawāriq-i-'ādāt*) from the folded pages of his record, each of them a mysterious herald loudly proclaiming in the reason's ear of mankind the glorious progression of his power, and by such revelations augmenting the felicity of mortals. One of the marvellous proofs of this is that when seven months complete had elapsed from his Majesty, the king of kings', auspicious birth, and when he had in his fortune and felicity entered on the eighth, a strange circumstance occurred. On an evening which was seized of the light of fortune's morn, Jījī Anaga—that cupola of chastity—
187 was nursing the first fruit of the garden of holiness, and grieving over the opposition to her by that veil of chastity—Māham Anaga, and by many others. She was very sad because they had represented to his Majesty Jahānbānī Jannat-āshyānī that Mīr Ghaznavī's wife (*i. e.*, herself) was practising incantations so that his Majesty, the prince of mankind, should not accept anyone's milk but her own. At this time, when none else was present, his Majesty, seeing that there was privacy, became vocal, and Messiah-like[2]

---

[1] *Lauḥ-i-maḥfūẓ*, Book of Destiny. D'Herbelot *s. v. Omm Alkitab*, & Lane, 2680c.

[2] Muḥammadans believe that Jesus Christ spoke in the cradle.

opened his wondrous mouth to comfort Jījī Anaga's afflicted heart. "Be of good cheer," he said, "for the celestial light of the *khilāfat* shall abide in thy bosom and shall bestow on the night of thy sorrow the effulgence of joy. But see that thou reveal this our secret to no one, and that thou dost not proclaim untimely this mystery of God's power, for hidden designs and great previsions are infolded therein." Jīji Anaga declared, "This life-fraught intimation brought me into rapture, and sorrow's knot was at once loosed from off my heart. This portent which gave me from the eternal throne the sole and undisputed charge of a child of light, expanded my heart, one becoming a hundred and a hundred a thousand.[1] Day by day the doors of joy and gladness opened wider and wider before me, and having established myself on thanksgiving for this great blessing, I addressed myself to my duties, heart and soul. The glory and dominion of two worlds were revealed to me. But I kept this mystery sealed up till that nursling of dominion became the throne-adorner of the regions of world-conquest. One day he had gone forth from Dihlī to hunt in the district of Pālam,[2] and there an enormous and terrific serpent, such as might move the heart of the daring,[3] appeared on the line of road. On this occasion his Majesty exhibited the miracle of Moses, and without the hesitation which comes even to generous hearts, put forth his white[4] hand and approaching the serpent, courageously and in the strength of a sacred intimation, seized its tail with his holy hand and quelled it. Yūsuf Muḥammad Khān,[5] brother of Mīrzā 'Azīz Kōkaltāsh beheld this token of power and in his astonishment came and told me. On that occasion I told my dear son that sealed and hidden-away mystery which I myself had seen and heard, and said, 'His Majesty did that wonderful thing in his tender years, 'tis not strange

1 Text, *Khāṭirikī*, but it should be *Khāṭir yakī*.

2 Jarrett II. 286. In the Dihlī district, and so apparently, different from Pālam in Kāngra.

3 *Arbāb-i-taḥawwur*. *Taḥawwur* means, according to Lane, a state in which one enters on rash enterprises, such as fighting with unbelievers more than double the number of the Muslim. Dict. 2906c.

4 An allusion to the Muḥammadan story of the white hand of Moses *cf.* Exodus iv. 6. The miracle of Moses above referred to seems to be the conversion of Moses' rod into a serpent.

5 Blochmann 323. Son of Jījī Anaga. He was the elder brother.

if in his maturity he has performed this miracle, for every act hath its time and every speech its season. The reason of my not mentioning this marvel till this point is that no one to whom I told it, would have believed it, but on the contrary would have taxed me with weakness of intellect. The taste of such a story would have been bitter to their wishes' palate. Moreover I was not at liberty to reveal it. Now, my son, that I have heard from you the story of the serpent, I have opened my lips to tell of the mystery which marked his tender years, while the other is a sample of his riper age. My honoured son! in that exhibitor of miracles such indications and stages of development (*'alāmāt ū maqāmāt*) are not
188 surprising." Though Abū'l-fazl, the composer of this noble record had heard these two anecdotes from a person of veracity, yet he also received them direct from that receptacle of chastity (Jījī Anaga). But what the writer has seen with his own eyes and has understood by his own contemplation, concerning the perfections and miracles of this nursling of Divine light, exceeds mortal conjecture and human comprehension. In truth what was recounted by the venerable mother of M. 'Azīz Kōka is astonishing to the exoteric (*aṣḥāb-i-ẓāhir*), but what this humble one hath witnessed is awe-augmenting to the esoteric (*arbāb-i-bāṭin*).

# CHAPTER XXIX.

## Departure of his Majesty Jahānbānī Jannat-Āshyānī for Qandahār, with the design of going thence to the Ḥijāz and of his resolution to enter Persia.

It is the Eternal will and the Divine design that when the glorious robe of a king's fortune is being embroidered with the fringe of perpetuity and the props of his throne of greatness and sovereignty made strong and glorious by the pillars of fixity and permanence, sundry accidents which have the appearance of retrogressions and withdrawals are brought in front of his path. In truth these are apparent and not real, and the impediments are in the end subjects of thanksgiving. The short-sighted regard such as defects and become astonished. But they of uplifted eyes recognise them as the mole on Fortune's cheek, and regard them as a note of the subjugation of the evil eye. The fortunate man regards every evil which comes in his way, as the complement of perfection, while the unfortunate man regards them as his destruction, spiritual and temporal, and collapses into the collar of lamentation. The retrogradations of the planets—the regents of the seven[1] celestial climes—are an illustration of this and typify the design. Though the world-illuminating sun be hid from sight by cloud and vapour, yet in truth 'tis no mighty screen which has been lowered over mortal eyes, nor has any defect reached those glorious halls (the sun's). When it seemeth to be a cause of concealment, the strong blast of Divine power casts the vapour headlong and relegates it to the black earth. The phenomena of sunrise and sunset too are torch-bearing indicators of this. For the status and condition of the Treasury of Light when in the East are identical with his status and condition when under the veil of the West. And the condition which he hath when

[1] The sun and moon were recognised as planets, thus making seven in all.

in the zenith and when in declination from the meridian, is absolutely the same as his condition when in the *nadir* of mid-night.[1] The difference is in the earth-born beholders and in the imaginations of the dwellers in a handful of clay. Assuredly the pinacles of his glory is all the holier because the thoughts of detrimental have touched its fringe. In accordance with these propositions, whoever cherisheth evil thoughts against tiara'ed lords of bliss,
189 and diademed lords of fortune, is caught at last by the exemplary punishment of his deeds, and becomes a primefactor of his own destruction. These truths are mirrored in the presage-full history of his Majesty Jahānbānī Jannat-āsẖyānī for in brief space was the skirt of his Majesty's fortune, which had been sullied by misfortune, washed and cleansed at the fountain-head of fruition, while all the ingrates received the punishment of their designs and deeds. The stack[2] of their lives and fortunes was consumed by the lightning of Divine wrath, and the note of the existence of those wretches was erased from the Book of Time. Accordingly the difficulties (*maṣā'ib*) and fatigues (*matā'ib*), of adversity (*'usr*) and the stations (*mawārid*) and ascensions (*maṭāli'*) of prosperity (*yusr*) are being set-forth in the order of their time and place.

In fine, as his Majesty Jahānbānī Jannat-āsẖyānī's holiness-expressing soul had grown aweary of this world's vain show, and had turned away her lofty contemplation from the territory of Sind, it occurred to his sanctified mind to offer peace to the ruler of Tatta and to march to Qandahār. When the sublime cavalcade should arrive there, he would commit his Majesty, the king of kings, and the elect ones of his Court to God's protection, would plant his own foot on the highway of asceticism and retreat and ascend the steps of ecstacy and rapture and phœnix-like (*humāwār*), pet the pinnacle of love 'neath the wings of genius. As he had gained spiritual abundance by circumambulating the altar of the heart, he would, by conveying the sacred litter (*maḥmil*)[3] to the *ka'ba* of clay at one semblance and substance. As the spiritual pinacothek had been constructed, he would also adorn the visible temple. Thus would

[1] *Watad-i-rub'-i-nisfu-l-lail.*

[2] *Kẖirman.* It also means parhelion or halo, and probably A. F. wished to take advantage of this double meaning.

[3] See Lane's Dict. 650*a*.

hearts be conciliated and a method of truthful guidance be furnished to the simple-minded followers of forms.

He was occupied with these thoughts when the ruler of Tatta on understanding his intention, recognised his own gain therein and despatched a petition for peace. As the soaring falcon of his Majesty's genius had spread her wings for the chase of the phœnix (*'anqā*) and had withdrawn her far-seeing gaze from lower game and let it fall on lofty eyries, his petition reached the place of acceptation. The Arghūniāns whose affairs were in distress, tossed the cap of joy to the skies on hearing the gladtidings of peace, and regarding the project as the goal of desire and as an unlooked for boon, forwarded a large present[1] and made various apologies.

His Majesty auspiciously and prosperously left Jūn for Qandahār *viâ* Sīwī (Sībī) on 7th Rabī'ul-ākhir, 950 (11th July, 1543). M. 'Askar on hearing of the approach of the royal cavalcade, and acting by M. Kāmrān's orders and from his own wickedness, strengthened the fort (Qandahār) and proceeded with evil intentions with a large body of troops towards the sublime camp in order that he might by help of villainy take his Majesty prisoner. Meanwhile Amīr Allāh Dōst, one of the learned of the age and who had on several
occasions acted as M. Kāmrān's Agent[2] (*vakīl*) and Shaikh 'Abdu-l 190
wahhāb[3] a descendant of Pūrān[4] were coming to solicit, in marriage on Mīrzā Kāmrān's behalf, the daughter of Shāh Ḥusain Beg Arghūn. On hearing of the approach of the sublime army, they took refuge in the castle of Sīwī. His Majesty Jahānbānī sent an exalted mandate to Mīr Allāh Dōst, summoning him to his presence, but he out of worthlessness, chose exclusion from the honour

---

[1] Shāh Ḥusain on the principle of making a golden bridge for a flying enemy, sent Humāyūn 30 boats and 300 camels. Badāōnī I. 442. See also Gulbadan 526 ff.

[2] This may be compared with *Tār. Sind.* Bābā Čūcak is also mentioned there as one of Kāmrān's ambassadors.

[3] The *Tār. Sind* has a good deal to say about this man. He was descended from Abū Sā'id Pūrānī, and was of an Arabian family, settled in Sind. He was a distinguished lawyer and perhaps A. F.'s remark about the eminence of Allāh Dōst was intended for 'Abdu-l-Wahhāb.

[4] Possibly Jalālu-d-dīn Pūrānī is meant. But more probably the reference is to a descendant of his, Shaikh Mīrak Pūrānī who was Shaikhu-l-islām of Tatta. See *Tār. Sind.*

of service and made the excuse that the garrison would not let him leave.

When the army came to the territory of Shāl, which is about 30[1] *farsakh* (150 miles) from Qandahār, Jalālu-d-dīn Beg, an officer of M. Kāmrān and who had a fief in the territory, had left people to capture any scouts and by them two of the royal servants who had gone on in advance to Sar-cashma[2] were arrested and brought in. One of them managed to escape from their clutches and came and reported what he had learnt of their evil designs by observing their ways and language. His Majesty Jahānbānī, on perceiving the ingratitude of this crew, gave up the idea of proceeding to Qandahār, and turned off towards Mashtang;[3] Pāyanda[4] Muḥammad Waisī took leave and went to Qandahār. With him was sent an autograph letter to M. 'Askarī, strong[5] in expressions such as might appeal to a little-loving, disloyal brother, and containing warnings and instructions. But where was the reason-harkening ear, and where the heart of right understanding? Treating these remonstrances as unheard, he continued to go on in his villainy. Qāsim Ḥusain Sulṭān,[6] Mahdī Qāsim Khān and many others of 'Askarī Mīrzā's servants remonstrated against his going lest his Majesty should grow desperate, and out of dire necessity proceed to Persia, and less great calamities should occur. Abū'l-khair and a number of wicked men uttered flattering, house-subverting words, outwardly specious but inwardly productive of evil and ruin, and confirmed him in his faulty resolves. On that day's

---

1 *Sih* in text, but the variant *sī* is right. Shāl is Quettah which is by compass about 130 miles south-east of Qandahār.

2 I presume this is the place marked on the survey map as about 60 miles N. by W. of Quettah.

3 See Errata of Text. Mashtang or Mastang lies about 30 miles, S. S. W. of Quettah and is between it and Khilāt. Both Mastang and Shāl are referred to in the *Āīn*, Jarrett II. 396, where they are described as east of Qandahār.

4 Apparently Pāyamda Khān Mughul, nephew of Hājī Muḥammad Kōka, and perhaps the part-author of one of the translations of Bābar's Memoirs, (Blochmann 387 and Ma'āṣir 394.)

5 Text, مصدّر *muṣaddar*, but most of if not all the MSS. I have consulted write مصدر without tashdīd and as if the word was *maṣdar*, theme or source.

6 Blochmann 348.

morning which was his downfall's evening,[1] the Mīrzā proceeded with evil intent towards Mashtang. When he had advanced one or two *kos*, he asked his servants, if any of them had been that way. Jai Bahādur Ūzbak, who was Qāsim Ḥusāin Sulṭān's servant and had on this expedition taken service with the Mīrzā, said, "I know this road thoroughly, and have repeatedly gone and come by it!" The Mīrzā replied that he was speaking the truth for he had been a 191
*jāgīrdār*[2] there, and he bade him go on ahead and lead the way. He objected that his pony was knocked up, and the Mīrzā signed to Tarsūn Barlās, one of his servants, to give him his horse. He objected about his own necessities but had to surrender the animal. Jai Bahādur, who had served the king in India, advanced a little by auspicious guidance and then putting his horse to the gallop, went off to Bairām Khān's tent, and unfolded[3] the facts of the case. Bairām Khān went with him to his Majesty Jahānbānī, whom he informed of the evil intentions of that ingrate ('Askarī). His Majesty sent to Tardī Beg and some others for horses. Those base, narrow-eyed men turned away from the perception of their good fortune (in thus having an opportunity of serving Humāyūn) and refused to give them. His Majesty wished to mount his horse (perhaps Jai Bahādur's) and go and give them a lesson. Bairām Khān deprecated doing this, as the moment was critical and there was no time for dallying. "Let the ingrates be left to God's vengeance, and let his Majesty follow his own course." On hearing this representation his Majesty, attended by a few devoted followers, took the road of the desert. He gave up the idea of Qandahār and Kābul and proceeded towards Persia (*'Irāq*) with the intention of going to the *Ḥijāz* (Mecca, &c.), and as a desert-traverser, entered on the path of separation (*firāq*). Khwāja Mu'aẓẓam, Nadīm Kōkaltāsh, Mīr Ghaznavī, and Khwāja 'Ambar Nāẓir were directed that his Majesty, the king of kings, was in the cradle of guardianship and under the protection of the

---

[1] A. F. plays on the double meaning of *shām*, evening and unlucky. 'Askarī *advanced* in the morning, but this was in reality the retrogression (*idbār*) of his fortune.

[2] Probably what is meant is that his master had been *jāgīrdār*.

[3] *Pardagushāy-i-ḥaqīqat-i-ḥāl.* A.F. seeks to convey the double meaning that Jai Bahādur opened the fold of the tent (as he is said by other authorities to have done) and also disclosed the truth.

Divine love, and that affliction's dust could not reach his fortune's skirt, but that they should by every possible means bring her Majesty Maryam-makānī to the king. Those right-minded ones made haste and performed acceptable service. After going a little way, night came on darker than the hearts of unacknowledging ingrates. Bairām Khān represented that his Majesty was aware of Mīrzā 'Askarī's lust for gold and property; that at this time the Mīrzā would be secure and at ease, and be sitting in a tent with two or three clerks, and looking at the list of the goods and chattels in his Majesty's camp. The proper thing for them was to rely upon the Divine favour, and to come suddenly on that tent, and settle his business. That though the Mīrzā had become alienated, all his servants had been brought up on his Majesty's salt, and that they would inevitably come forward and serve him. His Majesty approved of this proposal from the practical point of view,
192 but out of his pure nature and well-meaningness he declined to adopt it, and said they had now set out for a foreign land and had entered on a long journey, and that he would not give up his plans.[1] Once more he committed his Majesty, the king of kings, to the protection of the God of Glory, the repeller (*dāfi'*) of evils, and supporter (*rāfi'*) in dangers, and taking the eternal counsels as his guide and the everlasting favour as his helper in place and out of place, he fixed the saddle of dominion on the steed of enterprise, and the foot of forward-faring in the stirrup of trust and proceeded on his way.

When Mīrzā 'Askarī with his evil intentions approached Mashtang he sent on his *ṣadr* Mīr Abū'l-ḥasan that he might go to his Majesty Jahānbānī, and that if the latter was meditating departure, he might by trick and stratagem detain him. The Mīr arrived just when his Majesty Jahānbānī was mounting his horse, and sought to turn him by alleging sundry messages from the Mīrzā. His Majesty, by God's guidance, did not listen to his vain words, but rapidly went off. M. 'Askarī came up afterwards and sent Shāh Walad, Abū'l-khair and many others of his men to guard the camp and not let any one go out of it. He heard from the *Sadr* Mīr Abū'l-husain

[1] The meaning is that Humāyūn had begun his pilgrimage to Mecca and so would not turn back.

the story of Jai Bahādur's warning and of his Majesty Jahānbānī's departure. Tardī Beg Khān and the other faithless servants came and paid their respects to the Mīrzā who made them all over to trusty men of his own.

A short-sighted man, who does not reflect on the evil day or on a bad end and who enters on the path of wicked designs and of shamelessness, in reality strikes an axe into the foot of his own well-being, and prepares for himself misfortunes and heaven-sent adversities. These things are not hidden from the readers of the pages of the world's history! When Mīr Ghaznavī came and paid his respects to M. 'Askarī, the latter said, "We came to do homage to the king, wherefore has his Excellency gone off by the desert?" Then he inquired where the Prince was, meaning his Majesty, the king of kings. Mīr Ghaznavī said he was in his quarters. The Mīrzā said "Good, let a camel-load of fruit be taken to him from the commissariat (*rikāb-khāna*); I am coming too." At night he and one or two clerks examined[1] in his tent some of the things which had been brought from the royal stores (*sarkār*); they wrote them down and the state of affairs was exactly as Bairām Khān had conjectured and had represented. Next day at breakfast time (about 9 A. M.) he had his drums beaten and moved from his quarters to the royal encampment. He alighted at the door of his Majesty Jahānbānī's residence (*daulatkhāna*) and had all the men, one by one, small and great, arrested. He made over Tardī Beg Khān to Shāh Walad, and he put all the unfaithful servants in charge of his own men and took them off to Qandahār. Many of them he destroyed by hardships and torments, and from Tardī Beg Khān he took all his 193
hoard so that he soon got the retribution of his deeds. But no, no! how could this be retribution for such crimes? if we called this typhoon of evils one revolution (*girdī*)[2] in the descending of retribution, it would still not be appropriate.[3]

---

[1] Jauhar, who remained in the camp, describes how disappointed 'Askarī was to find that a heavy chest contained only stones.

[2] *Cf.* text I. 63, l. 5 where the same word *girdī* is used. But several MSS. have *nazl* نزل instead of *nuzūl* نزول as if the phrase was an atom (*girdī*) out of the abundance. Typhoon, *ṭūfān*, means etymologically a turning or revolving (*cf.* whirlwind) and hence is appropriately used here.

[3] Tardī Beg was eventually put to death by Bairān Khān.

*Verse.*[1]

If a wicked and ill-fated man
Become good by a teacher's instruction,
In the end the mystery is explained
For then his true nature is revealed.

It is clear to those who can discern the mysteries of fate, that when the fortunate hand of an eternally elected one be decked with sovereignty's signet, and the dominion-head be exalted by the *khilāfat's* diadem, the rays of glory are ever shining on the forehead of his career. One of the wondrous indications and celestial portents which occurred at this time in relation to his Majesty, the king of kings, was as follows. When Mīrzā 'Askarī came to the royal camp and began his improprieties, Mīr Ghaznavī and Māham Āghā[2] brought his Majesty the king of kings before him on the shoulder of honour and in the bosom of security. Though the Mīrzā directed his countenance towards him and had a jubilant[3] air and wore a forced smile, his Majesty, even then an aggregate of the perfections of a mature man of the world, spite of his tender years, was in no way elated (*shigufta*). Restraint[4] of spirit was manifested on his brow. The Mīrzā changed his tone[5] and said, "We

[1] The text has in the first line *kunad* instead of *kunish* and consequently is unintelligible. Most of the I. O. MSS. have *'kunish* كنش and I think this is unquestionably the right reading. The meaning is that the coltish nature will break through some day, or as Bābar expresses it, that everything returns to its original. It corresponds to the Horatian maxim about nature's returning even if expelled by a pitchfork.

[2] So in text instead of the Anaga sometimes used. Probably Āghā is right for it is also a term applied to a woman.

[3] *Dar maqām-i-shigaufstagī u zahrkhand āmad. Zahrkhand* is said by the *Bahār-i-'ajam* to be the opposite of *shukrkhand*. It means smiling or laughter out of anger or recklessness, *lit.* a poison-smile. A sardonic smile perhaps expresses the meaning.

[4] *Qabẓ-i-khāṭir*, repression or depression of spirit; قبض and بسط, says Lane 2482*b*, are terms applied by the investigators of truth among the Sufis, to two contrary states of the heart, from both of which it is seldom or never free; the former being an affection of the heart withholding it from dilatation and joys. See also Dict. T. T. II. 1198. There A. F. uses it in opposition to *shiguftagī* which literally means expansion.

[5] *Tarīq shuda.* This term is explained by the Bahār-i-'ajam to mean

can see whose this child is. Why should he be elated at seeing us?" The Mīrzā's ring was hanging from his neck by a red ribbon and after a little while the child in accordance with infantive ways—no! no! by Fortune's guiding hand, put his hand to the ribbon and sought to take it. The Mīrzā immediately took the ribbon from his neck and gave it to his Majesty, the king of kings. The acute in the assembly saw in this an auspicious prognostic that bye-and-bye the seal of dominion and the ring of sovereignty would bear his Majesty's name, and that water flowing from the fount of Divine bounties would become a river. From thence his Majesty the Shāhanshāh went, protected by the Divine aid, in company with M. 'Askarī towards Qandahār. Standing and sitting, sleeping and waking, rays of greatness and command streamed from his Majesty's forehead, and the lights of God's knowledge were manifested. On the road Kōkī Bahādur, one of M. 'Askarī's confidants, came near his Majesty's (Akbar) camel litter and said to Mīr Ghaznavī that if he made the prince over to him he would take him to the king. The Mīr replied that as the king himself had not taken him, 'twas evident there was a reason for leaving him; nor could he venture without high authority to take action. Bahādur said, "I've formed the desire to serve his Majesty and hence I come at such a time of desolation 194
to do so. I wanted to perform this service and now that you don't exalt me by this blessing, give me a token from his Majesty, the king of kings (Akbar), that I may give it to his Majesty." Mīr Ghaznavī gave to Bahādur his Majesty's cap,[1] the diadem of the moon of auspiciousness, and thereby exalted him.

M. 'Askarī brought his Majesty, the king of kings, to Qandahār on 18th Ramazān, 950 (16th December, 1543), and assigned him a residence in the citadel near himself. Māham Āghā, Jījī Anaga and Atka Khān were made eternally fortunate by serving him, and longed for the diffusion of the light of holiness. The Mīrzā made over this nursling of fortune who was growing up in the shadow of the

---

hanging down the head, or the reversal of a former condition. He quotes p. 216b A.F. for such use of it.

The *tāqīya* is properly the skull-cap worn under the turban, but perhaps this was all the child was wearing. It is very ridiculous that A. F. makes Bahādur speak of the infant as his Majesty Shāhanshāh, a title not invented for him till long afterwards.

Divine protection, to his own wife Sultān[1] Begam, and that cupola of chastity out of her abundant wisdom, lovingly and devotedly tended him. To appearance she watched over him, but in reality she was keeping herself alongside of light absolute, and so receiving illumination, and day by day she was beholding more and more the glory (*farr*) of greatness proceeding from the light-increasing brows of that world-blessing.

Evil thoughts respecting one who is God-supported and in whose person God-nourished light exists, can only terminate in good, and out of contrariety nothing can come except service and benefit. Accordingly Eternal Providence was tending him at that time when paternal affection and maternal love should have been responsible for his needments (*takafful-i-muhimmāt*) and he was in the hands of deadly enemies, so that the foot of loyalty of the far-sighted of wisdom's kingdom might be the more established, and that a guiding lamp might come into the hands of the short-sighted and simple, and that the facts of the Divine watchfulness and of heavenly guardianship might be manifest to friend and foe. I have heard from the sacred lips of his Majesty, the king of kings, as follows: "I perfectly remember what happened when I was one year old, and especially the time when his Majesty Jahānbānī proceeded towards Irāq and I was brought to Qandahār. I was then one year[2] and three months old. One day Māham Anaga, the mother of Adham Khān, (who was always in charge of that nursling of fortune), represented to M. 'Askarī, "It is a Tūrkī[3] custom that when a child begins to walk, the father or grandfather or whoever represents them, takes off his turban and strikes the child with it, as he is going along, so that the nursling of hope may come to the ground (*i. e.*, may fall down). At present his Majesty Jahānbānī is not here; you are in his room, and it is fitting you should perform this spell which is

---

[1] This lady went, after her husband's death, to Mecca in company with Gulbadan Begam and others in 1574.

[2] Fourteen months, *viz.*, from 15th October, 1542, to 16th December, 1543, or 14½ Muḥammadan months.

[3] Text, *rasm-i-buzurgān*, ancestral custom, but I. V. MS. A. 564, and 8308 and 3330 have Turkān, and this is most likely to be correct. Māham Anaga being a Turk or Uzbak might speak of Tūrkī customs to 'Askarī, but would hardly refer to ancestr customs.

like *sipand*[1] against the evil eye. The Mīrzā immediately took off his turban and flung it at me, and I fell down." "This striking and falling," his Majesty deigned to observe, "are visibly before me. Also at the same time they took me for good luck to have my head shaved[2] 195
at the shrine of Bābā[3] Ḥasan Abdāl. That journey and the taking off my hair are present before me as in a mirror."

What is there extraordinary about this or a hundred things like it, to any one in the blissful chambers of whose heart there is an enkindled lamp?

As the thread of the narrative has extended so far, it is unavoidable that for the moistening of discourse (*sīrābī-i-sukhan*), I say something about the remaining events of Sher Khān, about Mīrzā Ḥaidar's going to Kashmīr, about the condition of M. Kāmrān who went to Kābul, and M. Hindāl who hurried off to Qandahār, and Yādgār Nāsir Mīrzā who made opposition and remained in Bhakkar, so that the searcher after instruction may take warning, and by the strength of a happy fortune, spend his days prudently and righteously.

---

[1] Apparently *sipand* is not wild rue, but *mehndī*, *i.e.*, *Lawsonia inermis*, which yields henna.

[2] Probably what was cut off was a *cūnti*, or tuft. See Herbelot, pp. 21 and 180.

[3] There is a famous shrine of Ḥasan Abdāl in the Attock *tahsil* of the Rāwal Pindī district. See Murray's Hand-book for the Panjāb 268, the *Tuzak-i-jahāngīrī* 48 and Blochmann 575. Jahāngīr says that Shamsu-d-dīn Atka made a reservoir at Ḥasan Abdāl, and as he was Akbar's guardian and foster-father, it is possible that it was to this Ḥasan Abdāl that the child was taken. But the shrine is a long way off from Qandahār and it is doubtful if 'Askarī would have allowed Akbar to be removed so far. There is a shrine called Bābā Walī, and also Ḥasān Abdāl, in the outskirts of Qandahār (to the westward). It is mentioned *infra* text I. 238, eight lines from foot, and it is probably to this place that Akbar was taken.

I may note that there is a long account of the saint Ḥasan Abdāl in the *Tar. Sind.* Mā'ṣūm was a descendant of his, the saint's original home being Sabzwār in Persia.

## CHAPTER XXX.

### Brief account[1] of the evil-ending career of Shēr Khān.

It is known that Shēr Khān after crossing the Biāh (Beas) advanced slowly, and in spite of all his warlike equipment acted with great circumspection. He was greatly afraid lest the heroes of the royal army should coalesce and advancing into the field of warfare should exact vengeance from him and bring to nothing all his treacherous machinations. He had sent a large force ahead, but was very cautious about engaging. After some days, when the defection of M. Kāmran, and the opposition of the other brothers became known far and wide, he came to Lāhōr. From thence he advanced as far as Khushāb,[2] and was for some days in Bhera[3] and its neighbourhood. He sent a summons to Sulṭān Sārang[4] Ghakkar and Sulṭān Ādam who were leading landholders in that neighbourhood, but as they had been clients of his Majesty Gītī-sitānī Firdūs-makānī, and had prospered by the favour of that exalted family they did not listen to his overtures. He advanced to Hathīāpūr[5] in the Ghakkar territory and sent a large force against them. The Ghakkars fought bravely and defeated the Afghans so that many of them were captured and sold. Shēr Khān wished to march against them in person. He consulted his followers and they advised that as this tribe had strong mountains and remote (*zamīnhā-i-qalb*, heart, *i.e.*, internal) territories, they should be dealt with by degrees and by

[1] This and the two following headings do not occur in several MSS.

[2] Jarrett II, 323. In Shāhpūr, Panjab v. bank Jehlam, W. N. W. Lāhōr.

[3] Also in Shāhpūr, North-West Khushāb.

[4] See Delmerick, l. c. and Blochmann 486.

[5] Perhaps Hatiyār Lang, Jarrett II, 325. Named after Hātī Ghakkar; Bābar, 259, and Tuzak-i-Jahāngīrī, S. Aḥmad ed. 47, where the place is called Hatīya. It is between Rohtās and Rawal Pindi, and near a river called the Kāsī. Delmerick apud Blochmann, 487n.

policy. The proper course was to leave a large army in that
neighbourhood which could both watch the royal army and also
devastate the country of the Ghakkars. It was also desirable that
a strong fort should be built for the carrying out of these two
objects. Thus by a counter move these men would be impeded by
their own impediments (*az tanganāī-i-khud batang āmada*) and their
stubborn heads be brought low. For himself, the proper course was to
turn back and apply himself to the administration of the vast country
of India. In consequence of this advice he laid the foundations of 196
the Fort of Rohtās[1] and having left a large force there he marched
back and came to Āgra. From thence he came to Gwalior where
Mīr Abū-l-Qāsim was sheltering himself, but was obliged by want
of provisions to surrender. Shēr Khān became supreme, and divided
all India, except Bengal, into 47 divisions. He introduced the
branding[2] of soldiers' horses and carried into effect some of the many
plans of Sulṭān 'Alā'u-d-dīn which are set forth in the Tārīkh-i-Fīrūz-
shāhī,[3] and which he had heard of. After that he proceeded against
Pūran[4] Mal the Raja of Raisīn and Candīrī. He got the Raja out of
the fort by a dishonest treaty and promises and by the efforts of
sundry misguided lawyers[5] and wretched ignoramuses he destroyed
the very men to whom he had given quarter. Thence he came to

---

[1] I. G. s. v. Rotās. Named after Rohtās in Bihar; on the Kahan and in the Salt Range. For description see Murray's Hand-book, Panjab, 237. See also Tuzak-i-Jahāngīrī, pp. 46, 47.

[2] According to the Chronicle, Shēr Shāh claimed this as his own invention.

[3] Elliot III, 197 and also 179.

[4] According to one account descended from the Salhadī of Bābar's Mem. But 'Abbās calls him Bhāīa Pūran Mal and says he was only an officer under Salhadī's family.

[5] A. F.'s indignation is very creditable to him and he is apparently the only writer who expresses it, Niẓāmu-d-dīn, Badāōnī and Firishta tell the story without censure, and Abbās Khān seems to exult in it. Elliot IV, 402. But A. F. draws a veil over the fact, mentioned by the other historians, that the leading instigator or ratifier of Shēr Shāh's shameless breach of faith was a lawyer or rather theologian named Rafīu-d-dīn Ṣafavī of whose wisdom and learning A. F. speaks so highly in Chapter XXVI and in Jarrett, III. 423. Probably the reason for this reticence was that A. F.'s mother was the daughter or other near descendant of Rafī-ud-dīn. See Jarrett l. c. The reason the lawyers gave for the breach of the safe-conduct was that Pūran Mal had Muḥammadan women in his *harem* and had even made some of

Āgra and after the manner of the governors[1] (ḥukkām) of Bengal established serais on the roads at the distance of every *kos*.

After a dangerous illness in Āgra[2] he marched against Māldēō the lord of Ajmīr, Nāgor and many other cities. When he had by fraud and guile[3] disposed of that territory he hastened to Citūr and Ranthanbūr. There too he practised his juggleries so that the custodians of the forts sent him the keys. Having got rid of everything there he entered the territory of Dhundīra.[4] From there he went to the fort of Kālinjar and laying siege to it, he made covered approaches (*sābāthā*) and drove mines against it. On 10th Muharram,[5]

---

them into dancing girls. In a footnote to the text there is a passage which is too interesting to be omitted, supported as it is by two MSS. It is to the effect that on account of the breach of faith Quṭb Khān left Shēr Shāh's service and became a hermit. It is not clear who this Quṭb Khān was, but he could not have been Shēr Shāh's son for he had been shortly before killed in battle. 'Abbās Khān, Elliott, l. c. calls him Quṭb Khān Nabīt and says, as also does Badāōnī, that he was one of the negotiators of the treaty. The word which I have translated ignoramuses is *safīhān*. Could A. F. possibly mean to pun on Rafīu-d-dīn's title of Ṣafavī? For definition of safa, see Lane's Dict. 1377*b* and Dict. T. T. I. 724.

1 Referring to Ḥusain Shāh of Gaur, Stewart's Bengal 109.

2 According to 'Abbās the illness occurred on his way to Bihar and Bengal.

3 Alluding to the stratagem of the forged letters by which he is said to have deceived Māldēo. See Elphinstone's History. This is probably the Hādisa-i-Māldēo, Maldeo's catastrophe, to which A. F. refers in the *Āīn*, Jarrett III. 421 and note. It was this affair that drove A. F.'s father from Nāgōr.

4 This is Jaipūr in Ambar, the old name of which was Dhūndār. See Tod's Rajasthan.

5 This month and day are wrong. The date given by Ferishta and Khāfī Khān is 12 Rabī'u-l-awwal. A. F. says Shēr Khān reigned 5 years, 2 months, 13 days, which does not agree with the date 10th Muḥarram. Shēr Shāh is said to have assumed the title and to have struck coins after the battle of Qanauj. This occurred in the beginning of 947, 10th Muharram, whence perhaps A. F.'s date 10th Muḥarram 952, in order to make it an anniversary and point a moral. If we reckon that he ruled five years, *viz.*, 947–51 and died 12 Rabī-'ul-awwal we get the figures 5 2 12 or almost exactly A. F.'s. Indeed if he did not die till after sunset the 13 is right. A. F. refers to Shēr Shāh's death in the *Āīn*, Jarrett II, 159, 160. As pointed out by Erskine, A. F. later on, p. 336 of text gives another date for the death, *viz.*, 11 Rabī-'ul-awwal.

952, or 5th March, 1545, he was consumed by flames of fire which had spontaneously arisen out of the smoke-sighs[1] of the oppressed. The chronogram of his combustion was found in the words "(a)z ātish murd :" "Died from fire (=952)." Though in taking this splendid citadel his life came out of its elemental quadrilateral,[2] yet the fort came into possession. He governed Hindustan by fraud and craft 5 years, 2 months, 13 days. Eight[3] days afterwards his younger son Jalāl Khān took his place, and calling himself Islām Khān took the title of Shāh. He surpassed even his father in wickedness. As the sway of those two seditious impostors was alongside of the crescent-moon[4] world-lighting splendours of the standards of the everlasting dominion like the light of fireflies,[5] semblance without substance, the mysterious design of God for the sake of some purposes, which were infolded in His wisdom's ambushes, let it prank for a few days and then levelled it with the dust of ruin, and so the world escaped from the grip of the existence of those tyrannous mischief-makers.[6]

---

[1] The allusion seems to be to the Gulistān I, 27. *Dūd* means smoke, but is used metaphorically for the sighs or exhalations of the heart.

[2] A. F. plays upon the supposition that the human body is made up of four elements, and compares this quadrilateral to the four walls of Kalinjar.

[3] According to Niẓāmu-d-dīn and Ferishta Islām Khān succeeded on 15 Rabi-'ul-awwal, or the third day after the death.

[4] *Mahoa*, a crescent, or perhaps a ball representing a moon which was carried on the standards

[5] *Kirmakān-i-shabtāb*, tiny, night-gleaming worms, but apparently fire-flies are meant. I do not remember to have seen glow worms in India, and the reference to the failing to the ground shows that fireflies are intended, and Chalmers so translates the passage.

[6] *Mu'arbidān-i-satīzakār. Mu'arbid* is properly one who does not carry his liquor well, and so annoys his boon-companions. Lane 1995c

## CHAPTER XXXI.

### Brief account of M. Ḥaidar.

The story of M. Ḥaidar is as follows:—When he had got assistance from his Majesty Jahānbānī, he proceeded towards Kashmīr,
197 as already related. When he got to Naushahr,[1] the officers whose names have already been given, loyally came forward and did homage, and again showed him how he could enter Kashmīr and take possession of it. The Mīrzā advanced by the passes in reliance on the Divine aid and the royal fortune. Meanwhile a schism occurred in the Emperor's army. As has been already stated, Khwāja Kilān Beg either from his own inclination or at the instance of M. Kāmrān, abandoned the enterprise and joined M. Kāmrān, while Muẓaffar Tūpcī[2] went off to the Sārang[3] hills. None remained with M. Ḥaidar save a few old servants and the troops whom his Majesty Jahānbānī had deputed to his assistance. But as there was much strife and dissension and confusion and anarchy in Kashmīr, he was warmly supported by the eagerness of the Kashmīrīs, and on 22nd Rajab, 947 (22nd November, 1540), he entered by the pass of Pūnc[4] and conquered Kashmīr without a battle or a struggle. For at that time it had been long without an established ruler, and the ministers tyrannously held the country in their own possession, and while giving to one of the claimants the name of monarch, themselves exercised the authority. At that period a person called Nāzuk Shāh—having a name that was no name[5] was the

---

[1] *Tār. Rash.* 483. Naushahr is in Kashmīr and W. N. W. of Jammū. It is not given in the Ind. Gaz. It was the old capital.

[2] *Tār. Rash.* 483, Iskandar. And B. M. Add. 27, 247, Iskandar.

[3] The Ghakkar country S. W. of Kashmīr, Panüc.

[4] Text, but there is a variant Pūnc and Niẓāmu-d-dīn so writes it.

[5] A. F. puns on the word Nāzuk which means slight or slender, and calls it an *ism-i-bī-musammāī* (like the 'outis' of Ulysses). There is the variant Bārak (qu. Nārak), and the coins give Nādir. See Mr. Rodgers' paper, J. A. S. B. 1885, p. 114.

reputed sovereign. Under such circumstances in whatever direction there might not be union, or plan, or counsel, or judgment, to that quarter did the affairs of the country drift. It was the winter-quadragesima[1] and there was heavy snow. When Kācī Cak saw[2] that M. Ḥaidar was disposed to make himself independent, he, using the craft and perfidy which are indispensable to Kashmīrīs, left Kashmīr and went before Shēr Khān. For his object in bringing in M. Ḥaidar was his own aggrandisement and when that was not achieved, but when on the contrary things assumed a different shape, he withdrew his hand and entered on another scheme. He now tried another course and gave Shēr Khān the sister of Isma'īl, the son of Muḥammad Shāh.[3] When he had made himself acceptable by this means he took 'Alāwal Khān,[4] Ḥasan Khān Sarwānī and others to the number of 2,000 men and came to Kashmīr. Meanwhile Abdāl Mākrī, who was his backer, died of dropsy, and M. Ḥaidar having left his family in Andarkōt,[5] which is a very strong place, was in a protected position. The people of Kashmīr all deserted him and but few persons remained with him. He spent three months in the mountain defiles, and then on Monday, 20 Rabī'u-s-sānī, 948 (16th August, 1541), a battle took place, and by God's help he gained the victory. Though the enemy, consisting partly of Afghān auxiliaries and partly of faith- 193
less Kashmīrīs was more than 5,000 horse, yet as their action was based on faithlessness and disloyalty, it did not succeed and they were defeated. Many of the enemy were slain, and a party of them were made prisoner. Kashmīr came absolutely into the possession of the Mīrzā, and the Kashmīrī preacher (*khaṭīb*) Maulānā Jamālu-d-dīn Muḥammad Yūsuf found the chronogram *fatḥ-i-mukarrar* (victory repeated=948). Though the use of the word "repeated" (*takrār*)

---

[1] *Cilla-i-dai*, the forty days of *Dai*, a Persian month corresponding to December. Here *Dai* must be taken to mean winter as the month has 30 days only. The text has *bārān*, rain, but *Tār. Rash.* 485 shows that snow is meant.

[2] *Lit.* read on the brow of M. Ḥaidar's conduct the writing of independence (or absolute sovereignty).

[3] A former ruler of Kashmīr. Apparently he reigned four times and Nāzuk three. Jarrett II. 379, 380.

[4] Variant 'Ādil Khān and so in Firishta, but Niẓāmu-d-dīn has 'Alāwal.

[5] See *Tār. Rash.* 485 *n.* and Jarrett II. 370, but perhaps Indrakōt is the true reading.

might be applicable to the present expedition of the Mīrzā, yet as he himself has pointed [1] out in his history, the reference is to the fact that he once came [2] to Kas̲h̲mīr by the pass of Lār, as the agent of Sa'īd K̲h̲ān, the ruler of Kās̲h̲g̲h̲ar, and got possession of it on 4th S̲h̲a'bān,[3] 939 (1st March, 1533). But towards the end of S̲h̲awwāl of that year, (May 1533), he made peace with the Kas̲h̲mīr ministers, and with Muḥammad S̲h̲āh who was then the nominal ruler. The S̲h̲āh's daughter was given in marriage for Iskandar Sulṭān, the Mīrzā's son,[4] and the Mīrzā returned by the way he had entered.

When on this (last) occasion a providential victory was gained, and Kas̲h̲mīr was conquered, he for ten years zealously applied himself to its administration and clothed that charming land, but of desolated [5] appearance, with cities [6] and civilization. He sent for artists and craftsmen from all quarters and laboured for its renown and prosperity. Especially was music [7] in brisk demand and varieties of instruments were introduced. In short, the outward condition of that country, that is, its worldly state, acquired solidity. But owing to the Mīrzā's frigid [8] and insipid bigotries, the result of imperfect

---

[1] *Tār. Ras̲h̲*. 423.

[2] *Tār. Ras̲h̲*. 423 and Jarrett II. 363. Ḥaidar on that occasion entered Kas̲h̲mīr from Baltistān, *i. e.*, from the N. E.

[3] Apparently this is not the date of the victory, but of occasion on which the Kas̲h̲mīrīs rallied after their defeat, (*Tār. Ras̲h̲*. 437–39,) but Ḥaidar is not very explicit. In the *Āīn* A. F. wrongly gives the date as 930. Jarrett II, 390.

[4] Iskandar was not Ḥaidar's son, but Sa'īd K̲h̲ān's, (T. R.) 341, though Ḥaidar at Sa'īd K̲h̲ān's request regarded him as his own. In the *Āīn* A. F. correctly calls Sikandar (or Iskandar) the son of Sa'īd K̲h̲ān. See also *Akbarnāma* III. 552, l. 8. Probably *pisar-i-k̲h̲ud* is a copyist's error for *pisar-i-k̲h̲wānda, i.e.*, adopted son.

[5] *Ḥukm-i-k̲h̲arāba dās̲h̲t. Ḥukm* seems to be used here in the sense of appearance, *cf.* p. 127, l. 4 and 196, l. 5 from foot.

[6] Apparently an adaptation of the phrase used by Ḥaidar about his predecessor Zainu-l-'ābidīn.

[7] *Lit.* for music there was a bazaar (*hāt*).

[8] *Ta'aṣṣubhā-i-k̲h̲unuk-i-bīnamak. Ta'aṣṣub* has etymologically nearly the meaning religion. *Cf.* p. 334. l. 9. *K̲h̲unuk:* A. F. in the *Āīn* uses the word with reference to Sulṭān Sikandar, another ruler of Kas̲h̲mīr. He seems to contrast his bigotry and that of Ḥaidār with the liberal spirit of his son Zainu-l-'ābidīn.

development, the essentials for Kashmīr, *viz.*, unanimity and fidelity, found a bad market. And to this day there is an odour of bigotry about the Kashmīrīs, for there is a powerful influence in association, and especially is a strong impression produced by the ways of princes who are vigorous. It is to be hoped that by the blessing of his Majesty, the king of king's truth and chastity (*ḥaqīqat ū ḥaqqānīyat*) Kashmīr, spiritual and temporal, may attain unity, and that the articles of worship and religion may become current, unadulterated by hypocrisy and bigotry.

One of the capital and most inauspicious mistakes of the Mīrzā was that in spite of such victory he read the *khuṭba* and struck the coin in the name of Nāzuk Shāh after the fashion of the Kāshmīrī ministers. He should have fulfilled his duty of loyalty towards his Majesty Jahānbānī and have impressed the *darāhim* and *danānīr* and the pulpit *rostra* with his Majesty Jahānbānī's sacred name. Apparently he was temporising and was not giving currency to disloyalty, for when Kābul[1] was taken he honoured himself by having the *khuṭba* read in his Majesty Jahānbānī's sacred name.

In 958 (apparently October, 1551) he became, in a night attack 199
by the Kashmīrīs, a traveller to the region of non-existence. The short account of this is as follows :—

The Mīrzā transgressed the law of justice,—dominion's watchman,—and took to living for his own lusts and pleasures. He let fall from his hands prudence and the bearing of burdens, those two arms of felicity. The fraud and seditiousness of the Kashmīrīs which had been subverted by the Mīrzā's skill and sagacity, again stood up and the hypocritical and wicked faction took the road of deceit and in

---

See Jarrett II. 387, 388. It is clear from the *Tār. Rash.* that Ḥaidar was a rigid Muḥammadan of the Sunnī school and a persecutor of Sufīs, &c. See Elias & Ross, p. 436. He there takes exactly the opposite view to that of A. F. with regard to Sikandar and Zainu-l-'ābidīn.

[1] There are Kashmīr coins bearing Humāyūn's name and dated either 952 or 953. *Tār. Rash.* 24. Mr. Rodgers gives representations of three, of which one, No. 33, bears the date 950. Kābul was twice taken by Humāyūn, once in Ramaẓān 952, (November, 1545), and again in Rajab 955, (August, 1548). A. F. apparently refers to this second capture for he mentions that after this event an embassy arrived from Haidar. (A. N. I. 284).

friendly garb did the work of enemies. Their best stroke was the separating his army from him by stratagem, and the scattering of his capable servants. Some were sent towards Tibet, some to Paktī, and some to Rajaurī. 'Īdī Rīnā and Ḥusain Mākrī, son of Abdāl Mākrī, gained over Khwāja [1] Ḥājī, the Kashmīrī pedlar (*baqqāl*), who was the manager of the Mīrzā's affairs. They drew a great many to their side and marched against the Mīrzā. Ghāzī Khān and Malik Daulat Cak also joined them. Near Khānpūr, between Hīrapūr and Srīnagar, which last is the chief city of Kashmīr and the seat of government, they made a night-attack on the Mīrzā. He had approached the quarters of Khwāja Ḥājī to release Qarā [2] Bahādur, who was a prisoner. Suddenly he lost his life at the hands of Kamāl Dūbī,[3] though some say one of his own servants unknowingly hit him with an arrow.[4]

---

[1] *Tār. Rash*. 460 and 482.

[2] Ḥaidar's second cousin. See his biography in the *Ma'āṣir* III. 48 and in Blochmann 460.

[3] Text, *Dūlī*, but the variant *Dūbī* is right, for Niẓāmu-d-dīn speaks of Kamāl Dūbī as one of the persons who is supposed to have killed Ḥaidar.

[4] See *Tār. Rash*. App. A. 487 and Calcutta Review No.

A. F.'s account of Ḥaidar should be compared with Niẓāmu-d-dīn's and Firishta's and also with the *Tār. Rash*. and A. F.'s own statements in the *Āīn*. In the latter he is more favourable to Ḥaidar than in the *Akbarnāma*. The translation, (Jarrett II. 340,) does not seem quite correct. What A. F., text 584, 585, says, I think, is that the Kashmīrīs read the *khuṭba* in Nāzuk's name and that Ḥaidar at one and the same time recognised Humāyūn. The introduction of arts into Kashmīr which A. F. ascribes, in part, to Ḥaidar, is modestly attributed by the Mīrzā himself to Zainu-l-'ābidīn. *Tār. Rash*. 434.

# CHAPTER XXXII.

## Brief sketch of Mirzā Kāmrān's career.

As a short account of Mīrzā Ḥaidar has been given, I shall now record the actions of M. Kāmrān. On that ill-omened occasion when M. Kāmrān chose separation from his Majesty Jahānbānī and proceeded towards Kābul, he on arriving at Khushāb treated chiefship and pre-eminence (*sarī ū sarwarī*) as an affliction, and time,[1] the gamester, as his ally and had the *khuṭba* read in his own name. Improprieties of this kind will ever be manifested by him who maketh not far-seeing wisdom and instruction his counsellor and beloved associate. He knoweth not the duties of love nor the paths of generosity. He regardeth others' bane as his good, and scattereth evil seed in good men's fields. It is manifest what sort of crop will spring from such a sowing and tilling. And how shall the tree of his hopes yield the wished-for fruit? There is no permanency for him who takes no thought of the issue of things, nor any bond in fortune fastened to oneself by violence. What stability is there in a lofty palace wanting foundation; it soon falls to pieces like a minaret of ice! What fixity has a first night's moon which like a blinding flash of lightning vanishes in the twinkling of an eye? M. Kāmrān's sovereignty was quickly gone, like the freshness 200
of a rose, and his fortune departed like the soon-dying breeze of spring!

To be brief; he came by way of Dhankōṭ[2] to the bank of the Indus. Muhammad Sultān and Ulugh Mīrzā who had gone into the Multan territory but had been unable to maintain themselves there,

---

[1] That is, he regarded the whirligig of time whereby Humāyūn had been dethroned &c. as an advantage for himself.

[2] Jarrett II. 401 and note, and Bābar's Memoirs 140 where it is called Dīnkōt.

came and saluted M. Kāmrān on the river-bank. The Mīrzā tarried there for a while, and when the rebels fell into difficulties about corn, he made a bridge and crossed the river. Thence he came to Kābul and there he opened the gates of enjoyment in front of his own existence and spent his days in the indulgence of his pleasures and lusts. And Jamshīd[1] of Merv's saying, "Until the tiger leave the jungle, the pasturage is not open for the deer; nor till the falcon seek her nest, has the partridge freedom to fly," was verified in this instance. M. Kāmrān gave Ghaznīn and its territory to 'Askarī M. and sent Khwāja Khāwand Muḥammad on an embassy to Sulaimān M. in Badakhshān with the request that he would submit and make M. Kāmrān's style and coinage current in Badakhshān also. M. Sulaimān sent back the ambassador *re infectâ* and M. Kāmrān got enraged at this and led an army into Badakhshān. Near the village of Bārī[2] an engagement took place and when M. Sulaimān saw his own weakness and M. Kāmrān's strength he sent an envoy to knock at reconciliation's door. He caused the *khuṭba* to be read and coinage to be issued in M. Kāmrān's name; and the latter also took some Badakhshān territory from M. Sulaimān and gave it to his own men and then returned full of success. Meanwhile news came that M. Hindāl had taken possession of Qandahār. M. Kāmrān collected an army and marched against the city and besieged the fort for six months. M. Hindāl's supplies falling short, he asked for quarter and delivered up the fort. M. Kāmrān gave Qandahār to M. 'Askarī and returned to Kābul, bringing M. Hindāl along with him. For some days he treated M. Hindāl with severity but afterwards out of brotherhood and from hypocrisy in the guise of concord, gave him the fertile tract of Jūī Shāhī, which now bears the name of his Majesty the king of kings, and is called Jalālābād. The ruler of Sind also submitted[3] and now fortune was ministering the materials of negligence till M. Sulaimān broke his compact and seized of the territories which M. Kāmrān had

---

[1] Apparently the riddle-maker mentioned at text, 221 and Blochmann, 102.

[2] Chalmers. Mārī and Nārī in variant. Perhaps it is Paryān or it may be Barah which is marked on the map half way between Paryān and Chitral.

[3] Probably this refers to Shāh Ḥusain's giving his daughter in marriage to Kāmrān after refusing her to Humāyūn.

detached from Badakhshān. M. Kāmrān a second time led his army thither and a battle was fought near Andarāb.[1] M. Sulaimān was defeated and took refuge in Fort Zafar. M. Kāmrān followed him and besieged the fort. He stopped the coming of supplies and many of the inhabitants of Badakhshān came and did homage to him. As M. Sulaimān despaired of his soldiers, who were only eye-servers (*cashm-i-wafā dāsht*) and also as the fort was in difficulties from want of supplies, he was obliged to submit. M. Kāmrān left Qāsim Birlās, Mīrzā 'Abdu-l-lāh and many others of his 201
partisans under the charge of the said Birlās in Badakhshān, and himself went back (to Kābul). Khwāja Ḥusain[2] of Merv found the date of this occurrence in the words "*Jum'a hafdahum-i-māh-i-Jumāda'ṣ-ṣānī.*" (Friday, Jumāda II, 17th, 948=October 8th, 1546). He kept M. Sulaimān and his son M. Ibrāhīm in confinement. When he returned, he put the city into fête for a month, and spent his days in insouciance. He remembered not his God, nor did he deal justice to the oppressed. Till at length the fortune-star of his Majesty Jahānbānī's gracious heaven ascended, and coming with dominion and auspiciousness, lodged his punishment in his bosom, as will be related hereafter.

(M. Hindāl.)

Whoever behaves improperly to his benefactor and advances along the path of insincerity, receives the punishment of his actions in this world (*lit.* in the same condition). The account of M. Hindāl is of this tenor. He, at such a crisis and time of strife and sedition, left the service of his Majesty Jahānbānī, and taking the road of faithlessness proceeded towards Qandahār. When Qarāca Khān, who was governing Qandahār for M. Kāmrān, heard of the Mīrzā's arrival, he came out of the fort and respectfully embraced him. He made over the territory to the Mīrzā. Many days had not[3] elapsed when M. Kāmrān came and took possession thereof. He imprisoned

[1] Jarrett, III. 88. N. of Hindu Kush, South West Badakhshān.

[2] Blochmann, 574. A. F.'s somewhat disparaging remark about him there, may perhaps be due in part to his having celebrated a victory of Kāmrān. His odes on the births of Jahāngīr and Murād will be found at pp. 125 and 136 of Lowe's Badāonī.

[3] Kāmrān took Qandahār after a siege of six months.

the Mīrzā and treated him with severity, as has already been briefly stated.

(Yādgār Nāsir Mīrzā.)

It is certain that the end of the unfaithful, like the commencement of their deeds, is rejection by every heart (*mardūd-i-dilhā*). The wise do not place reliance (*i'tibār*) on unstable reliability (*i'tibār*). They wait in expectation of these ingrates receiving their portion so that they may be thankful and rejoice at their getting the punishment which is due for transgressions of rectitude, inasmuch as this will be a warning to mankind, and also an adminicle of the repentance of the wicked. Accordingly when Yādgār Nāṣir M. had been led from the right path by the deceit and perfidy of the ruler of Taṭṭa and had remained in Lohrī (Rohri), he stayed nearly two months there after the departure of his Majesty Jahānbānī. At last it became clear to him that the proposals of the ruler of Taṭṭa were all pretence, and his representations based on lies. Being helpless he abandoned his projects and proceeded towards Qandahār, though Hāshim Beg who was one of his truth-speaking well-wishers and well-pleasing (*rizā-jūī*) followers, told him that his joining M. Kāmrān and his leaving the service of his Majesty Jahānbānī were not approved of, and that the world was a place of retribution, and that he should reflect upon this. And it is a thing certain that the mind of him whose day of calamity is at hand, becomes darkened, that he displays audacity in injuring his benefactor, and that he reckons the advice of the right-thinking as wind and does not admit it into the ears of his understanding, and that he regards the weighty words of the wise as fables and fictions.[1] Accordingly Yādgār Nāṣir M. being unblessed, went toward Qandahār. He arrived at the time when M. Kāmrān had brought the fort of Qandahār to extremity, and did
202 homage to him; and accompanied him to Kābul. M. Kāmrān sent a person to the ruler of Taṭṭa and requested him to send with all respect her Highness Bilqīs-makānī Shahrbānū[2] and her son M. Sanjar, for they had separated from Yādgār Nāṣir M. and had remained in the Bhakkar territory. The ruler of Taṭṭa sent them in a suitable

---

[1] This is singularly like the *quem deus vult perdere*, &c.

[2] Of the household of Bilqīs, i.e., Queen of Sheba.

manner, together with a large number of persons who had separated from his Majesty Juhānbānī Jannat-āshyānī and were in that territory. By mistake or design it occurred that these people were sent by the route of the waterless and forageless desert. Many of them perished and when the remainder came to Shāl, fever broke out among them. Her Highness Bilqīs-makānī[1] died. Out of 2000 or 3000 men who were wandering in that caravan, only a few escaped with their lives and reached Qandahār.

---

1 Younger half-sister of Bābar and full-sister of Yādgār's father Naṣir. She married Junaid Birlās, and bore him Sanjar.

## CHAPTER XXXIII.

### March of the Sacred Band of his Majesty Jahānbānī Jannat-ashyānī to Khurāsān and Media ('Irāq), and account of what happened on the way.

Since the swift courser of the events-traversing pen has made some strides afield and has borne the words to their goal, let it now return to the track and resume its long journey. A brief account shall now be given of the finally victorious progress to Khurāsān and 'Irāq which came to pass to his Majesty Jahānbānī, and of his passing, with Providence for guide, through waterless deserts (*fayāfī*), saharas, and wastes.

When his Majesty, in accordance with the ordinance of the Eternal, planted his foot in the valley of resignation and took the path of the perilous wilderness (*cūl*), he honoured the attendants on his auspicious stirrup by the title of *Cūlī*.[1] By the infinite goodness of God, Malik Hātī Balūc, captain of the banditti, did homage in this howling wilderness (*cūl-i-pur-haul*), and conducting his Majesty to his abode, exerted himself in his service. He also became his guide out of that dread valley and brought him to the territory of Garmsir (*i. e.*, the warm region). Though Mīr 'Abdu-l-ḥai, the magistrate (*kalāntar*) of that territory, owing to unbefitting cautions, did not himself come forward and obtain the grace of service, yet he was assiduous in the performance of the rites of hospitality.

Khwāja Jalālu-d-dīn Maḥmūd[2] had come to that quarter to make

[1] Man of the desert; it corresponds to Badawī or Bedouin.

[2] Blochmann 384 and 527. At 527 he is mentioned as one of the viziers or finance-ministers. But perhaps this really was his younger brother Mas'ūd. There is a long biography of the Khwāja in the Ma'āṣir I. 615. He was put to death by Mun'im Khān, apparently in consequence of his unbridled tongue. The Ma'āṣir makes Bairam Khān primarily responsible for his murder, cf. A. N. II. 70, 71. It was Jalālu-d-dīn who conducted M. 'Askarī to Badakhshān when he was sent off

collections of revenue on behalf of M. 'Askarī. His Majesty sent Bābā Dōst Bakhshī to him to guide him aright and to bring him into his service. The Khwāja recognised this as a great opportunity and hastened to accept service. He poured out every thing he had in his store, in cash and in kind, among the troops. His Majesty Jahānbānī received him with favour and committed to his prudent judgment the duties of the *mīr-sāmānī-i-sarkār-i-khāṣa.*[1] His Majesty spent several days in this region giving charming counsels and instructions 203
to his faithful followers, and showing by heart-touching argument the world's faithlessness and the instability of external circumstances. He turned back their secular spirits from the pursuit of such things and directed them to the true goal and to the real point which it behoves the student of the masters of mind to pay attention to. His Majesty's lofty soul was engrossed by the thought that as the things belonging to detachment and seclusion increase day by day, he should seek some lonely corner, and withdrawing himself, outwardly and inwardly, from other matters should give himself up to God alone.

But his nobleness and humanity did not allow of his saddening the hearts of the followers of his fortunes by such mortification of desires. Nor did this faithful band withdraw their hand from service on account of these occurrences nor permit such a perfect personality, worthy of the true *khilāfat,* and whose like as a superintendent of things external and internal it would be hard to find in the course of revolving cycles, should restrain his arm from the world and amputate the series of everlasting sovereignty. All the aspirations of this family (*ṭabaqa*) are, inwardly for truth, and outwardly for humanity, and so it works for the production of universal concord. God be praised! the Unique Pearl of that abounding ocean, his Majesty the

---

to Mecca in disgrace—merely a cruel aggravation to 'Askarī's misfortunes. Jalālu-d-dīn is called Aubahī, i. e., from Aubah, a town near Herāt, by Bāyazīd who mentions to his credit—that by a timely remark he reclaimed Humāyūn from drunken habits. Bāyazīd mentions also that Jalālu-d-dīn was in the castle of Bābā Ḥājī when Humāyūn sent for him. The epithet *bujūq,* or half-nose, referred to by Blochmann, must have been given to Jalālu-d-dīn because 'Askarī had his nose cut or slit for improper language. See the story in Bāyazīd 55*a*.

[1] Stewardship of the Privy Purse. The expression *Sarkār-i-khāṣa* is used in Ṭahmāsp's letter p. 209, l. 17.

king of kings, to wit, hath attained such sway in full measure. In spite of the cares of conquering and upholding the visible world, he hath attained complete immersion in the billowy ocean of the empyreal and divine universe. And the step of his genius on the towering ascents of sublimity is firm and assured.

In fine, his Majesty determined, in accordance with the Divine will and his native nobleness to write a loving letter to the ruler of Persia and to turn the reins of intent towards that country. Should the ruler of Persia recognise hereditary right and show love and liberality, he would again give his attention to mundane matters and secure the hearts of his faithful band. Should it turn out otherwise he would in the liberty (*ikhtiyār*) of a hermitage, devote himself without liberty (*bī-ikhtiyār*) to his generous nature. Accordingly on Thursday, 1st[1] Shawwāl, 959 (28th December, 1945), he sent a letter by Cūlī Bahādur[2] to the effect that by order of the superintendents of destiny, who have attached so much deliberation and knowledge to every act, an urgent cause had arisen for procuring a speedy interview. After a brief sketch of his adventures this line was written under the cover.

*Verse.*

What has passed over our head, has passed,
Whether by stream, or hill, or wilderness.

His Majesty desired to spend some days in the Garmsir but Mīr 'Abdu-l-ḥai of Garmsir sent to represent to him that it was rumoured that M. 'Askarī had despatched a large force, and that possibly—which God forbid—they might come there, and things thus become irretrievable. If he went to the country of Sīstān, which belonged

---

[1] The letter is given in full in the ambassador Khur Shāh's history B. M. MS., No. 153, 58a, and the date of despatch stands there as 7th Shawwāl, 950 (3rd January, 1544). Perhaps A.F. did not quote the whole because, some phrases might be regarded as too abject. After the lines above-quoted Humāyūn went on to say that now the bird of desire was spreading his wings in order that he might be rewarded by beholding the sun of greatness and glory, *viz.*, Ṭahmāsp.

[2] Perhaps the Jai Bahādur formerly mentioned. As we have seen, Humāyūn gave the name of *Cūlī* to all who accompanied him across Balūcistān.

to the King of Persia, he would be protected from that reckless crew. 204
His Majesty reflected on the paucity of the sincere, and the plurality of the lords of opposition and discord, and recognised the fact that to stay in that country was to act carelessly, and so he proceeded towards Sīstān. He crossed the Hīrmand (Halmand) and halted at a lake[1] into which its waters flow. Aḥmad Sulṭān S̱ẖāmlū, the governor of Sīstān, recognised the advent as an unexpected blessing and tendered acceptable service and showed alacrity in offering hospitality. His Majesty spent some days in that pleasant country, the arena of the cavaliers[2] of fortune's plain, in the sport of catching waterfowl.[3] And in order to comfort his faithful comrades he busied himself with worldly matters and was a spectator of the wonders of destiny. Thence he proceeded to (the city of ?) Sīstān.[4] Áḥmad Sulṭān sent his mother and his wives to wait on her Majesty Maryam-makānī, and tendered all the revenues (*amwāl*) of his district as a present. His Majesty accepted a little of these in order to do him pleasure, and returned the remainder. In this halting place Ḥusain Qulī M. the brother of Aḥmad Sulṭān, who had come from Mas̱ẖhad to pay his respects to his mother and brother, in order that he might bid adieu to them before he went on pilgrimage, was honoured by an audience.[5] His Majesty questioned him about

---

[1] Lake Hāmūn. See Reclus 47 and 48. It is also called the Sea of Durra, or Zoreng. Elphinstone's Caubul II. 219.

[2] Alluding to the fact that Sīstān was Rustam's country. See Elphinstone's Caubul II. 219.

[3] *S̱ẖikār-i-qas̱ẖqaldāg̱ẖ*. This appears to be the coot (*fulica atra*). See Scully's App. to Shaw's Turk. Dict. p. 213 s.v. *qās̱ẖqāldāq*. See also P. de Courteille's Dict. s. v. *qasqāldāg̱ẖ* where it is translated "*plongeon noir*" and is said to be equivalent to Persian *mūg̱ẖ*. In Bāyazīd's Mems. 2 *b*. the word is spelt *qas̱ẖqaladāg̱ẖ*, and we are told that the *s̱ẖikār* or sport was carried on *ba-tarkāz*. Erskine in his MS. translation queries if this be stubble. Perhaps we should read *tīrgas* or harpoon, the *gas* being a double-headed arrow, and suppose that the sport was carried on in the manner described by Bābar, (pp. 153, 154) by means of a harpoon.

[4] I presume that this must be a city of that name for he was already in the district. Probably it is the place mentioned by Elphinstone under the name of Jalālābād. Bāyazīd has Qaṣba-i-Sīstān, the town of Sīstān. Raverty (*Ṭabaqāt-i-nāṣirī* 1122*n*.) speaks of Zaranj as being called the city of Sīstān.

[5] By the distinction of kissing the carpet.

religion and faith. He submitted that he had long studied the creeds of the Shī'as and Sunnīs, and had perused the books of both sects. The Shī'as maintained that the reviling and cursing of the Companions was meritorious and a means of religious progress, whereas the Sunnīs held that to blaspheme the Companions was an act of impiety. After consideration and meditation he had satisfied himself that no one can become impious by thinking he is doing right.[1] His Majesty much approved this remark, and with great kindness and condescension offered him the honour of service. As he was about to go on pilgrimage and had made his arrangements accordingly, he was debarred from this boon. Here also Ḥājī Muḥammad (son of) Bāba Qāshqa, and Ḥasan Kōka left M. 'Askarī and joined the noble army. They recommended that his Majesty should proceed towards Zamīn Dāwār because Amīr Beg, the governor, thereof was coming to serve, and Calma[2] Beg, governor of the fort of Bast, was also solicitous of the honour of employment; (and said also) that soon many men of M.
205 'Askarī would separate from him and enter his Majesty's service; and that Qandahār and its territory would come into the possession of the royal servants. When Aḥmad Sulṭān heard that they were giving this advice and were deterring his Majesty from going to Persia, he came to his Majesty and submitted, out of well-wishing and affection, that the expedition to Persia was worthy of his genius and that the faction which was dissuading him from going, was only actuated by fraud and treachery. As Aḥmad Sulṭān had by his devotion and sincerity established himself in his Majesty Jahānbānī's heart, his representations were accepted and acted upon. The Emperor determined to proceed to 'Irāq. On account of this affair Ḥājī Muḥ. Kōka was for some days excluded from the presence. Aḥmad Sulṭān attended on the stirrup, and wished to be a guide for the road, by way of Tabas[3] Kīlakī. As his Majesty had set his heart on visiting Herāt, he took the road by the fort of Ūk.[4]

---

[1] This story and much of the narrative of events in Sīstān are taken from Bāyazīd. See I. O. MS. No. 216, p. 3a.

[2] Afterwards a very distinguished officer. See Blochmann, 368.

[3] A town in Khurāsān. Jarrett III. 67. I insert the name Tabas in accordance with a variant and with Niẓāmu-d-dīn. For Tabas or Tubbas see Macgregor's Khurāsān I. 125. It lay on the road from Sīstān to Qaswīn (then the capital) and was a long way west of Herāt.

[4] See Raverty trans. *Tabaqāt-i-nāṣirī*, 34 and 1122*n*. He says Ūk lies

When the loving letter of his Majesty Jahānbānī Jannat-ashyānī reached Shāh Ṭahmāsp, he regarded his Majesty's auspicious advent as an unlooked for blessing and felt delighted. He wished that the glorious shadow of the auspicious *humā* (*humā-i-sa'ādat-i-humāyūnī*) might fall on the crest of his own fortune, and that the experience of this grace might form the inframing border for the record of the splendour of his family.[1] In acknowledgment of the blessing he bade the drums of rejoicing beat for three days in Qazwīn.[2] And he wrote a reply full of respect and veneration and of wishes for his Majesty's speedy arrival, with thousands of lands and *encomia*, and sent it along with various gifts and rarities by his special courtiers. This verse was written on the border (*'amwān*) of the letter.

*Verse.*

"A *humā* of auspicious soaring falls into our net,
If for thee there chance a passage to our abode.[3]

He sent back the messenger after doing him special honour, and expressed all manner of thankfulness and gratitude, and recalled old friendship. He also wrote to the governors of the cities and towns that at every city and halting-place where the august progress should rest, the leading men and the inhabitants, high and low, should keep the occasion as the *fête*, day of the royal family, and should go out to welcome his Majesty and should engage in royal feastings; also that they should provide at each stage proper materials and furnishings, food and drink, and fresh fruits, such as might be worthy of his Majesty's regard. An exact copy of the ordinance which was addressed to Muḥammad Khān, the governor of Herāt, is here set forth that it may be a code of regulations for the intelligent and that those alive to the ways of humanity may, by looking at this frontispiece of urbanity, act
with philanthropy, honouring and reverencing the unfortunate who 206

---

between Farah and Zaranj and has been in ruins for many years. Nāṣirī describes Ūk as N. E. of Shahristān, which is apparently the same as Zaranj.

1 Ṭahmāsp was only the second of his line.

2 D'Herbelot s. v. Caswin. Jarrett III. 83. It is 90 miles west-north-west of Ṭahrān. Milton refers to it in Paradise Lost X. 435:—

—or Bactrian Sophi, from the horns
Of Turkish crescent, leaves all waste beyond
The realm of Aladule, in his retreat
To Tauris or Casbeen.

3 This couplet is the beginning of an Ode of Ḥāfiẓ: No. 217, Vol. II, p. 138 Ed. Brockhaus.

have experienced fate in its heights and depths, and may not abate one jot of kindness towards them.

### ORDER (*farmān*) OF SHĀH ṬAHMĀSP TO THE GOVERNOR OF KHURĀSĀN.

This august order has been issued so that the asylum of dominion, workshop of Majesty and sun of power and prestige, Muḥammad Khān [1] Sharafu-d-dīn Ughlī Taklū, tutor [2] of our precious and upright son,[3] governor of Herāt,—the seat of sovereignty,—and *mīr dīwān*,[4] who hath been exalted by divers royal bounties and benefits, might know that the contents of his report, lately despatched to the court, the asylum of glory,—through Kamālu-d-dīn Shāh Qulī Beg, the asylum of nobility and brother of Qarā Sulṭān Shāmlū,[5] arrived on 12th Zī'l-ḥijja [6] (8th March, 1544), and that its distinguished purport has become known and understood from beginning to end.

---

[1] Blochmann, 426, and *Ma'āsiru-l-umarā'* I. 507, under title of J'afar Khān, his grandson who came to India and served under Akbar.

[2] *Lāla*. Blochmann, 426, remarks that the word does not occur in our dictionaries. Apparently it is a form of *lālā*, a *major-domo*, tutor, &c. Wollaston gives both *lālā* and *lallah*, s. v., tutor, but marks the last as vulgar.

[3] Sulṭān Muḥ. M. eldest son of Ṭahmāsp, and often called Muḥ. Khudābanda. He became king in 1578, but was a weak and unworthy ruler and soon disappeared. See Oliver. J. A. S. B. 1877, Vol. 56, p. 48.

[4] Apparently a translation of the Turkish title *beglar-begī* which occurs in the letter as given in B. M. MS., Or. 4678.

[5] According to Malcolm, Shāmlū means a son of Syria and refers to the fact that the tribe was brought from Syria by Tīmūr.

[6] Price points out that there is a difficulty about this date, for A. F. describes Humāyūn as reaching Herāt on 1st Zī'l-qa'da, or about 1½ months before Muḥ. Khān's letter was received by Ṭahmāsp. He suggests that the names of the months should be transposed. Probably the date in A. F.'s copy of the letter is altogether wrong, and the true date is that given in B. M. MS. Or. 4678, *viz.*, Tuesday, 5th Shawwāl, 950 (1st January, 1544). In the copy there given Ṭahmāsp describes himself as answering the letter on the same day. It was brought to him by Ḥasan Beg Taklū. Humāyūn wrote to Ṭahmāsp, according to A. F., on Thursday, 1st Shawwāl, 950, and probably Muḥ. Khān, the governor of Herāt, would write about the same time to his master. If Thursday was 1st Shawwāl, however, the following Sunday would be the 6th, not the 5th, unless we count, as the Muḥammadans do from sunset to sunset.

I have however found in the *Ma'ā-*

As to what has been written concerning the approach of the fortunate vicegerent (*nawwāb-i-kāmyāb*, i. e., Humāyūn), sphere-rider, sun-cupola, pearl of success and sovereignty's ocean, goodly tree ornamenting the garden of government and world-sway, world-illuminating light of the portico of sovereignty and glory, soaring cypress of the stream of auspiciousness and fortune, aromatic tree of glory and majesty's rose-garden, fruit of the tree of the *khilāfat* and of justice, king of land and sea (*barrain u baḥrain*), world-warming sun of felicity's heaven, exalted full-moon of the zenith of the *khilāfat* and world-rule, altar and exemplar of just princes, greatest and best of the *khāqāns*, the lord of majesty, high-born sovereign of supremacy's throne, exalted king of the kingdom of the dispensation of justice, khāqān of Alexander-type, glorious potentate, an enthroned Solomon, lord of guidance and assurance, world-guardian, lord of diadem and throne (*tāj u takht*), *ṣāḥib-qirān* (lord of conjunction) of the world of fortune and prestige, crowning diadem of famous *khāqāns*, the aided by God, defender of the Faith (Naṣīr-ud-dīn) Muḥammad Humāyūn Pādshāh. May the Almighty grant him greatness in accordance with desire until the last day! How may it be told what joy and delight have been caused by this.

*Verse.*

Good news, O courier of the morn,[1] thou bringest of the friend's advent.
May thy tidings be true, O thou ever the friend's intimate.
May that day come when, in the feast of meeting,
I shall sit, having my heart's desire, breathing in unison with the friend!

---

*ṣir-i-raḥīmī* (A. S. B. MS. p. 170*b*), a reading which seems to me to remove some difficulties and to be perhaps the right one. This is, that instead of *Ẕī'l-ḥijja* we have *Day-i-khujista*,—not ذي حجه but دي خجسته The date thus would be the 12th of the Persian month Dai, which corresponds to December. But if this is so the governor of Herāt must have written to his sovereign before Humāyūn actually entered Persia. Bāyazīd has Ẕī'l-ḥijja 949! I must admit here that though the *khujista* is plain enough in the Ma'āṣir yet the *dāl* of Dai is dotted ( ذى ) as if the copyist, at any rate, meant it for Ẕal.

[1] *Ṣabā*, rising; also east wind. Perhaps used here because Humāyūn was then in eastern Persia, and Ṭahmāsp was in the west, in Qazwīn.

Recognising that the untroubled progress and approach of this king, the angel of honour, are a great boon, be it known that, in guerdon of the glad tidings, we have bestowed the territory of Sabzwār[1] on that asylum of dominion (*i. e.*, Muḥammad Khān the addressee) from the beginning of Aries[2] of the year of the Hare. Let him send his *dārōgha* and vizier there, that the regular revenue and the extraordinary civil receipts thereof may be perceived from the begin-
207 ning of the current year, and be expended for the requirements of the victorious troops and his own necessities. Having acted, paragraph by paragraph, and day by day, in accordance with the procedure set forth in this edict (*nishān*), let there be no remissness concerning the paramount instructions.

Let him appoint five hundred prudent and experienced men, each of whom shall have a led[3] horse, a riding mule, and the necessary accoutrements, that they may go forth to meet the king, the lord of fortune,—with one[4] hundred swift horses which have been sent from the sublime court for the use of his Majesty, together with golden saddles; and let the asylum of dominion select from his own stable six swift horses, quiet, of good colour and strong, and such as may be fit for the riding of that royal cavalier of the field of glory

---

1 A town in Khurāsān, west of Nīshāpūr and between Mashhad and the Caspian. Blochmann, 55*n.* and Jarrett III. 85. But there is also a Sabzwār, south of Herāt, and probably this is the place meant. This Sabzwār is properly *Aspa-zār* or horse-meadow, and is so written in the copy of the Shāh's letter in the *Ma'āsir-i-raḥīmī*.

2 Text, *'amal*, but the Lucknow edition and three B. M. MSS. have *ḥamal*, and this seems correct. The Turkish, or Aighurian, cycle seems to have been used in official documents, &c., and began in Aries, as also did the Persian year. *Tushqān*, or the year of the Hare was the fourth of the cycle. Jarrett II. (I) 21.

3 *Asp-i-kutal* *Kutal*, or *kūtal*, is used to mean a second or substituted article. (Blochmann 109, 115.) The *Bahār-i-'ajam* explains it, when applied to horses, as meaning an animal strong enough to form part of the procession before a king's carriage, a processional horse in short. Such horses formed part of the *istiqbāl* which met the Persian-Afghān Mission on its approach to Mashhad. (Eastern Persia. Goldsmid and others. Macmillan, 1876. p. 357.)

4 Bāyazīd has *three* only and this is probably correct. Ṭahmāsp would hardly send 100 horses with golden saddles, nor if he did, would he be likely to tell Sharafu-d-dīn to add six. The six were probably added to the three to make the mystic nine.

and success; and let him place on them azure and embroidered saddles, with housings of gold brocade and gold thread, such as may befit the riding-horses of that majestic king; and let him make over each horse to two of his own servants, and despatch them. A splendid, special side-dagger ornamented with exquisite jewels which came to us from the fortunate vicegerent, the pardoned prince of sublime seat, the king our father—May God make his proof clear!—together with a golden scimitar (*shamshīr*) and a jewelled girdle, have been sent to the Alexander-principled king, for victory and conquest and good augury. Four hundred pieces of velvet and satin from Europe and Yezd have been sent, so that one hundred[1] and twenty coats may be made for the king's special use, and that the remainder may be for the servants attached to the victorious stirrup of that fortunate prince; also two-pile gold-brocaded velvet carpets and coverlets (*namad takya*[2]) of goat's hair with satin lining, and three pairs of large carpets twelve cubits (square?), four *Gōshkānī*[3] of fine silk,[4] and twelve tents, crimson, green and white, have been sent. May they arrive safely!

Let arrangements be made day by day for sweet and pleasant drinks, with white loaves kneaded with milk and butter and seasoned with fennel seeds and poppy seeds. Let them be well made and be sent to his Majesty. Let them also be sent for each member of his staff and for his other servants. Be it also arranged that at the places where his Majesty will halt, there be arranged and pitched, on the previous day, cleansed, pleasant, white, embroidered tents and awnings of silk and velvet, and also pantries and kitchens and all their necessary out-offices, so that every requisite apparatus be in readiness. When he, in his glory and fortune, shall direct a halt, let rose-water-sherbet and wholesome lemon-juice be prepared and poured out, after having been cooled with snow and ice. After the sherbet

---

[1] 120 were perhaps intended as a supply for a twelvemonth. Cf. Blochmann, 90, where it is stated that Akbar had 120 suits in his wardrobe, made up into twelve bundles.

[2] Blochmann, 55 and 96, *takyah-namad*.

[3] Gōshkān, or Jōshaqān, a town half-way between Kāshān and Ispahān, famous for carpets. (Blochmann, 55*n*).

[4] *Kurgī*, *kurk*, or *kurg*, is the fine short wool of the goat, nearest the skin. It also means fur. (Blochmann, 616).

let conserves of *maskān*[1] apples of Mas̲h̲had, water-melons, grapes, &c., with white loaves made as already directed, be tendered; and let care be taken that all the beverages be examined by the protector of sovereignty,[2] and that rose-water and grey ambergris be added to them. Each day let five hundred dishes of varied food be presented, together with the beverages. Let the asylum of dominion, Qazzāq[3] Sulṭān, and the acme of nobility, J'afar Sulṭān, together with your (other?) descendants and your clan to the number of one
208 thousand persons, go forth to offer welcome three days after the five hundred shall have set out. And during those three days let the said officers and the various troops be inspected. Be careful to give your servants *tipūcāq* and Arab horses, for there is no finer decoration for a soldier than a good horse; and let the uniforms of the one thousand be coloured and smart. And be it arranged that, when the officers come to wait upon his Majesty, they kiss the ground of service and honour with the lip of respect and render their service one by one. Be it seen to that, on the occasion of riding, &c., there be no altercation between the officers' servants and his Majesty's,[4] and that no annoyance of any kind happen to the king's servants. During the time of riding and of marching, let the officers remain with their own[5] troops and serve the king from a distance, but at the time of being on guard,[6] let each officer display his alacrity in the vicinity of the quarters which shall have been fixed (for the Emperor); and let them, having taken in their hands the staffs of service, serve in the manner that one would serve one's own king, and let them adopt and bring into practice the utmost attentiveness. Let this mandate be shown to the governor of every territory to which

[1] Text, *mas̲h̲kān*. The editors suggest *mas̲h̲kīn*, but according to *Bahār-i-'ajam*. *Mas̲h̲kān* is the name of a kind of apple grown in Ṭūs, *i.e.* Mas̲h̲had.

[2] *Salṭanat-panāh*. Bāyazīd has *ayālat-panāh* and in both cases S̲h̲arafu-d-dīn is the person meant. The special watch over the drinks of kings is characteristic of the East.

[3] Qazzāq Sulṭān was Muḥammad K̲h̲an's son, and J'afar was his grandson. Qazzāq, called in the *Ma'āṣir*, Qazzāq K̲h̲ān, rebelled against Ṭahmāsp in 972, and his son Ja'far emigrated to India. (Blochmann, 426).

[4] Lit. on no account let there be any unfriendly glances. *Wujūh* not *wuhūh* as in text.

[5] I adopt *k̲h̲ud* after *fauj*, from Bāyazīd.

[6] *Kas̲h̲āk* or *kas̲h̲īk*.

he (Humāyūn) may come, and care be taken that that officer render his service. Let entertainments be so conducted that the total of the food, sweetmeats and liquids be not less than 1,500 dishes. The service of, and attendance on the asylum of sovereignty, will be in charge of the asylum of dominion up to Mas͟hhad, the pure and holy. And when the officers aforesaid come to serve, every day there will be produced in the sublime banquet of that king, 1,200 dishes of varied food, such as may be fit for a royal table. And let each of the aforesaid officers, on the day when he is host, tender a present of nine horses, of which three will be for the king's special use, one for the chief *amīr* Muḥ. Bairām K͟hān Bahādur,[1] and the five others for such of the select officers as may be fitting. Let all nine horses be produced for his auspicious inspection, and mention which of them are for the fortunate *Nawwāb*, and also mention which is for such and such an officer,—that having been previously arranged by you,—for such statement, though it may appear improper, is right and will not look wrong; but by every possible means keep the servants in attendance pleased, and show the utmost sympathy and assiduity. Soothe the hearts of this body of men which have been clouded somewhat by the revolutions of unequal fate, with affection and sympathy, as is proper and pleasing at such seasons. Continue this practice throughout till they come to our presence. Thereafter, what is proper will be executed by ourselves. After food has been partaken of, let sweetmeats and comfits[2] prepared from candy (*qand*) and refined sugar (*nabāt*), and various conserves, and *ris͟hta-i-k͟haṭāī*[3]
(Chinese threads), which shall have been perfumed with rose-water, 209

---

[1] Bāyazīd has Bahārlū, which seems preferable.

[2] *Pālūda* or *fālūda*, the same as *ḥalwā*, except that the *sūjī* is boile in milk. Herklots. App.

[3] China or Cathay threads, apparently resembling vermicelli. See Vullers II. 39, and *Bahār-i-'ajam*. Steingass says they are a kind of paste lozenge eaten in soup, but this hardly agrees with the long description quoted by Vullers. They were made of rice flour, were very thin, like silk threads and were flavoured with almonds, pistachios, rose water, &c. In the B. M. Sloane, 4093, (Rieu I, 391*a*), which is a similar letter of Ṭahmāsp, but addressed to 'Alī Qulī K͟hān S͟hāmlū, the governor of Sīstān, the expression *ris͟hta-i-k͟haṭāī* is not used, but we have the apparently nearly synonymous phrase *ās͟h-i-māhca*. Vullers 1132*a*.

musk [1] and grey [2] ambergris, be brought in. The governor of the province [3] (*wilāyat*) after performing the duties of service and hospitality, shall put his mind at ease about his province, and escort (his Majesty) up to Herāt, the capital, not omitting the most minute points of service and attendance. When he shall arrive at twelve *farsakhs* from the said province,[4] the asylum of dominion (*i. e.*, the governor) will leave one of his experienced officers [5] in charge of our dear and excellent son, that he may take care of the city and wait on the son. The remainder of the victorious army from the city and province, and its boundaries, consisting of the Hazāra,[6] Nikodārī and others, to the number of thirty thousand, which number must be exact, shall go forth with the asylum of dominion to offer welcome. Tents, awnings and necessary furnitures will be conveyed by strings of camels and mules, so that a well-ordered camp may come under the Emperor's auspicious glance. When (the governor) is honoured by attendance on his Majesty he will, before making any other remarks, convey to him many prayers for his welfare on behalf of ourselves. And on the same day that he be distinguished by service he will halt in accordance with the rules (*tuzak*) and regulations of an army in camp. The asylum of dominion, when he has come on duty, will request leave, in order that he may entertain his Majesty, and will establish himself for three days in those quarters. On the first day he will invest all his (Humāyūn's) troops with handsome *khil'ats* of satin and brocade (*kamkhāb*) from Yezd, and of silk (*dārā'īhā*) of Mashhad and Khāf, and let them all have velvet cloaks (*bālāpōsh*),[7] and let there be given to every soldier and servant two Tabrīzī *tūmāns* [8]

---

[1] The musk here referred to seems to be a vegetable product.

[2] *'Ambar-i-ashhab*. This was the best kind. Blochmann 78.

[3] Probably a general order for the governors of all the provinces passed through.

[4] Apparently meaning, when Humāyūn arrives within 12 leagues, or about 50 miles, of the city of Herāt.

[5] *Uimāq*. Blochmann 371*n*, where it is stated that the word was originally the name of a Turkish tribe. See also Jarrett, II. 401*n*. 4 and III. 117*n*. The meaning here seems to be a confidential subordinate. Is Aimāq the right reading? Shaw gives this as a tribe near Herāt.

[6] Jarrett II. 401*n*. 4.

[7] The word also means a quilt, but here probably a cloak or upper garment.

[8] Wollaston, (App.), says the *tūmān* is a gold coin worth about eight shillings, but that it used to

for his daily expenses; and provide varied food in accordance with the rules already prescribed. And let there be a royal assemblage, so that tongues may speak in praise of it and shouts of approbation reach the ears of mankind. Let there be made a list of his troops, and let it be sent to the sublime court. Let 2,500[1] Tabrīzī *tūmāns* be taken from the funds of the Privy Purse which are coming to the said capital, and let them be spent for necessary purposes. Let the utmost zeal be displayed in service, and let the march from the said quarters to the city occupy four days, and let the entertainment of each day be the same as on the first. And it is proper that at every entertainment the honoured sons of the asylum of dominion bind, like servants and waiters, girdles of service on their loins and perform worshipful ministration, and that, in thanksgiving that such a king, who is a gift from the gifts of God, has become our guest, they display the utmost alacrity in service; and do not let there be any failure, for the more zeal and devotion are displayed in respect of his Majesty, the more will be the approval by us. And on the day before he will reach the city, let there be erected at the head of the avenue (*k͟hiyābān*) of the Bāg͟h 'Īdgāh tents with crimson satin on the inside, fine[2] linen between, and Ispahān linen (*miṣqālī*) on the top, which, during these days, was reported as being pre-
pared. And let care be taken that at every place where his 210
Majesty's gracious heart may take pleasure, and in every flower-garden that may be remarkable for its air, its streams, its amenities and delights, his Majesty be approached by you in an agreeable way, with the hand of respect placed servant-wise on the bosom, and that it be represented to him that that camp and army and all its paraphernalia are a present (*pēs͟hkas͟h*) to the fortunate Nawwāb. Also, while on the march, do you continually keep him pleased by conversation of a reassuring character. And do you yourself on the day before he will arrive at the city, leave that station

---

be worth much more, and in the time of S͟hāh 'Abbās I. was worth £3. Jahāngīr, quoted by Blochmann, 486, makes the Persian *tūmān* about equal to Rs. 33. If so, it might be compared with a gold mohur. But probably it was a silver coin that the soldiers received.

[1] The MS. has 10,500. The letter in Or. 4678 says that from first to last 10,000 *tūmāns* are to be expended.

[2] *Ṭaiyābī*. One MS. has Ṭabasī, *i. e.*, of the town of Tabas, and perhaps this is correct.

after obtaining your dismissal, and proceed to serve our son. Next morning bring out the dear son from his residence for the purpose of giving a welcome. Put on him the suit which we sent him last year on New Year's day, and leaving one of the grey-bearded confidential officers of the Taklū family (*Uīmāq-i-taklū*) who may be approved of and trusted by the asylum of dominion, in the capital, mount the son on horseback. And, for the time that he is proceeding to the city, let the asylum of dominion place Qazzāq Sulṭān on duty (with Humāyūn), and let[1] tents and camels and horses be presented, so that, when the fortunate Nawwāb mounts his horse next day, the camp may also march, and let the aforesaid[2] asylum of dominion be the guide. When the son shall come out of the city, strive that all the troops mount in the prescribed order,[3] and that they proceed towards the welcoming. When near that king, the Court of Majesty, *viz.*, when the space intervening be an arrow's flight, let the asylum of dominion advance and beg the king not to dismount. If he agree,[4] let him return immediately and dismount the happy son, and let the last go quickly and kiss the thigh and stirrup of that king of Solomon's Court and show all the points of service and respect and honour which are possible. Should the fortunate Nawwāb not agree, and should he dismount, let the son dismount before him and do homage and, his Majesty having first mounted, let our son kiss the king's hand and mount, and proceeding on thus, ride according to etiquette to the camp and the fixed quarters. And let the asylum of dominion be in attendance on the king, and close to the son, so that, if the king should put any questions to the son, and the son, out of bashfulness, be unable to reply, the asylum of dominion may make a proper reply. And in the quarters aforesaid let that son show hospitality to the king according to this routine, *viz.*, at about 9 A.M. let 300 dishes of varied foods be at once presented by way of refection. Between the two prayers (at midday) let 1,200 courses of varied foods be presented on *langarī* dishes known as *muḥammad*

---

[1] *Cādar*, perhaps veils or canopies for the women; as one does not see why tents should be required for the marching.

[2] Bāyazīd has "the asylum of dominion" (*i.e.*, Sharafu-d-dīn) *and* the aforesaid, *viz.*, Qazzāq Sulṭān, and this is probably correct.

[3] Text, *shān*, but most MSS. have *sān*, order or procession.

[4] Bāyazīd inserts here the word *fabihā*, *i. e.*, "good" or "Be it so."

*khānī*, and also on other plates of porcelain, gold and silver, placing covers of gold and silver over them. After that, let sweet conserves, such as may be available, and sweetmeats and comfits—be pre- 211
sented. After that let seven handsome and good horses be taken from the son's stables, and velvet and satin trimmings be placed on them, with girths of fine linen woven with silk, and let white girths be placed on red, and black girths on green velvet housings. It is proper that Ḥāfiẓ Ṣābir Qāq,[1] Maulānā Qāsim Qānūnī, the harpist, Ustād Shāh Muḥammad,[2] the hautbois player, Ḥāfiẓ Dōst Muḥammad Khāfī, Ustād Yūsuf *Maudūd*,[3] and other famous singers and musicians who may be in the city, be always present, and whenever his Majesty desire it, please him by singing and playing. And let everyone from far and near who may be worthy of that assemblage be in attendance so that he may be present when called upon, and that they may by every possible means make his hours pleasant to him. Further let gerfalcons[4] (*shunqār*), and hawks, saker[5] (*cargh*), sparrow hawks[6] (*bāsha*), royal[7] falcons (*shāhīn*), peregrine[8] falcons (*baḥrī*) and the like which may be in the son's establishment, or that of the asylum of dominion or his sons, be presented, and let all his servants have silk *khil'ats* of every kind and colour suitable to each—coloured velvets, waved silks (*khārā*[9]) and *takma-kalābattūn*,[10] and gold brocade. And on arrival at the quarters, let his servants be brought before our son, who shall, with the munificent ways which are hereditary with him from his ancestors, entertain them, giving each a suit of clothes and a horse befitting his condition, and let not the largesse (to each) exceed three *tūmāns*. Also let twelve times nine pieces of silk, includ-

---

1 Bāyazīd has Ṣābir Qāf. Does this mean one who has control over the Koran, *i.e.*, who knows it off by heart. The last three names in this list, *i.e.*, Ḥāfiẓ Dōst, &c., are not in Bāyazīd.

2 Blochmann, 613.

3 Apparently a *nom de plume* and meaning the beloved or the ecstatic :—from *wadd*.

4 Also spelt *shūnqār*,—the *Falco Hendersoni*, (Scully, App. 2, Shaw's Vocabulary.)

5 The Saker, or Cherugh of Jerdon.

6 *Accipiter nisus*; it is the female.

7 *Falco peregrinator* of Jerdon I. 25; it is the female.

8 Scully l. c. See also list of hawks in Burnes' Travels, and the account of hawking in the *Āīn*. (Blochmann, 293, *et seq.*)

9 Moirée antique. Blochmann, 92*n*.

10 *Kālābatūn* of Blochmann, 91*n*., who says it is a stuff with gold and silk threads.

ing velvet, satin, European and Yezdī *kamkhāb*, and *bāfta-shāmī* (Syrian cloth) and other choice materials (be taken), and let three hundred gold *tūmāns* be placed in thirty purses, together with the silk aforesaid, and let there be given to every soldier and servant [1] three Tabrīzī *tūmāns*, which are equal to 600 *shāhī*.[2] Let him spend three days in the Avenue and in the underground-channel country (*kārīzgāh*). And order that, during these three days, various artificers make a *cahār-tāq-bandī* [3] from the gate of the Cahār Bāgh which is a royal palace, to the Avenue which is in the Bāgh 'Īdgāh. And let one of the officers aforesaid be a coadjutor with each artificer, so that by their mutual rivalry every craft and excellent device may be executed. This is excellent that, as the king hath exalted this country by his distinguished advent, he should first come to a city which is the light of the eyes of mankind. Let there then be brought before his alchemic eye genial and sweet-spoken persons, such as are in this city, so that he may have cause for cheerfulness. On the third day when your mind shall be at rest with regard to the *cahār-tāq*, the City-Avenue, and the brightening up of the Cahār Bāgh let heralds
212 be appointed in the city, its wards, and the environs, and the neighbouring villages, to proclaim that all the men and women of the city shall assemble on the morning of the fourth day in the Avenue (*khiyābān*), and that in every shop and *bāzār*, where carpets and cloths shall be spread in order, the women and maidens [4] will be seated, and, as is the rule in that city, the women will eng‸ge in pleasant [5]

[1] The text does not seem quite correct here. All the I.O. MSS. have *lashkarī* and not merely *lashkar* and the proper reading seems to be *lashkarī u ba har nafar*. The account about the *tūmāns* is not clear. Perhaps the 300 gold *tūmāns* were a special present to Humāyūn. And perhaps the 30 purses were to be made of the silk.

[2] The *shāhī* is worth about a half penny, so that if the *tūmān* be reckoned at 8/8 three would be about equal to 600 *shāhī*. The figures in the text are, however, doubtful.

[3] An erection with four domes; a quadrangular tent, or canopy, apparently.

[4] Text, *beghi*, i. e., chiefs, but I take the word to be *baikahā*, i. e., maidens from بيكه *beka* which P. de Courteille renders *femme non mariée*.

[5] *Dar maqām-i-shīrīn kārī u shīrīn gūī dar āyand*. One of the meanings of *maqām* is a musical tone, and *kār* and *kāthā* are used by Bābar to mean airs or melodies. See his Memoirs, Erskine 197 and 198, and notes. So possibly all that is meant here is that the women were to recite

sayings and doings with the comers and goers. And from every ward and lane let the masters[1] of melody come forth, so that the like of it will not be seen in any other city of the world. And bid all the people come forth to offer welcome. After all this has been arranged, let the king be respectfully asked to put the foot of dominion in the stirrup of auspiciousness, and to mount on horseback. Our son will proceed alongside of his Majesty, but so that the head and neck of the latter's horse be in front.[2] You, the asylum of dominion, will follow close behind, so that, if he should put any questions about the buildings, the palaces, and gardens, you may make suitable reply. And when he shall come with auspiciousness to the city, he will visit the Cahār Bāgh. And let him alight in the small garden which was made at the time of our residence in that delicious city for the purpose of our living there and of reading and writing, and which is at present known by the name of Bāgh Shāhī. And make the baths in the Cahār Bāgh white and clean, and also the other baths, and make them fragrant with rose-water and musk, so that, whenever he is inclined, he may have a place for bodily repose.

On the first day our son will show hospitality with abundance of provisions, and when he shall have gone to his repose, you, the asylum of dominion, will display hospitality in the manner that will be described below.[3] When he (Humāyūn) enters the city, you will

---

and sing to the passers by. Most likely, however, the word *kārī* refers to dancing. See Vambéry's History of Bokhara, p. 242, note, where he describes a dance known as the Herātī. Mōhan Lāl, Burnes' *munshī*, rather maliciously observes that all the women of Herāt know how to sing and dance, but show these accomplishments neither to their husbands nor to their relations, but merely to their friends.

[1] This might mean women as well as men.

[2] The letter in B. M. MS. Or. 467 is still more explicit. The head of the prince's horse is to be on a line with Humāyūn's stirrup, and the head of the tutor's horse on a line with the prince's stirrup.

[3] A. F. appears to have missed out some words here. In Bāyazīd 96, we have "On the first day our son will show his Majesty abundant and excellent hospitality, and at night when he (the son) shall have gone to rest, the asylum of dominion (Sharafu-d-dīn) will call the great officers into his presence and direct that each one of them shall entertain the king who is favoured by God, one day in one of the gardens. On two other days, the son will entertain him, and after that the asylum of

make a report on the same day and despatch it to the sublime court. And let it be arranged that Mu'izzu-d-dīn Ḥusain *kalāntar* (magistrate), of Herāt, appoint a good writer who is a man of experience, to write a full diary from the day that the 500 make the reception (*istiqbāl*) to the day that he comes to the city, and let it be sealed and despatched by the asylum of dominion, and let all the stories and remarks, good or bad, which pass in the assemblage, be reduced to writing and be sent by the hands of trusty persons, so that we [1] be fully informed of all that occurs.

The entertaining by the asylum of dominion will be as follows :— Three thousand dishes of food, sweetmeats, syrups (*shīra*) and fruits will be prepared, and the necessary furniture will be arranged as follows :—*First*, fifty tents and twenty awnings, and the large store-tent [2] which was reported to have been prepared for his Majesty's special use, with twelve pairs of carpets of twelve cubits and ten cubits, and seven pairs of carpets of five cubits, nine
231 strings of female camels, 250 porcelain plates, large and small, and other plates and pots, all with bright covers, and also tinned (*qalqal'ī karda*), and two strings of mules let the asylum of dominion present on the occasion of his entertainment; and let the officers conduct their entertainments as follows :—Let them present food, sweetmeats and comfits to the extent of 1,500 plates, and also three horses, a string of camels and a string of mules, which shall have first been seen and approved by the asylum of dominion. The governors of Ghūrīān, Fūshanj,[3] and Karshū will show hospitality in their own country. The governor of Bākharz,[4] in Jām, and the governors of Khāf, Tarshīz,[5] Zāwahā and Muḥawwalāt [6]

---

dominion will himself entertain him according to the method which will now be described. When he (Hūmayūn) enters the city, &c."

1 The *iẓāfat* after *auẓā'* in text seems wrong. By the phrase *Nawwāb humāyūn-i-mā* Ṭahmāsp means himself. See text 207, 1.10.

2 *Cādar-i-buzurg alābata.* Qu. *ablat* or *abtāt*, Persian *batāt*, provisions. See Lane 148c. Perhaps it is what Abū'l-faẓl calls in the *Āīn*, (Blochmann, 48.) offices and workshops (*buyūtāt*).

3 Bushang of Yāqūt. Jarrett III. 87.

4 Macgregor's Khurāsān I. 253 and II. 146.

5 Blochmann 605*n*. and Macgregor's map, Jarrett III. 86*n*. It is a dependency of Nīshāpūr.

6 Macgregor II. 145, Muḥawwalāt etymologically means barren tracts.

will entertain at Sarāī Farhād which is five *parasangs*[1] from Mashhad.[2]

---

[1] Written *farsangī* here. It is *farsakhī* earlier in the letter.

[2] This letter seems to have been greatly admired and appears in several collections of letters. It also appears in the *Ma'āsir-i-rahīmī* but merely as a copy from the *Akbarnāma*. Erskine thinks that A. F. copied it from Bāyazīd, and this is very likely. There are occasional omissions and alterations in A. F.'s transcript which were probably made by him as improvements, or to show that he was not a servile copyist. Thus A. F. omits in one place the title *Jannat-āshiyānī* which in Bāyazīd is given by Ṭahmāsp to his own father, Ismā'īl, but which perhaps A. F. considered too sacred to be applied to anybody but Humāyūn. Then in the list of Humāyūn's titles at the beginning of the letter we have in Bāyazīd after the words "*'adl-gustarī*," (dispenser of justice), and before the words *khāqān-i-sikandar-nishān*—the jingling addition of *ṣāḥib-i-dev-u-parī*, lord of demons and fairies, which A. F. perhaps omitted as not being sufficiently dignified. On the other hand, A. F. gives the names of three persons who are to entertain Humāyūn, which do not occur in Bāyazīd.

Bāyazīd says the document was produced on 20th Rajab, 1000 H. by Mīr Mirdād Juvīnī, *dārōgha* of the records, and that he made an exact copy of it. Probably he did, for at the end he seems also to have copied an endorsement or other writing on the document to the effect that in 990 A. H. a copy was taken for the *Tārīkh-i-alfī*, (Record of a thousand years). Possibly, however, this was an endorsement made simultaneously with Bāyazīd's copy and meant to show that the copy was made for Bāyazīd's use in connection with the *Tārīkh-i-alfī*. The 990 may be the era of the *riḥlat* or death of Muḥammad which was adopted by Akbar for this work, and which began ten years after the Hijra. I have examined the copy of the second volume of the *Tār.-i-alfī* in the B. M. Or. 465, but the letter is not in it. Indeed the events of Humāyūn's reign are very cursorily referred to, and as if it was contemplated that they should be dealt with separately by A. F.

In his introduction to the letter, Bāyazīd tells us that Humāyūn took counsel with Aḥmad Sulṭān about visiting the Shāh, and that Aḥmad recommended him to go by Tabaskilakī as being the shortest, but that Humāyūn said that life was uncertain, and that as he had heard much praise of Herāt (perhaps from his parents) he would like to go that way. So he went by Ūk and there was met by 'Alī Sulṭān, a relation of Sharafu-d-dīn. Both Aḥmad Sulṭān and Sharafu-d-dīn wrote to Ṭaḥmāsp and received replies.

In B.M.MS. Or. 4678, Rieu's Cat. Supplement, there is at p. 117*b et seq.*, a letter from Ṭaḥmāsp to Sharafu-d-dīn which closely resembles that given by A. F., but still is

When his Majesty Jahānbānī Jannat-āshiyānī came near Farāh,[1] the Shāh's ambassador and his Majesty's messenger arrived, and his Majesty was made aware that the king of Persia regarded his advent as a great gain and was delighted at it. His Majesty, being a mine of courtesy, could not resist going to 'Irāq and so pleasing his faithful companions. He placed the foot of resolve in the stirrup of dominion and went on with a firm determination towards Herāt. At every stage some one of the notables and grandees of Khurāsān came out to meet him, and waited upon him as if he had been one of his own confidential courtiers. The sound of the royal cortege opened the gates of joy for the inhabitants, and the people of many towns, such as Jām,[2] Turbat,[3] Sarakhas,[4] Isfarāīn,[5] came to Herāt in expectation of the sublime advent. When the couriers of Tātār[6] Sulṭān, and of the nobles of Khurāsān, who had gone forth to welcome him, reported to Muḥammad Khān that the sublime procession had come near the Ziyāratgāh[7] the latter himself came out, accompanied by the nobles such as Wais Sulṭān, Shāh Qulī Sulṭān and the distinguished men of learning such as Mīr Murtaẓā Ṣadr, Mīr Ḥusain of Kerbalā and other excellent persons, and by the people generally. At the head of the Bridge of Mālān,[8] which is a famous resort in Herāt, they

far from being the same letter. It seems to be dated Wednesday, 5th Shawwāl 950, unless indeed that be the date of Sharafu-d-dīn's letter which is being replied to.

[1] Or Farrāh, 164 miles S. of Herāt. See *Tār. Rash*. 205 and Meynard's *Yāqūt*, 420. It is in Sīstān, and is now under Afghanistan. Hunter's I. G. I. 35.

[2] Halfway between Herāt and Mashhad.

[3] Probably Turbat-i-Ḥaidarī, S. of Mashhad.

[4] N.-N.-W. Herāt, on road to Merv and a long way from Herāt. Perhaps Carakhs is meant.

[5] This too is a remote place S. of Burjnaid and N. W. of Nīshāpūr. Also called Mihrjān, Jarrett III. 85.

[6] Not mentioned in Ṭahmāsp's letter as given by A. F., but in the copy in Or. 4678 Tātār Beg is directed to be sent out to welcome Humāyūn.

[7] There are many shrines near Herāt. I do not know which this is. See Yates's Notes on Herāt, J. A. S. B. 56 for 1887, p. 84.

[8] Bābar's Mem. 207*n*. Erskine says, Mālān is the name of the river that passes Herāt coming from the east. If so, it is another name for the Harī Rūd. It is also spelt Mālīn, Jarrett III. 87. Conolly II. 51 says, "Four miles from the city we crossed the Herirood by a long bridge of brick called Pool-i-Moulaun, which gives a name to the river. So much of the water had been drawn off

met him and conveyed to him the S͟hāh's felicitations and those respectful greetings which are magnanimity's essence. It had already been arranged that the roads should be swept and watered from the Mālān Bridge up to the Jahānārā Garden, and that the grandees and the ingenious men (*ẓurafā*) [1] of the city should come from either side and wait upon him. When the royal party arrived at a certain [2] stage Sulṭān Muḥammad Mīrzā came and welcomed him, and paid his reverential respects. That fortunate Prince and the other great officers treated him with all honour and respect. From the Ziyāratgāh 214
to Pul-i-Mālān, and from thence to the Jahānārā Garden—a distance of three or four leagues, the whole plain and the heights were filled with spectators from the city and the villages, and the crowd and the rejoicings were such as never occur but at the 'Īd and on New Year's day. On 1st Zīlqa'da,[3] 950 (27th January, 1544), he alighted at Bāg͟h Jahānārā. Muḥammad K͟hān gave a royal feast and tendered large presents. At the first assembly Ṣābir Qāq, the foremost reciter in K͟hurāsān and 'Irāq, chanted an ode of Amīr S͟hāhī [4] to the air *Sihgāh* [5] so that even rapt devotees were moved by it. In truth it was very appropriate and affecting. It began thus—

> "Blest the abode to which such a moon hath come,
> August the world where there is such a king."

When he came to the verse

> "Be nor grieved nor glad at terrestrial pain or pleasure
> For the world is sometimes this and sometimes that"

---

above, that the stream here was inconsiderable, but it was swift, and clear as a diamond." Mohan Lāl says it had 33 arches, but now only 27.

[1] I adopt the variant. The text has *s͟hurafā* nobles.

[2] Perhaps it should be "the stage of Darqarā."

[3] I have already remarked that this date seems wrong. It is also inconsistent with A. F.'s statement that the Persian New Year was near at hand for that occurs in the middle of March.

[4] A Persian poet of the first half of the 15th century. Rieu 640*a*.

[5] *Sih kāh* in text. *Sihgāh*, *i. e.*, three times, is the name of an air. *Vide* Vullers II. 354*b*. and the Burhān-i-Qāṭi'. Bābar p. 19 speaks of the Cārgāh key. I think the reference is to a musical air, but the words, which are *darmaqām-i-sih kāh*, may mean a place, *viz.*, the Kāhdastān, *Tār. Rash.* 206*n.*, and Bābar 207 who mentions both the bridge of Kāh and the Kāhdastān. For the use of the words *dar maqām*, to mean in the manner or fashion, see above p. 428, note 5.

His Majesty Jahānbānī was touched and deeply affected, and poured presents into the skirts of his hopes.

As Herāt and its sights pleased him much, and the New Year festival was at hand he stayed several days there. Whenever he rode out sight-seeing Muḥammad Khān was in attendance and paid his respects and scattered gold on each side of his Majesty. Every day he visited some famous spot, and on each occasion there was a joyous assemblage. Everything was managed on a prescribed plan. Sometimes his heart was solaced with the Kārīzgāh, (the place of underground channels) and sometimes the Bāgh Murād, the Bāgh Khiyābān, the Bāgh Zāghān,[1] and the Bāgh Safēd[2] were visited. In every flowering spot there were particoloured assemblages. Also on these days he visited the shrines of the great saints, especially that[3] of Khwāja 'Abdullāh Anṣārī, the Saint of Herāt. May his grave be holy! Ascetics, religious persons, lofty-souled men and famous men of learning were honoured by his company.

When the festivities of the New Year were over and the places of recreation had been visited, he proceeded towards Holy Mashhad by the way of Jām. At this time Aḥmad Sulṭān, Governor of Sīstān,
215 who had accompanied his Majesty hitherto, took leave to go to his own province. On 5th Zīlḥajja[4] he reached Jām and visited the shrine of His Highness Zhinda Pīl Aḥmad-i-Jām. When he approached Mashhad Shāh Qulī Sulṭān Istajlū who was the governor of the province, came out to welcome him, accompanied by the leading

---

[1] Bābar 207, *Tār. Rash.* 83.

[2] Bābar l. c.

[3] Yates l. c. p. 100, &c. It is at a place called Gazargāh (Bleaching ground) which is said by Major Raverty to derive its name from being a graveyard, *i. e.*, a place where bones are bleached. It is at the foot of the hills and some two miles north-east of the city. Yates, 83 and Conolly II. 24.

[4] =29th February, 1544, but I think this must be a mistake for 5th Muḥarram =29th March, 1544. We are told immediately below that Humāyūn arrived at Mashhad on 15th Muḥarram, and surely he would hardly have taken six weeks to get there from Jām. Besides we are told that he spent the Persian New Year at Herāt which he could not have done if he had left it in February. If the date given in J. R. A. S. for January, 1897, p. 47, be correct, Humāyūn must have paid a second visit to Jām some ten months later, for the date of the inscription put up by him there is 14th Shawwāl, 951= 29th December, 1544.

Saiyids, and all paid their respects. On 15th Muḥarram, 951, he reached Holy Mashhad and visited the shrine of (Imām) Rizavī,—may the blessing of God be upon him! He spent some days in the precincts of that noble building. Thence he went to Nīshāpūr. Shamsu-d-dīn 'Alī Sulṭān, who governed there, came with great and small and paid his respects, and was prompt with various services. His Majesty visited the turquoise[1] mines in that neighbourhood, and from thence went to Sabzawār and from thence to Dāmaghān. Among the marvellous things of that place is an ancient fountain[2] which has a talisman from of old, to wit, whenever any dirty thing falls into the fountain a storm arises, and the sky grows dark from the force of the wind and the dust. This too he examined with the eye of prescience. How many things are there not in the wondrous workshop of the Creator, the understanding of which does not come within the scope of our thoughts and imaginings? From Dāmaghān he went on to Bisṭām[3] and as the shrine of Baḥrṭamī[4] Shaikh Bayāzīd Bisṭāmī (may his grave be sanctified) was not on the line of road he turned aside to visit it. From thence he proceeded

[1] These still exist. Reclus ix. 225. They are at a place called Ma'din, *i.e.*, the mine, N.-W. Nīshāpūr

[2] D'Herbelot s. v. Bādkhaneh. In Eastern Persia by Goldsmid and others, p. 381. We find the following, "Ferrier has written of the high wind so prevalent here. The Persians say that it is occasioned by a mystic spring in the mountain about two *farsakhs* off which, the moment anything dirty is thrown into it, causes a tremendous gale to blow, which lasts several days, till the spring is purified, and a sentry is always kept at the well to prevent tampering with its waters. It is said that when the Shāh passed through Dāmghān *en route* for Mashhad, being incredulous of the story he ordered some of his suite to throw dirt into the spring when immediately such a wind arose that the royal camp was rolled up like so much paper, and the Shāh was compelled to have the cistern completely cleaned out and purified before the wind would cease." Dāmaghān is supposed to be the old capital of the Parthians, the Hecatompylos of the Greeks. It may be noted that Bābar, 149, tells a story about a fountain in Ghaznī, similar to that about the one in Dāmaghān.

[3] Jarrett III. 85*n*. and Meynard 104. It is N. Shāhrūd..

[4] *i. e.* swelling ocean. Bayāzīd belongs to the 8th and 9th century A.D. Jarrett III. 352 and 359, and Khazīna-al-Aṣfīyā I. 519. He was a very famous saint and the founder of a religious order.

towards Samnān [1] and halted at Ṣūfīābād [2] where is the tomb of Shaikh 'Alāu-d-daula Samnānī (may his grave be sanctified!).

Whether on the march or when halting, it was his Majesty's excellent practice to visit the shrines of Divine worshippers and to seek inspiration from the mental and physical circumambulation of the awakened of heart.[3] At every station that he reached the governors and grandees came forward to do him homage and on many occasions there came from the Shāh affectionate messages and splendid presents.

As the cavalcade reached Rey [4] the Shāh left Qazwīn with the intention of going into summer quarters and proceeded towards Sulṭāniya [5] and Ṣūrlīq. His Majesty Jahānbānī halted at Qazwīn,[6] which was at that time the Shāh's capital. The grandees and inhabitants generally came out to welcome him. He remained some days there, visiting the remarkable buildings and holy places in the city, and taking up his abode in the house of Khwāja 'Abdulghanī who was the city Magistrate (*Kalāntar*) and where the Shāh had for-
216 merly resided. From there he sent Bairām Khān to the Shāh, whose cortége had nearly reached its destination when Bairām Khān arrived. He conveyed his message and then returned from that stage [7] with joyful foot. Thereafter his Majesty proceeded to Sulṭāniya. The Shāh was encamped between Abhar [8] and Sulṭāniya. When his Majesty arrived near that residence the great officers came, one after the other, and paid their respects. After that Bahrām Mīrzā and

---

[1] Jarrett III. 85 and Meynard 317.

[2] Apparently there is some mistake here. Ṣūfīābad lies far to the east of Samnān and Bisṭām, and would naturally be reached by Humāyūn before them. It is N. Sabzawār and N.-W. Nīshāpūr.

[3] Jarrett III. 376. He was a famous Ṣūfī and author of a book on religion, and also of one on general history. He died 736 A.H. (1336); see Rieu Cat. I. 413*a*.

[4] Meynard 273 and Jarrett III. 84. It is the Rāgas of the Book of Tobit.

[5] Jarrett III. 83.

[6] Meynard 441.

[7] Firishta calls the place Bīlāq-i-Qadār (the name of the son of Ishmael). There is unconscious irony in A. F.'s remarks. If Jauhar's account, Stewart 62, is to be trusted, Bairām had cause to be glad that he got away safely from the Shāh's presence.

[8] Bāyazīd says the meeting was in Zangān. Badāonī I. 444, calls it Ilāq Sūrtāq. Abhar is W. Qazwīn and is described by Chardin. See also Meynard 11 and Jarrett III. 83.

Sām Mīrzā, the Shāh's honoured brothers came and welcomed him. In Jumāda-al-awwal, 951 (July, 1544), the Shāh himself welcomed [1] him with all the observances of respect and honour, and had an interview with him in which all the conditions of reverence and veneration were fulfilled. In a noble palace, on the gilding of which skilful artists had long been engaged and in which they had displayed miracles [2] of craftmanship, an enchanting picture-gallery received its inauguration by the interview with his Majesty Jahānbānī. A regal assemblage took place, and in accordance with the canons of magnanimity and the requirements of condolence and exalted inquiries after welfare there was sympathy and mutual discourse. The gates of sincerity and honouring having been unclosed, those of sociability and gaiety opened of themselves, and high converse ensued. Mīrzā Qāsim [3] of Gūnābād in his book of poems (Masnavī) in which the Shāh is celebrated has spoken as follows of the interview between those two illustrious potentates:—

*Verse.*

Two Lords of Conjunction in one banquet-hall
Made a syzygy like the sun and moon,
Two lustrous visions for Fortune's eye,
Two blessed 'Īd for month and year,
Two stars making heaven resplendent
Side by side in one spot like the Farqadain, [4]
Two eyes of the world in companionship
Joining in courtesy like two eye-brows,
Two auspicious portents in one sign (*burj*),
Two glorious pearls in one casket (*darj*).

---

[1] *Istiqbāl farmūda*, as if Ṭahmāsp had gone forward to meet Humāyūn, but according to Jauhar, who was probably an eyewitness, the only *istiqbāl* made by Ṭahmāsp was his advancing to the edge of the carpet.

[2] *Yad-i-baiẓā*, lit. a white hand, the reference being to the transfigured hand of Moses.

[3] A Persian poet with the title of Qāsimī. Rieu Cat. 660*a* and 661*b*, and Blochmann 591. Gūnābād is the Jūnābiz of Yāqūt, Meynard 165. It belongs to the province of Nīshāpūr. The form Gūnābād is said to be wrong. It lies S. Nīshāpūr and nearly due W. Herāt. Qāsimī wrote a poetical history (Shāhnāma) of Shāh Isma'īl and another of his son Ṭahmāsp.

[4] The two calves, the name of two bright stars near the Pole, $\beta$ and $\gamma$ of Ursa Minor. Lane 2387*a*.

The Shāh observed "The glorious Creator and Bestower of Worlds made the conquest of India, achieved by his Majesty Gītī-sitānī Firdūs-makānī, the key of the treasure-house of universal sway for your world-compassing sword. Every failure and infirmity which hath in these days appeared in administration and world-rule arose from the disservice and discord of disloyal brothers. Over this you had no control. In mundane affairs fraternal unanimity is
217 of high import, and is a disentangler of perplexities. In this present regard ourselves as your younger [1] brother and know us to be a helper and a supporter, for—our life on it—we shall succour you to the height of your desire. We acknowledge old ties, and shall fulfil whatever assistance may be necessary. Should we be required to go in person as your auxiliary we will go." He spoke many sincere words and such as bore the impress of magnanimity. For several days they held Cyrus-like festivities. His Majesty the Shāh entered personally into all the arrangements, and every day had a novel entertainment. There was increase of formal and spiritual beauty, and day by day he waxed more and more friendly and affectionate. How can feasts be described when so great a Shāh was in his own person the caterer? What gold-embroidered velvet and silken [2] canopies there were and what numbers of wrought pavilions and lofty tents there were!

Far as the eye could reach, silken rugs and precious carpets were laid [3] out and thereby were spread pleasure and joy. What account can be given of how in the important matter of the distribution of presents and rareties he gave his personal attention to the subject? How tell of the choice horses of Media with embroidered and golden saddles and the splendid housings and trappings, of the adorned mules of Bard'a,[4] of the strangely [5] shaped camels, male or female, with valuable coverings, of the many scimitars and daggers set with jewels and the like, of the fine linen, and the robes (*pōstīn*) of the marten (*kesh*) and the red [6] fox, the ermine (*sanjāb*), and

---

[1] Ṭahmāsp was about eight years younger than Humāyūn.

[2] *Tāja bāf*, a kind of silk, Blochmann 93.

[3] There is a play on words here. Joy was spread out like a carpet.

[4] Apparently the name of a district in Persia.

[5] *Badī' paikar*. In *Āīn*, text I. 146, Blochmann 143, A. F. calls the camel *shigarf paikar*.

[6] *Jalghāra* in text, and there is

the squirrel[1] (*tīn*), and also the dresses of gold brocade, velvet, silk (*tāja*), satin, figured silks from Europe (*mushajjar-i-Firingī*), and Yezd, and Kāshān? Many basins, ewers, and candlesticks of gold and silver set with rubies and pearls, many gold and silver dishes, ornamented tents, grand carpets, the marvel of the age for size and beauty, and other regal articles were brought one by one before his Majesty's holy glance. Money and goods were distributed to all the followers, and royal courtesies were interchanged.

His Majesty Jahānbānī on the day of the great festival presented to the Shāh as the gift[2] of a traveller a diamond[3] of great value—worth the revenues of countries and climes, together with 250 Badakhshān rubies. Without a doubt, all the expenditure which the Shāh, whether from his privy purse, or through his officers, incurred on account of his Majesty Jahānbānī from the time of his entering the country to his exit therefrom was hereby repaid more than four times over. From thence they went to Sultāuīya and there held
Cyrus-like festivities. In the intervals between these glorious seasons 218
of fortunate conjunctions a cloudiness of heart was created on both sides through the instigation of sundry strife-mongers,[4] but the turbidity did not last long, and was washed away by the waters of cleansing. His Majesty the Shāh made every day new arrangements for pleasure and joy. Among other things he ordered the amusement of a hunting-drive (*shikār-i-qamargha*), and his army drove the beasts of the plain a ten days' journey up to a spring known as the Sāvūq Bulāq[5] which is the first stage of the Zailāq Bīlāq.[6] His

---

the variant *chalghāwa*. P. de Courteille has in his Dict. چلقاوه and translates "renard rouge, pelisse faite avec sa peau."

1 In Shaw's Turkī Dict. تیین tiyin is given as a Kazzāk word for a squirrel.

2 *Ba rasm-i-armaghānī*. See Burhān-i-Qāti'.

3 No doubt this was Bābar's diamond and probably the Koh-i-nūr. B. M. MS. Or. 153, p. 58*b*, says it was Bābar's diamond, and that it weighed 6½ misqāls, and that Shāh Tahmāsp afterwards sent it to Nizām Shāh ruler of the Deccan.

4 Referring to Bahrām Mīrzā, the Shāh's brother and also to some disloyal servants of Humāyūn. See Nizāmuddīn, Ferishta, Jauhar and also Badāōnī I. 444.

5 Bulāq means a spring in Tūrkī. Perhaps the correct name is Sūj Bulāq, *i. e.*, the cold spring. This is near the Takht-i-Sulaimān which is mentioned by Jauhar as the scene of a hunt.

6 Bīlāq means a garden and also

Majesty Jahānbānī and the Shāh entered the hunting-ground together and gave new lustre to the arts of horsemanship and game-slaying. After that Bahrām Mīrzā, Sām Mīrzā, and after them Bairām Khān, Ḥājī Muḥammad Kōkī, Shāh Qulī [1] Sulṭān Muhrdār (seal-keeper, or chancellor), Rōshan Kōka, Ḥasan Kōka, and many others of his Majesty Jahānbānī's trusty followers were permitted to enter the *qamargha*. Several of the Shāh's officers were bidden to enter, such as 'Abdālla Khān Istajlū, son-in-law of the great Shāh Isma'īl, Abūl Qāsim Khalfā, Sīūndak [2] Sulṭān, Qūrcī Bāshī Afshār, Badar Khān Istajlū and some others. After a time a general permission to enter was given. Everyone of the soldiers and troopers engaged in seizing and binding [3] the game. Meanwhile Bahrām Mīrzā, who had a grudge against the Khalfā intentionally [4] shot an arrow at him so that he died. Out of consideration for the Mīrzā no one mentioned this to the Shāh. After this troops were sent away in order that a fresh *qamargha* might be made at Sulaimān's [5] Pool (*Ḥauẓ-i-Sulaimān*). When they assembled, hunting, *more majorum*, was resumed, and here they spent some time also in playing [6] polo and in archery.[7] On this day as the archery was keen (lit. the *qabaq-*

an underground building used to avoid the heat.

[1] There seems some mistake here, for this man is mentioned by Bāyazīd as a servant of the Shāh. Blochmann has several Shāh Qulīs, but none of them is entitled Sulṭān. A. F. however later on, I. 266 gives this title to the Shāh Qulī who was Bairām's sister's son and became Khān Jahān. But he can hardly be the Shāh Qulī of the hunt for he had not then come from Qandahar. It would seem from Bāyazīd 176 that the person meant is Ḥusain Qulī brother of the Governor of Sīstān. Bāyazīd states that Humāyūn made him his seal-keeper when at Qandahar.

[2] Bāyazīd calls him Sūndak.

[3] The Lucknow ed. has *kushtan*, "killing."

[4] *Cf.* Elliot V. 219. Considering how easily an accident could occur (*vide* the story of Adrastus in Herodotus), and the dislike of Humāyūn's party for Bahrām, who seems to have given his brother good advice about Humāyūn, one feels inclined to think this charge of murder unfounded. Bāyazīd does not tax the Mīrzā with it. Nor apparently did Ṭahmāsp suspect his brother, and yet he must have heard of the occurrence.

[5] See Reclus ix. 185 and 252.

[6] *Caugānbāzī*. See A. F.'s account of the game in Blochmann 297.

[7] *Qabaqandāzī*. A kind of tilting at the ring, but the weapon used was an arrow. There is an allusion to this game in the Gulistān III. 27. See Vullers II. 710 for a full description of it, and also Dozy's Dict. s. v.

*bāzār* was hot) Bairām Beg received the title of Khān and Ḥājī Muḥammad Kōkī that of Sulṭan. At the close of this reunion the list [1] of the 12,000 [2] horse who had been designated to march with the Shāh's son Prince Murād as the king's auxiliaries was presented to his Majesty together with the list of supplies which were to be despatched along with his Majesty Jahānbānī. The following is the list of the exalted persons who were appointed to take part in the great expedition :—

*List.*

1. Mīrzā Murād.
2. Badāgh Khān Qājār,[3] the Mīrzā's tutor.
3. Shāh Qulī Sulṭān Afshār, governor of Kirmān.
4. Aḥmad Sulṭān Shāmlū, son of Muḥammad Khalīfa.
5. Sanjāb Sulṭān Afshār, governor of Farāh.
6. Yār 'Alī Sulṭān Taklū.
7. Sulṭān 'Alī Afshār.
8. Sulṭān Qulī [4] Qūrcībāshī a relation of Muḥammad Khān (governor of Herat).
9. Ya'qūb Mīrzā, *taghāī* (maternal uncle) of Sulṭān Muḥammad Khudābanda (Ṭahmāsp's eldest son).
10. Sulṭān Ḥusain Qulī Shāmlū, brother of Aḥmad Sulṭān governor of Sīstān.
11. Adham Mīrzā, son of Dēō [5] Mīrzā.
12. Tahamtan Mīrzā, son of Dēō Sulṭān. 219
13. Ḥaidar Sulṭān Shaibānī.[6]
14 & 15. His sons 'Alī Qulī and Bahādur.
16. Maqṣūd Mīrzā Ākhta Begī, son of Zainu-d-dīn Sulṭān Shāmlū.

---

303*a*. *Qabaq*, it seems, properly means a gourd. Humāyūn's servants would be proficient at the game for they played it in India before the days of Sher Khān. See Khwāndamīr's Humāyūnnāma 149*b*, of B. M. MS. Or. 1762 Rieu Cat. 1024*a*.

[1] *Ṭūmār*. Possibly it here means review. Bāyazīd says that the *ṭūmār* of the stores was made over to Humāyūn's lieutenants (*wukalā*).

[2] 10,000 in Bāyazīd.

[3] Text *Qācār*.

[4] The 'Alī Sulṭān of Bāyazīd.

[5] 11 and 12 were brothers according to Bāyazīd so that Dēō Sulṭān and Dēō Mīrzā are one and the same person.

[6] Several MSS. have Sīstānī.

17. Muḥammadī Mirzā, grandson of Jahān Sh̲āh Mīrzā,[1] known as Sh̲āh Yezdī[2] Beg.

18. Kacal Iṣtajlū.

19. 'Alī Sulṭān Culāq,[3] sister's son of Muḥammad Kh̲ān.

20. Abū'l-fatḥ Sulṭān Afsh̲ār.

21. Ḥasan Sulṭān Sh̲āmlū.[4]

22. Yādgār Sulṭān Mōṣlū (*i. e.*, of Mōṣul).

23. Aḥmad Sulṭān Alāsh̲ Agh̲lī Istajlū.

24. Ṣāfī Walī Sulṭān, descendant[5] of the Ṣūfīs, Kh̲alīfa of the Rūmlū.

25. 'Alī Beg Ẕūlfiqārkush̲.[6]

26. Muḥammadī Beg Kitābdār (librarian) Qājār.

Likewise there were nominated 300 cuirassiers of the Sh̲āh's bodyguard[7] with fitting equipments. After the conclusion of this reunion an order was given that there should be a third hunt[8] in Āq-i-Ziyārat which is the last stage before the summer-quarters of Sūrlīk.[9] Various rejoicings and festivities occurred, and all the paraphernalia of delectation were gathered together. In the charming

---

[1] Bāyazīd has Bādsh̲āh instead of Mīrzā after Jahān Sh̲āh's name, no doubt because he was the son of Qarā Yūsuf of the Black Sheep. He was killed in 1467. See D'Herbelot art. Jehan Sh̲āh.

[2] Apparently Birdī or Bardī is the true reading, Erskine II. 294. If so he was apparently Sh̲āh Birdī Bayāt the brother of Bāyazīd, and the man who renounced the world and became a religious poet under the style of Bahrām Saqqā. See Bāyazīd 19*a*.

[3] *Julāq* in text, but *culāq*, which means "one-handed," is probably correct.

[4] Rūmlū in Bāyazīd.

[5] *Walad-i-Ṣūfīān Kh̲alīfa Rūmlū.* The passage is not clear. Rūmlū seems to mean the people to Rūm or Asia Minor, but the name does not appear among the seven Turkish tribes whom Timūr released at Ṣadru-d-dīn's request.

[6] "The slayer of Ẕūlfiqār." Ẕūlfiqār was a Kurd who became Sulṭān of Mōṣul and took possession of Bagdad. Ṭahmāsp when about 14 made war upon him in 1527, and during the siege 'Alī Beg murdered him. See Malcolm's Persia I. 566 and B. M. MS. Or. 153, Rieu 110*a* and 40*b*.

[7] *Qūrcī-i-kh̲āṣa.* The *Qūrcī* were the Sh̲āh's household cavalry, and were descended from the 2,000 prisoners released by Timūr to Ṣadru-d-dīn. See Denison Ross J. A. S., April '96, p. 292, and Vullers 748*a*.

[8] *Sh̲ikār-i-qamargh̲a.* See Badāōnī, Lowe's translation, p. 93 for a graphic description of such a hunt.

[9] Surlaq in text but clearly the Sūrlīq of p. 215 and of the Ṭabaqāt.

spot of Miyāna,[1] which is famous for its salubrity, the Shāh came to his Majesty Jahānbānī's quarters, and wished him god-speed and the two sovereigns bade adieu to one another with mutual respect and in an auspicious hour.

His Majesty Jahānbānī proceeded from thence to Ardabīl and Tabrīz in accordance with the precedent[2] set by his Majesty Ṣāḥib Qirānī. The litter of her Majesty Maryam-Makānī, together with her attendants, was sent by the straight road towards Qandahār, Ḥājī Muḥammad Khān being put in charge of the troops and sent to wait on the litter of the cupola of chastity. The 12,000 horse who had been appointed to attend on the victorious stirrup were sent away to get their accoutrements, &c., so that when his Majesty Jahānbānī arrived at the Hilmand the Prince (Murād) might join him there with the army. His Majesty Jahānbānī first proceeded to view Tabrīz, and when he came near it the governors and grandees came out to welcome him at a dam[3] which Mīrzā Mīrān Shāh had constructed on the stream which comes to Tabrīz from the slope of the Sahand.[4] In accordance with the Shāh's orders the governor put the city in fête, and decked[5] her for his Majesty's enlightened gaze, and himself performed the rites of hospitality. The games of hockey[6] and wolf running[7] for which Tabrīz was famous, but which had been inter-

---

[1] Jarrett III. 82. The Mianah of Reclus who gives it a very bad character for salubrity. This is taken partly from Col. Monteith's account in the R. Geo. S. J. for 1833 who speaks of Miana's being infested by a poisonous bug. The famous traveller Thévenot the younger died here in 1667.

[2] Alluding to the visit paid by Tīmūr to Ṣadru-d-dīn Ṣūfī, the founder of the Ṣufī dynasty, at Ardabīl.

[3] *Saddī*. Mīrān Shāh was a son of Tīmūr. The dam was probably made to supply Tabrīz with water, and the stream either the Māhrūd of Meynard 133*n*. or the Ajī Cai (river).

[4] A mountain south of Tabrīz and 11800 feet high. The *izāfat* after Sahand in text seems wrong.

[5] *Jilwa dād*. Cf. Revelations xxi. 2, "The holy city made ready as a bride adorned for her husband."

[6] *Caugān*, but in Tabrīz played on foot, for A. F. adds the word *piyāda*.

[7] *Gurg-dawānī*. The dictionaries do not make it clear what this sport was. *Gurg-daw* means trotting or running like a wolf, and *Gurg-bāzī* is explained as a game current in Kāshān, and consisting in letting a wolf loose, &c. Bāyazīd speaks of *Gurg-dawānī* and also of a sport called Armanī-Musalmān, apparently Armenians against Muḥammadans. From

dicted on account of riots, were revived by the Shāh's orders for his Majesty's delectation. His Majesty visited the splendid buildings, the memorials of ancient kings—and the pleasure-parks of the city. Fresh illustrations were thereby brought to his mind of the bypast (*guzashtagān*) monuments of the earth, of the revolutions (*sargashtagān*), of the mansions of the skies, of the passing away (*guzashtagī*) of the inconstant universe, and of the breaches (*gusistāgīhā*)[1] of the
220 unstable earth, and they brought to his lips truthful words about compassing the favour of the Creator. He became wrapt in some old verses, and in ecstacy he recited aloud this quatrain:—

*Quatrain.*

Alas that substance hath slipped from the palm,
And that many hearts (*lit.* livers) have bled at death's hand;
None cometh[2] from that (other) world that I might inquire
How it fared with the travellers thereto.

Mullā Quṭbu-d-dīn[3] Jalanjū of Bagdad waited upon him in this illustrious city and attended him as far as Holy Mashhad. The exquisite and magical Khwāja 'Abdu-ṣ-ṣamad[4] shīrīnqalam (sweet pen)

---

the following passage in Chardin it appears that the pastime in question was really that of dancing wolves:—

"La place de Tauris est la plus grande place de ville que j'aye vue au monde, elle passe de beaucoup celle d' Ispahan. Les Turcs y ont rangé plusieurs fois trente mille hommes en bataille. Le soir cette place est remplie de menu peuple, qui vient se divertir aux passe-tems qu' on y donne. Ce sont des jeux, des tours d' addresse et des bouffonneries, comme en font les Saltimbanques, des luttes, des combats de taureaux, et de beliers; des recits en vers et en prose, et des dances de Loups. Le peuple de Tauris prend son plus grand divertissement a voir cette dance, et l'on y améne de cent lieues voir des loups qui savent bien dancer. Les mieux dressey (?) se vendant jusqu'à cinq cent ecus la pièce. Il arrive souvent pour ces loups de grosses emeutes qu' on a bien de la peine a appaiser. Voyages I. 184, ed. of 1741.

[1] Alluding to the earthquakes by which Tabrīz has been so often shattered.

[2] "That bourne whence no traveller returneth."

[3] We learn from Bāyazīd 24a that this Mullā was the father of Qāẓī 'Alī Bakhshī, Blochmann 411 and 528, and that Humāyūn sent him an invitation from Badakhshān, but that he was unable to accept it.

[4] Famous as a painter and calligraphist. Blochmann 107 and 495. He afterwards joined Humāyūn at Kābul. He was a poet and a mem-

also entered into service in this city, and was much esteemed by that connoisseur of excellence. But from the hindrances of fate he could not accompany him. One of the wonderful good omens was this that when his Majesty came to Tabrīz, as he was very keen about astrolabes, spheres[1] (*kura*) and other instruments of observation, he bade his equerry Paik Muḥammad search diligently in the city for spheres (*kura*). That simpleton brought some colts (*karra*) with their mothers![2] His Majesty was pleased and purchased them as a good omen. After leaving Tabrīz he went to Ardabīl. When he arrived at S͟hammāsī[3] all the S͟hāik͟hzādas and the other grandees and nobles came and paid their respects. He stayed a week in Ardabīl and then went to K͟halk͟hāl[4] and from thence to Ṭāram[5] and from thence to K͟harazbīl.[6] As the air and fruits of that place were remarkably excellent, especially the seedless[7] pomegranates, he remained there three days. In Sabzawār he rejoined his camp. Here her Majesty Maryam-Makānī gave birth to a daughter.[8] From the beginning of his march towards Kābul and Qandahār, at every stage that he came to, the rulers and grandees tendered presents and exercised hospitality. At this stage Mīr S͟hamsu-d-dīn 'Alī Sulṭān performed acceptable service, and on the day of the entertainment rope-dancers exhibited their skill. When he came to Mas͟hhad the

---

ber of the Divine Faith. Blochmann 209. There is an account of him in Bāyazīd 24a *et seq.*

[1] Apparently celestial globes and not armillary spheres. Jarrett II. 2.

[2] *Mādiyānhā*, *lit.* "mares."

[3] *Samāsī* in some MSS., evidently a place in the environs of Ardabīl and occupied by descendants of the Ṣafī saint. See J. R. A. S. for April 1896, p. 262, where S͟hammāsī is mentioned as a village near Ardabīl.

[4] Two days' journey from Ardabīl, Meynard 210.

[5] Tārūn in Jauhar, 75. Apparently the Tāram طارم of Yāqūt who describes it as a large district between Qazwīn and Gīlān, Meynard 131.

[6] Khardabyl of Jauhar, 75.

[7] A. F. notices seedless pomegranates as one of the productions of the Tūmān of Nēknihāl near Jalālābad, Jarrett II. 405. Chardin, speaking of pomegranates, says "Il y en a dont le pepin est si tendre qu'on ne la sent presquepas sous le dentet il y en a qui n' ont point de membrane ou pellicule entre les grains. Il vient des granades de Yezd qui pesent plus d'une livre. At p. 97 of Vol. II. he says he has never seen pomegranates better than those of Miyāna.

[8] I have found no further mention of this child. She was not Bak͟hshī or Yak͟hs͟hī Bānū.

Holy the Governor and nobles strove to do him honour. He waited some time in this city to allow for the gathering of the Shāh's army. From here he sent one 'Abdu-l-fattāḥ Kurkīrāq[1] to demand the subsidy[2] (sāwarī) which had been assigned upon Herāt, and the latter died on his way back. From the same place he sent Maulānā Nūru-
221 d-dīn Muḥammad Tarkhān to summon Shaikh Abū'l-qāsīm Jurjāni and Maulānā Ilyās of Ardabīl who were adorned with external and internal excellencies. At Kābul they came into his service. He was greatly pleased by the arrival of these two distinguished men with whom he discussed the Durratu-l-Tāj.[3] And during the time he was in Mashhad he continually held discourses with the learned and eloquent who waited upon him and were benefited by the alchemy of his companionship, Maulānā Jamshīd[4] the enigmatist, who was an aggregate of excellencies, repeatedly had the honour of visiting him. One day Mullā Ḥairatī[5] presented the following to the amending glance of his Majesty :—

*Verse.*

Whiles my heart, whiles my liver is consumed from love of the fair,
Every moment love makes a fresh scar ;
My state is like that of the moth and the lamp,
For if I approach my wings (*bāl-ū-param*) are burnt away.

His Majesty who was a genuine artist (*khallāq-i-ma'ānī*) and a paragon of acuteness, gave this excellent turn (*taṣarruf*) to it :—

---

[1] This is the word which Blochmann was unable to explain satisfactorily, 72*n*. and 616. Here it is used as a title. *Kurk* means fur and *īrāq* accoutrements. A. F. gives few dates in this part of his history. We learn from Bāyazīd that Humāyūn reached Mashhad at the end of Ramaẓān, *i.e.*, 15th December, 1544. From the inscription furnished by the lamented Mr. Ney Elias J. R. A. S. for January 1897, p. 47, it appears that Humāyūn was at Turbat-i-Jāma few days later, *viz.*, on 29th December.

[2] "Present dont en fait homaje." See Vullers and Quatremère, Not. et Extraits XIV. 27.

[3] "Pearl of the diadem." It is an encyclopædia of philosophical sciences by Quṭbu-d-dīn Shīrāzī a disciple of Naṣīru-d-dīn Ṭūsī. Rieu 434*a*. The parenthesis is rather out of place if they did not come till he was in Kābul.

[4] Blochmann 102.

[5] A Persian poet. He died at Kāshān in 961 A.H. 1554. Blochmann, 187*n*. Bāyazīd tells the story

*Verse.*

I go forward though my wings be burnt.

The Maulānā sincerely prostrated himself before his Majesty's exquisite emendation. From Mashhad he went to the caravanserai of Ṭarq [1] and from there he went by way of the fort of Gāh [2] to Sīstān. Here the Prince and the Shāh's officers joined him. From thence they went to Garmsīr. Mīr 'Abdu-l-Ḥai of Garmsīr came out of the fort of Lakī [3] with a quiver bound round his neck and did homage and excused himself for his offences and for his shameful conduct in remaining aloof from service on the occasion of his Majesty's march (into Persia). As his Majesty's disposition was forgiving and benevolent, he accepted his apologies and encompassed him with favours.

Since the narrative has proceeded so far, it is indispensable that something should be said of the officers who served the State during their exile.

The head of the faithful servants was Bairām Khān, who throughout waited on the stirrup of his Majesty Jahānbānī Jannat-āshiyānī as if he were his good Fortune (*cūn sa'ādat*). The second was Khwāja Mu'aẓẓam who was the uterine [4] brother of her Majesty Maryam-Makānī. From the beginning of his career he was not free from turbulence of brain and heat of disposition. Gradually his forwardness (*bibākī*) and bloody-mindedness (*saffākī*) increased beyond bounds. His last action will be described in its proper place. The third was 'Āqil [5] Sulṭān Uzbeg, son of 'Ādil Sulṭān, who by his

and calls Humāyūn's emendation a *dakhl* which is a technical term for a repartee or antistrophe.

[1] The Raut Ṭarq of Jauhar 76. Yāqūt describes it as 10 *farsakhs* from Ispahan, Meynard 392.

[2] Jauhar 76. The place seems to be Kākh, Reclus IX. 227. It is described by Macgregor 1. 155.

[3] On right bank of Helmand, Erskine II. 304.

[4] *Ukhuwwat-i-akhyāfī*, brother by the same mother but by a different father, Lane 832c. Other writers apparently regard him as the full brother of Akbar's mother, Maāsiru-l-Umarā I. 618 and Blochmann 524. One would be glad to think that he was not the full brother.

[5] His mother was Shād Begam, the daughter of Sulṭān Ḥusain of Herāt by Pāyanda Sulṭān Begam. Bābar, 180. 'Ādil Sulṭān was son of Mahdī Sulṭān. Bābar 363. 'Āqil Sulṭān is mentioned by Bāyazīd, 18a as one of the officers who marched with Humāyūn from Qandahār to Kābul.

mother's side was a grandson of Sultān Ḥusain Mīrzā. Though in the beginning he was among the subsidised officers, in the end he was named among the excluded (*baḥirmān mausūm gasht*).

The 4th was Ḥājī Muḥammad [1] Kōkī, the brother of Kōkī who was
222 one of the great officers of his Majesty Gītī-sitānī Firdūs-makānī. Ḥājī Muḥammad was of singular courage and the Shāh often said that kings stood in need of such a servant. On the day of the *qabaqandāzī* he hit the *qabaq* and received a (*jaldū*) present from the Shāh.

5th, Rūshan Kōka, foster-brother of his Majesty Jahānbānī Jannat-āshiyānī. On the journey the jewellery was entrusted to him. As he proved unfaithful in this trust it was necessary to put him in prison for some time. He was pardoned and released.

6th, Ḥasan Beg, brother of Maḥram Kōkī. Though he was foster-brother of Kamrān Mīrzā he was long in the service of his Majesty Jahānbānī. He was of generous nature, affable, and a confidant. He was drowned at the Causā ferry.

7th, Khwāja Maqṣūd [2] of Herāt—a man of pure disposition and of integrity; he was noted for his trustworthiness and sincerity, and was one of the tried servants of her Majesty Maryam-Makānī. He was ever assiduous in her service. He had two auspicious sons who were foster-brothers of the king of kings. One was Saif [3] Khān, who drank the wholesome cup of martyrdom in the year of the conquest of Gujrāt. The other was Zain [4] Khān Kōka, distinguished for fidelity and intelligence, and who became the object of the favour of the king of kings and one of the great officers.

8th, Khwāja Ghāzī of Tabrīz. He was a skilful accountant and also acquainted with histories and chronicles. When the sublime army left Lahore for Sind he separated from M. Kāmrān and joined his Majesty. He was appointed Mushraf-i-dīwān [5] (accountant).

[1] In spite of his services, Humāyūn eventually put him to death. Jauhar 109 and A. N. I. 311.

[2] Possibly the Maulāna Maqṣūd the engraver of Blochmann 52, who in index calls him Khwāja.

[3] Blochmann 350.

[4] Blochmann 344.

[5] Blochmann 263, Blochmann VII., describes the office as higher than that of the Dīwān but lower than that of the Vakīl. Jauhar 88 refers to Khwāja Ghāzī as Dīwān. He fell into disgrace on account of his conspiring with Rūshan Kōka to steal Humāyūn's jewels. Jauhar 68 and 72 and Gulbadan's Memoirs.

After that he was for a long time excluded from the Court. At the end of his life, when the vigour of his understanding was impaired, he was admitted to the Court of the king of kings.

9th, Khwāja Amīnu-d-dīn [1] Maḥmūd of Herāt who surpassed all the world in the science of accounts (*fann-i-sīyāq*) and who also wrote in *shikasta* admirably. He was very subtle (*mūshigāf*, lit. hair-splitting) in matters of business and knowledge of arithmetic.

His Majesty made him for some time Bakhshī to the king of kings. At the time of the latter's sovereignty he attained to high office and was exalted by receiving the title of Khwāja Jahān.

10th, Bābā Dōst Bakhshī. He also was distinguished for his knowledge of accounts and always displayed great aptitude in the affairs of the dīwānī.

11th, Darvesh Maqṣūd Bangālī. He came from the Ziyāratgāh of Herāt and was a man of integrity. He was left behind with Jahāngīr 223
Qulī [2] Beg in Bengal and was the only one who escaped. His Majesty Jahānbānī Jannat-ashiyānī was especially gracious to him, and afterwards his Majesty the king of kings showed him great favour. He spent a long life in the ranks of offerers up of prayers (for Akbar).

12th, Ḥasan [3] 'Alī Ishak Āqā. He was distinguished for courage and activity. He had done good service, but one Ya'qūb [4] by name who was a favourite of his Majesty Jahānbānī having used improper language, some evil-disposed Qizilbāshis (Persians) laid an ambush for the young man in a deserted [5] village near Tabrīz and assassinated him. As there was a coolness between him and Ḥasan 'Alī it was

---

1 Blochmann 424 and 528 and Elliott V. 384. It is curious that A. F. does not mention *shikasta* in his chapter on writing in the *Āīn*. Badāōnī calls him *Wazīr-i-mustaqall* (absolute Vizier) and speaks much of his influence. Lowe's trans. 189-90. M. Quatremère has a note about the precise meaning of the word *sīyāq* and refers to this passage in the A. N.

2 Killed in Bihār when fighting with Sher Khān.

3 He had a Balūcī wife who was one of the two women who accompanied Humāyūn in his flight to Persia, and she was useful on the desert journey as an interpreter. Jauhar, 52 and 53.

4 He was Humāyūn's butler. An account of this murder is given by Jauhar 76.

5 *Mauẓa'-i-kharāba.* According to Jauhar, Ya'qūb was killed a long way from Tabrīz and between Qazwīn and Sabzawār. Erskine calls the place Kila Ders. II. 296n.

reported that the latter had instigated the murder. On this account he could not accompany the sublime army but remained in Persia. When Kābul became the royal residence he was allowed to kiss the threshold.

13th, 'Alī Dōst Bārbegī,[1] son of the aforesaid Ḥasan 'Alī. He came afterwards and joined in Holy Mashhad. From first to last he was distinguished in Herāt (?) for service and devotion.

14th, Ibrāhīm Ishak Āqā. He was a devoted servant of the Court.

15th, Shaikh Yūsuf[2] Cūlī who called himself a descendant of Shaikh Aḥmad[3] Yasavī. He was a humble-minded man of agreeable qualities.

16th, Shaikh Buhlūl[4] who claimed to be descended from the Turkī Shaikhs. He was a good servant.

17th, Maulānā Nūru-d-dīn.[5] He was acquainted with mathematics, astronomy and the astrolabe. He had entered into the service of his Majesty Gītī-sitānī Firdūs-makānī along with Qāẓī Burhān[6] of Khāf. He was one of the courtiers of his Majesty Jahānbānī. His Majesty the king of kings exalted him by the title of Tarkhān.

18th, Muḥammad Qāsim Maujī. He enlisted into the service of his Majesty Jahānbānī Jannat-āshiyānī in Badakhshān. He was related to Mīr Muḥammad Jālabān,[7] and in Badakhshān he acted as a raft-conductor (jālabānī). In India in the reign of his Majesty

[1] The 'Alī Dōst Khān of the Ṭabaqāt, Blochmann 533 and n. The reference to Herāt is not intelligible. Perhaps the word is *harāt* and means in all matters. One MS. has *derustayīn*, *i.e.*, well-principled. He also served under Akbar.

[2] Perhaps the Shaikh Yūsuf Harkan of Blochmann 539.

[3] Aḥmad Yasavī belonged to the Naqshbandī order and was one of the great saints of Central Asia, Vambéry's Boohara 246*n* There are short accounts of him in the Khazīnatu-l-Aṣfiyā I, 531 and in the Safīnatu-l-Auliyā, Newal Kishore ed. Lucknow, 76. He was born at Yasī now known as Turkistān, Reclus VI. 533 and which is a town in Turkistān about 150 miles north of Tashkend. He died in 562 A. H. or 1176 A. D. See also A. F.'s account of the Yasavī sect. Jarrett, III. 358.

[4] Perhaps the Buhlūl of Delhi mentioned in the Ṭabaqāt lith. ed. 392.

[5] Blochmann 541, Badāonī III. 157 and 197.

[6] Qu. The Shaikh Burhān of Blochmann 539?

[7] Bābar, Mem. 395 refers to Mīr Muḥammad Jālabān as deserving great rewards for the skill with which he had constructed a bridge over the Ganges. See also *ibid.* 417.

the king of kings he was admiral. He had a charming residence on the bank of the Jumna, and there too he brought the ship of his life to the shore of extinction.

19th, Ḥaidar[1] Muḥammad Ākhta Begī, (in charge of the geldings). He was an old servant.

20th, Saiyid Muḥammad Pakna[2] (the stout ?). He was a brave man and good at his hands (*Ṣāḥib-i-qabẓa*). In Herāt he carried off the *qabaq*.

21st, Saiyid Muḥammad[3] Qālī. In Bakkar he was for some time Mīr 'Adl. He had the right to sit in the illustrious assembly.

22nd, Ḥāfiẓ Sulṭān Muḥammad Rakhna. He came to Bakkar in the garb of a faqīr and entered into service. He recited touching verses.[4] Gradually he was numbered among the envoys[5] and obtained honour in the time of his Majesty the king of kings. At Sahrind 224
(Sirhind) he made a charming garden worthy of being celebrated.

23rd, Mirzā Beg Balūc, whose father had been in Khurāsān hazāra-i-Balūc.

24th, His son Mīr Ḥusain. Both were excellent servants.

25th, Khwāja 'Ambar Nāẓir,[6] a confidential eunuch of his Majesty Gītī-sitānī Firdūs-makānī. From his Majesty the king of kings he got the title of I'tibār Khān (the trusty Khān). He was attached to the litter of her Majesty Maryam-makānī.

---

[1] Blochmann 384 and 432*n*. Maujī means whimsical or emotional but was perhaps assumed with reference to his naval duties, *mauj* meaning a wave. Maujī was his poetical name and under it he is described by Badāōnī III. 324 who gives extracts from his poetry and says he died in 979H. or 1572 A. D. See also Maāsiru-l-Umarā III. 203.

[2] Apparently also known as Shēr Muḥammad because he had killed a leopard. A. N. I. 287. He took part in the blinding of Kāmrān.

[3] Blochmann 438. If so, he was of Amrōha. Possibly هروی (*haravī*) which occurs in one MS. is a mistake for امروی. Badāōnī, Lowe, 214 and 224.

[4] The Lucknow ed. reads *dū bait*, two quatrains. In *Āīn* A. F. speaks of the garden of Ḥāfiẓ Rakhna as the delight of all beholders, Jarrett II. 281.

[5] *Īlciyān*, but the reading is very doubtful. Some MSS. appear to read *yakjihatiyān*, *i.e.*, single-minded or loyal. One MS. has *yakhcakiyān* and another has *dākhil-i-maḥāfil*. Bāyazīd 39*a* mentions him as a *gōyindā* or reciter and as present at the interview between Humāyūn and his brother at Tālīqān.

[6] Blochmann, 403.

26th, 'Ārif Tūs̲h̲akcī. He was on the list of purchased (or captured) slaves, but claimed to be a Saiyid. By favour of his Majesty the king of kings he obtained the title of Bahar[1] K̲h̲an and rose to high office.

Among the faithful servants and slaves were Mihtar K̲h̲ān, treasurer (*k̲h̲azīnadār*), Mihtar Fāk̲h̲ir Tūs̲h̲akcī, Mullā Balāl, librarian, Mihtar Taimūr in charge of the sharbats (*s̲h̲arbatcī*), Mihtar Jauharī[2] ewer-bearer, Mihtar Wakīla, treasurer (*k̲h̲azāncī*), Mihtar Wāṣil, and Mihtar Sumbul Mīr Ātas̲h̲ (Master of Ordnance). Others were Sulṭān Muḥammad Qarāwal-begī (huntsman), 'Abdu-l-wahhāb in charge of the pantry, Jabāī Bahādur, Tūlaq Yātis̲h̲navīs.[3]

Bravo! Oh fortunate ones of lucky star who with good intention and firm foot came forward in the paths of testimony and in stations of Divine trial, and served their benefactor.

*Verse.*

I know not why helpers are backward,
For by service men attain to position.

[1] Apparently the Bahār K̲h̲ān Muḥammad Aṣg̲h̲ar of Blochmann 405. B. M. MS. Add. 6544 calls him Bahādur K̲h̲ān.

[2] The writer of the memoirs.

[3] Writer who keeps the lists of the night-watch; generally spelt *yātis̲h̲*. See P. de Courteille's Dict.

# CHAPTER XXXIV.

## Return of his Majesty Jahānbānī Jannat-āshiyānī from Persia, and the coming of his Majesty the Shāhinshāh from Qandahār to Kābul.

When the grateful (*lit.* shade-scattering) [1] report of the approach of his Majesty Jahānbānī became vivid, and the news of his army was spread in Kābul and Qandahār, the blowing of these spring-breezes of victory caused the hope-buds of expectants to open and a current to set in the resolution-stream of the irresolute.

*Verse.*

Eternal bounty from measureless store
Cast to the city a report of his advent.
The hope-field of the hopeless smiled,
The success-garden of the success-less grew verdant.

The loud reverberation overset M. Kāmrān, and as the season of awakening and of contrition was past, he advanced further in evil ways, and gave way to wicked thoughts. In the first place he sent 225
Khiẓr Khān Hazāra's brother and Qurbān Qarāwalbegī (head of the vanguard) to bring the nursling of light, to wit, the Shāhinshāh from Qandahār to Kābul. When they arrived M. 'Askarī took counsel with his associates about sending his Majesty. All who were of sound sense said it was not right to send him and that when his Majesty Jahānbānī Jannat-āshiyānī approached the proper thing to do was to send to him with all reverence the child of dominion so that by means of this fair nosegay of fortune's parterre he might obtain for himself forgiveness of his offences. Some others said it was proper to send him to M. Kāmrān so as not to lose his favour, for, as regarded the other suggestion, it was too late now for a reconciliation with his Majesty Jahānbānī. In the end the Mīrza

---

[1] There is a play here on Humāyūn's name. He is represented as casting his shadow over Afghānistān like the Humā or phœnix.

put aside the sound advice and sent his Majesty Shâhinshâh in the depth of winter, and in snow and ice to Kābul. His sister Bakhshī Bānū Begam[1] was sent with him, and also Shamsu-d-dīn of Ghaznīn who had received the title of Atka Khān, Māham Anaga, mother of Adham Khān, Jījī Anaga, mother of M. 'Azīz Kōkaltāsh and a number of other servants. In order that they might not be recognised, the nursling of light was called Mīrak on this journey, and his sister Bīja.[2] When they arrived at Qilāt (*Kelat-i-Ghilzai*) they put up at night in the house of a Hazāra. Owing to the radiance (*far*) and majesty which were manifest on his Majesty's forehead, men recognised him as soon as they saw him, and in the morning there rose to the lips of the master of the house the statement that the prince had been brought there. As soon as Khiẓr Khān's brother heard this remark he set off at once, and hurried on to Ghaznīn. The attendants beheld, hour by hour, and moment by moment, notes of greatness in the prince from his earliest years and marvelled at the Divine Creation while watching the wondrous lights of his development. Among them was this that when they had marched from Ghaznīn and had come to their halting-place, the lamp in the house went out and the place was in darkness. His Majesty, the essence of whose nature had affinity with light, fell a-weeping from horror of the darkness and though *Anagas* and nurses did their best they could not succeed in soothing him. But as soon as they brought a lamp his heart grew pacified, and the lights of joy showed themselves
226 in his cheeks. This was a clear proof of light-augmenting and darkness-dispelling, both internally and externally. When his Majesty the Shāhinshāh came to Kābul from Qandahār, M. Kāmrān brought that nursling of fortune's garden to the house of the cupola of chastity Khānzāda Begam, sister of her Majesty Gītī-sitānī Firdūs-makānī. Next day he held a grand assembly in the Shahr-ārā garden and did homage to his Majesty.

1 Half sister. She was first married to Ibrāhīm, son of M. Sulaimān, and afterwards her brother gave her in marriage to Sharafu-d-dīn Ḥusain, Blochmann, 322.

2 There is a variant, Bīca, but apparently Baca, child, as the true reading. *Mīrak* means princeling.

# CHAPTER XXXV.

## Victory of his Majesty the Shāhinshāh in a wrestle with Ibrāhīm Mīrzā, and his felicitous beating of the drum of prestige.

When M. Kāmrān beheld that true cypress of fortune's rosarium in the Shahr-ārā garden he was, from the lucklessness of his fate, confused and astonied at the sight of that lustrous forehead whence streamed the glory of eternal dominion and success. And as God the world-adorner was willing the joy of the lord of dominion and the spiritual and temporal defeat of the Mīrzā, whatever the latter thought to be matters of his joy, proved to be materials of vexation. For instance, on a day when the Mīrzā held a feast and had for his own glorification sent for his Majesty the Shāhinshāh, it chanced that on the occasion of the Shab-i-Barāt[1] they had, according to the custom, brought a decorated kettle-drum for his son Ibrāhīm Mīrzā.[2] His Majesty the Shāhinshāh took a fancy to it, in accordance with the principle that the orchestra of world-conquest must strike up in his name, and the drum of world-rule and universal adornment must give forth a loud sound on the roof of his residence. The uncomprehending Mīrzā did not wish to let him have it, and reflecting that M. Ibrāhīm was the elder of the two, and apparently the stronger, he made the taking of the drum a pretext for a trial of strength and a

[1] The night of record, 14 Sha'bān = for 952, 22nd October, 1545. Apparently the wrestling must have taken place long after Akbar was removed to Kābul for that was in winter and so presumably in end of 1544 or beginning of 1545. But possibly Sha'bān 951 is meant, in which case the wrestling took place on 1st November, 1544. If this be so, however, Akbar must have been removed to Kābul long before Humāyūn had left Persia. There is an account in Herklots of the feasting, &c., on the Shab-i-barāt.

[2] One MS. has Abū'l-qāsim, and Ferishta, lith. ed. p. 264, states that Kāmrān had one son Abū'l-qāsim, and that Akbar imprisoned him in Gwālyār in 964 (1556), and afterwards put him to death at the time of the rebellion of Khān Zamān in 1567.

wrestling-match. Whoever conquered was to have the drum. His Majesty who was aided by heaven, and sustained from all eternity and who regarded not the pomp of M. Kāmrān nor the superior age of Ibrāhīm Mīrzā, rejoiced on hearing the condition, imposed by the Mīrzā for his own enjoyment, and became a means of augmenting the Mīrza's sorrow. Despite his tender years, which made such actions very surprising, he, by Divine inspiration, and celestial teaching, without hesitation girt up his loins, and rolled up his sleeves, and with strong arm, which was strengthened by eternal power, stepped bravely forward. He grappled with Ibrāhīm Mīrzā according to the canons of the skilful and of the masters of wrestling and
227 putting his hand before his waist so lifted him up and flung him on the ground that a cry burst forth from the assemblage, and that shouts of Bravo arose from far and near. This was the beginning of the beating of that drum of victory and conquest of his Majesty the S̲h̲āhins̲h̲āh, the Shadow of God, which came to be beaten above the loftiest pinnacles of earth, and beneath the green vault (*sipihr-i-k̲h̲aẓrā*) of heaven. M. Kāmrān who had thought of this wrestling bout as a test of the issue of his contest with his Majesty Jahānbānī took a bad omen from the result and became dejected, while the well-wishers and intimates of his Majesty the S̲h̲āhins̲h̲āh expanded with joy and exulted at the happy omen. His Majesty beat the drum which he had gained by the strength of his arm, and the joyous sound gladdened the hearts of the royal servants. The Mīrzā, as things had turned out adversely,[1] and the throw of the dice revealed an omen contrary to his desire, gave way to evil designs against the altar of fortune (Akbar), one of these being that he ordered his Majesty, who was still sucking,[2] to be weaned. He was oblivious of the fact that he who drew milk from the breasts of the Divine favour and obtained nutriment from a celestial nurse could come to no harm from such acts, and that he who had the True Protector for his guardian could receive no detriment from these evil imaginings.

---

[1] *Az baski ṭarīq s̲h̲uda būd.* For a similar phrase see p. 193 of text, *l.* 14.

[2] Akbar must have been then two, if not three years old, and surely it was time to wean a child who could lift up another child older and bigger than himself and cast him to the earth.

## CHAPTER XXXVI.

### ARRIVAL OF HIS MAJESTY JAHĀNBĀNĪ JANNAT-ĀSHIYĀNĪ'S ARMY AT THE GARMSĪR AND THE TAKING OF THE FORT OF BAST.

It is not unknown to the observers of facts and contemplators of occurrences whose watchful eyes are open, and have been smeared with the antimony of alertness that when the lofty standards of his Majesty Jahānbānī and his Persian auxiliaries arrived at the Garmsīr, 'Alī Sulṭān Taklū and a number of devoted men were sent to take Bast[1] which belongs to the Garmsīr and appertains to Qandahār. Shāham 'Alī Jalāīr, father of Tīmūr Jalāīr, and Mīr Khalaj who were there as feudatories of M. Kāmrān had strengthened the fort which was now besieged by the royal army. In the course of the siege a musket ball from the fort struck 'Alī Sulṭān and deprived him of life. His soldiers appointed his twelve years old son in his room and pressed forward the siege more and more. These facts were reported to the king of Persia and after some time there arrived a rescript ratifying the arrangement. Gradually the garrison got into straits and no help coming to them they begged for quarter. Owing to the imperial clemency they received this, and delivered up the fort. When it had come into the possession of the royal servants his Majesty Jahānbānī encamped in the neighbourhood, and Shāham 228
'Alī and Mīr Khalaj tied quivers round their necks and came out and did homage. His Majesty in accordance with his innate benignity forgave their offences, and enrolled them among his servants. At the same place a report was spread that M. 'Askarī was about to fly with his treasure to Kābul. A number of the Persians and

---

[1] Jarrett III. 68n. Meynard 100 "Near the confluence of the Arghandāb with the Helmand," Erskine II. 304. It is on the east side of Helmand and is marked on map as Kila Bist, in ruins. Yākūt says Bast belongs to Kābul and Meynard remarks that he and the author of the Lubb-al-lubāb are the only writers who say this. Ibn Ḥaukal (Ouseley 207) places it in Sijistān and A. F. does not put it in Qandahār in the Āīn.

of the king's servants pressed for leave to pursue him. Though his Majesty Jahānbānī had ascertained by truthful scouts that the report was false, and that M. 'Askarī meditated to fight and to defend the fort of Qandahār, and moreover even on the supposition that the report was true his Majesty from his innate kindness was unwilling that 'Askarī should be pursued, yet they brooked[1] not restraint and having obtained a sort of permission to go they hurried off lest the Mīrzā should escape them. When after making great haste they arrived in disorder at the environs of Qandahār, they found that the report of the Mīrzā's departure was false. A large body came out and fought with them, while cannon and muskets were discharged from the fort. A large number of Persians and others were killed, and many were wounded. Khwāja Mu'azzam, Ḥaidar Sulṭān, Ḥājī Muḥammad, son of Bābā Qushqa, 'Alī Qulī, son of Ḥaidar Sulṭān, Shāh Qulī Nāranjī[2] and a number of the Caghatāis and Persians gave proofs of their courage and drove the enemy back to the Fort. Although Jamīl Beg,[3] one of Mīrzā 'Askarī's trusted servants, sent a message to the Mīrzā to come down in person as but a small force remained and that it would be easy t. dispose of those who had once already been defeated, the Mīrzā did not assent, and despatched a message to the effect that "they know the numbers and quality of our men, and will not restrict their troops to the same number as before, on the contrary they probably have a reserve in hiding by whose help they will do for us. We shant let ourselves be gulled, but will make the fort strong, and not give battle till M. Kāmrān arrive." As God befriended the army of his Majesty Jahānbānī, M. Kāmrān did not make his appearance, and some victories were obtained which were the prelude of countless successes. In these days Bābā Sihrindī who was one of M. Kāmrān's distinguished officers, and who belonged to the Qandahār garrison was killed.

---

[1] *bē jalūī karda*, not heeding the rein?

[2] Blochmann 480.

[3] Bāyazīd tells us that he was a younger brother of Bāpūs and that he was killed by a musket shot at the second siege of Kābul.

# CHAPTER XXXVII.

## ARRIVAL OF THE ARMY OF HIS MAJESTY JAHĀNBĀNĪ JANNAT-ĀSHIYĀNĪ AT QANDAHĀR, ITS SIEGE AND CAPTURE.

When the heroes had gained such a victory his Majesty Jahānbānī Jannat-āshiyānī returned thanks to God, and reached Qandahār 229 five days after the joyful event on Saturday, 7th Muḥarram, 952 (21st March, 1545), in an auspicious hour which was compounded of favourable aspect. He halted by the side (*dar ẓila'*) of the gate Māshūr[1] and encamped in the garden of Shamsu-d-dīn 'Alī the Qāẓī of Qandahār. The batteries were allotted and the captains distributed. There were daily combats between the brave men on both sides. One day Ḥaidar Sulṭān and his two sons 'Alī Qulī Khān[2] and Bahādur Khān, and Khwāja Mu'aẓẓam drove the enemy from the front of Khwāja[3] Khiẓr to the shrines near the old city and the barricade[4] (*kūca band*), and displayed great deeds. Ḥaidar[5] Sulṭān was in advance of all the others and the leader in the attacks. A remarkable circumstance was that Bābū Dōst Yasāwal was standing with a number of men among the shrines and was shooting arrows. Ḥaidar Sulṭān thought to slay him with his lance and raised his arm to do this, and at the same moment an arrow reached his armpit. Isma'īl[6] Sulṭān of Jām, whom M. Kāmrān had sent as an auxiliary, was standing on the white (*āqca*) Tower which faces the tombs, beside M. 'Askarī and was

1 Apparently the weavers' gate, *māshūr* or *māsūr* meaning a weaver's reed or spindle.

2 Afterwards the famous Khān Zamān, Blochmann 319 and 328.

3 This seems to be the name of a shrine. See Jarrett II. 404. Bāyazīd speaks of the dāman-i-Khwāja Khiẓr.

4 Perhaps what is meant is that it was a cul de sac.

5 Apparently he was not severely wounded for we find him taking part in the expedition against Rafī'. He died of the pestilence on the march to Kābul.

6 Apparently the Isma'īl Qulī Beg Duldāī of Blochmann 388 and Ma'āṣir I. 64. He deserted to Humāyūn at Qandahār (Bāyazīd).

watching the fight. Though he was too far off to distinguish the features, he remarked that "the man from whose hand the lance has fallen may be Ḥaidar Sulṭān for once I went with 'Ubaidu-l-lāh Khān[1] to the city of Tūs, and Ḥaidar Sulṭan and I were comrades[2] in an attack and I lost these two fingers. From the mode of fighting I guess that this is he." When they brought in the lance afterwards his (Ḥaidar's) name was found written on it. When they read it, they praised Isma'il's conjecture. In this engagement many men of rank were wounded, the first of all to be wounded being Khwāja Mu'aẓẓam, but who succeeded in returning. About this time news was brought that Rafī' Kōka, the foster brother of M. Kāmrān, was stationed[3] behind a hill towards Zamīndāwar on the bank of the Arghandāb with a force of Hazāras and Nakodars.[4] Bairām Khān, Muḥammad Mīrzā, Ḥaidar Sulṭān, Maqṣūd Mīrzā Akhtabēgī, the son of Zainu-d-dīn Sulṭān Shāmlū and a number of others were sent against him. By good fortune Rafī' Kōka was made prisoner, and great store of provisions, cattle and weapons was seized and the scarcity in the camp was changed to plenty. Other battles were also fought by the brave warriors with successful results.

230 As M. 'Askarī had from his own backsliding let the thread of performance fall from his hand, and was persistently contumacious it occurred to his Majesty on account of his general benevolence and his fraternal affection that he should send to M. Kāmrān the Shāh's[5] letter together with an admonitory firmān of his own. Perchance he would awake from the sleep of neglect and take the straight road and by dint of good acts make reparation for his offences. In this way many persons might escape from unnecessary

---

[1] The great Shaibānī's nephew and Ḥaidar M.'s brother-in-law. See *Tar. Rash.* 283. The battle was probably that fought between the Uzbegs and Persians at Zūrābād near Jām on 25th September, 1528. Bābar, Mem. 390 and 397 and Erskine's Hist. II. 491.

[2] The text has *hamrāh*, but perhaps it should be *hamrū* and the meaning be that Isma'īl encountered Ḥaidar as an opponent. It is hardly likely that Ḥaidar would be on the Uzbeg side. But perhaps the text means that Isma'īl was opposed to 'Ubaidu-l-lāh.

[3] Bāyazīd has *sangar* (in an) entrenchment.

[4] Jarrett II. 401*n*.

[5] It appears from Bāyazīd that Bairām took to Kāmrān letters both from Shāh Ṭahmāsp and Humāyūn.

destruction, and brotherly concord might result in great deeds which were brooding in his right-thinking soul. Accordingly Bairām Khān was despatched to Kābul as an ambassador. When he reached the pass of Rūghnī [1] and the Āb-Istāda,[2] which is between Qandahār and Ghaznīn a number of Hazāras blocked the way. At the close of the day there was an engagement and the king's servants were victorious and chastised the worthless Hazāras. Many of them were slain. When Bairām Khān arrived near Kābul, Bābūs and many others came and welcomed him and took him with them. M. Kamrān held a reception in the Cahār Bāgh and sent for Bairām Khān. The latter rightly thought that it would not be proper to give the two rescripts to the Mīrzā when he would doubtless be sitting down, and it was very unlikely that he would stand up and pay respect to them as was proper he should do. Having considered the matter, he took the Koran in his hand and tendered it as an offering. The Mīrzā on seeing the Koran stood up out of reverence towards it, and at this moment Bairām Khān presented the two rescripts. Thus the device procured respect for them. The king's and the Shāh's gifts were duly presented and Bairām sitting down beside the Mīrza uttered words of truth and sincerity. At the close of the meeting he took leave to pay his respects to the Shāhinshāh. He also obtained permission to see M. Hindāl, M. Sulaimān, Yādgār Nāṣir Mīrzā and Ulugh Beg Mīrzā. The Mīrzā (Kāmrān) dismissed him and appointed Bābūs to accompany him at the interview. Bairām Khān first went to kiss the threshold of his Majesty the king of kings who was in the bāgh-i-maktab (school-garden) with that cupola of chastity Khānzāda Begam, elder sister of his Majesty Gītī-sitāni Firdūs-makānī. Māham Bega who was his Majesty's nurse (*anaga*) brought out the nursling of Divine light from the inner chambers. The visitors performed [3] their obeisance, and acquitted themselves of their embassy to him. It was a great joy to Bairām Khān and his companions to have the privilege of beholding his auspicious Majesty. The witnessing of the divine lights which were manifest on 231

[1] I cannot find this pass.

[2] *I. e.*, standing or stagnant water. It is a salt-lake south of Ghaznī, I. G. I. 33 and Bābar's Mem. 149. The lake is 7000 feet above the sea.

[3] The account of Bairām's visit to Kābul, &c., seems taken from Bāyazīd. He gives more details, for he was one of the party.

his Majesty's forehead glorified their vision, and they returned thanks to Providence. Taking leave from them they went and visited M. Hindāl who was in the house of his respected mother Dildār Begam and was under surveillance. They presented to him a gracious *firmān*, a robe of honour and a horse. With like ceremonies they next day visited M. Sulaimān [1] and M. Ibrāhīm who had been imprisoned in the fort in the house of Qāsim [2] Mukhliṣ. On that day they were by M. Kāmrān's orders brought out from there into the garden of Jalālu-d-dīn Beg which is near the Shahr-Ārā [3] garden. Bairām Khān embraced these two grandees in that garden and gladdened them by conveying to them the gifts and favours of the king and the Shāh. Taking leave from them he went to *jalka* [4] Siyāh Sang, where Yādgār Naṣir had settled, and gave [5] him hopes of the pardon of his offences, and the forgetting of his faults, and of his receiving various royal favours. In like manner he visited and conveyed hopes to Ulugh [6] Mīrzā and other grandees, and gave them, as was proper, soothing messages. M. Kāmrān kept Bairām Khān under surveillance for more than a month, having neither the strength to resist, nor the grace to submit. He remained in these perplexities, until after hundreds of solicitations he let him (Bairām) go after a month and a half. He also by entreaties prevailed upon her Highness Khānzāda Begam to go to Qandahār ostensibly to persuade M. 'Askarī, who, he pretended, was not under his influence, to make over Qandahār to his Majesty Jahānbānī's servants, but in reality in order that if things should go ill with him, who was holding out, and was maintaining the fort under M. Kāmrān's orders, and he should have to give up the fort, that cupola of chastity might

[1] It appears from Bāyazīd that one reason for visiting Sulaimān was to give him a letter from the king of Persia, and also to explain the fate of the horse which Ṭahmāsp had sent him.

[2] Kāmrān's artillery-officer (Bāyazīd).

[3] Jarrett, II. 404.

[4] See Vullers 525a. Siyāh Sang, i.e., Blackstone, is an *ūlang* or meadow east of Kābul, Bābar, 139.

[5] Bāyazīd says Bairām was with Yādgār till 3 watches of the night as they were old friends in India. If Bairām spoke soothingly to him with Humāyūn's consent, it seems base and treacherous of the latter to have put Yādgār to death shortly after his submission.

[6] Blochmann, 461, 462. He was a Timuride, a son of M. Sultān Mīrzā and grandson of Sulṭān Ḥusain of Herāt.

be an intercessor for M. 'Askarī and might procure him his liberty. As M. 'Askarī had left the right path and in his devotion to M. Kāmrān had given up the rein of intention to the hand of rebellion and hostility, he applied himself to strengthening the fort, and placed guns and muskets all over it. The fort too was very strong, for it was of mud and so the breaching (*qila' ū qama'*) of it was very difficult. The breadth of the wall was sixty yards[1] (*gaz*). Though the heroes of the victorious army were few in number, yet they strove manfully 232
so that the Turkomans were astonished, and became jealous of them.

One day his Majesty Jahānbānī had a select party, and there his confidential intimates opened the door of recitals and took into their hands the thread of narrative. The assembly became delightsome from the flow of pleasing anecdotes and joyous tales. By the elixir of the words of the brave the coin of the courageous was tested and increased, and a stock of valour accrued to those whose supply was small. On this occasion there came to his mind the loving remembrance of his Majesty the Shāhinshāh. What may be the condition of this young cypress of the stream of the Caliphate, separated now from friends and surrounded by foes? And what are the thoughts of the envious, the foolish and the evil-minded about this auspicious rose-bush? With a heart rent in twain and a soul divided 'twixt hope and fear, he opened the hand of supplication before the great Temple which granteth the desire of the afflicted and distressed and prayed for the happiness and long life of that goodly tree of the Sultanate. In this way he relieved his blistered heart.

*Verse.*

Lord: keep Thou this royal pearl
Far from the molestation of the wicked,
Grant him water from wisdom's stream,
Grant him heat from perception's sun.

The sun hath trod many circuits in heaven
That this Light might issue from the veil,
Many a star hath displayed benign aspects
That this Moon might put aside his looks.

---

[1] So in all MSS. apparently, but perhaps A. F. wrote *shash* (6) and not *shast* (60).

High Heaven trod many a round
That the horizons might share in this light,
May eternal splendour be his portion
May his lightsome heart ne'er be darkened!

And in order to comfort his capacious soul he called for the horoscope which is the guarded tablet of mysteries of the fortune-favoured one and carefully perused it. In that frontispiece of auspiciousness he read personal safety, long life, ascension of the grades of fortune, ruin of enemies, and failure of the evil and crooked thoughted. Joyfully lifting up his head he exclaimed "God be praised, my heart is wholly at rest from these anxieties. There is hope that bye and bye I shall be made happy by a sight of that divine nursling, and shall, by the star of that auspicious one become victorious over all my foes." Having returned thanks to God he set himself to conquer the fort. M. 'Askarī used all diligence in holding it, and made changes in the garrisons of the batteries every
233 day and every night, lest proffers of reconciliation should be made by the besiegers[1] and there should thus be less vigilance on the part of the defence.

As the siege was protracted, and none of the king's servants came and joined him, the Persian officers relaxed their exertions and meditated a return home. His Majesty Jahānbānī read this design in their demeanour, and redoubled his efforts to take the fort. One night he moved out from his battery, and approaching the gate from the side of old Qandahār—the place is called Cahār Dara—he came within a stone throw of it, and there established a battery. Next morning when the Turkomāns saw this, they felt encouraged to take the fort, and they all moved forward; and narrowed the lines of circumvallation. M. 'Askarī was astonished, and showed signs of despair, and besought with many entreaties that as the cupola of chastity (Khānzāda) was approaching, he might have a respite till her arrival so that he might be reassured by her and might be enabled to serve (Humāyūn). He sent his petition through Mīr

[1] The passage is rather obscure, but I think the word *mūrcal* in the last part of the sentence must refer to the siege-batteries. The expression *ḥar-yak-jihatī darmīyān andāḵẖta* may be compared with that at p. 153, l. 8 of text.

Ṭāhir, brother of Khwāja Dōst Khāwind. His Majesty Jahānbānī, who was a mine of liberality and clemency, accepted his prayer and stayed the siege-operations for some days, The wicked Mīrzā outwardly assumed the airs of a suppliant, but secretly exerted himself to strengthen the fort, and when her Highness and Bairām Khān arrived he renewed his opposition. Though the noble lady endeavoured to restrain M. 'Askarī from evil designs and to induce him to kiss the holy threshold, he from his disordered brain would not accept her counsels, but continued obdurate and would not suffer her to leave the fort and go to his Majesty's camp. Thus the Mīrzā's contumacy and villainy were revealed even to his Majesty Jahānbānī. Relying therefore on the favour of God, who is the surety of those who commend themselves to Him, he strenuously endeavoured to take the fort. Meanwhile Ulugh Mīrzā, son of Muḥammad Sulṭān Mīrzā, who was descended from Sulṭān Ḥusain through a daughter, Sher-afkan[1] Beg, son of Qūc Beg, and Faẓāil Beg, brother of Mun'im Khān, Mīr Barka and Mīrzā Ḥasan[2] Khān, sons of Mīr 'Abdullāh, who 234
belonged to the Saiyids the Banī-mukhtārs of Sabzawār, and many others came from Kābul by the guidance of a happy star and did homage. The cause of their escaping was this. M. Kāmrān was keeping Ulugh Beg in confinement, and out of precaution he made him to a different custodian every week. When it came to Sher-afkan's turn, it happened that he too was afraid of the Mīrzā. He joined with the others and brought out Ulugh Mīrzā, and enjoyed the blessing of service. His Majesty Jahānbānī received this party with favour and gave them robes of honour, and assigned Zamīn Dāwar to M. Ulugh Beg. Though Qāsim Ḥusain Sulṭān came out with them, he lost his way one night and fell among the Hazāras. After some days and after being robbed he arrived on foot and with blistered soles. His Majesty remarked to him "There must have been something wanting in your loyalty for you to have lost your way and become involved in such troubles." After that Dawa[3] Beg Hazāra came in with his tribesmen. Petitions too arrived from the Kābul officers. The arrival of this party, and the receipt of petitions from officers and nobles caused great joy in the camp. The Qizilbāshī,

---

[1] Blochmann, 455.

[2] Blochmann, 439.

[3] See Erskine, the text has Dada.

(Persians) who had been uneasy in their minds, became tranquil and displayed alacrity in carrying on the war while the leaders of the garrison began to waver, and the foot of firmness slipped from the battlement of defence. The dwellers in the fort wrote daily accounts of M. 'Askarī and shot[1] them down from the walls. Their purport was that the garrison was in difficulties, and that the besiegers should press on, and not relax their efforts. At last it came to this that the officers of M. 'Askarī's army flung themselves out of the fort one by one, and that the gunners and infantry did the same. First, Khiẓr[2] Khwāja Khān threw himself down from the fort in the vicinity of his Majesty's battery, and seizing the collar of supplication with the hand of contrition fell at the holy feet of his Majesty Jahānbānī. After him Muayyad[3] Beg let himself down by ropes from the fort, and was exalted by doing homage. Then Isma'īl Beg, who was one of Gītī-sitānī Firdūs-makānī's officers and was distinguished for counsel and courage arrived, and Abū'l-Ḥusain Beg, brother's son of Qarāca Khān, and Munawwar Beg, son of Nūr[4] Beg, came with him. One night Khiẓr Khān Hazāra flung himself down from the fort, and two or three Hazāras took him on their backs and went off with him towards Kōt Laka (?). Inasmuch as the work of defence had got out of hand, and M. 'Askarī could neither make up his mind to remain in the fort, nor had he the face to come to the world-protecting Court, Khiẓr Khān Hazāra desired to betake himself to the cell of safety
235 and to come to strive out of these dangers. In the morning news came to the camp that he had left the fort and taken to flight. A number of people hastened to search for him. He had gone some distance and then hidden himself behind a rock. Some reliable persons relate that Khiẓr Khān Hazāra used to tell how the men who had been sent to catch him passed close to him and how once a man touched the skirt of his garment and thought it was an animal, while

[1] *Bartāftand*, explained by Erskine as meaning the fastening of letters to arrows and then shooting them down.

[2] Also called Khiẓr Khān Sulṭān. He was husband of Gulbadan the daughter of Bābar and authoress of Memoirs.

[3] According to Niẓāmu-d-dīn he was a prisoner in Qandahār. He died shortly after the taking of Kābul to the great joy of everybody, says Bāyazīd, as they regarded him as a Satan and the cause of Humāyūn's losing India.

[4] One of Bābar's officers. Mem. 424, 425.

Khiẓr Khān held his breath from fear. When night came on he emerged from under the rock and reached a place of safety.

As the daily increasing success of his Majesty Jahānbānī was patent, and it became clear to the garrison that owing to the good fortune of his Majesty Jahānbānī and the zeal of his devoted servants it would be impossible to maintain the defence, M. 'Askarī awoke from the sleep of carelessness and became disturbed in his mind, and could neither advance nor stay where he was. At first he asked to be allowed to surrender Qandahār and to proceed to Kabul, but his Majesty Jahānbānī did not agree to this, and the Mīrzā's crude idea came to nought. Out of necessity he had to send her Highness Khānzāda Begam to his Majesty to beg forgiveness of his offences. At the request of that cream of chastity's family the writing of forgiveness was drawn over the register of his offences, and on Thursday, 25th Jumāda-l-ākhir (3rd September, 1545), of that year (952) he came out of the fort, contrite and repentant, and in the train of the cupola of chastity. His Majesty Jahānbānī had formed an assemblage in the dīwānkhana and the Caghatāī and Persian officers were drawn up in line according to their rank. In accordance with the royal orders Bairām Khān hung the sword round M. 'Askarī's neck and introduced him. His Majesty Jahānbānī, in spite of all the mortal injuries which he had received from him, put aside the canons of sovereignty and with native kindness and excessive clemency accepted the intercession of the cupola of chastity and drawing the pen of forgiveness over the schedule of his deeds, he encompassed him with the curtains of favour and with exceeding affection. After returning thanks to God for this beginning of success, he gave orders for the removal of the sword from the Mīrzā's neck, and after he had paid his respects bade him be seated. After that Muḥammad Khān Jalāir, Shāham Khān, Muqīm Khān, Shāh Qulī Sīstānī, Tūlak Khān Qūrcī and others to the number of thirty persons were brought forward with swords and
quivers round their necks[1] to make their obeisance. Out of these 236
Muqīm Khān and Shāh Qulī Sīstānī were ordered into confinement with fetters[2] on their legs and wooden boards on their necks.

---

[1] Niẓāmu-d-dīn says they carried their shrouds in their hands.

[2] *Zūlāna* i. q., zāwalāna. See Burhān-i-Qāti' under Zūlāna and Vullers under zāwalāna.

From the close of day up to early dawn, which is the time of the arrival of the glory of heaven, there was a delightful assembly. Instructive events were described, and Mīr Qalandar and other reciters and players discoursed excellent music, thereby removing the rust from his Majesty's world-adorning soul. During the assembly they in accordance with his Majesty's orders presented M. 'Askarī with an exact copy of the letter which he had written to his Balūcī followers at the time when his Majesty was proceeding to a strange land by way of the desert. The Mīrzā's life was embittered, and mirth became melancholy. At last, out of necessity an order was given that he should be kept under surveillance, and that he should be brought from time to time to make his obeisance so that while his offences had, out of innate kindness, been forgiven, he might for some days take counsel with himself in bondage. Next day the night-illumining crescent of victory lighted up those who sat darkling in the citadel. Muḥammad Murād Mīrzā and the Caghatāi and Persian officers came to the city in attendance on his Majesty. For three nights and days the city was brightened by the light of his Majesty's august advent, and was in peace and tranquillity. On the fourth day it was, in accordance with the secret workings of his Majesty's comprehensive mind, presented to Muḥammad Murād Mīrzā, and his Majesty took up his quarters in the Cār Bāgh of his Majesty Firdūs-makānī, which is on the bank of the Arghandāb, and was refreshed by its pleasant groves. In that charming spot the official accountant laid before him a detailed list of the properties of M. 'Askarī, which had been brought together from all quarters, but his Majesty did not regard them as worthy of consideration and distributed them among those of his brave soldiers who were in want.

When M. Kāmrān heard of the conquest of Qandahār and of his Majesty Jahānbānī's coming against Kābul, he was agitated and troubled, and had his Majesty the Shāhinshāh brought from the house of the cupola of chastity Khānzāda Begam to his own, and made him over to his chief wife Khānam Begam. He also confined Shamsu-d-dīn Muḥammad Ghaznavī, commonly called Atka Khān, in an unworthy place, and took counsel with his officers as to what he should do with M. Sulaimān. Mullā 'Abdu-l-Khāliq, who was Kāmrān's teacher, and Bābūs, who had charge of political affairs, advised that the Mīrzā should be dealt gently with and be allowed

to go to Badakhshān so that he might be useful in time of need. Fortunately for M. Sulaimān it happened that Mīr Naẓar 'Alī, Mīr Hazār Teshkānī, Mīr 'Alī Balūc, and others had combined a few days before and had seized Fort Ẓafar, and put Qāsim Barlās and 237
other officers into confinement. They sent a message to M. Kāmrān that if he sent M. Sulaimān, they would make over Badakhshān to him, otherwise they would put their prisoners to death and hand over the country to the Uzbegs. Accordingly Mīrzās Sulaimān and Ibrāhīm and Ḥaram[1] Begam were sent off to Badakhshān. When they had got as far as Pāī Minār and Ma'mūra village, M. Kāmrān repented of having let M. Sulaimān go and sent persons to recall him, alleging that he had something to say to him. M. Sulaimān suspected this message and wrote a letter of excuse in reply to the effect that as he had taken leave in an auspicious hour, it was not proper to return, and that he trusted M. Kamrān would be so kind as to write to him what he wished to confer about and to send the letter by a confidential servant when he would act in accordance therewith. Meanwhile he hastened on to Badakhshān. As soon as he reached Badakhshān he broke his agreement. At this time too Yādgār Nāṣir Mīrzā fled from Kābul towards Badakhshān. And as fate desired that M. Kāmrān should receive the recompense of his deeds, the materials for this were being prepared daily. Of the Mīrzās no one remained with him except Hindāl. Him he flattered and appointed to pursue and capture Yādgār Nāṣir, promising him that he would give him one-third of all he now possessed or should afterwards acquire, on condition that he should not deviate in any way from loyalty and fraternal feeling. Having made this compact he sent off the Mīrzā whom he had kept under surveillance. M. Hindāl, who had been brought into difficulties by Kāmrān's ill treatment verbally agreed for he regarded his escape from his claws as a great relief. But when he came to Pāī Minār, he under a wise guidance proceeded towards his Majesty Jahānbānī. M. Kāmrān was astonished on hearing of this affair, and lost the thread of his counsel. He had no servants or companions who would consult his welfare or tell him the truth.

---

[1] According to Bāyazīd, p. 16a, Sulaimān was released before the fall of Qandahār. He also says that his wife Ḥaram or Khurram Begam bribed the officers with her jewels to advise his release.

Most of his servants had their eyes veiled, and the vision of their intelligence was troubled by the ophthalmia of neglect. They beheld not the way of salvation nor the straight path. Those who did see what was proper, had not the power to express their sentiments. This was due to two circumstances:—(1) Some had not the courage to make representations. (2) Some were of such a nature that they studied the temper of the Mīrzā, and did not consider truthful representations advisable, for they were certain that from
238 his self-sufficiency he would not accept good advice, but would be displeased on the mere mention of it. And his displeasure would cause injury to the influence and position of the speaker. The condition of fidelity is that in such matters one should not delay or have regard to one's language, nor spend one's time in negligence or delay. For the evil of this falls in the end upon all, and is as ruinous to the general prosperity. And the results of treacherous counsel, which is the greatest and worst of treacheries, come forth. And the mole of untrustworthiness and flattery, which is the blackness[1] of disloyalty and unpropitiousness, reveals itself on the cheek of their procedure. It behoves such men, if they feel afraid of not suppressing the truth or of uttering honest but disagreeable remonstrances to recognise the fact that such opportunities are part of their good fortune, and to rejoice thereat, and not to let the wrinkle of contraction form in the forehead of frankness. For though in appearance the great may be disgusted, yet in reality the noble mind approves of hearing both sides. And though such advisers may appear to run counter to the opinion of their masters, yet in fact they will at once be relieved from responsibility and have discharged the duty of good service, and also be lauded in word and deed by those who consider the end and regard the final termination. M. Kāmrān, in fact, went from blunder to blunder from want of warning wisdom, and the absence of sound counsellors.

---

[1] *Nīl. lit.* blueness, blue being the colour of mourning and misfortune.

# CHAPTER XXXVIII.

## March of his Majesty Jahānbānī Jannat-Āshiyānī's army from Qandahār to conquer Kābul, and victory over that territory.

When his Majesty was freed from anxiety about Qandahār he placed before himself the conquest of Kābul, and with this intention left his Majesty Firdūs-makānī's garden and halted at the Gumbaz Safēd (the white dome) above the shrine of Ḥasan Abdāl. The thought of the expedition continually occupied his mind, and he was perpetually holding conferences about it with far-sighted loyalists and devoted friends. Many of the Persians were wearied of their long expatriation and went off without leave, while some departed after obtaining leave by importunity. Budāgh Khān and the others who were in attendance on the Shāh's son opened, from want of consideration, the hand of tyranny and oppression over the subject population, and thought of increasing their own substance by such unhallowed proceedings. High and low used to come from the city, imploring justice, and his Majesty Jahānbānī was in a difficulty for if he were to rebuke the oppressors, the Shāh would be vexed, 239
while, if he did not execute justice, the hand of the unjust would not be withdrawn from the subjugated, and this would call down the Divine displeasure. As the time was not convenient, he remained perturbed, and put off remedying the evil till another season.

When the expedition to Kābul had been determined upon he was compelled to ask Budāgh Khān [1] for accommodation for some of his ladies and for his goods and chattels. He candidly acknowledged that in accordance with his promise he had made over Qandahār to the Persians, but said that he could not set the foot of resolve

---

1 The name seems Turkish and is also spelt Būdāq. See Blochmann 371, but the person there mentioned is probably not the Budāgh Khān of the text.

in the stirrup of toil until he had disposed of his people,[1] and his mind were at ease concerning them. Budāgh Khān in his ignorance of affairs made objections and unlike a wise man was neither alert in carrying out the Shāh's orders, nor in obeying the king's mandate, which was the root of the matter. The chief officers represented that they had a great enterprise in hand, and that there was nothing for it but to seize Qandahār. They would thus undertake whatever was before them with a light heart. His Majesty referred to the kindnesses of the Shāh and declined to vex the latter's servants, and thought they must submit to their unreasonable conduct. He began to consider if he should go to Badakhshān and should join M. Sulaimān to himself before attacking Kābul. But as a strong motive for haste in conquering Kābul was his desire to behold the Shāhinshāh and to share to the full in that light of the garden of the Khilāfat, knowing that by heaven's decree all providential victories depended on the auspicious existence of that splendour, his eager desire to attain that object revealed itself from time to time. Just then the Shāh's son became a beholder of the gardens (*riyāẓ*) of mercy, and a visitor of the pools (*ḥiyāẓ*) of pardon (*i.e.*, he died). The confidential officers represented that winter was at hand, and that it was impossible for them to convey the women and children and the baggage (*partāl*) along with them into the hill-country.[2] The Shāh's son was dead, and it was not right to leave Qandahār to the Turkamāns, especially when they were so headstrong and were by their tyranny ruining the country and casting down the pillars of peace. Moreover, though they had been commissioned to bind constantly the girdle of service on their souls' waist, and to serve continually the sublime expedition they had been perverse and been drunken with the wine of negligence, and had not shown zeal in submitting to orders. On the contrary they had transgressed the supreme commands, and had openly and secretly gone into opposition and had suspended over their countenances the veil of
240 shamelessness. It behoved his Majesty to shorten their oppressive

[1] *Mardān-i-khud*, meaning his harem.

[2] Perhaps referring to Humāyūn's project of marching into Badakhshān, but more probably to the hills north of Qandahār through which they would have to march to Kābul as Ghaznīn was still in the hands of the enemy.

arms so that they should not reach the skirt of the poor and needy in this city which was the first fruit of the Divine favour. God forbid that such a proper design should produce a cloud in the mind of the Shāh. Inasmuch as it was a long march to Kābul and the Hazāra and Afghāns were more numerous than ants or locusts, and as they (the Persians) were stumbling-blocks in their path, and above all, as they were intriguing[1] with M. Kāmrān, the first thing to do was to get hold of a refuge so that their minds should be at rest. At this moment there was no place better for this purpose than Qandahār. It was therefore in accordance both with reason and justice that Budāgh Khān be told that he must, *nolens volens*, give up Qandahār. If he did not comply, the city must be besieged and taken possession of; and let a loving letter be written to the Shāh, explanatory of the facts of the case and the necessities of the position, and replete with candour and friendship. As the noble Shāh was a mine of wisdom and justice he would regard the transaction as one to be approved of. The leading spirit in this matter was Ḥājī Muḥammad, the son of Bābā Qushqa. His Majesty Jahānbānī said "I admit it all, but 'twere base to lay siege to the place, to unsheath the sword of battle, and to put a whole party to death. Though they 've left the path of moderation (*i'tidāl*), I do not approve of immoderation (*bē-i'tidāl*) on the part of my servants. If this course be taken Budāgh Khān's men will perish, and such a result will look ill in the eyes of good men. It is much better that you devise some plan whereby we may get possession of the fort without war or tumult." Accordingly he sent a messenger to Budāgh Khān, with the request that as they were marching against Kābul he would keep M. 'Askarī in prison in Qandahār so that his Majesty's mind might be at rest. Budāgh Khān thought the proposal advantageous to himself and agreed to it. It was arranged that the courageous heroes of the battlefield should proceed to the environs of Qandahār and lie in ambush there and then suddenly, when they got an opportunity, should enter the fort. Bairām Khān and a body of troops were told off for the Gandigān[2] Gate,

[1] I think these two clauses must refer to the Persians though there does not appear to be any evidence that they were plotting with Kāmrān.

[2] The text has Kandikān but probably the gate was named after the village of Gandigān W. of the modern city of Qandahār, and the battle-field

while Ulugh Mīrzā, Ḥājī Muḥammad and another body of troops were deputed to the Māshūr Gate, and Muayyad Beg and others were stationed near the New Gate. Those tigers of the jungle of courage made a rapid night-march and lay in ambush near Qandahār. When the "true dawn" appeared Ḥājī Muḥammad presented himself before all the others at the Māshūr Gate. By chance[1] some forage-camels were going in; he advanced under their cover, and tiger-like[2] suddenly entered the gate. The warder saw him and challenged him. He said that he was bringing M. 'Askarī by Budāgh Khān's orders so that he might be confined in the Fort. This pretext
241 did not avail, and the warder was about to shut the gate when Ḥājī Muḥammad severed his arm with a blow of his sword. Some others came up from behind, and all the Persians who were there, and offered battle, were killed. Bairām Khān entered by the Gandigān Gate, and the Fort came into the possession of the King's servants. The Persians fled and took refuge in the citadel. At midday his Majesty Jahānbānī arrived and having entered by the Gandigān Gate took post at the Āqca (white) bastion. Thus that fortunate city became by the glory of his arrival an aligting stage of peace and tranquillity and a station of justice and beneficence. All, small and great, raised pæans of joy at this happy advent. Budāgh Khān came forward, through the intervention of Ḥaidar Sulṭān, and paid the homage of ashamedness and apologised for his offence. His Majesty encompassed him with princely favours and dismissed him. He made over the city to Bairām Khān and wrote to the Shāh that as Budāgh Khān had acted contrary to the Shāh's orders, and been slack in his duty, he had taken Qandahār[3] from

---

of 1st September, 1880. Lord Roberts' 41 years in India II. 368, Map.

[1] Khāfī Khān, I. 130, has a more detailed account of the stratagem.

[2] A. F. compares Ḥājī Muḥammad to a tiger stalking his prey.

[3] Elphinstone has some just remarks on Humāyūn's treachery and A. F.'s canting defence thereof. But he is not correct in saying that the people of Qandahār had never been subject to Humāyūn. He was certainly their suzerain through his brothers, and he was justified in regarding all Afghānistān as belonging to his family from the day of his father's conquest. Bādāonī I. 447 gives four reasons for taking Qandahār from the Persians, and as may be supposed, he is more vigorous and more to the point than the lumbering A. F.

him and made it over to Bairām Khān who was a dependant[1] of the Shāh.

Meanwhile M. 'Askarī, unmindful of the royal clemency, and of his life's having been spared made his escape. After some days an Afghān came and reported that the Mīrzā was in his house, and asked that some one might be sent to seize him, but without letting it be known from whom the information came. His Majesty Jahānbānī appointed Shāh Mīrzā and Khwāja 'Ambar Nāẓir and they brought him out of the Afghān's house from under a woolen carpet (*palās*), and conducted him to the Presence. His Majesty from his innate clemency, and his observance of his Majesty Gītī-sitānī Firdūs-makānī's testament[2] which was made for all mankind and especially for the brothers, forgave anew his crimes and faults and made him over to Nadīm[3] Kokaltāsh who was one of his Majesty's special confidants. He divided the territory of Qandahār among his officers. Tīrī[4] he gave to Ulugh Mīrzā, and the parganas of Lahū he assigned to Ḥājī Muḥammad for his maintenance. Zamīn Dāwar was given to Isma'īl Beg, Qilāt[5] to Sherafkan,[6] Shāl to Ḥaidar Sulṭān. In this manner all the officers got jāgīrs appropriate to their positions. Khwāja Jalālu-d-dīn Maḥmūd, who had committed extortion[7] in the city on M. 'Askarī's men and on others, was delivered over to Mīr Muḥammad[8] 'Alī.

---

1 *Ta'alluq bashāh dārad.* Bairām was a Turkoman and a *persona grata* with Ṭahmāsp. But perhaps the meaning is "the city remains dependent on the Shāh."

2 The reference as to Bābar's dying request that Humāyūn would always forgive his brothers.

3 The author of a MS. life of Akbar in the possession of Colonel Hanna, and who, as a grandson of 'Azīz Kōka and great-grandson of Jījī Anaga, was likely to know, states that Nadīm was the husband of the famous Māham Anaga.

4 N. Qandahār, on the Helmand, the Tarīn of the *Āīn*, Jarrett, II. 398. The text has Tiprī.

5 Probably Qilāt Banjārah, Jarrett, II. 397.

6 Bāyazīd, 17*b*, says it was given to Qāsim Ḥusain Khān Shaibānī.

7 *Ṭama' karda būd, lit.*, had behaved avariciously. The allusion to Jalālu-d-dīn is puzzling for he was in Humāyūn's service. But he had once been 'Askarī's servant and perhaps he abused his opportunities when the troops entered Qandahār. Erskine's paraphrase of the passage in his history hardly agrees with the text.

8 No doubt Muḥammad 'Alī Taghāī, the maternal uncle of Humāyūn, and who afterwards was governor of Kābul.

When the holy heart was relieved of the affairs of Qandahār, and when, by the blessing of Divine aid, and by the royal efforts, destiny and deliberation had come into accord (*taqdīr muāfiq-i-tadbīr āmad*), he in an auspicious hour left her Majesty Maryam-makānī in Qandahār and addressed himself to the subduing of Kābul. One
242 of the endless bounties and unexpected favours was that a large caravan had come from Hindustān and the merchants had made good bargains by purchasing 'Irāq horses from the Turkomans (the Persian auxiliaries of Humāyūn). As the lights of prestige were streaming from the cheek of circumstance, the leaders of the caravan came and represented that if their horses were taken into the service of the grand army and an order be given for payment after the conquest of Hindustān they would be greatly pleased and would feel that they were fortunate. "Glorious will be our fortune," they said, "if by giving this aid we may come to be numbered among the loyalists of the sublime dynasty." His Majesty Jahānbānī regarded the proposition as a heavenly aid, and a providential contribution, and having acceded to their request, he ordered that purchase-bonds for the horses should be written out at the rates desired by the vendors and be given to them. He himself came to the ridge near Bābā Hasan Abdāl and ordered Ulugh Mīrzā, Bairām Khān, Sherafkan and Haidar Muḥammad Ākhta Begī (master of the horse), to set apart the horses for the royal stables, and then to select those for the officers and others according to their rank. One thousand horses purchased by the privy purse (*sarkār-i-khāṣṣa*) were given away in accordance with each one's requirements. The hearts, both of the merchants[1] and the soldiers, were soothed and gladdened. Dawa Beg Hazāra, wishing to be distinguished for serving both in person and property, led[2] the way by night to the fort of Tīrī, where his clan was. When the army arrived there, the headmen brought according to their ability horses and sheep as presents. They did good service, and as the place had pleasant pastures (*alanghā*) his Majesty remained there for several days to recruit and to enjoy himself. Her Highness Khānzāda Begam fell ill here,

[1] Jauhar gives another and more probable account of this affair.

[2] *Rāh sarkarda burd*, perhaps the meaning is that he went by night in advance of the army.

and the illness lasted, and she died.[1] His Majesty performed the rites of mourning, and grasping the strong rope of patience, the glory of the awakened of hearts and the mark of the intelligent, he engaged in charities and works of beneficence such as befitted a princely family and might be a sweet savour to the soul of that generous matron. He then marched under the guidance of a lofty fortune towards Kābul. Near Qandahār M. Hindāl did homage and was received with unbounded kindness. His Majesty was much delighted at his coming, which was the preface to the advent of many others. Officers hastened from Kābul in troops. But by reason of contrariety and mingling of air-currents a sickness and pestilence
broke out on the march in the camp, and there were many travellers 243
to the city of annihilation. Among them was Ḥaidar Sulṭān. As the untowardness of the atmosphere was great, and the force became small M. Hindāl represented that they ought to return to Qandahār for the winter and march against Kābul in the beginning of spring and after making the army efficient. His Majesty said nothing to his face, but when the meeting was over he sent him this verbal message by Mīr Saiyid Barka: "When I did not know that you would come, or that Yādgār Nāṣir Mīrzā would leave[2] (Kāmrān) I proceeded towards Kābul in reliance on the Divine favours, why should I delay now because an unforeseen circumstance (the pestilence) has occurred? If this thought has come into your mind on account of the fatigues and pains of your men you can go and repose this winter in Żamīn Dawar which I have given to you, and when

---

1 Gulbadan Begam says she died after three days' illness. She calls the place Qabalḥak (?) and says the body was buried there but removed three months afterwards to Khānzāda's brother's (Bābar) sepulchre. In all probability Qabalḥak is a copyist's error for Ghilcak (غلچک) in Bābā Ḥasan Abdāl. Bāyazīd, p. 69, says that there was a garden there which Humāyūn visited several times.

2 It would seem from Jauhar, Stewart 81 and Erskine II. 322 that it was only at Tīrī that Hindāl joined Humāyūn. Erskine says Yādgār Nāṣir also joined here, but from the text and also from A. N. I. 248 and Bāyazīd 21b it would appear that Yādgār though he left Kāmrān did not immediately join Humāyūn. He went to Badakhshān, and then to Qandahār (after Humāyūn had marched) and did not join Humāyūn till at Kābul when he came along with Humāyūn's *harem*. No doubt he went to Qandahār because his old friend (see Bāyazīd) Bairām was there.

the knot of Kābul has been untied you can rejoin our service." The Mīrzā was greatly ashamed on getting this message and begged forgiveness. His Majesty advanced with good intent and a confident hope, and braced up his heart to carrying through the business. On the march Jamīl Beg, brother (younger) of Babūs, whom M. Kāmrān had made guardian of Āq[1] Sulṭān his son-in-law and had placed in Ghaznīn, came and kissed the threshold, and begged the forgiveness of Bābūs' offences. His request was granted.

When the army halted at the station (*yurt*) of Shaikh ʿAlī, which is in the neighbourhood of Paghmān (*naʿmān* in text) and Arqandī, M. Kāmrān became disturbed at the approach of the world-conquering standards and sent forth Qāsim Barlās with a body of troops. He ordered his artillery-officer, Qāsim Mukhliṣ Tarbatī to take his arsenal to Jalka Daurī near Bābūs Beg's house, and to draw it up there. He also brought inside the fort all the men's families who were living outside. When he had strengthened the fort he came out from Kābul with pomp and insouciance and encamped near the quarters (*yurt*) of Bābūs Beg. He employed himself in reviewing and marshalling the troops. Qāsim Barlās had proceeded with a body of troops to Takīya Khimār[2] when Khwāja Muʿaẓẓam, Ḥājī Muḥammad and Sherafkan hastened from the royal camp and displayed their superiority. By the Divine aid—which was the vanguard of conquering fortune—Qāsim Barlās could not withstand them and turned to flee. When only a small space remained between the two forces M. Hindāl was at his own request appointed to the vanguard. The army had passed the defile of the "Khwāja's ridge" and had halted in the neighbourhood of Arqandī
244 when Bābūs and Jamīl Beg and a number of their men, and with Shāh Bardī[3] Khān who held Gardēz, Bangash and Naghz came

[1] Younger brother of Khizr Khwāja the husband of Gulbadan Begam. Āq Sulṭān, the White Prince, is his sobriquet, his name, according to Bāyazīd 19*b*, being Ḥasan Daulat Sulṭān. He was married to Ḥabība one of Kāmrān's daughters. But he afterwards offended his father-in-law who had his wife taken away from him. See Gulbadan's Mem.

[2] *Camār* in text. *Khimār* means vintner. Stewart read *ḥimār*, an ass, and this is a more likely name.

[3] This is the man who afterwards became a saint and water-carrier and wrote poetry under the style of Bahrām Saqqā. He was elder brother

and submitted. They were received with unbounded favours. After that, Muṣāḥib Beg, son of Khwāja Kalān Beg, came with many men and enjoyed the fortune of service, and was exalted by princely favours. Meanwhile Bābūs represented that it was no time for dallying and that his Majesty should mount his horse as all the men were coming over. His Majesty Jahānbānī mounted the swift steed of fortune. On this occasion he sent for 'Alī Qulī Safarcī and Bahādur the sons of Ḥaidar Sulṭān who were in mourning for their father and loaded them with favours and kindnesses. After a time Qarāca Khān came and did homage. M. Kāmrān read his own downfall in the pages of the royal fortunes and sent Khwāja Khāwand Maḥmūd and Khwāja 'Abdu-l-Khāliq to apologise for his offences. He made sundry requests through the Khwājas, who arrived when the two armies were less than a mile apart. His Majesty accepted [1] his homage and postponed decision on his petitions. He promised further favours to the Khwājas and dismissed them with honour. Out of humanity and kindness he ordered a suspension of hostilities. The object of the Mīrzā in sending the Khwājas was to cause delay and make the king's soldiers slacken their march and to get time for himself, and he was waiting for the darkness of night so that he might by making a long night-march remove himself to a distance. When then the veil of nocturnal gloom had darkened the earth he from an obscured understanding and a benighted soul could not resolve upon experiencing the pleasure of doing homage and withdrew in all haste into the citadel. Then he took his son M. Ibrāhīm and his wives and went off to Ghaznīn by Bīnī [2] Ḥiṣār. When his

of Bāyazīd the memoirs-writer. His proper name was Shāh Bardī Biyāt. M. Kāmrān had by this time taken his districts from him, and given them to Khiẓr Khwāja Hazāra. Kāmrān gave him in exchange Ghōrband, &c., Bāyazīd 19*b*.

[1] I think the meaning is that he postponed decision on Kāmrān's requests until he came forward and did homage in person. According to Bāyazīd Humāyūn rejected all Kāmrān's proposals. Gulbadan Begam says Humāyūn made presents of food and clothes to the Khwājas.

[2] See Jarrett II. 404*n*. and *Āīn* text I. 592. The words in Bāyazīd 21*a* appear to be Bīnī-Kōhī. Lord Roberts in his "Forty-one years in India," II. 223 says "Beni Hissar, a considerable village, surrounded by orchards and gardens, and only two miles south of the far-famed citadel of the Bala Hissar." The name means "nose (or ridge) of the fortress."

Majesty Jahānbānī heard of his flight he sent Bābūs with a number of trusty men to Kābul to prevent any molestation of the inhabitants or sepoys, and to make them all hopeful of the royal favour. He appointed M. Hindāl and a body of troops to pursue the Mīrzā and proceeded himself to Kābul with victory at his foot and fortune as his stirrup-companion. In an auspicious moment the drummers of dominion beat high the great drum (*kūrāka*) of prestige and the standard-bearers of victory advanced the stelliform [1] standards of glory to the starry sphere. On the night of the 13th of the Jalālī month of Āzar corresponding to the night of Wednesday, 12th [2] Ramaẓān, 952 (18th November, 1545), the conquest of Kābul, the beginning of countless victories, was accomplished by heavenly aid, and the gates of joy and success opened to the hearts of mankind. Two

---

[1] *Kaukaba*. This is a play on the double meaning of the word *kaukab*, meaning both a star and the globe surmounting the standard, and this is all the neater from the fact that the march was at night.

[2] There is a good deal of confusion about the year. See Erskine II. 325*n*. Niẓāmu-d-dīn prefers 953, though some, he says, give it as 952. As pointed out by the *Bib. Ind.* editors the first chronogram given by A. F. yields 954, and the second, or metrical one, 952. I am of opinion that 952 is right. 12th Ramaẓān, 952, appears to be a Wednesday and corresponds to 18th November, 1545. Other authorities give the date as 10th Ramaẓān. A. F. gives the date of the commencement of the siege of Qandahār, 7th Muḥarram, 952, or 21st March, 1545, but does not give its termination. The omission is supplied by the Bādshāhnāma I. 64, which says that Qandahār was taken on Thursday, 25th Jumāda-l-ākhir, 952, or 4th September, 1545, and that Kābul was taken on Wednesday, 12th Ramaẓān, of the same year. The idea that the year was 953 seems to have arisen from supposing that Akbar was over four when Kābul was taken. Bāyazīd and Ferishta say this, but he was just over three if the capture was in 952. We know that Humāyūn was at Mashhad on the day after the Ramaẓān of 951 and at Jām on 21st Shawāl (see inscription in R.A.S.J. for 1897). He was then on his way to join the Persian army and so he might arrive at Qandahār in the beginning of 952 and take Kābul about 9 months later. The difference between the authorities as to the day of the month of the capture of Kābul may be due to some reckoning the day of Kāmrān's flight as that of the capture, while others have taken the date of Humāyūn's triumphal entry. Gulbadan Begam who was in Kābul at the time gives the night of 12th Ramaẓān as that of Humāyūn's entry. Perhaps A. F. copied this.

hours of the night had passed when his Majesty exalted the plain
of Kābul by the radiance of his advent. Navīdī[1] found the chrono- 245
gram of this victory to be *Kābulrā girift*, He took Kābul. Another
is the hemistich "*bē jang girift mulk-i-Kābul az we,*" "without a
battle he took the country of Kābul from him."

When the gates of joy and gladness opened at the glorious indications of the personality of his Majesty the S͟hāhins͟hāh, and the foundations of dominion were thereby renewed, his Majesty Jahānbānī regarded not the defeat of M. Kāmrān, nor the conquest of Kābul, but abode in expectation of the blissful footsteps of his Majesty the S͟hāhins͟hāh until they brought to him, in an auspicious moment, that world-intelligence who at that time was, so far as regarded the existence of his bodily elements aged three years[2] two months and eight days. His Majesty obtained spiritual and temporal felicity by beholding that blisful nursling of light divine, and prostrated himself in thanksgiving for the safety of the young shoot of fortune's garden, and for the glorious acquisition of the lamp of the family. In the presence of this glorious fortune, and before this abundant bliss he opened the gates of liberality and beneficence for all mankind. On the morning after that world-illuminating day his Majesty Jahānbānī sat on the throne of fortune and attainment, and received the homage (*kōrnis͟h*) of the pillars of the state and of the soldiery and servants, while at the same time the nations were made fortunate by kissing the threshold, and raising the hands of supplication implored from God the enduring glory of the K͟hilāfat, and the uprearing of the standards of empire. His Majesty threw open the gates of justice and beneficence before all people and tranquilly spent the winter aloft in the citadel in serving the Creator and in

---

1 Apparently this is the *nom-de-plume* of K͟hwāja Zain-al-'Ābidīn, a Persian poet. Rieu Supplement No. 307. He afterwards called himself 'Abdī and died in Ardabīl 988. Perhaps he is the Bābā 'Abdī mentioned in the Haft Iqlīm as having settled at Qandahār. See Ethé's Cat. 470, art. No. 1222.

2 The text has 2 years but this is clearly wrong. Akbar was born on 5th Rajab, 949, or 15th October, 1542, and Kābul was entered on 12th Ramaẓān, 952, so that according to the Muḥammadan calendar Akbar was then 3 years 2 months 8 days old, or 3 years 1 month according to the solar calendar. Bāyazīd says he was then between 4 and 5 which would make the year of the capture 953.

comforting His creatures. Of the events which happened about this time there were the deaths of Yūnus 'Alī and Mūyid[1] Beg who were leading officers of the Court. At the same time it came to the ears of his Majesty that Khwāja Mu'aẓẓam was plotting to run away in company with Muqaddam Beg,[2] and to convey themselves to M. Kāmrān. This vexed greatly his noble heart. He exiled Muqaddam Beg to Kashmīr and discarded Khwāja Mu'aẓẓam. By the felicity of his Majesty's presence and his bounteous shade the country of Kābul became an abode of security and peace and a resting-place of Divine mercy.

---

[1] Bāyazīd 21*b* says that the death of this man caused universal joy.

[2] He did good service by facilitating Humāyūn's escape after the battle of Qanauj, and probably for this reason he was only punished by banishment. He was a Kōka or foster-brother and had been one of Kāmrān's officers. He seems to have afterwards come back to Humāyūn. Text I. 296 and 300.

# CHAPTER XXXIX.

CELEBRATION OF THE SHĀHINSHĀH'S CIRCUMCISION, ILLUMINATIONS; 246
AND MANIFESTATION OF MARVELS BY THE TENDER
PLANT OF GLORY'S GARDEN.

'Tis ever the way of noble grantors of desires and auspicious-minded lords to seize opportunities for liberality, and to fulfil a choice worship, whose acmè is the conquest of affections, under the guise of Use and Wont—a course whereby they are protected from the dulled vision of blear-eyed mortals. Accordingly now that fortune's breeze was blowing afresh, and the rose-garden of attainment had bloomed anew, the custom of circumcision, as applied to the new growth of fortune's garden, and fresh offshoot of the palm of glory and grandeur, was made an occasion for the contentment and enrichment[1] of mankind. In the prime of spring, when the spirit of plants was in motion and the nightingale of delight was on the wing—

*Verse.*

"Violets raised their head from the stream's lip
Earth was ambergris-perfumed from the fragrance of flowers,
The fragrant breeze of morn, let us say
Carried a thousand musk-bags in her bosom."

He ordered that an encampment should be made in the Urta[2] Bāgh, a most delightful spot, and that affection might all the more be won—and this in truth is the giving of thanks to the Almighty, he threw open the gates of joy and pleasance, and in renewal of the splendours of Kaikāūs and of Kaiqubād it was directed that their

---

[1] Gulbadan Begam describes Humāyūn's bounties on this occasion to the widows and orphans of those who had fallen at Causa, &c.

[2] ارته. The word is Tūrkī and more commonly written اورته. It means middle so that Urta Bāgh might mean the middle or inner garden.

Highnesses the Begams should grace the entrancing garden with their presence, according[1] to their ranks and conditions, while the Amīrs and the city-magnates should occupy the Cār Bāgh. All the Amīrs bound the girdle of endeavour on the waist of joy and undertook these arrangements. The city magistrates, and leading men exerted themselves in an admirable fashion, while the artists and craftsmen vied with one another in decorating the shops, and in promoting the briskness of the bazar. Soon there was such ornamentation as exceeds description. Every day his Majesty Jahānbānī came and adorned the banquet, and he distinguished everyone by sympathetic expressions suitable to their rank and condition. Before the festival (of the circumcision) took place Qarāca Khān, Muṣāḥib Beg, and other familiars of the Court, who had been sent to convey her Majesty Mariam-Makānī, arrived from Qandahār, and her blissful advent increased the rejoicings.

247 It occurred to his Majesty Jahānbānī that he should make manifest to great and small the touchstone-capability (*'iyār-i-dānish*) of the Shāhinshāh, from whose brow there streamed while yet of tender years, thousands of rays of light divine. He therefore arranged a princely festival in the pavilions of chastity. All the great ladies attended in the gynaeceum.[2] For the instruction of the spectators his Majesty the Shāhinshāh was brought in on the shoulder of respect and placed on the auspicious Divan, and in conformity with orders her Majesty Mariam-Makānī entered in the train of the other ladies, and without being distinguished in any way. The design of the king was that the prince (*lit.* the light of the eye-pupil of the Sulṭānate) should single out his honoured mother from the crowd of ladies. By light divine his Majesty, without difficulty, hesitation, or mistake, and in virtue of his abiding intelligence and innate discernment took refuge with his saintly mother, and put himself into her arms. On beholding this glorious act—surprising to the minds of the superficial and to persons who

---

[1] The meaning seems to be that the ladies' tents were arranged in order according to their ranks.

[2] *Bārgāh-i-ḥarīm*, which, perhaps, only means private audience-hall. It is not clear to me from A.F.'s language whether the ladies were veiled or not, but presumably this would make little difference to Akbar who had not seen his mother since he was an infant.

are swayed by what is usual—a shout arose among the spectators, and they recognised the power of the eternally-nourished one, and prodigy of fate's worship. All perceived that this was not the work of the bodily senses which put a difference between childhood and adolescence. Rather it was nought but spiritual intuition and Divine teaching. 'Twas holy light breaking forth from its ambushes by the instrumentality of this nursling of Fortune's garden.

Of a truth, the veil of distance can be no hindrance to what is eternally conjoined, nor apparent remoteness any impediment to spiritual propinquity. And when we consider the matter what room is there for remoteness? For, in this firstling of Life's rosebush there is perfect contact with the Primæval, and the diffusive lights of being, the perfecting (*takmīl*) of the bodily frame, and the burnishing (*taṣqīl*) of the senses assume form *pari passu* (*darja ba darja*). And there is close relation with the glorious world of the Holy and the Absolute to whose verge there is no entrance for the darkness of ignorance, or the plethora of heedlessness. Nor is it hidden from those who can look far into the world of mystery that though this sublime Master seemeth to have been engendered amid bodily elements and from protoplasm (*mawadd-i-hayyūlānī*) yet as regards the source of his nature and the root of his being his forefathers and foremothers have been procreated from him so that spiritually and in an esoteric sense he is the Father of Fathers. And to his Majesty Jahānbānī—that curtain-raiser of celestial mysteries—it was manifest that the Cosmoplast of the outer world had brought this nursling of Creation's Spring into the field of actuality in order, firstly, that he might experience the stages of mortal life, and secondly, that he might bring together and compose the distractions of the world. In short he (Humāyūn) under the guise of the rite of circumcision offered thanksgiving to the Bestower of spiritual and temporal blessings. Each day there 248
was a novel, royal feast, and thanks were returned to the world-adorning Creator. The great ones of realm and religion came from all parts, and were made happy by royal gifts. Among these, Yādgār Nāṣir Mīrzā had the honour of performing obeisance. The brief account of him is that on the first[1] uprearing of fortune's

[1] If this means that Yādgār Nāṣir deserted Kāmrān on Humāyūn's first appearance before Qandahār, it is wrong, for we know from Bāyazīd,

standards on the borders of Qandahār he separated from M. Kāmrān, as has already been described, and proceeded to Badakhshān. As he could not succeed there, he set off in order to enter his Majesty Jahānbânī's service. At the time that the sublime army proceeded from Qandahār to conquer Kâbul, the Mīrzâ after experiencing the world's hardships arrived at Qandahār. Bairâm Khān showed him every hospitality there, and then in accordance with orders he had the felicity of paying his respects to his Majesty Jahānbānī at that joyous time (the circumcision festival). He had the good fortune also to do homage to the Shāhinshāh and to be made fortunate by the glances of favour.

During this joyful season, which was the time of the adorning of pleasure's springtide, and the period of decking the garden of dominion and prestige, at a moment when the constellations were shedding light from favourable aspects upon mortals the meeting for the decorating of the young plant of the Divine rose garden, to wit, for the circumcision of his Majesty the Shāhinshāh, was held with thousands of rejoicings. The materials (*asbāb*) for the joy of mankind were brought together, the gates (*abwāb*) of joy were opened for mortals. Small and great shared in the princely gifts, and high and low experienced the royal favour. The world's pains (*kulfathā*) ended in pleasure (*ulfat*) and the world's differences changed into unison. The captains presented their gifts, and were exalted by grand favours. In the midst of these celebrations his Majesty for the cheering of hearts, which is a great buttress of sovereignty, proceeded towards Khwāja Reg Rawān,[1] and ordered festivities. A world obeyed order was issued that the amīrs should wrestle[2] with one another. His Majesty himself by means of the balance of inspection picked out equally-matched antagonists. His Majesty wrestled with Imām[3] Qulī Qūrcī and M. Hindāl did so with

---

whose statement A.F. has elsewhere copied, that Yādgār was at Kābul when Bairām went there on a mission.

[1] Moving sand. See Bābar 146 and Jarrett II. 409 and especially Wood's Journey to the source of the Oxus, p. 115. The moving sand is in the upper end of the Kōh Dāman, and on its eastern side.

[2] The account of the wrestling is taken from Bāyazīd 216.

[3] Perhaps the Imām Qulī Shighālī of Blochmann, 512. The word Shighālī is probably derived from Shighāwal. Shaw's Turkī Dict. 134.

Yādgār Nāṣir M. After that he went to Khwāja Se[1] Yār to visit the *arghawān* groves. Then he returned and bade preparations be made for a great feast. He distributed fiefs, presents, and robes of 249
honour to the servants of the threshold in accordance with their deserts. M. Hindāl obtained Ghaznīn and its dependencies while Zamīn Dāwar and Tīrī were given to Ulugh Mīrzā. All those connected with the Court received gifts in proportion to their conditions, and the tribes of mankind abode with tranquillity and ease of heart in the shade of abundance, and the light of favour.

Among the events which occurred during the festivities was the arrival of the ambassadors of Shāh Ṭahmāsp. They brought congratulations on the victory and delivered suitable gifts. At their head was Walad Beg whom his Majesty welcomed with princely favours. Another was the arrival of Shāh[2] Qāsim Taghāī who brought a petition and gifts from M. Sulaimān. But the Mīrzā's excuses for not coming in person had not the honour of being accepted by his Majesty, and a peremptory order was issued for his attendance and he was informed that his reputation for sincerity and loyalty depended upon his appearing in person[3] to do homage. Another thing which happened about this time was the arrival of Mīr Saiyid 'Alī who was eminent in Afghānistān and Balūcistān for his possessions and for his honesty. He resided near Dūkī which is an appurtenance of Sind.[4] He greeted the threshold with the foot of integrity and the head of sincerity, and became a recipient of royal favours. Dūkī was awarded to him. About the same time Lavang Balūc, who was a leader among his people, came along with his brethren and did homage. His Majesty received him likewise with favour and granted him Shāl and Mastang. These visitors were granted their desires and dismissed rapidly lest the wild nature

---

1 The fountain of the Three friends, Bābar 147 and Jarrett II. 409*n*.

2 Sulaimān's maternal uncle, Bāyazīd 22*a*.

3 Jauhar, Stewart, 83.

4 The text has Hind but I adopt the variant of Sind as Dūkī is used by Bābar, 152 and 3, for the south-eastern hills of Afghanistan which is near Sind. In the *Āīn*, Jarrett II. 397, Dūkī is given as the eastern division of Qandahār. Erskine, Hist. II. 327, accepts the Hind of the text and remarks in a note that Dūkī was probably dependent on Multan.

of such dwellers in clachans (*rūstā parwardān*) should prove too strong for them, and delay be inimical to their constitutions.

Among the things which happened about this time there was this, that Yādgār Nāṣir Mīrzā from an ill-fatedness and an inward wickedness made a confused jumble of all favours, past and subsequent, and placed them in the alcove of oblivion and contumaciously took his stand on the path of wickedness and perversity. He gave ear to wretches of whom Muẓaffar the foster-brother of M. 'Askarī was the ringleader, and continually harboured evil thoughts. When these facts came, one after the other, to the knowledge of his Majesty,
250 and were confirmed by honest intelligencers, especially when 'Abdul Jabbār Shaikh, who was a most trustworthy person, and was intimate with one of the plotters and shared his counsels, came and detailed the circumstances after inquiry, the holy heart of his Majesty Jahānbānī Janna-t-āshiyānī became disgusted and he had Muẓaffar Kōka seized and put to death. Then he sent for Yādgār Nāṣir M. and reproached him by the mouth of Qarāca Khān. The substance of the rebuke was as follows: "We thought that when we had passed over your grievous offences, and had bestowed boundless favours on you, you would take warning and atone for your transgressions, past and present, and that even the ungrateful might have a limit and some discretion." The Mīrzā cast aside shame, and sometimes was silent and sometimes denied or feigned ignorance. His Majesty, after making categorical[1] statements (of his offences) and after royal reproofs, directed Ibrāhīm Isḥāk Āqā and others to confine him in the Kābul citadel (the Bālā Ḥiṣar) near the room where M. 'Askarī was imprisoned.

One of the things that happened at this time was the death of Caghatāī Sulṭān, who was a young Mogul prince and the unique of the age for beauty and character. His Majesty Jahānbānī regarded him with affection and distinguished him by favours. He felt his loss deeply, but reflecting on the Divine decree which hath assigned existence absolute to the other world, and to this world

[1] This expression (*ḥisābī*) seems to refer to the statement in Bāyazīd 22*a*, that nearly 30 charges were formulated against Yādgar, one being an act of disrespect committed by him so long ago as at the taking of Cāmpānīr.

only contingent existence, he wisely took refuge in submission and self-surrender. Mīr Amānī uttered this chronogram.

*Verse.*

Sulṭān Caghatāī was the rose of Beauty's rosarium,
Of a sudden, Death led him to paradise,
In the rose-season he designed leaving this garden,
Hearts were ingulphed in blood from grief for this likeness of a rosebud,
I sought his date from the bereaved nightingale,
Sighing he said "The rose hath left the garden."[1]

---

[1] *Gul az bāgh bīrūn shud.* Bāgh=1003 and gul=50 so that 1003 − 50=953, which is the date of the death. Amānī composed an equally ingenious chronogram on the death of Hindāl. See *infra.* According to Rieu, Tūrki Cat. 301, there were five poets of this name. The one in question is probably the second on Rieu's list, Mīr Amānī of Herāt who according to the Bodleian Cat. of Persian MSS. p. 219, used to live at Kābul and was killed at Jaunpūr by a fall from his horse in 981 A.H. A.F. his apparently taken the lines from Bāyazīd 22*a*, but the third line there is

دل غنچه صفت در غم او غرقهٔ بخون شد

Badāōnī has a similar chronogram about Bairām Khān's death. Lowe, 14 and text I. 46.

## CHAPTER XL.

### March of his Majesty Jahānbānī Jannat-Āshiyānī's army for the conquest of Badakhshān, the victory over that country, and what happened during that time.

When the disaffection of M. Sulaimān became confirmed, and it was made certain that he had twisted away his head from the burden of commands, and that the idea of sovereignty was paining it, and that he was inwardly troubled by this vain imagination, his Majesty
51 Jahānbānī, in the beginning of 953 (March 1546), turned the rein of intention towards Badakhshān. One of the Mīrzā's rebellious acts was that after the taking of Kābul he laid hold of Khūst and Andarāb, which were in the possession of M. Kāmrān,[1] and had been assigned to one of the royal servants. As moreover, by theory and practice the whole of Badakhshān did not belong to M. Sulaimān, his Majesty desired also to take away Qandūz and its dependencies and to make them over in fief to one of his followers, and bade him be contented with what his Majesty Gītī-sitānī Firdaus-makānī had given to his father. When his Majesty's dominions should be enlarged, his fief too would be increased. In consideration, however, of the Mīrzā's circumstances Qandūz was left as it was. The Mīrzā ignorantly averted his face from his benefactor, and openly smote the door of opposition, and had the *khutba* read in his own name. His Majesty resolved to extinguish the flames of disaffection. He left his Majesty the Shāhinshāh under God's protection and set out in a propitious hour, and halted at Yurat Cālāk.[2] He took M. 'Askarī along with him. He had anxieties about Yādgār Nāṣir Mīrzā, and when the army reached the Ulang of Qarā Bāgh[3] he determined

1. Kāmrān is not mentioned, but I think he must be meant. All the MSS. however have only the word Mīrzā so that perhaps A.F. really meant Sulaimān.

2 Bāyazīd seems to make Khwāja Rīwāz the first stage.

3 There is a Qarā Bāgh west of Ghaznīn called by A.F. in the Āīn the Qandahār Qarā Bāgh, but the

that he would relieve him of the pangs of existence and thereby give peace and security to the State. For the match of his strife, and the spark of his contentiousness were like to consume all the families. An order to this effect was sent to Muḥammad 'Alī Taghāī who had charge of Kābul. He out of complete simplicity and want of perspicuity returned for answer, "I have never killed a sparrow, how can I achieve the killing of the Mīrzā." His Majesty passed over his simplicity and charged Muḥammad Qāsim Maujī with this most proper service and he in the night-time sped the arrow of death by a bowstring.[1] When the holy heart was at rest from the malevolence of the Mīrzā, his Majesty marched under the Divine guidance towards the Badakhshāns (*Badakhshānāt*). When he arrived at Andarāb and had encamped at the garden of 'Alī Qulī Andarābī, M. Sulaimān owing to his evil fortune advanced to offer battle and drew up at the village of Tīrgirān[2] which is a dependency of Andarāb. When his Majesty heard this, he sent forward M. Hindāl, Qarāca Khān, Ḥājī Muḥammad Khān and a number of other brave men. A great battle ensued between the royal army and the 252
Mīrzā. The latter protected himself by a trench and stood firm, while Mīrzā Beg Barlās and a body of archers discharged their arrows from behind it. M. Hīndāl, Qarāca Khān and Ḥājī Muḥammad Khān displayed their valour and Khwāja Mu'azzam and Bahādur Khān were wounded by arrows, and had to dismount. Walad[3] Qāsim Beg, Ja'far Beg and the bodyguards, and Aḥmad Beg, and Dūghān[4] Beg who belonged to the Shāh's special bodyguard and who in company with the ambassador served his Majesty in this fight, came to the ground in consequence of their horses falling. The result hung in

Qarā Bāgh of the text must be the place about 25 miles north of Kābul and near Istālāf.

[1] In plain language the unfortunate Mīrzā was strangled. A.F.'s account seems taken from Bāyazīd who gives specimens of the charges brought against the Mīrzā. He says Mun'im Khān suggested the employment of Muḥammad Qāsim. Bāyazīd represents the execution as taking place before Humāyūn left Kābul and this seems probable. The Mīrzā's body was buried is a high ground opposite the citadel-gate and near a pond, but was afterwards removed to Ghaznīn, to his father's sepulchre.

[2] Bāyazīd 25*b*.

[3] Bāyazīd has Dalū Qāsim, brother of Walad Beg.

[4] Tāghān in Bāyazīd.

the balance till a body of devoted servants such as Shaikh Buhlūl, Sulṭān Muḥammad Fawrāq, Laṭīfī of Sabrind, Sulṭān Ḥusain Khān, Muḥammad Khān[1] Jalāīr, Muḥammad Khān Turkamān, M. Qulī Jalāīr, M. Qulī,[2] brother of Ḥaidar Muḥammad Khān, and Shāh Qulī Nāranjī[3] relying on the invisible Opener attacked M. Beg. And having by God's help crossed the trench, they raised their swords and briskly attacked the foe. The latter could not maintain themselves or abide the onset and fled, reckoning dispersion and route as a gain. On every side the braves of the field of action and lions of battle's jungle advanced on the plains of victory. Ere his Majesty had mounted his swift steed the reverberation of victory sounded in his ears. The voice of exaltation burst forth. M. Sulaimān did not remain firm but went off towards the defiles of Khōst by way of Nārīn[4] and Ishkamish. Tūlak of Ṭāliqan, M. Beg Barlās,[5] and Avīs Sulṭān who was a scion of the kings of Moghulistān separated themselves from M. Sulaimān and did homage. M. Hindāl and a body of heroes were ordered to seize the fugitives and his Majesty himself took part in the pursuit. Many Badakhshānī horses fell into the hands of the brave warriors, and his Majesty arrived by the Pass of Shāshān[6] at the valley of Khōst. M. Sulaimān fled miserably with a few followers to Kūlāb.[7] The Badakhshān nobles and soldiers came in crowds and did homage and everyone of them was treated with consideration and with favours suitable to their position. On account of the abundance of fruits his Majesty remained several days in Khōst[8] and was the accom-
253 plisher of the wishes of the people. For the purpose of hunting waterfowl and partridges and for fishing he proceeded to Warask.[9]

[1] Blochmann 411.

[2] Blochmann 385.

[3] Blochmann 480.

[4] Nārī in text.

[5] Bāyazīd calls him the ruler of Ghōrī (qu. Ghōr).

[6] Sāsān in text, but the variant is right. It was north of Tīrgirān and Andarāb.

[7] Beyond the Oxus.

[8] It would seem that Māham, the mother of Humāyūn, came from Khōst, for Bāyazīd, 26*a* says that Humāyūn stayed in Khōst for several days in the society of his maternal grandparents. The Khwāja Muḥammad 'Alī mentioned in Bābar's Mem. as the ruler of Khōst, is probably either Māham's father, or her brother. If the latter he must be the Mīr Muḥammad 'Alī whom Humāyūn put in charge of Kābul.

[9] So in Bāyazīd. Text has Darask. The place has already been

There he practised the netting[1] of birds (*ganjishk*) which is a speciality of that place. From thence he went to Kalāōgān[2] and from there to Kishm.[3] M. Sulaimān did not think it advisable to remain in that neighbourhood and so had crossed the Āmū and was there in perturbation with a few followers. One thing that happened at Kishm was that a servant of Shāh Ṭahmāsp named Khusrū[4] had fled and entered his Majesty Jahānbānī's service. He had used some improper language about the Shāh, and Dūghān Beg, Ḥusain Beg and Ja'far Beg of the Shāh's bodyguard and who were in attendance on his Majesty, on hearing of this met Khasrū in the Kishm bazaar and killed him. His Majesty disapproved of this lawlessness and imprisoned them, but after some days he, at the intercession of Ḥusain Qulī Sulṭān Muhrdār, drew the line of forgiveness over their offence.

When the affairs of Badakhshān had been settled, Qandūz and its dependencies were given to M. Hindāl, and much of Badakhshān was divided in fiefs among the officers. Mun'im Khān was made taḥṣīldār of Khōst, and Bābūs was sent to collect the revenues of Ṭālīqān.[5] His Majesty resolved that for the better management of the affairs of Badakhshān and for the comfort of the subjects and soldiery he would make Qil'a Ẓafar his winter-quarters. He therefore proceeded in that direction; but when he came to Shākhdān, between Kishm and Qil'a Ẓafar, he fell ill and so had to halt there for nearly two months. At the beginning of this illness he lay unconscious for four days, and on this account unpleasing rumours became rife, and men left their fiefs and came in. M. Hindāl left his post with improper ideas and in concert with other officers came as far as the bank of the Kōkca, and the partizans of M. Sulaimān raised their heads here and there. But Qarāca Khān came with a number of loyalists and pitched his tent in the royal courtyard and

---

mentioned as Warask in text I. p. 99 near foot. It is probably the Varsack of Wood, 160*n*., and if so, is the river on which Kishm stands.

1 See Bāyazīd, 26*a* & *b*, and Bābar, Mem. 153.

2 The Kalagān of the maps. It is west of Kishm.

3 Bāyazīd says Humāyūn stayed 3 or 4 months in Kishm.

4 Bāyazīd calls him Khusrū Pādshāh and says Qāsim Jangī was his slave.

5 Ṭālqān in text, but see Bāyazīd 27*a*.

confined M. 'Askarī who was likely to be seditious, bringing him into his own tent. Qarāca acted as a personal attendant, and waited on his Majesty during his sickness. No one entered the Presence except Khwāja Khāwand Maḥmūd[1] and Khwāja Mu'īn.[1] On the fifth day, which was the beginning of the convalescence, his Majesty showed signs of improvement, and Mīr Barka entered and paid his respects. When his Majesty's glance fell upon him, the Mīr became agitated and showed a desire[2] to sacrifice himself as a thanksgiving
254 for his Majesty's recovery. His Majesty said "Mīr,[3] God hath spared (*bakhshīd*) me." The Mīr gave some hints of the confusion of affairs and of the rectitude of Qarāca Khān. His Majesty had him called, and spoke benignantly to him, and expressed his sense of his services. At the same moment he sent a rescript of favour to the ornament of dominion, the tender plant of the stream of sovereignty, the head and trunk of fortune's springtide, to wit, his Majesty the Shāhinshāh, by the hands of Fażīl Beg, lest any evil tidings should have reached there and have dimmed the radiant heart of that nursling of Divine light, or should have caused commotions in that country. By a happy coincidence Fażīl Beg arrived with the *firmān* of favour on the morning after the night on which the distressing news of his Majesty's illness had reached Kābul. The coming of the glad tidings dispelled grief and was productive of universal order and steadfastness. The flames of discord died down; and M. Hindāl hastened back to his place, and everyone else went back to his *jāīgīr*.

---

[1] They were father and son. There is an account of Mu'īn, the son, in Blochmann. He is perhaps the same as the Mu'īn who was Qāẓī of Lahor, Blochmann, 545. Mu'īn's son was Sharafu-d-dīn who married Bakhshī Bānū, Akbar's sister, and became afterwards a rebel. The family was descended from Khwāja Aḥrār the famous saint of Samarkand.

[2] Perhaps the meaning is: Changed his intention of devoting himself into thanksgiving for Humāyūn's recovery.

[3] Mīr Barka was the son of Mīr 'Abdullāh and is several times referred to in the Akbarnāma. According to Jauhar it was Cūcak Begam who waited on Humāyūn during his illness and was rewarded by seeing him open his eyes when she squeezed some pomegranate juice into his lips. Bāyazīd praises the attention of Fāṭima Begam the Urdū Begī whose daughter married Khwāja Mu'aẓẓam and was killed by him. Perhaps it was the same Fāṭima who married Bāqī Khān. Badāonī, II. 61.

Among the occurrences of this year was the killing of Khwāja Sulṭān Muḥammad Rashīdī[1] who held the office of Vizier. The short history of this event is as follows: Khwāja Mu'aẓẓam in conjunction with sundry vagabonds, whose brains were ruined, adopted some bigoted[2] phrases of the religious views of some heretical, worthless fools who had no power of reflection in their natures, and were entangled in wordy wranglings, whose nostrils took in naught of the fragrance of truth and justice and in the tree of whose understanding there was no fruit produced by the flowers of knowledge, and having conceived faithless bigotry to be faith he came into the quarters of the Khwāja on the night of 21st Ramaẓān, 16th November, 1546, just as the day's fasting was over, and broke his fast by giving him of the water[3] of the sword of ignorance for his final draught. Then fearing the wrath of the king, which is typical of Divine chastisement, he took to flight. When this news came to the ears of his Majesty he sent men to seize him and his companions, and a strict order was despatched to the authorities in Kābul, which was the residence of those ill-starred ones. Muḥammad 'Alī Taghāī, Faẓīl Beg and others, who were in the service of his Majesty the Shāhinshāh, and were managing the affairs of Kābul, on receiving the command seized Khwāja Mu'aẓẓam and his companions and imprisoned them.

When there appeared at Shākhdān signs of convalescence in 255
the burning frame (*mizāj-i-wahhāj*) of his Majesty Jahānbānī he seated himself in the guarded litter of the Divine favour and proceeded towards Qil'a Ẓafar. Maulānā Bāyazīd who was an eminent physician and had been nominated as tutor to his Majesty

---

[1] Bāyazīd calls him in his list "Dīwān," and there spells his name as Rashīd.

[2] Bāyazīd 27*b*, describes the murder, but says nothing of bigotry's having been the motive. It was committed by sundry Persians in concert with Mu'aẓẓam and apparently cupidity had to do with it for when they fled they carried off some of Shāh Ṭahmāsp's presents from Takht-i-Sulaimān (*qu.* the place mentioned by Wood 160). Niẓāmu-d-dīn mentions that the Khwāja came with Humāyūn from Persia. Probably therefore he was a Shī'a and this may have made him obnoxious to Khwāja Mu'aẓẓam.

[3] *Āb* meaning both water and glitter and applied to the wave-markings on a sword.

the Shāhinshāh, and whose grandfather had been in the service of that Alexander[1] and Aristotle (Sikandar-Makānī Aristō-Nishānī) Mīrzā Ulugh Beg, and had been distinguished among all the mathematical observers, performed excellent service during this illness. When his Majesty reached Qil'a Zafar he soon recovered his health, and his equilibrium was restored. By the completion of the recovery of his Majesty Jahānbānī joy and delight came into the hands of the desires of mortals. In accordance with orders a grass[2] house was built and he often distributed justice and happiness therefrom. From it Sherafkan, the son of Kūc Beg, received investiture of Kahmard, Zuhāk and Bāmiān. And from excess of kindness his Majesty announced that when the army arrived at Kābul he would add Ghōrband to his fiefs. His Majesty took the pleasure of *tasqāwal*[3] —hunting which in the Badakhshān language is called *shikār-i-nihilam*.

---

[1] The epithet Sikandar-Makānī may serve to illustrate that of Mariam-Makānī applied to Abkar's mother. Ulugh Beg's real name was Muhammad Turghāī according to Vambery. The two astronomers who helped him in the composition of his tables were Ghiyāsu-d-dīn Jamshīd and the Qāzīzāda (Salāhu-d-dīn). One of them was perhaps Bāyazīd's grandfather (see D'Herbelot's articles, Ulugh Beg and Zig, and Jarrett II. 12, No. 85). The person meant may however be 'Alī Koshjī, said by D'Herbelot to be the Qāzīzāda's son. See Erskine's Bābar 51*n*. 4.

[2] *Khāna-i-kān*, the khāna-i-kānī of Bāyazīd. Bāyazīd, from whom A.F. borrows, tells us that the house was built by Jalālu-d-dīn Mahmūd who was then Mīr Buyūtāt or Barrack-master. The time was winter. Bāyazīd tells a story in connection with this house, of Humāyūn and some intimate courtiers (*ahl-i-nishast*) having cooked *bughrā* (macaroni?) there. He also tells of Sherafkan's visit. When he first came he was drunk and Humāyūn seeing his state from behind the screen (*cīgh*), ordered him off. When he came again some days afterwards, Humāyūn behaved with great delicacy towards him and granted him certain districts. Kān means a mine and also a sheath, and so may mean a screen, but I incline to think that the کانی kānī of Bāyazīd is a copyists' error for کاهی *kāhī*, made of thatch or straw.

[3] Neither *tasqāwal* nor *nihilam* occurs in the dictionaries. A.F. here copies Bāyazīd who describes, p. 28*b*, an expedition to the mountains on the other side of the Kōkca. They arrived at the hills, which were excessively steep, at midnight, and hunted the deer next morning. They passed so near and so quickly that they could not be shot with arrows and had to be caught by the hand. The word *nihilam* is used by Bābar,

The dread residence of his Majesty in Badakhshān wrought dismay in all Tūrān. The Usbeks gathered together and were full of apprehension, and could find no suitable remedy for their fears.

---

Mem. 28, and Erskine (or Leydon) says that he does not know what animal it is. In reality *nihilam* is not the name of an animal, but of a method of hunting, *viz.*, driving. Its synonym *tasqāwal* is Tūrkī and the last part is perhaps اول awal, meaning an enclosure. (Redhouse).

## CHAPTER XLI.

### Unveiling the mysteries of Design in the strife-stirrings of M. Kāmrān, and account of his rule over Kābul.

'Tis an ancient canon and an established ordinance that when God the Creator of the world wills to set an elect one on the throne of sway over mortals and by establishing him on a kingdom-adorning seat to place in his mighty hand the bridle of men's hearts, He maketh him in the beginning of his course the alighting-place of divers difficulties and the receptacle of sundry afflictions to the end that he may the more fully appreciate the force of the unending favours which stand ready for him in the hidden world; so that by becoming conversant with the varied stages of existence he may come to know personally Grace and Wrath, expansion and contraction, joy and sorrow. All this is clear to those who are familiar with ancient records, and are cognisant of old stories. But inasmuch as the personality of the holy product of the meeting[1] of the two seas of the Divine Power (*Jalāl*) and the Divine Beauty (*Jamāl*), his Majesty the Shāhinshāh, to wit, is by virtue of the Eternal Decree designated for all the stages of knowledge, and as the world-
256 adorning Deity created him a wise-hearted[2] Teacher and an illuminated, farseeing soul needing not the instruction of any of the sons of men, the apparition of those calamities was not to acquaint him with Grace and Wrath, nor to burn away carnalities and mortalities. Rather did the order of the manifestations of the glories of opposing qualities and the notes of conflicting attributes unveil themselves as of course and in their full perfection. And there was an illustration[3]

---

[1] *Mujma'-i-bahrain.* Explained as meaning the meeting of salt and fresh water. It was the title given by the ill-fated Dārā Shikōh to his book which was intended to reconcile the Hindū and Muhammadan religions.

[2] *Cf.* Faiẓī's verses, Badāōnī, II. 261 and Lowe, 277.

[3] Referring to Akbar's refusal, when a child, to learn his lessons. See *infra*, p. 519.

of this in his early years, for at that time his holy soul kept aloof from inappropriate teaching. These truthful remarks will make it clear to the wise and the admonished that it is in the eyes of the superficial that such facts[1] are regarded as arising from abundance of instruction and a surplus of knowledge, while in the eyes of those who see the truth they are but the inevitable refulgence of a personality imbued with wisdom from of old. And whenever the bitter[2] waters of affliction are to be poured into the lips of one who stands afar off from the courts of Unity, and is a bewildered wanderer in the desert of astoniedness, there is in the first place a curve (*lit.* a fold or wrinkle) of magnificence cast into his forehead[3] of acceptance and he is made the originator of divers act of ingratitude, and the shower-forth of varieties of injustice and tyranny, till he be flung into eternal wrath and everlasting punishment. This is a figure of the condition of M. Kāmrān who fell out with his benefactor and elder brother, his eternal superior, chosen one of God, king of the age, and just ruler, and wrought the destruction in life, estate and honour, of many a servant of God.

In fine, a strange disaster occurred during this time of enjoyment, when the capacious soul of his Majesty was a palatial garden of mirth and rejoicing. A desolating report came that M. Kāmrān was strife-mongering and that he had suddenly fallen upon the city of Kābul and brought it into his possession, and that Sherafkan had, heedless of the end of things, gone over to the Mīrzā. His Majesty Jahānbānī's sanctified heart was troubled, firstly, by the fate of his Majesty the Shāhinshāh; secondly, by sympathy for the citizens and subjects, who are a trust from the Creator, and who should be tended not less carefully than the children; thirdly, by the rebellious proceedings of the Mīrzā and the results thereof. He addressed himself with celestial genius to the remedying of these disturbances, and displayed suitable solicitude for putting an end to the outbreak.

---

1 Apparently the fact referred to in Note 3.

2 Referring to the bitter lakes met with in a desert, the Marah of the Hebrews.

3 *Nāṣiya-i-qabūlash*. Meaning, I suppose, that Kāmrān was offered the choice of greatness, and that his wickedness was enhanced by his misuse of his opportunities for well-doing.

And Abūl Faẓl, the writer of this noble record, turns away from amplitude of language, in order that he may give an account of events, and hastens towards narration, and gives a brief and parenthetical account of the circumstances so that the lips of those athirst for the waters of words may be satiated.

257 The description of the occurrence is as follows. When the army of fortune took Qandahār and came to the environs of Kābul, and all the Kābul army and all the people of that country were delighted at the good tidings of his Majesty Jahānbānī's advent, and separated from the Mīrzā and came in crowds and did homage, the Mīrzā turned away from the path of advice and the road of obedience and loyalty and becoming a bewildered wanderer in the desert of perturbation and want took the road to Ghaznīn. He forsook the blessing of service and absconded. M. Hindāl, Muṣāḥib Beg and a number of others were sent after him, as has been related in the account of the taking of Kābul. But when no trace of him could be found, and it was not known which way he had gone (*lit.* no dust rose up from his path) the pursuers returned in obedience to the royal commands and came to Kābul. This Mīrzā brought himself in all haste to Ghaznīn. The rulers and inhabitants of that place were favoured by fortune, they strengthened the fort and did not open the gate of inclination for him. The Mīrzā's false representations were unsuccessful; so he hastened from these to the house of Khiẓr Khān Hazāra. He treated the Mīrzā with hospitality and brought him to Tīrī, and from thence to Zamīn Dāwar. Ḥisāmu-d-dīn 'Alī, the son of Mīr Khalīfa, was in Zamīn Dāwar. He strengthened the fort and fought bravely, and courageously guarded the fort. When this news was brought to his Majesty he made over Ghaznīn to M. Hindāl and Zamān Dāwar and its appurtenances to M. Ulugh, giving him also a standard, a kettle-drum and a *tuman tūgh*. He also sent an order to Bairām Khān to join Yādgār Naṣir M., who had come there (Qandahār) to act loyally, to M. Ulugh and to send them against M. Kāmrān. He also sent a rescript to Yādgār Nāṣir M. to act in concert with M. Ulugh in putting down M. Kāmrān and by means of this service to move upwards on the steps of amendment of his past crimes. The Mīrzās went together from Qandahār to Zamīn Dāwar, and when the news of their approach reached the Mīrzā's camp, the Hazāras dispersed into the wilds and M. Kāmrān withdrew. He

hurried off to Bhakkar and took refuge with Shāh Ḥasan Arghūn. M. Ulugh Beg took firm possession of his fief; and Yādgār Nāṣir M. made as it were, a pilgrimage to the service of his Majesty. In Kābul he learnt the bliss of service as has already been stated. M. Kāmrān came to a halt in Sind and married the daughter of the Ruler of Tatta, who had already been betrothed to him. He had stayed there for some time devising mischief when the news came of his Majesty Jahānbānī's illness, which had occurred in Badakh- 258
shān. After that there came other bad news. The Mīrzā asked help from the Ruler of Tatta and resolved to go to Kābul. The ruler of Tatta thought this a great opportunity and sent a body of troops with the Mīrzā. Some were of opinion that he should first seize Qandahār, and then go to Kābul. But as Qandahār was secure under the control of Bairām Khān, Kāmrān set before himself the capture of Kābul and boldly hastened there. Near Qilāt he fell in with a number of Afghān merchants who were bringing horses. He arbitrarily took the horses from them and gave them to his men. From thence he hastened to Ghaznīn, and arrived there unexpectedly. Zāhid Beg was holding the fort for M. Hindāl and was spending his time in drunkenness and negligence. He was completely intoxicated on the night when the Mīrzā arrived. By the help of the butcher 'Abdu-r-raḥmān, the Mīrzā's men secretly ascended, and got possession of the fort. Zāhid Beg was brought drunk before the Mīrzā, and the wretches cast him in his drunkenness from the pinnacle of life into the abyss of annihilation. The Mīrzā left his son-in-law Daulat Sulṭān in Ghaznīn, and leaving there also a number of men from Bhakkar under the leadership of Mulk Muḥammad, who was a confidential servant of the Ruler of Tatta he went as rapidly to Kābul. He arrived there at dawn without warning. He first went to the headdress-maker's gate. He learnt that Muḥammad Taghāī was in the hot bath, and it would appear that there too (referring to what occurred at Ghaznīn) drunkenness had brought him into the stupor of cropsickness. 'Alī Qulī Ūghlī, one of the Mīrzā's bodyguard, entered the bath and brought out Muḥammad 'Alī naked. The Mīrzā gave him his ablution with the water of the sword, and entered the fort. Pahlwān Ashtar, who had charge of the Iron Gate, opened it in accordance with a compact, and the Mīrzā entered the city, which now came into his possession. On the morning when

this occurrence took place, Ḥājī Muḥammad 'Asas[1] came and saluted the Mīrzā. The latter said 'How have I gone and how have I come back'! 'Asas replied "You went in the evening and you came in the morning." The Mīrzā went up to the citadel and took up his quarters there. Shamsu-d-dīn Muḥammad Khān Atka brought his Majesty the Shāhinshāh with all reverence before M. Kāmrān. The Mīrzā, on beholding that theatre of miracles involuntarily became gracious and gentle. He shewed him various favours, but from short-sightedness put his Majesty, who was under the shadow of the protection of God, into the charge of his own men.

When M. Kāmrān had brought Kābul into his possession, he practised various kinds of cruelty and opened his hands to shed people's blood and to seize their property. He caused Mihtar Wāṣil
259 and Mihtar Wakīl, who were special royal slaves, to be blinded. Ḥisāmu-d-dīn 'Alī, son of Mīr Khalīfa, whom his Majesty had summoned to his personal service, and whose fief he had transferred to Ulugh Mīrzā, had come about this time to Kābul and Kāmrān in revenge for his firmness at Zamān Dāwar had him castrated and put to death in a most horrible manner. Cūli Bahādur too, who was a loyal and approved servant, was put to death, and Khwāja Mu'aẓẓam, Bahādur Khān, Atka Khān, Nadīm Kōka and many other household servants were put into prison. The Mīrzā thus prepared for himself spiritual and temporal ruin, and an evil name in realm and religion. He was continually tempting and ruining men by deceitful letters.[2] Among such was Sherafkan who was induced to desert; and Ḥasan Beg Kōka and Sulṭān Muḥammad Bakhshī were by lies brought to separate themselves (from Humāyūn). Insincere, low dispositioned ones of narrow capacity for the idea of a small advantage put the dust of the world into the cup of their avarice and trod the path of disloyalty. And it appears that the main cause of the capture of Kābul was the discord of men and their negligence and want of vigilance and circumspection. For at that time Muḥammad 'Alī Taghāi was Dārōgha of the city for his Majesty Jahānbānī, but he continually took the path of carelessness, and did not apply the

---

1 Ferishta says that 'Asas was Bābar's jester. He adds that 'Asas went on to quote a verse in Kāmrān's honour.

2 *Cf.* Gulbadan's Memoirs. She mentions that Kāmrān tried to make her write a letter to her husband, inviting him to join him.

rules of wariness. Fazīl Beg too set up for himself a separate scheme (*lit.* a separate shop) in the city and had ideas of becoming independent (of Muḥammad 'Alī). From smallness of capacity and inefficiency they opposed one another and struck an axe on their own foot. When Kābul fell into the hands of the Mīrzā he set about collecting troops and in arranging for sedition. A large number collected round him. One day he was seated on the top of the citadel, and Walad Beg, Abūl Qāsim and many others of the Shāh's bodyguard, who had got leave and were proceeding towards Persia, came to pay their respects to the Mīrzā. His Majesty the Shāhinshāh was also adorning the Mīrzā's banquet with the light of his presence. All the Mīrzā's confidential servants were set upon rapacity (*darpai akhz ū jar*), and the men round about, who were like flies at the stall of a sweetmeat-seller, were falling upon one another. A good service presented itself to Abūl Qāsim, and he whispered to Walad Beg that it would be a loyal act if they who were thirty active men should do a brave deed in unison, finish off the Mīrzā, and glorify this young plant of the springtide of dominion and fortune, to wit, his Majesty the Shāhinshāh. Walad Beg, who was not a man of war, showed backwardness towards this proposal and said "We are travellers, why should we intermeddle"? As the top-thread of every act is bound to some special point of time what possibility was there of its appearing before that?

## CHAPTER XLII.

260 MARCH OF HIS MAJESTY JAHĀNBĀNĪ JANNAT-ĀSHIYĀNĪ FROM BADAKHSHĀN TO KĀBUL, AND THE SIEGE THEREOF.

When the news of M. Kāmrān's strife and sedition reached the ears of his Majesty Jahānbānī he resolved, in spite of the extreme cold, and the abundance of ice and snow, to hasten by the defile of Ābdara,[1] and to extinguish the flames of sedition. His first step was to send a gracious missive to M. Sulaimān, pardoning his offences and restoring that dismayed desert-wanderer to house and home, and exalting him by conferring on him the territories which his Majesty Gīti-sitānī Firdaus-makānī had bestowed on his father. He confirmed M. Hindāl in possession of Qandūz, Andarāb, Khōst, Kahmard and Ghōrī and its neighbourhood, and thereupon he, under the guidance of God, and in a most auspicious hour, turned the reins of intent towards Kābul. On account of the protracted continuance of the ice and snow he stayed for some days in Ṭālīqān.[2] The Uzbegs looked upon his Majesty's return as a great gain and a grand escape, and one and all abode in peace and tranquillity. In fact the whole of Tūrān was relieved from the dread of the grand army. When the snow had abated his Majesty moved from Tālīqān towards Qandūz. M. Hindāl showed him hospitality there, and in order to gratify the Mīrzā his Majesty took up his quarters near the town in the garden of Khusrū Shāh. After the 'Īd-i-Qurbān[3] he marched by the pass of Shibartū[4] to the pass of Rēgak,[5] and halted at Khwāja Seh Yārān

[1] A pass in the Hindu Kush leading from Badakhshān to Kābul, and according to Babār, Mem. 139, the only one open in the winter. It was by it that Babār went to Qundūz in the winter of 1510 when he heard of the death of Shairbānī. Tār. Rash. 237 and note. Apparently the name is not known now. See also Jarrett II. 400 and note.

[2] Ṭālqān in text which agrees with Marco Polo's spelling.

[3] This festival takes place on 10th Zi'lḥajja the last month of the Muḥammadan year, so if the year in question was 953, the date of the festival was 1st February, 1547.

[4] "Usually called Shibr or Shaber nowadays," Tār. Rash. 76n.

[5] Bāyazīd has, 296, Kotal Rekak

(Three Friends). Sher 'Alī, who posed as one of the trusty and sincere followers of the Mīrzā, had strongly fortified the Ābdara defile; but what can outward force do against inward (*i.e.*, Divine) aid? or human strength against the Divine support? He fled before M. Hindāl and Qarāca Khān, but when the victorious cortége had passed through he came up from the rear and fell upon the baggage and the tents. When his Majesty had encamped at Cārīkārān, a large number, heedless of favours and of promises and covenants, deserted and joining M. Kāmrān obtained dignities (*darajāt*, lit. ascendings) which in reality were degradations (*darakāt*, lit. descendings). Among these were Iskandar Sulṭān and M. Sanjar Barlās son of Sulṭān Junaid[1] Barlās, sister's son of his Majesty Gītī-sitānī Firdaus-makānī. His Majesty stayed in the borders of Zamzama, and exerted 261
himself to strengthen the weak-hearted and the wavering. By compacts and covenants he knit up the hearts of the disheartened and convened a council. Those who received permission to speak represented that as M. Kāmrān had enclosed the city and made himself strong the proper course for them was to leave Kābul and to encamp at Būrī and Khwāja Pushta, so that they might be able to provision the troops. All agreed to this, and they marched from Zamzama. When they had gone a little way it came into the inspired mind of his Majesty that it was not advisable to go to Khwāja Pushta for many of the men had their families in the city, and would desert in consequence. And many perhaps would think that the army was going to proceed to Qandahār. The proper thing to do was to summon up one's courage and take possession of the enclosing lines (*shahrband*). If the Mīrzā came out to fight, so much the better; and if he did not, the men would not desert, and also they would be sheltered to some degree from the inconveniences of the rainy season. He sent for Ḥājī Muḥammad Khān and communicated to him this secret inspiration. He approved of the plan and it was settled accordingly. Ḥājī Muḥammad Khān with a body of troops proceeded by the way of the Minār pass while his Majesty set out

and says it is above Cārīkār. Perhaps it is the Khawak pass, which is at the top of the Pangshīr valley, and the pass by which Wood entered Afghanistan. See his Journey to the Source of the Oxus, 272.

1 Junaid was married to Shahrbānū, a younger sister of Bābar and is often mentioned in the Memoirs.

by the Payān pass to conquer the city. The victorious troops had, under the leadership of M. Hindāl, reached the neighbourhood of Dēh-Afg͟hānān and were near the shrine of Bābā S͟has͟hpar when Sherafkan came out at the head of a large body of M. Kāmrān's best men, and a hand to hand fight took place. Many of the imperial troops did not stand their ground. But M. Hindāl remained firm, and gave proof of courage and devotion. When this state of things became apparent to his Majesty he directed Qarāca K͟hān, Mīr Barka, and many others of the stamp of S͟hāh Qulī Nāranjī[1] and the like to advance and give a lesson to the rebels. They went forward, Mīr Barka being ahead of them all, and meanwhile Ḥājī Muḥammad K͟hān, and the body of men who had been dispatched in the direction above mentioned, came up, and the enemy was defeated. S͟herafkan was made prisoner and brought before his Majesty. He being a mine of grace and gentleness was willing to confine him for some days so that he might get a lesson while in chains and return to his duty. But at the request of Qarāca K͟hān, and the urgency of all the loyalists who were enraged at his ingratitude and insincerity, he was put to death. His Majesty then proceeded towards Kābul by the way of the k͟hiyābān[2] (avenue) while the im-
262 perial braves pursued the fugitives and arrived at the Iron Gate. Mīrzā K͟hiẓr K͟hān and a number of the Arg͟hūniān troops went off to the Hazārajāt. The wall (*shahrband*) fell into the possession of the imperialists, and his Majesty halted that day in the garden of Qarāca K͟hān. Many of the evil-disposed rebels, who had been made prisoners on the field of battle, were executed and S͟her 'Alī was disconcerted[3] and took refuge in the citadel. Those who were distracted[4] there obtained repose.

His Majesty Jahānbānī visited afterwards the Dīwānk͟hāna and Urta Bāg͟h gardens, and took up his quarters on the hill of 'Aqābīn[5]

[1] Blochmann 480 and 596. He was from Kurdistan, near Bagdad. He was a wrestler, Blochmann 253.

[2] Ouseley, Persian Travels III. 389 renders this word by "paved causeway."

[3] *Sarāsīma*, but there is the variant *berāha*, *i.e.*, the erring or the vagabond.

[4] Perhaps this refers to the ladies of Humāyūn's family who were shut up in the fort, but most probably it only means that the garrison were relieved by seeing S͟her 'Alī re-enter.

[5] A.F. says, Jarrett II. 404, that it overlooked the fort.

which is over against the fort.. Guns and culverins (*ẓarbzanhā*) were placed in position and discharged. Every day M. Kāmrān's men came out and had hand to hand conflicts. Mahdī Khān, his relation Calma Beg,[1] Bābā S'aīd Qibcāq, Ism'aīl Kūz,[2] Mullā Mabtalāī Aujī, and some other ill-fated ones fled from the victorious army, and joined the Mīrzā. His Majesty Jahānbānī ordered Qarāca Khān, Ḥājī Muḥammad Khān, and a number of others to seek for an encamping ground in front of the Yārak gate[3] for that was the proper place for taking post. He also directed that the siege-operations should be brought nearer to the fort, and that the charge of the batteries should be distributed, and the Mīrzā be pressed more closely. The persons deputed were searching for a site when 30 or 40 men came suddenly out from the Yārak gate. Ḥājī Muḥammad Khān attacked them and as they were not able to keep their ground they fled towards the fort. Meanwhile Sher 'Alī came from inside the fort and engaged Ḥājī Muḥammad Khān, and inflicted a severe wound on his right arm. During this conflict the imperialists pressed forward and drove Sher 'Alī inside the fort. They lifted up Ḥājī Muḥammad Khān, who was faint and powerless, and carried him to his quarters. He was ill for a long time, and it was reported that he was dead. His Majesty sent a messenger to him requesting that he would get on horse-back and come to the batteries. He mounted his horse in obedience to the request, and the market of the foes-joy fell flat. One day M. Sanjar son of Sulṭān Junaid who had gone off with the brand of faithlessness on his brow came out and attacked. His horse became unmanageable[4] and carried him as far as the Violet-Garden. He was made prisoner and brought before his Majesty who granted him his life, but sent him to prison. Muḥammad Qāsim[5] and Muḥammad Ḥusain who were sisters' sons of 263

[1] Apparently this is the man who afterwards behaved so nobly. Blochmann 378.

[2] Text, *kūr*, but the variant *kūz* is probably right for it is a synonym for *khars*, wine-jar, which we know from text p. 278 l. 7 was Humāyūn's nickname for Ism'aīl.

[3] There is the variant Bārak.

[4] *Sikh jalū*. B.M. MSS. Add. 27, 247 and 17926 and No. 564 I.V. have *shakh jalū*, hard-bridled, *i.e.*, hard-mouthed, and doubtless this is the true reading. It is *shakh jalū* in Bāyazīd from whom A.F. probably took the expression.

[5] Blochmann 380 and 485. It was Qāsim who built the Agra Fort.

Pahlwān Dōst Mīr Barr[1] and who are now among the great officers, and have attained to high rank, threw themselves down from a bastion between the Iron Gate and the bastion of Qāsim Birlās, and in the 'Aqābīn received the blessing of doing homage and like a brace of eagles[2] (*'aqābīn*) clutched the prey of everlasting good fortune.

While this fighting was going on a large caravan arrived from abroad (*wilāyat*)[3] at Cārīkārān. There were many horses in it and other goods. M. Kāmrān sent Sher 'Alī with a body of trusty adherents to take possession of those goods, though Tardī Muḥammad Jang Jang, who was one of the Mīrzā's trusted followers, protested, and plainly said that if his Majesty Jahānbānī should hear of it and send his men and block their way so that they should not be able to rejoin the Mīrzā, they would be lost, and at the same time the Mīrzā's purpose would not be affected. The Mīrzā had his eyes fixed on the goods and would not receive this warning, and sent his men under the leadership of Sher 'Alī. As soon as the news reached his Majesty Ḥājī Muḥammad Khān was appointed to the service of restraining those tyrants from their plunder. Ḥājī Muḥammad represented that the force had gone off at night and had done their work, and that if they followed them and failed to meet with them, they would escape. He suggested that the points commanding the roads and fords should be seized so that they should not be able to get inside the fort. His Majesty Jahānbānī agreed and himself came down from the hill and gave directions for occupying the stations and places of access. Sher 'Alī and Tardī Muḥammad Jang Jang and the others who had reached the merchants forcibly took possession of their goods, and much thereof was plundered. On returning they wanted to enter the fort, but found the roads and fords closed against them. Tardī Muḥammad and Sher 'Alī had an altercation and Tardī Muḥammad Jang Jang said "See, my words have come true"! Though they looked right and left, they could find no way of re-entering. They were dumbfounded and withdrew, and waited for an opportunity of getting in by stratagem.

[1] Blochmann 485 and VI where it is stated that the title means superintendent of the Imperial Forests.

[2] A.F. puns on the name of the ridge where Humāyūn was.

[3] Bāyazīd says the horses came from Balkh.

One day Bāqī Ṣāliḥ, who was one of the valiant men of the garrison, eagerly brought M. Kāmrān near the Iron Gate, and boastingly said that by one sally he would bring Sher 'Alī in by this gate. When they opened the gate a number of the Mīrzā's braves came out. The men of the battery, such as Muḥammad Qāsim Khān Maujī, Qāsim Mukhliṣ, and Jamīl Beg came forward and showed alacrity and courage. Sumbul Khān and 60 or 70 slaves did good execution with their muskets. Jamīl Beg was martyred, and Bāqī Ṣāliḥ, who was the cause of this disturbance, was killed[1] 264
by a bullet, and Jalālu-d-dīn Beg, who was one of the Mīrzā's confidants, was severely wounded. Many others also were wounded. They failed in their object and closed the gate of the fort. Sher 'Alī despaired of entering the fort and hurried off to Ghaznīn. His Majesty Jahānbānī despatched after him Khiẓr Khwāja Khān, Muṣāḥib Beg, Ismāil Beg Dūldāī, and a large body of troops in order that they might by dint of courage make those luckless ones prisoners. They came up with Sher 'Alī at the Sajāwand pass, and an engagement took place. The imperialists were victorious, and many horses and goods fell into their hands. Many prisoners were also made. Sher 'Alī escaped with a few men to the Hazārajāt and took refuge in the house of Khiẓr Khān.[2] The imperialists returned victorious with much booty and were rewarded by boundless favours. The plundered merchants, who had taken protection at the holy court, were told to take whatever goods and horses they recognised, and thus many horses and goods were restored to their owners. This occurrence was a revival of fortune. The rebel prisoners were brought in front of the batteries and publicly put to death with varied punishments so that those who were slumbering on the bed of error might be aroused.

When there was no entrance or egress by any gate, and by no door could he obtain victory[3] for his designs, and no road was open save that of failure, M. Kāmrān set himself in his evil mind to punish

---

1 According to Niẓāmu-d-dīn, he deserted to Humāyūn along with Jalālu-d-dīn Beg, Elliot, V. 225. The lit. translation of A.F. is a musket-arrow fell as fire on the harvest of his life.

2 This must be Khiẓr Khān Hazāra.

3 *Bar Kāmrānī*. A.F. plays upon Kāmrān's name and his recent failure to get Sher 'Alī re-admitted.

sheltered striplings and innocent children and to defile pure-skirted ones. He made over[1] the wife of Bābūs to the people of the bazaar, and spilled upon the ground, with cruel tortures, the blood of his three boys, one of whom was seven, the other five, and the third three years old, and flung them down from the top of the fort to near the batteries of Qarāca Khān and Muṣāḥib Beg. He also hung upon the battlements Sirdār Beg the son of Qarāca Beg and Khudā Dōst the son of Muṣāḥib Beg, and sent a message to them to come and see him, or to let him depart, or to withdraw the king from the siege. Otherwise he would kill their sons as he had done those of Bābūs. Qarāca Khān, who was then prime minister, cried out with a loud voice, "God save His Majesty the king. Our houses and homes and our children must one day perish, and their non-existence cannot be avoided. What better thing can there be than their coming to an end in the path of their master and benefactor. What are children when our lives are a sacrifice for His Majesty. Depart from those vain thoughts, and come and humbly submit, which will prove your salvation and be the ornamentation of your life, so that as your well-wishers we may do for you the utmost in our power. Why do
265 you frighten us by killing our children? If our children be really put to death, revenge for that is at hand." His Majesty sent for Qarāca Khān and Muṣāḥib Beg and soothed them by sympathetic words and favours. The Mīrzā struck at men's honour and reputation by most unseemly conduct towards their women and children. He suspended the wife of Muḥammad Qāsim Khān Maujī by the breasts[2] (*pistān basta*). And inasmuch as the Mīrzā was sick with vexation and envy, every opposition which he in appearance made against His Majesty Jahānbānī was really resistance and opposition to the Almighty Creator. Every act of such a tyrant must inevitably fail of success, and in the end becomes the cause of his temporal and spiritual ruin.

---

1 Bāyazīd says he made her over to an improper man (or men), *ba mardum-i-nā-munāsib sipurd*, and killed the two sons, aged 10 and 12.

2 Bāyazīd says she was hung up over the Iron Gate.

# CHAPTER XLIII.

## Display of Great Marvels on the part of His Majesty the Shāhinshāh, and the taking of Kābul.

M. Kāmrān in his folly and want of wisdom brought, for the sake of his own protection, that nursling of the garden of sovereignty and that new fruit of the springtide of the Khilāfat—*viz.*, his Majesty the Shāhinshāh—in front of the guns, and kept him in a place where it was difficult, on account of the marksmen (*qadr-andāzān*) of the victorious army, for an ant or a grasshopper to pass. What humanity was this? Or what beast of prey or demon has such principles? Why did the tongue of him who gave such an order not grow dumb, and the arm of him who executed it not refuse its office when it encompassed that tree of fortune and planted it for such a purpose? The eye which could not see the manifest claims of his Majesty Jahānbānī—an elder brother, a venerated father's representative and a benefactor—; how could it perceive the world-adorning beauty of his Majesty the Shāhinshāh when concealed within the veil of honour, and when it was immature and in the dawn? How shall a heart which from the anguish of envy is trodden under foot of sorrow and is at enmity with Almighty God, perceive the rays of Divine light when enclosed in a human form? How shall he who cannot see the right path for himself divine the proper course for another? And inasmuch as the Divine Wisdom watched over that exhibition of hidden lights and kept him in the shelter of guardianship and the shadow of protection from evils and perils, and was surety for the safety of that Unique of the Age, it did not bring those wicked tyrants in a moment to the punishment of their deeds. Rather the design and intent of Providence with regard to those regardless ones had predetermined that they should be tossed about in the world and cast into the ashes of calamity and contempt, and by the revolutions of Time, degree by degree, and step by step, be brought[1] into

[1] There is the variant *guzārish*, payment or retribution, and this is

dissolution (*gudāẕish*), and that the wicked actions of that oppressor should be flung gradually into the bosom of retribution, so that
266 by beholding the final retribution other wrong-doers might take warning. Assuredly, when such things are looked upon with a purged vision, the recompense and retribution which comes into evidence by degrees and step by step is severer and more fatal in its exhaustive torments!

When the evil act (the exposure of Akbar) of this unspeakable crew was executed, the hands of the marksmen trembled, the arrows flew crooked, and the lintstocks congealed. Sumbul K͟hān, the master fireworker, felt his ardent soul grow cold, and thought within himself, "What can have happened"? God be praised! What evil-thoughted ones imagine to be failure and so press on in their wickedness becomes a means of perfection and an adminicle of security! This was instanced here. Firstly, that by being protected in so perilous a place by God from the strokes of seldom-missing marksmen, and of wondrous musketeers, shame was wrought for the wicked and blackhearted, and the beauty of instruction was conferred on the seekers after righteousness; and, secondly, that the miracle of fires displaying coldness and of lintstocks not becoming alight was manifested. When Sumbul K͟hān's eyes fell on the object-spot (*masqaṭ-i-tīr*, the lighting-place of the arrow), his powers of vision were quickened and he recognised his Majesty the S͟hāhins͟hāh. The horror of the sight almost drove the souls out of the bodies of the spectators, and the gunners became as dead men (*qālab tahī kunand*, emptied their bodies). The mystery became revealed to Sumbul K͟hān, and he understood why the fires had gone out. In a moment he withdrew his hand from the battery, and the dejected crew of traitors (*firqa-i mutafarriqa-i bāg͟hīa*) were respited for a time from the severity of the royal artillery. Wherever God's protection stands sentinel o'er His Chosen One, what power have human stratagems to do him wrong? Though fools exhibited the unbecoming act, yet the Divine plan required the revelation of the mystery and was the exponent of this truth, so that mortals might have an explanation of the miracle and that every one might, in proportion to his intellect and capacity, reflect upon its nature and might, according

supported by B.M. MSS. and is probably right. But I.O., No. 564, has *gudāẕish*.

to the measure of his understanding, comprehend good and evil. In short, wicked men compassed this event in order to lighten their sufferings and the pressure which was upon them, but the far-seeing and discriminating reckoned the move as causing the speedy downfall of those workers of iniquity.

In the meantime, M. Ulugh Beg came from Zamīn Dāwar and Qāsim Ḥusain Shaibānī[1] from Qilāt, and Khwāja Ghāzī, who had remained in the Shāh's camp, and Shāh Qulī Sulṭān,[2] who was related to Bairam Khān, came from Qandahār, and a number came in from Badakhshān. H.M. assigned them a battery by the Yārak Gate. Those right-minded men girt up their loins for service and the valiant heroes displayed more and more alacrity and energy and 267
pressed the Mīrzā more and more closely. When all his schemes failed, he turned like a fox to fawning and to feline hypocrisy and came forward with protestations of shame and repentance and with blandishments. He represented through Qarāca Khān that he regretted the past and was desirous of entering into service and of making amends for the past, so that he might win over his Majesty's appreciative heart by acceptable services. Might now his life and estate be under the o'ershadowing protection of his Majesty's clemency as the offering of his shame and penitence. His Majesty by virtue of his noble nature accepted his statements and ordered the siege-operations to be slackened. As M. Hindāl, Qarāca Khān, Muṣāḥib Beg and many of the other officers had not freely quaffed the sweet waters of loyalty they, from regard to their own interests, which is a note of old, discord-loving service, did not wish the Mīrzā to make his submission. Why should I mention sincerity and loyalty? These are priceless jewels and rarely-found gems. If they be scarce among Turanians, in whose country they have long ceased to be procurable, what marvel is it? But they had not even the practical sense, which is the surety for one's own loss and gain, to do good in return for good. Those blind-hearted ones returned evil for good. Worse than this; they perpetually prepared the element of bloodshed and trouble for mankind, with the evil

---

1 Bāyazīd says he was brother of Ḥaidar Sulṭān.

2 Apparently the No. 45 of Blochmann 359. The Maāsir-i-Raḥīmī 288b, calls him Shāh M. Qandahārī and says he held Qandahār for Bairam.

idea that thereby their own greatness and affluence would be increased. How were their thoughts linked together, or what consistent ideas did they possess? If they had understood even the lowest stages of loyalty, which carries with it so many blessings, they had never approved of thus endamaging themselves. If they were unacquainted with the sanctuary of loyalty, what had become of the bazaar of common sense that this faction did not come to know of it? If the ear of their understandings did not tell them of this, would that they had known the depression of sorrow and so not have struck so sharp a hatchet into their own feet.

At length that faction for their own evil designs terrified the Mīrzā, and sent a message to him saying, "with what hope do you remain in the fort, or with what hope will you come to the Presence. Day by day the siege-operations are becoming more and more complete, you should get out quickly by a certain battery;" and they referred him to the battery of Ḥasan Qulī Āqā. The Mīrzā, in accordance with this advice, came out by the Delhi Gate at the place which they had pointed out to him, on the night of Thursday, the 7th Rabīʿ al-awwal 954, 27th April, 1547, and absconded. He went towards Badakhshān, thinking that he might perhaps do something
268 with the help of M. Sulaimān, or, failing that, might be helped by the Uzbegs. His Majesty Jahānbānī appointed Ḥājī Muḥammad Khān and a body of troops to pursue him, and entered the city of Kābul, which had been a wilderness of rebellion, and made it by his advent a pleasant home of friendliness. His Majesty the Shāhinshāh, a station of endless marvels, went forth to meet him and was made fortunate by entering the Presence. The chaste ladies also did homage. His Majesty Jahānbānī on beholding his Majesty the Shāhinshāh, displayed in heart and countenance fresh light and glory. What greater blessing could there be than this, that the eyes of a Jacob should be brightened by the beauty of a Joseph? Or what sublimer repose could there be than that the heart of such a sage (*ṣāḥib dil*) should be comforted by union with such a darling? In thanksgiving for the safety of the holy personality (Akbar), and for his well-being, he made vows, prayers, and alms, and applied fresh balm to the wounded hearts of mankind which were bleeding from the oppression of circumstances. Each one was soothed and comforted by manifold sympathies and consolations, and the distractions

of pained hearts were changed into concords.[1] His Majesty Jahānbānī and his Majesty the Shāhinshāh took their seat with the lustre of dominion and the magnificence of prestige on the throne of victory and the *masnad* of honour. Though Ḥājī Muḥammad and the others who had been sent in pursuit of M. Kāmrān came up with him, they out of the glamour and fascination of old and disloyal service, let him[2] go as if they had not seen him. The Mīrzā slipped away but Āq Sulṭān[3] and a number of other followers were made prisoners. They were subjected to a just scrutiny and each received a punishment suitable to his offences. Among them, Sulṭān Qulī Atka, Tarsūn Mīrzā, a relation of 'Abdullāh Mīrzā, Ḥāfiẓ Maqṣūd, Maulānā Bāqī Īrghū,[4] Maulānā Qadam Arbāb, and many others who were the ringleaders of strife and sedition were punished capitally. M. Kāmrān resolved upon flight, and arranged with his men that he would take refuge at the hill of Istālif, and that he would collect troops and prepare war. At the end of the night he went secretly towards Badakhshān along with 'Alī Qulī Qūrcī by the way of Sanjad Dara. After a thousand (*hazār*) distresses he passed on from the Hazārajāt with thousands of disgraces and ignominies towards Badakhshān. M. Beg, who was one of his confidents, and Sher 'Alī joined him with a few men near Ẓuḥḥāk. When they got to Ghōrī he sent a message to M. Beg Birlās the ruler of that place and summoned him to his presence. He replied that disloyalty, the note of the wicked, would not come from him. The Mīrzā wished to pass by Ghōrī but one of his servants (*qalaqcīān qu. qalūqcīān*) 269
abused him and said, "Why do you go with this fellow, (meaning

[1] This seems to be taken from Gulbadan Begam's Memoirs.

[2] According to Jauhar it was Hindāl who came up with Kāmrān as he was escaping on a man's back and who out of brotherly compassion let him go and supplied him with a horse. Niẓāmu-d-dīn says Ḥajī Muḥammad turned back on account of some Turkī words used by Kāmrān. What they meant is rather obscure, but apparently he ironically asked Ḥājī if he had killed his father that he should be so keen in pursuing him. See Elliot V., 227, and Badāonī, Ranking's translation, p. 581.

[3] Kāmrān's son-in-law and Gulbadan Begam's brother-in-law. Her account is that he afterwards left Kāmrān and retired to Mecca.

[4] Or *yārghū*. It is a Turkish or Mongolian word, and one of its meanings is prefect. See Vullers s.v.

the Mīrzā), who if he was the son of his Majesty Gītī Sitānī and had a drop of his spirit would never have let off the governor of Ghōrī so tamely or have left him scatheless." The Mīrzā was stung by his taunts and said, "Why do you talk so idly and why don't you reflect? I am acting in this way because of your want of preparation; would I have let the thing pass in this way if you were equipped for war"? The madman again spoke roughly to the Mīrzā, and he turned back and fought with the governor of Ghōrī. The latter was defeated and Ghōrī fell into the Mīrzā's hands. Thus he got possession of some munitions of war. He left Sher 'Alī there and went on to Badakhshān. He sent a messenger to M. Sulaimān and M. Ibrāhīm, inviting them to assist him, but they wisely did not give up their loyalty to the king, and were on their guard against helping the Mīrzā.

M. Kāmrān, being led away by his vain thoughts, went on towards Balkh in order that he might take refuge with Pīr Muḥammad Khān and with his help get possession of Badakhshān. His Majesty Jahānbānī appointed Qarāca Khān to the Badakhshānāt, so that he might in concert with M. Sulaiman and M. Hindāl and the other officers get possession of M. Kāmrān or drive him away. Qarāca Khān came to Badakhshān and went to Ghōrī along with the Mīrzās. Sher 'Alī and some of M. Kāmrān's men were garrisoned there. Brave fightings took place and gallant men on both sides were killed. Among them was Khwāja Nūr, who was one of M. Hindāl's great men. Mullā Mīr Kitābdār, who was a favourite of M. Hindāl, also obtained martyrdom. At last the besieged could resist no longer and fled, and the fort fell into the hands of the king's servants. Meanwhile news came that M. Kāmrān and Pīr Muḥammad Khān had arrived from Balkh. The Mīrzās did not engage, but turned back into the defiles while Qarāca Khān proceeded towards Kābul. His Majesty Jahānbānī on hearing of the confusion in Badakhshān turned his rein in that direction. When he reached Ghūrband, Qarāca Khan came and did homage. But as Qarāca Khān's baggage had been plundered on the way [1] back (to Ghūrband?) by the Aimāqs, he was permitted to go to Kābul in order that he might collect materials and quickly join. His Majesty, on his account

[1] *Dar murāja'at*, on the return journey, from Badakhshān and Ghōrī, I presume.

marched from Ghōrband and halted at the village of Gulbihār and occupied himself in making excursions and in hunting till Qarāca Khān arrived. After Qarāca Khān came, though the season was
over, his Majesty adhered to his first resolve and proceeded towards 270
Badakhshān. As the designs of Providence were not in accordance with this expedition, the passes of the Hindu Kōh were made difficult by snow, and a strange confusion occurred in the pass so that it was difficult to cross. In accordance with expediency, he returned to Kābul, resolving that in spring he would turn towards Badakhshān.

## CHAPTER XLIV.

### THE PUTTING[1] HIS MAJESTY THE SHĀHINSHĀH TO SCHOOL, AND OTHER EVENTS WHICH HAPPENED AT THIS TIME.

As it is fixed and recorded in the Academy of Divine knowledge, which is the "guarded tablet" of sempiternal writings—and all the arts and sciences in that sanctuary of the presence are the offspring of instruction's school—that the possessors of the new

---

[1] There is a reference later on, text I. 316, to Akbar's teachers. We are told of them that 'Aṣāmu-d-dīn the first teacher was removed for his addiction to pigeon-flying. This was a taste which he communicated to his pupil, if indeed the boy did not inherit it from his great-grandfather 'Umar Shaikh, and did not lead astray his luckless preceptor, for we are told, Blochmann 299, that when Akbar was very young he was fond of pigeon-flying and that he took up the pursuit again in mature life. There is also in the Maāṣir-i-Raḥīmī MS. A.S.B., p. 808*b*, *et seq*, a long letter about pigeons from Akbar to the Khān-khānān. Akbar's second teacher was Maulānā Bāyazīd, a physician and a descendant of one of Ulugh Beg's astronomers, but he too was objected to, and finally Humāyūn drew lots as to which of three persons should be his son's tutor. The result was that Maulānā 'Abdu-l-Qādir was appointed. He belonged to Tabrīz and was brother of Abul Qāsim who became Dīwān of Gujrāt, Blochmann 485 and 545. But 'Abdu-l-Qādir seems to have been superseded in his turn for we find that in the second year of his reign, that is, when he was 15, Akbar made Mīr 'Abdu-l-laṭīf his tutor. Niẓāmu-d-dīn mentions in his list of the learned men a Mullā 'Alā'ūd-d-dīn as Akbar's tutor. He also mentions that Mullā 'Abdu-l-Qādir retired to Mecca after having for years discharged with credit the duties of Akbar's teacher. The truth, as far as it can be seen through the maze of A.F.'s rhetoric, seems to be that Akbar was an idle boy, fond of animals and out-door amusements, and that he would not learn his lessons. This is corroborated by Jahāngīr's description of him as an unlettered man, and one who in his youth was fond of the pleasures of the table. It seems probable too that Akbar never knew how to read and write. This seems extraordinary in the son of so learned a man as Humāyūn, but apparently the latter was not to blame for this. See text I. 316.

material of reason are to be brought, on the emergence of articulate speech, to learn the combinations of letters (*ḥurūf-i-murakkaba*) and to acquire general knowledge, *viz.*, that which has been put together by united cares and intellectual essays, and by special progressions and classifications to walk in the beaten paths of reason, so this scholar of the Divine Academy and graduate of God's college was, in compliance with use and wont, taken to man's school on 7th Shawwāl of this year, 20th November, 1547, being the fourth[1] year, fourth month and fourth day of the eternity-conjoined life of his Majesty the Shāhinshāh. The weighty office was conferred on the Mullāzāda Mullā (teacher the son of a teacher) 'Aṣāmu-d-dīn Ibrāhīm. Though in the eyes of the superficial his Majesty was taken to be taught, yet according to the view of the far-seeing he was carried to the lofty position of teacher. A strange thing was that his Majesty Jahānbānī, who was acquainted with celestial sciences and versed in the mysteries of the stars, had fixed, in consultation with acute astrologers and time-knowing astrolabe-conners, a special hour for the initiative of his Majesty's instruction, such as might happen once during cycles and lifetimes, but when the master-moment arrived that scholar of God's school had attired himself for sport and had disappeared! In spite of all endeavours and of sedulous search on the part of royalty, no trace of him could be found. The enlightened-hearted perceived from this wondrous mystery that the design was that this lord of lofty wisdom and special pupil of God should not be implicated and commingled with ordinary human learning, so that at the time of the revelation of this *Khedive* of subtlety it might be apparent to mankind that the knowledge of this king of knowers was of the nature of a gift, and not of an acquirement. In spite of this truth, however, letters and the current sciences manifest themselves gloriously in his Majesty's sanctified mind, whether they be those committed to writing by scientists, or such niceties and secrets as come from Wisdom's source without the intervention of teaching and being

[1] The year must have been 954 for we are told in a previous chapter that Humāyūn left Qandūz in the last month of 953, and Akbar was at this time 5 years, 3 months, and 2 days old, for he was born on 5th Rajab, 949, or if we take the Gregorian calendar he was 5 years, 1 month, 5 days old, *viz.*, from 15th October, 1542—20th November, 1547.

taught (*ta'līm ū ta'allum*). Accordingly when masters of wisdom, lords of the mathematics, those possessed of exoteric sciences, and the inheritors of all the arts, whether general or specific, reach the carpet of the holy Presence, they from a consciousness of their own ignorance sink the head of ashamedness in the collar of hesitancy, and abide in amazement. The inspired nature of his Majesty is strongly drawn to the composing of Hindī and Persian poetry and is critical and hair-splitting in the niceties of poetic diction. Among books of poetry, he recites off-hand the Maulavī's[1] Masnavī and the Dīwān of the "mystic-tongue," and takes delight in their verities and beauties. The following weighty verse is a product of his Majesty's meditations.

*Verse.*

'Tis not the chain of insanity on the neck of the afflicted Majnūn;
Love hath laid a loving hand on his neck.

He has also strung glorious thoughts in the Hindī language, which may be regarded as masterpieces in this kind.

*Verse.*

Oh Thou congeries of excellencies, how may I express thee!

In fine, after they had kept him for some time with that meritorious teacher, engaged in recitations which were worse that none, those who only regarded externals dwelt upon the inefficiency of the tutor and set themselves to get rid of him. That helpless one was superseded, and Maulānā Bāyazīd was appointed. They did not know that the taskmasters of creation were taking care that the inspired mind of this nursling of Divine light should not become

---

[1] This is Jalālu-d-dīn Rūmī, and the mystic-tongue is Ḥāfiẓ. The passage about the Hindī and Persian poetry is omitted in the Lucknow edition. It seems discrepant from Blochmann, 548, where A.F. tells us that Akbar did not care for poets. But see also *id.* 103, 104. Nor does the passage occur in B.M. MSS. 27, 247, 17, 926, 5610 and 6544. It is also absent from the I.O. MSS. Nos. 4 and 564, and is, I think, undoubtedly spurious. The passage to be omitted begins on last line of p. 270 of Bib. Ind. ed. at *ū ṭaba'* and goes down to *alqiṣṣa* on 7th line of 271.

the reception chamber of inky impressions or the alighting-stage of the sooty types of the exoteric sciences.

During this auspicious time his Majesty Jahānbānī was in Kābul arranging for the distribution of provinces and for an expedition to Badakhshān, and for bringing to an end the affair of M. Kāmrān. M. Kāmrān came to despair of help from M. Sulaimān and M. Ibrāhīm, and went off with evil thoughts to Balkh in order that he might with Pīr Muḥammad[1] Khān's help obtain possession of Badakhshān. When he arrived at the village of Aibak[2] the Governor thereof received him courteously, but kept him under surveillance, and reported the circumstance to Pīr Muḥammad Khān. The latter regarded the Mīrzā's advent as a boon and sent trusty persons to welcome him. He conveyed the Mīrzā with all respect to his own house, and showed him hospitality. He also accompanied him to Badakhshān. The Mīrzās, in accordance with their resolve, retired to the mountainous borders of Badakhshān, and much of that country came into the possession of M. Kāmrān. Pīr Muḥammad Khān left a body of troops for M. Kāmrān's assistance and returned to his own country. The Mīrzā came to Kishm and Tāliqān, and sent Rafīq Kōka, and Khāliq Bardī with a body of Caghatāī and Uzbeg troops to Rūstāq. M. Sulaimān and M. Ibrāhīm collected the people of Kūlāb and came against Rūstāq. They came from Qil'a Ẓafar and Khamalinkān[3] and fought bravely against Rafīq Kōka and the others, but by heaven's decree they were defeated and had to withdraw to the hill country. His Majesty Jahānbānī was pleasing his enlightened heart in Kābul, and his determination was that he would go to Badakhshān. As his servants' hearts were not sincere, this design abode under the veil of dilatoriness and delay (*ta'awwuq ū tawaqquf*), and meanwhile Qarāca Khān, who had rendered good service and had become a station for endless favours, let the goblet of his understanding brim over, for the vessel was tiny and the wine plenteous, and without reflecting on his performances, rank, and condition, and on the lofty position of his master, set his foot outside

---

1 He was the son of Jānī Beg and uncle of the famous 'Abdullāh Khān. He died in 974 (1566). See Vambéry's Bokhara and Howorth, Part II. pp. 724, 726 and 729.

2 The Hiibak of the maps. Perhaps it is named after Quṭbu-d-dīn Aibak.

3 Bābar's Mem. 167, where it is spelt Khamalingān.

of the path of moderation. So at length out of the stupidity which is natural to the immoderately exalted he uttered words which even the drunk and mad do not use. Among them was the expression of his wish that Khwāja Ghāzī, who as a reward for his abilities and good service had been appointed to the office of Dīwān, should be sent to him bound in order that he might put him to death,[1] and that his office should be given to Khwāja Qāsim Tūla.[2] As such a measure did not commend itself to his Majesty Jahānbānī, who was a spring of justice and compassion, Qarāca Khān, who in his vain thoughts imagined himself to be the pillar of the victorious dominion, seduced, in the blackness of his fortune, and inversion of his horoscope, a large body of men from the path, and went off towards Badakhshān. Bābūs, Muṣāḥib Beg, Ismāīl Beg Duldāī, 'Alī Qulī[3] of Andarāb, Ḥaidar Dōst Moghal, Shaikham Khwāja Khiẓrī and Qurbān Qarāwal with nearly 3000 veteran horsemen, all of whom had been enticed by him, went off by Kotal Minār *en route* for Badakhshān and so trod the wilderness of error.

When his Majesty heard of this he wished to go off at once in person after those ill-fated ones who had turned away from the altar of auspiciousness. From observance of the favourable hour (for starting), he delayed setting out himself and despatched some of his followers to pursue the wretches. According as each of his loyal servants came up he was sent off, and so Tardī Beg Khān, Mun'im Khān, Muḥammad Qulī Barlās, 'Abdullāh Sulṭān and other loyalists hastened off, one after the other. Near midday, when the auspicious moment had arrived, his Majesty Jahānbānī mounted the horse of victory. A number of gallant youths pressed forward, and coming up with the rearguard of those headstrong ones, engaged them and overcame them. At the end of the day they came to close quarters with Qarāca Khān at the river;[4] night interposed to save the lives of those black-hearted ones, and they fled under its protection. They crossed by the Ghorband bridge, breaking it down

1 Jauhar and Bāyazīd give the reason for Qarāca's animosity. He had issued an order to Khwāja Ghāzī for the payment of 10 tūmāns, and the latter, who was treasurer, or finance-minister refused to honour the draft.

2 Tūla may mean weighman. Bāyazīd calls him Khwāja Qāsim Buyūtāt.

3 Blochmann 432.

4 Presumably the Ghorband river.

afterwards. Those who had followed them returned, and did homage at Qarā Bāgh. His Majesty Jahānbānī's world-adorning mind decided
to return to Kābul, and there to make preparations and to proceed 27
against Badakhshān. The short-sighted fugitives left Tamar 'Alī Shighālī, who was Qarāca Khān's vakil, in Panjshīr, that he might collect news there of affairs in Kābul, and having crossed a pass in the Hindū Kōh joined M. Kāmrān in Kishm. His Majesty Jahānbānī returned next day and refreshed the Urta Bāgh by the sunshine of his presence. He gave appropriate nicknames to all those sordid ones who had not recognised their duties to their king, and had been unfaithful to their salt. Thus he styled Qarāca Qarā Bakht (black fortune), Ismāīl Khirs (bear), Muṣāḥib Munāfiq (hypocrite), and Bābūs Daiyūs[1] (wittol). And he sent orders to M. Hindāl, M. Sulaimān, and M. Ibrāhīm to make preparations and to await the coming of the grand army. An order was also issued for Ḥājī Muḥammad Khān's coming from Ghaznīn to the Presence.

During this time when the preparations for an expedition against Badakhshān were engaging his mind, he was continually consulting prudent old men and wise young men, in whose foreheads there shone the jewel of sincerity. All those who had neither stout hearts nor clear vision urged the marching to Qandahār in order that preparations might be made there, and that thereafter they might proceed to quell the sedition of M. Kāmrān. Those who held in their hands the diploma of wisdom with the emblazonment of valour supported the royal idea of proceeding to Badakhshān. One day he said to Muḥammad Sulṭān,[2] "What do you say"? He replied, "M. Kāmrān is uplifted by the desertion of those ingrates. It seems likely that he will anticipate us and come into these territories. It appears to me that if the imperial army cross the Hindū Kōh first it will be victorious, otherwise—God forbid it—the dice will fall in another fashion." His Majesty Jahānbānī said "The downfall of

---

1 Perhaps a bitter allusion to the fact that Bābūs was rejoining a man (Kāmrān) who had given over Bābūs' wife to the people of the bazar. See *supra*. Probably *khare*, a winejar, was the nickname of Ism'aīl, rather than *khirs*, for A.F. has previously called him *kūs*, i.e., flagon.

2 A grandson of Sulṭān Ḥusain of Herāt. Blochmann 462.

the uplifted has been repeatedly witnessed. "If he be uplifted, we are supplicants at God's Court." He also repeated this verse.

*Verse.*

Let no one exult in his own strength,
For pride casts the cap from the head ;

and he concluded, "What sense is there in delaying, God willing, we'll at this very[1] moment cross the pass."

---

[1] This story is told by Jauhar, and with more point. Humāyūn is represented there as saying "God willing, we shall cross the hills first."

# CHAPTER XLV.

## Departure of His Majesty Jahānbānī Jannat-Āshiyānī's World-Conquering Army for Badakhshān, and its Victorious Return to Kābul.

When the expedition had been determined upon—and the measure was a most necessary one, they set off at an auspicious hour 274
on Monday, 5th Jumādā-al-awal, 955, 12th June, 1548, and encamped at Alang Cālak.[1] After two or three days, they moved from there to Qarā Bāgh, where they remained ten or twelve days on account of some state-affairs. In spite of some rumours about his disloyalty, Ḥājī Muḥammad Khān came as a well-wisher, and Qāsim Ḥusain Sulṭan, who was in Bangash, also came and did homage, and was favourably received. At the same stage, M. Ibrāhīm under the guidance of an auspicious star came post-haste and paid his respects. The lights of special favour were shed on the forehead of his fortune. One of the wonderful things which were the heralds of countless victories was that when he was about to proceed to Badakhshān, his Majesty was standing in the ewer-room. Suddenly it occurred to his sanctified mind that "if this white bird (referring to a cock which was always in the room) come upon my shoulder and crow, it will be a sign of victory." As soon as he had this thought, the auspicious bird came flying and flapping its wings like a *humā*, perched on his shoulder, and cast an auspicious shadow over the head of fortune. His Majesty returned thanks, and ordered that a silver ring be put on the bird's foot.[2]

Among the occurrences which were suitable preludes to victory was this that when M. Ibrāhīm arrived at Panjshīr[3] Tamar Shighālī

---

[1] The *alang* or meadow of Cālāk is mentioned by Bābar, Mem. 138 as being one *kos* from Kābul. He says it is extensive, but that the mosquitoes greatly annoy the horses.

[2] This story is told by Jauhar who adds that Humāyūn used to feed the bird with raisins.

[3] Jarrett II, 399 n. and 411, and Bābar 145.

intercepted him. Malik 'Alī of Panjshīr joined the Mīrzā with his clan, and M. Ibrāhīm bravely engaged Tamar 'Alī Shighālī, and routed him. He brought Malik 'Alī of Panjshīr along with him as a precautionary measure, and introduced him to his Majesty Jahānbānī. This simple-minded well-wisher of the State was incommoded by having to travel with M. Ibrāhīm, on account of groundless anxieties about his lands,[1] and after a quarrel it came to fighting. Though the Mīrzā had but few men with him he displayed great superiority and conducted his own party to the Presence. Next day Malik 'Alī sent his brother and preferred excuses for his offence, and he also sent the head of Tamar 'Alī. His Majesty rewarded the messenger with a robe of honour and other presents, and sent a soothing letter to his brother. He wrote that the Mīrzā had not
275 understood him, that his hereditary[2] loyalty was patent to his Majesty's heart, and that when his Majesty came to his territory he would treat him with royal favours; his Majesty also treated M. Ibrāhīm with much favour and called him his son. After bestowing royal benignities on him he gave him leave to depart in order that he might go and get M. Sulaimān ready with his army, and the munitions of war. He was to await the arrival of the royal army near Badakhshān. When it reached Tāliqān, they were to come and join. The noble lady Miriam-Makānī and his Majesty the Shāhinshāh, the light of the eyes of the Sulṭānate and the rose tree (*gulbun*) of the rose garden of the spring of the Khilāfat, were sent off from the village of Gulbihār[3] to Kābul. Muḥammad Qāsim Maujī was appointed governor of Kābul and sent with them. He was to continually serve his Majesty the Shāhinshāh, and also to manage thoroughly the district. When his Majesty had halted at the village of Bāzārak[4] in the Tūmān of Panjshīr, Ḥājī Muḥammad (son of)

---

[1] *Bafiqr-i-nāqiṣ-i-samīndārāna.* I presume that this is the meaning, but it may mean that Malik 'Alī was too independent to go with another man, and that too one who was only an heir-apparent.

[2] Perhaps he was a Yusufzai and a relative of Shāh Manṣūr, son of Malik Sulaimān, whose daughter Bābar married. Mem. 250.

[3] Gulbān in text, but it is Gulbihār in Lucknow ed., and this is probably correct as it agrees with Bābar 154. See also 219, where Bābar has some verses about Gulbihār. It lies N. of Kābul, and as usual A.F. puns on the name.

[4] Jarrett, 399 and 400 n. 1.

Bāba Qus͟hqa, Qāsim Ḥusain Sulṭān, Tardī Beg, Muḥammad Qulī Barlās, 'Ali Qulī Sulṭān, Mīr Laṭīf, and Ḥaidar Muḥammad Cūlī were sent as an advance-guard.[1] As soon as they had crossed the Hindū Kōh, Mahdī Sulṭān,[2] Tardī Muḥammad Jang Jang, and the party who were in the fort of Andarāb, fled. In accordance with the royal orders, Tardī Beg and Muḥammad Qulī Barlās hastened to K͟hōst in order to seize the families of the fugitives which were there. M. Kāmrān, being drunk with the wine of arrogance, was in Qil'a Ẓafar. Though the runaway officers in Tālīqān requested the Mīrzā to guard the roads, and to block the route from Kābul, they were not successful. Mullā K͟hirad Zargar, who was then in close contact with M. Kāmrān, and was a constant sedition-monger, made great efforts in this respect, but could not attain his object. At last Qarāca K͟hān and his party took the precaution to send Muṣāḥib Beg to bring the families from K͟hōst, lest a force should come from Kābul and make them prisoners. Just at this time Tardī Beg and Muḥammad Qulī arrived at K͟hōst, and Muṣāḥib Beg took off the families to Tālīqān. Apparently this was done by the connivance which is the result of long service.

When the royal standards approached Andarāb, M. Hindāl arrived from Qandūz, and brought in S͟her 'Alī as a prisoner. His Majesty Jahānbānī honoured the Mīrzā with various favours. Among these was that he should pay his respects on horseback.[3]
The short account of the affair of S͟her 'Alī is that before the arrival 276
of the imperial troops in the Badak͟hs͟hānāt, and when M. Kāmrān was in power there, S͟her 'Alī in his arrogance always behaved disrespectfully to the Mīrzā, and urged the taking of Qandūz and the bringing in of M. Hindāl. At last the Mīrzā appointed him to Qandūz, and M. Hindāl by the royal good fortune succeeded in making him prisoner. The thing happened thus. One night many of the infantry soldiers of Qandūz surrounded his house (tent?).

---

[1] *Ba rasm-i-manqulā.* But the meaning is that they were sent on in advance of the main army, and the word is properly *mang͟hulāī* and is Mongolian.

[2] Apparently this was a brother of Gulbadan's husband K͟hiẓr K͟hwāja. Tār. Rash., 401.

[3] Jauhar states that Hindāl arrived a watch after nightfall. He saw Humāyūn afar off, and wanted to alight from his horse, but Humāyūn made him keep his seat.

He fled and flung himself into the river, and broke his arm, and was caught in his own snare. When the Mīrzā brought him before his Majesty Jahānbānī, the latter did not regard his improper actions, and drew the pen of forgiveness over his offences, and having given him a robe of honour nominated him to Ghōrī. For his far-seeing mind looked to his nature and his capabilities, and as he found in him manliness and administrative ability, he passed over so many great crimes, each of which was deserving of condign punishment, and distinguished him by favours. For in the scales of appreciation he found that the subjects of reward were more than those of retribution.[1]

After M. Hindāl had been honoured by royal favours, an order was issued that Ḥājī Muḥammad Khān and a number of others should advance as a vanguard (*manqulā*), and that the Mīrzā should head them. All were to obey the Mīrzā—who would always be a supporter of dominion—and not to fail in good service, so that each might be rewarded in proportion thereto. In the middle of Jumādā-al-ākhir 955, 22nd May, 1548, the camp reached the Qāẓī's Alang, which is a village of Andarāb. The Qāzī of Andarāb and the men of the Tūqbāī[2] and Sālqāncī tribes, and the Balūcīs and a number of soldiers and of the Aimaqs of Badakhshān, and of the servants of Muṣāḥib Beg did homage, and received royal favours. From thence the army proceeded, march after march, to Tālīqān. Most of the fugitive officers, as well as Mīrza 'Abdullāh and a number of M. Kāmrān's men, were in garrison there. An order was issued to M. Hindāl and the officers with him to cross the Bangī[3] river and engage. Just then M. Kāmrān[4] hastily brought his men from

---

[1] Bāyazīd tells us that Sher 'Alī had been a servant of the unfortunate Yādgār Nāṣīr.

[2] This is an Afghān tribe, Jarrett, II. 403. I have not found the name Sālqāncī mentioned.

[3] The text has Tangī, but the variant Bangī is right. The Bangī or Bungī is a tributary of the Khairābād river, which again is a tributary of the Oxus. The Bangī flows south of Tālīqān. See Wood's Journey to the source of the Oxus, p. 152.

[4] Jauhar says Kāmrān marched 25 *kos* from Qil'a Ẓafar (Kāmrān seems to have been famous for his rapid movements), and that it was not till after sunrise that he was recognised. He drove back Ḥājī Muḥammad, but when he heard Humāyūn's drums he cried, "I've lost the game," and retreated into Tālīqān.

Qila' Zaffar and Kishm and joined the unholy crew. On Saturday, 15th Jamāda-al-ākhirī[1] an engagement took place on a rising ground which they call khalsān (?) The royal army had not yet crossed 277
the river and there was some distance between the advance-guard and the main body. In accordance with the Divine Will, the imperial vanguard was turned back and had to recross the river. The enemy proceeded to plunder.[2] M. Kāmrān was stationed on the same rising ground with a few men. Meanwhile his Majesty Jahānbānī arrived on the river bank and wished to cross in front of the enemy. Sundry faithful informants represented that the river was in a pool[3] there, and that a mile higher up there was a mill, and that as the place was stony, it would be easy to cross there. They went there, and when they got nigh the mill, Shaikham[4] Khwāja Khizrī, the kalantar (headman) of the Khwāja[5] Khizrīs was brought in a prisoner. The *tinqatārs* who were by his Majesty's rein were bidden to strike the faithless runagate. They so fisted and kicked him that the spectators felt certain that his black soul could no longer have connection with his body. In that place they captured Ismāīl Beg Dūldai and brought him to the presence. His Majesty granted him his life, forgave him his offences at the intercession of Mun'am Khān, and made him over to him. His Majesty then proceeded to the height where M. Kāmrān was. He appointed Fatah Ullah Beg, brother of Rūshan Kōka to the vanguard, and sent forward with him a number of

[1] As the army arrived at Andarāb in the middle of the month and then made several marches there is probably a mistake in this date.

[2] Jauhar mentions that after the plundering was over, and the enemy had retreated to Tālīqān, it was reported to Humāyūn that the library was safe. He was much pleased, saying, "God be praised that things which cannot be replaced are safe! As for other things, they were a small matter."

[3] *Āb jamjama ast*, *jamjama* means a skull in Arabic. Perhaps all that is meant here is that the waters of the river were collected together in the place.

[4] He had deserted along with Qarāca Khān. Bayāzīd says the millers took him up and cared for him and that he became kalāntar again and lived for several years. He was beaten with the stocks of muskets, &c. According to Jauhar, Humāyūn ordered him to be split into nine strips; 42 wounds were inflicted on him, but at night he went off to his own house.

[5] This is mentioned as a clan in Bābar, 277.

devoted heroes. A gallant engagement took place, and Fataḥ Ullah was unhorsed. Just then the royal standard (*kaukab*), which is the preface of conquest and the advance-guard of victory, made its appearance; the Mīrzā gave up heart and had no power to resist. He fled to the fort of Tālīqān, and set himself to strengthen it. The imperial army proceeded to plunder. A dispute arose among the attendants (*qalaqcīān*) about the goods, and his Majesty gave orders for *haral*,[1] *i.e.*, that every one should keep what came into his hands, and others had no claim to it. In that victory no one had even a hair of his head injured, excepting 'Alī Qulī Khān. Isaḥaq[2] (Isaac) Sulṭān, Tardī Beg, the son of Beg Mīrak, Bābī Jūjak, and a number of others who had boldly followed the victorious were made prisoners. M. Hindāl and Ḥājī Muḥammad brought their prisoners to the Presence, and his Majesty treated them according to the laws of justice and equity, and distributed favour and chastisement suitable to their deservings. And he returned thanks to the Court of the True Disposer, who is liberal without stint and bounteous without solicitation.

Next day he commenced the siege and distributed the batteries.
278 One day a shot from the battery which was in charge of Mun'am Khān, Muḥammad Qulī Barlas and Ḥusain Qulī Sulṭān Muhrdār, struck Mubāriz Beg and killed him. His Majesty, who was a mine of compassion, lamented[3] greatly and exclaimed, "Would that his brother Muṣāḥib Beg had been killed in his stead." With brotherly feeling, or rather out of general amiability, he, in spite of M. Kāmrān's many crimes, became kindly disposed to him and sent him an admonitory *firmān* which might be an armlet of dominion and fortune and

---

1 Bayāzīd writes *hūral* and says the result of the order was that some lost Rs. 2000 and did get one back, and that others who had not ten rupees got 10,000.

2 Tār. Rash. 451. He was son of Shāh Muḥammad Sulṭān, who was grandson of Bābar's maternal uncle Muḥammad Khān, and his mother (Khadīja Sulṭān) was a daughter of Bābar's younger maternal uncle Aḥmad Khān. Isaḥaq's sister Muhtarīm was married to Kāmrān and afterwards to Ibrāhīm, the son of M. Sulaimān, Blochmann 312. She was Ḥaidar M.'s wife's sister, and was married to Kāmrān through his influence.

3 According to Jauhar, Humāyūn was affected, not so much by the death of Mubāriz, as by his having felt it necessary to put a number of prisoners to death.

a neck-charm of grace and favour. After various high-thoughted counsels this was written, "O evil brother and beloved war-seeker, refrain from courses which are productive of conflict and cause the affliction and destruction of countless men. Have compassion on the men of the city and of the army. To-day they are all killed; to-morrow is the judgment.

*Verse.*

The blood of that race is on thy neck,
The hand of that crowd upon thy skirt,
'Twere[1] far better to think on peace
And bring to pass the ways of gentleness.

He sent this auspicious rescript along with Naṣib Rammāl.[2] As the Mīrzā, being drunk with folly, had turned away from fortune and put dominion behind his back, the sage advices were of no avail. In reply to that roll of grace and preamble of knowledge, he uttered[3] the following verse—

*Verse.*[4]

Who'd to his bosom strain dominion's bride
Must kiss the gleaming falchion's lip.

Naṣīb Rammāl conveyed to the royal hearing the account of the Mīrzā's recalcitrance and an order was given for strengthening the batteries. Meanwhile, Mīrzās Sulaimān and Ibrāhīm arrived with all their forces and were made partakers of royal favours. Cākar K͟hān, son of Wais Qibcāq also arrived with the men of Kūlāb and formed a supplement to the army of fortune. During this period of one[5] month of the siege the gates of victory opened more and more for the imperialists, while the knot of affairs grew tighter for M. Kāmrān, and he became more and more straitened. At last he became hopeless of the success of tricks and stratagems, and also

1 These last two lines are not in Jauhar and would be better away.

2 *I.e.*, a diviner or soothsayer.

3 Jauhar says that when Kāmrān received Humāyūn's letter he read it and was silent for a while, and then quoted the verse.

4 This couplet is said by Ḥaidar Mīrzā to have been sent by S͟haibānī to S͟hāh Ism'aīl. Tār. Rash. 233.

5 Jauhar has two months, but if A.F.'s other dates are right the siege did not last even one month.

came to despair of the help from Pīr Muḥammad Khān Uzbeg, which he in his short-sightedness looked for. Involuntarily he put his hands to the saddle strips (*fitrāk*)[1] of obedience and submission. By means of this device he saved himself this time from the whirlpool of danger and brought the ship of safety from out the tumult of the waves to the shore of salvation. With this design, he made various supplications and cries for help. One day he fastened a letter to an arrow and shot it into the camp. Its purport was that he had not recognised the claims of his Majesty to reverence. "I have seen what I have seen, and now I repent of the past and wish that leave may be granted to me to circumambulate the Holy K'aba so that I may be cleansed from the sin of rebellion and the
279 anguish of ingratitude, and may become fit for proper service. My hope is that this boon may be granted to me through the intervention of Mīr 'Arab[2] of Mecca." The Mīr was distinguished among all the devotees of the age for honesty and transparency and had applied himself to alchemy. His Majesty Jahānbānī Jinnatāshiyānī had a regard for him, and on this expedition he kept close to the royal stirrup and was adorning the army of prayer (*lashkar-i-du'ā*). When the petition of supplication reached the royal hearing, he sent for the Mīr and spoke to him about it. The Mīr said that he would write an answer and send it into the fort. He wrote as follows.[3] "Know, O men of the fort, that salvation is in sincerity and safety in submission, and peace be upon whoever followeth the right path." When M. Kāmrān had understood the purport of this writing, he wrote back by the same method that he would submit to whatever the Mīr should order His Majesty Jahānbānī, inasmuch as kindness and benevolence were of his nature's essence, sent off the Mīr, who proceeded to the fort and expounded the doctrines of verity which in reason's reservoir are more sweet than limpid streams, but more bitter to the sensual taste than the juice of the colocynth. In his exposition and application he did not leave out a single point, and at every sentence of reproof the Mīrzā, as he had received a lesson from

1 Explained by the Lucknow edition by the word shikārband. The *fitrāk* are the cords attached to the saddle and used for tying game to.

2 Can this be the Muḥammad 'Arab mentioned by Bayāzīd 11*b*, and who was Ṭahmāsp's Imām?

3 It was in Arabic and A.F. gives the original and also a translation.

the crapulous headaches following on his debauches, held down the head of submission and cried, "I've sinned, I've sinned, I'll do whatever you order." The Mīr said, "The atonement is that you arise and with a sincere soul and contrite heart come with me and do homage." The Mīrzā, either from sincerity or deceit set off, but when they got near the gate, the Mīr, who could perceive the temporary nature of the feelings, became aware that they were without root.[1] He stopped, and said to the Mīrzā, "As you have set out to kiss the threshold and have emerged from the circle of sedition, and have escaped from a state of rebellion, the proper thing for auspiciousness and repentance is that you send the runaway officers to the Court with their necks bound, that you yourself recite the khuṭba in his Majesty's name, and that you secretly depart and go off to the Ḥijāz." The Mīrzā accepted the advice and agreed to everything, but added,[2] "Entreat his Majesty to suffer Bābūs to depart along with me, for he is an old servant, and I am desirous of atoning to him on this journey for what I have done to him." When the Mīr returned and reported the circumstances to his Majesty, he asked pardon for the Mīrzā's offences, and his Majesty, on account of his constitutional kindness, forgave him and ratified all that the Mīr had arranged.

On Friday, 12th Rajab, 955, 12th August, 1548, Maulānā 'Abdul Bāqī the Ṣadr recited the khuṭba in his Majesty Jahānbānī's name,

---

1 These words are followed by the clause, "and this amount of submission is sufficient in the outer world," and this is put as if it were part of the Mīr's reflections. But I believe it is a parenthesis of A.F.'s own.

2 This and much else is taken from Bayāzīd. It is strange that Kāmrān should have thought it possible for him to atone to Bābūs, but perhaps Bābūs' return to him shewed that he had condoned the outrages. Kāmrān's begging that Bābūs might be allowed to go with him was a sign of grace, for it saved him from the probable fate of the other officers. Niẓāmū-d-dīn says distinctly that he begged forgiveness for Bābūs. Bayāzīd says that Kāmrān begged off Bābūs saying he had killed his sons and that by taking him to Mecca he would obtain absolution (*bahilī ḥasil karam*), and that Humāyūn agreed, saying that he did not want cuckolds (*dewūs*) in his camp. According to Firishta, Humāyūn was so elated by his victory that he broken out into poetry in the fataḥnāmā, or proclamation which he sent to Bairām Khān. Firishta gives the verses and also Bairām's quatrain in reply.

280 and his Majesty went off from there to a garden[1] in the neighbourhood. The batteries were dismantled, and an order was given that Ḥājī Muḥammad should be present with a body of troops, that the Mīrzā was departing with a few men, as had been arranged, and that until his exit from the dominions they should guard the borders. 'Alī Dōst Khān Bārgbegī, 'Abdal Wahhāb, Sayid Muḥammad Pakna, Muḥammad Quli Shaikh Kamān, Laṭifī Sahrindī and a number of others were appointed to guard the gate of the fort and to bring in the runaway officers and to let the Mīrzā pass with the sanctioned companions. The Mīrzā came out in accordance with the compact. On the way, one of M. Ibrāhīm's servants recognised as his own a horse which one[2] of M. Kāmrān's servants was riding, and told this to M. Ibrāhim, who sent people to bring away the horse. When this was brought to his Majesty's ears, he, in his courtesy, disapproved of the proceeding and censured M. Ibrāhīm, and he, out of shame and narrowness of disposition went off without leave to Kishm. Ḥājī Muḥammad, too, was blamed as the insult to the Mīrzā had been committed with his knowledge. A gracious firmān containing apologies, with a robe of honour and a horse were sent along with Khwāja Jalālu-d-dīn Maḥmūd the Mīr Bīyūtāt (to Kāmrān). When the night was somewhat advanced, Qarāca Khān was produced with a sword tied to his neck. When he came in front of the torches an order[3] was issued for removing the sword; his guilt was forgiven, and he was honoured by being allowed to do homage. And his Majesty said[4] in Tūrkī, "'Tis the fortune of war, such accidents as

---

[1] Apparently the garden of Mīr Tūlaq (Bayāzīd).

[2] Bayāzīd says it was a *dāh*, or maidservant who was on the horse. This would make the insult the greater. A.F. probably uses the word khidmatgār as at I. 44 line 7 to mean a female servant.

[3] Bayāzīd says that when Humāyūn caught sight of Qarāca he said, "He is a white-bearded man, and I called him father, take off the sword from his neck."

[4] *'Ālam-i-sipāhigarī ast.* Apparently Humāyun kindly intended to console Qarāca for his defeat by representing that he had only suffered from the mistakes or accidents inseparable from war, and drew a veil over the treachery of his behaviour. We find in Bayāzīd, Humāyūn using a similar expression in the moment of his defeat at Balkh in order to hearten his men. The words there are *Ḥazrat anwā' dildārīhā mīdād and ke 'ālam sipahgīrīst 'aiba nadarad.* "His Majesty was using various encouragements, saying it is the fortune of war, there is no disgrace."

this must happen." He was ordered to stand on the left, below Tardī Beg Khān.

Next they brought Muṣāḥib Beg with a quiver and a sword at his neck. When he came near the torches an order was given for removing the weapons. Similarly they brought Sardār Beg the son of Qarāca Khān. His Majesty said "'Tis the elders' fault, what fault have the children committed?" In this manner the other officers were brought in one after the other and heard the news of pardon. Last, came Qurbān Qarāwal, a personal servant of his Majesty and with shame and downcast looks did obeisance. His Majesty said in Tūrkī, "What ailed *you*, and what made *you* go away." He replied in the same language, "What is the use of inquiring about the complexion of those who have been made black by the hand of God's power"?[1] Ḥasan Qulī Sulṭān Muhrdār, who was always allowed liberty of speech, recited this verse in the assembly.

*Verse.*[2]

When a lamp has been lighted by God
Who puffs at it burns his own beard.

All the officers felt uneasy at the appropriateness[3] (of the quotation) to Qarāca Khān who had a long beard. Next day his Majesty marched from there and encamped in a pleasant meadow on the bank of the Tālīqān[4] river. On Wednesday, 17th Rajab, M. Kāmrān came back, under divine guidance, and did homage. The 281
explanation of this remarkable occurrence is as follows. In Bādām-darah[5] M. Kāmrān was expatiating to M. 'Abdullah in thanksgiving for the royal favours and was expressing his surprise at his Majesty's

---

[1] Bayāzīd says that on hearing Qarbān's reply Humāyūn smiled and told his *dīwāns* that if Qarbān's jāgīr had been resumed, it should be restored to him.

[2] This verse as stated by Vambéry, Hist. of Bokhāra, 256, to have been quoted by the unfortunate Khwāja Abūl Makārim (*see* Bābar's Mem. 65), to Shaibānī in 1501 when questioned as to why he had shaved off his beard.

[3] Probably the better rendering is that given by Erskine in a note Hist. II. 357. "All the rebel lords, but especially Qarāca, felt much ashamed.

[4] Apparently the Bangī river, which is called by Niẓāmu-d-dīn the Tālīqān river.

[5] Niẓāmu-d-dīn, Lucknow ed. 215, says Kāmrān had gone two leagues (*parasangs*) when he turned back. Erskine's copy, *see* Hist. II. 358, had *ten* and not two leagues, and this is in all probability correct.

passing over so many crimes and acts of disrespect. M. 'Abdullah asked him what he would have done if he had been in his Majesty's place. Kāmrān replied that he would not have forgiven or forgotten Then, said M. 'Abdullah, you have an opportunity of making atonement, how would it be if you availed yourself of it? The Mīrzā asked what he meant, and M. 'Abdullah[1] said, "We are this day in a place where the king's arm cannot reach us. The right thing is for us to go post haste with a few men and make our submission, return thanks to his Majesty and beg pardon for our offences, and render acceptable service." M. Kāmrān approved of the idea and set off with a few men; when he came nigh the camp he sent Bābūs to do obeisance and to report his coming. His Majesty Jahānbānī rejoiced at the coming of the Mīrzā and ordered that first Mun'im Khān, Tardī Beg Khān, Mīr Muḥammad Munshī, Ḥasan Qulī Sulṭān Muhrdār, Bāltū Beg, Tuwācī Begī, Tākhcī Beg and many others should go forth, and after them that Qāsim Ḥusain Sulṭān Shaibānī, Khiẓr Khwāja Sulṭān, Iskandar Sulṭān, 'Alī Qulī Khān, Bahādur Khān and many others should go, and thirdly, that M. Hindāl, M. 'Askarī, and M. Sulaimān should go to welcome him. And on the same day he ordered that the chains should be taken off M. 'Askarī's feet.

Next morning the princes and officers came and paid their respects in accordance with forms which his Majesty had prescribed, and his Majesty Jahānbānī took his seat on the throne and held a general audience. M. Kāmrān hastened forward to kiss the carpet and paid the obeisances of supplication and the prostrations of sincerity. His Majesty Jahānbānī graciously observed, "The ceremonials of reception (*dīdan-i-tōra*) have been observed, now come and let us embrace like brothers." Then he clasped the Mīrzā to his bosom, and wept so violently that all those present were touched to the heart. The Mīrzā after making profound obeisances sat on the left[2] in accordance with the royal indication. His Majesty said in

[1] This is the 'Abdullah Khān Moghal of Blochmann, 396. He was Kāmrān's brother-in-law, and Akbar afterwards married his daughter.

[2] Jauhar says, "on the right hand," but all the A.N. MSS. have "left." Though Humāyūn was very generous and forgiving he was also a great stickler for propriety and it was probably to mark Kāmrān's previous misconduct that he was not put on the right hand like Sulaimān the son of his father's cousin. Erskine, however, Hist. II. 358 seems to imply that the left was among the Turks the place of honour.

Turkī "Sit close by." The right side was pointed out to M. Sulaimān. In like manner the princes and officers sat on the right and left according to their degree. All the intimate courtiers, such as Ḥasan Qulī Muhrdār, Mīr Muḥammad Munshī, Ḥaidar Muḥammad, Maqṣūd Beg Akhta sat close together (*dar dingal*). A great festival was held. Qāsim Cangī, Kocak Ghicakī, Makhlaṣ Qabūzī, Ḥāfiẓ Sulṭān Muḥammad Rukhna, Khwāja Kamālu-d-dīn Ḥusain, Ḥāfiẓ Muhrī and others of this enchanting band took their seats near the festive circle[1] 282
(*qūr*) and discoursed delightful music. Among the younger men (*īkkahā*) there were Kākar 'Alī, Shāham Beg Jalāir, Tūlak Qōcīn and others standing behind the circle (*qūr*). Fruits and varied dishes were set out in royal fashion. In this assembly Ḥasan Qulī Muhrdār said to M. Kāmrān, "I have heard that it was stated before you that some one had said in Pīr Muḥammad Khān's presence that whoever did not cherish hatred as big as an orange against Martwẓa 'Alī was not entitled to be called a Musalmān, and that you remarked thereupon that it behoved a servant of God to have such hatred as big as a pumpkin." The Mīrzā became very angry and said, "Then it seems people take me for a heretic"[2] (*khāriji*). There was general conversation (?) and his Majesty Jahānbānī scattered pearls of speech. The meeting lasted till the end of day. In this joyful assembly M. 'Askarī was made over to M. Kāmrān, and allowed to go to his quarters. As the Mīrzā had come in a hurry, tents, &c., were erected

[1] Bayāzīd says, behind the *qūr*. The word has several meanings, the most common being that of "flags and other ensigns;" Blochmann 50 note. But here the word seems to have the meaning given in P. de Courteille's Dict. "cercle de gens qui sont en fête."

[2] A.F. seems to have taken this story from Bayāzīd, and as usual, he rather spoils it. According to Bayāzīd the remark was first made in the Court of 'Ubaidu-l-lāh, and this is the way the story is told in Shāh Ṭahmāsp's Memoirs. See Dr. Teufel's paper on the Z.D.M.G. and Dr. Horn's translation, Strasburg, 1892, p. 37. See also the paper on Bayāzīd's Memoirs J.A.S.B., LXVI. Part I, No. 4 for 1898. Dr. Teufel quotes a somewhat similar mode of comparison from Herodotus. Kāmrān had married an Uzbeg wife, and was no doubt desirous when at Balkh of ingratiating himself with the Uzbegs, who were Sunnīs like himself. The story therefore is probably true. In reply to Kāmrān's angry denial Ḥasan excused himself by saying that he was only repeating what he had heard and by using the proverb that the quoting of infidel-expressions does not make one's self an infidel.

for him near the royal residence. Next day a counsel was held with the princes and officers about an expedition against Balkh. Everyone spoke according to his opinions. His Majesty ordered that when the army arrived at Nārī whatever appeared proper should be carried into execution. Nārī is a village from which there is a road to Balkh and another to Kābūl.

On the fourth day they marched from this delightful station and at night encamped at the spring of Bandgasha which is near Ishkamish where a joyful assembly was held. To that memorable place his Majesty Gītī-sitānī Firdūs Makānī had come in former times, and Khān Mīrzā and Jahangīr Mīrzā had presented themselves there and placed the head of obedience on the line of command. And his Majesty Firdūs Makānī had in commemoration of his having halted there, and of the coming of his brothers and of their making their submission recorded the date on a rock. His Majesty Jahānbānī Jinnat Āshiyānī who had come to this delightful spot in accordance with H.H. Gītī-sitānī's precedent also recorded the date of his coming, and of the homage of M. Kāmrān, and the assembling together of the brothers. And these two dates of two mighty kings on one stone-tablet are like the writing of the portico of time on the page of night and day, being two closely intertwined memorials.[1] From thence his Majesty proceeded to the village of Nārī[2] and proceeded

---

[1] The meaning seems to be that the two inscriptions followed one another like day the night. But I think that A.F. has misread his authority (Bayāzīd) and is in error in thinking that Bābar and Hūmayūn's inscriptions were at one and the same place. Bayāzīd says Bābar engraved his on his return from Samarqand. The inscription then is probably that mentioned in Bābar's Memoirs p. 101, but that was put up at a place north of the Oxus, viz., at Ābburdan in the Masīḥa or Masīkha hill country and near Ūratīpa and Farghāna. Ishkamish or Ishkāmish lies S. of the Oxus and S.E. Qandūz. If Bābar was ever there and put up an inscription, it is an event not mentioned in his Memoirs. There is also an Ishkashm in East Badakhshān near the ruby mines. According to Gulbadan Begam the meeting of the brothers was at Kishm, but this is east of Tālīqān and out of Humāyūn's way. *Bandgashā* or more properly Bandkasha means a bolt or bar and probably was a name given to the place on account of the reunions that took place there. Bayāzīd tells us that Humāyūn carved the letters with his own hand.

[2] Though Kāmrān was pardoned at Tālīqān, his retirement to Mecca

to distribute the territory of Badakhshān. Khatlān,[1] which is commonly known as Kūlāb, was given to M. Kāmrān as far as the (river) Mūk[2] and Qarātigīn. Cākār Khān was M. Kāmrān's prime minister and was sent along with him. 'Askarī M. was also sent 28
along with the Mīrzā, and Qarātigīn was given to him as his fief. Though M. Kāmrān was not satisfied with his fief yet in consideration of his having been granted his life he did not make any objection.[3] Qila' Zaffar, Tālīqān and several other *parganas* were assigned to Mīrzās Sulaimān and Ibrāhīm. Qandūz, Ghūrī, Kahmard, Baqlān, Ishkamish and Nārī were conferred on M. Hindāl, and Sher 'Alī was sent along with him. It was arranged that the expedition against Balkh should take place next year. After the princes had thus been

---

was apparently still contemplated. So probably he took no part in the discussion at Tālīqān or its vicinity about the expedition to Balkh. As he had been helped by Pīr Muḥammad the Khān of Balkh, (Erskine, Hist. II. 368, thinks this was one reason for the expedition), and had an Uzbeg wife it is hardly natural that he should have been consulted. Jauhar is probably wrong in saying that Humāyūn contemplated giving Balkh in exchange for or in addition to Kūlāb. It was not till after the army got to Nārī (or Nārīn) that the change was made by which Kāmrān gave up his pilgrimage and accepted Khatlān or Kūlāb. At Nārī Kāmrān set off on his expedition to Mecca and had gone half a *kos* when Ḥasan Qulī overtook him, and in accordance with Humāyūn's instructions induced him to return and to accept Kūlāb. Thus then Kāmrān turned twice back, once at Tālīqān and again at Nārīn.

1 For descriptions of Khatlān and Qarātigīn see the Introduction to Erskine's translation of Bābar's Memoirs. See also Yule's Essay, prefixed to Wood's Journey, p. lxx. They are both remote places, and mountainous tracts, N. of the Oxus, and no doubt this is why they were given to Kāmrān and 'Askarī. Cākar Khān was the son of Sulṭan Wais Qipcāq (Bayāzīd 36*a* and A.N. I. 278).

2 The Mūk or Mūksū is a river, Reclus VI. 332. It flows northwards, and falls into the Surkhāb river (which again is a tributary of the Oxus) in the east of Qarātigīn. See also Yule's Essay, prefixed to Wood's Journey, p. lxx. text and note.

3 According to Jauhar, Kāmrān even after he went to Kabūl expressed a desire to be relieved of his government, and to be allowed to go on pilgrimage. Humāyūn invited him to Kabūl, but he would not go and quoted a couplet of Khāqānī to the effect that after thirty years he had discovered that sovereignty was beggary (*darweshat*) and beggary sovereignty. But, says Jauhar, he was not sincere in the bottom of his heart.

made recipients of royal favours his Majesty decided upon going to Kābul. In a final meeting, agreement and engagements, which are the passwords of those who arrange temporal affairs, were interchanged and everyone having been committed to God, the Disposer of men whether great or small, was permitted to depart, but of brotherly affection he called for a cup of sherbat and after taking a little of it he tendered it to M. Kamrān, and an order was given that each prince should in his turn partake of the royal draught (*ālūsh*, see Vullers *s.v.*), and pledge themselves to unity and concord. In accordance with the lofty command they together with the bond of brotherhood tied the knot of sincerity and friendship. Each prince received a standard and a kettle drum, and thereby was proclaimed to have obtained the dignity of a confidential relationship. Mīrzās Kāmrān, Sulaimān and Hindāl were honoured with *tamantoghs*[1] and went off from here to their fiefs. The royal cortege marched to Khūst and halted in that delightful spot. His Majesty then went on by Parīān towards Kābul. Parīān is a fort of which his Majesty Ṣaḥib-qarānī laid the foundations after he had chastised the Hindus of Katūr.[2] His Majesty repaired it and gave it the name of Islāmābād. When the victorious standards arrived there Pahlwān Dost Mīr Barr was ordered to repair the broken down fort, and the task of supervision was assigned to various officers. His Majesty remained there ten days and by Pahlwān's exertions the fort received shape in the course of a week, and was furnished with gates, battlements and embrasures.[3] His Majesty left Beg Mīrak in charge of it.

When the world-adorning mind was relieved from the business of the fort he turned his attention to the silver mines, but it appeared that the receipts did not equal the working-expenses. From there he proceeded and encamped on the bank of the Panjshīr river near the pass of Ushtar Karām.[4] He reached the environs of Kābul in the beginning of winter when the ground had become white with snow and waited there for some days in expectation of a suitable time and

---

1 Blochmann 50. The *tamaatōgh* was composed of the tails of the yāk and was a flag of the highest dignity.

2 See Tār. Rash. 103 note.

3 *Sangandās*, properly places where stones, &c., were thrown down on the enemy.

4 Major Raverty has kindly informed me that this should be Grām, village, the name meaning the camel's village.

propitious hour. His Majesty the Shāhinshāh in whose coming there were thousands of prosperities and good omens came out to welcome him. The Atgah Khān and a number of the courtiers tendered 248
their service. His Majesty exulted and expanded at the auspicious sight of that eye-pupil of the *Khilāfat* and new moon of glory, from whose temples there shone the auspiciousness of the two worlds, and prostrated his forehead in thanksgiving to Almighty God. On Friday, 2nd Ramẓān, which was the auspicious time, he, attended by victory and conquest, cast the shadow of his advent over the city, and prostrated himself on the floor of prayer. Blessings and congratulations arose from the people, and at this time Samandar[1] came from Kashmīr with petitions and presents from M. Ḥaidar. In the letter were eloquent praises of the climate, of the spring and the autumn, of the flowers and fruits of Kashmīr, and pressing entreaties that he would visit that lovely region. There were also fitting expressions about the conquest of Hindustan, and incitements were held to the world-conquering genius. His Majesty out of the abundance of his goodness sent a diploma of victory full of favourable expressions to the Mīrzā. And he mentioned therein his secret designs upon India. He was constantly engaged in plans for strengthening the Khilāfat and for improving the affairs of the State, and applied his intellect to this object in accordance with the methods which the times called for. Among them was his dismissing to the Ḥijāz Qarāca Khān and Muṣaḥib Beg who were ringleaders in hypocrisy, and deserving of all kinds of punishment. His idea was that perchance in times of exile, which is a file of the immoderate in spirit, they might think of the time of fortune, and recognising its blessings to some measure might refrain from following evil. They went off and stayed in the Hazāra country, and at length the clemency of his Majesty Jahānbānī accepted the inaudible[2] excuses of those ingrates.

---

[1] Apparently Samandar was Humāyūn's servant and presumedly had been sent by him to Kashmīr. See former mentions of him in A.N. 178 and 179, where also he is spoken of as an ambassador. There is nothing about him in the Tār. Rash. Perhaps he was sent at the time when Maqdūm Beg was exiled to Kashmīr in 952. A.F. has already mentioned that Ḥaidar read the khuṭba in Humāyūn's name when Kābul was conquered. Qu. was this in 952 or 954?

[2] *Namasamū'* unheard, meaning I suppose, that they were too far off to be heard, perhaps=unspoken.

At the same time he sent Khwāja Jalālu-d-dīn Maḥmūd on an embassy to Persia along with gifts and rarities in order that the foundations of affection might be renewed, and love be confirmed.

Among the occurrences of this year was the martyrdom of M. Ulugh Beg, the son of Muḥammad Sulṭān. The brief account of this affair is that the Mīrzā was proceeding from Zamīn Dāwar, which was his fief, towards Badakhshān in order to pay his respects to his Majesty Jahānbānī, Khwāja M'uaẓẓam also accompanied him from a desire to kiss the threshold, and to atone for his offences. When they came near Ghaznīn the news of the grand army's victory arrived
285 and Khwāja M'uaẓẓam prevailed upon the Mīrzā to go against the Hazāras so that they might attack and harry a tribe who were always practising plunder and robbery. From the inconsiderateness which is the natural stock of youthful arrogance and is the madness of pride they did not observe proper strategy and showed rashness in fight. The Mīrzā drank the last draught from the goblet of the scimetar, and his Majesty exalted Tardī Muḥammad Khān by assigning Zamīn Dāwar to him as his fief and sent him off in order that he might bring that country into order. In the same year the ambassadors of 'Abdu-r-rashīd Khān, son of Sulṭān Saīd Khān, the ruler of Kāshghar arrived bringing valuable presents. They were welcomed with favours and allowed to return quickly. At the same time 'Abbās Sulṭān, one of the Uzbeg princes, gained auspiciousness by kissing the threshold, and was received with favour. His rank was exalted by his marriage with the chaste Gulcihara Begam, a younger[1] sister of his Majesty.

Among the occurrences of this year was the martyrdom of M. Shāh, brother of M. Ulugh Beg. He was coming from Ushtar Karām, which was in his fief, with the intention of paying his respects, but when he reached the pass of Minār, Shāh Muḥammad, brother of Ḥājī Muḥammad, in revenge for M. Muḥammad Sulṭān's having killed Kōkī, the paternal uncle of Ḥājī Muḥammad in India, lay in ambush and shot him with an arrow at the top of the pass, and raised the Mīrzā on that summit to the glorious degree of a martyr.

---

1 She was Humāyūn's half-sister, being an elder sister of Gulbadan Begam. This was her second marriage. 'Abbās soon ran away, see next chapter. The lady was no longer young, being probably over thirty.

# CHAPTER XLVI.

## March of his Majesty Jahānbānī Jannat-Āshyānī from Kābul to Balkh, and his return owing to the discordance of M. Kāmrān and the hypocrisy of the officers.

Though the conquest of India and the removal of weeds from that garden held a foremost place in his Majesty's mind, and though he was also anxious to visit Kashmīr, he postponed these enterprises and undertook[1] the expedition to Balkh, which had been previously determined on, and for which preparations had been made.

In the beginning of 956[2] (February, 1549), when the season had become milder, he sent Bāltū Beg, one of his confidants, to M. Kāmrān with the information that he was proceeding against Balkh in accordance with agreements, and that M. Kāmrān should co-operate in this and meet him when he should arrive at the borders of Badakhshān. Orders were also sent to Mīrzās Hindāl, 'Askarī, Sulaimān and Ibrāhīm to make arrangements for carriage and to prepare their men and join quickly.

The grand expedition started, but because of arrangements and 286
the disposal of business and the coming of Ḥājī Muḥammad Khān from Ghaznīn, there was a delay of nearly a month in Cālāk.[3] From this stage Khw. Dōst Khawānd was sent to Kūlāb to bring in M. Kāmrān.

Khw. Qāsim Buyūtāt, a former vizier, Khw. M. Beg, who was *dīwān-i-ḥāl,*[4] but owing to whose want of guiding-power (*bī rashidī*)

---

[1] According to Firishta, Bairām Khān had an old quarrel with the Uzbaks and so urged on the expedition against Balkh.

[2] 956 H. began on January 30th. Bayāzīd says that Humāyūn started in the beginning of spring; perhaps A.F. was reckoning by the Persian year.

[3] It is only about two miles north-west of Kābul. (Bābar, 138).

[4] I have not found this title, if title it be. Perhaps it implies that M. Beg was the existing vizier or

Khw. Ghāzī had seized the charge of affairs—and Khw. Maqṣūd 'Alī who was M. Kāmrān's *factotum*, made with others an inquiry, through the instrumentality of Mīr Barka, into the affairs of Khw. Ghāzī and Rūh. Allāh. Mun'im Khān, Muḥammad Qulī Khān Barlās, Farīdūn Khān and Maulānā 'Abdu-l-bāqī, the *ṣadr*, were appointed to audit the accounts. Husain Qulī Sulṭān[1] who was one of his Majesty's intimates, was the superintendent in this affair. The result of the inquiry was that Khw. Ghāzī and Rūḥ Allāh and a number of other condemned[2] clerks were held to ransom. Muḥammad Qulī Sulṭān was appointed to take an account of Khw. Ghāzī's property, and Khw. Sulṭān 'Alī, who, by the favour of his Majesty,[3] had received the title of *Afẓal* (most excellent) Khān, was raised from the position of *mushrif-i-buyūtāt* to that of *dīwān-i-buyūtāt*.

At this time, M. Ibrāhīm came post and did homage and was welcomed with favours.

When his Majesty's mind had been set at rest about the necessary arrangements for the expedition, he marched to Istālif. Here 'Abbās Sulṭān[4] Uzbak absconded. His Majesty marched slowly, as he waited to be joined by the Mīrzās. When he heard that they had started, and that M. Kāmrān was getting ready, he went by Panjshīr and encamped at Andarāb. In imitation of his Majesty Ṣāḥib-qirānī, he halted for three days at a stage[5] where that fortunate prince had laid foundations. Thence he went to Nārī, where there is a meeting of the ways. Having crossed the Nārī Pass, he traversed the plain of Nīlbar,[6] the spring beauty of which is famous and pre-eminent above that of other parts of Badakhshān. Near this flowery spot, Mīrzās Hindāl and Sulaimān did homage and were encompassed with favours. Here at M. Sulaimān's request, M. Ibrāhīm was permitted

---

*dīwān* and did not perform the duties M. Beg was a nephew of Khw. Jahān Amīnā of Herāt and a poet who wrote under the name of Shahrī. (Blochmann, 424).

[1] Sister's son of Bairām and known by the title of Khānjahān. Blochmann, 329).

[2] *Mataghallibrā gīrāndand.* Cf. text. 241 for use of this verb. Apparently the same Muḥammad Qulī or 'Alī was employed in both cases.

[3] Blochmann, 376. *Niẓāmu-d-dīn* says Akbar bestowed the title.

[4] He had recently married a sister of Humāyūn.

[5] Probably Pariān.

[6] Apparently contracted from *nīlūfar*, the lotus or water-lily.

to go to Badakhshān[1] that he might protect the country and look after the local army.

From the neighbourhood of Baqlān,[2] Mīrzās Hindāl and Sulaimān and Ḥājī Muḥammad Khān and a number of experienced and energetic men were sent on in advance, that they might set free from the Uzbeks the town of Aibak, a dependency of Balkh which is famed for its cultivation, the abundance of its fruits, and the excellence of its climate.

At this time, Sher Muḥammad Pakna—one of the personal 287
attendants (*yasāwalān*) killed a leopard with an arrow and presented it. Ḥusain Qulī *muhrdār*, represented that the Turks regarded it as unlucky to kill a leopard when on an expedition, and said that, at the time when Bairām Ughlān[3] made him prisoner and brought him before Kistan Qarā,[4] the ruler of Balkh, and they were making preparations in Jajaktu[5] and Maimana for marching to Herāt, someone killed a leopard and for this reason the expedition was stayed. His Majesty paid no heed[6] to this story, and held firmly to his resolution of going to Balkh.

Next day the advance force arrived at Aibak. Pīr Muḥammad Khān, the ruler of Balkh, had sent his guardian, Khw. Bāgh[7] and a

---

[1] Apparently here used to denote Kishm, the capital. They were already in Badakhshān.

[2] It is west of Nārīn and south of Qundūz.

[3] Called by Blochmann (464) the "well-known Bairām Oghlān." It appears from Bāyazīd that he was maternal uncle of Muḥammad Hakīm.

[4] An elder brother of Pīr Muḥammad and his predecessor in Balkh. He was a son of Jānī Beg (Vambéry's Bokhara, 282*n.*) and seems to have died in 955 H. See Shāhid Ṣādiq 235*b*.

[5] The text omits the conjunction between these names but a variant gives it and it occurs in Bāyazīd, and the *Ḥadīqatu-l-aqālīm* gives the names as those of two towns. Vambéry (l.c. Introd. XXIX *n.*) speaks of Tchichektu and Almar (modern Maimana). Maimana lies about half-way between Balkh and Herāt. The Jajaktu of the text seems properly to be Chichaktu and is so spelt in the map appended to Captain Yate's "England and Russia face to face. (1887)." It lies west-south-west of Maimana.

[6] Bāyazīd says that Humāyūn remarked that the Uzbeks were his enemies and that what was a bad sign for them was a good one for himself.

[7] Text, Māq; but Bāyazīd, whom probably A.F. is copying, has Bāgh Māq may however be right for it

number of experienced men such as Īl M., Ḥusain Sa'īd Bai,[1] Muḥammad Qulī M. and Jūjak M. to guard Aibak and provide for its defence. They reached it at about the same time as the imperial army and had no resource but to enter the fort of Aibak and secure themselves there. His Majesty arrived and set himself to take the fort and distributed the batteries. In two or three days the garrison asked for quarter and came out and did homage and Aibak fell into the hands of the imperial servants.

His Majesty held a royal festival and consulted with the *atālīq* about the conquest of Transoxiana. The *atālīq* represented that he was not a fit person to consult about such matters, but his Majesty replied that he bore marks of honesty, and that he should, without hesitation, say what he thought. Then the *atālīq* said that as the serviceable men of Pīr Muḥammad Khān had fallen into his Majesty's hands, he should put them all to death and go on in the career of victory, for Transoxiana would fall into his hands without a battle. His Majesty replied that it is ignoble to break one's word and that this is especially so in the case of princes; that he had granted quarter and could not recede from this. The *atālīq* replied that if his Majesty did not approve of this plan, he might keep him prisoner and make a treaty to the effect that all the country on this side of Khulm should be his own and that an auxiliary force should be supplied (*i.e.*, by Pīr Muḥammad) whenever the expedition against India should take place. As the eternal will and stablished decree had gone forth against these two propositions, what was written by the pen of fate appeared to the Lord of Purpose to be preferable.[2]
288 His Majesty stayed there several days. Though the climate of Aibak and its abundance of fruit were a motive for staying, yet the chief reason was the non-arrival of M. Kāmrān. The wise and far-seeing used to insist that if this delay had not taken place, Pīr Muḥammad

means praise in Turkī and might be part of a proper name while Bāgh does not seem part of a man's name. It seems not impossible that Māq is an abbreviation of Imāq.

[1] See Wood's Journey, 224, where he says that Bai has the same significance as Khān amongst the Afghāns.

[2] A good instance of A.F.'s turgid style. Instead of simply stating that Humāyūn rejected the apparently sound proposition of the *atālīq*, he says that as another course had been decreed by fate, Humāyūn also preferred it.

Khān would not have been able to resist, and would either have been put to the rout or obliged to make peace on such terms as his Majesty chose. For 'Abdu-l-'azīz Khān[1] and the other Uzbek Khāns would not have been able to come to help. Since there was long delay, they had time to come to the assistance of the enemy. The Uzbek officers who had been taken prisoners, were sent to Kābul with Khw. Qāsim *makhlas*, one of the trusted of the Court, but his Majesty took the *atālīq* with him and marched by way of Khulm. Two or three days later, they passed Khulm and halted at Bābā Shāhū. Next day they encamped near the shrine[2] which is a well-known landmark, and scouts brought information that a large body of Uzbeks had arrived under the leadership of Waqqāṣ Sulṭān and Shāh Muhammad Sulṭān Ḥiṣārī.[3]

His Majesty drew up his troops and set his foot in the stirrup of victory. A slight engagement took place between the advance guards and, at the time of encamping, Shāh Muḥammad Sulṭān Ḥiṣārī attacked the camp with a large force. Brave men like Kābulī Khān,[4] brother of Muḥammad Qāsim *maujī*, Sher Muḥammad Pakna and Muḥammad Khān Turkmān distinguished themselves. Kābulī fell and the enemy being unable to resist took to flight. Ūkīn Ughlān, a man of distinction among the Uzbeks, was made prisoner and brought to the presence. A dispute arose between Muḥammad Khān Turkmān and Saiyid Muḥammad Pakna, each claiming the honour of this feat. His Majesty asked Ūkīn who had brought him down. He pointed to Muḥammad Khān and said, "He first aimed a blow at me and the wind of it unhorsed me. When I recovered myself and stood up, this other man," pointing to Saiyid Muḥammad

[1] As stated in text, he was a son of Ubaidu-l-lāh, the brother-in-law of Ḥaidar M. He began to reign in Bukhāra in 1540.

[2] The Mazār-i-sharīf of the maps. It is the shrine of Shāh Auliya, *i.e.*, 'Alī, Muḥammad's son-in-law, his tomb having been discovered there, it is said, during the reign of Sulṭān Ḥusain Baiqrā. There is an account of its discovery in the *Ḥadīqatu-l-aqālīm s. v.* Balkh. *Cf.* too Wood's Journey, 135.

[3] Perhaps another son of Jānī Beg and brother of Pīr Muḥammad. Bāyazīd calls him a son of Barandūq Sulṭān. The *Tār. Rash.* (161 and 452) also mentions a Shāh M. Sulṭān who was a grandson of Sultān Maḥmud Khān.

[4] Bāyazīd tells us he was killed and his head cut off and taken to Balkh

Pakna, "struck me on the face with his sword." His Majesty blamed Saiyid Muḥammad saying, "He was thrown down by Muḥammad K͟hān; you were ungenerous to strike another's catch (*said*)." He gave the prize of valour to Muḥammad K͟hān and made over Ūkīn to Pīr Muḥammad *akhta* to be cared for.

In spite of the signs of victory, hypocritical, disloyal officers continued to show faint-heartedness and were continually uttering false reports about M. Kāmrān and spreading them among themselves. Though everything disgraceful which they ascribed to the Mīrzā had the appearance of truth, for he was capable of it and of more, yet in this instance, they fastened false charges on him.

289 In fine the Uzbeks gave battle next day in great force and tried to gain the victory, 'Abdu-l-'azīz K͟hān, son of Ubaid K͟hān, being in the centre, Pīr Muḥammad K͟hān on the right and Sulṭān-i-ḥiṣār on the left. His Majesty also drew up his army, he himself occupying the centre, M. Sulaimān the right wing and M. Hindāl the left, while Qarāca K͟hān, Ḥājī Muḥammad K͟hān, Tardī Beg K͟hān, Mun'im K͟hān and Sulṭān Ḥusain Beg Jalāïr with his brothers were in the van. After mid-day the armies encountered one another and a great battle raged till evening. Brave men trod the field of courage and drove off the enemy's front ranks across the canals and into the outer defences (*kūcaband*) of Balk͟h. His Majesty in the strength of his mental vigour and wisdom, wished to pursue and to take his standards across the canals. His hypocritical followers while pretending to agree, gave wrong advice, and ignorant friends supported their opinion out of ignorance, and thereby made the opinion of enemies to prevail. They did not permit the crossing of the canals and uttered timorous speeches, sometimes alleging the paucity of their men and the number of the enemy; sometimes speaking of M. Kāmrān's going to Kābul and of their fears lest the soldiers' families should be made prisoners, and sometimes urging that they ought to wait for M. Kāmrān. Pressing these and other matters, they recommended a retreat. At length, after a thousand struggles with his spirit, it was agreed to proceed to Daragaz which is a strong position, and to stay there some days and collect the Aimaqs and other soldiers and so to get together the materials of victory. During that delay accurate news of M. Kāmrān would arrive. In the event of his having marched against Kābul, it was not proper for

them to torment themselves (*kāftan*)[1] in these parts. At a future time, they could with whole heart, conquer Balkh, nay, Transoxiana and, by the help of God, they had been constantly successful up to this day and would continue so. For every reason it was right to withdraw and proceed to Dara-gaz. His Majesty seeing the general feeling, was helpless and ordered a march in that direction.

Thus the already captured Balkh was let go on account of the discord of the disloyal. Shaikh Bahlūl was sent to turn back the van which had crossed the stream and driven back the Uzbeks and entered the fortifications (*shahrband*). M. Sulaimān and a number of other valiant men were appointed to be the rear-guard.

As the whole aim of the disaffected and black-hearted was to 290
confound the army, this compulsory retreat to Dara-gaz, which happened also to be on the route to Kābul, was represented as a return thither, and the march of M. Kāmrān was on every-one's tongue. Men lost heart and separated in different directions. Though his Majesty Jahānbānī sent Ḥusain Qulī Sl. *muhrdār* who was one of his confidants, and a number of others also, to turn back the disheartened crowd, it was of no avail, as proposition and disposition did not coincide (*taqdīr mūāfiq-i-tadbīr nabūd*). And in fact the decree of the Omnipotent was to this effect in order that the vast country of India might be sheltered from the mischief of tyrants and the inflictions of oppressors and become the descension-point of the blessings of a holy personality, and the abiding-throne and theatre (*takhtgāh-i-abd dastgāh*) of his Majesty, the *Shāhanshāh*, the Shadow of God; and that many thousands of good seeds might be shed over the wide fields of earth and the hope-plots of the sincere. To sum up; God, the World-adorner, revealed such a victory as this under the guise of conditions which might prove a lesson and a warning to the wise, and thereby brought to pass the things of counsel and wisdom. For had this disaster not occurred, the work of the helpless ones of India would have been hindered by the undertaking of the conquest of Transoxiana; and the setting-in order of those lands which are a haven for the pilgrims of the seven climes, had sunk under the veil of delay.

---

1 *Kāftan* means to split or cleave and the sense seems to be that now their minds were divided; afterwards they could in comfort *ba khaṭir-i-jama'*, lit. with united heart, conquer Balkh, etc.

In brief, when the enemy became aware of the unpleasing occurrence (*i.e.*, the retreat), they put their own confused affairs in order and came in pursuit. His Majesty Jahānbānī displayed splendid courage and performed achievements whose eulogy might be the frontispiece to the model-battles of the world. In that jungle of tigers of war, his world-traversing dun-coloured [1] steed which bore the name of *tasarru-n-nazirīn* [2] and had been presented to him by Muḥammad Khān,[3] the governor of Herāt and which he was riding, fell from being wounded by an arrow. Ḥaidar Muḥammad *akhta* presented that leader of faith and dominion with his own horse and was exalted by this piece of service. As the Divine protection was hovering over that Lord of Sovereignty's throne, he was brought into a place of safety. Most of his followers, when they beheld symptoms of defeat, dispersed in all directions in a cowardly and ignominious manner.

The names of the chief officers of the army are as follows: Mīrās Hindāl and Sulaimān, Qarāca Khān, Ḥājī Muḥammad Khān, Tardī Beg Khān, Mun'im Khān, Khiẓr Khw. Sl.,[4] Muḥammad Qulī Khān Jalāir, Iskandar Khān, Qāsim Ḥusain Khān, Ḥaidar Muḥammad *ākhta-begī*, 'Abdu-l-lāh Khān Uzbek, Ḥusain Qulī Khān *muhrdār*, Muḥibb 'Alī Khān

---

[1] *Zarrīn fām*, golden-coloured. Bāyazīd calls the horse, *asp-i-qula*, dun-coloured.

[2] *Tasarru-n-nāẓirīn*. It delights beholders. This is an Arabic expression and is used in the Korān to describe the kind of cow which Moses told the Israelites to sacrifice. The reading of the text is probably correct, but it differs from the word in Bāyazīd, in the copy in the India Office though it would seem that it is from Bāyazīd that A.F. has taken the story. There the word looks like nazzar, but Erskine in his MS. translation has nashtar so perhaps he took the word to be nastar, or nasrīn, *i.e.*, the narcissus. This might be an allusion to the yellow colour of the horse.

Bāyazīd who was evidently fond of horses and proud of his powers of managing them, as a later story of his shows, is careful to tell us that Humāyūn's horse afterwards died of its wound. He adds that the horse given by Ḥaidar to Humāyūn was *ṭūraqī*, bow-legged, or weak-kneed.

[3] Most MSS. seem to have Sharafu-d-dīn after Muḥammad Khān.

[4] Gulbadan Begam's affection induces her to represent her husband as behaving in heroic fashion during the retreat, by turning back to search for Hindāl. But Bāyazīd names him as one of those who refused to stand when called upon to do so by Ḥusain Qulī and he says it was Shāh Qulī Nāranjī who went back to look for Hindāl. A.F. seems to include in his list both the leaders who behaved well and those who ran away.

of) Mīr Khalifa, Sl. Ḥusain Khān, Bāltū Sl., Muṣāḥib Beg, Shāh 291
.h Khān, Shāham Khān Beg Jalāīr, Shāh Qulī Nāranjī, Muḥammad
.n *maujī*, Laṭafu-l-lāh of Sihrind, 'Abdu-l-wahhāb Aujī,[1] Baqī
-Muḥammad *parwānci*, and Khaldīn.[2]

Three days later, his Majesty halted at the top of the pass[3] of the Four Springs and here Muḥammad. Qulī Shaikh Turkmān[4] who had hit on the right road, heard of the royal party and joined it.

From this place, his Majesty wrote an affectionate epistle to his Majesty the *Shāhinshāh*, and to the chaste ladies who were in Kābul, the abode of peace and sent it by Beg Muḥammad *ākhta-begī*. He also sent a friendly letter to Rashīd Khān, the ruler of Kashghār who had always shewn loyalty and devotion, informing him of his arrival and telling him how his evil-minded brother, M. Kāmrān, had by constraint of his natural character, elevated the hideousness of discord over the beauty of concord and so had completely depressed the side of love and loyalty. Many of his followers too had shewn a want of

---

1 Perhaps this epithet means that he was a native of Aujān in Āzarbaijān. (Jarrett III. 81 and Ouseley's Travels). But most MSS. have Audajī, *e.g.*, B.M. 27, 247 and 5610.

2 Probably the Khaldīn Dōst Saharī mentioned in text (316) in the list of Hindāl's servants.

3 Text, *bar sar-i-yakh*, on the top of the ice, but reference to Bāyazīd and to various MSS. of the A.N. has convinced me that the proper reading is *bar sar-i-pal*, top of the pass or mountain. Bāyazīd has *bar sar-i-kutal* and *kutal* has the meanings of *paj*. It is true that he also has the expression in the same passage ماربيچ *mārpēc*, a convolution or winding road, and that possibly this may refer to the winding road taken by Humāyūn as distinguished from the *rāh-i-rāst*, straight road, taken by Kāmān. (According to Steingass the phrase *rāh-rāst* means "a great distance.")

It seems to me that in several parts of this narrative, A.F. and Bāyazīd have copied from the same source.

Cahar Cashma is marked in the Government map of Afghānistān as S.W. of Haibak and near Dara-yusaf. Bāyazīd speaks of four wells,—two, apparently at the top of the pass, and two lower down. He describes then as near Aibak.

4 Text, *kamāl*. Several MSS. have Kamān but Bayazīd seems to have Turkmān, and evidently the man meant as the M. Qulī Turkmān Afshān of Blochmann 474. *See* Bāyazīd 47*b*, 48*a* and 75*a*. MSS. have *kamān*. The expression in text is not clear. Bāyazīd says the Shaikh was going along on the right or straight road. M. Qulī brought the welcome news that the Uzbeks had discontinued the pursuit.

courage. Certainly the expedition had not redounded to the joy of well-wishers; on the contrary, it had been a cause of sorrow and distress. In the same letter, he expressed his thanks for his safety and he inserted excellent counsels such as might comfort a loving heart.

Leaving that place, he arrived after one night's interval, at Ghūrband and on the next night, at Khwāja Sīyārān. Thence he went to Qarā Bagh and thence to Ma'mūra.[1] His Majesty, the *Shāhanshāh*, came out to meet him here and was affectionately received. From this place he went in an auspicious hour to Kābul.

M. Sulaimān went off to Badakhshān and M. Hindāl to Qundūz. Mun'im Khān accompanying him. All the other officers followed his Majesty to Kābul. Shāh Bidāgh Khān who had given proofs of courage, remained a prisoner with the enemy, as did also Mīr Sharīf *bakhshī*, Khw. Nāṣiru-d-dīn 'Alī *mustaufī*, Mīr Muḥammad *munshī*, Mīr Jān Beg *dārogha-i-'imārat*, and Khw. Muḥammad Amīn Kang. All the other servants were safe.

When the *atālīq* and other Uzbeks who had been made prisoners at Aibak, were released and went to their own country, and gave account of the royal kindness and liberality, Pīr Muḥammad Khān was astonished, and sent his prisoners in a humane manner to Kābul.

His Majesty, recognizing that his return was really advantageous, set himself to arrange his kingdom and engaged in the conduct of
292 things spiritual and temporal. Khw. Jalālu-d-dīn Maḥmūd had been sent on an embassy to the king of Persia, but from various causes had delayed in Qandahār and he was now recalled. Khw. 'Abdū-ṣ-ṣamad and Mīr Saiyid 'Alī who were celebrated for their skill in painting, came with the Khwāja and were graciously received. Khw. Sl. 'Alī, known as Afẓal Khān, was raised[2] from the position of *mashrif-i-khizāna* to that of vizier; while the whole charge of the *dīwānī* was made over to Khw. M. Beg.

The account of M. Kāmrān is as follows. When his Majesty, out of his kindness and affection, forgave his grave offences and gave him Kūlāb and appointed Cākar Beg of Kūlāb, the son of Sl. Wais

[1] *Dih-i-ma'mūra*, near Kābul. (Jarrett II. 404).

[2] It is not clear whether this is the promotion recorded above (text 286) or a still higher one.

Beg, as his co-adjutor and went to Kābul, no long time intervened before the Mīrzā behaved badly to Cākar Beg and drove him out: He placed the great favours which had been bestowed on him in the niche (*ṭāq*) of forgetfulness and giving way to evil thoughts, watched for his opportunity. During the time that His Majesty Jahānbānī was in Kābul, he was continually making false promises that he would come; and His Majesty, out of his candid nature and straightforwardness,—which are the characteristics of magnanimous natures,—believed his false words and went off to Balkh. The Mīrzā looked upon this opportunity as fair gain and again determined in his perfidious heart, that he would go to Kābul. The rebellious designs which were leavening his mind, came near the surface, and at his instigation, narrow-minded and disloyal officers practised various hypocrisies in that expedition, as has already been related. But as His Majesty returned and cast the shade of his justice on Kābul, M. Kāmrān left M. 'Askarī in Kūlāb and went off to fight M. Sulaimān. The latter hastened away without fighting from Tāliqān to Qil'a Ẓafar.

M. Kāmrān made over Ṭāliqān to Bābūs Beg and proceeded towards Qil'a Ẓafar. Mīrzās Sulaimān and Ibrāhim not thinking it expedient to fight left Isḥāq[1] Sultan in Qil'a Ẓafar and went off to the defiles of Badakhshān. They took post in the village of Jirm and awaited the Divine retribution. M. Kāmrān, having disposed of M. Sulaimān went off to Qundūz. He began by making false pretences to M. Hindāl and proposed a union with him. M. Hindāl did not hearken to him and stood by his obligations, whereupon M. Kāmrān laid siege to Qundūz. M. Hindāl neglected no point in defending the fort and when M. Kāmrān could not succeed, he joined the Uzbeks and asked their assistance. A large body of 293
Uzbeks came to help him and joined him in the siege. M. Hindāl in order to cause confusion and deceive the foe, which in fact is a guidance on the high road of success, devised an excellent plan, *viz.*, he wrote a letter as from M. Kamrān to himself, full of a renewal of peace between them and of deceiving the Uzbeks, and after the manner of experts, he gave this false document to a courier who was intentionally to throw himself into the hands of Uzbeks. When, on searching the courier, the letter was found, and when it appeared

[1] A brother-in-law of Kāmrān.

from its contents that the two Mīrzās were going to act in concert and make the Uzbeks a target for the arrows of evil, the latter were confounded and withdrew from the siege and set off for their own country. The affair of the fort remained unaccomplished and just then, news came that Cākar Beg was besieging Kūlāb and that M. ʻAskarī had been defeated and was shut up therein. Also that M. Sulaimān had joined with Is͟hāq Sl. and had got possession of Qilʻa Z̤afar and had then imprisoned Is͟hāq Sl. M. Kāmrān was bewildered at this news and withdrawing in despair from Qundūz, he sent Yāsīn Daulat and Bābūs with a body of troops against M. Sulaimān and himself hastened to Kūlāb and made Cākar Beg retire. M. ʻAskarī came out and did homage to M. Kāmrān who took him with himself, and went off to put down M. Sulaimān. They had halted near Rūstāq, when a large force of Uzbeks who had come on a plundering expedition (*yurtāwalī*)[1] under the leadership of Saʻīd Beg, passed by the encampment and made a raid on it. Mīrzās Kāmrān, ʻAskarī and ʻAbdu-l-lāh Mug͟hal escaped with a few men to Tālīqān. When the Saʻīd afore-named knew the rights of the matter, he sent back the baggage[2] to the Mīrzā with all respect and apologized for the plundering. Mīrzās Hindāl and Sulaimān thinking the opportunity favourable, set out to put down M. Kāmrān who not deeming it advisable to remain in Badak͟hs͟hān, went off to K͟host in order that he might, by the route of Z̤uḥḥāq and Bāmīān withdraw into the Hazāra country. There he would learn the real state of Kābul and either proceed there or go elsewhere.[3] As the disloyal officers of His Majesty Jahānbānī were always urging the Mīrzā to come to Kābul, he fraudulently sent ambassadors to the Court and represented that his object in coming was to apologize for the past and to serve his

---

1 P. de C. gives in his Dictionary, یورتول as meaning "troupe qu'on envoie pour faire une razzie, coureurs.

2 See *errata* to text. The word is really اغرلق *ag͟hirliq*. It probably included Kāmrān's wives and daughters for Gulbadan says they were captured. Bāyazīd says it was Pīr Muhammad K͟hān of Balk͟h who sent back the plunder. It would appear from Gulbadan, that he was the son of a brother of one of Kāmrān's wives.

3 Bāyazīd says Kāmrān's idea was to go to Bhakkar and it is very likely —(having regard to his relations with the ruling family of Bhakkar), that *dīgar* of the text is a mistake for Bhakkar.

Majesty. His hope was, he said, that His Majesty would with royal kindness, forgive his crimes and sins.

*Verse.*

I've come again to worship the dust of tny feet,
If submission be ordered, I'm ready to pay it.

"My hope is that on this occasion, I may by good service, obtain release from the heavy burden of shame." His Majesty from the purity of his own nature, regarded his gold-incrusted copper as genuine, and accepted it according to the standard for fine gold.

---

## CHAPTER XLVII.

### 294 March of His Majesty Jahānbānī Jannat-Āshyānī from Kābul, and fight with M. Kāmrān; and other instructive occurrences.

When the arrival of M. Kāmrān at the borders of Kābul was approaching, a number of the loyal and farseeing represented that there should be a limit to simplicity and optimistic views of persons. Seeing that the fraud, lying and disaffection of this ingrate had been tested many times, it was right and proper that caution should not be thrown away again, and that the army should be ordered to march out, and the banners of victory be unfurled for the suppression of the rebellious. If indeed the Mīrzā had repented of his evil deeds, and had entered on the path of concord, and were desirous of doing homage, he would receive distinction from the royal favour (in going out to welcome him), and if on this occasion also he was persistent in perversity, the rules of precaution would be observed on our side. On hearing these weighty words His Majesty determined to march towards Ghūrband, which was the Mīrzā's route, and he set out in that direction in the middle of 957 (June-July, 1550). He left His Majesty the Shāhanshāh as prince in Kābul and put Qāsim Khān Berlās at the head of affairs. Qarāca Khān, Muṣāḥib Beg and many others, white without and black within, who were always stirring up strife, were rejoiced and wrote seditious letters to M. Kāmrān, pressing him to come to Kābul and saying that they, and many others, would welcome him and would disperse the King's well-wishers by unfitting suggestions, and that Kābul would easily fall into his hands.

'Tis marvellous how actions which, with complete inconsistency, they regarded as improper when practised on themselves by equals and associates, *viz.*, promise-breaking, evil-devising, and lying, should all be performed by them against their Master and benefactor! Their blinded eyes opened not to the hideousness thereof, nay, they regarded its repulsiveness as a beauty, and counted it as part of their wisdom of strategy. Though they understood loyalty and right dealing and looked for them in their servants, yet they were so overcome by their own baseness as to play the game of deceit and infidelity against such a pure-hearted Master! And what wrongheadedness also! I can imagine that they could not comprehend the glorious merits of this holy personality, but where was their common sense! That which they expected from their own servants they would not render to that aggregation of benevolences and to that bestower of so many favours, any one of which deserved a life's devotion, but on the contrary they acted in the very opposite way to one who was their Master and benefactor, and requited him with negligence and wrong advice. But alas! What marvel is it that he who has been kneaded of strife and malice, should show such behaviour? What joy have the born-blind in the glory of the sun? The sincerity's eye of this crew has been filmed over with hypocrisy and become void of light, and their breast of love has been narrowed by the tumour of pride! How can such recognise a Master's rights to gratitude, or perceive the beauties of a benefactor? What place then is there for thanksgiving for boundless favours? The wild steeds of the o'er mastering passions of such self-pleasers have not such docility[1] that their bridles can be tightened by the band of chiding, or their reins turned by the outspread fingers of counsel!

295

At length His Majesty, in accordance with the decrees of fate, marched from Kābul and encamped at Qarā Bāgh. From thence he went to Cārīkārān and from there to the river Bārān. It happened that there was a stream on this stage and that His Majesty crossed it on horseback, whilst his followers went off in different directions seeking for a safe passage. His Majesty did not approve of this and instanced in reproof of this disaffected crew, the conduct of the devotees of Shāh Ism'āīl Ṣafavī, who flung themselves down from a sky-high mountain to seize his handkerchief and made for themselves a lofty foundation of fame and life-sacrifice. Such was His Majesty's sound opinion of his followers on this occasion, and such was their pusillanimous circumspection. In fine Qarāca Qarābakht and Muṣāḥib Munafiq and others, who were burning torches of sedition, represented, directly and indirectly, that they had to do with mountains, and

---

[1] *Khudrāī*, which is short for *Khud-dārī*. *See* Vullers I. 714a.

that there were many defiles; that the Mīrzā would have few men with him, and that the loyal should be stationed on different roads, so that the Mīrzā should not be able to come out. The whole idea of these evil-minded ones was to disperse the army so that M. Kāmrān's purpose might be effected. His Majesty Jahānbānī, who in his noble
296 nature only believed good of men, thought the plan of these traitors a good one and sent Ḥājī Muḥammad Khān *Kōkī*, Mīr Barka, M. Ḥasan Khān, Bahādur Khān, Khw. Jalālu-d-dīn Maḥmūd, Calpī Beg, Muḥammad Khān Beg Turkmān, Shaikh Bahlūl, Ḥaidar Qāsim Kōhbar, and Shāh Qulī Nāranjī to Ẓuḥḥāq and Bāmiān, and appointed Mun'im Khān and a large body of troops to Sāl Aulang. Qarāca, and Muṣāḥib, Qāsim Ḥusain Sl. and a number who remained with His Majesty, drew up daily an account of His Majesty's position and sent it to M. Kāmrān, and were continually representing to His Majesty that this time the Mīrzā had no other idea but to serve him.

When there were few loyalists in attendance, and the convention of hypocrites was powerful, M. Kāmrān, who had been confounded by the royal pomp and the large army and had been unable either to quit the service (of the king) or to go forward and do homage, having become acquainted by the brokerage of the hypocrites with their treachery, turned off from the road by Ẓuḥḥāq and Bāmiān towards Dara Qibcāq [1] which is a dependency of Ghūrband. Yāsīn Daulat, Maqdum Kōka and Bābā Sa'īd led the advance, while he himself was in the centre. His men were arranged in two bodies. It was midday when His Majesty was apprised by a peasant [2] of that quarter of the coming of M. Kāmrān, and of his evil intentions. Qarāca who was the ringleader of the ill-disposed, represented that if one listened to the tales of a man like this and placed reliance on such false rumours, hearts would be divided, and the people (Kāmrān's followers) would become apprehensive. Should there be a desire to give battle on account of this news, and should warlike preparations be made, certainly when M. Kāmrān heard of them, he would desist from his

1 This pass is marked on the map appended to Yule's introduction to Wood's Journey. It is also called Cārdār and lies S.E. of the Dandān Shikan. See also Bābar's Mem., p. 139.

2 Bayazīd says a servant of the Mīr Munshī brought the news and made such an uproar that Humāyūn, according to Erskine, had him put to death, but perhaps the words only mean that he was beaten.

desire of entering into service. Meanwhile the news of the Mīrza's coming and of his wicked intentions became stronger and more continuous. Wondrous to relate, the hypocrisy and inmost thought of those hypocrites had not yet been revealed on the mirror of His Majesty's mind. Nought entered his holy heart save good thoughts of people, till at length it become established that the enemy was coming and coming with a hostile intention. An order was given that all who were with him should mount their horses. He himself put the foot of courage in the stirrup of enterprise and in a short time there was a hot engagement. Pīr Muḥammad *ākhtā*, who was one of the devoted followers and Muḥammad Khān Jalāīr and many other brave men moved forward. Pīr Muḥammad *ākhtā*, who was athirst for the stream of life-sacrifice, brought his foot into the circle of conflicts and so watered the sword of battle in slaying the foe, that he himself was swept
away by the foam. M. Qulī made his steed so rush about in the 297
field of contest that after slaughtering crowds of wretches he, in the press and confusion, fell wounded[1] from his horse. His son Dōst Muḥammad could not endure to see him in the power of the foe, and ran to his help. While his father yet lived, he killed his adversary, and had such combats that he too was swept away, and disappeared. His Majesty Jahānbānī got upon a rising ground and calculated the strength of friend and foe. By seeing the manner in which some of his servants were killed, and by seeing others go in crowds over to the enemy, the truth of the fraud and treachery of those scoundrels became apparent to him. His native valour and intrepidity were stirred up, and seizing a lance he himself rushed against the foe. They were scattered before him, but an arrow wounded his horse and Beg Bābāī of Kūlāb came from behind, and

---

1 From A.F.'s account it would appear that M. Qulī was killed, as well as his son. According to the Maaṣir I. 557 and Blochmann 385 M. Qulī did not die till 983 but the M. Qulī of the battle of Qibcāk is not the M. Qulī who was Ḥaidar Muḥammad's brother. The Tabaqat, Elliot V. 232 calls the son Aḥmad. Bāyazīd says, 51*b* that Pīr Muḥammad was killed by an arrow, that M. Qulī's horse was killed, and M. Qulī's leg broken. Then he adds, "Imam Qulī and his son belonged to the body-guard. The son ran to his father to put him on horseback, but he too suffered martyrdom." This looks as if Bāyazīd regarded M. Qulī and Imām Qulī as the same person. The M. Qulī who was killed has the title of Cūlī. *See* Erskine's history.

knowingly[1] or unknowingly struck him a blow with his sword. His Majesty turned round and gave him an angry look which caused him[2] to stumble. Mihtar[3] Sakāī known as Farḥat Khān came and put that wretch to flight, and M. Nijāt tendered his piebald horse to His Majesty who took it and gave the Mīrzā his. Meanwhile 'Abdu-l-wahhāb, one of the *yasāwal* came and telling how the officers had joined with M. Kāmrān, seized His Majesty's rein. "What time was it," he said, for fighting. The bucket of success must at one time come up full from the waters of hope and at another, it must, by a revolution of the wheel, go down empty."

Hail! eternal fate! which rules the beggar and the king, and directs the cycle of fortune and misfortune, which holds the key of deliverance for those in bonds, and causeth the exalted to fall. Until men have passed through the dark night of the hours of affliction, they know not the glory of the world-warming sun, and until the thirsty lips have sought the desert mirage, they are not watered at the spring of desire. This event is a proof of this, for on that day there was the apparition of the eventual salvation of His Majesty. He proceeded to Ẓuḥḥāq and Bāmīān whither he had sent many of his loyal officers. 'Abdu-l-wahhāb, Farḥat Khan, Muḥammad Āmīn, Sabdal[4] Khān and others accompanied him. Muḥammad Āmīn and 'Abdu-l-wahhāb were ordered to form the rear guard. On account of weakness and of the distress from his
298 wound, he took off his cuirass and made it over to Sabdal Khān who, out of stupidity, flung it away. Next day many of his servants joined him. One day he sent Shāh Budāgh Khān, Tūlak Qūcīn, and Majnūn Qāqshāl—ten in all,—towards Kābul to serve as a rear guard and also to keep a look out, but Tūlak Qūcīn only returned. He was received with favour on that market day of testing and raised to the office of *Qūrbegī*. The confidential servants were summoned and a council was held. Ḥājī Muḥammad Khān whose fief

---

[1] *i.e.*, either he recognised him or he did not.

[2] From the Iqbālnāma it would appear that the word *dast* should be separated from *tes*, and that the phrase is, dast az pa khaṭa*kard*, meaning that Beg Bāba grew confused, lit. did not know his hand from his foot.

[3] Blochmann 438. From Jauhar it would appear that he was an Abyssinian slave.

[4] Blochmann 441.

was Ghaznīn, and on whose heart's fireplace dissimulation was pre-eminently concocted, recommended a march to Qandahār. This however was not approved of. A number of the right-thinking recommended marching to Badakhshān, and then proceeding to Kābul along with Mīrzās Sulaimān, Hindāl and Ibrāhīm. A party of devoted heroes suggested that to-day M. Kāmrān was intoxicated with the mischievous wine of the hypocrites and narrow-souled ones and off his guard, while they had the good fortune to be at the feet of His Majesty. On what other day would they be successful?[1] The proper thing was that they should all with one heart march to Kābul. There was a confident hope that they would be able to dispose of M. Kāmrān without going to Badakhshān. As recent evidence had been obtained of the deceit and hypocrisy of very many of the nurslings of the Court, reliance was not put upon this opinion and the cautious course seemed to be to proceed to Badakhshān. Accordingly he ordered a march by the route of Yekka Aulang. At such a time as this Ḥājī Muḥammad obtained leave for his brother Shāh Muḥammad and his men and sent them to Ghaznīn! His Majesty with his own holy hand wrote a letter to His Majesty the Shāhinshāh announcing his safety and made it over to him (Shāh Muḥammad) in order that he might by every possible[2] means convey it to him. He also sent verbal messages of victory and promises of his coming. And he bade him (Shāh Muḥammad) go quickly to Ghaznīn and make every effort for keeping it safe till his return which, he trusted, would soon occur. Though the loyal represented that to separate hypocrites from himself at such a time was to put the reins of hypocritical actions into the hands of these unreliables and forward the schemes of the seditions, and though every one represented, either openly or by hints, that he (Ḥājī Muḥammad), was sending his brother to M. Kāmrān, and that he himself was seeking to be a household-spy and a deceiver of simple believers, His Majesty did not give heed and granted leave to Shāh Muḥammad. Next day

[1] This is evidently the Alanjak of Stewart's Jauhar, 98. It was an Aimāq settlement and lies about thirty miles S.-W. of Bāmīān. (Bābar's Mem., 211n.).

[2] Shāh Muḥammad's route to Ghaznīn would probably take him near Kābul.

he proceeded towards Kahmard. Many faithless ones separated from his service, but all who observed the limits of loyalty and were careful of their good name, stayed with him and bound the girdle of service on the waist of fidelity.

299 After[1] travelling three days on this road, Tūlakjī and Sānqājī, the headmen of the Aimāqs who live there, brought horses and sheep to the utmost of their power and presented them. They rendered acceptable service. His Majesty encamped at night near one of their settlements. When he mounted his horse in the morning, news was brought that a large caravan had arrived under the charge of Mīr Saiyid 'Alī of Sabzawār. Merchants from Irāq and Khurāsān had many horses and other goods with them and were on their way to India. At the end of the day the chiefs of the caravan were admitted to the Presence. The providential arrival of this large party was the beginning of celestial victories. The prudent and farseeing merchants recognised a great auspiciousness for themselves in the favour of so great a prince, and in assisting him; and tendered all their horses and goods as a present. His Majesty perceived that this was an aid from heaven and took[2] a portion of the goods at four or five times their value, and divided them among his followers and intimates. He also set aside presents for each of the princes of Badakhshān. The remainder he returned to them that they might sell the articles wherever they chose. Next day he arrived at Kahmard. Ṭāhir Muḥammad, son of Mīr Khurd was there. He recognised the arrival as a great favour and paid his respects, but either from meanness or not having materials, he could not with regard to his entertainment, succeed in wiping the sweat of shame from the face of his service. From there after two days and a night (*shab darmīyān*) they arrived at the bank of the river Bangī. From the other side a man[3] called out "O men of the caravan," have you any news among you of the King? When His Majesty heard him,

---

[1] From this point A.F. seems to follow Jauhar. Bāyazīd was not with Humāyūn in the retreat, he having fled towards Kābul. Perhaps the names Tūlakjī and Sānqājī are those of tribes and not of individuals. Sānqājī looks to be a variant of the tribal name Sālqāncī mentioned at Text, p. 276, 8 lines from foot.

[2] *dah cahal u dah panjāh*. Cf. Bābar's Mem., 138.

[3] See Jauhar, Stewart, 98.

he forbade any one to give news, and asked the man who he was, and who had sent him, and what news there was among them about the King. The man answered that he was sent by Naẓarī of Sāl[1] Aulang to get news of the King, and that the report among them was that the King had come out of the battle wounded, and that after that no one had seen him. The Mīrzā's men had found the royal *jība* (cuirass or corselet) which the King had worn on that day and had brought it to the Mīrzā who had rejoiced thereat, and had instituted feasts. His Majesty summoned him to his presence and asked him if he knew him. He replied that the Divine effulgence does not remain hid. His Majesty said, "Go and convey the good tidings to Naẓarī, and tell him to make himself ready, so that at the time of my return he may perform acceptable service." Next day he crossed
by a ford and reached the village of Auliyā Khanjān.[2] Here M. 300
Hindāl joined him and was exalted by tendering presents. After that he encamped at Andarāb. Mīrzās Sulaimān and Ibrāhīm did homage and formed the part of loyalists.

As the narrative has proceeded so far, it is necessary that before His Majesty Jahānbānī shall have assembled his army and marched to the conquest of Kābul, the pen should take up the account of M. Kāmrān from the beginning of his treachery till his coming out from Kābul, which was the beginning of his punishment, so that the lips athirst for the wine of words, may be moistened from the watering place of this supplement.

When the stewards of destiny brought forth from a hidden quarter, for the confirmation of the royal, ever-during dominion, and for the confounding of the masters of hypocrisy, such a victory in the guise of defeat, and such joy in the garb of sorrow, and when His Majesty Jahānbānī proceeded by the arrangement of devoted loyalists, towards Ẓuḥḥāq and Bāmīān, M. Kāmrān was amazed at

---

1 This, seems to be the Saulah-Aulang (between Panjhū and Ghūr-band) of Jarrett II. 400*n*. Naẓarī is perhaps the Mīr Naẓarī of the Turkish admiral Sīdī 'Alī, Vambéry, 65 and 66.

2 The Khinjān of the maps, W.S.-W. of Andarāb. But the river when the conversation with Naẓarī's servant took place, can hardly have been the Bangī. The text has Ādī Khinjān. In the government-map of Afghānistān, the town is called Khinjān Waliān. They appear to be two places. See Bābar's Mem., 139, and Jarrett II. 400.

the appearance ot so wondrous an event, such as he had never imagined as likely to happen. The hypocrites joined him in crowds, and that foolish one was excited and delighted by the coming of those triflers and stretched out the arm of oppression upon the faithful who were firmly grasping the pinnacle of fidelity to the king. On the very field of battle Bābā Sa'īd brought Qarāca Qarabakht wounded before the Mīrzā. The latter was gracious and inquired about his evil-ending condition. He replied that Bābā Sa'īd had wounded him unawares and the Mīrzā proceeded to console that cheat by baseless favours. After that Bābā Dōst *yasāwal* and a number of others brought forward Ḥusain Qulī *muhrdār*, who was one of the devoted loyalists, that evildoer struck with his own sword this faithful servant and ordered him to be cut to pieces in his presence. Thus this fundholder[1] in loyalty's treasure-house sold in his benefactor's service a fleeting life and a contingent existence for the coin of fidelity, and thereby became for ever a sharer in the banquet of the true and the loyal. They also brought in Tākhjī Beg who was a Caghatāī officer and reckoned among the faithful. Him too they put to the sword without hesitation. After that Beg Bābāī of Kūlāb came forward and told the story of the wounding of His Majesty. The Mīrzā was jubilant and sent Yūsīn Daulat and Maqdum *Kōka* and a body of men in pursuit. Qāsim Ḥusain Sl. had on this day shown treachery and blindness of heart. From the trepidation and fear which cling to the skirt of the disloyal, he took refuge on the side of the mountain and in his confusion did not know whether to advance or fly. Ḥasan *Ṣadr* and a number more were sent to him and they, by soothments and encouragement, brought him in. The Mīrzā left the field of battle and came to
301 Cārikārān. Here a man brought His Majesty's special corselet to the Mīrzā who was so exultant that he could not contain himself for joy (lit. his clothes were not large enough for him). He marched from thence and besieged Kābūl. Qāsim Khān Barlās was in the service of His Majesty the Shāhinshāh, and was looking after the security of the fort. Though the Mīrzā made false promises to him, he would not sever the strong cord of fidelity which bound him to

---

1 No doubt Ḥusain Qulī's title of *muhrdār*,=sealer, and also gold *muhr* holder has suggested this simile to the author.

His Majesty Jahānbānī, till false rumours were spread and the corselet (*jība*) was sent. The fort was taken by dint of hundreds of false promises and by staking lying tales. The new fruit of the garden of creation and nosegay of the spring of horizons, *viz.*, His Majesty the Shāhinshāh who was perfuming the nostrils of the age, and from whose brows of fortune there radiated the light of the Divine *Khilāfat*, was made a prisoner. But the Divine protection, which is ever near him, watched in the old fashion over that prince, outwardly small but grand in reality.

M. Kāmrān having taken possession of Kābūl, set about arranging his affairs and organising his army. He gave in fief to M. 'Asharī, Jūī Shābī which is now known as Jalālābād, in accordance with the auspicious title of the Shāhinshāh. It is a delightful spot and a partition (*barzakh*) between India and foreign countries, being replete with the advantages of the one and exempt from the evils of the other. It was Munīm Khān who gave it its holy apellation and who colonised it. Ghaznīn and its territory were given to Qarāca Khān and Ghūrband and its neighbourhood to Yāsīn Daulat. In this manner fiefs and grants were made to his followers. The royal servants were laid hold of, Khw. Sl. 'Alī the dīwān being imprisoned, and the hand of oppression was opened and money and goods were taken from him and used for evil purposes. But the Mirzā was ever in dread of the approach of the royal army, and could not pass his days in tranquillity. The direction of affairs was with Qarācā Khān and Khw. Qāsim the *Mīr Buyūtāt*, and by means of oppression and tyranny materials which in fact were no materials were got together, forgetting the verse :—

*Verse.*[1]

Who take *dirams* by force and give gold for ornamentation,
Dig up the foundation of the mosque[2] and gild the palace-roof.

About three months were spent in this way till the sound of the approach of His Majesty Jahānbānī from Badakhshān rose high in the province of Kābūl. The Mīrzā collected soldiers and

---

[1] The Lucknow editor illustrates this verse by a quotation from Sa'dī.

از رعیت کسیکه مایه ربود
پای دیوار کنود و بام اندود

[2] *'Amr* which means both life and mosques.

*zamīndārs* from the Hazāras and others and set off with a full equipment. He left Bābā Jūjak and Mullā S̲h̲afāī in Kābūl, and took His Majesty the S̲h̲āhins̲h̲āh,—the marks of auspiciousness in whom
302 were apparent, and were acknowledged by small and great and by friend and foe,—with him, either to bring himself good fortune or for greater security. Nor was he aware that God, the giver of life and adorner of the world, had assigned the benign influences of both worlds which were implanted in this holy personality to his friends, not to his foes. What lustre does antimony give to the blind?

Now that this parenthetical narrative has been completed, we must return to our subject and briefly describe the remaining occurrences of His Majesty Jahānbānī.

# CHAPTER XLVIII.

## RETURN OF HIS MAJESTY JAHĀNBĀNĪ JANNAT-ĀSHYĀNĪ FROM BADAKHSHĀN, AND HIS BATTLE WITH M. KĀMRĀN, AND ARRIVAL IN KĀBUL AFTER THE VICTORY.

When His Majesty Jahānbānī had encamped at Andarāb and the Mīrzās had waited upon him, as has already been related, he, in a short time, got together an army and prepared to march through the passes of the Hindū Kōh. As there were a number of traitors and false-hearted ones in attendance, His Majesty, in order to conciliate and to give repose to the exoteric, came down from the heaven of his nature (*fitrat*)[1] and took his seat on the earth of the spirit (*tabī'at*) of the age and brought forward the proposition of an oath, which is regarded by the worshippers of form as of great weight, suggesting that he should administer a special oath to each section (*girōh*) to the effect that they would accompany him with one heart and will. And he observed that, though the creative, Divine pen was the recorder of duties, and though it was the Divine help which caused and stablished in the right way the actions of the loyal, and though his own empire-viewing mind was at rest with regard to them all, yet he desired to in some measure enlighten the hearts of worldlings who could see nothing except what was symptomatic (*sabab*) and that the countenance of truth might display her perfect beauty in the mirror of their actions.[2] Upon this Ḥājī Muḥammad Khān *Kōkī*, who had no reverence and no sincerity of heart,

---

1 "The difference between فطرت and طبيعت is that the former signifies the essential nature of the individual man, the latter the super-induced accidents of temperament which are more under his control." (Jarrett III. 403 note).

2 The meaning is that though Humāyūn was satisfied of their fidelity, yet for the sake of outsiders he wished them to take an oath so that their loyalty should thereby be evidenced.

represented that in accordance with orders they would all take the oath, let His Majesty take an oath also, to the effect that he would listen to and carry into effect what they, the loyalists, should in their right thinking perceive and should represent to him. M. Hindāl who was imbued with devotion and had a knowledge of affairs, said "Ḥājī Muḥammad, what sort of story is this you are saying, and what kind of oath is this? Never have servants said such words to their masters, or slaves to their lords." His Majesty who was a mine of urbanity—and a sea of generosity, said, "So be it. We shall do whatever Ḥājī Muḥammad wishes and shall, in his loyalty, suggest." After making confirmatory oaths and agreements, they marched from that place.[1]

When the grand army came near Ushtar Grām M. Kāmrān, according to his wont and in his folly, made preparations for war and having collected a body of troops marched against the royal army. When there was only a little distance between the two armies His Majesty Jahānbānī in adherence to his affectionate nature sent M. Shāh,[2] a relative of Mīr Barka who belonged to the illustrious Saiyids of Termiz, to the Mīrzā, and conveyed weighty advices such as might be earrings for the ears of men of fortune and prestige. The gist of them was that to take always the path of opposition and to abandon the high-way of concord was remote from wisdom. God forbid that all this contention should take place about Kābul. Respect obligations, old and new, and observe the ways of peace and candour, and be of one heart and accept companionship in the conquest of India. The Saiyid performed his mission, and peace was agreed upon, but on the condition that as Qandahār belonged to His Majesty, Kābul should belong to Kāmrān; upon these terms he would enter into service and take part in the conquest of India. As His Majesty was kind and affectionate, he sent the ambassador a second time, along with Maulanā 'Abdu-l-bāqi *Ṣadr* and sent r

[1] See the interesting remarks of Erskine on this incident. (Hist. I. 387-90). Jauhar (Stewart 99), mentions it and says that Humāyūn had fasted all the day in order to give the ceremony more solemnity.

[2] Erskine says he was related t the imperial family. Perhaps he was descended from Mīr 'Alā-ul-Mulk of Termīz who had married Fakhir-jahān, a daughter of Abū Sa'īd.

message that if Kāmrān was sincere and really wished to take the road of concord, he should give his dear daughter in marriage to the unique pearl of the *khilāfat, viz.*, His Majesty the Shāhinshāh, so that His Majesty might bestow Kābul upon them, and that they two (Humāyūn and Kāmrān) might unite in destroying the darkness of the great country of India, and might make that last which had become the stage of wicked men and of calamities, an abode of peace and tranquillity. Both Kābul and Hindūstān would then in reality belong to the two of them. The Mīrzā wished to accept these wise suggestions but Qarāca Qarābakht, who was the centre of his power, did not agree and said "Our heads[1] and Kābul."

In fact on that day the Eight Stars[2] were in front of the Mīrzā and, according to astrologers, to fight under these circumstances is to be defeated, and so the Mīrzā by stratagems put off the fight to another day. The victorious army (Humāyūn's) was anxious to engage, but Ḥājī Muḥammad did not want this, and His Majesty in deference to him, delayed to give battle. Meanwhile *Khw.* 'Abdu-ṣ-Ṣamad and many others who had gone to a distance during the battle of Qibcāq, took advantage of their opportunity and joined His Majesty, and brought tidings of the vacillation and confusion in the hostile army. Half the day had passed when His Majesty put the foot of firmness in the stirrup of intent, and having drawn up his forces, and arranged them in right and left wings, centre and van- 304
guard, ordered an advance. The centre derived glory from his own presence, the right wing was made illustrious by M. Sulaimān, and the left wing by M. Hindāl. M. Ibrāhīm had charge of the vanguard. Ḥājī Muḥammad Khān and other tried heroes had charge of the reserve.[3]

---

1 *Sir-i-mā u Kābul.* Erskine says this is equivalent to death in Kābul. Perhaps the meaning rather is that their heads and Kābul were equally dear, and that neither could be given up. Or perhaps that the only two conditions of peace were that they should save their heads and also keep Kābul.

2 *Sakizīldūz.* See Steingass *s.v.* and Bābar's Mem., 92. It appears to be an old name for the constellation of Virgo, and to be the same word as the Secdeidos of Ābū-M'āāshir of Balkh. See Ideler's Untersuchungen, 1809, and Athenaeum of 19th May, 1900.

3 التمش *Ilmish*, given in Meninski as meaning sixty and so equal to veteran. But it is the reserve, apparently, of the front-ranks or vanguard. As Mr. Irvine has pointed

On the other side, M. Kāmrān was in the centre, M. 'Askāri on the right, Āq Sulṭān on the left, and Qarāca Khān on the vanguard. The two armies moved on, in appearance like two iron mountains, and approached each other. Mihtar Sahbāka and a number of faithful servants who had after the affair of Qabcāq entered, from necessity, the service of the Mīrzā, galloped off and joined the victorious army. Near the river Mūrī, M. Ibrāhīm in his high courage, took the lead. The soldiers on both sides fought bravely. At this time the head of Qarāca Khān was brought before the world-traversing steed (of Humāyūn) and all were freed from the malice of that troublesome traitor. An order was given that the guilty head of that faithless one should be stuck up at the Iron gate of Kābul so that it might be a warning to the seditious. Thus the words which he himself had uttered "Our heads and Kābul," were brought to pass. I have heard from reliable persons that a low follower of the Mīrzā seized the traitor and wished to take him before His Majesty Jahānbānī as an atonement for his offences and that Qambar 'Alī Sahārī[1] who was a servant of M. Hindāl and whose brother had been killed in Qandahār by Qarāca, was following and that he took off his (Qarāca's) cap (*ṭāqīya*) and struck him on the crown of the head with his sword, splitting it, and then cutting off the head brought it to His Majesty.

During this conflict and tumult, in which the royal servants fought with devotion, knowing that it was the end of the contest, M. Kāmrān could not maintain his ground and took to flight. He went off to Afghānistān by the Pass of Bādpaj[2] (the windy pass). The victorious army betook itself to plunder and got hold of much property. The enemies of the State were seized and put to the sword, many of them lowered the veil of shame over their faces and made the tears of repentance their intercessors and after a thousand reproaches, were enrolled in the list of servants of the State. M. 'Askarī fell into the hands of the heroes of the army (*'Askar*). A victory such as might be the introduction to countless victories, was obtained

out to me it is used by Khāfī Khān II. 876. *See* also P. de Courteille and Zenker.

[1] Text, Sahārī, but there is the variant Bahārī, and this is the word in Niẓāmu-d-dīn. Sahārī however appears to be right. There was a Sarkār of that name in the Agra division. See Jarrett II. 195.

[2] Bābar's Mem., 142 note 4. By Afghānistan is meant the country east of Kābul.

and was the subject of thousands of rejoicings. But the heart of 305
His Majesty was very anxious about the safety of the jewel of empire's diadem, *viz.*, His Majesty the S͟hāhins͟hāh, for he had heard that on this occasion M. Kāmrān had brought him with him. His Majesty could get no comfort from his distraction until Ḥasan *Āk͟hta* brought that rosebush of fortune's rose-garden, and cypress of the parterre of sovereignty before him. Recognising his advent as the beginning of fortune, he returned thanks to God for his safety and the realisation of his hopes, and with excessive joy, he clasped that Divine nursling to his bosom. After his devotions he distributed charities,—which are the practical form of thanksgiving,—and drew to himself the hearts of the poor and the widowed and orphaned by abundant presents. And he rewarded every one of the devoted servants either because of the happy issue of events with regard to the eye-pupil of the *K͟hilāfat* or as a guerdon (*jaldū*) for good service. His Majesty Jahānbānī announced that in future he never would be separated from this new fruit of the garden of the *K͟hilāfat*,—for thousands of good auspices were infolded in his footsteps,—and he recognised that the glorious victory came from the blessing of the advent of this sublime pearl. At this joyous time two camels loaded with boxes and without drivers were seen on the field of battle. His Majesty said "every one is having his plunder, let mine be these two camels!" He went himself and taking their nose-strings, ordered that they should be made to kneel and that the boxes should be opened, so that he might see what was inside. By a beautiful coincidence it was found that the special, royal books which were lost at the battle of Qibcāq were in these boxes and in perfect condition. This was the occasion for a thousand rejoicings. K͟hw. Qāsim Mīr buyūtāt, who was the kindler of the fire of strife, was consumed in the flames of this battle by the fire of his own deeds, and so commotion and depravity were set at rest. On this day a joyous assemblage was held in Cārīkārān.

When by the favour of God, the gates of victory had been opened and the seditious had been punished, Kābul became on the following day the alighting place for blessed feet and a station of everlasting auspiciousness. First, His Majesty entered the citadel and had the joy of receiving his chaste ladies. After that he, according to his wont, proceeded to the Ūrta Bāg͟h and freshened it

by his fortunate presence. There he made arrangements for his subjects and dominions, rewarding the good servants and punishing the bad. Dīndār Beg, Ḥaidar Dōst Mughal Qānjī, and Mast 'Alī[1]
306 Qūrcī who had on many occasions shown disloyalty, were capitally punished in accordance with their deserts, and the public benefit. He exercised his genius in the distribution of justice. M. Sulaimān was loaded with gifts and dismissed to Badakhshān. M. Ibrāhīm remained for some days, as a special mark of favour, and then was sent to Badakhshān. And it was settled that in an auspicious hour he should be married to His Majesty's daughter Bakhshī[2] Bānū. His Majesty's world-adorning heart engaged in the arrangement of affairs and exalted all the servants by his affability and benevolence.

[1] Bāyazīd says Mast 'Alī's offence was his refusing to fight at Qibcāq on the plea that a bad cuirass had been given to him, that Haidar Dost Mughal Qānjī was punished for inciting Qarāca to rebellion, and that Dīndār was punished for offences committed in India.

[2] Akbar's half-sister. After Ibrāhīm's death she married Sharafu-d-dīn Ḥusain (Blochmann 322). In Gulbadan's Memoirs the name is spelt Īkhshī ایخشی which is a Turkī word meaning good, and possibly this is the proper spelling. Redhouse gives it the meaning of beautiful.

# CHAPTER XLIX.

## ASSIGNMENT OF THE VILLAGE OF CARKH[1] TO HIS MAJESTY THE SHĀHANSHĀH, AND THE PROGNOSTICATIONS THEREFROM OF THE FAR-SEEING.[2]

At this time, when, by God's help, Kābul had become the seat of the thrones of sovereignty and the spot irradiated by the lights of the *Khilāfat*, the village of Carkh—which belongs to the *tūmān* of Lahūgar,—was assigned to His Majesty the Shāhanshāh. The enlightened drew an omen from this mysterious gift, and beat the drum of rejoicing high o'er the nine spheres (*carkh*). His Majesty gave to Ḥājī Muḥammad the office of household-administrator (*wakālat-i-darkhāna*, mayoralty of the palace), which is a very great post,—and bade him mend his ways. But as, owing to his narrow understanding, he was intoxicated with his courage and proud of his reputation, evil thoughts continually held him in the prison of affliction (*gham*), and he was always ungrateful and showing improper desires. His Majesty Jahānbānī, from his lofty nature and a tolerance which was boundless, used to pass this over; for the excellent principle of this ruler was that the plant of the human life,—which is the product of the Divine workmanship and the fruit-bearing growth of the garden of fate, should not be pulled up for every defect, especially in the case of one who was distinguished among his equals for wisdom or courage or for any other fine quality. But that evil-constituted wretch thought, in his folly and wrong-headedness, that this was a weakness (in Humāyūn), and so made it an incitement to still greater madness; while His Majesty always winked at such conduct and loaded him with favours. At this auspicious time, His Majesty continually kept open the gates of justice and distributed favours

---

[1] See Bābar's Memoirs 148, and Jarrett II. 406. It is S.E. of Kābul. A.F. puns on the meaning of the word carkh, *infra*.

[2] This heading is very inadequate.

upon which the administration of the terrene and terrestrials depends, and knit together the distractions and dispersions of the time.

M. Kāmrān, after his defeat, went off from the village of Ushtar-
307 grām, in the most wretched circumstances,—such as were the just result of his ingratitude and the fruit of his oblivion of benefits,—with eight followers (*viz.*, Āq Sl.,[1] brother of Khiẓr Khw. Khān, Bābā Sa'īd Qibcāq, Tamar Tāsh *atga*, Qatlaq Qadam, 'Alī Muḥammad, Jōgī Khan, Abdāl, and Maqṣūd *qūrci*),—by way of Dih-i-sabz, and joined the Afghāns. M. Hindāl, Ḥājī Muḥammad Khān, Khiẓr Khw. Khān and the others who had gone in pursuit, did not exercise proper diligence and returned. The Afghāns blocked the Mīrzā's path and plundered him, and he, fearing lest he should be recognized, shaved all the hair from his face (*cār ẓarb zada*) and came, disguised as a *qalandar* to Malik Muḥammad of Mandraur, one of the leading men of the Lamghānāt, who recognized old obligations and tended him. M. Kāmrān was not in the least awakened by all these disasters,—every one of which was, in the eyes of the wise, a strong whip of warning and of arousing from the sleep of negligence,—but again stretched himself out in slumber. A number of soldiers who had the form of men but neither the heart to perceive what was right nor the eye to feel shame and who were always practising sedition and treachery, gathered round him.

When this news came to the sublime camp, the market of hypocrites grew brisk and the loyal were distressed. At such a time as this, when the flame of sedition and strife had become tongued, Ḥājī Muḥammad Khān went off to Ghaznīn without leave. His Majesty Jahānbānī, from desire to temporize and also from his perfect appreciation (of the man), regarded this disgraceful proceeding as love of opposition (? *nāzjang*)[2] and did not approve of it. He appointed Bahādur

---

[1] According to Gulbadan Begam, he left Kāmrān (who was his father-in-law) about this time and was, in consequence, deprived of his wife. He was a younger brother of Gulbadan's husband, Khiẓr.

[2] The reading and meaning are uncertain. The Bodleian MSS. appear to give *nāskhunuk*, i.e., coldness of love, or *nāsḥakk*, the erasing of love. If may also be *nāqkhang*, love of depravity. The I.O. MS. No. 4 has *nāz-khunuk* quite clearly. Most probably the true reading is *nāz-khang*, wickedness, for A.F. has other similar uses of *khang*. (See I. 198 l. 15 and 334 l. 9, where we have the word *khang* following *ta'aṣṣub* and used in the sense of evil bigotry.

Khān, Muḥammad Qu'lī Barlās, Qīdūq Sl. and a number of heroes to suppress M. Kāmrān. When the army of fortune came near the Mīrzā, he withdrew to the defiles of 'Alīgār and 'Alīshang. The officers followed him and he, leaving that country, sought protection with the Afghān tribes of Khalīl and Mahmand. The vagabonds who had gathered round him, were again dispersed. The victorious troops turned back at the village of Ghazū-i-shahīdān. Now that His Majesty's mind had obtained a respite from the wickedness of M. Kāmrān, he, in order to increase the sympathy of M. Sulaimān and to do him yet more honour, proposed a marriage to him. Khw. Jalālu-d-dīn Maḥmūd and the chaste Bībī Fāṭima were sent to ask for the hand of Khānam, the daughter of M. Sulaimān, for when this should be arranged, His Majesty's mind would be at rest as regarded Badakhshān and M. Sulaimān would be conciliated. M. 'Askarī was also sent with Jalālu-d-dīn to be made over to M. Sulaimān. And an order was issued to M. Sulaimān that he should send on M. 'Askarī to the Ḥijāz by way of Balkh. M. Sulaimān recognized the coming of the envoys as a distinction and neglected nothing that could do them honour.[1] In obedience to the royal 308
order, he sent off M. 'Askarī towards Balkh. The Mīrzā could not, from shame and repentance, settle there but set off on his long journey, taking with him the travelling-companion of impatience. The measure of his days became full between Syria and Mecca in the year 965.[2] M. Sulaimān agreed that the marriage with His Majesty Jahānbānī should take place on the arrival of the begams (of Humāyūn's court) and the nobles, and on his daughter's becoming older: and he respectfully dismissed the embassy with letters full of apology and submission.

---

[1] A.F. perhaps does well to emphasize the respect paid to Humāyūn's envoys by Sulaimān. Bāyazīd tells a different story of their treatment by Sulaimān's wife, Khurram Begam.

[2] Firishta, 961 H. He says that 'Askarī left one daughter whom Akbar married to Yūsuf Khān of Mashhad, the later governor of Kashmīr. (Blochmann 346). The chronogram of 'Askarī's death given by Budāunī is incorrect (I. 453) Apparently it is that of his birth for it yields 922. All the MSS. of the A.N. which I have examined have 965. If this be right, 'Askarī survived all his brothers.

## CHAPTER L.

### Expedition of His Majesty Jahānbānī to Extinguish Another Time the Seditious Flames of M. Kāmrān.

Inasmuch as habit is, as they say, a fifth[1] humour of the body,—whoever is addicted to evil ways is like the scorpion, and in stinging is without the power of self-control. How much more they who are constitutionally bad and in whom habit accords with nature. Accordingly M. Kāmrān again inclined towards his disposition and practice and made his evil deeds the instrument of his own punishment. He gathered together a number of Afghāns from the Khalīl and Mahmand tribes and a troop of vagabonds who could not distinguish good from evil, and set about plundering and ravaging. His Majesty Jahānbānī, who was the giver of peace to the world and the age, recognized that the ending of such tumults was a part of worship, and he resolved to act in accordance therewith. He sent Khw. Ikhtīyār and Mīr ʿAbdu-l-ḥai, who were confidential courtiers, to Ghaznīn, to convey a gracious letter to Ḥājī Muḥammad and recall him from the darkness of evil thoughts to the light of recognition of duty. While His Majesty was making his preparations, he heard that M. Kāmrān was besieging, with a number of vagabonds, a fort near Cārbagh, in the vicinity of Jalālābād. He therefore did not wait for Ḥājī Muḥammad Khān, but went off with all rapidity towards Jalālābād. When M. Kāmrān heard this, he was amazed and fled. He again betook himself to the defiles and went off from there by Bangash and Gardīz, thinking that he might join Ḥājī Muḥammad. For this perverse wretch held with M. Kāmrān.

The story of Ḥājī Muḥammad is as follows. As the time of his ruin approached, evil thoughts came forth more and more from his

---

[1] Muḥammadans reckon that there are four humours in man. See Lane S. v. خلط 788b. They derived the notion from Hippocrates and Galen.

impure heart, and he dismissed the royal ambassadors with pretences and false promises of his coming. At the same time he sent a messenger to M. Kāmrān, asking him how long he was going to wander about in the hills and deserts, and telling him to come quickly in his own direction so that they might act in concert. By chance Bairām Khān, who was going to Qandahār in His Majesty's service, arrived at Ghaznin. Ḥajī Muḥammad, who was longing for the Khān (*bā khān tawaqān būd*), went out to meet him and fawned upon him, seeking to bring him into the fort under the pretext of a feast and to shut him up there. The Khān proceeded towards the fort when Mīr Ḥabash, who was with Ḥājī Muḥammad Khān, gave a signal to the Khān, and he, being put on his guard, thereby made an excuse and renounced his intention of entering the fort, and encamped at a fountain outside the city. There he soothed Ḥājī Muḥammad and prevailed upon him to accompany him to Kābul. He sent the news of his own arrival and of the bringing of Ḥājī Muḥammad; and His Majesty, having heard that M. Kāmrān was coming to the territory of Kābul, proceeded to Kābul with all haste. M. Kāmrān advanced to within one stage of Kābul and then, when he heard of the arrival of the Khānkhānān and of his having Ḥājī Muḥammad Khān with him, he again withdrew in confusion to Lamghān. One day Ḥājī Muḥammad wished to enter Kābul by the Iron Gate, but Khw. Jalālu-d-dīn Maḥmūd, who was in charge of Kābul, would not permit him to enter the fort and sent him a harsh message. That face-blackened one became suspicious and went off to Qarā Bāgh, under pretext of hunting; and then, passing by the Kutal-i-minār went to Bābā Qucqār (*i.e.*, Bābā ram); then by the Däman-i-kōh of Bihzādī and Lalandar,[1] went quickly off to Ghaznīn. Just then the victorious standards of His Majesty Jahānbānī, who had gone towards Kābul to quell the disturbance of M. Kāmrān, arrived at Sīāh Sang. Bairām Khān was exalted by paying homage. His Majesty Jahānbānī ordered that no one should enter the city, for he was going in pursuit of the Mīrzā, so that he might, once for all, free God's creatures from daily disturbance. But as his mind was not at ease about Ḥājī Muḥammad, the officers were unanimous that he should be secured about him and

309

[1] *Bilandarī*. Erskine reads Alindar. I adopt the variant Lalandar which is supported by B.M. MSS. and by Jarrett II. 404.

then set out after the Mīrzā. His Majesty came to the city and appointed Bairām Khān to look after Ḥājī Muḥammad and instructed him to act with dissimulation and by every contrivance possible to bring him in.

Bairām Khān tamed Ḥājī Muḥammad by suitable devices and after promises and oaths, he came to the village of Gulkār[1] and embraced the Khānkhānān. The latter brought him to the presence of the forgiving prince and begged for the remission of his offences.
301 Four or five days later they all went together towards the Lamghānāt which was the retreat of the Mīrzā. In spite of the recent forgiveness of so many crimes, Ḥājī Muḥammad acted as if he had never committed them, and again had the audacity to enter on still worse schemes. He shewed disgraceful conduct and disgusted the holy heart. His Majesty went off with a large body of men, and when the standards of fortune reached Jalālābād, the Mīrzā retreated to the defiles of Kanūr and Nūrgal, and all sedition-mongers crept away. The Khānkhānān was appointed to follow the Mīrzā, and the latter, not being able to maintain himself in Kanūr[2] and Nūrgal went off to the Indus (*Nīlāb*). The Khānkhānān returned and did homage in Daka.[3]

At this time His Majesty took into consideration general utility and the public tranquillity, and ordered the arrest of Ḥājī Muḥammad and his brother, Shāh Muḥammad—who was capable of being Ḥājī Muḥammad's instructor in wickedness. And these two ungrateful brothers—who in their service looked to nothing but material advantages and their own credit; who were given over to cupidity and ingratitude; who looked for a great price in exchange for their inferior goods, and who were unmindful of benefits, were caught by their own wickedness. His Majesty, in accordance with his just nature, ordered that the services which the low-thoughted service-sellers had voluntarily or involuntarily rendered during their careers, should be entered by them in a list, and that one of the honest servants should write out their offences, so that by putting them into the balance of justice, the real facts about these two evil-doers

[1] Gulkina, a suburb of Kābul. See Bābar 137 and Jarrett II. 404 and note.

[2] Kanūr (read by Chalmers Katūr), Nūrkal. These are two distinct places. Bābar's Mems. 143 and Jarrett II. 392.

[3] At the end of the Khaibar

might be patent to mankind. The record[1] of their good deeds remained unwritten, while their sins came to 102 great culpabilities,—each one of which might have been a ground of imprisonment and death and degradation. Good God! there is one man who after good service is trembling and downcast, lest his (Akbar's) glance fall upon his work and there be a suspicion that he, a simple-minded man, is selling his services, or that he is ill-conditioned. And the more honest his service, the greater his apprehensions! And there is another kind of man who sells things not done at the rate of things done; who passes off bad deeds as good ones; who after tricking out his blemishes,[2] looks for favours, and indulges himself in self-commendation.

When by this thorough investigation it was proved to the world that these two disloyalists deserved the punishment of their own wickedness, and that it was time the skirt of the age should be cleansed from the dirt of their existence, their fierce and brutish natures—which infected them in the cage of the raw material of 311
humanity,—were drawn forth by a halter from human shape, and consigned to a fitting place, and they, or rather the world, was granted deliverance from their hideous nature. Ghaznīn was assigned to Bahādur Khān and his (Ḥājī Muḥammad's) other fiefs were distributed among the (royal) servants.

The winter was spent in that neighbourhood, in travelling and hunting, and in feasting and rejoicing. In the beginning of spring, when the humours are in a state of equilibrium, general receptions were held, and after petitions and tendering of gifts, a number were enrolled in service. The dust of the Mīrzā's strife and disturbance was laid, and His Majesty Jahānbānī went by Bādpaj to the river Bārān. On the night that the army was near Bādpaj, there was much rain and snow and many suffered. When hunting and sight-seeing were ended, Kābul was made the seat of dominion, and

[1] *Cf.* Jauhar, Stewart 107. He places their punishment in 961 (1553).

[2] ابله طرازي. This compound is not to be found in the dictionaries. Some MSS. read آبله *ābila*, a blister or pimple, and this, I believe the true reading, ابله folly, does not seem applicable here nor at text, 336, l. 16, where the phrase occurs again. I think the expression corresponds to the English "plastering the boil" and means covering over and adorning a sore, so as to make it look like a beauty.

Bairām Khān was sent to administer the affairs of Qandahār. Khw. Ghāzī was sent with him to convey presents and to go on an embassy to the ruler of Persia. Ghaznīn, Gardīsh, Bangash and the *tūmān* of Lahūgar (Logar)[1] were bestowed on M. Hindāl. Qundūz, which belonged to the Mīrzā, was conferred on Mīr Barka and M. Ḥasan. M. Hindāl was granted leave to go to Ghaznīn and Mīr Barka received permission to go to Qundūz. Jūī Shāhī and its territory were assigned to Khiẓr Khw. Khān. Before Mīr Barka reached Qundūz, M. Ibrāhīm got possession of it by trickery from Muḥammad Ṭāhir Khān, and Mīr Barka returned to Kābul. His Majesty Jahānbānī allowed the good services of the Mīrzā to be an atonement for his action and left him in possession of Qundūz. At this time, Abū'l-ma'ālī was introduced into the service through 'Abdu-s-samī.' Shāh Abū'l-ma'ālī traced his descent from the *saiyids* of Termiz. His personal beauty made the good and right-thinking look for goodness of nature, and his forwardness was tolerated on account of his courage. Consequently he became a favourite with His Majesty Jahānbānī. Some of his insolencies and extravagancies will be related in their proper place.

---

[1] *Āīn*, Lōhgar. Jarrett II. 406.

# CHAPTER LI.

## Another Expedition of His Majesty Jahānbānī Jannat-Āshyānī to Quell the Disturbance caused by M. Kāmrān; and the Martyrdom of M. Hindāl.

M. Kāmrān spent some days in the cell of contempt and disgrace, and then hearts which had been set at rest, were again agitated by 312
the news of his strife-mongering; and wayfarers reported to His Majesty that he had come back from the Indus (*Nīlāb*) and had again raised the head of sedition in the district of Jūī Shāhī, in concert with a band of vagabonds. His Majesty summoned M. Hindāl from Ghaznīn and issued marching-orders to the neighbouring *jāgīrdārs*. In a short time M. Hindāl did homage, and the devoted and dutiful followers gathered round. His Majesty Jahānbānī ordered an expedition to extinguish the flames of sedition, and M. Kāmrān, on hearing of this, retreated unsuccessful. When the victorious standards had neared Surkhāb, Ḥaidar Muḥammad *Ākhtā-begī*, who was in the advance-guard, had, with many devoted men, gone ahead of the royal camp and halted on the banks of the Siāh Āb, which is between the Surkhāb and Gandamak. M. Kāmrān, who did not find himself able to engage in a pitched battle, made a night attack on him. Ḥaidar Muḥammad showed lion-like courage and made a gallant fight, and received conspicuous wounds, which are in appearance and in reality red-lettered diplomas (*ṭughrā*). He remained firm and did not give up his ground. Though many things were plundered, the Mīrzā failed and had to return disconcerted. After some days when the village of Japrīār, which belongs to the *tūmān* of Neknahār,[1] had been made the camping ground,—inasmuch

[1] Or Nēknihal, Jarrett II. 405. It lies S. of the Kābul river. *See* also Bellew's Races of Afghānistān 64. The Japrīar of text is written Jaryār by Erskine. Bayāzīd speaks of Caryār and Hindālpūr; and Raverty, (Notes on Afghanistan, 55) says Jiryār or Jabīryār belongs to Nangnahar and is also written Jabīrhār and lies on the slopes of the Spinghar Range.

as vigilance and caution are the components of alertness,—batteries were arranged and a trench and bulwark made. At the end of the day two Afghāns brought word that M. Kāmrān intended that night to make an attack with a large body of Afghāns. His Majesty Jahānbānī brought the rules of circumspection to bear and stationed men at every point. On the night of Sunday, 21st Zi'l-qa'da, 958 (20th November, 1551), when a quarter of the night had passed away, M. Kāmrān fell upon the camp with a large body of Afghāns. His Majesty Jahānbānī mounted his horse and stood on a height behind his tent, and summoned to his presence the glory of foreheads and the great pearl of the diadem of the *Khilāfat*, to wit, His Majesty the Shāhanshāh. The servants of the exalted threshold were all in the entrenchments and doing their duty bravely. The flames of battle were blazing. In the midst of this tumult and confusion 'Abdu-l-wahhāb *yasāwal*, who was in the entrenchments, was struck by a bullet and became a martyr. The market of conflict grew hot until the shining moon,—which is the mirror-holder of the world,—raised her head from the quarter of fortune and brightened the earth with her effulgence. The light
313 of victory radiated from the brows of dominion, and the adversary sought safety in flight. The imperialists were victorious and raised the standards of composure. The hearts of all had become tranquil when suddenly an unpleasant report came to the royal hearing, that M. Hindāl had left this evil world. Joy became bitter and exaltation was changed into abundance of sorrow. Alas! 'tis the way of this transitory world that if a breath go forth in joy, next moment the smoke of grief ascends from the breast of the afflicted.

*Verse.*

Never is heaven's eye brightened by the morning,
Without the evening twilight's suffusing it with blood.

There is neither capability of dallying for enjoyment therein, nor permission for persistent grief. Though the Mīrzā left this unstable world and departed from this unenduring hostel, he gained the glory of martyrdom and at once acquired a good name in the visible world and an exalted rank in the world of reality. Hail! O Thou little-receiving and much-giving who, on the departure of borrowed life, hast given such permanent grandeurs! His Majesty who was a mine of gratitude, was so affected and sorrowful at the death of so noble a brother that his feelings cannot be described or hinted at. But as he was wise and farseeing, he turned from lamentation to resignation and sought comfort in the pleasant abode of submission to the Divine Will.

The account of this melancholy affair is as follows. When M. Hindāl heard of the projected night attack he put the entrenchments in order, and he had gone to take some repose, when the noise of the Afghāns arose. An indescribable number of Afghāns came into each battery, and many entered the Mīrzā's. The night was dark. The Mīrzā addressed himself to the repulsing of the wretches, while his own men were confused and hastened to look[1] after their horses. Meanwhile the Mīrzā came face to face with the Afghāns. Nūrm[2] *Kōka* and many others behaved badly. The time for using bow and arrow passed and he grappled with one of the foe, and by main force overthrew the born villain. The brother of that wretch, Jaranda[3] by name and belonging to the Mahmand tribe, sent the Mīrzā to the other world by a poison-stained spear. Some of M. Kāmrān's companions used to relate that that evil-natured Afghān got hold of a case which contained the Mīrzā's special thumb-stalls and brought it before M. Kāmrān, not knowing with whom he had played this disastrous game. He described the occurrence. When the Mīrzā's eye fell on the thumb-stall case, he knew what misfortune had happened and flung his turban on the 314
ground, saying that M. Hindāl had been martyred.

In short the soul of the Mīrzā travelled on that dark night to the abode of annihilation without its being known, and his body remained where it fell. Meanwhile some of his servants were coming back, when Khw. Ibrāhīm Badakhshī observed that there was a black cuirass (*qalmāq*) on the body. As it was dark and the tumult still continued, he did not approach it. Then it occurred to him that M. Hindāl had been wearing a black cuirass. He turned round and looked at it and recognised the Mīrzā. In accordance

[1] Gulbadan's account is that none of them dismounted.

[2] This name seems to mean *my light* and to be formed like Māham, my moon. He was foster-brother of M. Ibrāhīm, Akbar's half-brother, Blochmann 526.

[3] The Iqbālnāma has Farīd.

with patience and deliberation which are the watchwords of the wise, he carried[1] off the body to the Mīrzā's tent and made it over to the doorkeepers; and he wisely took steps to conceal the melancholy occurrence so that the enemy might not rejoice nor be encouraged, and also that the imperial servants might not be disheartened. He reported that the Mīrzā was much fatigued, and was also slightly wounded, and that no one should make any noise or tumult close by. He himself went up on the rising ground and conveyed congratulations on the victory as from the Mīrzā. The illuminated soul of His Majesty Jahānbānī received a ray of intelligence from this statement. In fine the Mīrzā's bier was deposited in Jūī Shāhī, and after some time was brought to Kābul. The body was placed in the Guzargāh, near the holy tomb of His Majesty Getī-sitānī Firdūs-makānī, and buried at his feet. Mullā Khurd Zargar who was in the Mirza's[2] service, composed an elegy of which the first couplet was,—

*Verse.*[3]

One night sorrow made a night-attack on the apple of mine eye,
Owing to the onset of blood, my beloved departed.

---

[1] Gulbadan says Mīr Bāba Dōst carried in the body.

[2] From a previous reference (Text I. 275) it appears that Mullā Khurd was in Kāmrān's service, so that the word Mīrzā here probably refers to Kāmrān. He is mentioned in the *Tabaqāt-i-akbarī*, Lucknow Ed., p. 405, under the name of Mullā Khurd Zargar. His poetical name was Fanāī and Nizāmu-d-dīn says he was originally a servant of M. 'Askarī. *See* also Blochmann 426, but perhaps this is a different Fanāī.

[3] *Lit.* One night the blood of the liver made an attack on my eye-pupil.
Owing to the coming and going of blood the black-eyed one pitched his tent outside.

The text has *sipāh-dīda* and this may be correct, the meaning being the sentinel, or the soldier-eye. But there is the variant *siāh dīda* meaning black-eyed, and a mistress; and this reading I adopt. Probably the poet wanted to take advantage of both readings for *sipāh* agrees with the expression "pitched his tent outside. Possibly he had in his mind the passage in Bābar's Memoirs, (Leyden and Erskine, p. 33), where we are told that Baisanghar had to shift his pavilion three times on account of the number of executions that took place in front of it. The quatrain which follows is said by A.F. to be also by Mullā Khurd, but Badāōnī (I. 454) gives it as the composition of Maulānā Ḥasan 'Alī

This chronogram is also his,—

*Verse.*

Hindâl Muḥammad, a king of glorious title,
Suddenly, in the dead of night, became a martyr,
As a night-attack (*shabkhūn*) caused his martyrdom,
Seek the chronogram from *shabkhūn*[1] (958).

Mīr Amānī uttered this enigmatical chronogram,—

*Verse.*[2]

A cypress left the garden of glory.

The Mīrzā was born in 924[3] (1518) and so it was said :—

*Verse.*

The chronogram was *kaukab-i-burj-i-shāhanshāhi* (924), (the *kaukab* of the king of kings' tower).

Next day His Majesty Jahānbānī went from there to Bihsūd, where he encamped in order that he might, once for all, set his world-adorning heart at rest with respect to the strife of the seditious and then make Kābul, by the glory of his sublime court, an abode of peace and tranquillity.

---

Kharās. He also gives some other lines in which the same chronogram appears.

[1] *Shabkhūn* makes, by *abjad*, 958 (1551).

[2] The cypress stands for the letter *alif*, on account of its straight shape. If *alif* be removed from the words *būstān-i-daulat*, the other letters amount by *abjad* to 958.

[3] Erskine (II. 404 *n.*) says he was born in 925, and this agrees with Bābar (250). *Kaukab* means both a star, and a golden ball, and *burj* means both a tower and a sign of the Zodiac. The Memoirs of Gulbadan Begam also go to show that Hindāl who was her full brother, was born in 925.

## CHAPTER LII.

315 Assignment of the Territory of Ghaznīn to His Majesty the Shāhinshāh, and Elevation of some to his Service.

As, from his early years, the notes of greatness and the glory of government shone from the lustrous brows of that new fruit of the tree of sovereignty and that splendour and nosegay of the garden of the *khilāfat* and fortune,—to wit, His Majesty the Shāhinshāh,—at this time, when he was ten years old, all the servants of M. Hindāl, together with all his *Jāgīrs, viz.*, Ghaznīn, *etc.*, were assigned to him, so that, by the practice of rule, he might exhibit favour and severity in the management of men; and by administration of a part, he might become accustomed to administer the whole. One of the wonderful things of fate was that some days earlier, the turban of this light of the eyes of dominion came off in a crowd when he was riding in the service of His Majesty Jahānbānī. M. Hindāl was there and from perfect reverence, he took off his own fortunate cap (*tāj*) in the midst of that crowd and placed it on the star-brushing head (*i.e.*, of Akbar). The far-seeing drew the omen from this that the time when the Shāhinshāh would wear the diadem and wield authority, was nigh at hand. The Almighty, in recompense for this deed, elevated the Mīrzā to the rank of martyrdom which is equivalent to life and joy eternal. His Majesty the Shāhinshāh—who is the Divine nursling,—shewed such marks of greatness, graciousness and appreciation of men, in winning hearts, that grief for the Mīrzā left men's souls and they became possessed of constant joy.

*Verse.*

O God! so long as the world hath lustre and colour,
The heavens gyration and the earth stability;
Grant him enjoyment of life and youth;
Above all, give him abundance of existence.

The names of the principal servants of the deceased Mīrzā who entered into the service of the Shāhinshāh, are as follows;—(1). Muḥibb 'Alī Khān; (2). Nāṣir Qulī; (3). Khw. Ibrāhīm; (4). Maulānā 'Abdu-l-lāh; (5). Ādīna Tuqbāī; (6). Samānjī; (7). Qarghūjī; (8). Jān Muḥammad Tuqbāī; (9). Tāju-d-dīn Maḥmūd *bārbegī*; (10). Tīmūr Tāsh; (11). Maulānā Ṣānī, now known as Ṣānī Khān;[1] (12). Maulānā Bābā Dost[2] *ṣadr*, who was highly regarded by the Mīrzā; (13). Mīr Jamāl[3] who was also a favourite with the Mīrzā; (14). Khaldīn 316
Dōst Sahārī. Bābā Dōst was also a servant of the Mīrzā but, as in the educational canon, nothing is worse than bad company, he, on account of his bad character was not taken on. Though Muḥammad Ṭāhir Khān was an old servant of the Mīrzā, yet, inasmuch as he had not been able to keep charge of Qundūz,[4] he was excluded from the glance of the truth-discerning eye, and was not made a companion on this auspicious expedition. As the Court of this bestower of glory on the earth, was a test of the jewel of humanity, the condition of every one of these men who was of good disposition and pure character, became better day by day, and they attained lofty positions. And it is to be hoped that they will remain to the end in that condition. Everyone who was evil had the veil stripped from his acts and was so dealt with as to be a warning to all who were evil or negligent.

As the village of Bihsūd became the camp of the pavilions of fortune, an order was given to build a strong fort. His Majesty the Shāhinshāh was sent off[5] in order to strengthen the city of Kābul and that he might there practise the methods of spiritual and temporal sovereignty. His Majesty himself remained at Bihsūd under the Divine aid and exercised vigilance with regard to M. Kāmrān. The army remained there for four or five months. The Mīrzā, from want of sense, (*az bī istiṭā'atī*) was each day the guest of a clan and each night took refuge with a landholder. From a defect of

[1] Blochmann 476 and Badāonī III. 206.

[2] Qu. father of Ḥamīda Bānū Begam. *See* Gulbadan Begam's Memoirs. Perhaps he was also known as 'Ali Akbar and perhaps Badāonī was mistaken in giving this as another name of Sānī Khān.

[3] Probably this was the brother of Bābar's Afghān wife, Bībī Mubārika.

[4] A reference to his allowing himself to be over-reached by M. Ibrāhīm.

[5] Humāyūn seems to have forgotten his vow never again to be separated from Akbar.

nature, he remained veiled in self-conceit and excluded from the auspicious service and fellowship of such a benefactor, and was for ever indulging in seditious thoughts.

At this time, a set of superficialists who were in the service of His Majesty the Shāhinshāh and were oblivious of an internal abode of wisdom, wrote to His Majesty Jahānbānī and complained about his Highness. His Majesty, notwithstanding that he was aware of the inner light of the Shāhinshāh, had regard to externals, and sent a gracious letter containing instructions and admonitions, full of kindness and paternal affection and not at all of a censuring or cautioning character. For what need has he who has been taught at the Divine school,—of human instructions? or what concern has the nursling of Heaven with such didactics? In that letter this verse of Shaikh Niẓāmī was quoted.

*Verse.*

Sit not idle, 'tis not the time for play :
'Tis the time for arts and for work.

He was first taken before Mullāzāda Mullā 'Aṣāmu-d-dīn to be taught. As this teacher was devoted to pigeons, the servants reported against him. His Majesty discharged him and made over the
317 duty of outward instruction to Maulānā Bāyazīd. He performed this duty, but as the world-adorning Deity did not wish that His own special pupil should become tainted by exoteric sciences, He diverted him from such pursuits and made him inattentive to them. The shallow thought it was the fault of the teachers and reported against them, but as the latter were right-thinking and of good character, the complaints were not accepted or acted upon. At last His Majesty had an inspiration, to wit, that for the purpose of instructing that pupil of the Divine school, lots should be cast between Mullā 'Abdu-l-Qādir, Mullāzāda Mullā 'Aṣāmu-d-dīn, and Maulānā Bāyazīd, so that he, on whom the lucky chance should fall, should be exalted by being made the sole teacher. It happened that the lot fell on Maulānā Abdu-l-Qādir, and an order issued for the removal of Maulānā Bāyazīd and the appointment of Maulānā 'Abdu-l-Qādir.

It is not hidden from the wise and acute that the appointment of a teacher in a case like this, springs from use and wont, and does

not pertain to the acquisition of perfections. For him who is God's pupil, what occasion is there for teaching by creatures, or for application to lessons? Accordingly his holy heart and his sacred soul never turned towards external teaching. And his possession of the most excellent sciences together with his disinclination for the learning of letters were a method of showing to mankind, at the time of the manifestation of the lights of hidden abundancies, that the lofty comprehension of this Lord of the Age was not learnt or acquired, but was the gift of God in which human effort had no part. His Highness in that period assimilated external glory and temporal dominion in abundance, but feigned ignorance of inward perfections and spent much time in sport, and practised wisdom under a veil of concealment, so that even the farseeing failed to notice it.[1] But, as his genius was soaring, he was making a perfect veil for himself out of grand external performances. And he put his heart into acts so that though their beauty was not evident to the superficial yet the profound perceived the designs. Among them was his continually giving his attention[2] to that wondrous creature the camel and his delight in the marvels of Divine power. He used to observe and contemplate the strange make and ways of camels, which were the biggest animals in that region and, under the guise of amusement and metaphor, made serious reflections on the *darvish*-like constitution of those beasts—their endurance and patience; submission and resignation, their passive obedience even should the leading cord be in the hand of a child,—their being satisfied to eat thorns, and their endurance of thirst. He also applied his thoughts to the delight in an Arab horse which is a grand subject of dominion and exaltation, and carried off the ball of 318
excellencies and of philosophy (*hunarpardāzī*, love of science) with the polo-stick of the Divine help and of sempiternal instruction. And sometimes he opened the wings of his genius in the spacious atmosphere of meditation upon God and brought his contemplative mind to study the sport of pigeon-flying.[3] He scattered grain in order to allure their timid breasts and proceeded from the superficial joy and

[1] The text omits the negative, but the variant *namīuftād* makes better sense and is supported by two B.M. MSS. Nos. 27,247 and 5610.

[2] This may be compared with the remarks in the *Āīn*, Blochmann 143.

[3] *Cf.* Blochmann 298.

ecstacy of these handfuls of wings and feathers to the recuperative and visible raptures of the lords of perfection, and thereby participated in the joys of the spiritual world. He carried his heart from the flying of these aerial fliers to the lofty soaring of the swift-winged ones of holy heaven, and under the guise of sport performed the work of adoration. Sometimes he would apply himself to coursing with dogs and thus occupy himself with sensuous things. Outwardly it was cynegetics, inwardly it was quickening the senses. Apparently his heart was fixed upon dog-fancying, in reality he was conducting his companions in the methods of government. And[1] although he was pursuing his quests under the veil of irrecognition and kept himself attired in the garb of superficialists, he could not hide his sweet savour or his brilliancy. Divine glory ever shone from his lustrous brows, and the attributes of spiritual and temporal leadership were conspicuous in the irradiated countenance of that elect of God!

One day he was engaged in hunting on the slope of the Safīd[2] Sang hills and had put hunting-dogs into the charge of his immediate attendants in order that they should lie in[3] wait. And certain men

---

[1] *Cf.* the remarks about hunting, Blochmann 282.

[2] There is a Safīd Sang south of Kābul, but probably what is meant is the Safīd Koh or Spīnghār range S.W. of Jalālābād.

[3] *Ke tūsqāwal bāshind.* The word tūsqāwal is not in the dictionaries. It occurs once before, *viz.*, at Text, p. 255, l. 11. That passage is founded on Bayāzīd I.O. MS, 28*b* and he says that *tūsqāwal* is called *nihilam* in Badakhshān. Now Bābar has the word *nihilam*, p. 28 of Memoirs, and speaks of his uncle Sulṭān Maḥmūd Mīrzā's being very fond of hunting the *nihilam*. That is, this is how Leyden has understood the passage, and P. de Courteille has followed him. But it would appear from the passage before us that *tasqāwal* according to A.F. means a particular kind of hunting and is not the name of any animal. Apparently it refers to the practice of driving game past a shelter or shooting box. The Lucknow edition of the Akbarnāma says in a note to the passage, at p. 238 that *tasqāwal* is a Turki word and means a hunter who remains on the low ground in ambush. It may perhaps be connected with the Turqī *qarāwal* a hunter, or it may be Arabic and a derivative from تقليد and ثقل and mean one who feigns inactivity. Bābar's remark that his uncle took to the pursuit in the latter part of his life seems to imply that the sport was not of an active kind. In the Persian of Bābar's Mem., as given in the Bombay lithographed edition, *nihilam* appears as *bahilam*.

Since writing this note I have

had been sent up the mountain to drive the deer down into the plain. When the deer came to the obstacles, the servants had been caught by the dog of carnal appetite, and as in their folly they thought only of His Highness's tender years and boyish appearance, they had set themselves to eat and so did not slip the dogs in time. When he became aware of this, his inward sovereignty was aroused, and he issued an order that their necks should be bound with cords as if they were dogs, and they be led round the camp. He so sate on the *masnad* of severity that the old and experienced were amazed and placed the finger of surprise in their mouths. When this occurrence came to the ears of His Majesty Jahānbānī, his heart was greatly delighted and he remarked that he would soon come to great sovereignty and attain everlasting dominion.

Shāham Khān Jalāir used to tell how one day His Majesty Jahānbānī bade him go and see what the new fruit of fortune's springtide was doing. "When I went," he said, "I found him lying down. His lustrous countenance was serene and he looked as if he were asleep. In truth he was holding converse with the holy ones of heaven's court (the angels). His blessed hand moved occasionally as is seen in the recuperative states of the lords of contemplation. From time to time there fell from his pearl-dropping tongue such
expressions as "God willing, I'll bring the cream of earth's surface 319
under my sway and fulfil the desires of the sorrowful of the seven climes." "The Khān used to say that when he saw this condition and heard these words, he became amazed, and great awe fell upon him, so that he could not stand. He went aside and remained stupefied. Several times did he (Akbar) speak in this fashion.

A laudable behaviour of His Highness at this time and one which showed his lofty and farseeing nature was that whenever any flatterers or black-hearted persons, who see nothing but their own personal loss or gain, or rather think their[1] loss is their gain, would

---

found the word *tūsqāwal* توشقاول in the Turkish-Persian dictionary of Mīrzā 'Alī Bakht, and which is known as the Farhang Aṣafarī. This dictionary is in the Mullā Fīrūz Library, Bombay, and is No. 27, p. 54 of Rehatsek's catalogue. It explains *tūsqāwāl* as the shutting up of a road. *Tasqāwal*, or *nihilam* then was a kind of hunting analogous to "driving" and was perhaps such a sport as Akbar is said to have engaged in at the Deer-tower of Fateḥpūr Sīkrī.

[1] Perhaps it should be *zīān-i-digar* the loss of others, but all the MSS. seem to have *Khud*.

say "May you soon be king of the seven climes" or "May you be the Lord of the Age" he would be much displeased and say "Those people in their little sense want to show themselves wellwishers. God forbid that they know anything of the palace of wellwishing! They are imagining evil for me in thinking of the decease of His Majesty Jahānbānī, and are gathering my temporal good from my spiritual ill. Or rather they are casting trouble into the country of welfare and raising the head of sedition. For the spiritual and temporal good fortune of children lies in their hopes and wishes being always for the preservation of their august fathers, and they wish them long life. For he who does not act rightly by his temporal God how shall he conduct himself properly towards his spiritual God?" Let men admire the lofty understanding, the pure nature, and the right thinking of this spiritually and temporally great one (Akbar)! In fine, greatness and glory shone in every action of His Highness. What the mature and experienced attained to by thought and care, this cherished one of God's glance acquired with small application in the beginning of his career. And every knowledge and science that the learned and the studious gathered with difficulty, came into the hands of this exhibitor of wondrous powers without meditation or care. Ripe wisdom made the hope-eye of the world shine on beholding this light of the eyes of sovereignty, and made men exult in the firm wisdom and deep knowledge of this nursling of God. But till the time of the revelation of the *Khilāfat*, it was veiled and hidden, and he passed his time under God's protection and free from the mischief of the deceit and treachery of ill-wishers.

## CHAPTER LIII.

### EXPEDITION OF HIS MAJESTY JAHĀNBĀNĪ JANNAT-ĀSHYĀNĪ FROM BIHSŪD AGAINST THE AFGHĀN CLANS,—AMONGST WHOM WAS THE AMBUSH OF M. KĀMRĀN'S STRIFES,— AND FLIGHT OF THE LATTER TO INDIA.

When winter came to an end in the village of Bihsūd and the violence of the cold was over; and when it was known that M. Kāmrān, with a few retainers, was spending his days amongst the Afghān clans, most of the officers were of opinion that, as the Mīrzā had now no power of opposition, His Majesty should leave there a 320
body of troops, and should proceed to Kābul. But a party of the far-seeing represented that as the weather was now temperate, it was advisable to attack and plunder the Afghāns; and that it was improper to return until this faction,—the material of strife and sedition;—had been thoroughly subdued. Thus both M. Kāmrān who was secretly living amongst the tribe and who was making ready the constituents of dissension, would fall into their hands, and also, the root of the disturbers would be dug up.

His Majesty Jahānbānī preferred this view, and guided by victory, mounted the steed of fortune in order to fall suddenly upon the clans and pour the dust of defeat on their heads. A number of impetuous heroes and wielders of the sword, such as Muḥammad Khān Jalāir, Sl. Muḥammad Fawāq, Shaikh Bahlūl, Shāh Qulī Nāranjī, were appointed under the leadership of Sl. Ḥusain Khān to go forward in advance. The wind was very cold that night and the way was long, so they halted mid-way to ease their men and cattle. In the morning they mounted and went on.

As the tribes had scattered here and there, it was not known in which the Mīrzā was. In this time of perplexity, Māham 'Alī Qulī Khān and Bābā Khizārī who were on the way from M. Kāmrān to Malik Muḥammad of Mandraur, fell into the hands of the royal servants. They asked in which tribe the Mīrzā was. Māham 'Alī

led the inquirers astray and indicated a tribe other than that in which the Mīrzā was. Bābā said, "He is frightened, he does not know what he is saying. The Mīrzā is in such and such an encampment and I will show the way." The advance-guard reached the place at early dawn, attacked it, sent many to the abode of annihilation and captured a number of women and children. Some of the heroes entered the tent where the Mīrzā was sleeping, and Shāh Qulī Nāranjī declares that he was one of them and that there were two persons within. One of them was caught and the other con-
321 trived to escape. In the morning, it was seen that the captive was Beg Mulūk whom the Mīrzā always kept in his sight, and that it was the Mīrzā who had gone out. Some of the vagabond Afghāns, such as Shaikh Yūsuf Kararānī and Malik Sangī, stood up to fight and then flung the dust of disgrace on themselves by running away. Their goods fell into the hands of the royal servants. The victory was won before the arrival of the royal standards. The Mīrzā was not able to remain in those parts and went to India.

When His Majesty's heart was freed from the business of chastising the rebellious and when, by God's favour, a great victory had been gained,—such as might be a preface to victories,—he left the district and returned to Bihsūd. When it was ascertained that the Mīrzā had escaped, under circumstances befitting thankless ingrates, and had gone to India, His Majesty Jahānbānī went to the Bāgh-i-ṣafā[1] which is the delight of hearts and may be styled a cleanser (*ṣafā-bakhsh*) of the picture-gallery of the soul, and there made a festival with pomp and splendour.

As the days were lengthening and there was the beginning of the splendour of spring and of the freshness of avenues (*khiyābān*) and of the delights of the heart opening streams, he sent a number of special individuals under charge of 'Alī Qulī of Andarāb to Kābul to fetch that spring-blossom, His Majesty the Shāhinshāh, together with the chaste ladies; so that he might, by beholding the wonders of early spring and by reading the pages of the rose-garden, gain

[1] The Bāgh-i-ṣafā was at Cār Bāgh which is marked in maps as W. of Jalālābād and higher up the Kābul river. See Raverty, "Notes on Afghānistān," p. 53, and Jarrett II. 405. The Bāgh-i-ṣafā is distinct from the Bāgh-i-wafā'.

admittance to the enclosure of recognition of the Divine artist and might lay the foundations of thanksgiving.

Their Highnesses arrived in a short time, and His Majesty gave endless thanksgiving gifts, which are a means of attracting yet more favours from the true Benefactor. After a time of enjoyment, he proceeded in an auspicious hour, to Kābul.

## CHAPTER LIV.

### His Majesty the Shāhinshāh goes to Ghaznīn, and exaltation of that place by his dwelling there.

As His Majesty Jahānbānī perceived that the splendours of guidance and of capacity for affairs of His Majesty the Shāhinshāh were increasing daily, he determined, now that things were quieted,
322 to separate him for a few days from his person in order that his greatness might be tested, that all might know his abilities, and also that he might have practice in the art of rule. For whoever in his youthful years, and also when by himself, shall make prudence his guide, and show magnanimity in all his ways, and who shall, without pluming himself on his own grandeur, exercise justice and equity to the humble and needy, and he whom real union (with his parent or guardian) shall suffice and whom physical remoteness shall not make sad,—assuredly he it is who can become the Unique Pearl of the *Khilāfat*. As the glories of such qualities were believed to be, or rather were known with certainty to be, written on the tablet-forehead of His Majesty the Shāhinshāh, he was sent to Ghaznīn in the beginning of 959, (end of December, 1551). The *Atka Khān*, Khw. Jalālu-d-dīn Maḥmūd and all the servants of M. Hindāl were attached to him in this happy enterprise, the general management being with the Khwāja aforesaid. He spent six months there in vigilance and prosperity, and as spiritual and temporal supremacy was ever visible in him, right actions and laudable manners, such as are not seen in mature and experienced men, displayed themselves in this fortunate and happy-starred youth. And he was continually winning hearts by his right ways and his worship of the right. He always strove to comfort the distracted. He was always bent upon pleasing that class of men who expend themselves in the domain of privation and who, having girt up the loins of effort for the purification of manners and the knowledge of God, have taken the path of poverty and renunciation, turning aside from ease and sorrow, and

the praise and blame of worldlings, and concerning themselves solely with the Unique and Companionless One (God).

At that time there was in Ghaznīn Bābā Bilās[1] who was one of the enthusiastic God-knowers and immersed in the sea of contemplation and who spent his days in the cell and the hermitage of obscurity. His Highness frequently went to see him. And that seer of the workshop of holiness read temporal and spiritual supremacy in the lines of his forehead and congratulated him on his external and internal kingship, and gave him the good news of long life, and lofty distinctions. When it was near the time that he should obtain respite from the hunting and travelling in Ghaznīn he, in accordance with an indication from His Majesty Jahānbānī Jannat-āshyānī, set about his return. The reason of his recal was that His Majesty Jahānbānī was ever engaged in business in Kābul. All his time was divided and apportioned, and not a moment of night or day was spent in frivolities or idleness. But together with his dispensing of justice, and comforting the brokenhearted and surveying the work of the kingdom, he took pleasure in travel and field-sports. One day he had gone riding to Zama[2] which is one of the delightful villages of Kābul, and had accidentally fallen from his horse, and sustained bodily injuries. As prudence is closely associated with 328
dominion, he, out of precaution and reflection on the end of things, sent a letter recalling His Majesty Shāhinshāh. By the happy influence of his advent His Majesty attained a perfect recovery.

---

[1] A variant gives Palās and this is the form used by Bayāzīd. He tells how Humāyūn unsuccessfully tried to evade the saint when he visited Ghaznīn on his way to Qandahār; and how the saint questioned him about his having put Ḥājī Muḥammad to death. Erskine MS. trs. p. 40.

[2] Called Zamzama at p. 260 last line. It lay N. of Kābul.

## CHAPTER LV.

### EXPEDITION OF HIS MAJESTY JAHĀNBĀNĪ JANNAT-ĀSHYĀNĪ TO BANGASH. AND CHASTISEMENT OF THE REBELLIOUS; REARING THE STANDARD OF INTENTION FOR INDIA; CAPTURE OF M. KĀMRĀN, AND RETURN TO KĀBUL, ETC.

In the winter of the end of 959 (November, 1552), His Majesty Jahānbānī determined upon proceeding to Bangash which is a winter-quarters for Kābul. The design of this expedition was both to chastise the rebels of that quarter, and also to recruit his army. For the sake of auspiciousness, he took with him His Majesty the Shāhinshāh, as being closely connected with his good fortune, and proceeded towards Gardīz and Bangash. The Afghāns received proper punishment, and their goods fell into the hands of the soldiery. The first tribe attacked was the 'Abdu-r-raḥmānī,[1] the last was the Barmazīd. Fatḥ Shāh [2] Afghān,—who in his folly and unwisdom thought himself wise and led others astray,—fled from the onset of the victorious army, and on his way fell in with Mun'im Khān and a body of troops who were marching to join the king. All his goods and chattels came into the hands of the soldiery and he was wounded and forced to take flight. During this turmoil the delegates (*wukalā'*) of Sl. Adam Gakhar, the chief of the Gakhar clan, arrived with a letter and were graciously received. The contents of the letter were that M. Kāmrān had come in distress to his territory; that Sl. Adam, in whose head was the breath of loyalty, did not wish the Mīrzā to spend his days in this vagabond fashion; that if His Majesty would come, he would produce the Mīrzā in order that the latter might make amends for his crimes and become a

1 Jarrett II. 407.

2 Erskine says that he was reputed to belong to the *Cirāgh-kash* (lamp extinguishing) sect. This is derived from Bayāzīd (82*a*), who adds that he lived in Tīrāh.

servant of dominion's threshold; and that Sl. Adam himself would also do homage.

Be it known that the Gakhars are a numerous clan and that they live between the Bihat (Jehlam) and the Indus. In the time of Sl. Zainu-l-'ābidīn of Kashmir, there came a Ghaznīn officer, named Malik Kid,[1] a kinsman of the ruler of Kābul, and took this country 324 by force from the possession of the Kashmīrīs. He was succeeded by his son, Malik Kalān, and he again by his son Bīr (or Pīr).[2] After him came Tatār Khān who had much contest with Sher Khān and his son, Salīm Khān. He regarded himself as attached to His Majesty's family, for at the time when His Majesty Getī-sitānī Firdūs-makānī conquered India, he entered his service and did good work. He was especially devoted in the war with Rānā Sānkā. He had two sons, Sl. Sārang and Sl. Adam. After Sārang the headship of the tribe fell to Sl. Adam. The sons of Sārang Kamāl Khān and S'aīd Khān submitted but were secretly disaffected. Jōgī Khān, a confidential servant of M. Kāmrān, arrived with as Sl. Adam's ambassador and tendered a petition from the Mīrzā, full of smooth and baseless words.

Abū'-i-fazl, the writer of this compendium of wisdom, and the chronicler of the deeds of this noble family, has his mind fixed on the history of His Majesty the Shāhinshāh and on the diffusion of information concerning his glorious rule. It is to satisfy the thirsty readers of this precious chronicle that he has given,—as a side-piece,—an account of the lofty line from Adam down till now, which is the era of the heir of the universe. It is indispensable to tell briefly the evil acts of M. Kāmrān and of his receiving retribution therefor by his own acts.[3] Although the dignity of this noble record is too exalted for the entry of such matters, yet in order to complete the narrative, it is impossible to avoid treating of the low as well as of the high.

Let it not be hidden from the listeners to these strange occurrences,—every one of which is a sermon from a sacred pulpit,—that when that morning, as has been related, M. Kāmrān was defeated and escaped with a thousand risks from the hands of the swordsmen,

---

1 Blochmann 456.

2 The Gakhars say Tatār was grandson of Bīr and son of Pilu.

3 A.F. means that he was blinded because he had blinded others.

he was unable to remain in any one place. From the ruin of his understanding,—the fruit of ingratitude,—and notwithstanding reverses, each of which might have guided him to the highway of auspiciousness,—he did not submit himself to a master so gracious and forgiving, when the dust of remorse and repentance should have covered his face and when he should have come, with shame and apology, to kiss the threshold and atone for his crimes,—but he, the destined pervert, went off to India for the purpose of presenting himself before Salīm Khān, son of Sher Khān, (who in addition to inborn ingratitude, had his brain perturbed by the wine of insouciance and the ferment of pride), and to obtain from him auxiliaries for his disloyalty. Good God! what kind of reason had he
325 to go to his deadly foe to compass the ruin of so great a friend? Why should he submit to indignities to this end? and wish him (Salīm) to assist him to contend with his benefactor? To sum up; evil thoughts brought the Mīrzā to this, and with a few followers, he took the road to India. From the neighbourhood of the Khaibar, he sent Shāh Budāgh Khān to Salīm Khān who was in Ban,[1] a town of the Panjāb. The Mīrzā's ambassador arrived there and performed his mission. Salīm Khān perceived that the success of the Mīrzā's wishes was beyond his (Salīm's) power and therefore dissembled. He sent some money for expenses by the envoy and arranged that he (Kāmrān) should wait where he was, and he promised to send him help, and to assign him an income. Before the ambassador had returned to the Mīrzā, Alī Muḥammad Asp also was sent to Salīm Khān. To sum up this long story, which might better have been shortened;—when the Mīrzā arrived within four *kos* of Ban, Salīm Khān sent his own son, Āwāz Khān, Maulānā 'Abdu-l-lāh of Sulṭānpūr and a number of his officers to welcome him. The Mīrzā was received by the Afghān leader (*i.e.*, Salīm) in a manuer unfitting for enemies or street-dogs.[2] His companions were Bābā Jūjak, Mullā Shafāī, Bābā

[1] The Bīn of Erskine. Perhaps it is Bain in the Bannū country which is marked in Thoburn's map. It lies south of Edwardesābād. See too Jarrett II. 393. Raverty (Notes, etc., p. 354), mentions Ban as 19 miles north-east of Sīālkōt and 8 miles south-west of Jammū. It is on the east bank of the Cenāb. There is a "Bone" in the Salt Range. (Wanderings of a Naturalist, Adams, p. 134).

[2] Text 325. *See* Erskine II. 408 for an account of Kamrān's humiliating reception.

Sa'īd Qibcāq, Shāh Budāgh,[1] 'Ālam Shāh, Raḥmān Qulī Khān, Ṣāliḥ *dīwāna*, Ḥājī Yūsuf, 'Ali Muḥammad Asp, Tāmartāsh, Ghālib Khān, Abdāl Kūka and many other broken men whose names had better not be given. As the acts of ingrates and the thoughts of the unfaithful are not for good and meet with disaster in the end, whatever happened to them was the consequence of their actions. The Mīrzā was disgusted with the bad manners of this ignorant crew (*i.e.*, the Afghāns) and continually reproached Shāh Budāgh in private, who had instigated him to come.

When Salīm Khān's mind was at rest about the affairs of the Panjāb, he set off for Dihlī, taking the Mīrzā with him under false promises. He kept saying that he would let him go but did not do so. His idea was to imprison him in one of the strong forts of India. When the Mīrzā perceived how things were, and that there was no hope of assistance nor of his own release, he resolved to escape. He sent Jōgī Khān, his trusted servant, to Rāja Bakhū who was twelve *kos* from Māciwāra and asked for help. The Rāja received the messenger kindly and promised his protection. One day when Salīm Khān had crossed the Māciwāra river, the Mirza left Yūsuf 326
*aftābcī* in his (Kāmrān's) sleeping suit and arranged with Bābā Sa'īd to go on for a long time reciting something so that it might be supposed the Mīrzā was lying down. He himself changed his clothes and put a veil over his face and then went out by the enclosed side and hastened to the refuge which had been agreed upon. The Rāja gave him a proper reception and when it was reported that an army was coming to search for him, sent him on, to the Rāja of Kahlūr whose was the safest place in the neighbourhood. He too, from fear of enemies, sent the Mīrzā on, giving him a guide to Jammū. But the Rāja of Jammū from the cautiousness of a landholder, would not allow him to enter his territory. Dismayed and confused, the Mīrzā went off to Mankōt. There he was almost captured, and again changing his apparel, he went on, in woman's garb, towards Kābul, in the company of an Afghān horse-dealer. Meditating evil, he went to Sl. Adam Gakhar thinking that perhaps he might induce the Gakhar tribe to act with him and to do things which ought not to be done. But Sl. Adam approved of loyalty. He kept the Mīrzā, by

[1] Blochmann 371. See also Raverty "Notes on Afghānistān," 359.

various pretexts, under surveillance and sent to represent the matter at the sublime Court. The Mīrzā also, when he saw disappointing indications in the behaviour of the tribe, was compelled to adopt feline ways and to send a petition, as already stated. Though he tried to induce the Gakhars to join him, he had no success. He did not trouble himself about escaping because he had no refuge; moreover owing to the guard kept over him and to his own fatigue, he saw that it would be difficult to get away. He was obliged to subsist with this people and he learnt that every harmful thought becomes null and void which is entertained by the ill-wisher to a dominion adorned by the Divine splendour and safe-guarded by its protection; and that such an ill-wisher sinks into eternal punishment.

When the envoy of Sl. Adam had represented the state of affairs, His Majesty determined to make an expedition into India as far as the Gakhar country. He sent Khw. Jalālu-d-dīn Maḥmūd to guard and govern Kābul and marched on himself, taking the Shāhinshāh with him, for the furtherance of good fortune. He bound the girdle of determination on the waist of energy that he might end the affair of M. Kāmrān and ease the world from his strife and sin. When the standards of victory reached the Indus, he sent Qāẓī Ḥamīd, the chief judge of the victorious camp, to Sl. Adam, requesting his
327 presence. He also sent the Mīrzā sage counsel and exhortations, to the effect that he should scour from his heart the rust of opposition and discord. When later, he crossed the Indus, there was no sign of Sl. Adam who apparently was affected by the misplaced apprehensions of a landholder. His Majesty despatched Mūn'im Khān to soothe him and bring him in. He also sent a few words to the Mīrzā such as might guide him to fortune. Mūn'im Khān was moreover to ascertain from their actions and manners what were their secret thoughts and to report accordingly. He displayed his abilities and after cajolery and stratagem, Sl. Adam brought the Mīrzā and did homage near Parhāla. His Majesty gave a feast which was kept up all night. Spite of so many crimes,—each one deserving condign punishment,—M. Kāmrān was encompassed with favours. All loyal officers and prudent well-wishers represented that though the kindness and benevolence of His Majesty always required that in his Court, the mantle of pardon should clothe great criminals,—yet foresight and firmness demanded that the oppressor and injurer of

mankind should receive his deserts, so that the dust of wickedness might be wiped from the face of men's safety. Fore-casting care made it proper that the outward appeasement of one man,—and he an ill-wisher,—should not be preferred to the satisfaction of many distinguished loyalists. What shock would there be to the wall of justice if, to bind up the broken-hearted and heal the wounds of lacerated breasts, the portrait of a tyrant were erased from the world's picture-gallery? Especially when this course involved thousands of advantages. The obliteration of this worthless figure would be in every way pleasing to God and in accordance with general laws. Such ingratitude and rebellion were not of the character to give hope of security or to permit his actions to be regarded as not done. The matter had passed beyond bounds; it could no longer be coped with (*ṭāqathā ṭāq shuda*). It was advisable for him and for all that he should become a traveller to the world of non-existence, that so God's creatures might be saved from thousands of ills and the record of his deeds become no blacker. People's goods had long been subject to plunder and rapine through the turmoils of this wicked rebel: their property and honour had gone to the winds of strife and the lives of so many men had been valued as dust; and the jewel of sincerity,—which is the neck-ornament of the virtues,—had been lost in the mists of trouble. Now the proper
course was to release such a man from the claws of final retribution 328
and to give mankind tranquillity, under the shadow of justice.

His Majesty Jahānbānī looked to the wisdom and benevolence of the Causer of causes (God), and declined to engage in this affair. (Nor would he believe) that the world-adorning Initiator would, in spite of his omnipotence, make a man so unutterable, (*i.e.*, as M. Kāmrān). Besides taking this profound view, his discerning eye approved of the admonitions of His Majesty Getī-sitānī Firdūs-makānī and would not agree to the proposition. His officers, who had witnessed the various bloodsheds and strife caused by this insolent shedder of blood,—were again firm in their request: they took legal opinions which were attested by the law-officers; and they brought a paper signed by the great of realm and religion and laid it before His Majesty. These documents His Majesty sent to M. Kāmrān who having read the record of his deeds and the punishment (proposed), returned the message that those who to-day had put their seals for his death, were the men who had brought him to this pass. The spirit of clemency moved His Majesty and, spite of the general insistance and of the existence of so many reasons, would not let him shed the Mīrzā's blood. At length for the general welfare, a special order was issued and they deprived the Mīrzā of sight. 'Alī Dōst *bārbegī* (master of the ceremonies), Saiyid Muḥammad Pakna and Ghulām 'Alī *shash-angasht*[1] were told off for this duty.

They entered the Mīrzā's tent. He thought they had come to kill him and at once ran at them with his fists. 'Alī Dost said, "Mīrzā, compose yourself: the order is not for death. Why are you agitated? As justice demands,—for you blinded Saiyid 'Alī[2] and many other innocent persons,—you will behold in your own eyes the retaliation thereof." On hearing this, the Mīrzā agreed to submit to the royal commands and endured the insertion of the needle. They blinded both his eyes,—the sentinels of a seditious heart. These loyal servants took the precaution of using the lancet many times. The Mīrzā being thankful that his life was spared, uttered no remonstrance. With his natural kindness, His Majesty expressed his regrets and marched onwards. Many affectionate and loving words rose to his lips. This catastrophe occurred in the end of 960 (Nov.-Dec., 1553). Khw. Muḥammad Mūman of Farankhūd[3] found the chronogram, *nishtar* (lancet) = 960).

On the same day, the Mīrzā sent to Mun'im Khān to request him by all means in his power, to obtain for him from His Majesty the services of Beg Mulūk. The petition was at once granted and Beg Mulūk was sent. The Mīrzā,—owing to the great affection he bore
329 him,—took his hands and placing them over his own sightless eyes, recited this verse;—

Though a veil be drawn over my eyes,
I behold thee with the eye which has oft seen thy face.

After this occurrence, His Majesty set off to chastise the Jānūhā[4] who were vagabonds and impediments of the road. The

---

[1] *i.e.*, six-fingered or -toed.

[2] Kāmrān did this at Tīrī after returning from Sind and before capturing Ghaznīn.

[3] Text 328. Farakhūd is mentioned by Yāqūt as a village near Samarkand. See too Blochmann 434*n*.

[4] Blochmann 456*n*. They inhabited the Salt Range. Their proper name is Janju'āh.

wretched rebels slipped their necks from the collar of obedience and were killed fighting with the heroes of victory. K͟hw. Qāsim Maḥdī and others of the army of fortune attained the glory of martyrdom.

His mind being at rest about this affair, His Majesty resolved to go to Kas͟hmīr, an intention he had cherished for years. His officers thought it inadvisable and abused Kas͟hmīr, likening it to a well[1] or prison, in order to induce the holy heart to renounce the enterprise, for, they said, "The noise of the march of the army of fortune has caused commotion in India and Salīm K͟hān is coming to the Panjāb with great preparation; whilst on our side, there has been no due preparation." "If we go forward and the Afg͟hān army approach us, how can we pass it and go on to Kas͟hmīr? Perhaps the Kas͟hmīrī affair will be a long one and if so and black-hearted Afg͟hāns secure the passes, what will be the end of it? The proper thing is to give up the idea of the expedition and to return to Kābul now that the traitor has been removed from our midst. When military preparations have been made, we will set the foot of courage in the stirrup of energy and by the might of daily-waxing success, shall easily destroy the Afg͟hans." His Majesty heard these words, and gave them no heed but despatched His Majesty the *S͟hāhins͟hāh* with many officers to protect Kābul and turned his own rein towards Kas͟hmīr and desired to set forth. Acting on the evil teaching of their huckster-natured officers,—who looked to nothing but their own profit,—most of the servants and soldiers left their masters and set out for Kābul. Except officers, none remained to serve His Majesty. By this shameful conduct,—far removed from the path of loyalty and obedience,—the composure of the noble soul was disturbed. He ordered the trusty by all means to turn back the men and not to hesitate, if necessary, to put any to death. Meanwhile he sought an omen from the glorious Koran. It chanced that the story
of the faithful Joseph came up. Those who had leave to speak, set 330
themselves to explain this and considered it carefully. K͟hw. Ḥusain of Merv submitted that what had been said about Kas͟hmīr,—*viz.*, that it was like a well or a prison,—was true; for the story of Joseph names both these things.

---

[1] Alluding to its girdle of mountains.

When disunion showed itself amongst those with him, His Majesty, being compelled to abandon his intention, moved towards Kābul. When he was encamped on the Indus, M. Kāmrān petitioned to be allowed to go to the Ḥijāz. As His Majesty was now desirous of giving him pleasure, he consented. On the night of dismissing the Mīrzā[1] on his journey, he went with a number of chosen followers to his quarters. After paying due respects, the Mīrzā recited this verse.[2]

The fold of the poor man's turban brushes the sky,
When the shadow of a monarch like thee falls on his head.

Later on, this verse was on his tongue ;—

Whate'er comes on my life from thee is cause for thanks,—
Be it shaft of cruelty or dagger of tyranny.

Although the second couplet inclines to thanks, a critic can see that it runs over with censure. His Majesty who was a world of compassion and gentleness, took no heed of this but expressed commiseration. With his inspired tongue he said, "He who knoweth secrets and things hidden, is aware how much ashamed I am of this thing which did not come about with my goodwill[3] Would that

---

[1] A.F.'s account of this interview seems to be taken from Bayāzīd (I.O. MS. 64*b*.) but though he is often a servile copyist, he is rarely quite an accurate one. As I understand Bayāzīd, Kāmrān said, "If people consider that His Majesty has dealt kindly with me, I attest the fact (*sijl kardam*). Possibly a negative has slipped out here for it would be more to the point if Kāmrān said, "Should people think His Majesty has *not* dealt kindly by me, I attest the contrary." A.F. makes Kāmrān say, "If I were innocent, I would take the opportunity of this visit to attest my innocency." The text has *baḥal kardamī*, "I would absolve him :" and this is Erskiṇe's reading of the passage. (A.N. MS. trs.). But after referring to Bayāzīd and other sources, it seems to me that *sijl* and not *baḥal* is written. This agrees with the context ; "Were I innocent, I would take advantage of this public opportunity to assert the fact, but I well know I am guilty." It will be observed that Erskine renders the passage differently in his History (II. 417) and in his MS. trs.

[2] Imitated from the Gulistān III. 19. Blochmann quotes the lines (179).

[3] I do not feel sure of the meaning, but I think that Humāyūn was gently hinting that as Kāmrān, when in power, had blinded several people, he might, if successful against his brother, have blinded Humāyūn

you had done it to me ere this happened." The Mīrzā woke from the slumber of negligence and comprehended both the measure of his crimes and the extent of the princely mercies. He fell into a state of shame and supplication and asked Ḥājī Yūsuf what persons were present. Ḥājī Yūsuf named them, *viz.*, Tardī Beg Khān, Mun'im Khān, Bābūs Beg, Khw. Ḥusain[1] of Merv, Mīr 'Abdāl-ḥai, Mīr 'Abdu-l-lāh, Khanjar Beg and 'Ārif Beg. The Mīrzā said, "Friends, be ye all witnesses that if I knew myself innocent, I would assert the fact at this time of distinction when His Majesty visits me; but I am certain I was worthy of death. He has granted me life and has given me leave to depart to the Ḥijaz. For the beneficence and favour of His Majesty, I offer a thousand thanks because he has not exacted retribution commensurate with my wickedness and misconduct." After this he passed on to recommendations for his 331
children. His Majesty gladly promised to care for them. Having encompassed the Mīrzā with kingly favours, he bade him adieu. It had been stipulated that the Mīrzā should not lament in the presence and he therefore restrained himself, but, as soon as His Majesty had gone towards his own tent, he wept and lamented.

Next day an order was issued that any of the Mīrzā's servants who wished to accompany him, might do so. No one came forward. Those who had boasted of their affection, abandoned it. Calma kūka,[2]—(who by his perfect loyalty and fidelity to His Majesty the *Shāhinshāh* obtained the title of Khān 'Alam and who gave his life for his benefactor and the master of mortals, as will be told in its place),—was standing there. He was His Majesty's table-servant (*safarcī*) and the recipient of royal favour. His Majesty Jahānbānī asked him whether he would go with the Mīrzā, or stay with him. The excellence of Court service and the abundance of royal favour notwithstanding, he preferred the path of fidelity to temporal delights and answered, "I see that it befits my position[3] to serve the Mīrzā in his dark days of helplessness and black nights of loneliness."

---

Chalmers translates, "Would that I had been the sufferer and you the author of the evil."

[1] See Badāonī III. 176, for account of this poet and also *Ṭabaqāt-i-akbarī*, Luck. ed. 396. Niẓāmu-d-dīn says he was son of a vizier and died in Kābul.

[2] Blochmann 378.

[3] He was son of Hamdam a foster-brother of Kāmrān, so that his fidelity was to the "milk-brotherhood."

His Majesty who was the touch-stone of knowledge of men and their accurate balance, highly approved of his faithfulness and though he set value on his services, he let him go. He made over to him the money and goods fixed upon for the expenses of the journey and sent him to the Mīrzā. Beg Muluk, notwithstanding his close connection with the Mīrzā went with him some stages only and then returned,—a proceeding exceedingly disapproved by His Majesty and, notwithstanding external agreeableness,[1] he became disregarded.

The Mīrzā went by the Indus to Tatta and thence to his destination (Mecca). He performed the pilgrimage three times, and on the 11th Ẕī'l-ḥijja, 964 (5th. Oct., 1557), at Mecca,[2] he was borne away to non-existence, uttering these words, in response to the Divine call, "Here I am for Thee."[3]

As the series of words about M. Kāmrān has now been folded up, I hasten to my proper subject, and record that, as the evil Afghāns had destroyed the fort at Bikrām, known as Peshāwur, where His Majesty was encamped, he determined to rebuild it and leaving a body of his well-wishers in it, to proceed to Kābul:—for the completion of this fort would be the beginning of the conquest of India. The officers wanted to get back to Kābul and were unwilling on any account soever to delay in this place. His Majesty Jahānbānī set himself energetically to the task and in a short time, had the fort rebuilt. Pahlwān Dost *mīr barr* divided the work, according to orders, amongst the officers and it was soon finished.
332 Sikandar Khān Uzbak was left in charge and His Majesty moved towards Kābul.

Later on, the Afghāns made a great attack on the fort but Ṣikandar Khān defended it manfully, and they were repulsed. In

---

[1] *Baqabūl-i-ṣuratīki dāsht, mardūd-i-naẓarhā shud.* This is from Bayāzīd, 65a whose words are;—*u ān bī sa'ādat Beg Mulūk, cand manzil ki hamrāh-i-mīrzā raft, bī rukhṣat judā shuda āmid in bawajūd-i-maqbūlī mardūd-i-khāṣṣu 'āmm shud.* It would seem from text 1. 368 that he must have afterwards repented and gone upon the pilgrimage.

[2] منا Minnā in text, that being a valley in Mecca. The three *ḥajj* will be those of 961–963. That of 964 could not have been completed. See Asiatic Quarterly Review, July, 1899, p. 164.

[3] See Hughes' Dictionary of Islām s.v. *talbīyah*. *Labbaik* may be said to correspond to Colonel Newcomb's *Adsum*.

the beginning of 961 (Dec., 1553), Kābul was made glorious by the arrival of His Majesty. The ladies came to wait upon him and offered congratulations. He however said that congratulations had their proper place and that the affair of M. Kāmrān was not one for congratulation because it was as if he had struck at his own eyes. Gracious letters were issued to the officers. One was sent also to 'Abdu-r-rashīd, ruler of Kashghār, who had all along been mindful of kinship and amicably disposed. The letter told what had occurred and was sent by prudent hands. While His Majesty was superintending affairs of state and distributing rewards and punishments, a son was born to him from the chaste womb of Māh Jūjak Begam, in this year, on the night of Wednesday, 15th Jumāda'l-awwal (19th April, 1554), and after the passing of two *dāng* [1] of the sign Sagittarius. His Majesty named him Muḥammad Ḥakīm. As the chronograms [2] of his birth were both Abū'-l-mafākhir and Abū'-l-faẓāil, he received both patronymics (*kanyat*). The gates of joy were opened and thanks were rendered to God. At about the same time, Khānish Begam, daughter of Jūjūq M. of Khwārizm, gave birth to a son whom they named Ibrāhīm Sl. He soon went to the blessed country (*'ālam-i-qads*).

*Verse.*

He was a flash from high heaven :
Birth and death touched.

---

1 Apparently meaning one-third of a degree.

2 Both names yield 961 (1554).

## CHAPTER LVI.

### His Majesty Jahānbānī's Journey to Qandahār and his return therefrom.

In the beginning of the winter of this year, His Majesty determined to go to Qandahār rather than to India, as a number of strifemongers had made false representations about Bairām Khān. Accordingly he went there. The government of Kābul was entrusted to 'Alī Quli Khān of Andarāb, and the Divine nursling, eye-pupil of
383 the *Khilāfat*, prop of glory, His Majesty the Shāhinshāh accompanied his father as far as Ghaznīn. The prince's *vakils*, who were in charge of Ghaznīn, were assiduous in discharging the duties of hospitality. When the royal standards moved onwards from Ghaznīn, the prince returned to Kābul. Bairām Khān recognised the advent of the king as a great favour and returned thanks for it, with a heart full of loyalty, he did homage at the village of Shorāndām, ten[1] leagues out from Qandahār, and His Majesty was convinced that the reports about him were not true. He arrived at Qandahār in an auspicious hour. Splendid feasts were held. Among the distinguished servants present there were Shāh Abū'l-ma'ālī, Mun'īm Khān, Khiẓr Khw. Khān; Muḥibb 'Ali Khān, (son of) Mīr Khalīfa, Ism'aīl Dūldai and Ḥaidar Muḥammad ākhta-begī. Of the Ahl-i-Sa'ādat (learned or literary men) there were Khw. Ḥusain of Merv, Maulānā 'Abdu-l-bāqī the *Ṣadr* and others. Bairām Khān neglected no punctilio of civility and the whole winter was spent in Qandahār in enjoyment. And during this time, whatever was necessary for the king's privy purse, was all defrayed by Bairām Khān. He had all the court servants brought into the houses of his own servants, where their entertainment was provided for. All this time His Majesty Jahānbānī enjoyed sensual and mental recreations[2] and pleasures spiritual and temporal and had feasts and entertainments and visited the

1 Some MSS. read "two leagues."

2 *Tanazzuhāt* which has for one of its meanings, walking about in gardens.

hermitages of dervishes and the cells of pure religionists, and distributed largesse in accordance with their conditions. Among others, he frequently visited Maulānā Zainu-d-dīn Maḥmūd *Kamāngar*[1] (the bow-maker) who was one of the determined opponents of sensuality, and holy words were spoken on both sides. There were conversations about the attainment of desires in time and eternity.

K͟hw. G͟hāzī, who had gone on an embassy to Persia and had come to Qandahār with presents before His Majesty had arrived there, returned to employment and was, on account of his meritorious services, raiṣed to the lofty office of dīwān. About the same time Mu'aẓẓam[2] Sl. came from Zamīn-Dāwar and entered into service. Mihtar Qarā, who was one of the trusted followers of Muḥammad 334
K͟hān of Herāt also came with valuable offerings and was received into service. He brought representations of fidelity and was encompassed with favours. And for the sake of the State and for the delight of hearts, he had a *qamarg͟ha* hunt in the neighbourhood of Shōrāndām. This pleased the officers and His Majesty took an omen from it for the capture of his desires.

One of the evil things which happened in Qandahār was the killing of S͟her 'Alī Beg by S͟hāh Abū'l-ma'ālī. A brief account of the affair is, that about this time, S͟her 'Alī Beg, the father of Qarā Beg *mīr s͟hikār*, came without leave from S͟hāh Tahmāsp, the ruler of Persia, and entered the royal service. S͟hāh Abū'l-ma'ālī, being intoxicated by Court-favour and by his honours and courage, set his foot outside the circle of moderation, and did extravagant things. And as the evil bigotry of rebellious people had damaged the brain of his faith, he frequently and openly said in the court of His Majesty Jahānbānī, that he would kill this heretical fellow. Out of the favour he bore him, His Majesty regarded this as a pleasantry and gave no heed to the matter. At length, Abū'l-ma'ālī, being drunk with the wine of bigotry, one night attacked that stranger and poured his blood upon the ground! His Majesty was much displeased, but the close, though superficial relationship[3] was a veil of faults and prevented him from punishing the evil deed.

---

[1] Blochmann, 539. Badāōnī III. 151. The fullest account of him is at Badāōnī I. 455. The saint really was a maker of bows. He was a native of Bahadā in K͟hurāsān.

[2] Humāyūn's brother-in-law.

[3] Hūmāyūn called him "son."

When the excellent loyalty of Bairām Khān was made clear and it became apparent to all that his foot was firm in the path of obedience and good service, His Majesty confirmed him in the government of Qandahār which it had been his recent intention to give to Mun'im Khān. He took Zamīn-Dāwar from Khw. Mu'aẓẓam and gave it to Bahādur Khān, the brother of 'Alī Qulī Khān. His mind being now at rest about the affairs of his kingdom, he returned to Kābul with the intention of conquering Hindustān. He gave leave of absence to Bairām Khān in order that he might make preparations for this expedition and join him as soon as possible. His Majesty took Walī Beg[1] and Ḥājī Muḥammad Sīstānī with him because people were continually telling tales of them and putting together the materials of strife. Near Ghaznīn, he was met by His Majesty the Shāhinshāh and it was a meeting like the conjunction[2] of favourable planets. Muḥammad Qulī Khān Barlās and Atka Khān (Shamsu-d-dīn) and many others did homage and at the end of 961 (Oct., 1554), Kābul received celestial glory by his advent.

335 At this time, Mun'im Khān was raised to the office of guardian of His Majesty the Shāhinshāh. Though, from use and wont, His Majesty gave the name of guardian (*atālīq*) to the elder man, yet in reality he sent him like a child, to learn wisdom from that exhibitor of universal reason. Mun'im Khān returned thanks to Heaven for this great gift and prepared a glorious feast. He also tendered fitting gifts and arranged the materials of his own exaltation. In this year, Ulugh Beg, the son of Halhal Sl. arrived on the part of the ruler of Persia, and tendered gifts which were a cause of increasing joy. His Majesty continually looked after the administration of justice and also engaged himself in preparations for the conquest of Hindūstān. At this time one of the dervishes who was famous in foreign lands (*wilāyat*) had sent a pair of boots as a gift: His Majesty Jahānbānī said that he drew an omen from these boots favourable to the conquest of Hindūstān for it was a common saying that Turkistān is the head, Khurāsān the breast and Hindūstān the foot (of the

[1] Blochmann, 374 and 518. Walī Beg was apparently a grand-nephew of Ḥājī Muḥammad Kōka.

[2] An allusion to Amīr Khusrau's poem on the meeting of Kaikūbād and his father, Nāsiru-d-dīn. Elliot III. 524.

world). He said this omen was like that mentioned by His Majesty Ṣāḥib-qirānī, *viz.*, that in the year in which he moved from Transoxiana to conquer Khurāsān and when he arrived at Andarkhūī, a village in which lived a dervish named Sangī Atā[1] who was famous for purity of heart and for his miracles,—His Majesty Ṣāḥib-qirānī went to visit him. By way of already-made (*mā ḥaẓar*) breakfast, the dervish placed before him the breastbone of a sheep. His Majesty (Tīmūr) observed to his courtiers that he drew an omen, from this breast, for the conquest of Khurāsān because Khurāsān was called the breast of the world.

Bairām Khān arrived on the day following the feast of Ramẓān (the 'Īd,—2nd Shawwal,—31st August). His Majesty, for the sake of giving greater pleasure and out of the affection he bore him, had the feast repeated and gave an entertainment more splendid than that of the 'Īd. On this joyful day, which was made the test day for horsemen and dextrous archers, the royal cavalier of the plain of fortune and nursling of the spring of glory, to wit, His Majesty the Shāhinshāh, felt disposed to engage for a time in shooting at the *qabaq* and to show his archer's skill to the generality and thus to lead them on the way of devotion. The first time he aimed at the *qabaq*,[2]—which experienced marksmen had failed to hit,—his arrow struck the ligature of the golden ball. At this all the people shouted. Such a thing appeared wonderful to the superficial, but what marvel was there in it to those who have beheld with awakened eyes the real spectacle 336
of the mysteries of the lord of the world. How is it strange that he who is a mine of substantial wonders, should display external marvels? Bairām Khān composed an excellent ode on His Majesty's

[1] The *Ẓafarnāma* (Bib. Ind. ed. I. 310) gives the name of the dervish as Bābā Sankū. See also Pétit de la Croix's trs. ed. 1722, II. 315. The occurrence took place at Andarkhūī west of Balkh. The dervish did not exactly place the bone before Tīmūr as a *mā ḥaẓarī*, for he flung it at Tīmūr's head. A.F. speaks of the story as having been told by Tīmūr. In Tīmūr's Memoirs (trs. Stewart, p. 38) there is an allusion to an omen taken from a sheep bone but nothing about a saint. Nor indeed is it necessary to regard A.F. as referring to the personal Memoirs. His words,—*ān tafā'ulī ki Ḥaẓrat Ṣāḥib-qirānī farmūda būdand* may mean only "the omen which Tīmūr explained."

[2] For account of this sport see Bābar's Mems. Erskine, 21*n.* and Vullers *s.v.*

*qabaq*-shooting and presented it at the feast. The opening couplet is as follows;—

> Thine arrow has snatched the fastening of the ball from the crook:[1]
> It has made the curve like a meteor grazing the Pleiades.

During this time of enjoyment when the thought of the conquest of Hindūstān was lighting up the hearts of loyal servants,—petitions came from the faithful in Hindūstān and brought to the royal ears news of the death of Salīm Shāh and of the confusion of the country.

---

[1] The *kajak* is the wooden crook which in the game of *qabaq*-shooting was attached to the pole and on which balls of gold or silver, or gourds were suspended. Bairām's verses are quoted, with variation, in the *Bahār-i-'ajam* s.v. *kajak*. The second line of the couplet is obscure. Amongst others, *hilāl* has the meanings of the young moon and of a spear-point: I presume it also may mean an arrow. Indeed *hilālī* means a crescent-headed arrow. The Lucknow editor understands by *hilāl*, the half-moon of the thumb nail which is contiguous to the thumb-stall (*zihgīr*) of archers. The *ṣūrat-i-parwīn* of the couplet he explains as being the balls of the *qabaq*,—for it seems that several were sometimes used: He would seem to understand the line, as "Thy finger has made the balls assume the appearance of the Pleiades, brushed by a meteor." Maulvi Abdūl Haq Abīd understands by *hilāl* the curved end of the *kajaks* or suspending rod. Badāōnī (I. 480) quotes Bairām's lines and says they, as well as similar ones by Jāhī Yatmān, are derived from an ode by Nigārī of Tūn. See also Ranking's translation, 622. He states that the crescent moon is compared to an erasing-knife.

# CHAPTER LVII.

## BRIEF ACCOUNT OF THE EVENTS AND MISFORTUNES WHICH TOOK PLACE IN HINDŪSTĀN DURING THE DAYS OF CONFUSION.

As the thread of the story has been drawn out so far it is necessary that the chronicles give a short account of India so that the condition of impatient awaiting may not befal the intelligent members of the congregation of understanding. The brief account is, that when on 11th Rabī'u-l-awwal, 952 (23rd May, 1545), Sher Khān, after having established his power by wickedness and tyranny and having ruled five years, two months and thirteen days,—went to the abode of nothingness, his younger son, Salīm Khān, eight days afterwards, took his father's seat by the instrumentality of the officers. He ruled eight years, two months and eight days. For some time he had to carry on a war with his elder brother 'Ādil Khān and with Khwās Khān. This last was one of Sher Khān's slaves, and obtained[1] a reputation for sanctity among the commonalty by making a fair show, (*āblatarāzī*, perhaps, "plastering the boil") by trickery (*gurbzat*) and by seizing men's property and by distributing the acquisitions of the learned among the base and ignorant. As contention with one's own master,—even though he be worthless,—does not prosper, the schemes of those strifemongers did not succeed. Salīm Khān also contended for a time with the Niyāz tribe who ruled the Panjāb, their leader being Haibat Khān. They were overcome and in the defiles of the mountains of Kashmīr fell into the abyss of destruction. He also was occupied for some time in fighting with the Gakhars, and did not prevail, for his servants could not get the better of them, and they (the Gakhars) were loyal to the holy family (the Tīmūrids). He completed the fort

[1] See Erskine's translation of this passage, and his account of Khwās Khān. (II. 460). It would not be uncharitable to suppose that Khwās Khān had not shown favour to A.F.'s father and family.

of Rohtās which Sher Khān had begun, and he had a presage of evil when he was in the Siwālik hills and founded the fort of Mānkōṭ as a refuge for himself. For a long time he laboured under apprehensions on account of the Afghān vagabonds and his own bad life, and spent his days in the fort of Guāliār. Though he dealt equitably
337 with the peasantry, he treated the soldiers very harshly. On 22nd Zī'l-qa'da, 960 (October 30th, 1553), he died from a malignant ulcer which formed in one of his lower members owing to the issue of corrupt matter. According to his will, Fīrūz Khān, who was of tender age was appointed his successor, but after a few days Mūbāriz Khān, who was Fīrūz's maternal uncle, put that innocent one to death, and himself assumed the sovereignty, taking the name of Muḥammad 'Ādil. He was the son of Niẓām Khān, younger brother of Sher Khān. This Niẓām had one son and three daughters, and a strange thing was that the son became a ruler and the husbands of the three daughters rose to high rank,—for one was Salīm Khān, another Sikandar Sūr, and the third was Ibrāhīm Sūr. A brief account of these last two will be given hereafter. Hīmū who, by evil speaking, evil plotting and calumny which, as rulers have to study mankind, gives them pleasure, and this to such an extent that the pleasure hides from their penetrating gaze constitutional faults and innate wickedness,[1] rose from low degree to high rank and became the prime minister of that tyrant, who spent all his time in sport and amusement and bodily lusts, and neglected affairs. Confusion was produced in the world. Now that we have come so far it is proper that a brief account should be given of Hīmū.

## Account of Hīmū.

Let him who searches out the marvels of God's power take a long view and get an instructive warning from the account of Hīmū. Outwardly he had neither rank (*ḥasb*) nor race (*nasab*), nor beauty of form, (*ṣūrat*) nor noble qualities (*sairat*). Perchance the incomparable Deity raised him to high position for some occult reason which was hidden from the eyes of the acute, or perhaps He sent one worse than themselves to chastise the wicked of the age. In short

[1] A.F. means that rulers have from their position to welcome evil-speaking as it is the only way in which they can get information. A true reflection upon despotism but strange to come from A.F

that evil-looking one of puny form and lofty designs was ranked among the petty hucksters of Rewārī[1] which is a township of Mewāt. For his family, (*nasab*), he belonged to the Dhūsar tribe which is the lowest class of hucksters in India. At the back of lanes he sold saltpetre (*nimak-i-s̲h̲ōr*) with thousands of mortifications (*ba hazārān bīnimakī*) till at last he by means of astuteness, became a government huckster under Salīm Khān, of whom a short account has already been given. By masterpieces of feline trickery, he gradually made himself known to Salīm K̲h̲ān by evil-speaking and business capacity. He was always getting people into trouble. Apparently he was behaving loyally towards his master, in reality he was seeking his own ends, and decking his own household with the goods of the op- 338
pressed. Avaunt; avaunt! he was preparing destruction for his lord and striking the axe into his own foot. Here the great ones of the world[2] made a big mistake for these much-occupied ones from their wishing to know about men give place to wicked talebearers, either in order to learn hidden things about them or to punish evildoers. Though they make an engagement with themselves that they will not use the information for attacking the reputation and honour of the good and loyal, yet the outwardly well-seeming but inwardly base crew of men seize their opportunity and for their own advantage attack the loyal with their smooth tongues,—while the great sometimes, owing to the multiplicity of business, forget the engagements with themselves and become suspicious of the loyal and raze the foundations of their own power.

In short this wicked man soon got a place in Salīm Khān's affections by misrepresentation, and obtained a footing in the administration. When the measure of Salīm K̲h̲ān's life was full, and the period of the sway of the evildoers of India had come to Mubāriz K̲h̲ān aforesaid who was Salīm K̲h̲ān's cousin, Hīmū found him careless of worldly affairs and annexed the whole of the administration and rose to lofty offices. Nothing remained to Mubāriz K̲h̲ān, who was commonly known as 'Adlī (tyrant), except the name (of king). Hīmū undertook all appointments and dismissals, and the distribution of justice. In his foresight he got possession of

[1] In the Gūrgāon district and a railway-junction.

[2] The text has *dīnī*, of faith, but surely this is a mistake for *danyā*, though it seems that *dīn* may also have a temporal meaning.

the treasures of Sher Khān and Salīm Khān and of their elephant-stud. He was freehanded in disposing of their accumulations. His base debtors worshipped him and did his behests. For some days he took the title of Rāi and then he fastened the title of Rāja on himself and assumed the style of the Rāja Bikramājīt. Thus did he in his folly apply great names to himself. From foresight he preserved the nominal sovereignty for 'Adlī and waged great wars against his opponents. By his valour and daring he was victorious and performed great deeds. He became famous for courage and capability. By degrees he advanced so far as to venture to encounter the sublime army of His Majesty the Shāhinshāh. But as this holy personality was the touchstone of the good and bad, his counterfeit coin was tested and his black existence annihilated by the lights of world-illuminating justice! This will be related in its proper place.

Now that one out of a thousand of Hīmū's evil behaviours has been described, I proceed to a brief account of Hindūstān.

When the sovereignty came to Mubāriz Khān, the affairs of
339 India became worse than before. In fact both father and son (*i.e.*, Sher Khān and Salīm) behaved properly in the management of affairs. Alas! that they should have spent their days in disloyalty and ingratitude! If these two had been servants of the sublime threshold of His Majesty the Shāhinshāh, and if the home administration had been entrusted to the father, and the guardianship of the marches to the son, they would have been encompassed with royal favours, and have gained, by good service, an existence which the wise regard as real life. Such workers deserved such a master. As for the vulgar form of rule which is brought about by rebellion, it is regarded by the wise as an existence inferior by many degrees to death.

In short when Salīm Khān died, Mubāriz Khān showed such behaviour as may no other person evince! Aḥmad Khān Sūr the sister's husband of Salīm Khān who had charge of the Panjāb, became a claimant for the sovereignty and styled himself Sikandar Khān. And Muḥammad Khān, who was nearly connected with Sher Khān and was the Governor of Bengal, aimed at general supremacy. Ibrāhīm Khān Sūr who was also a relation, set about obtaining the rule of India while Shaj'at Khān, who was commonly known as Sajāwal Khān, raised his head high in Mālwa. The vagabond Afghāns gathered together and caused confusion. Sikandar

collected the army of the Panjāb and other vagabonds and meditated an attack upon Āgra. Mubāriz Khān and Ibrāhīm advanced with the same intention. At last by the wishes of Hīmū, Mubāriz Khān went off to the eastward, and a battle took place near Āgra, between Sikandar and Ibrāhīm. Ibrāhīm was defeated and had to retire, while his father Ghāzī Khān Sūr, who governed Bīana, sheltered himself in the fort. Sikandar's affairs became prosperous, and he got possession of the country from the Indus to the Ganges. He collected an army and wished to march eastwards to dispose of the claimant to the throne and to become sole monarch. At this time the reverberation of the advance of His Majesty Jahānbānī Jannat-āshyānī for the conquest of India rose high. Tātār Khān and Ḥabīl Khān and a large body of troops were appointed to defend the Panjāb. Muḥammad Khān, the Governor of Bengal, determined to rid himself of Mubāriz Khān and other competitors. After some other events, a great battle took place near Capparghatta between him and Mubāriz Khān and Hīmū, and Muḥammad Khān fell. The treasures of Sher Khān and Salīm Khān came into Hīmu's hands. He sank into the enjoyment of corporeal pleasures, and in appearance his circumstances improved. At this time he fought battles with Ibrāhīm and other competitors. He was everywhere victorious. 340
And though he did not know how to ride a horse and was always carried about in an elephant-box (*ṣindūq-i-fīl* qr. *hauda*) he in his courage and audacity freely spent the money which had come of itself into his hands, and did great deeds such as men could not conceive. As Sikandar was established in Āgra, he went off to Bihār and Bengal. Khiẓr Khān, the son of Muḥammad Khān took his father's place and assumed a great title, calling himself Sl. Jalālu-d-dīn. He applied himself to the management of Bengal. Mubāriz Khān and Hīmū determined to go to Bengal, but spent some time in getting rid of their opponents. But I leave these details, which I have no inclination to describe in the closet of neglect, to proceed to my legitimate subject.

## CHAPTER LVIII.

### Expedition of His Majesty Jahânbânî Jannat-âshyânî for the conquest of India, and victory thereof by the dominion-increasing auspices of the King of Kings (Akbar).

Let it not be concealed from those waiting for strange impressions and the listeners for glorious news, that when the truth about the confusion in India and the tumult and uproar in this centre of peace and tranquillity, of which some hints have been already been given, again came to the hearing of His Majesty Jahānbānī Jannat-āshyānī, he addressed himself to the expedition, already determined upon in the recesses of his foreseeing mind, and having committed all the chaste ladies of his family in Kābul to the Divine protection, he appointed S̲h̲āh Walī *bakāwal-begī* the guardian of M. Muḥammad Ḥakīm. The service of the ladies and the affairs of the province of Kābul were entrusted to Mun'im K̲h̲ān, and His Majesty set out in the middle of Ẕū'l-ḥijja 961, (about 12th November, 1554), in a propitious hour and at a time which the heavenly motions made glorious, and the aspects of the stars made supreme. The nursling of Divine light, His Majesty the S̲h̲āhins̲h̲āh to wit, was then, as regards his elemental life, twelve years and eight[1] months old. The perfect understanding of that great one of both worlds was beyond computation. He was made the forefront of the army of spiritual and temporal victories. On the day of starting an omen was taken from the *dīwān* of Ḥāfiẓ. As a great work was being unveiled the heralds of glad tidings from people and places spake loudly and with thousands of tongues. Among them this holy

[1] Text, *hasht*, but probably A.F. wrote *shash*, six, for Akbar was then barely 12¼ lunar years old. According to our calendar he was only 12 years and 1 month old.

master-couplet (*shāhbait*) on the front of the noble page emerged as a preamble of victory and was like the writing on the forehead of dominion.

*Verse.*

"Ask dominion from the auspicious bird (*murgh-i-humāyūn*)
and from his shadow
[1]For the crow and the kite have not the master-plume of
genius (text, *himmat*, but Ḥāfiz, apparently wrote *daulat*).

Though the practically wise applied this truthful verse to the dominion and victory of His Majesty Jahānbānī, the far seeing of wisdom's Court understood it as announcing the great *khilafat* and the supreme sovereignty of His Majesty the Shāhinshāh and waited at the gate of the expectation of the upward [2]flight of the holy bird. His Majesty Jahānbānī laid firm hold of the strong hand of the Divine favour and grasped the stout cable of heavenly tidings and went off with few men—they did not amount to 3000,—but with large help from the armies of Providence, which could not be calculated by intellectual accountants. Bairām Khān obtained leave 341

[1] The lines come from an ode of Ḥāfiz beginning *kzstagānrā aoṭalab bashid-u-quwwat nabūd*, Ed. Brockhaus II. 137 No. 216. The crow and the kite are taken to represent India See Elliot. Hist. III. 546*n*. where we are told that the expression "cawing crows" is used by Badl Chād and Amīr Khasrū to signify Hindūs. No doubt the allusion as to their complexion, and Elliot's note may also explain an obscure passage of Ḥaidar Mīrzā's (*Tar Rash*, Elias and Ross 399) where we are told that Khwāja Nūrā changed Humāyūn not to cast his shadow over a land where the parrot was less common than the kite. The translator's note to this passage seems erroneous. Though the parrot is common in India yet it is not so common as the kite, and apparently the Khwāja meant to warn Humāyūn against going to Sind or remaining in India. He cannot have meant Persia, for Humāyūn went there, and Ḥaidar says that he did not go to a country where the parrot was rarer than the kite. See also the line of Qāsim Kāhi (Badāonī III. 173) where he says that he is not a kite or a crow that he should adorn India. The lines quoted by Ḥaidar Mirzā are given also by Badāonī (II. 49) and are applied by him to India. They come from an ode by Ḥāfiz which begins *Khūshast khilwat agar yār yār-i-manbāshid*, Brockhaus' ed. II. 109, No. 189.

[2] Apparently this means that they waited in expectation of Humāyūn's death.

for the purpose of setting some royal matters, and of arranging his equipment and remained in Kābul. His Majesty Jahānbānī went from Jalālābad[1] down the river on a raft, and encamped at Bikrām (Peshawar) in the end of Muḥarram 962, (near end of December, 1554). Sikandar Khān Uzbak who had done good service, was made the subject of favours and on that day was raised to the rank of Khān. On 5th Ṣafar, (31st December, 1554), the bank of the river Sind, known as the Nīlāb, was made the camping ground, and three days were spent there. Here Bairām Khān arrived from Kābul, and with sundry intelligencers brought the good news that Tātār Khān Kāshī[2] who had been appointed with a large force to guard the fort of Rohtās had, in spite of the strength of the fort etc., fled merely on hearing of the uprearing of the royal standards on the borders of the Indus. His Majesty took into account the good offices, old and new, of Sulṭān Adam Gakhar and sent him a gracious letter inviting him to come and do homage. As he had not a happy star, he made landholder-like excuses and represented that he had concluded a treaty with Sikandar who had taken his son Lashkari along with him. Should he come and do homage, he would both break his compact, and incur the risk of having his son killed. The imperial servants represented that it was proper to order the victorious army to look after him (Sulṭān Adam) before advancing further, and that it was not wise to move on and leave such a disaffected person behind. His Majesty, who was a mine of gentleness and generosity, said that he belonged to a family which was faithful from of old, and that recently he had done good service, as already related, and that to punish him now was not in accordance
342 with prestige, especially as he had used humble language and had made apologies.

When the grand army crossed the Indus, the Afghāns who were collected in the neighbourhood of Rohtās retreated and the army continued to advance. Every day a delightful spot presented itself, and cities and villages came under the shadow of justice and enjoyed the luxury of tranquillity. And now that we have come so far,

---

[1] Similarly Wood went on a raft from Jalālabad to Peshāwar, p. 280.

[2] Bāyazīd calls him Iskāndar Sulṭāni Quzāq. Many MSS. including Badāonī's, have Kāsī.

it is proper, before detailing events, to give the names of such of the companions of the stirrup of victory as were of high rank.

List.[1]

When the army arrived at the auspicious town of Kalānūr, Shihābu-d-dīn Aḥmad Khān, Ashraf Khān and Farḥat Khān were sent to Lahore to have the glorious name (of Humāyūn) proclaimed from the pulpit and placed upon the coinage, and also to give the

---

[1] The list is short compared with Bāyazīd's, I.O. M.S. 72 ff.)

1. Bairam Khān.
2. Shāh Abū'l-ma'ālī.
3. Khiẓr Khw. Khān (Bāyazīd, Khiẓr Sl. Mughal.)
4. Tardī Beg Khān.
5. Sikandar Khān.
6. Khiẓr Khān Hazāra.
7. 'Abdu-l-lāh Khān Uzbak.
8. Mīrzā 'Abdu-l-lāh.
9. Muṣāḥib Beg.
10. 'Alī Qulī Khān Shaibāni (or Sistānī).
11. Muḥammad Qulī Khān Barlās
12. Khw. Mu'aẓẓam.
13. 'Alī Qulī Khān Andarābī.
14. Ḥaidar Muḥammad, *ākhta-begi*.
15. Bābūs Beg (Blochmann, 389)
16. Isma'īl Beg Dūldai.
17. Mīrzā Ḥasan Khān.
18. Mīrzā Nijāt.
19. Muḥammad Khān Jalāīr.
20. Sl. Ḥusain Khān.
21. Qandūq Sl.
22. Muḥammad Amīn *dīwāna*.
23. Shāh Qulī Nāranjī.
24. Tulak Khān.
25. Kākar 'Alī Khān.
26. Bāqī Beg *yātīgh-begī* (head of the guards).
27. La'l Khān Badakhshī (Bāyazid, an officer of Sulaimān).
28. Beg Muḥammad *ākhta-begī*.
29. Khw. Pādshāh *Murīẓ* (? sickly. Blochmann 459),
30. Kīcak Khw.
31. Khw. 'Abdu-l-bārī.
32. Khw. 'Abdu-l-lāh.
33. Mīr Mu'īn.
34. Mīr Ghanī.
35. Shāh Fakhru-d-dīn.
36. Mīr Muḥsin *Dā'ī*.
37. Khw. Ḥusain of Merv.
38. Mīr 'Abdu-l-Ḥai.
39. Mīr 'Abdul-l-lāh *qānūnī*.
40. Khanjar Beg (Bāyazīd, a relation of Tardī Beg).
41. 'Arif Beg.
42. Khw. 'Abdu-ṣ-ṣamad.
43. Mīr Sayyid 'Alī.
44. Mullā 'Abdu-l-qādir.
45. Mullā Ilyās (Elias) of Ardabīl (astronomer).
46. Shaikh 'Abu-l-qāsim Jorjānī. (Bāyazid, Asterābādī).
47. Maulānā 'Abdu-l-bāqī.
48. Afẓal Khān, *mīr bakhshī*.
49. Khw. 'Abdu-l-majīd *dīwān*.
50. Ashraf Khān *mīr munshī*.
51. Qāsim Makhlaṣ.
52. Khw. 'Aṭā-u-llāh, *dīwān-i-bayūtāt*.
53. Khw. Abū'-l-qāsim.
54. Shihābu-d-dīn Aḥmad Khān.
55. Mu'īn Khān Farankhūdī (Blochmann 434).
56. Khw. Amīnu-d-dīn Maḥmūd.
57. Mulk Mukhtār.

inhabitants of that great city an order of protection from the mischief of strifemongers. Bairām Khān, Tardī Beg Khān, Iskandar Khān, Khiẓr Khān Hazāra, Ismā'īl Beg Dūldai and a large troop were sent against Naṣīb Khān Panj Bhaiya (?) who was stationed
343 at Harhāna (Harīana) while His Majesty himself went on to Lahore. The nobles of that country came forward to welcome him. They offered up thanks for this glorious favour and gave large presents. High and low were treated with royal favours according to their degree. On the 2nd Rabī'-ṣ-ṣānī, (24th February, 1555), the illustrious city of Lahore, which is in fact a great city of India, was made glorious by his advent, and all classes and conditions of men were freed from the evils of the times, and attained the objects for which they had been long waiting on hope's highway.

In the end of this month news came that an Afghān named Shāhbāz Khān had collected a number of Afghāns in Dīpālpūr and was indulging in evil intentions. His Majesty Jahānbānī sent to that quarter Shāh Abū'-l-Ma'ālī 'Alī Qulī Khān Shaibānī, 'Alī Qulī Khān Andarābī, Muḥammad Khān Jalāīr and a number of brave officers. A hot engagement ensued, and both sides exposed their lives. The Sayyidzāda Abū'-l-Ma'ālī who was intoxicated with the world and proud of his beauty, got into difficulty but 'Alī Qulī Khān and other heroes performed wonders. The enemy was defeated and many of them were levelled with the dust. The imperial servants returned victorious. Now that I have proceeded so far it is necessary that I give a brief account of the victorious army which was placed under the leadership of Bairām Khān.

Let it not be hidden from the inquirers into events that when Bairām Khān arrived near *pargana* Harhāna (Harīāna), Naṣīb Khān Afghān made a small resistance—suitable to his nature,—and then fled. Great booty in money and goods fell into the hands of the heroes. Families also were captured. As Bairām Khān had heard from His Majesty Jahānbānī that he had vowed there should be no imprisonment when he should, by God's help, conquer India, and that the servants of God should not be confined, he got on horseback and collected together all the families of the Afghāns and sent them with trustworthy people to Naṣīb Khān. And he sent as the proceeds of this victory, which might be regarded as the preface to countless others, presents of elephants, etc., with a petition of his

own to the world-protecting court of His Majesty Jahānbānī. Having 344
offered up thanks for this agreeable victory, he left that place and advanced further. When he came near Jalandhar, the Afghāns thought it prudent to fly, and owing to the disputes which occurred in the victorious army, they were able to save their lives and the best of their property. The short account of this is that Tardī Beg Khān wanted to go after the dispersed Afghāns and Bairām Khān did not approve of this and did not give him permission. Tardī Beg Khān sent Bāltū Khān to Bairām Khān in order that by all means possible he might get leave to pursue them. Bāltū Beg came and delivered his message and Khwāja Mu'aẓẓam Sulṭān spoke harshly and abused him. Bāltū Khān retorted and the Khwāja used his sword and wounded Bāltū Khān in the arm. When His Majesty heard of this he wrote a letter of admonition and sent Afẓal Khān to explain matters. He conveyed His Majesty's counsels to the officers and brought about a reconciliation. Bairām Khān halted in Jālandhar, and assigned *parganas* in the neighbourhood to the various officers and sent them to their several posts. Sikandar Khān was appointed to Māciwāra. He went and thinking he had it in hand, advanced further, and took possession of Sihrind. Much property fell into his hands. Meanwhile Tātār Khān, Ḥabīl Khān, Naṣīb Khān, Mubārak Khān and a number of Afghān soldiers arrived from Delhi. Sikandar Khān did not think it prudent to remain in Sihrind and came to Jālandhar. Bairām Khān did not approve of this and was angry. He said that Sikandar should have kept his ground at Sihrind and have sent word to him. After much discussion the great officers took hold of the saddle-straps of the royal, everduring fortune and advanced from Jālandhar. When they came to the borders of Māciwāra, Tardī Muḥammad Khān and many officers did not think it advisable to cross the Satlaj. As the rainy season was near at hand the proper thing to do, they said, was to secure the ferries and to halt. When the violence of the rains was over, and the air had become temperate, they could cross the river. Bairām Khān and the farsighted perceived that it was right to cross the river and spoke properly in this sense. At length by the exertions of Mullā Pīr Muḥammad, Muḥammad Qāsim Khān of Nīshāpūr, Walī Beg and Ḥaidar Qulī Beg Shāmlū, Bairām Khān crossed the river. Tardī Beg Khān and the other officers were obliged to

do likewise. The army of fortune was divided into four bands.
345 The centre was controlled by Bairām Khān, the right wing by Khiẓr Khān Hazāra, the left wing by Tardī Beg Khān, while Sikandar Khān and a number of active men were appointed to the vanguard. As the desires of the prince of the world were limited to the laws of justice and were in accordance with the Divine Will, the work of his ministers was daily more and more victorious. When the Afghāns heard of the smallness of the victorious army and of its having crossed the river, they hastily came up with a large force. The two forces encountered one another towards evening and a great battle took place. The farseeing soldiers chose a place near Bijana[1] (?) for the battle field and stood firm. All distinguished themselves, but at last night intervened. Even then they continued to discharge arrows. By a happy chance, which was the beginning to the victory, fire broke out in a very large village of thatched houses and this was like the lighting of thousands of lamps for the guidance of the troops. It was found on inquiry that this Divine aid was wrought by the exertions of the enemy. And what they had thought was for their advantage turned to their loss. In fact by means of this illumination, which was the vanguard of victory, the conquering heroes obtained information concerning the position of the enemy and were enabled to work havoc with their arrows. The foe did not know the position of the victorious army and shot in the dark and at random. When about three watches of the night had passed, the enemy was unable to resist any longer and took to flight. A great victory was gained. Elephants and much other property fell into the hands of the imperial servants. The chief of the booty was sent with a loyal petition to the Court. Next day they advanced and halted in Sihrind and 'Alī Qulī Shaibānī who had come up with the rear, was sent on with a body of troops.

One of the wonderful things was that when His Majesty heard that Tātār Khān had arrived with a large and well equipped army

[1] Mācīwāra is on the S. bank of the Satlaj. Firishta says they crossed the river and halted on the bank of the Pacwāra stream. Is Pacwāra the name of the side of the river opposite Mācīwāra? *Jab* means a trench and this may be the meaning here. Price read *baḥrī*, as some MSS. have it, and translates "by the side of a considerable fresh water lake." It is probably a place-name.

at Māciwāra, he remarked to a number of eager spirits that the place was a great distance off and that whatever the Divine Will intended would take place before they could arrive. The best thing therefore was for them to take refuge at the sublime threshold and to implore victory from the almonry of Divine aid. At the same moment he raised high the hands of supplication and asked for the success of the advance forces of the royal army. Many days had not passed when the official report of the victory arrived and much booty was brought to the Court. On consideration, it was found 346
that the day of prayer and the day of victory coincided. He paid the devotions of thanksgiving for the Providential victory and opened the hand of liberality for mankind.

When Sikandar heard what had taken place, he marched against the royal army with 80,000 horse and a complete equipment. Bairām Khān with abundant prudence and courage remained firm in Sihrind and took measures to defend the fort. He sent representations one after the other requesting the advance of His Majesty. As the latter was at that time suffering from cholic, he sent in his room the parterre-adorner of the *khilāfat*, viz., His Majesty the Shāhinshāh who always had victory at his stirrup. The cortēge of this *khedive* of the world had not gone far from Lahore when His Majesty Jahānbānī perfectly recovered, and on account of the distress of separation, and also out of precaution joined in the march. He directed that Farhat Khān should be the *shiqdār*[1] of Lahore, Bābūs Beg the *faujdār* of the Panjāb, M. Shāh Sulṭān the *amīn* and Mihtar Jauhar the treasurer. On the night of 7th Rajab, (29th May, 1555), the territory of Sihrind was illuminated by the royal advent. The officers did homage, and the drums of rejoicing were beaten. For fifteen days the officers had kept their ground in the face of such a large army and had occupied themselves in garrison-work. The royal tents were erected in a garden near the city. The arrangements for battle were suitably made and the army was distributed into four divisions. One was called by the honoured name of His Majesty Jahānbānī; another by that of His Majesty the Shāhinshāh; a third by that of Shāh Abū'-l-Ma'ālī; the fourth was entrusted to Bairām Khān. Each division bound the girdle of effort on the waist of their lives. The heroes displayed a willingness to risk their lives, and on

[1] Revenue officer, Jarrett II. 49.

each side men drank the last draught in the cup of the sword. On both sides humanity and gentleness were practised so that the bodies of those who had sacrificed their lives, were reverently made over to their friends. The shortsighted looking to the plurality of the enemy and the paucity of the king's forces, became pale from unbecoming apprehensions, but the farsighted read the inscription of victory on the countenances of the imperial[1] servants and daily became more and more steadfast. Especially did His Majesty Jahānbānī, who was a world of resolution, hearten every one by fitting behaviour, and inspire them with courage.

[1] *Aulīyā-i-daulat*, servant of the State, but here probably a periphrasis for Humāyūn and Akbar. See Lumsden's Persian Grammar, Calcutta, 1810, II. 363.

# CHAPTER LIX.

APPEARANCE OF GREAT MARVELS; AND THE ANNOUNCEMENT OF GOOD NEWS ON THE PART OF HIS MAJESTY THE SHĀHINSHĀH; AND OTHER FORTUNATE OCCURRENCES. 347

Though His Majesty the Shāhinshāh used his tender age as a veil and lived secluded, yet, as God the Creator willed that the real state of this great one of the age should be made manifest,—involuntarily did wondrous works, each of which was a competent witness to his lofty nature (*shāhide ast'adil*), hasten to the world of manifestation. Among the unusual things which at this time revealed themselves on the part of His Majesty the Shāhinshāh, was this, that he came out on the roof of a house in the city and contemplated with his clime-comprehending glance the hostile army. It was so great an army that no one could imagine its being defeated, but he said that in a short time "our" men would disperse it. His entourage who knew of his far-sight and had often beheld his marvels, rejoiced at this tidings, and offered thanks to God. Things like this look strange to custom-worshippers and formalists. But the worshippers of truth, and the esoteric do not regard this occurrence or hundreds like it as strange when coming from one so eminent temporally and spiritually.

At this time Khwāja 'Ambar Nāẓir, who was an old servant, came from Kābul and applied for employment. His Majesty Jahānbānī made him over to the nursling of Divine light. Forthwith he entered into his service and used to explain to him the manners and customs of India, and he brought Indians before the Unique of the age. As the star of the men of India was powerful, their ways became pleasing to him. This was the first time that he conceived an inclination for hunting with the *cīta* (hunting leopard), and the first place where he saw the sport. For Walī Beg the father of the

Khān Jahān[1] presented as peshkash a *cīta* which had come into his hands from the Afghāns at the battle of Māčīwāra and was called Fateḥbāz (the gamester of victory). The farseeing who were in his entourage made conjectures about countless victories on seeing this strange form. The keeper of this *cīta* was called Dūndū and on account of his good qualities, he received the title of Fateḥ Khān.[2] And at this day when the insignificant well-wisher, Abū'l-fazl, is writing this noble volume with a pen perfumed with sincerity,
348 Fateḥ Khān is in the service of His Majesty the Shāhinshāh and reckoned among the especial huntsmen. His Majesty who always dressed himself in outward disguises, and clothed himself in other garb, and kept his splendour hidden under various veils, made another screen for his beauty by his regard for this strange animal. But the rays of the sun and the fragrance of musk cannot be hid. On that day when fortune drew me to learn wisdom and to beatitude, and when by having the blessing of service, I became cognisant of the perfections of this chosen one of God, what prostrations of thanksgiving did I not perform, and what successes did I not obtain from this auspicious service! I was exalted spiritually and temporally, and I cleansed the chamber of my heart from superfluous desires. Now that the time of thanksgiving has arrived and that I wish to record my impressions—so that I may both give thanks and that a lamp of vision may be put in the path of the walkers in darkness, I am unaffectedly disturbed by the fact that I am in service and that there is a commercial nexus. Would that I had no outward acquaintance (with Akbar), and that I were not in the list of visible servants! so that the outwardly-seeing but inwardly-blind might not reckon this individual among the crowd of flatterers, and that men might, through my apparent exclusion be led to the goal and attain felicity. Good God! panegyrics have been written of old about ascetics who had not a tithe of the tenth part of the excellencies of this Khedive of the Age, nay, many of them had naught but external semblance, and yet, because there was no reciprocity in the matter, men void of insight imagine that these are not flatteries but are representations of the truth! But now, at this day, when the story of the Leader (*peshwā*) of mankind, whether

---

[1] Ḥusain Qulī, Blochmann, 329.

[2] Blochmann, 528.

spiritual or temporal, is about to be told, I who have tracked the spirit of the age must bear on my heart's shoulder the burden of men's ill-understanding! But forasmuch as my first thought was to pay in some small measure my debt of gratitude, I am not saddened by this man-troubling burden (*bār-i-mardamāzār*). And wherefore should I be? And now rejoicing in my good intention I pass on as a swift nocturnal linkman! Many have gained the Truth and ta'en the highway of loyalty! I now leave this subject, to which there is no end, and return to the point in my narrative where I was.

In fine, His Majesty Jahānbānī waged a masterly war for about forty[1] days, and by taking thought, and by making preparations gave support to the hearts of the loyal and enabled them to adorn the field of battle. At length, on 2nd S͟h'abān of the year in question (962), 22nd June, 1555, which was the watch-day (*naubat-i-taraddad*)[2] of the servants of His Majesty the S͟hāhins͟hāh K͟hwāja Mu'aẓẓam, Atka K͟hān and others went forth and did manfully. On
the other side Kālā Pahār, brother of Iskandar, came forward and 349
fought. Though it had not been intended that on that day there should be a general engagement, yet as something was to emerge from the curtain of fate, gradually the flames of conflict burst forth and rose high. The victorious troops advanced from all sides and steadily took post, so that there was a glorious battle-array.

*Verse.*

Two iron mountains moved from their places,
You'd say earth was moved from top to bottom,
Two armies drew their poniards in front of each other,
The centre and wings were drawn up in line,
The rush of arrows and the clash of swords,
Tore the marrow of elephants and the entrails (*zehra*, lit., gall-bladder)[3] of tigers.

---

[1] Humāyūn had been less than thirty days at Sihrind for he arrived there on the night of 7th Rajab.

[2] I am not sure of the meaning of the word *taraddad* here. It usually means reiteration or returning *Naubat* means relieving guard. Apparently the meaning here is that the duty of keeping guard was with Akbar's division on that day. See Badāūnī I. 460 who uses the word *yazak*.

[3] The gall-bladder is supposed to be the seat of courage, and Jahāngīr

By the auspicious influence of the fortune of His Majesty the Shāhinshāh, a great victory was gained, and much booty fell into the hands of the imperial servants. A large number of the luckless foe went to the world of non-existence. Sikandar went off with his men to the Dāman-i-kōh of the Panjāb. Khwāja Musāfirī,[1] one of the gallant men, came in his path. When Sikandar saw that a man was going to attack him, he turned, but though he put his hand to his sword, he could not draw it. After many attempts he disengaged himself from him and came away from that dangerous place. What else but this can happen to those intoxicated with the world and proud of their glory? His Majesty Jahānbānī in the midst of the worldly success, which is a wine that overthrows men, was wise and made supplications to God. And he conducted himself with perfect wisdom towards all classes. What marvel then that he was successful! Obedience to wisdom the Sulṭān (Sulṭān-i-khird) fits the work to the desire. Firstly; it makes the intention good. Secondly; effort is made in work suitable to one's condition. Thirdly; when good results are obtained the credit of them is not given to oneself. And no author is recognised except the omnipotent God. In fine His Majesty in order to teach the superficial, and in order to show respect to the various degrees of supplication, did not confine himself to inward thanksgiving, but had recourse to external acts, and prostrated himself in prayer to God. Though when India was last conquered, the victory of His Majesty Gītī-sitānī Firdūs-makānī was a masterpiece, as has been already described, yet the wise and acute know that it was not like this present marvel. In fact[2] there have been few instances in past times of such a victory as this which was obtained by few against many and which came solely from the great throne of God. Just at the time of this victory there was an excessive storm of wind and rain. As this caused the destruction of a number of oppressors and ingrates, it may be regarded as belonging

---

speaks in his Memoirs of dissecting a tiger and a leopard in order to discover the source of their vigour.

[1] Apparently this is the Bābā Dost Khwāja Khiẓr Musāfirī mentioned by Bayāzīd at p. 82*a* as taking part afterwards in the defence of Kābul.

[2] See translation, *supra*, p. 246. The account given in the present chapter about the battle's being fought on the day assigned to Akbar's division explains the expression at p. 246 about the blessing of Akbar's personality.

to the successes of the servants of the State, and as a mark of the 350
destruction of the contumacious. But as it prevented a pursuit of the fugitives and gave them after a thousand agonies a release from danger it may be regarded as a respite to an ill-fated crew.

When by Divine aid such a great gift had been revealed, His Majesty sat on the throne of justice and appraised the services of the loyal and devoted. In order to bring out the jewel of the sincere from the potsherd of service-sellers the question arose, in whose name should the proclamation of victory be recorded? An order was given that everyone should lay in his claim. S̲h̲āh Abū'l-ma'ālī, who was drunk with the wine of negligence, wished that the record of the glorious victory should be in his name. Bairām K̲h̲ān who was conscious that the coming to India was by his exertions, and who, up to the time of the victory, had, in opposition to a crowd of men, supported the world-adorning views of His Majesty Jahānbānī and had conducted the conquest of the countries and the uprooting of foes, was keenly desirous that the proclamation should bear his name. The farseeing and wise who knew that the victory was due to the felicity of His Majesty the S̲h̲āhins̲h̲āh and nursling of Divine light, opened their eyes and ears in surprised contemplation of the speakers, and the experienced and the just, knowing that this great victory which had shed its rays on the day assigned to the watch (*naubat-i-manṣūbān*) of the light of the garden of the *k̲h̲ilāfat* was due to the presence of his Majesty the S̲h̲āhins̲h̲āh, were astonished at the utterances of those men (Abū'l-ma'ālī and Bairām). At last, His Majesty Jahānbānī became by inspiration cognisant of the truth, and ordered the victory to be inscribed in the name of His Majesty the S̲h̲āhins̲h̲āh and thereby gratified the loyal far and near.

One of the strange occurrences of this time was the arrest of K̲h̲wāja Mu'aẓẓam. The brief account is that a letter containing some lines by the K̲h̲wāja came to hand. In his contemptible understanding and wickedness, he had written improper things to Sikandar and had represented himself as his well-wisher. His Majesty was greatly surprised and called upon the K̲h̲wāja for an explanation. As he could not deny, he said[1] that his well-wishing (*daulat-k̲h̲wāhī*)

[1] Apparently he maintained that the expressions in the letter about loyalty referred to Humāyūn and not to Sikandar. Price in his Retrospect gives a different rendering. His view is that Mu'aẓẓam said he

referred to His Majesty and that he had purposely contrived that the letter should come into His Majesty's hand in order that he should show him more favour, and cause him to be the performer of good
351 service. His Majesty ordered him into confinement and placed him in charge of Mīr Qālī. After arranging the matters of Sihrind, His Majesty proceeded by way of Sāmāna towards Delhi. When he came to Sāmāna he sent Abu'l-Ma'ālī with a number of officers such as Muḥammad Qulī Khān Birlās, Ismā'īl Beg Dūldai, Muṣahib Beg, Ibrāhīm Khān Uzbek, and others to Lahore so that if Sikandar should come out from the hills, they might hold him in check. The charge of the Panjāb was made over to Shāh Abū'l-ma'ālī. On account of the pleasant climate of Sāmāna, and the violence of the rains ordered a halt there for some days. While then, a report came from Sikandar Khān Uzbek, stating that by God's help he had come to Delhi and that the enemy had not withstood him, but had fled. The proper thing now was to exalt the site of India's throne by establishing there the *masnad* of the Lord of the Age. On receipt of this news His Majesty marched from Samāna, and on Thursday 1 Ramaẓān, 20th July, 1555, alighted at Salīmgaṛh which is on the north of Delhi and on the bank of the Jamūnā. On the fourth of the same month he entered the city and became established on the throne of the *khilafāt*.

On this day and while on the march His Majesty the Shāhinshāh struck a *nīlagāo* (an antelope, *portax pictus*) with his sword and took it as a prey so that the huntsmen were surprised,[1] while the acute obtained a sign of his capturing the booty of a sublime intention, and were made glad. His Majesty Jahānbānī who from the beginning of this blessed campaign till he came to Delhi and conquered India had given up the eating of animals now turned his thoughts towards the making a beginning (of eating flesh). On this day he rejoiced exceedingly and ordered that a piece of the *nīlagāo* be dried and kept in order that when after the Ramaẓān he should be disposed to eat animal food, he might make his first meal from this flesh. He then returned thanks to God.

---

wrote disloyally in order to give Humāyūn an opportunity of exercising his favourite virtue of forgiveness. Mīr Qālī may mean the head-cook.

[1] B.M. MS. Add. 27,247 has *ghiza* instead of *hairat-afzāī* so that the meaning would be "it became food for the huntsmen."

All the servants of the threshold of the *Khilafāt* received high offices and noble fiefs. Sirkār Ḥiṣār and its neighbourhood were given as a *jāgīr* to the servants[1] of His Majesty the Shāhinshāh. Omen-takers recognized this as the fort[2] for the distresses of the world, and again drew a presage for the daily increasing dominion of His Highness. Bairām Khān was presented with Sihrind and various other *parganas*. Tardī Beg Khān was sent to Mewāt, Sikandar Khān to Agra, 'Alī Qulī Khān to Sambal, and Ḥaidar Muḥammad Khān Ākhta Begī to Biāna, which is near Agra. By the blessing of the royal advent, and the beatitudes of the spiritual and temporal khedive, India was made a garden of dominion and auspiciousness. Mankind attained good fortune. His Majesty stayed in the fort of Delhi and was continually engaged in pleasing God, and he watered the rose-garden of sovereignty with the stream of justice. He 352
forever kept before him obedience to the Creator, and the prosperity of his creatures and so adorned the throne of the *khilāfat*.

Among the occurrences which were the cause of increasing his joy, was the arrival of Shāh Walī[3] Atka from Kābul. He brought news of the health of the chaste ladies, and also many details. He gave the joyful news that God had given a son to Māh Jūjak. His Majesty returned thanks to God for this good news and gave a feast and poured the coin of desire into the lap of mankind. He gave that rose of fortune the name of Farrukh Fāl, and rewarded Shāh Walī for his news by the title of Sulṭān and sent him back to Kābul with presents. He also gave him letters of greeting and affection.

Among the occurrences of this time was the arrival of Rustam Khān who was a leading man among the Afghāns. The brief account of this affair is that when the Atka Khān and a number of the royal servants proceeded towards Ḥiṣār, they halted on the day of Khūrdād 6th Shahryūr=Wednesday, 25th Ramẓān, two kos from Ḥiṣār. Rustam Khān, Tātār Khān, Aḥmad Khān, Pīr Muḥammad of Rohtak, Bījlī Khān, Shihāb Khān, Tāj Khān, Ādam Khān Qiyām Khānī and

---

[1] The meaning is that Ḥiṣār was given as an appanage to Akbar.

[2] B.M. Add. 27,247 has *iḥṣār* in which case the meaning is "the shutting off or restraining the evils of the world."

[3] Perhaps this is the Walī Beg mentioned in Blochmann 518. He was son of Payanda (the part-translator of Bābar's memoirs?) and nephew of Ḥājī Muḥammad Koka.

a number of Afghāns came out of Ḥiṣār and prepared to fight. Though the Afghāns were nearly 2,000 in number and the royal servants about 400, a great engagement took place and by Divine help the victory was gained, and seventy of the enemy were killed. Rustam Khān fled and strengthened the fort of Ḥiṣār. The contenders of fortune besieged it for twenty-three days. When Rustam found himself in difficulties he came to terms. He was sent to Court along with about 700 men of note in the charge of Mīr Laṭīf and Khwāja Qāsim Makhlaṣ, and he did homage along with many others. After some time an order was given that he should get a proper *jāgīr*, but on the condition that his sons should be guarded in Bikrām in order that they might enter on the path of favour and also that the road of vigilance and caution might not be abandoned. That simpleton rejected this condition, which was a means of confirming his obedience, and was about to abscond. When this was found out, he was imprisoned and committed to the charge of Beg Muḥammad Ishak Āqā.

353 One of the occurrences of this time was the affair of Qambar Dīwāna. The short account is that he was one of the common men or rather of the unknown men of the camp. When after the victory of Sihrind, the royal standards went on to Delhi, this Qambar gathered together a number of his own set of vagabonds and indulged in plunder and rapine. Booty was contiuually coming into his hands, and was distributed by him, and out of cunning, he was continually sending petitions to the Court. Proceeding from Sihrind he went fighting on and got possession of Sambal. There he established himself and sent his adopted son, who had received the name of 'Ārifu-l-lāh to Budāōn. Rai Ḥusain Jalwānī, who was a leading officer among the Afghāns, was there and was got rid of without a struggle. From there Qambar 'Alī went on to Kānt Gōla[1] and devastated that country. There he fought an irregular (*bītuzukāna*, without method) battle with Rukn Khān a leading Afghān and was defeated. From there he came to Budāōn. Though this madman was always sending petitions and making representations of obedience and good

[1] Kānt o Gola, Blochmann 373. They are in Rohilkand, and nearly correspond to Shāhjahānpūr. Elliot V. 498 note, and his Supp. Glossary II. 167.

service, his words and his deeds did not agree. He extended his foot beyond his carpet and made men Khāns and Sulṭāns of his own motion, and gave them standards and drums! Frenzy took possession of him and often from madness or assumed madness and fraud, he gave up his own house to be plundered. There continually appeared in him irregular proceedings which were allied to madness. When then facts repeatedly came to the notice of His Majesty he issued an order to 'Alī Qulī Khān Shaibānī to send him to Court, and to punish him if he resisted. Just when the madman, having been defeated by Rukn Khān, had come to Budāōn, 'Alī Qulī Khān after having settled the affairs of Mīrat came to Sambal. After arranging matters there he came to Budāōn. Though he sent a person to call him, Qambar did not appear, and said "Just as you are a slave of the king, so am I one of the office-bearers of the expedition, and I have got this province by the sword." At last 'Alī Qulī Khān took to arms and when Qambar was defeated, he took refuge in the fort of Budāōn, and sent a petition to Court. When His Majesty got this account of him, he sent Qāsim Makhlaṣ to encompass him with favours and to bring him to kiss the threshold. Before Qāsim had reached Budaōn, and brought this message of deliverance, 'Alī Qulī Khān had killed him. The short account of this is that when Qambar strengthened the fort, and the siege was being protracted, 'Alī Qulī Khān sent to him Muḥammad Beg Turkamān and Mullā Ghiāṣu-d-din. He imprisoned these envoys, and they secretly won 354
over a number of people to their side and having by craft overcome the garrison, they made Qambar a prisoner. 'Alī Qulī Khān sent his head to Court. The just heart of the king was grieved at this and he sent a firmān of rebuke to 'Alī Qulī Khān. He asked why he went to war when he (Qambar) was making proffers of obedience and wished to submit, and why did he kill him without orders after getting him into his power? His Majesty repeatedly said to those near him that he had wished to see this man and that if he had found on the tablet of his forehead truth and rectitude, he would have shown him favour and have educated him.

One of the occurrences of this time was the ingratitude of M. Sulaimān. The brief account of this is that when the royal standards went off to India, Tardī Beg Khān, who held Andarāb and Ishkamish in his *jāgīr*, was ordered to join. Muqīm Khān remained behind to look after the *jāgīr.* M. Sulaimān thought this a good opportunity to get hold of the territories. First, he tried craft, and sought to win over Muqīm Khān to his side. When this failed, the Mīrzā threw off the mask and besieged Andarāb. Muqīm Khān was compelled to come out with his family, and by fighting his way through he got away from that dangerous spot and came to Kābul. One of the occurrences of this time was the killing by Ḥaidar Muḥammad Khān Akhta Begī of Ghāzī Khān[1] the father of that Ibrāhīm who had had an itching desire for a throne. The story is as follows: When Ḥaidar Muḥammad Khān was sent to Biāna, Ghāzī Khān, who was the governor, could not resist and took refuge in the fort. Relying upon the promises and engagements which were held out by Ḥaidar Muḥammad, he came out; but Ḥaidar Muḥammad fixed his eyes on his goods and chattels and broke his promise, and put him to death with the sword of injustice. When His Majesty Jahānbānī heard of this, it did not commend itself to his just mind. As he (*i.e.*, Humāyūn) was at a distance, and had only recently come to India he ostensibly refrained from inflicting punishment on him but he announced that Ḥaidar would never again bind[2] on his belt. And in truth what the fate-interpreting tongue had uttered remained in force till he left this world. Shihabu-d-dīn Aḥmad Khān who was the Mīr Bīyūtāt (*i.e.*, officer in charge of buildings, &c.), was sent to inquire into the matter and to appraise the property. His Majesty went on, in ways well-pleasing to God, in taking care of his subjects, in building up the world, and in giving repose to mankind.

---

[1] In B.M. Add. 27,247 the words are differently and more grammatically arranged. The Ibrāhīm here referred to is the Ibrāhīm Khān Sūr who is described in text p. 339 as having contended for the throne of India with Sikandar and as having been defeated by him near Agra.

[2] Apparently the prophecy was that his arm would wither. Bayāzīd tells us that Ḥaidar's arm became useless. Perhaps this was ascribed to Humāyūn's prophecy or curse, but Bayāzīd says it was in consequence of a wound that he received in Afghanistān. It seems that Humāyūn was regarded as one who had the power of imprecating disaster on those who had offended him. Another instance is given by Jauhar and Gulbadan Begam as having occurred in Sind.

# CHAPTER LX.

## Expedition of His Majesty the Shāhinshāh to the Panjāb in accordance with the orders of His Majesty Jahānbānī Jinnat Āshayānī. 355

During this time that the world-conquering soul of His Majesty Jahānbānī was managing with justice the territories of India, unpleasant reports about Shāh Abū-l-Ma'āli came to the effect that being intoxicated with the harmful wine of the world he was troubling the people, and was conducting himself in ways contrary to the king's commands. As His Majesty Jahānbānī had a special regard for him he considered such reports as contrary to the truth and as inventions of the envious and malignant. But at length it was noised in the royal camp that Sikandar had come out from the hills and it became certain that this infatuated *Sayyidzāda* had without authority severed Farḥat Khān from the governorship of Lahore and had appointed one of his own creatures in his room. Also that he was laying hands on the royal treasure. By Divine inspiration the resolution became fixed in His Majesty Jahānbānī's holy soul, which was a mirror showing what was right for country and empire, that the Panjāb, which is one of the great provinces of India, should be made illustrious by the blessing of the protection and government of His Majesty the Shāhinshāh, and that, if it seemed proper, Abū-l-Ma'ālī should have Ḥiṣār[1] and its neighbourhood. Moreover as he was sending about this time for the chaste ladies from Kābul it was right that the Panjāb should be in the possession of His Majesty

---

[1] Ḥiṣār, we are told in the previous chapter, had been conferred on Akbar, and the meaning apparently is that if Akbar (and Bairām) thought proper, Ḥiṣār might now be given to Abū-l-Ma'ālī, in exchange for the Panjāb.

the Shāhinshāh's servants. Though the army was large enough to quell Sikandar yet for political and personal reasons the name "auxiliary" was used. In the beginning of the year 963, November, 1555, in an auspicious hour which befitted the accession to the throne of the seven climes, His Majesty the Shāhinshāh the Divine nursling was appointed (to the Panjāb) according to the rules of sovereignty and splendour. Bairām Khān was nominally appointed as guardian of His Highness, but in fact the education of that support of dominion was committed to the fortunate auspices of His Majesty the Shāhinshāh. A number of loyal and faithful followers attended on his stirrup.

When they arrived at Sihrind the royal servants who were in Ḥiṣār Fīrūza obtained the blessing of service and were delighted. In that auspicious station Ustād 'Azīz Sistānī who for his good service and loyalty had received the title of Rūmī Khān [1] and had no equal in pyrotechny and in shooting with guns had the felicity of entering the Shāhinshāh's service. It was here that his shooting began and in a short time he became a master in this strange craft,
356 just as he is a master in every act and science. And wondrous masterpieces, such that volumes could not contain the accounts of them, were displayed by this exhibitor of perfections in this as in other acts. What shall I say or what shall I write about the totality of this holy personality? For without exception when any person who shall have studied some particular art or science, whether with mature scientists, or with master craftsmen, and whether in whole or in part, and have acquired practice therein by studying for years with able teachers enters the service of this scrutinising intellect and universal genius, he gets lost in contemplating his abundant knowledge and is struck with astonishment. And he thinks to himself that apparently His Majesty has spent all his time in nothing but this art. But afterwards he says no one could acquire such skill, it must be the gift of God! And one of the wonderful things is that he enters into contradictory dispositions and varied characters in one and the same *seance*, for this is not difficult to the world-adorning mind. What capacity have philosophers, or learned men,

---

1 Perhaps the Rūmī Khān Ḥalabī, *i.e.*, of Aleppo, mentioned in Blochmann 441.

or artists to keep his company except for a time and on their own subject? Such lofty understanding and such wide intelligence are not within human powers. Rather the power of an angel would not suffice. May Almighty God long preserve this glorious pearl for the alignment (*intizām*) of mortals!

## CHAPTER LXI.

### Brief account of His Majesty Jahanbānī Jannat Āshayānī, and description of some of his remarkable inventions and regulations.

As the affairs of the Panjāb had been happily arranged by the expedition of His Majesty the Shāhinshāh there, His Majesty Jahānbānī remained in Delhi and employed himself in the work of political administration. He gave his attention to the reconstruction of the territories, the extirpation of enemies and the conquest of other provinces. He repeatedly said that he would make several seats of government, and labour for the regulation of India. Delhi, Agra, Jaunpūr, Māndū, Lahore, Qanauj and other suitable places would be chosen and in every place there would be an army under the charge of a prudent, farseeing, subject-cherishing, and just officer, so that there should be no need then for an auxiliary force. And he would not keep more than 12,000 horse attached to his own person. He also used to say that he would have embroidered gold and silver seats prepared to be used in the public assemblies by the princes and by such men of his entourage as were to be exalted by special honour so that they might sit upon them when an order to that effect was given. For it was likely that the affections of the great and worldly,
357 who had not reached the palace of loyalty but still remained in the bazar of traffic, and of loss and gain, would not be captured merely by gifts of property, and that until their honour and prestige were increased they would not be won over.

From the beginning of his career till now his mind was exercised in strange inventions and in showing forth recondite truths. Among these was this that at the time when His Majesty Gētī Sitānī Firdūs Makānī proceeded from Kabul to Qandahār he left His Majesty Jahānbānī in Kābul to look after affairs. One day His Majesty was riding in the environs of the city and exploring the plains and meadows. On the way he said to Maulānā Rūḥ Ullāh, who was his teacher, "it has occurred to me to take an augury from the names of three persons whom I may find on the road, and I shall build the foundations of my dominion (*daulat*) thereon." The Maulānā said the name of one person would be enough. He replied "A secret inspiration has communicated itself to me." After going a little distance a wayfarer of mature age appeared and when they asked him his name, he replied "Murād Khwāja." After him another man appeared who was driving an ass loaded with wood. When they asked him his name he said "Daulat Khwāja." Upon this the inspired tongue (of Humāyūn) said that "if the name of the next person that comes be Sāādat Khwāja it will be a strange and beautiful coincidence, and the star of joy (*murād*) will ascend from the horizon of auspiciousness (*sa'ādat*)." At that very moment a man (a boy, in Khwāndamīr's account) appeared, who was grazing some cattle, and when they asked him what his name was he replied "Sa'ādat Khwāja." The servants in attendance were astonished at this marvel, and all felt assured that the lord of auspicious fortune would by Divine favour attain to lofty rank and become possessed of dominion.[1]

When these mysterious glad tidings were fulfilled and the rose garden of hope was made fresh and verdant by the stream of justice he founded his affairs, sacred and secular on joy (*murād*), dominion (*daulat*) and auspiciousness (*sa'ādat*). And he divided all the servants of the fortunate threshold, or rather all the inhabitants of his dominions into three classes. He called his brothers, and other relatives, his officers, his viziers, and all his soldiers *Ahl-i-daulat*. For it was clear that without the help of this body of men the ladder of dominion and fortune could not be climbed. He called the philosophers, the 'ulamā, the chancellors (*ṣadūr*), the sayyids, the shaikhs, the Qāzīs, the poets and the other learned men, the judges, nobles and skilful persons *Ahl-i-sa'ādat*, because the honouring of these auspicious persons, and the association with them were a means of gaining everlasting auspiciousness. He called architects, painters,

[1] This story is given in Elliot V. 118 and 236 who remarks that it first appears in Khwāndamīr. Niẓāmu-d-dīn and Ferishta assign it to the period just before Humāyūn's conquest of India. Khwāndamīr calls the teacher Maslīhu-d-dīn Rūḥu-lla

358 musicians and singers *Ahl-i-murād*, because they were the delight of all the world. Similarly he divided the days of the week among the *Ahl-i-daulat, sa'ādat and murād*, to wit, Saturday and Thursday belonged to Ahl-i-sa'ādat, and on these two days his attention was given to the regulators of knowledge and devotion. The reason of appropriating those two days to the *Ahl-i-sa'ādat* was that Saturday is assigned to Saturn, and Saturn is the patron of shaikhs and ancient families. Thursday is Jupiter's day, and that is the star of learned men and of other noble orders. Sunday and Tuesday were assigned to the *Ahl-i-daulat*, and on them, royal affairs, and the management of world-government were transacted. The reason for thus assigning these two days was that Sunday appertains to the sun whose rays regulate rule and sovereignty, while Tuesday is Mars's day and Mars is the patron of soldiers. Monday and Tuesday were days of joy (*murād*). On these days boon-companions and favourites and others of the *Ahl-i-murād* were treated with special favour. The point in selecting these two days was that Monday is the Moon's day, and Wednesday is Mercury's. Both of these have a special connection with household matters (*amūr-i-biyūtat*). Friday (*jam'a*), in accordance with its name, applied to all objects, and on it all the classes of humanity participated in the royal bounty.

One of the arrangements which characterised the *dīwān*-days was that when the throne of the *khilāfat* was set up and His Majesty being seated thereon was advising the *Dīvān*, information was given to the people by beat of drum, and when he left the *Dīvān*, cannoniers announced the fact to the subjects by the discharge of cannon. And on these days keepers of the wardrobe [1] would bring several suits of apparel, (*dast-i-khelāt*), and the treasurers several bags of gold near to the palace, so that their might be no stoppage to the gifts and largesses. Several brave men stood armed, and with cuirasses on their breasts.

Another of his inventions was that of three golden arrows which were an allusion to the three divisions [2] of *sa'ādat, daulat* and *murād*. Each of these was assigned to one of the leaders of the three classes in order that he should supervise the works thereof. And it was provided that so long as each of the holders of these arrows

---

[1] *Karkīrāqcīān*, Blochmann 87 *n.* 2 nd 616.

[2] *Sahm* which means both a division or segment, and an arrow.

exerted himself in the management of the duties appertaining to that division (*sahm*), which consisted in acting according to the will of God and in loyalty, he should be the subject of favour and should be secure on the *masnad* of authority. But if ever he should become intoxicated by the wine of grandeur and transgress the path of justice, or from some evil motive should avert his eyes from loyalty,
and should restrict his zeal to the acquisition of wealth, the arrow of **359**
his design would not reach the target of success and the writing of deposition would be drawn on the page of his condition, and he would meet with a fitting retribution. Mīr Khwānd the chief chronicler (*Mīr Muwarrikh*) has recorded in his *Qānūn-i-humāyūnī*[1] that in the time of his service the arrow of *sa'ādat* was entrusted with absolute authority to the most excellent of the masters of learning and perfection—Maulānā Farghali,[2] and the opening and shutting, the contraction and expansion, of the affairs of Sayyids, Shaikhs, 'Ulamā, Qāẓīs, and teachers, and the inquiry into the claims of ecclesiastics (*arbāb-i-'amāīm, lit.* wearers of large turbans), and the appointment and removal of those entrusted with the works of religion, and the assignment of stipends and *siyūrghāls* were all in his charge. The arrow of *daulat* was with the prop of sovereignty—Āmīr Hindū Beg, and the shutting and opening, the binding and unloosing of the great affairs of the officers and viziers, and of all the government-clerks, and those entrusted with civil affairs, and the fixing of the pay of the soldiers, and the appointment of the household servants rested with him. The arrow of *murād* and of the works of architecture was assigned to Amīr Waisī. He had to look after the buildings and the arrangement of matters of pomp and pageantry and to care for the perfecting of the things of splendour and glory.

Another of his inventions was the distribution of arrows into twelve classes. Each order of men was assigned to an arrow. The arrangement was as follows: The twelfth arrow, which was of the finest gold, was reserved for the royal quiver, *i.e.*, for Humāyūn and Akbar. The eleventh was for the brothers and other kinsmen and such of the sons of kings as were servants of the threshold of dominion. The tenth arrow was for the Sayyids, the Shaikhs, and the

---

[1] *Cf.* Elliot V. 116 and B.M. MS. Or. 1762, and Add. 30,774.

[2] This is the man of whom Haidar Mīrzā writes so severely, and who was drowned at Causā.

'Ulamā. The ninth for the great officers. The eighth was for the intimates (*maqarrabān*) and the *ankaciān* who held *manṣabs* (offices). The seventh for the other *ankaciān*.[1] The sixth for the heads of[2] clans. The fifth for the distinguished young volunteers. The fourth for the cashiers (Blochmann, 45). The third for the soldiers (*jūānān-i-jargah*). The second for artificers.[3] The first for doorkeepers,[4] watchmen, and the like.

Another of his inventions was his dividing the department of State into four classes corresponding to the four elements, *viz.*, Fire, Air, Water, and Earth. And for the transaction of the business of

---

[1] The word in text is unintelligible and is no doubt corrupt. A footnote says that on the margin of one MS. there is written ایچکی īckī, which is explained as meaning head-writer. Perhaps the copyist thought of, or wrote bitikciān, official writers, see Jarrett II. 47. The *n* in the text is clearly wrong, and this letter does not occur in A.F.'s original, *viz.*, <u>Kh</u>wāndamīr, who has ایچکیان Zekiān, B.M. MS. Or. 1762, p. 138, Zeker gives ایچي meaning a brother-in-law, and perhaps this is the word, or it may be connected with ایچکار īckār, inner, and consequently intimate, or ever with ایچکی Ickī drink, or with ایچکره meaning elegant, slender. From its following *maqarrabān* it clearly means intimate associates of some kind.

[2] *Sar<u>kh</u>ailān-i-qabāīl*. Elliot V. 123, renders the corresponding passage of <u>Kh</u>wāndamīr "the *harems* and the well-behaved female attendants." But <u>Kh</u>wāndamīr's words are *mat'alliq ast ba sar<u>kh</u>ailān qabāīl u yuzbakīān* (*i.e.*, Uzbeks) and apparently the 12 divisions had reference only to males. The fifth which Elliot renders young maidservants is in A.F.'s text *ikka jūānān-i-bahadur*, and perhaps means the volunteers or independent warriors (*Ekkahā*) referred to in Erskine's Supplementary Remarks, Hist. II. 541, as men who joined the service, either alone, or with a few followers, as volunteer] soldiers of fortune. Perhaps these Ekkahā were the men afterwards called Ahadī or Aḥadī in Akbar's time, see Blochmann, 20*n*. and 161. Ika یکه is a Mongolian word, and means great. Quatremére N. and E., XIV.

[3] *<u>Sh</u>āgird pe<u>sh</u>agān*. This expression is often used for civilians or laymen attached to an army, such as shopkeepers, citizens, and the like.

[4] <u>Kh</u>wandāmīr has the word *darbānān* but he has not the word *pāsbānān*. Instead of *pāsbānān* he has *sārbānān*. See B.M. MSS. Or. 1762, p. 133 and Or. 5850, p. 196. The pages which should contain the account of the arrows are wanting in the translation in the B.M. MS. Add. 30774. There is a gap after p. 76 or 49*b*. A note at the end of Or. 5850 makes the curious mis-statement that the work is by Gulbadan Begam!

each of these four departments a vizier was appointed. The artiller and the arrangements of armour and arms and of other things with which fire had to do were called the Fire Department. Khwāja 'Abdu l-Mulk was appointed to be vizier of it. The wardrobe (*karqirāqkhāna*), the kitchen, the stable, and the necessary management of the mules and camels was called the Air Department. The charge of it was given to Khwāja Laṭif Ullāh. The arrangements 360
of the *Sharbatkhāna*, the wine-cellar (*sūcīkhāna*), and of canals was called the Water Department. Khwāja Ḥasan was appointed the vizier thereof. The affairs of agriculture and of buildings[1] and the administration of exchequer-lands (*ṣabṭ-i-khāliṣāt*) and of some of the buildings (*biyūtāt*) were called the Earth Department. The vizier was Khwāja Jalālu-d-dīn Mīrzā Beg. In every one of the departments one of the Amīrs was employed. For instance, Amīr Nāṣir Qulī was the Mīr Sarkār, or head-officer, of the Fire Department and always wore red.

Another of the inventions of this time was that four large barges were set in the river Jamūna (Jumna) and that the master-carpenters constructed[2] on each of them a *cārṭāq* (a square house) of two storeys and of very elegant shape. The barges were so joined together that the *cārṭāqs* faced one another. Between every two of these four barges another *ṭāq* (platform) was made[3] and thus there appeared an octagonal reservoir between the barges.

---

[1] *'Imārāt.* Perhaps the word here means colonization or the settling of ryots, for we have buildings (*bīyūtāt*) mentioned immediately afterwards.

[2] The text says that the carpenters made the barges too, but I presume that the skill of the *ustādān-i-najjār* was chiefly shown in constructing the houses upon them. The *cārtāqs* are perhaps square buildings or they may be buildings with four pillars, see Vullers *s.v. cārṭāq*. But, as Quatremére points out N. and E., XIV. 498, the word *cār*, four, is often vaguely used.

[3] *Lit.* were by the field of power made into fact. A.F. has been simply copying Khwāndamīr, and I confess I do not fully understand the description, or how the tank or reservoir was octagonal. I suppose, however, that the four barges formed a square and that the space between them, which was probabl planked over, made a portion of the river into a tank. The corresponding passage of Khwāndamīr is thus translated by Munshī Sadasūk Lāl, p. 90, of B.M. MS. Add. 30, 774:—

"The four boats which, according to royal directions, were made by the most clever carpenters in the water of the Jumna. In each of these boats there was made a large room

Another of his excellent inventions was his arrangement of shops and the putting up of a bazar on boats. This increased the amazement of the rare of intellect. In the year 939, 1532-33, when His Majesty went from Fīrūzābād-i-Dihlī (*i.e.*, Delhi) to Agra, the capital, by way of the river, and was accompanied by most of the Amīrs and pillars of the State and all the *īkcīān*[1] and officers, a bazar of this kind was made and carried down the Jamūnā. Everyone could get what he wanted in that bazar.

In like manner the royal gardeners made, in accordance with orders, a garden on the river.

Another of his inventions was a movable[2] bridge.

Another of his wonderful inventions was a movable palace. This palace was composed of three storeys which were of cut beams. The master-carpenters had so joined the pieces together that whoever looked at them thought that the whole was of one piece. Whenever they wanted they could take it to pieces and convey it to any country. And the ladders (or steps) to the upper storey were so constructed that they could be opened out or shut up at pleasure.

One of the wonderful inventions of that holy mind was a cap (*tāj*) which was alike magnificent and agreeable to wear. The border (or margin) which went round the *tāj* had two divisions (*furja*), and each of these was in the form of the figure seven (V), and thus by there being two figures 7 (VV) the number 77 was produced, which

(having four doors or pillars) of two storeys exceedingly nice. The boats were joined together in such a manner that the four apartments stood opposite each other, and by the junction of each two boats another apartment was produced and between all the four a figure resembling a reservoir of octagonal form was made." Price says: "The four vessels were connected by a strong platform or some species of gallery in such a manner that the pavilions were placed in a situation exactly opposite to each other, perhaps in the form of a lozenge, and between each of the vessels was interposed an additional pavilion, making altogether the number of eight and forming in the centre of the whole a beautiful tank or pond of water of eight sides."

[1] This is the word *ankacīān* already referred to. Possibly it may be here a mistake for *bitikcīān* or writers.

[2] This is described at length by Khwāndamīr, p. 139*a*, of Persian text and 112 of translation. It is perhaps characteristic of A.F. that this, perhaps, the only really useful work of Humāyūn, is left undescribed by him.

was the numerical value of the word *'izz*. Here it was called the *tāj-i-'izzat* or cap of honour. This was invented in Badakhshān [1] and 361
when His Majesty came to Agra and appeared before His Majesty Getī Sitānī Firdūs Makānī the latter was much pleased.

Another of his inventions was a tent (*khirgā*) which had twelve partitions corresponding to the signs of the Zodiac. Each mansion (*burj*) had lattices (*pinjarahā*) [2] through the interstices of which there shone the light of the stars of dominion. And there was another tent [3] which was like the Heaven of Heavens which encompasses the heaven of the fixed stars. This surrounded the other tents and as the crystalline sphere (*i.e.*, the Heaven of Heavens) is undotted (with stars) so this tent was without lattices.

One of his pleasure-increasing inventions was the "carpet of mirth" (*basāṭ-i-nishāṭ*). This was a round carpet corresponding to the orbits of the spheres and the elemental spheres. The first circle which corresponded to the crystalline sphere was white, the second blue (*kabūd*), the third black, like Saturn, the fourth, which was the house of Jupiter, was light brown (*ṣandali*), the fifth, which was related to Mars, was ruby-coloured, the sixth, which was the house of the Sun, was golden, the seventh, which was the house of Venus, was bright green, the eighth, which was the station of

---

[1] The *tāj-i-'izzat* according to Khwāndamīr was not used only by Humāyūn, but was for the nobles also. Only Humāyūn's was all of one colour, whereas their's were of several colours. He may have invented it in Badakhshān, but the chronogram of its construction, *tāj-i-s'aādat*, given by Khwāndamīr yields 939, or two years after Bābar's death.

[2] Blochmann 225, account of *pinjarahsāz*, or lattice-work.

[3] Khwāndamīr's description is at p. 122 of translation and 140 of Persian text. "A large tent which like the empyrean heaven that covers the inferior ones surrounded all the petty tents and took them within itself like a cover. Like the crystalline sphere, on which there are no spots of the fixed stars and the planets, this had also no lattice or balcony round it." Khwāndamīr explains that the outer tent was distinct from the inner one and could be used separately. The inner tent which represented the twelve signs of the Zodiac was perhaps the tent mentioned by Gulbadan Begam and called by her *mihr-āmīz*, *i.e.*, associated with the sun. The word which Sadasūk Lāl has translated balcony is *qan'aāt*, so perhaps the outer tent had no flaps or side-walls.

Mercury, was bluish (*sūsanī, i.e.*, lily, or iris-coloured). For the nature of Mercury is composite and when blue and rose are mixed the result is *sūsanī*. And the reason why *sūsanī* was chosen in preference to other colours was that several philosophers have called the colour of Mercury that of collyrium (*kuḥlī*), and the *sūsanī* is nearer to collyrium than other mixed colours are. The ninth circle, which was the station of the Moon, was white. After the circle of the Moon came the region (*kura, i.e.*, globe or sphere) of fire and air, then that of earth and water. The inhabited quarter of the earth was divided into seven climes. He himself occupied the golden circle (*i.e.*, the one consecrated to the Sun) and there he adorned the throne of the *k͟hilāfat*. Each section (or group) was ordered to sit in accordance with the one of the seven planets which was appropriate to it in the circle which corresponded therewith. Thus, the Indian officers sate in the circle of Saturn, while the Sayyids and the 'Ulamā sate in the circle of Jupiter. The persons who occupied each circle made use of dice, on each side of which there was represented a human figure in a different position. According to each one's throw he assumed a position which corresponded to the figure that turned up. For example, if a standing figure turned up he stood, if a seated, he sate down, and if a reclining one he lay down. This was a means of increasing mirth.[1]

Another of his excellent devices was the wearing of clothes each day corresponding to the colour of the planet of that day. Thus on Sunday he wore a yellow robe, which is the colour appropriated to the Sun, who is the regent thereof. On Monday[2] he wore

---

1 Perhaps some will think that Humāyūn's courtiers, like Mr. Peter Magnus' friends, were easily amused. This carpet is described by K͟hwāndamīr, Persian text 155, translation 206: It appears to have been of enormous size, for, he says, that each of the seven circles had 200 grades (?) so that in all 1,400 persons could sit in it. The bright green, *sabzrōs͟han*, which is given as the colour of the circle of Venus, is said in the dictionaries to be the name of a kind of pigeon. Blochmann, pp. 294, 299, renders *sabz* by "bluish." Sadasūk Lāl renders *sūsanī* by violet. The expression *umrā-i-Hindī* used with reference to the circle of Saturn means Indian-born officers whether Hindus or Muḥammadans, for K͟hwāndamīr says that the *Mas͟hāīk͟h* also sat there.

2 K͟hwāndamīr says that when the moon was near the full Humāyūn wore white.

green, which is appropriate to the Moon, and so on. Another of his inventions was the drum[1] of justice. If the claim of anyone related to some dispute he beat the drum once. If his grievance consisted 36
in the non-receipt of stipend, or wages he struck twice. If his goods and chattels (*māl-u-jihāt*) had been seized by oppression, or had been stolen, he complained by beating the drum thrice. If he had a claim of blood against anyone he beat the drum loudly four times.

The notes of the inventive genius of this *khedive* of holy type are many, but the above are enough to enable the understanding and the acute to comprehend the rare jewels of his soul. It is now better to abridge words and to come to the proper subject.

---

[1] This is an institution as old as Nūshirwān. Khwāndāmir makes the next sentence more intelligible by prefixing the word *andak* small to the word *mukhāṣamat*, dispute or suit. In the Lucknow Museum there are a number of large drums which came from Agra, and are said to belong to Akbar's time. Perhaps they are the remains of one of Humāyūn's institutions.

## CHAPTER LXII.

### INCIDENCE OF A FLASH OF INDICATION OF A JOURNEY TO THE WORLD OF HOLINESS ON THE INWARD MIRROR OF HIS MAJESTY JAHĀNBĀNĪ JINNAT ĀSHIYĀNĪ, AND HIS DEPARTURE FOR THAT WORLD.

Let it not be concealed from inquiring minds that at about the time when His Majesty the Shāhinshāh, the young shoot of the parterre of insight, obtained leave to go to the Panjāb, there frequently rose on the lips of His Majesty Jahānbānī Jinnat Āshiyānī the mention of a departure to the world of holiness. Contrary to his laudable habit of regarding such references as unbecoming (*makrūh*), as being repugnant to the management of affairs, and of avoiding them in conversation, he now took pleasure in speaking on the subject. Seemingly the flash had pictured itself in the antechamber of his mystery-knowing heart. Among such references there was this that one day he quoted with commendation the true words of His Majesty Getī-sitānī Firdūs-Makānī, when he remarked in a meeting of friends that a servant of his used to say that whenever he saw the graves in Ghaznīn[1] he felt an inclination to die. Following up this, His Majesty would say that when he contemplated[2] Delhi and its shrines the words recurred to his memory, and he thought how sweet they were! At about the same time and when he was proceeding towards the eternal world he said to several of his familiars: "This day after paying my morning devotions a mysterious thing occurred and a secret inspiration brought this quatrain on my lips:"—

[1] "Here (Ghaznīn) is the last resting-place of Ḥakīm Sanāī and many other saintly personages." A.F. in Āīn, Jarrett, II, 408.

[2] Probably Humāyūn was referring to a visit which he paid to the shrines and graves in and round Delhi in company with Sidi 'Alī shortly before his death. See p. 53 of the Admiral's book.

*Verse.*

"O God, make me wholly Thine.
Acquaint me with Thine attributes.
Tyrannous Reason hath crippled my soul.
Call me Thine own madman[1] and set me free."

Tears fell from his truth-seeing eyes while he was reciting these lines, and complete detachment was manifested on his irradiated brows. About the time, too, when the Court was at Delhi, the eye-brightener of the *khilāfat*, to wit, His Majesty the Shāhinshāh, one night beheld in a dream that someone was pulling up his[2] musky (*i.e.*, black) locks. When he awoke he told the dream to Māham 363
Anaga, the mother of Adham Khān. She summoned all the skilled interpreters and asked them what the dream portended. When this question was put to His Majesty Jahānbānī he said: "Evil will be far from his (Akbar's) head." Afterwards he told them quietly of his own inevitable doom, and administered consolation to them. Constantly during those days he was uttering words which had for the organs of the farseeing among the courtiers the savour of a passage from this transitory world which all must quit, and which divided[3] the joints and marrow of the faithful of soul. Among other things, he wrote with his own hand on the arch of his portico these opening lines of a poem by Shaikh Āẕarī:—[4]

[1] *Cf.* Erskine, Hist., 535, note. His translation and account of the circumstances differ somewhat from the text. Apparently the poet contrasts the cold light of reason with the ecstacy of madness (or love). The translation in Erskine's version of the Akbarnāma in the B.M. is nearer the original.

[2] The text has *ānḥaẓrat*, which presumably stands for Humāyūn, but a footnote says that several MSS. have *īshān*, and all the MSS. that I have examined in the B.M., I.O., and R.A.S. have *īshān*, and so has the Lucknow edition. I have therefore adopted the variant. I think that what Akbar saw must have been the pulling of his own locks, otherwise there would have been no cause for alarm on his account, and it is hardly likely that his father, then a man of 50, would have black hair.

[3] I have paraphrased the passage. The literal translation is: "The faithful of soul were cut to pieces."

[4] The poetical name of Jalāl-ud-dīn Ḥamza of Isfarain or Mihrjān near Nīshāpūr. He died in 866 A.H. Beale's Or. Dict., 90. See also Rieu., Cat. I, 43*a*. According to the account there Āẕarī, who took his poetical name from the month of his birth, was born at Marv and died in 866 A.H.=

*Verse.*

I've heard that on this gilded dome (the sky) 't is writ
The end[1] of all things is praiseworthy.

He also when near his departure reduced his consumption of opium, so much so that he said to his intimates "We'll see for how many more days two or three pellets (*habb*) will suffice." He had seven days' divided supply and wrapped in paper, and made over to his body-servants, and he said to them "this is all the opium we shall eat." On the day which was the first stage of his journey to the region of holiness and detachment, there remained four pellets. He sent for these, and partook[2] thereof in rosewater.

At the close[3] of Friday Rabī'-al-awwal 963, Shāh

1461-62. Badaūnī, III, 193, says that Maulānā Bekasī is the authority for this story. He quotes the couplet.

1 Another rendering might be: "To meditate on the end of all things is praiseworthy." Price translates: "Of all mankind the end is happy."

2 The meaning is not quite clear. Probably A.F. means that Hūmāyān took one of the four pellets along with rosewater. It is hardly likely that he would take four all at once. The day when he sent for the opium is clearly, I think, the day of the accident, and not of the death, and the time would be in the course of the day and before the accident, which occurred at evening. Probably the number four is dwelt upon as indicating that Hūmāyūn had set aside the exact number of pellets that would last till his death. If Friday was the day of the accident and he took one pill on that day, and survived till Monday, as Sidi 'Alī says, this would be the case. According to other authorities he died on the evening of Sunday, the 26th January, or 13 Rabī'-al-awwal. This is the date given in the Bādshāhnāma of 'Abdu-l-Ḥamīd, Bib. Ind. ed., p. 63.

3 *Akhir-i-rūz.* But perhaps the īẓāfat is wrong, and the translation should be: "At length, on Friday," &c. A.F. does not give the day of the month; but, as he says later on, that the officers concealed the accident (or at least its seriousness) for seventeen days and then proclaimed Akbar on 28 Rabī'-al-awwal, we may take it that the fall occurred on Friday, the 11th Rabī'-al-awwal, corresponding to 24th January, 1556. See Mrs. Beveridge's translation of Count Noer's Akbar, I. 67, note. The date, 11 Rabī'-al-awwal, given at the end of Stewart's translation of Jauhar is not in the original, and the whole sentence is an addition. There is a good deal of discrepancy about the dates of Humāyūn's fall and death, and on these points reference may be made to the note above quoted and also to Mr. C. J. Rodgers' note in the J.A.S.B. for 1871, Vol. XL, p. 133, and to Mr.

Budāgh,[1] 'Ālam[2] Shāh, Beg Mūlak,[3] and others who had returned

Blochmann's remarks thereon. A.F.'s statement that the fall occurred on a Friday is supported by the circumstance that a number of worshippers were assembled at the adjoining mosque, as would naturally be the case on a Friday, and also by the testimony of Kātibi-Rūmī, the Turkish admiral, Sīdī 'Alī Rëīs. He was in Delhi at the time; and, though he does not expressly say so, he was apparently present at the last audience. His words (Vambéry's translation, Luzac, 1899, p. 55) are: "All was ready for the start (the Admiral's). Humāyūn had given audience on Friday evening, when, upon leaving his castle of pleasure, the Muezzin, announced the Ezan just as he was descending the staircase. It was his wont, whenever he heard the summons, to bow the knee in holy reverence. He did so now, but unfortunately fell down several steps, and received great injuries to his head and arm." Truly the proverb rightly says, 'There is no guarding against fate.'

"Everything was confusion in the palace, but for two days they kept the matter secret. It was announced to the outer world that the sovereign was in good health, and alms were distributed amongst the poor. On the third day, however, that was on the Monday, he died of his wounds."

It seems to me probable that the Turkish Admiral is the person referred to by A.F. as Caghatāī Khān. No officer of Humāyūn's or Akbar's of that name is mentioned anywhere, and Sīdī 'Alī may have got the sobriquet of Caghatāī Khān on account of his proficiency in the Caghatāī language. See the Turkish publisher's preface, Vambéry, l.c., p. XVII. Sīdī 'Alī, too, had just come from Gujrāt. Another reason for believing Friday to be the day, is that Friday was Humāyūn's day for holding receptions and granting audiences. *See* A.N.Cap., LXII. On the whole then, unless it can be established astronomically that Venus did not rise on Friday, 24th January 1556, I think we may take that to be the day of the accident. This date is further corroborated by Sīdī 'Alī's statement that he left for Lahore on a Thursday in the middle of Rabī'-al-awwal. He did not leave till after the death, and Thursday would be the 17th Rabī'-al-awwal. Vambéry's translation, contrary to that of Diez, makes Thursday the day of the Admiral's arrival at Lahore, but this is clearly wrong.

With regard to the place and circumstances of the accident there is

[1] Blochmann, 371 and 382.

[2] If this was Khān 'Ālam Calma Beg, Blochmann, 378, he must have returned from Mecca before Kāmrān's death. But perhaps it is not. 'Ālam Shāh is mentioned at p. 325 of text as one of those who accompanied Kāmrān to India.

[3] It would seem from this as if Beg Mūlak had repented and gone after Kāmrān.

from the Ḥijāz, and Caghatāī Khān and some men from Gujrāt came and made reports. Also Pahlwān Dōst Mīr Barr, and Maulānā Asad came from Kābul with representations from Mun'im Khān. At the end of the day he came out on the roof of the library which had recently been fitted up, and gave the people who were assembled at the chief mosque the blessing of performing homage (*kornish*). For a considerable time he asked questions about Holy Mecca and about Gujrāt and Kābul.

After that he sent for all the mathematicians, for it was expected that Venus would rise on that night and he wished to observe her.

---

a good account by Mr. Rodgers in the paper already referred to. He corrects the mistakes of Elphinstone and Marshman. I visited the place in September, 1899. The building is known as the Sher Mandal from having been built by Sher Shah and is described by Syed Ahmad in his Aṣār Ṣanādīd (*see* also Garçin de Tassy's translation). It is an octagonal building of red stone and has two storeys. But the first is now solid, *i.e.*, has no room in it. It has inside stairs leading up to the second storey, which is an octagonal room fitted with niches (*ṭāq*), which perhaps were used as bookshelves. From this two separate flights of steps lead up to the roof, on which there is a small open cupola supported on eight pillars. One of the flights is shown by the guides as that from which Humāyūn fell. There is a turn in the stairs and the steps are of granite, a foot high, and steep and narrow. The stairs open out, it should be stated, in the body of the roof, so that Humāyūn fell through the roof rather than off it. He certainly did not fall over the parapet. " The stairs come up on both sides of the cupola, in the space intervening between it and the parapet." (Rodgers). Presumably Humāyūn's intention was to sit down on the part of the roof which formed the first step of the stair, and to rest his feet on the second step *(Zīna-i-duwam)*. It was the cold weather and so he would naturally be wearing a long dressing-gown. The guides say that the body was wrapped in cotton. As we know from the Maaṣir Raḥīmī it was brought away from Delhi when Hīmūn defeated Tardī Beg and got possession of the city. It was kept for a time at Sirhind and then brought back and kept near the Purāna Qila' till the grand tomb, built by Humāyūn's widow, Ḥājī Begam, was ready.

The Sher Mandal is to the south of Delhi and about four miles from the railway station. It is near the Jamna and was still nearer it in old times. Hard by, is the Jama' Masjid of Sher Shāh, and Humāyūn's tomb is not far off. The reason probably why Hūmāyūn was then residing at the Sher Mandal was because that neighbourhood is the site of the city of Dīnpanāh, which was founded by Hūmāyūn in earlier and happier days.

It was his excellent intention that when Venus rose and the moment became auspicious he would hold a grand assembly and make promotions of officers. At the beginning of the evening he wished to descend and when he came to the second[1] step, a reciter (*muqrī*), by name Miskīn (wretched), raised an untimely call to prayer. His Majesty, out of respect to the call, wished to sit down where he was. As the steps *(darjāt)* of the stair *(zīnā.)* were sharp *(tez)* and the stones slippery *(laghzanda)* his blessed foot caught in the skirt of his robe at the moment of sitting down and his good staff slipped. He lost his feet and fell upon his head, his right temple receiving a severe blow, so that some drops of blood issued from his right ear. As he possessed a heart acquainted with mysteries he immediately, and in order that he might give comfort and also make dispositions for the world, sent an affectionate dispatch containing a report of his wel- 364
fare to the nursling of the light of fortune by the hands of Naẓr[2] Shaikh Cūlī.

One of the wondrous flashes of his (Akbar's) intelligence was that in the middle of that very day (the day of the accident, not of the announcement) he had[3] said to some of his suite that a great misfortune would happen to an eminent man and that probably he would die.

The loyalists who were on the spot endeavoured to conceal[4] the

---

1 *Zīna-i-duwum.* The exact meaning of the expression is doubtful. Naturally one would think that it referred to the second step of the top stair, but *zīna* means a stair rather than a step, and the word *darjāt* as used just below to mean the steps. Perhaps A.F. means the second flight of steps counting from below, or he may have supposed that the fall was from the lower or second flight of steps. The stairs are certainly very steep and awkward and might easily cause a nasty fall.

2 "The recital of the *āẓān* must be listened to with great reverence. If a person be walking at the time he should stand still; if reclining sit up." Hughes' Dict. of Islam, 286.

3 Bayāzīd enters him on his list as Shaikh Naẓr Cūlī Turkistānī and says that after the conquest of India Akbar made him Mīr 'Ādl. Presumably Naẓr was his name, and Cūlī his title, from having been with Humāyūn in the desert. The Mīrāt-i-'Ālam, B.M. Add., 7657, p. 971a, gives a copy of the letter which Naẓr Shaikh conveyed. See translation of it in Blochmann's remarks on Rodgers' paper l.c..

4 *Mīfarmūdand.* This is the formula used by A.F. when mentioning Akbar's utterances.

dreadful occurrence and took measures to send information to the heir-apparent of the *masnad* of the *khilāfat* and to collect the principal officers who had obtained leave to various parts of the kingdom. With extreme prudence they kept this life-destroying event from the public for seventeen days. Those who were present at court and the counsellors of the threshold of the *khilāfat, viz.*, Khizr Khwāja Khān, 'Alī Qulī Khān, Laṭīf Mīrzā, Khizr Khān Hazāra, Qūndūq Khān, Qambar 'Alī Beg, Ashraf Khān, Afẓal Khān, who were in the list of helpful ministers *(wuzrāī kifāyāt pēsha)* and Khwāja Ḥusain of Merv, Mīr 'Abdu-l-Ḥai, Pēshrau Khān, Mihtar Khān, and after some days Tardī Beg Khān, who inscribed on his heart's tablet the office of Amīr-al-Umarā [1] (Blochmann, 240) assembled together and on the 28th of the same month, 11th February, 1556, they recited the *khuṭba* in the famous name and lofty titles of the *khedive* of the age, and so healed and mended the distracted world and gave the terrene and terrestrials a message of enduring restoration. The stewards of heaven, who had been in expectation of this, rejoiced, and the desires of the administrators of the natural world were accomplished. Mīr 'Abdu-l-Ḥai Ṣadr recited this couplet:—

*Verse.*

If the world's new year be destroyed,
Let the hundred-leaved red rose remain.

Several persons had recited this verse, and it had become well known and had been made the subject of conversation at assemblies. A strange thing was that at the same time one of the literate *(fazlā)* had found the second line [2] to give the date of the accession of the *Khedive* of the Age, but this was by writing the word *gul* with an ī, *gulī,* though in one sense the ordinary orthography does not lend itself to this form. And during the days of concealing this fatal affair they on one occasion dressed up Mullā Bēkasī [3] in the clothes

---

[1] That is, no doubt, they endeavoured to conceal the gravity of the accident. This agrees with what Sīdī 'Alī tells us.

[2] The second line yields 953 and if ī be added it yields 10 more or 963. I think the meaning is that 'Abdu-l-Ḥai uttered the verse without any thought of its being a chronogram, and that the strange thing was that it was afterwards found that a slight alteration made it into a chronogram.

[3] Sīdī 'Alī Reis, the Turkish ad-

of the deceased *(lit:* that pardoned pinnacle) and brought him out on the top of the terrace *(aiwān)* which was His Majesty's place of sitting, and showed him to the people with his face towards the river. The people performed the *kornish* and were in some measure relieved from their distress and confusion.

When the sad misfortune was made known a great disturbance and trouble, such as was natural at a crisis like this, arose. The officers exerted themselves to soothe hearts and give people confidence and did what was proper at this time of dispersion both in 365
respect of friends and of foes. They did what they could to mend the breach and to cement the crack. And how could the bond (*'aqd*) of the eternal fortune of this noble family not attain corroboration and shape when the world-adorning glory of the personality of His Majesty the Shāhinshāh, the true heir of sovereignty, had seized the summit of the throne of the *khilāfat* of the terrene and of terrestrials. Good God! How could it enter into the circle of the thoughts and imaginings of the farseeing that a being so wondrous in his perfections and so befriended of fortune, at once the arranger of the visible world and the acquirer of spirituality, should so soon leave this earth? But as the time had come when the Creator would give rejuvenescence to the old world and give a new education to mankind,—a time which had not arrived in many cycles of the past,—of necessity He designed to exhibit the nobly-constituted and consummate paragon who should be the perfection of mortals. Con-

---

miral, l.c. 57, tells this story and confirms A.F.'s account. He calls the representative Mullā Bī and says he bore a striking resemblance to Humāyūn, though he was of slighter ("shorter," in Diez) make. Sīdī 'Alī says the deception took place on the Tuesday, and he gives himself the credit of having suggested the concealment. But Gulbadan Begam tells us that the same thing was done when her father died. Badāūnī, III, 192, has an account of Bēkasī, i.e., I presume the orphan or destitute one, but singularly enough he says nothing about his impersonation of Humāyūn. Bēkasī seems to have been a native of Ghaznīn and he died at Peshawar in 973, 1566. He was a poet, and Badāūnī gives specimens of his verses. It is interesting to find Sīdī 'Alī confirming A.F. in the small matter of the impersonation's having taken place on the riverside.

In F. H. Diez's translation, in his Denkwürdigkeiten von Asien, Berlin, 1815, p. 209, the name is given as Mullā Bikjiesi. His translation seems to be better than Vambéry's.

sequently the occurrence of this unavoidable event, though in the eyes of the superficial a subject of mourning and sorrow, might be reckoned by the eyes of the mature of vision as a treasury of glory and beauty. For by the bounteous presence of this sublime pearl of sovereignty the visible and invisible worlds became again glorious, and the market-square of dominion, spiritual and temporal, became active. And as the lofty intelligence of this lord of the age was come to perfection, and the constituent elements of the rule of this great-thoughted one had been put in order and the die of dominion had turned up inscribed with his name, seeing that with real ancestorhood he wore the vesture of sonship, if the ruler of the age (Humāyūn) had on account of his right-seeing and good qualities been preserved in the prison of visible life, it must have followed that, on account of the submission to the noblest, which is proper according to the rules of wisdom, this eminent one of the age (Humāyūn) should submit to the nursling of light (Akbar). But as the robe of fatherhood is an imposing one and cometh from God, it could not harmonise with obedience to the offspring. Also the happiness of children cannot be recorded in the book of fate except when they submit to their fathers and obey their behests. Consequently it was unavoidable that the beginning of the feast of fortune should be the lord of the earth's leaving this world.

In fine, after giving consolations and congratulations, the imperial servants who were collected in Delhi separated in order to unite distracted hearts, and each hastened to his own place. Tardī Beg Khān, who in concert with them was at Delhi, in order to arrange the affairs of this city, sent the insignia of sovereignty along with Ghulām 'Alī Shaçhangasht and other trusty servants to the world-protecting court and made declarations of obedience and devotion. M. Abū-l-Qāsim,[1] the son of M. Kāmrān, was also sent to do homage.

[1] This apparently is the same person as the Ibrāhīm mentioned as having, when a child, wrestled with Akbar. He probably had his name changed when he became father of a son. I regret to say that Akbar afterwards had him put to death in Gwālīār.

## CHAPTER LXIII.

### OF THE DOMINION-INCREASING ACTS OF HIS MAJESTY THE SHĀHINSHĀH FROM THE TIME OF HIS FELICITOUS SETTING OUT FOR THE PANJĀB TILL HIS SACRED ACCESSION. 366

The brief account of the fortune-encompassing condition of His Majesty the Shāhinshāh from the time of his being dispatched to the Panjāb till his glorious accession is that when the standards of fortune were turned towards the Panjāb the Atka Khān and other servants came from Hiṣār Fīrūza and met him on the way, in accordance with an intimation to that effect, and had the honour of paying their respects. When fortune's equipage arrived at Sihrind all the king's[1] servants who had been appointed as auxiliaries to Shāh Abū-l-M'aālī, such as Muḥammad Qulī Khān Barlās, Muṣāhib Beg, Khwāja Jalālu-d-dīn Maḥmud, Farḥat Khān, Ṭāhir Muḥammad, son of Mīr Khurd, and Mihtar Taimūr Sharbatai, came away without leave (from Abū-l-M'aālī) on hearing of the advance of His Majesty the Shāhinshāh, and hastened to obtain the bliss of service, for they had been troubled by the evil fellowship of that ill-regulated young man. They were favourably received. Sikandar, who had come out of the hills, withdrew to them again before the victorious army had encamped. The infatuated Mīr who had marched out to put him down hastened back to Lahore. When it became certain that the province had been given to His Majesty the Shāhinshāh, and that he was proceeding thither, Abu-l-M'aālī felt constrained to come with a body of troops to the bank of the Sulṭānpūr river (the Bīās) and to do homage. His Majesty out of kindness, and in order to ratify the favour that had been shown by His Majesty Jahānbānī himself indicated to Abū-l-M'aālī that he should take a seat

[1] That is, Humāyūn's servants. The Atka Khān and others who came from Ḥiṣār were Akbar's special retainers.

in the high assemblage, and encompassed him with favours. But inasmuch as the easily intoxicated Mīr had been made drunk by one gulp of the world's wine he, after obtaining leave and returning to his quarters sent a message that "my position[1] with His Majesty Jahānbānī is universally known; and especially your Highness may recollect that at the *qamargha* (ring-hunt) in Jūī[2] Shāhī I ate with His Majesty Jahānbānī in the same place and off the same plate; you were present, and had your portion (*alūsh*) sent to you. Taking then my position into consideration, why, when I came to your habitation, was a separate rug put down for me, and why was there a separate tablecloth? "His Majesty a mine of sense and urbanity, smiled at his ignorance, and said to Ḥājī Muḥammad Sīstānī who had brought the message "Tell him the regulations of State and the laws of love are distinct, you have not with me the position that you had with His Majesty Jahānbānī. 'Tis strange that you have not discriminated between these two positions, and have complained." The Mīr was greatly abashed.

His Majesty went on towards the hills in order to extirpate Sikandar who was stated to be in Mānkot and its neighbourhood.

When the army of fortune encamped near Harīāna a swift courier arrived and apprized Bairām Khān of His Majesty Jahānbānī's fall. Bairām Khān did not think it expedient to advance further, and moved the army to Kalānūr in order that they might halt for some days in that pleasant place. Near Kalānūr Nazr Shaikh Cūlī arrived and produced the sublime mandate[3] (*firmān*). Just about this time the tidings of the inevitable events reached the royal hearing, and His Majesty displayed the weeping and lamentation which befitted the condition of affection and love. The distress and internal affliction which were experienced by that lofty-souled one exceeded human conception. Bairām Khān, Atka Khān and Māham Anaga essayed to comfort him, but as his sorrow sprang from excessive love what they regarded as topics of consolation only augmented his grief. This

[1] Humāyūn used to call him son.

[2] This was Akbar's appanage, which makes the favour shown to Abū-l-M'ālī the more striking.

[3] The Mirāt-i-'ālam B.M. Add. 7657, p. 271*a*, gives what purports to be the substance of the letter. There is a translation of the passage in J.A.S.B., Vol. XL. for 1871.

chosen one of God expends such sorrow of heart and consideration for individual men ! How grieved and afflicted he is at the death of any one who has a savour of sincerity, devotion, and ability ! It was fitting that such a disposition should show itself in his holy personality under circumstances which were in old times motives for rejoicing among the unthinking so that men of the world who regard only what they perceive by their senses may acknowledge the true grandeur of this great one, and that such acknowledgment may be a means of guiding all mankind, and that the guidance may result in general enlightenment and charity. If it were not for this reason, how could the wide domain of the knowledge, piety and devotion of this nursling of the light of glory permit that such censure of the decrees of Providence should contract the law of submission ? At length by the assistance of far-reaching reason he conveyed himself to the asylum of patience and employed hismself in alms-giving and in other good works, which may benefit those who have travelled to the abiding world. Poets and sages composed elegies and chronograms. Among them was Khwāja Ḥusain of Merv who made a *tarkībband* in an elegy, about that cupola of pardon, some lines of which are as follows :—

*Verse.*[1]

O heart, thou too must hear the sound of death.
Death's morning must blow on thy life's ascension,
As the order for tasting death is for all men.
Be sure that the sherbet of death must be drunk.
This name of life which they imposed upon you.
Is a name that must be carried on to the side of death.

---

[1] A note to the Lucknow edition says that a *tarkībband* is a composition in which the metre changes after seven or more verses. According to Dr. Ranking's book or Prosody, Bombay, 1895, p. 12, this is the definition of *Tarjiband*. Khwājah Ḥusain made a famous poem about the birth of Jahāngīr. He is said to have died at Kābul in 979. It is singular that the verses do not occur in most MSS. The editors of the Bib. Ind. edition say in a note that they are only to be found in the Lucknow edition. They do not occur in any of seven MSS. in the B.M. which I have examined. Unfortunately the editor of the Lucknow lithograph (1284 A.H.) does not tell us the sources of his text beyond vaguely stating at p. 8 of his preface that he was supplied by his publisher with several good copies of the book.

Be not proud of this rose and garden of life.
Autumn's breeze must blow on this rose and garden.
368 Thou hast heard with thine own ears that such an one remaineth not
Others's ears must receive tidings of thee likewise.

Mīr 'Abdu-l-Ḥai found this chronogram :—

*Verse.*

Alas, Alas ! My king fell from the roof. (963).

Maulānā Mas'aūd of Ḥiṣar composed this :—

*Verse.*

Hūmāyūn Pādshāh was united to God. (963).

But this was by writing the sacred name (Hūmāyūn) without *alif*. Maulānā Qāsim Kāhī made this chronogram :—

*Verse.*

Hūmāyūn Pādshāh fell from the roof. (962).

This chronogram is one year short. A difference of one or two years may be allowed in the case (of the dates) of buildings, but not in obituary chronograms.[1] A number discovered this chronogram :—

[2] *Verse.*

Let Jalālu-d-dīn be the kingdom's heir. (963).

The spiritual and physical perfections and the notes of reason

---

[1] A.F. means that as buildings are often begun in one year and finished in another, an error of a year or two in the chronogram is not of importance. For an account of Qāsim Kāhī, see Blochmann, 209, and 566, and Ṭabaqāt Akbarī, Lucknow ed., 396.

[2] Dr. Ethé gives in his catalogue of the Persian MSS. in the India Office, No. 1441, p. 793, a chronogram by Hijrī which deserves to be recorded. It is :—

حیف زان پادشه عارف دانای حکیم

Alas ! for the king, the saint, the sage (963).

With reference to A.F.'s statement that Qāsim Kāhī's chronogram is defective by a year, it may be remarked that many seem to have thought that 962 was the year of the death. Bayāzīd, 81*a*, gives this date and so does Jauhar B.M. MS., 16, 711, p. 145*a*. It is also the date given in the verses engraved under the cornice at Sikandar. The stanza is :—

ز نهصد فزون بود شصت دوسال
که شاه اکبر آن مایهٔ ذو الجلال
بیالاے زرین مسند نشست
که بر نهصد او گشته افلاك پشت

and knowledge in this unique one of the world were greater than can be recorded. He was thoroughly versant in various sciences, rational and traditional (*'aqlī u naqlī*). Especially was he distinguished in the mathematical sciences. He always consorted with philosophers. Illustrious mathematicians obtained bliss at the foot of his throne. He desired to establish observatories and had collected the equipments thereof. He had fixed upon several sites for observatories. He also regarded with favour poetry and poets. And as he had a metrical turn he spent the intervals of time, between spiritual and temporal obligations, in composing poetry. The *divan* of his poems is in the grand library. The following quatrains are taken from that frontispiece of marvels:—

*Quatrain.*

Oh! heart, fret not in presence of the rival,
Tell not thy heart's condition to any physician.
What has happened to thee from that tyrant
Is a woeful tale, and a very strange event.

*Another.*

Oh! heart, rejoice in the presence of the friend,
In his service faithfully consume thyself.
Each night sit rejoicing in the thought of the friend,
Each day make a New Year by meeting him.

*Another.*

Oh thou, whose tyranny is a world's flag,
The day when I see not oppression from thee is oppressive.
The sorrow that comes from the tyrannous sphere,
What sorrow is it to me when there is the sorrow of love for thee?

---

though possibly this may be explained as only meaning that 962 years were completed.

In the Tārīkh Alfī, I.O. MS. No. 3293, p. 430*b*, 963 is given as the date, and no doubt this is correct, but perhaps many people were misled by Akbar's introduction of the Faslī year and counted 963 as beginning with the vernal equinox of the year of his accession. It, therefore, seems unnecessary to have recourse to the emendation of the chronogram suggested by Mr. Rodgers, in his valuable paper on Eastern Chronograms, R.A.S.J., for 1898 p. 718.

84

God be praised! the exposition of this noble catena which, like the catena of the skies, is upheld by God and hath a holy refuge, and of which one extremity is bound to Adam Ṣafī, the morning of Creation, while the other is linked with the ascension of the sun of
369 the Shāhinshāh's personality, has been set forth with concision and brevity and in a fresh style other than that coming from the tainted pen of the deckers (*basmacīān*) of epistolary models. By drawing up this grand catalogue and glorious preamble, Abū-l-faẓl—that airy particle—has obtained benediction, and many mysteries and points of wisdom have found insertion as ancillaries. Were these truths, and mysteries separated from the main chronicle, they would form a choice book brimful of the marrow of wisdom.

*Verse.*

I made a cup of wine out of my blood.
Not a jar of vinegar that blisters the breast.
There are many truths in each dot of it,
Who does not perpend them, comprehends them not.

Though in so far as regards ordinary readers what I have recounted up till now of the events of the ancestors may seem superfluous and a flux of words, yet the great society of truth-knowers is well aware that into this book of Divine praise—may no evil eye approach it!—I have not introduced, from the beginning to the end, a single superfluous letter. An account has been given of divers screens—veils of the sacred Shāhinshāh-beauty,—and behind each screen there is the bridal face of genius. Away, away! Where is the screen, and where is the secluded bride? One beauty there is which assumes several manifestations, and within these is one genius which is full of radiance and which informs [1] the world-illuminating Beauty.

*Verse.*

He who knows speech knows
What kind of speech this is.

How can I, whose heart is pawned in one place, turn towards the two worlds? What profit is there in the writing of histories? Two swords will not lie in one scabbard, or two purposes in one heart.

---

[1] I adopt the variant *girū* which I believe to be the Turkish کیرو *gīrū*.

Do not take into consideration the distracted souls of the inconstant, for where is the heart of those heartless, earthly-natured ones that can be subjected to consideration? But for the sage inquirer into causes the truth is illustrated by the ascent of His Majesty the Shāhinshāh, and so the afflicted world of secondary causes has been brought into the noose of design. And by profound contemplation and good fortune, the stewards of fate, who, owing to the happy auspices of this individual, have brought the chapters of felicity to a conclusion, have revealed the world-adorning beauty of the Shāhinshāh in the exponents of this sublime catena, so that the genuine love for that unique one of the divine temple has given zeal for the writing of this lengthy chronicle. The convention of discourse has been made animated, and the rose garden of ornaments been watered. Neither has there been any flagging in the single-heartedness of this desert-traverser. The progressive beauties of the true beloved have been set forth, and the degrees of love's sciences have received their full ascension.

Now what the vulgar and the superficial have regarded as a digression has been concluded and the time has come for what both sections (of readers) regard as the true object. I hope I may obtain 370
my wish in the noble enterprise.

*Verse.*

My pen whose point is a mysterious tongue,
Is the treasure-opener of a secret mine,
From him who regards it with gravity
I ask justice, not acclamation.

*Verse.*

May this work be worthy applause!
May God grant that so it may be.

END OF VOLUME I.

*Errata and Addenda*

1. P. 3, n. 3. Aḥmad 'Alī Khān, keeper of the Rāmpūr Library Rohilkand, showed me a passage in a commentary on Anwarī's Odes, which offered an explanation of the phrase, 18,000 worlds. It said that *alf* had the meaning of perfect, or complete, because one thousand was the highest number used in *abjad*, or alphabetical numeration, and that therefore 18,000 meant only 18. This latter number was arrived at by adding together the four worlds, *viz.*, the *'Aālam jabarūt*, *'Aālam malakūt*, *'arsh*, and *kursī*, the seven heavens, the four elements, and the three *mawālid*, مواليد ثلاثة, *i.e.*, the animal, vegetable, and mineral kingdoms. The commentary was by Abūl Ḥasan Firāhānī, and gave as the authority for the statement 'Abdu-r-razzāq Kāshī Sulṭān-al-'Aārifīn's Tawīlāt. The passage occurs at p. 82*b*, of the Rāmpūr MS. and is an explanation of a verse where Anwarī plays on the two meanings of the word *alf*, *viz.*, 1,000 and also the first letter of the alphabet. It also occurs in B.M. MS., Or. 361 p. 43*a* Rieu 556*b*.

2. P. 5, last line. The best translation of the epithet *istīsqā bakhsh* seems to be "answerer of the prayer for rain." "See Lane 1355*b*. The reference is to Akbar's alleged miracle of causing rain to fall, and also to his satisfying the thirst of all who wander about, panting after the truth. Blochmann 164.

3. Do., n. 4. See Āīn text I, 158 where the lover ('Aāshaq) and the loved (Māshūq) are described as one.

4. P. 6, n. 2. See Tennyson's paraphrase in his "Akbar's Dream."

5. P. 7, n. 2. Several of the lines occur in Faizī's Marka-i-adwār, B.M. MS., Add. 7795 p. 25, Canto on Speech.

6. Verse, Delete capital in Thy. Niẓāmī's lines are addressed to an earthly prince, and A.F. employs them in the same sense.

7. P. 11, n. 3. I.O. MS. 4 has *zā*.

8. P. 12, l. 6. Perhaps the following is a better translation, "Rather the aim of praise is to place this vain, self-adorning, self-auctioning, carnal soul on the threshold of submission and the pedestal of supplication and humility, and to cast it out of sight so that

inward happiness may be graced by outward surrender, and the inner and outer natures may be decked with lowliness and be fitted to the modesty of the bosom of purpose and become the praise of the life-giving creator."

9. P. 12, n. 4. See Faiẓī's Nal Daman, last Canto, p. 138 of Newal Kishore's ed., 1893.

بر طاق نظر کشیدم این دیر
که جلوه‌ء بینش سبک سیر

" I drew (or erected) this dome on vision's arch.
To be the glory of the swift-rolling eye.

See also for use of the phrases *khudārāī* and *khweshtan-gazīnī*, A.F.'s description of the initiation of a novice in the "Divine Faith," *Āīn*, text I, 160 and Blochmann 166.

10. P. 16, l. 7. These two epithets occur in the beginning of the 'Iyār dānish.

11. P. 16, n. 1. Maulvī Abdul Ḥuq Abīd informs me that the meaning here is that Akbar provided food for his people. The phrase "servants of God" means here mankind, or at least all Muḥammadans.

12. L. 13. Perhaps the translation, children of Noah, and n. 2 are wrong, for the word in the text is نوع and not نوح.

13. P. 20, l. 9. Maulvi A. H. A. informs me that I have missed the point here. The meaning of *khūrda-anges* is " to find fault with," and the translation should be " his equity finds defect in the evenness of Farwardīn, his courtesy derides the breeze of Ardibihisht," *i.e.*, his equability surpasses that of Farwardīn, and his sweetness smiles superior to the zephyrs of Ardibihisht. See for similar hyperboles the description of Spring in Vol. II, p. 81.

14. P. 21. Notes 3 and 4. R.A.S., MSS., 116 and 117 have *taḥrīr* and perhaps this is a preferable reading to *tajabbar*. The reference may be to the cancelling of bonds by tearing the top of the document, or to the shrouds with which malefactors provided themselves when suing for mercy.

15. P. 28, four lines from foot. The word in text is *harfsard* fluent, but this does not make good sense. I should be inclined to prefer *ḥarfsard*, which is apparently the reading of R.A.S. MSS., Nos. 117 and 119. See Bahār-i 'Ajam-ed, Newal Kishwar 1894

s.v. *ḥarfsard*. *Ḥarfsarā* however like the word *sakhn-sarā* used later on by A.F., may mean a word-twitterer, *i.e.*, one who indulges in empty verbiage. Maulvi A. H. A. thinks that *ḥarfsarā* is right.

16. P. 24, l. 14. *Az rāh-i-mijāz mīdān-īd*, etc. Read, "this follower of the truth knows from observation of the outer world."

Do. last line. The words "what strength has Saha," etc., ending with the word atom, form a quatrain, and should have been printed as such. The literal translation of the last clause is "less than an atom."

17. P. 25, n. 3. Possibly A.F. was thinking of the Anwar Suhailī. That contains 5 or 6,000 verses and A.F.'s chief mode of abridging it in the 'Iyār dānish is to omit them.

18. P. 26, last line and n. 2. The most correct translation of *b'azz-i-murād* seems to be "with respect to desires." A.F. intimates that he is not ambitious. See also p. 374 of this translation, note 1.

19. P. 27, n. 2. The expression about wearing the cap on the crown of the heart may remind us of the passage in the Anabasis II. 5, where Tissaphernes says to Clearchus that the help of the Greeks will enable him to wear his diadem lightly on his heart. See Grote, 4th ed., VII, 240.

20. P. 29, n. 4, l. 6. For 227 read 247.

21. P. 32, n. 2. Read *Shahristān*.

22. P. 33, n. 3. For Fardōs read Firdūs. It may be noted here that Gītī in Gītīsitānī is pronounced Getī in India, and is so spelt by Blochmann.

23. P. 35, l. 4. Perhaps *tamīz* here means, to cleanse.

24. P. 35, l. 5. *Tan-i-Wāḥid* is perhaps explained by A.N., II, 43, where we have the word *akhshijān*, *i.e.*, possessed by the four elements. It is applied here to ordinary mortals in whom the constituents are not fused together and unified, but are at war with one another.

25. P. 42, second para. According to the Tabaqāt Akbarī, end of account of the 23rd year, the dream occurred on the night of the birth. Lucknow ed. 339. 'Ārif Qandahārī says it occurred on 4 Rabī'-al-awwal 947.

26. P. 45, last line and n. 5. Perhaps *ḥarf-i-namūdār darmyān būd* merely means that the subject of the *namūdār* was under

discussion. *Cf.* text 162, l. 5, where ḥarf-i-*rukhṣat darmiyān award* means he introduced the subject or leave.

27. P. 53, m. l. 6. For 43c read 43*a*. In the same note for pistadin read pistachio, and spot for South, do for Hajrī read Ḥijrā and add, Ḥijrī was the *takhallaṣ* of a poet. See Budāūnī III, 386 and Tabaqāt Akbarī, Lucknow ed. 401. He was long in the service of M. Hindāl and was descended from Aḥmad Jām, and so would be a relative of Ḥamīda. His *dīvān* is in the A.S.B. library, Cat. p. 117, and also in the I.O. library, Ethé No. 1441 of p. 793. It contains odes in praise of Akbar and a chronogram for Humāyūn's death, but I could not find any interesting historical allusion in the poems, or any reference to Ḥamīda.

28. P. 53, n. I think it clear that A.F. means that K. Mu'azzam was only the half-brother of Ḥamīda. At p. 55 he uses the word a'yānī to denote a full-brother.

29. P. 54, n. 2, last sentence. For Procyon read Sirius, and delete the last four words. The epithet applied to Procyon is ghamīza, the obscure (?)

30. P. 55. According to local tradition, Akbar was born in the fields about a mile outside of the fort. See a paper by N. V. Mandlik read 8th March, 1855, and published in his writings and speeches, Bombay, 1896, p. 199, and also the Calcutta Review for January 1900. Possibly the old fort stood where the Akbar memorial now stands, for V. N. Mandlik says that the old fort was destroyed and a new one built by Nur Muḥammad Kulhara in 1746.

31. P. 58, second line. Though *ṭāūs* means a peacock it also means a handsome man or woman and the root is *ṭūs*, beautiful. A.F. applies the term to Rūpmatī II, 137. It seems to have been a title in use among the Afghans. See the story of Kāmrān's reception by Selim Shāh in Budaūnī (Ranking), and see also Bābar's Memoirs where Ṭāūs Khān is given as the name of an Afghan chief.

32. P. 58, verse third, last line. The correct translation appears to be: "Easily carried away the hearts of lovers of the difficult," meaning, I presume, the critical and not easily pleased.

33. P. 62 near foot. For "rouse" read "roused."

34. P. 66, n. Yes; Allāh has properly three ls, so that 66 is right.

35. P. 66, n. 1. For 3436 read 343*b*.

36. P. 66, n. 2. For Jafar Ṣadiq read J'āāfar Ṣādiq.

37. P. 69, n. 2. For Taṣhīlāt read Tasahīlāt. It means, simplifications, or easy lessons.

38. P. 73, n. 1, col. 2, line 11th. For 711 read "7 lines."

39. P. 77, n. 2. Alcochoden is evidently the same word as *Kadkhudā* with the article prefixed.

40. P. 82, n. My remark about the Canon Masudicus is, I believe, erroneous. From Rehatsek's description it would seem that there is no astrology in the work. The copy in the Mulla Fīrūz library is in good condition, and very legible. There is also a copy in the Nawab of Rāmpūr's library.

41. P. 83, n. In last para. delete the repetition of the words "et ex hoc adorogen," and substitute "dorongen." In last sentence of same paragraph read "A difficulty arises."

42. P. 91. For Carden read Cardan.

43. P. 92, l. 1. It seems probable that 22 was regarded as a mystic number from its being that of the letters of the Hebrew, Syriac, and, presumably, of the ancient Arabic, alphabets.

44. End of last para. Substitute the translation "Alas! I have no brother to rise high in my service," delete note 4 and substitute "آرزو is here used in the sense of regret."

45. P. 96, n. 1. Delete comma after Shīraz. In this note I have mixed up two distinct princes. The Buyide 'Azad-ad-daula ruled in Bagdad. Alp Arslān whom Col. Jarrett calls 'Azad-ad-daula belongs to the 12th century. Fatḥulla whom Budāūnī calls Shāh Fatḥulla came to Akbar's court in 990 A.H. See Budāūnī, Lowe, 326. There is a long account of him, taken chiefly from Budāūnī, on the Darbār Akbarī of Azād.

46. P. 111, n. 3. Humāyūn's death and Akbar's accession occurred when the sun was in Gemini. Can *hashtam-chaharam* mean the 32nd degree? B.M. M.P. Add. 27, 247 has *hashtam dar chaharam*, *i.e.*, 8 by 4. In the Bādshāhnāma Bib. Ind. I, 66, Akbar is said to have been born when the sun was in Scorpio. I think now that the proper translation is "As the 8th and 4th Houses are Gemini with respect to the degrees."

47. P. 112, l. 18. Delete comma after Mars, and insert one after Jupiter.

P. 117, second para. For "copied in sketch" read "exactly copied."

P. 117, n. 3. The word occurs again in A.N. II, p. 11, l. 16.

P. 123. The account of Humāyūn's dancing seems to be taken from the Tārīkh Alfī, though there the circumstance is said to have only occurred once. The passage occurs in the description of the events of 949 A.H. and at page 572*a* of B.M. MS. Or. 465 and is as follows:—

یکی از مقربان صادق القول آن حضرت نقل کرده که اکثر اوقات بخلوتی در آمده ملاحظه زایچه طالع میفرمودند نوبتی بی اطلاع آن حضرت چون نزدیک آن خلوت رفته شد آواز پای مسموع گشت چون دیگری دران خلوت راه نداشت بعد از امعان نظر معلوم شد که آن حضرت از غایت شوق دست افشانی میفرمودند و بعد از وقوف بر اطلاع غیر فرمودند که سبب رقص شوقی است که از ملاحظه زایچه طالع این فرزند سعادتمند بدل راه یافته •

48. P. 130, five lines from foot. Dāya Bhāwal means the nurse Bhāwal, and the word dāya is used immediately before with reference to Jījī. Dāya Bhāwal is evidently the same person as Bhāwal Anaga who is mentioned soon afterwards, and A.F.'s meaning is that though there is a statement that Bhāwal was the first nurse, the ascertained fact is (*taḥaqīq ānast*) that Akbar was first of all suckled by his mother, then by Fakhr-i-nisā, then by Bhāwal. Bhāwal or Behāwal is probably a form of the Persian word *bahāwar* precious and which is sometimes spelt *bahālū*. Presumably A.F. by speaking of her as a special servant, *khidmatgār-i-khāṣ* of Humāyūn, means that she was one of his concubines, and of course she must have been a mother. Possibly she was Māham Anaga. Māham, as I have stated elsewhere, means "my Moon" and is a common appellation of women. The author of the Darbārī Akbarī, p. 749, makes the curious statement that Bhāwal Anaga was the daughter of one Jogā Barhār,* and that she was introduced into the harem of Humāyūn by his father Bābar. There her attractive face and manners captivated Humāyūn, but her star paled before the sun of Miriam-Makīnī's presence, and the king made her over to Jalāl Koka (?). Still she remained in the harem, and became one of Akbar's nurses. No authority is given for these statements, and I do not know where the author found them. It

* Qu. Parihār?

looks as if he meant to identify her with Māham Anaga, and to represent the latter as a Hindu. This view might coincide with Budāūnī's remark that Akbar was from his earliest years associated with low Hindus. I cannot find the tribe or caste Barhār either in Crooke, or Sherring, though there are some names nearly approaching to it, and I was told in Upper India that there was such a caste. A.F. mentions (A.N. II, 210, top line), the caste Parihār in describing Gondwāna. He also mentions there one Jogī Dās a younger brother of Sangrām Sā. The Parihārs were Rajputs and were rulers of Bandelkhand before the Candels, Sleeman's Rambles ed. 1893, I, 175 note. It is possible that the Jalāl Koka of the Darbārī Akbar may be another name for Nadīm Koka, and that the facts stated there may be a solution of the mystery of Adham Khān's parentage. There certainly is, as Elliot remarks, a mystery about the paternity of Adham Khān and it may be that though his mother was married to Nadīm Koka, Humāyūn was his father.

49. P. 132, last line. Maulvī Abdul Haq Abīd informs me that the meaning of the words sākinān-i-majāma-i-uns is "the dwellers of the gathering places of Divine love, or, the members of the congregations of Divine love," *i.e.*, the angels.

50. P. 134. In an article in the R.A.S.J., for January 1889, p. 99, I endeavoured to show that Māham Anaga was the wife of Nadīm Kokaltāsh. The mention of his name at p. 135 as one of those left at 'Umarkot in charge of Miriam-Makānī perhaps supports this view. It appears from a note by Garcin de Tassy at p. 11 of his abridged translation of Syed Aḥmad's book on the Delhi monuments, Paris, 1861, that the author of Colonel Hama's MS., noticed in the article above referred to, was probably Mīrzī Hidayat Ullah for it is stated by Garcin de Tassy that Hidayat Ullah was a grandson of Mīrzā Koka and wrote a Tārīkh or chronicle in 1070 A.H. or 1659. See also p. 129. Hidayat Ullah's chronicle is not in the B.M. or I.O., and I have been unable to find out where it is, for Garcin de Tassy does not tell us and there is no reference to the MS. in Syed Aḥmad's book. Hidayat Ullah's name occurs in Beale's Oriental Biographies. See below p. 475, n. 3. To the remark about Adham Khān's age at end of note in p. 134 it may be added that A.F. describes Adham as taking a prominent part in the beginning of the seige of Mānkot. He could hardly have done

this if he had been no older than Akbar who was then only fourteen.

51. P. 139, last lines. The late Mr. Rodgers states, R.A.S.J., for 1898, p. 729, that this chronogram is by Faiẓī, but this seems to be a mistake. A.F. does not ascribe it to his brother, and the latter was not born till some years after Akbar's birth.

52. P. 154, n. 3. Probably this is the correct translation. A.F. means apparently that previous works, though voluminous, have not treated the subject in a satisfactory manner.

53. P. 166, n. 8. For Īfan read Ifīn.

54. P. 180, last sentence. The expression *dar parda ārāī* receives elucidation from its recurrence in text I, 347, top line. This, I think, disposes of the suggestion inserted by Dr. Bloch in a note at the end of this fasciculus. See also II, 42 of text, l. 10 and do. 43, l. 10. By the expression, remaining behind the veil, A.F. not only means the period before Akbar's birth, but also the time before he revealed himself to the world. *Cf.* Blochmann, p. 124, n. 1 and p. 13, line 12.

55. P. 182, verse. These lines occur in Sharafu-d-din's preface to the Ẓafarnāma, *i.e.*, in his Tārīkh Jahāngīr.

56. P. 201, n. 2. There is a mistake in this note. The Prolegomena says ten, but only gives five names.

57. P. 204, l. 10. Read *Shāhnishānī.*

58. P. 217, n. 2. Gauhar Shād's death is described in the Maṭla' Sa'ādain, and the date given is 9 Ramẓān. Sām Mīrzā in his anthology R.M. MS. Add. 7670, p. 46*b*, says Qatalu-d-dīn Muhammad Duānī was the author of the chronogram. He gives the quatrain.

59. P. 218, l. 14. For "gave" read "give."

60. P. 222, l. 6. For "then" read "these."

61. Do. Shahrbānū's name is also omitted in Shīrāzī's text, and in the Alwar MS. only four daughters are mentioned. Shahrbānū apparently means the Moon-lady. For "Bābar's," p. 222, n. 1, read "'Umar Shaikh's."

62. P. 223, beginning of chapter, and n. 2. For "king of the four quarters and of the seven heavens" read king of the throne of the seven worlds." The word *cahār* is often used, as Quatremère has shown in his notes to the Maṭla' Saādain without really meaning four. *Cahār bālish* really only means the pillows of the *divān,*

or the *divān* itself. By the *haft manzar* is meant here probably the seven climes, or the seven heavens, or the seven planets. It is however worthy of notice that the Quṭb of Delhi was known as the Mināa-i-haft manẓar, *i.e.*, the minaret of seven stories. See Garçin de Ṭassy's translation of Syed 'Aḥmad's work on Delhi, Paris 1861, p. 86. As Delhi was Bābar's capital, it is possible that here A.F. is alluding to the Quṭb.

63. P. 223, n. 4. For Jānī read Jāmī.

64. P. 228, two lines from foot. Text and MSS. have Bektūb. Erskine, 170, has Bektob.

65. P. 232, n. last sentence, read *Khālazāīd*. It means "full aunt." Bābar in the account of his father's children speaks of one daughter as being *hamshīrazāīd, i.e.*, full sister, of Nāṣir.

66. P. 233, line 18. Before 917 read "in the month of Rajab."

67. P. 234, top line and n. 1. Usually called Najm Ṣānī from his having succeeded Najm Zargar Gīlānī. His real name was Yār Aḥmad Ispahānī. The Haft Iqlim I.O. copy 329*b* says he was put to death by Ubaid Ullah on 3 Ramẓān 918. These occurrences are detailed in the T. Alfī B.M. MS., Or. 465, 514*b* and also in the Ḥabību-s-siyar, and in the lives of Ismāīl and Ṭahmāsp by Khwāndamīr's son Maḥmūd, as well as in the anonymous author of the life of Ism'aīl, B.M. MSS., Or. 2939 and 3248. A.F. is correct in saying that Bābar had at first won the victory; Ubaid Ullah lay in ambush and turned the victory into a defeat. The victories which Babar previously gained occurred near Ḥiṣār and were won against Shaibānī's sons Ḥamza and Mahdī Sulṭāns. See Shaibānī' letter B.M. MS., Or. 3482 68*b* where a list of his children is given.

68. Do., n. 1. In the anonymous life of Ism'aīl, p. 215*a*, it is stated that one ward of Karshi was exclusively occupied by Caghatais, and that they begged for Bābar's protection. He interceded for them with Najm Ṣānī, but it was in vain. On the day of the battle Najm Ṣānī put Babar in the reserve. When Bābar saw that the battle was lost he fled to Ḥiṣār.

69. P. 238, n. 5, for "taken" read "taker." The derivation here given seems correct, and is supported by Gulbadan Begam's Memoirs, p. 8*c*, where Qāsim Beg is described as writing to Bābar that a new prince had been born, and suggesting that his name should be

made a prognostic of the conquest of India, *ba shagūn* fatḥ-i-*Hind u takht alimash.* The last word is Turkī and means "taking." In consequence of this letter Bābar called his son Hindāl.

70. P. 241, top line. Read Biban.

71. Do., n. 3. A.F. is evidently copying S͟haik͟h Zain here. He has B.M. MS., Or. 1999, 51*b*, "*ba zinjīr u k͟hām-i-gāo.*"

72. P. 243. n. 1. See S͟haik͟h Zain 88*a*. The page is misplaced in MS. and should come after 57*b*.

73. Do., l. 14. For *tūlg͟hāma* read *tūlaqma*.

74. P. 244, n. 5. Possibly Bābar does not name Taimur because he was not a *bādshāh*, but only an Amīr. But most likely it is because Taimur did not acquire the sovereignty of Hindustan. He merely plundered the country and returned. A.F. reckons Taimur, for at p. 245 he calls Bābar the fourth conqueror.

75. P. 244. The comparison with Taimur's forces is taken from Shaikh Zain, B.M. MS., pp. 53*b* and 55*a*. Zain has naukar-turk Turkish servants instead of naukar-i-naukar. He also gives 18,000 as the number of horses who can occupy a *farsang* though he reckons Taimur's total force at 72,000.

76. P. 246, note 278. More probably the reference is to the battle of Pānīpat with Hemū though Akbar had little personal share in the victory. Instead of " many rebellious chiefs " read "so many refractory chiefs."

77. P. 247, n. 4. Zain l.c., pp. 63*c* and *b* says Alaūddīn brought a diamond to India. Mūtamed K͟hān says in the Iqbālnāma that Alau-d-din got diamond from Vikramāditya. In this he is merely copying A.F. My opinion now is that it is not certain that Bābar means that his son got the diamond from Vikramāditya's heirs. His language is vague and perhaps all he means is that the diamond was one of the things that Humāyūn got when he was investing the fort. At any rate Bābar's account is not that of an eyewitness. Zain makes Humāyūn the spokesman to his father. He says the diamond was reckoned worth 2½ days of the world's income. The word in Add. 27, 247 is خراج and I am sure that income is a better translation than expenditure.

78. P. 248, beginning of para. Zain has Tuesday the 29th.

7 [illegible]. 249, n. In Persian quotation read in second line ا و سک و صدد in third خواست and in fourth line first word وزع

intead of واخ and also دارند for دارد and فرد for او مرد to complete the sentence should be added و زن یک شاهر خرانعام شود.

80. P. 257, last para. and n. 4. Shaikh Zain, p. 98*b*, says that Ibrahim's mother was sent to Kābul and the Tārīkh Maḥmadi B.M. Or. 1824, p. 57*a* says that on the road the lady flung herself into the Indus and drowned herself. The author gives as his authority for this statement the Iqbālnāma of Mūtamed Khān, and I have verified the reference. It also appears from the Iqbālnāma that the lady's name was Bava بوا. But this was only a sobriquet, and perhaps was the name by which Bābar called her. It means in Hindi, sister and paternal aunt.

81. P. 264, verse. For cap read veil.

82. 266, n. 5. It appears from Bābar's Memoirs, Erskine 274, that Khān Mirzā was alive on 4th September, 1519, or Ramaẓān 925, for the Jān Nāsir there mentioned as coming from his government seems a clerical error for Khān Mīrzān; O, p. 272; we see that Kipak had been sent to him, and presumably this was to summon him to his presence.

83. P. 272, n. 2. Insert comma after him, and delete comma after Ḥaidar.

84. P. 273, n. 1. Probably Alwar is correct. The child probably was born at Alwar which was his brother Hindāl's appanage afterwards, and received his name from the place.

85. P. 277, near foot. Read "He bade adieu to this faithless world on 6 Jamāda-ul-awwal 937 in a garden (cārbāgho) in Agra, on the banks of the Jamna, which that springtide of fortune had made verdant."

Add. note 2*a*. The local tradition is that Bābar was temporarily buried in the Rāmbāgh (originally perhaps[1] Ārāmbāgh) on the left or east side of the river, about two miles above the railway bridge. Mr. Keene says in his guide to Agra, p. 1, that according to the Akbarnāma Bābar was buried in the Cārbāgh some miles lower down the river and nearly opposite the Tāj. But the Akbarnāma says nothing about where the body was buried, and A.F.'s words are that the death occurred in a *Cārbāgh*. Any laid out garden is called a *Cārbāgh*, meaning perhaps that it is rectangular, or divided into

[1] Rām may however be the original form. Rām is an abbreviation of Ārām and here has nothing to do with Rām the Indian hero. See Hyde, p. 263 and Steingass s.v. *rām*.

squares by paths. Bābar's body remained in the garden for several years, and perhaps would never have been removed if Humāyūn had not been driven out of India. Bābar tells us that the east bank of the Jamna was called Kābul by the Indians in allusion to its gardens. Perhaps this gave rise to the story that Bābar desired to be buried in Kābul, or it may be that his son satisfied his conscience by thinking that his father's body was deposited in a place known as Kābul. At all events it seems to have lain there till after the battle of Kanauj and the consequent flight from India when Bābar's widow Bīka Begam performed the pious duty of removing it to Kābul. See the story in Jauhar (Persian text) and in Erskine's History II, 325 n. It is clear from Jahāngīr's reference to Bīka Begam in the Tuzuk, p. 51, lith. ed. that she was Bābar's widow and that consequently it was not Bābar's daughter M'asūma, or Humāyūn's wife Ḥājī Begam who removed the bones.

There does not appear to be now any trace of the grave in the Rām Bāg͟h, as the Cārbāg͟h is now called. The garden seems also to have been known as the Gul-afs͟hān. There is a long account of the making of the Cārbāg͟h in Bābar, Erskine 341, and also in Shaik͟h Zāin's Tārīk͟h Bābārī B.M., Or. 1999, p. 83*b*. It was on the east side of the Jamna, and opposite the fort. S. Zāin calls it Cārbāg͟h-i-has͟ht bihis͟ht, a name which also occurs in Bābar. S. Zāin gives a poem about the garden, ending in the chronogram خانهٔ کعبهٔ آفاق. These three words K͟hāna kāaba āfāq, *i.e.*, house of the Kaaba of the horizons yield 935.

86. Nizāmu-d-dīn calls Mahdī K͟hwāja "*dāmād*," but "*dāmād*" means husband of the king's sister and husband in general as well as son-in-law. Gulbadan Begam, who is a better authority on the point, calls Mahdī K͟hwāja *izna*, *i.e.*, brother-in-law (it may also mean son-in-law) of Bābar. In the Ḥabīb-as-siyar B.M., MS. Add. 16,679, p. 370*a*, line 16, it is stated that Mahdī K͟hwāja was the husband of Bābar's elder sister K͟hānzāda Begam. The entry refers to the year 922. In the Bombay lithograph and in B.M. Add. 17,925 the name K͟hānzāda is not given but it is stated that Mahdī K͟hwāja was married to two sisters of Bābar, that he was the son of Mūsa and grandson of Mīr Murtaẓa, and that on the mother's side he was descended from Abul K͟hair K͟hān (S͟haibānī's grandfather). In the Majālis Nafais of 'Ali S͟her, a K͟hwāja Mūsā is described as a rich man who bought

verses from poor poets and passed them off as his own. Apparently Ibrāhīm Qanūnī a famous musician who is also mentioned in the Majālis as well as in Sām M. Taḥfat B.M. MS. 7671, p. 64*b* was a son of Khwāja Mūsā.

87. P. 278, *Cf.* A.N. III, 580. The 34th year corresponds to 997-998 A.H. or 1588-89. The Memoirs were partially translated before this, first by Shaikh Zāin, and second by Payanda Ḥasan Ghaznavī and Muḥammad Qulī Moghal in 994 *et seq.*, *i.e.*, 1585. It also seems to me from a MS. in the Alwar Palace-library that the so-called 'Abdurraḥīm's translation existed in Humāyūn's time. See Asiatic Quarterly Review for July and October 1900.

87*a*. Do., n. 2. For Tempel read Teufel.

88. P. 279, Verse. This quatrain is given in a Persian MS. of the Shaw collection in the Indian Institute, Oxford, No. 309 and called the Jām'a-al-muqāmāt, "collection of assemblies." The circumstances under which Bābar came to compose it are also given there. We are told that he won the victory over Rānā Sanga owing to the mysterious aid of Maulāna Khwājaga Aḥmad, otherwise known as Maqdūm 'Aāzim. So he sent Darvesh Muḥammad Sārbān to him at Dahbād near Samarkand with presents and this verse. The saint is said in return to have written part of the Risāla-Bābarī. (Bābar's Memoirs ?)

89. P. 280. Mr. Blochmann has given a translation of this passage at p. 220 of the Proceedings A.S.B. for 1874. There are several mistakes in my rendering. For the account of Shāikh Zain this should be substituted. "Shāikh Zain Ṣadr, great-grandson of (*ba do wāsṭa*, two removes) Shāikh Zainu-d-dīn Khwāfī. He had acquired a knowledge of science, was of quick parts and was skilled in poetry and the art of letter-writing. He was distinguished by his long association with His Majesty, and became an Amīr in the time of His Majesty Jahānbānī Jinnat-Āshiyānī." See at p. 219 l.c., the inscription on S. Zain's mosque at Kachparwa.

90. Do., line 12. For "paternal" read "maternal."

91. Do., Fārighī. For an account of him and specimens of his poetry see Budāūnī, Ranking 616. Budāūnī says that he and his nephew died in the same year (940 A.H.)

92. P. 281. Mr. Blochmann has "surkh widāī kuhnah, a little-known poet." The word which I have rendered "inartificial" is

*be-ta'yīn*, and should be rendered "obscure." He is mentioned in 'Alī Sher's Majālis, p. 41*a*, of Persian translation.

93. Do., l. 6. Insert indefinite article before *masnavī*.

94. P. 285, n. 2. Māham most probably means "My moon." It was apparently a common appellation for women. *Cf.* Māham Anaga, and the name of Taimur's wife. See Schuyler's Turkistan II. 97, ed. 1876, where we are told that a beautiful lady who was executed at Bokhāra was commonly known as "My moon of Kenin ghaz." *Cf.* the proper names Nuram, and Shāikham, *i.e.*, My light and my Shāikh. If Maham be regarded as a Turkī word it should from the law of the sequence of vowels be spelt Māhim as in P. de Courteille.

94*a*. The fullest accounts of this worthless character, M. Zamān, Mirzā are to be found in B.M. MSS., Or. 2939 and 3248. He was married to Bābar's daughter in Kabul in 921 or 922, and a few months afterwards his father-in-law sent him back to Balkh as governor. He was not a success there, and could not resist the Uzbegs. In 934 Bābar summoned him to India and settled a large estate upon. He ended his days by being drowned at Causa.

95. Do. According to the Mirāt Sikandarī four letters passed between Humāyūn and Bahādūr; verse I, p. 293, belongs to Humāyūn's first letter, and verse II to the second, *viz.*, that which was written on receipt of Bāhādūr's first reply. The M. Sikandarī Bombay lithograph 237 gives Humāyūn's second letter, and at 235 Bahadūr's reply. The latter is very insolent in tone and it is no wonder that it offended Humāyūn. It blames him for his treatment of M. Zamān and taunts him with boasting of the deeds of his seventh ancestor (Taimur) while having nothing of his own to show. It winds up with a verse to this effect. The translation in Bayley's Gujrat, p. 374, is very erroneous. A translation of the M. Sikandarī has lately been published at Bombay by Faẓl Ullah. The correspondence will also be found in B.M.'s MS., Or. 3482, pp. 104-106. I do not think Bayāzīd was M. Zamān's custodian. More probably he was his fellow-prisoner.

96. P. 295, Verse. See also T. Alfi, p. 115, of B.M., Or. 465. The second couplet is from Ḥāfiẓ, Brockhans, p. 141, Ode 220.

97. P. 296, 2nd line. The figure 1 is misplaced. It refers to "weak head" on top line.

98. P. 297, n. 4. In a letter to Erskine, Mountstūart Elphinstone,

see his life by Colebrooke, comments on what appears to be Bābar's suppression of facts about the Prince of Hind, whose name he seems to have used. I presume Elphinstone refers to Alāūddīn whom Bābar used as a tool.

99. P. 298, n. second col. For 960 read 96 n.

100. P. 302, n. 1. There were at least three Rūmī Khāns, *viz.*, 1ts. The man whom the Portuguese called Khwāja Sofar, who built the fort of Surat, and whose head was carried off by a cannon ball at the second siege of Diu in June 1546. 2nd. His son whom the Tārīkh Muḥammadi calls Khwāja Maham, who was killed in the same siege, just at its close in November 1546. See Tevius, p. 441. 3rd. Rūmī Khān, Bahādur's artillery-officer who deserted to Humāyūn and was poisoned after the taking of Cunār. Some information regarding Rūmī Khān the artillerist and Khwāja Safar will be found in the Barq-al-Yamān of Quṭbu-d-dīn of which De Saçy has given an abstract in N. et E. IV. It appears from it that Rūmī Khān the artillerist's real name was Mastafa Beg and that he was the son of Bairam and nephew of Sulaimān. He came to India in the Turkish fleet commanded by his uncle in 936. Khwāja Safar came at the same time and both were well received by Bahādūr, Mastafa getting the title of Rūmī Khān and the governorship of Diu, and Safar being made governor of Surat. The story of Rūmī Khān's being poisoned is confirmed by Quṭbu-d-dīn. Erskine, Hist. II, 82 n., says that the first Rūmī Khān is buried at Surat, and Tevius, p. 385, of his commentaries, seems to say that his obsequies were celebrated at Diu. 'Aārif Qandahārī gives the verses in which the chronogram of the building of Surat fort occur, see Blochmann 354, and says they were written by Aḥmad Shīrāzī known as Raẓaī. The name of the builder of the fort is given in the verses as Khān 'Aāẓim Khān Khudawand Khān.

101. P. 306, n. 2. Dele *dīn*.

102. P. 307, three lines from foot. Read "Aghazwār," (like Aghaz or Oghuz'). He was Governor of Herat and also Atāliq.

103. P. 309, three lines from foot. Read "Gawars."

104. P. 314, 11 lines from foot. For "wrong" read "strong."

105. Do., n. 1. The page reference is wrong.

106. Do., n. 2. For Monday read Tuesday.

107. P. 316, n. 3. After Nariād insert "and Aḥmadābad."

108. P. 317, second line and n. 1. We are told in the M. Sikandarī that Humāyūn called him a "black slave" *Ghulām-i-siah.* 'Imād-ul-Mulk is stated, Bayley's Gujrat p. 400, to have been the son of Tawakkal chief of the royal *Khāsah* Khailān. He was put to death at Surat by Khudawand Khān Rūmī in 1545, l.c , 435 and 436.

109. Do., second last para. For Nansārī read Nausārī.

110. P. 321, n. 1. Ferishta calls it Ghāt Karcī and an article by Mohan Lāl Vishnu Lal Pandia in J.A.S.B. for 1897, p. 167, states that Ghāt Karcī is the name of a town close to the town of Bānswāra.

111. P. 323, 13th line for "reporting" read "repenting."

112. P. 323, n. 3. Sofar or Sofarus of the Portuguese, probably the epithet refers to Rūmī Khān's complexion as the word means the pale or yellow. Sofar however is a proper name and may have been Rūmī Khān's real name or it may have been given to him on account of his Greek origin, for the Greeks are called the sons of Asfar (the superlative of safar. Lane 1699*b*). According to Damian a Goes, who calls him Khwāja Coffarus, he was born of a Turkish mother and a Christian father in the island of Chios. See Damian's Diensis Oppugnatio, Cologne 1602, published by Birckmann, p. 279.

113. P. 329, n. 2. This genealogy is also given in A.N. II, 64. I am inclined to think that Nūru-d-dīn first married Gul-barg, a daughter of Bābar not named by Gulbadan, and had by her Selīma, and that then in Humāyūn's reign, and probably after the death of her first husband Ishān Taimur, he married Gulrang. It is Pashā, not Pāshā Begum. Nūru-d-dīn belonged to the Naqshbandi order.

114. P. 331, second para. *Cf.* Jarrett II, 122, where it is said that the Bengalis make boats so high that when attached to the shore they overtop the walls of a fort. Rūmī Khān then seems to have adopted a Bengali stratagem.

115 P. 338, n. 2. Beale, O.B.D., p. 265, of ed. 1894, says that Shaikh Phūl or Bahlūl's tomb is on a hill near the fort of Biāna. Mammed Bakhshī is said to have buried him there. The brothers were descended from Farīdu-d-dīn-'Attār, and their father's name was Qiyāmu-d-dīn, and he is buried at Ghāzīpūr.

116. P. 341, n. 2, l. 3. For "East" read "West." Narhan is probably correct for Bayāzīd, 148*b*, speaks of Narhan as a ferry near Tājpūr where Khwajah Zechariah and others had a *Jāgīr*.

There is a pargana Tájpūr mentioned in the Āīn Jarrett II. 130 as in Sarkār Tāndha. Of course this is not the Darbhanga Tājpūr.

117. P. 344, 5 lines from foot. Dele the word "learned" within brackets.

118. Do. n. 2. For *Shihna* read *Shahna*.

118*a*. Do. n. 4. For Roebach read Roebuck.

119. P. 352, seven lines from foot. For *ābrūyān* read *beābruyārn.*

120. P. 357, n. 1. A Sārang Khān is mentioned in Taimu's. Institutes, Davy and White, as a brother of Matu Khān and as ruling in the country of Multan.

121. P. 360. There is an obscurity about Ḥamīda Bānu's parentage. In B.M. M.S. Add. 7688, which is a collection of letters, there are three addressed by Nawāb Bilqīs Makānī Miriam Beg to her mother and sister. They also appear in the similar collection, Or. 3842, 147*b*. Apparently the writer is Ḥamīda Banū, for they belong to her time, *viz.*, the reign of Ṭahmāsp, and they are such as she might write in a foreign country. They also immediately follow the correspondence of her husband, Humāyūn. Bilqīs Makānī is a name given to Ḥamīda in the T. Sindh, and Miriam Beg may be Miriam Makānī. In the first letter the writer calls her mother Sultānam and begs her good offices for one Ṣafī Khān, whom she describes as being the son of her *lala* or guardian. The second is to her sister, Zainab Begam, and is to the same effect. The third is to her mother and consists of inquiries after her health. It is forwarded by one Khwāja Rizwān who had come to explain his offences. The compiler of the book describes these letters as addressed to the writer's own mother and sister, and if so, we learn that her mother was called Sultānam and her sister Zainab. But possibly they are addressed to ladies of Ṭahmāsp's family whom she may have adopted as her mother and sister. Ṣafī Khān is described in the letters as a Saiyid of noble family, and he may be the Amír Ṣafī mentioned in Sām Mīrzā's Taḥfat Sāmī B.M. MS. P. 45, as belonging to a noble family of Saiyids and as coming from Nīshāpur. He was a caligraphist. The three letters are written in high-flown Persian. It is, however, possible that the writer was the niece of Ṭahmāsp and daughter of M'asūm Beg whom Humāyūn is said to have married in Persia. Jauhar 75.

122. P. 360, n. 2. He is also probably the Bāba Dost Bakhshī whom Bayāzīd in his list p. 74c. calls Bābā Dost Cūlī (because he accompanied Humāyūn across the desert) and who, he says, acted as Humāyūn's Bakhshī on the way to Persia. Bayāzīd mentions Bābā Dost Bakhshī and his son, Dost Muhammad, several times in his account of the siege of Kabul by M. Sulaimān. He praises the valour of the son and describes, 85b., how Bāba Dost Bakhshī had the command of a battery during the siege and how he laid a trap for M. Ibrahim. At p. 92б Bāyāzīd tells how when Mun'im Khān decided that he would not go to India on account of Bairām Khān's being all powerful, he bade Bāyāzīd go back to Kābul. Bazzāid said he could not go back alone, and when Mun'im insisted on his return he begged and obtained that Bāba Dost Bakhshī should be sent back with him. This seems to show that Bāba Dōst was a *persona grata* with the Begams.

123. P. 362, n. 1. The source of the Maaṣir's information (and consequently of Mr. Blochmann's) is the Tabaqāt Akbari Lucknow ed. 339. The presentation of the record is placed there in the end of the 23rd year. 'Mīr Ali Akbar was afterwards disgraced and imprisoned.

124. P. 364, n. 2. Read Ḥijrī. His poetry is not religious. There were two poets of this name, and the *divāns* of both of them are in the I.O.

125. P. 369, n. 1. The passage is explained in T. Alfī p. 570*a* of B. M. MS. Or. 465, where it is stated that 'Abdu-l-Ghafūr said what he should not have said about the distressed condition of Humāyūn's army. "*Sakna cand ke namībāyīst guft az pareshānī lashkariān Ḥazrat guft.*"

126. Do. n. 2. The story is also told in the T. Alfī 570*a*. The unfortunate men took refuge with Humāyūn. Yādgār Nāsir said he wanted to settle revenue accounts with them and induced Humāyūn to send them to him. Humāyūn sent them with a guard, but Yādgār Nāsir got rid of the guard and then sent the zamindārs to Shāh Ḥusain. Possibly the story is another version of that told by Ṭāhir Nasyānī. See his Tārīkh of which there is a copy in the Rampore Library, and also Elliot I, 253.

127. P. 372, n. 2. The Mirāt-i-'Aālam B. M. MS., p. 261, says expressly that the diamond was the one obtained by the victory over

Ibrāhīm. It also says, later on, that this was the diamond given by Humāyūn to Ṭahmāsp.

128. P. 376, n. For "author's" read "author."

129. P. 378, n. 3. Another division is noted by Mut'amid Khān in the preface to his Iqbālnāma. According to it the first volume is an account of Akbar's ancestors, as in Bib. Ind. ed. The second comprised the occurrences of 47 years, and was divided into two parts, *viz.*, the first thirty years, making a *qarn*, and the second part extending from the 31st to the 47th year and unfinished. See the translation of passage in preface to Gladwin's translation of the Āīn.

130. P. 382, n. 4. I am now inclined to think that Hardwār must be wrong, though it is difficult to say what the right word is. Possibly it is merely a copyist's blunder, Hardwār هردوار having been written for حدود ḥadūd, boundaries, which occurs in other narratives of the occurrence, where we are told that Bairām came *az ḥadūd-i-Gujrāt.*

131. P. 385. With reference to this story see the quotation from the Dabīstān in Blochmann 163 n. The informant referred to therein is 'Azīz Koka's own mother Jījī, and not Ḥamīda.

132. P. 402, n. 5. Apparently there is no pun, A. F. merely means that Nāzuk was only a king in name.

133. P. 404, n. 8. Read "nearly the meaning of the word religion."

134. P. 405 l. 6. For "chastity" read "charity" and for 'king of king' read 'king of kings.'

135. P. 413, n. 2 top line. For "merely" read "surely."

136. The letter is also given in the collection B.M. MS. Or. 3482, p. 104. The letter is in very humble terms. Tahmāsp's quotation from Ḥāfiz about the *humā* was happy, for *humā* is part of Humāyūn's name and in his letter Humāyūn had compared himself to a bird or moth flying towards the sun.

These collections also contain a long and interesting letter from Humāyūn written after the defect of Balkh and detailing Kāmrān's misconduct, etc. There is also a very long letter from Ṭahmasp to Sulaimān, the Sultan of Turkey (which, however, was never sent), in which he holds up Humāyūn as an instance of pride going before a fall, and tells a story of a dream that Humāyūn had while in India.

137. P. 416, n. 4. It has been suggested to me that Shahristan is a mistake for Shahr-i-sīstan, the city or capital of Sīstān. But it appears from Yāqūt, Meynard 253 and 301, that the old capital of Sijistān was called Rām Shahristan, and was three *farsakhs* from Zaranj.

138. P. 417, end of first para. For "'amwān" read *'anwān*.

139. P. 427, l. 8. The Mirāt al 'Aālam has Sābir Daqāqq, *i.e.*, a fuller.

140. Do. n. 1. For "three" read "two."

141. P. 443, last line read "For the world's law is sometimes this, sometimes that." Amīr Shāhī's ode will be found at p. 18*a* of B. M. MS. Add. 7788, and at 37*b* of Add. 23,612. The lines which follow the last distich quoted by A. F. are not very intelligible. Amīr Shāhi was originally of Sabzāwār. There is a full account of him in Daulāt Shāh's work, Browne's ed.

142. Do. n. 5. Read p. 198 for p. 19. The word *cārgāh* is *cārkāh* in Ilminsky. Add. 27,247 of B. M. has Sābir Qulī for Sābir Qāq. and *dar muqām* sairgāh, *i.e.*, theatre or place of recreation for *sihgāh*. Qāq seems to be right, for the 'Aālam Ārāī has the jingle *Ḥāfiz Sābir Qāq ke nādira wy a fāq*. Add. 27, 247, seems to be the only MS. which has *sairgēh*, but it also occurs in the Afzal-at-Tawārīkh p. 122*a* of B. M. MS. Or. 4678, and in the Aalam Ārai Rein, Cat., supplement 7654, p. 173*a*. See also the *dar muqām panjgāh* of Budāunī I, 481, where Dr. Ranking's translation, p. 622, seems to be wrong.

143. P. 434, n. 3. Read Yate for Yates.

144. P. 438, four lines from foot. Though Barda' or Barza' be the name of a place in Azarbaijān, yet the word here probably means "packsaddle."

145. P. 442, n. 5, l. 3. For "to" read "of."

146. P. 444, n. Olearius' account of Tabrīz may also be consulted.

147. P. 445, n. 8. Probably one of the two daughters who died in the second year of Akbar's reign during Miriam Makānī's journey from Kabul to India.

148. P. 446, n. 3. See also Ethe's Cat. I. O. MSS., p. 1210, No. 2219.

149. Do. See Badāūnī, Ranking, 619, for another correction by Humāyūn.

150. P. 447, third line from foot. For "forwardness" read "audacity."

151. P. 451, line 4 and n. Dele. figure 1.

151*a*. P. 459. For Babū Dōst read Bābā Dost.

152. P. 465, l. 22. Insert the word "over."

153. P. 470, l. 14. Last word. Dele the word "as."

154. P. 475, n. 2. For "as" read "is."

155. P. 477, n. 1. For "in" read "near" Bābā Ḥasan Abdāl. Possibly the place is the Qibcāq pass of Jarrett II, 400.

156. P. 481. The editors of text point out in a note that both these chronograms are wrong, one yielding 954, and the other 955 and they observe that 952 as the true date.

157. P. 491. n. For Istālāf read "Istālif."

158. Do. n. 1. For "is" read "in."

158*a*. 489, note, last line. For I. 46 read II. 46.

159. P. 494. Line 4, and note. The Mūīn who was Qāzī of Lahore is probably the officer mentioned at Vol. II, p. 163, as appointed to Malwa, and seems to have been different from Sharafu-al-din's father.

160. P. 497 n. For "Leydon" read "Leyden." Deerstalking is described by Bellew, Journal of Mission to Afghanistan, p. 327, as a favourite amusement of the Afghans.

161 P. 500 line 19. For "this Mīrzā" read "the Mīrzā."

162. P. 502, line 18. For "Zāmān" read "Zamīn."

162*a*. P. 504, n. For "Shaīrbānī" read "Shaibānī."

163. P. 505, n. Apparently Junaid was also called Amīr Qutlaq Qadam. See Mahmūd's life *Of* Ṭahmasp. B. M. MS. Or. 2939, 129*b*., and T. Alfī 536*a*. line 7.

164. P. 508, *l*. 5. *aqābain* if it is the dual.

165. P. 521, n. 2. For Hiibak read Heibak.

166. P. 530, text and note 1. *cf.* Bayley's Gujrat 446 Suṭṭān Maḥmūd had commanded his officers to give up the house of anyone guilty of either of those offences to *halan*, *i.e.*, to plunder. See also Bombay lithograph of Mirāt Sikandarī p. 302. The reference to Bayāzīd is p. 35*b*. of his memoirs.

167. P. 2. 537, n. 2. For "on" read "in".

168. P. 539, n. Erskine's opinion is confirmed by Humāyūn's letter to Ṭahmāsp B.M. MS. Add. 7688 p. 105*b*.

169. P. 545, n. 3. There is a good deal about Bairam Oghlān in Mahmūd's lives of Ismāīl and Ṭahmāsp. He was an Uzbeg and governor of Balkh under Kisten Qara. The Aḥsan Tawārikh 101b. speaks of Bairam's attacking Herat. He had been ruler of Gurjistan and was eventually killed in battle. See l. c. pp. 129b and 133a.

170. Do. n. 7. In Humāyūn's letter to Ṭahmāsp giving an account of the expedition to Balkh he is called Khwāja Bāqī.

171. P. 557. I have not found this story about Ism'aīl's handkerchief in the anonymous life of that prince, but there is a sensational account of his crossing with his troops the rivers Kūr and Aras (Araxes), *vide* p. 55a. But the story is told at length by D'Herbelot with only this difference that it was a slipper which Ism'aīl threw into a trench.

172. P. 576, n. 1. For ایلچی read خدمت

## *Additional Errata and Addenda.*

1. P. 59, n. 3. For Ilahad Faiẓ read Ilāhdād Faiẓī, and for No. 1890 read B.M. MS., Or., 1890.

2. P. 117, n. 2. *Bajins* probably means here "accurately, in facsimile."

3. P. 119, n. 3. For Cholgīl read Cholgii.

4. P. 160, n. 4. For Farāj read Faraj.

5. P. 163, l. 8. For "Domes of Haramān" read "ancient domes."

6. P. 192, l. 14. "The Jāmūqa tribe" should apparently be "Jāmūqa's tribe," see p. 193.

7. P. 200, 7 ll. from foot. For Īsū Mangū read Īsū Manga.

8. P. 203, last sentence. There is a variant which makes it the Amīr who honoured the saint.

9. P. 218, l. 3. For Abū Bakr read Abā Bakr.

10. Do., l. 6. For Bābī read Bābāī.

11. P. 225, last line. For "or" read "and."

12. P. 227, l. 3. Put comma after "killed."

13. P. 229, l. 10. See Sām Mīrzā's Taḥafat, B.M. MS. Add. 7670, p. 44, for an account of the origin of the name Khwāb-bīn.

14. P. 233, n. 1. For Maḥmūd Ḥasan read Muḥammad Ḥusain

15. P. 234, l. 9. Insert figure 5 after Jām.

16. Do., l. 13. "The country of Hindustan." Akwardly expressed, for Bābar was not then seeing Hindustan. But the akwardness is in the original and is apparently due to the fact that Bābar wrote his Memoirs after conquering India. The word both in the Turkī and the Persian is *Nawāhī*, and this is rendered by P. des Courteille "les abords."

17. Do., n. 4. For Barīk-al read Bārik-ab.

18. P. 236, five lines from foot. For "his six brothers" read "six of his brothers."

19. P. 237, n. 4. The remark near the end of this note is wrong, for the Muhammadan Ararat is not what Europeans call Ararat, but

is a mountain called Jūdī Dāgh belonging to a range south of Lake Van and east of Jazīra-b. Omar. It lies a long way S. S. W. of what is now known as Mount Ararat.

20. P. 239, l. 4 from foot. Akwardly expressed, for of course Humāyūn arrived before Lahore was taken. There should be a full stop after "taken," the word "and" should be deleted, and "on" made On.

21. Do., n. 4. The Bāgh Wafā was at Adīnapur (Jalālābād), the Bāgh Ṣafā was higher up the river near Cār Bāgh, and there was another Bāgh Ṣafā in the Salt-Range.

22. P. 242, top line. For gabions substitute *tūrās*. They were not gabions, but light wattles (?) which the soldiers carried as they marched. See Bābar 86, and P. de. Courteille 151.

23. P. 248, l. 15. The words "according to their rank" are misplaced. They should come after "presents."

24. P. 253, 4 lines from foot. Perhaps Qāẓī Ziā is the Zīau-d-dīn Nūr Beg of Khwandamīr's Humāyūn-nāma, and who, he says, got the title of Amīr-i-Zakāt.

25. P. 254, l. 3. Insert H.M. before Jahānbānī.

26. P. 256, l. 20. Jājamū'. This town is in Unao, Oude.

26*a*. P. 260, n. 1. Cancel note. Beg Mīrak was not Niẓāmu-d-dīn's grandfather.

27. P. 262, l. 3. For Urdū Shān read Urdu Shāh.

28. P. 265, l. 18. For Kram read Karim.

29. P. 267, l. 11. Insert comma after Qāsīm.

30. P. 277, Verse. The whole verse is given by Khwandamīr in his Humāyūn nāma. See translation by Sadu Sukh Lāl, p. 45, of B.M. MS. Add. 30,774.

31. P 281, last sentence. Perhaps this Kīcak or Kūcak was the brother whom Khwāja Kilān left in Qandahār, when he deserted his post, and who surrendered to Ṭahmāsp. The Afẓal Tārīkh B.M. MS. Or. 4678, p 96*a* says he was a brother of Khwāja Kilān. The Aḥsān T.B.M. MS. Or. 4134 calls him, p. 107, Kachī Khān and Maḥmūd Or. 2939, p. 1831 calls him Kechak khān.

32. P. 285, Verse. For the first two lines substitute

The year of his auspicious (*humāyūnash*) birth is "May Almighty God increase thy stature."

The second line is a chronogram. In n. 4, for *qadran* read *qadrā* and for *Zādakallāhu* read Zādak Allah. Perhaps Sāmānī only means that he was a native of Sāmāna (in India).

33. P. 293, l. 4. Read Kanār for Kānār.

34. P. 294, n. 1. Abū Turab's account shows that Bahādur was present at the battle of Pānīpat, though he did not take part in it.

35. P. 295, Verse II. This comes from Ḥāfiẓ Ode 220. Brockhaus 141.

36. P. 296, l. 9. Abū Turāb says in history of Gujrāt, p. 13*a*, that the twenty krors of old coinage were equal to 30 krors, 50 lakhs *murādi*. *Murādī* is explained in dictionaries as meaning small money.

37. P. 302, n. 1. Abū Turāb, p. 79, also gives the title of Khudāwand Khān to Khwāja Ṣafar.

38. P. , last line. Khwāndamīr gives his full name, p. 72 or 47, as Maulānā Muhīu-d-dīn Muḥammad Farghārī.

39. P. 315, n. 1. For *Kaifu* read *Kaif*. But I doubt if Humāyūn suspected any play on the word. The real explanation of Humāyūn's anger seems to be that the chapter of the Elephant is a denunciatory and terrifying one, and used in compositions which convey threats. Perhaps Humāyūn remembered that it was so used by Shāhrukh, the son of Taimur, in a threatening letter which he addressed in 833 or 835 A. H. to Barsbāī, the Sulṭān of Egypt. See the story in the extract from Makrīzī given in De Sacy's Chrestomathie Arabe II. 84. Instead of the letter beginning with Bismillah, it began with the Sura of the Elephant, and quoted the whole of it. The rest of the letter was filled with menaces. Barsabāī replied in similar style.

40. P. 316, n. 4. Apparently the 'Alam Lūdī here mentioned is 'Alaū-d-dīn, the uncle of Ibrāhīm Sulṭān.

41. P. 317, n. 1. Yes, Khudāwand Khān was a very old man. Abū Turāb says, 28*b*, that he was Akhūnd of Sulṭān Moẓaffar and had been Vizier and Vakīl of four Sulṭāns. Férishta says he was the father of Cingīz Khān, not the son, and Abū Turāb makes the same statement.

42. P. 320, l. 7. Asāwal is spelt Ashāwal in Sir Theodore Hope's book on Aḥmadābād, and is the spot where the original chieftain was defeated by Qāsim.

43. P. 324, l. 10. Abū Turāb tells this story, but he does not give his informant's name. He only says that he was an Akhūnd and

had been Bahādur's teacher and that in this way he had become acquainted with him. Nor does he say anything about his informant's taking an oath. Qu? is the Quṭbu-d-dīn of A.F's story Abū Turāb's uncle?

44. P. 325, n. 2. I have seen somewhere that there was a mosque in Aḥmadābād called Masjid Ṣafā, but that it was not built till 994 A.H.

45. P. 336, l. 19. For Bābā Khān read Bābā Beg.

46. P. 341. I now incline to think that Narhan is correct. It is a well-known ford and is mentioned in the 2nd volume. But though A.F. has written Narhan, it does not seem likely that Humāyūn went so far east.

47. P. 359, l. 17. For 'Abdu-l-Mākrī read Abdāl Mākrī.

48. P. 368, n. 1. Shāh Ḥusain had a son by Gulbarak B. who died young.

49. P. 396, n. 1. For J. V. read I. C.

50. P. 407, n. 2. See Burnes' Cabool, 1842, p. 115. He says the correct name is Dingote, and that it is 6 m. above Kālā Bāgh.

51. P. 408, l. 10. After Khāwand, for Muḥammad read Maḥmūd.

52. P. 416, n. 4. The following note by George P. Tate, Esq., of the Indian Survey, has been kindly furnished to me by Mr. Irvine:—

" Qila'-i-Ūk. Ūk is the ancient name of a small district to the north of the Hamūn-i-Helmand, and therefore of Seistān, the chief towns of which are Lāsh and Juwain. The names of these towns are existing at the present day, but the name of the district has apparently fallen into desuetude, as it does not seem to be generally known. Qila'-i-Ūk would therefore merely mean the principal fort, or capital of the district, the name of which, if it had one, was not generally known. A similar case can be found not far off from that locality. In the Zafarnāmah the author writes of the capital of Seistān as Shahr-i-Seistān, and does not mention it by name. This practice still holds good. The word " Shahr " is used, as we use the word " town," with reference to London. Rarely, or never, is the " Shahr " or capital, spoken of by its name of Nasratābād. This is the modern capital. The site of the ancient capital of Seistān is at a short distance to the N.-E. of the modern capital. Ūk, judging from its propinquity to Seistān, probably was subject to the (Kāiānī) Maliks of Seistān, from whose country it was divided by the Helmand, if the Helmand at that time did not find a more southerly outlet for its waters, which seems to me to have possibly been the case.

"Humāyūn, if he passed through Ūk on his way to Persia, took a route which at the present day lies within the Afghan border, and the reason of his adopting this route would probably have been the evil reputation for lawlessness earned by the inhabitants of the Kohistān, that is, the country around Neh and Birjand, through which the trade route (now in use) between Seistān and Mashhad passes. This would probably have been the shortest route to Mashhad, had it been safe to use it."

53 P. 434, n. 3. For Gazargāh read Gāzargāh.

54. P. 439, last line. For Zailāq read Yailāq. Yailāq means summer-quarters, and the translation should apparently be "first stage of the summer-quarters"

55. P. 436, n. 7. For Qadār read Qīdār. See Genesis xxv. 13.

56. P. 440, n. 1. For Bayāzīd 176, read Bayāzīd 17*b*.

57. P. 442, n. 2. This identification is wrong.

58. P. 443, n. 2. For Ṣāfī read Ṣafī.

59. Do., n. 3. For Saddi read Sadd.

60. P. 445, l. 6. For Paik Muḥammad read Beg Muḥammad.

61. P. 448, last para. It would seem from Gulbadan Begam's Memoirs that either he or his relative Kecak or Kucak wrote an account of Humāyūn's adventures in Sind. Kicak is said to have been a brother of Khwāja Kilān, so that Khwāja Ghāzī was related to him also. Note 5 is not altogether correct. Khwāja Ghāzī and Rustam Koka fell into disgrace in Persia for stealing Humāyūn's jewels, but he got over that and was made accountant when Humāyūn returned to Afghanistan. But there he was dismissed for defalcations, see p. 544. In the passage of the Āīn referred to by me as Blochmann VII, A.F. is represented as saying that the office of Mashrif was higher than that of *dīwān*, but surely there must be some mistake, for at p. VI., last line, Blochmann translates Mashrif as clerk, and at p. 544 we are told that Afẓal was promoted from being Mashrif to being diwān. Perhaps the word at p. VII is not Mashrif, but Masharrif-i-diwān, *i.e.*, the exalter of the diwān or the Diwān *par excellence*.

61.* P. 448, l. 4. Brother (*barādar*) seems a mistake here for brother's son (*barādarzāda*), see p. 542, last para., where Kokī is described as the paternal uncle of Ḥājī Muḥammad.

62. P. 448, l. 13. The description here evidently refers to Maḥram and not to Ḥasan.

63. P. 548, near foot. For Bābā Sihrindī read Bābāī Sihrindī.

64. P. 460, near middle. For Muḥammad M. read Muḥammadī M.

65. P. 466, l. 20. For Kot Laka read Kohlakā, and translate "hill-country." Lakā means country.

66. Do. 7 lines from foot. For "strive" read "strove."

67. P. 475, n. 3. Nadīm Koka is called Nadīm Beg by K͟hwandamīr in his Humāyūn-nāma, p. 149*b*, and is described as a Turk and as in high favour with Humāyūn, and the recipient of a k͟hilat. He calls him *janāb amārat s͟h'aār fark͟handa iṭwār* Nadīm Beg *muhrdār* (sealer).

68. P. 482, n. 2. For "come back to Humāyūn" read "gone back to Kāmrān."

69. P. 520, l. 7. Insert marginal number 271, and p. 521, l. 5, from foot insert 272.

70. P. 522, n. 2. A.F. calls him Buyatāt at pp. 543 and 565.

71. P. 526, n. 3. For Gulbān read Gulbār.

72. P. 529, l. 10. The word "*jamjhama* is used again in text II. 117, and clearly means there a morass or collection of water.

73. P. 530, l. 11. For Bābī read Bāba, and in next line insert "army" after victorious.

74. P. 534, l. 6. For Bārgbegī read Bārbegī.

75. P. 540, n. 1. For tamaatogh read tumāntog͟h.

76. P. 541. For marginal number 248 read 284.

77. P. 543, last para. This is an interesting paragraph and requires elucidation. It appears from the Āīn, Blochmann VI, that the words Vizier and Diwan are synonymous. The meaning, then, seems to be that K͟hwāja Qāsim Buyatāt had been made the Vizier or head of the department, and that then Mīrzā Beg had been appointed in his room. He was a poet and apparently inefficient and consequently K͟hwāja G͟hāzī exercised unlimited power. That he was a dishonest man is proved by Gulbadan Begam's Memoirs, where we learn that he stole Humāyūn's jewels. Apparently the investigation was undertaken at the suggestion of Mīr Barka, who belonged to Sabza-

wār, and is called in the Āīn Sayyid Barka. Ḥusain Qulī was made *muḥassil* of the affair, *i.e.*, apparently reporter of the findings of the committee. The word *mutaghallib* is given in Steingass as meaning victorious or powerful, but here it seems to be used in the sense of embezzling, and it is so understood by the Lucknow editor, who says the Khwājas were found guilty of *taghallab, i.e.*, embezzlement. I think we should render the passage here "the fraudulent clerks."

78. P. 543, l. 4 from foot. For Khawānd read Khāwand.

79. P. 544, n. 1. This note is wrong. The Ḥasan Qulī meant is probably the sealbearer often mentioned by Bayāzīd. See p. 440, n. 1.

80. P. 544, l. 9. For "condemned" read "defaulting."

81. Do., l. 11. Insert Jahānbānī after "His Majesty."

82. P. 551, l. 6. *Dele* stop after Muḥammad.

83. P. 68, l. 16. Insert on margin 303.

84*a* n. 2. *Dele* last sentence. The word in the Memoirs is Bakhshi.

84. P. 599, l. 17. *Dele* word "as." This last sentence, about Jogī Khān, has no connection with the account of the Gakkars, and should have been put into a separate paragraph and prefaced by the words "In fine."

85. P. 600, l. 9. Possibly the clause within brackets refers to Kāmrān and not to Salīm Khān. Substitute at l. 11, "assistance for his own ruin" for "auxiliaries for his disloyalty.

86. P. 608, n. 3. For "Newcomb" read Newcome.

86*a*. P. 612. According to the Darbār Akbarī, p. 312, it was 'Abdullah Sulṭānpurī who sent the boots and also a whip.

87. P. 614. For Salīm Shāh read Salīm Khān. A.F. is always careful not to style Sher or his son Salīm, Shāh.

88. P. 623. The list is A.F.'s not Bayāzīd's and should not have appeared as a note.

89. P. 665. Ferishta says that he, after search, found Humāyūn's *divān*, and he gives extracts from it.

# DEDICATION

In Memory of

J. H. B.

M. T. B.

L. S. B.

# PREFACE TO THE FIRST VOLUME.

When the Asiatic Society of Bengal did me the honour of inviting me to translate the Akbarnāma, I replied that I doubted my ability to make a complete translation, and suggested that I might edit the manuscript version by Lieutenant Chalmers. My suggestion was accepted, and I accordingly obtained from the Royal Asiatic Society the loan of the Chalmers' manuscript and permission to print it. I soon found, however, that the translation was too abridged to be made the basis of my work, and that it was necessary to execute a new version. Chalmers' manuscript was of great service to Elphinstone and Count Noer, and it has also been of much use to myself, but there are many gaps in it, and Abul Faẓl's language has throughout been greatly compressed. One gap near the beginning extends to over ninety pages of the printed text, and has the effect of omitting the account of Akbar's birth, with the prognostics and horoscopes appertaining thereto, as well as the notices of his ancestors from Adam down to his grandfather (Bābar). The reader may judge of the extent to which abbreviation has been carried, when I state that the Chalmers MS. consists of two thinnish volumes of foolscap, and that the Bibliotheca Indica edition of the Persian text, occupies three large quartoes which aggregate 1,600 pages.

The task of translation has occupied me several years, and the work has not been very congenial, for Abūl Faẓl is not an author for whom one can feel much sympathy or admiration. He was a great flatterer and unhesitatingly suppressed or distorted facts. His style, too, seems—at least to Western eyes—to be quite detestable, being full of circumlocutions, and both turgid and obscure. He is often prolix, and often unduly concise and darkly allusive. His one merit—and it is one which he specially claims for himself—is his laboriousness. He was an unwearied worker, and when we blame him and lament his deficiencies we shall do well to consider what a blank our knowledge of Akbar's reign would have been, had not Abūl Faẓl exerted himself during years of strenuous effort to chronicle events and institutions. His work also has the imperishable merit of being a record by a contemporary, and by one who had access to information at first hand.

I regret that the work of translation has not devolved upon a better Persian scholar than I am. I have endeavoured to do my best, and I have sought assistance in many quarters. I now desire to express my gratitude to my friends, Maulvi Abdul Haq Abid, the late Mr. J. Beames, Mr. A. G. Ellis of the British Museum, Mr. Irvine and Mr. Whinfield, and to the translation of the Āīn-i-Akbarī, by Professor Blochmann and Colonel Jarrett, and the works of Major Price. I am also indebted for much literary assistance to my elder brother, Mr. David Beveridge. There are, I am sure, many mistakes in my translation and notes, but there would have been many more but for the assistance of my friends. I regret that I have been obliged to make two long lists of Errata and Addenda. In part this has been due to the translations being made in England and printed in India, and in part to increase of knowledge. The translation of the second volume, which carries on the history of Akbar's reign to the middle of the seventeenth year, has been completed by me, and I am about to begin the translation of the third and last volume. The translation has been made from the Bibliotheca Indica edition of the text, but I have consulted many MSS. in the British Museum, the India Office, and the Royal Asiatic Society's Library, &c. The Bibliotheca Indica edition is by no means so good as it might have been, for the learned native editors* were destitute of geographical or historical knowledge. Hence they have often made mistakes in the names of persons and places. They have also no explanatory notes. In their preface they are severe upon the Lucknow edition. No doubt that edition has many faults, but it was the first in the field, and it is on the whole a creditable monument of the enter-

* It is stated in the Persian preface that nine MSS. and the Lucknow lithograph were used in the preparation of the edition. None of the MSS. was of an early date.

prise of the publisher, Munshi Newal Kishor, and of the liberality of the Maharajah of Patiala. The editor, Maulvī Ṣādiq 'Alī, also deserves honourable mention. He has added numerous notes, and though many of these are trivial, yet there are also many which are really enlightening.

Since completing the translation, I have seen a remarkable MS. of the first volume of the Akbarnāma in the possession of Saiyid 'Alī Bilgrāmī. This is evidently a rough draft and contains several things which do not occur in the MSS. of the finished work. Among them are one or two letters of Humāyūn. I have given an account of this MS. in R. A. S. J. for January 1903, p. 115.

H. Beveridge.

*4th September 1902.*

# INDEX

TO THE

## FIRST VOLUME.

The numbers refer to the pages ; *n* stands for " footnote."

* Also at Cīr Bāgh above Jālālābād Raverty's notes 58, and Bayāzīd 109*a* last line also Babar's Memoirs, 291 (the new garden), 594 and *n* 1.

### I.

J.

K.

## T.

## U.



## V.